The Art and Science of Child Custody Evaluations

The Art and Science of Child Custody Evaluations

Jonathan W. Gould
David A. Martindale

The Guilford Press
New York / London

© 2007 The Guilford Press
A Division of Guilford Publications, Inc.
72 Spring Street, New York, NY 10012
www.guilford.com

Printed in the United States of America

This book is printed on acid-free paper.

Last digit is print number: 9 8 7 6 5 4 3 2 1

Library of Congress Cataloging-in-Publication Data

Gould, Jonathan W., 1953–
    The art and science of child custody evaluations / Jonathan W.
Gould, and David A. Martindale.
        p. cm.
    Includes bibliographical references and index.
    ISBN-13: 978-1-59385-488-1 (hardcover : alk. paper)
    ISBN-10: 1-59385-488-9 (hardcover : alk. paper)
    1. Custody of children—United States—Evaluation.   2. Parent
and child (Law)—United States.   I. Martindale, David A.
II. Title.
    KF547.G675 2007
    346.7301'73—dc22

                                                    2007016019

About the Authors

Jonathan W. Gould, PhD, practices forensic psychology with a specialization in issues related to family law, including child custody, and is board certified in forensic psychology by the American Board of Professional Psychology. He performs court-appointed custody evaluations and consults with attorneys and psychologists in the areas of child custody, Child Protective Services evaluations such as termination of parental rights, and professional ethics and standards. Dr. Gould also consults with attorneys in the areas of criminal child sexual abuse and other forms of child maltreatment. With David A. Martindale, he is a principal in the consulting group Child Custody Consultants.

David A. Martindale, PhD, is board certified in forensic psychology by the American Board of Professional Psychology. He performed court-appointed custody evaluations for 16 years in New York state and served as the Reporter for the Association of Family and Conciliation Courts' *Model Standards for Child Custody Evaluation.* Dr. Martindale's practice is now limited to consulting with attorneys, psychologists, and psychology licensing boards in the areas of child custody and professional ethics and standards. With Jonathan W. Gould, he is a principal in the consulting group Child Custody Consultants.

Preface

When Jon wrote his 1998 book about conducting scientifically crafted child custody evaluations, he began the book with the following sentence: "Forensic child custody evaluations are in their infancy" (Gould, 1998, p. 1). Today, the research, scholarship, and professional practice of child custody evaluations have grown into a healthy early adolescence. Over the past 10 years, the field of child custody has witnessed the development of professional practice guidelines (American Academy of Child and Adolescent Psychiatry, 1997b; American Psychological Association, 1994) and professional practice standards (Association of Family and Conciliation Courts, 2006; Martindale, 2005b) that guide the field. There has been an increasing consensus expressed in the literature about a common set of methods and procedures to be used in crafting a scientifically informed, reliable, and relevant child custody evaluation (Austin, 2002; Austin & Kirkpatrick, 2005; Amundson, Duda, & Gill, 2000; Baerger, Galatzer-Levy, Gould, & Nye, 2003; Galatzer-Levy, Baerger, Gould, & Nye, 2002; Gould & Bell, 2000; Gould & Lehrmann, 2002; Gould & Stahl, 2000; Kirkland, 2002; Kirkpatrick, 2004; Martindale & Gould, 2004).

We have witnessed the growth of several important journals that focus attention on issues related to child custody, such as *Family Court Review*, the *Journal of Child Custody*, the *Journal of Forensic Psychological Practice*, and the *American Journal of Forensic Psychology*. Historically, the field of child custody has been viewed as a stepsister to more traditional forensic psychological endeavors such as those in the area of criminal competency, criminal responsibility, or personal injury. We believe that the work of child custody evaluators is gaining greater status among more traditional forensic psychologists, as witnessed by child custody articles appearing in mainstream forensic psychology journals, such as *Psychology, Public Policy, and Law*; *Law and Human Behavior*; and *Behavioral Sciences and the Law*. Journals that publish articles about psychological tests and measures, such as *Psychological Assessment*, have also begun to accept and publish research on normative data for child custody litigants on different tests and measures.

Mental health journals that address areas of special interest to child custody evaluators have proliferated, for example, *Child Maltreatment*, *Child Abuse and Neglect*, *Violence Against Women*, the *Journal of Interpersonal Violence*, the *Journal of Child Sexual Abuse*, and *Trauma, Violence, and Abuse*.

With increasing frequency, legal journals—such as *Family Law Quarterly* and the *Journal of the American Association of Matrimonial Lawyers*—have also begun to publish articles about child custody. Judges' journals have also shown an increasing interest in child custody works, as evidenced in the *Juvenile and Family Court Journal* and the *Court Journal*.

Professional organizations from a variety of disciplines offer workshops in many areas of child custody, from basic courses in forensic methods and procedures applied to child custody evaluations to more advanced courses on cross-examining an expert witness and factors to consider in relocation cases.

Through use of the Internet, several custody-related listservs and bulletin boards have emerged. Among them is the child custody listserv to which we both belong and to which we both actively contribute. The American Bar Association's listserv focusing on child custody and domestic violence issues is also an important contributor to professional exchange.

Like the body of an adolescent, the field of child custody assessment gives the appearance of maturity, and in many ways it is. There are also many ways in which the field of child custody assessment still needs to grow. If Jon's first book helped define the infancy of this dynamic and growing field, this present work helps define its early adolescence.

A Call for Standards

Other scholars have noted the increasing maturity in both research and professional practice in the child custody field. Examining the current state of the art in child custody, Kirkpatrick (2004) has argued that "forensic mental health evaluators, family courts, and family law practitioners know enough, or should know enough, by now to identify *minimum standards of practice for the conduct of child custody and visitation evaluations* (CCEs)" (p. 62, emphasis in original). He concludes that the time has come "for the establishment of a set of minimum standards for CCEs" (p. 62).

We agree with Kirkpatrick's view that there is overwhelming consensus in the child custody field supporting methods and procedures that include the use of semistructured interviews, psychological tests and measures, direct parent–child observations, collateral interviews, and record reviews. We also acknowledge that there are differences between the emerging scientifically informed model (e.g., Ackerman & Kane, 1999; Gould, 2006; Martindale & Gould, 2004) and those of other authors (e.g., Benjamin & Gollan, 2002). Some of these differences help stimulate debate and crystallize positions (Benjamin, Gould, & Rotman, 2005; Martindale & Gould, 2006). From our perspective, the scholarly discussion of differences helps move a field forward. Scholarly debate is the essence of scientific growth.

In this book, we offer a definition of the forensic model. We have noted elsewhere (Martindale & Gould, 2004) that no one yet has operationally defined the concept of the forensic model as applied to custody work. In our "Ethics and Methods" chapter here (Chapter 3), we provide what we believe is a useful, operational definition of the forensic model. We use the term "forensic model" throughout the book to refer to the manner in which child custody evaluations ought to be conducted and the manner in which forensic evaluators ought to approach their investigative task.

Kuehnle (1998a) described the *scientist-practitioner model* to require conclusions based upon "empirically established relationships between data and the behavior of interest" (p. 5). We wish to acknowledge Kuehnle's influence in our development of the *forensic model*. Kuehnle's application of the scientist-practitioner model to the investigation of child sexual abuse allegations rests upon the Boulder scientist-practitioner model (Committee on Training in Clinical Psychology, 1950) that has dominated most training programs in clinical and counseling psychology over the past 50 years. Use of the forensic model does not stifle the creativity of the evaluator. The model identifies minimum expectations for professional practice and it identifies a common set of general methods and procedures aimed at gathering reliable and relevant information about a family under investigation. We believe that our definition of the forensic model adds to Kuehnle's scientist-practitioner model by building specifically on the relationship between psychology and law that is the fabric of forensic psychological practice.

We began writing this book with the intention that it would teach mental health professionals how to conduct child custody evaluations. That is, we wanted to build upon Jon's earlier text. As we became more involved in organizing the current behavioral science research applied to child custody, we made several decisions. First, we decided that there were several useful scholarly works already available that clearly articulated the forensic model in general (e.g., Goldstein, 2003; Heilbrun, 2001; Melton, Petrila, Poythress, & Slobogin, 1997) and that there were several useful scholarly works already available that clearly articulated how the forensic model could be applied to child custody work (e.g., Ackerman, 2001; Ackerman & Kane, 2003; Baerger et al., 2003; Galatzer-Levy et al., 2002; Gould, 2006; Gould & Bell, 2000; Gould & Stahl, 2000; Gould & Lehrmann, 2002; Otto, Buffington-Vollum, & Edens, 2003). In writing this book, we endeavored to distinguish it from other books already available, including the second edition of Jon's earlier work (Gould, 2006).

Our secondary intention was to write a book that provided both a strong endorsement of the forensic model applied to child custody evaluations and scientifically informed opinions about current and controversial areas of assessment often seen in child custody work. In particular, we were interested in bringing together ideas found in the literature on domestic violence, child sex abuse, trauma and maltreatment, child alienation, and child and women's advocacy that heretofore had not been incorporated into mainstream writing about child custody evaluations. We turned our attention to integrating bodies of literature that had previously been discrete works of scholarship not well integrated into the child custody literature. We wanted to write a book that would help the sophisticated evaluator think through some of the more challenging and perplexing issues that are part of our everyday work.

We make no claim that this book sets a new standard. We have labored to analyze and to synthesize areas of literature applied to child custody work that have not been included in previous books. We have brought together a vast array of information about domestic violence, sexual abuse, child maltreatment, and alienation dynamics, with the intention of creating awareness among evaluators of the need to create a uniform assessment model. We have assembled information about the forensic interview of children that has yet to be presented in child custody books. We have synthesized information about the use of specific psychological tests and measures, and we have elaborated upon investigative protocols that should impose a structure upon the forensic evaluation of complex issues in child custody assessment.

We both wish that the underlying scientifically informed assessment methods and procedures used in forensic assessments were more mature in many areas of forensic practice. We also wish that the empirical foundation for scientifically informed psychological opinions offered to the court had more robust empirical support. Nevertheless, we are convinced that the current state of the art in child custody assessment is strong enough to justify a call for child custody evaluators to uniformly embrace the forensic model. Accordingly, we believe that as a profession, we can no longer justify choosing to endorse and use assessment methods that have no empirical support in the literature (Martindale, 2006; Martindale & Gould, 2006).

It seems obvious to us that forensic psychology must finally do more than pay lip service to the forensic model. The stakes for doing so are higher now than they have ever been. Science informs practice. Practice does not inform science. This book is another step toward outlining the extensive literature across several disciplines that addresses issues associated with the application of current research and current forensic methods and procedures to an understanding of the best psychological interests of the child.

Our hearts are with the children of divorce. Our concerns are with the families and their struggles to create healthy binuclear families. We wish to find ways to reduce divorce-related conflict, and we wish to find ways to encourage the nonlitigious settlement of custodial disputes. Not one of these interests, concerns, or motives is in conflict with the desire to utilize the science and scholarship of our respective disciplines, and not one of these interests, concerns, or motives is in conflict with the desire to conduct forensic mental health assessments dispassionately.

Contents

PART III

The Science of Child Custody Evaluations: Factors to Assess in Child Custody Evaluations

PART IV

The Art and Science of Child Custody Evaluations: Assessing Allegations of Maltreatment

PART I

Child Custody Evaluations and the Best Interests of the Child

CHAPTER 1

Introduction

This book focuses on the evolving and dynamic interdependence between the behavioral sciences and family law in child custody evaluations and, more specifically, the role of the forensic evaluator when allegations of child maltreatment arise in child custody disputes. In many ways, this should be the healthiest dialogue between the two disciplines because the role boundaries and expectations applied to the evaluator role are more clearly delineated in the published literature than for other forensic mental health roles (Ackerman & Kane, 1998; Galatzer-Levy & Krauss, 1999; Gould, 2006; Greenberg & Shuman, 1997; Greenberg & Gould, 2001). This book teaches mental health professionals who conduct child custody evaluations to make such evaluations more useful to the courts and more valuable to the families who are engaged in the evaluation process. We contend that a scientifically informed child custody evaluation that is designed to meet at least the minimum legal standards of admissibility as a scientific work product best serves both courts and families.

There are many challenges within the field of child custody work for mental health practitioners. One challenge is created by the failure of both graduate schools and internship programs to prepare clinicians for work within an adversarial context. Another challenge is the apparent lack of understanding of what an expert is and how mental health professionals have a moral as well as an ethical obligation when they agree to serve as experts to meet the demands of that role competently. Other challenges includes learning how to craft an evaluation so that the information gathered will meet the standards of admissibility required by the legal system and finding an effective means by which to maintain one's expertise (an endeavor that demands keeping abreast of changing statutes and case law, research findings, and developments in assessment methods and procedures).

The Purpose of a Child Custody Evaluation

The primary purpose of a child custody evaluation is to provide information to the court and the family about the best psychological interests of the child or children. In Chapter 2, we explore the meanings and definitional limitations surrounding the concept of the best psychological interests of the child. In this chapter, we discuss what defines a child custody evaluation and provide a brief historical overview of conceptual frameworks that have been developed and refined to assist mental health professionals in constructing child custody evaluations.

The American Psychological Association's child custody guidelines (1994) made a subtle yet substantial modification when they added the adjective *psychological* to the definition of the best interests of the child (Guideline 14, p. 679). Mental health practitioners are encouraged not to provide testimony about the ultimate legal issue because of the limitations inherent in a psychological investigation. For example, we often are asked not to examine the financial issues involved in equitable distribution of property and its effect on children while recognizing that such a factor may play a role in the judge's decision. Similarly, factors outside the scope of behavioral science research such as questions about morality or theology may affect the judge's decision making and be outside the sphere of expertise of a psychologist. We need to recognize and respect what is and is not within the scope of our professional expertise and stay within its limits.

The Relationship between Law and Psychology

Historically, the relationship between law and psychology has been somewhat difficult to manage, in part because the rules and expectations of the mental health practitioner's role within the legal system have been poorly defined. This poor definition has resulted in controversies within the field of psychology about what constitutes ethical and appropriate involvement in the legal system, and concern about this ambiguity has stimulated efforts to define better role differences between clinical and forensic functions (Greenberg & Shuman, 1997, 2007; Heltzel, 2007) as well as efforts to delineate better for judges and attorneys the appropriate boundaries of testimony offered by treating therapists working within a forensic context (Greenberg & Gould, 2001; Greenberg, Martindale, Gould, & Gould-Saltman, 2004). There has been an unfolding dialogue between the courts and custody evaluators focusing on the nature and quality of testimony by forensic psychological experts as contrasted with testimony by treating practitioners (Shuman, Greenberg, Heilbrun, & Foote, 1998; Krauss & Sales, 1999, 2000). Additionally, both within the courts and within the profession of psychology, increased concern has been expressed regarding the offering of clinical opinions masquerading as scientific knowledge (Gould & Martindale, 2005; Shuman & Sales, 1998, 1999; Tippins & Wittmann, 2005).

These evolving dialogues have resulted in some interesting interdisciplinary demands, such as when a clinician receives a subpoena to testify about ongoing treatment. Often, the clinician is an unwilling participant in litigation. The court (or an attorney) believes that the clinician has information that cannot be obtained through other avenues of testimony. The clinician is directed to disclose to the court information obtained during treatment that was never intended to leave the therapy office and certainly never considered appropriate for placement in the public record. In circumstances such as these, the role boundaries and expectations placed on the clinician by the court are often poorly defined. Providing testimony about treatment when the initial therapy contract did not anticipate forensic involvement may assist the court, but it may also serve to undermine an effective therapeutic relationship by forcing the clinician to offer an opinion in open court that would never have been spoken otherwise.

When clinicians provide court-ordered treatment, the dialogue between the clinician and the court is often more cooperative and collegial, but there are still tensions between the clinician's need to protect the privacy rights of the therapy client and the content of the treatment sessions and the court's need for complete and accurate information. Recent writings have suggested a model for conducting treatment in a forensic context and have called upon the profession of psychology to develop a set of professional practice guidelines that might assist clinicians in performing their clinical roles within the context of ongoing legal involvement (Gould & Greenberg, 2000; Greenberg & Gould, 2001; Greenberg, Gould, Gould-Saltman, & Stahl, 2001; Greenberg, Martindale, Gould, & Gould-Saltman, 2004). Similarly, Barsky and Gould (2002) have proposed a set of steps to help the nonforensic clinician understand how to navigate the legal system. The evolving dialogue in these areas of psycholegal practice is increasingly focused on developing a foundation for ethical and competent clinical testimony within the legal system.

Although the discussion of clinical treatment within a forensic context is a rich topic for examination, it is not the focus of this book. The topic is included because, often, those involved in the practice of child custody work are also involved in providing treatment services to families in transition and/or are asked to contribute to the analysis of the best psychological interests of the child in a critical evaluation for the court of treatment services offered by others. These references are offered as a starting point for further readings and thought about this complex issue.

A Very Hot Kitchen

Forensic psychology in general and child custody evaluations in particular have been a draw for many mental health practitioners seeking to avoid the long arm of managed care. One result of the intrusion of managed care into the previously autonomously run practices of psychologists is that more and more clinicians are offering to perform services in nonclinical specialties as a means to escape the tentacles of the current health care system (Gould, 2006; Goldstein, 2003). Mental health practitioners entering the child custody field are stepping into a very complex and formidable area of work. As Kirkland and Kirkland (2001) state,

> The area of child custody evaluations is potentially one of the most stressful and difficult for psychologists because of high levels of emotionality and acrimony associated with the process and the participants. . . . It is speculated that child custody evaluations are among the most dangerous and risky endeavors for psychologists, owing to high levels of stress, threat of litigation, risk of board complaints, and even the possibility of personal harm. (p. 171)

Despite these apparent risks, mental health professionals are increasingly entering the forensic arena. Some are skilled in forensic thinking and the application of forensic methodology and procedures to psycholegal questions. Others step into the forensic arena with a poor understanding of the differences between clinical and forensic roles and responsibilities (Greenberg & Gould, 2001; Greenberg & Shuman, 1997) as well as of standard forensic methods and procedures (Gould, 2004; Kirkpatrick, 2004; Martindale & Gould, 2004). Many lack basic forensic training, while others do not know about admissibility standards for expert witness testimony such as the implications of *Frye* (*Frye v. United States*, 1923), *Daubert* (*Daubert v. Merrell Dow Pharmaceuticals*, 1993), or *Kumho Tire* (*Kumho Tire Company Ltd. et al. v. Carmichael et al.*, 1999) rulings on courtroom testimony.

The arena of child custody work is complex and requires effort to stay current. Kirkland and Kirkland (2001) suggested several defensive steps that the wise evaluator should take in anticipation of "an eventual and inevitable complaint" (p. 174). Among the recommended defensive steps is to ensure that one's work reflects a thorough compliance with all specific state and national guidelines. Kirkland and Kirkland encourage examiners to "stay on top of the developing ethical and procedural literature" and to "avoid any role conflicts or even possible sources of perceived bias" (p. 174). They stress the importance of using collateral interviews and multiple data sources and recommend not addressing the ultimate issue before the court and carefully considering test interpretation, taking particular care not to over- or underinterpret psychological test data.

Stop and think about the Kirkland and Kirkland (2001) suggestion that child custody evaluators should construct their forensic practice in anticipation of an eventual and inevitable complaint. Evaluators would be wise to heed the caution of Kirkland and Kirkland. Simply stated, child custody work can be both demanding and anxiety producing. Mental health professionals who enter the forensic arena as it is currently structured need to be prepared for participation in an adversarial process.

Attorneys receive training in the art of adversarial exchange. Those who learn well and who are by temperament comfortable with oral battle become active litigators. The others handle matters of law that do not bring them in to the courtroom. Litigators are prepared to spend days or weeks in the courtroom battling with their colleagues over issues of law. They challenge. They argue. They play strategic games with the facts. During their courtroom time, attorneys zealously advocate for their clients' positions and work hard at undermining the credibility of witnesses offering testimony not supportive of their positions before the court. When it is over, most attorneys shake hands and leave the adversarial spirit in the courtroom.

Probably as a result of having been trained as clinicians, many mental health professionals seem to have thinner skin. We are not trained in the art of advocacy nor do we spend our professional time in an adversarial setting. We expect empathy, honesty, concern, and support from our colleagues. Our training compels us to be gentle, compassionate, understanding, forgiving, and constructive in our criticism.

When mental health professionals offer their services as custody evaluators, sometimes they will be required to function in a work environment that is foreign to them: the courtroom. The task of experts, regardless of the manner in which they are being compensated for time expended, is to assist the trier of fact—to function as educators. Effective expert witnesses must develop the ability to maintain their composure and to focus on the task of communicating useful information to the court while attorneys treat the courtroom as though it were a battlefield. Forensic psychological experts must be able to endure aggressive (and, in some cases, deliberately nasty) cross-examination. Just as our teaching colleagues cannot allow their concentration to be impaired by disruptive students, we must stay focused on our educative function in the court. Cross-examining attorneys are ethically obligated to do whatever they can to cast doubt on evidence that is unfavorable to their clients. It is not personal.

The advisory report filed at the conclusion of a child custody evaluation should provide the trier of fact with a rational and scientific foundation for the interpretations, conclusions, and recommendations offered to the court. In preparing their reports, evaluators must focus on the objective: providing pertinent information about the family system. While denigration, criticism based on personal values, and reprimands are counterproductive, so is excessive concern for the emotional comfort of the litigants. Evaluators must recognize that they are obligated to articulate what data-gathering methods were utilized, what data were obtained, how those data bear upon the criteria that are collectively referred to as the *best interests standard*, and the logical nexus between the data and the opinions and recommendations offered.

There is a very interesting movement developing across the United States called *collaborative law*, in which conciliation and negotiation replace aggressive advocacy (e.g., Fagerstrom, 1997; Tesler & Thompson, 2006). It is beyond the scope of this book to discuss collaborative law except to observe that it is interesting, progressive, and potentially of greater use to certain families than the current adversarial system.

We would welcome a change in the current system that would call upon mental health professionals to prepare for participation in one of the legal system's most highly contentious arenas. We believe that within the emerging concept of collaborative law, mental health professionals may play an important role in providing useful information about family functioning that can be used to assist the family in better managing their transition from an intact family to a binuclear family (Ahrons, 1987). It will likely be many, many years (if ever) before the collaborative law movement replaces the current system of advocacy.

The reality of today's legal system and the ways in which mental health professionals participate in that system suggests that we need to be prepared for an adversarial process. Kirkland and Kirkland (2001) remind us that, after successfully negotiating the litigation process in which reports are used, evaluators often are the subject of licensing board investigations resulting from the "acrimonious complaints of an angered party" (p. 172). Their study found that a child custody complaint is "unlikely to result in a finding of formal fault or in a revocation, but this is little joy for the practitioner whose license is in administrative purgatory during the response and defense period of the complaint" (p. 174).

A well-researched and well-written report is an important step in helping the family understand how to rehabilitate itself and how to assist specific family members in gaining the management skills and emotional competencies needed to help children move toward their psychological potential. A well-crafted report can provide relevant and useful information to the court, the attorneys, and the family while preserving the dignity of the family so that postdivorce healing can take place more effectively. Mental health professionals help promote understanding and change. We neither encourage nor support conflict with the intent of facilitating one party's litigation strategy. Our job is to paint a picture of a child's life within a binuclear family context. The task of the forensic psychological evaluator is to describe with clarity, knowledge, objectivity, and compassionate understanding the struggles each family has endured in moving from a stable, intact nuclear unit to a binuclear unit in which the children need to learn how to accept and cope with their changing world.

Whether the information contained in an advisory report encourages settlement or is utilized as an instrument in litigation, a report should be scientifically informed in order to provide the best possible specialized knowledge for the family, the attorneys, and the court. An appropriately prepared report outlining the findings of a scientifically informed evaluation should be useful either in settlement discussions or in litigation. In either case, we must focus upon the reliability, relevance, and helpfulness (Krauss & Sales, 1999) of the information contained in the report.

Changing Paradigms

One might argue that the field of child custody evaluations is undergoing a paradigm shift (Kuhn, 1969). When paradigms change, conflict is inevitable. There is conflict over the nature of the change, over the direction of the change, and over the speed of the change. We believe that the paradigm shift is from a clinically based model emphasizing the clinical judgment of the evaluator (Calloway, 2002) to a forensically based model (Martindale & Gould, 2004) emphasizing the gathering of reliable data from independent sources and using reliable methods and procedures from which is sought convergence between or among independent data sources that may be used to confirm or disconfirm specific hyphotheses.

Across the United States, there are battles occurring in some communities over how to conduct child custody evaluations. One side argues that child custody evaluations are clinical exercises, limited to testing and in-office clinical interviews. The other side stresses the need to conduct child custody evaluations as forensic evaluations are conducted. Child custody evaluations utilize a five-pronged methodology, including semistructured interview questionnaires, psychological tests, self-report measures, direct behavioral observation, and extensive collateral record review and collateral interviews (Austin, 2000d, 2002; Austin & Kirkpatrick, 2004; Gould, 1998, 2006; Heilbrun, 2001; Heilbrun, Warren, & Picarello, 2003; Otto, Buffington-Volkam, & Edens, 2003).

Those who encourage the use of conventional forensic methods and procedures find support among the major professional organizations that have published guidelines (e.g., American Academy of Child and Adolescent Psychiatry, 1997b; American Psychological Association, 1994) or standards (Association of Family and Conciliation Courts, 2007) as well as from workshop providers who offer training in child custody evaluations through organizations such as the American Academy of Forensic Psychology, the American Psychological Association, and the Association of Family and Conciliation Courts. Judging from a review of the literature and the contents of workshops offered across the United States, there seems to be little question that the movement toward a scientifically informed model of child custody evaluations has taken hold (Bow & Quinnell, 2002; Kirkland, 2002; Kirkpatrick, 2004; Tippins & Wittmann, 2005). Those who continue to endorse the older, clinical model (e.g., Calloway, 2002; Trubitt, 2004) are, in our view, failing to meet their ethical responsibility to provide forensic services at the highest level of professional competence (Committee on Ethical Guidelines for Forensic Psychologists, 1991) because of the potential impact that an expert's opinion may have on the decision-making process in a custody trial. As discussed later, those who rely solely upon clinical methodology and clinical judgment and fail to utilize reliable and relevant forensic methods and procedures may be conducting themselves in a manner inconsistent with the ethical obligations of their profession and undermining the credibility of all psychological experts who serve the court (Tippins & Wittmann, 2005; Weissman & DeBow, 2003). There is an emerging awareness of the critical distinction between providing expert witness testimony based upon clinical opinion and providing expert witness testimony based upon information drawn from forensic methodology (Shuman & Sales, 1998). The competent evaluator needs to be aware of these important issues.

Limitations of Clinical Judgment in a Forensic Context

Clinicians entering the world of custody evaluations encounter references to a controversy concerning the use of clinically versus scientifically informed methods. The concern about clinical judgment used in a forensic context is reflected in several recent articles. Summarizing the controversy, Shuman and Sales (1998) make the following points:

1. While some expert testimony by people with scientific degrees is derived from research the accuracy of which can be validated, much other expert testimony advances opinions derived from judgments in which accuracy rests on the experts' nonvalidated theories and skills.
2. These untested opinions are commonly referred to as "clinical" judgments and are defined by their reliance on personal experience rather than on statistically analyzed data drawn from valid and reliable research.
3. Use of the term "clinical" refers to a method or approach of making judgments or decisions.
4. The growing literature on human judgment and decision making helps explain the inherent unreliability of clinical judgment and decision making.
5. Expert judgments that are clinically derived are as susceptible to error as lay judgments and involve the use of strategies in arriving at decisions that contribute to the error rate.
6. Clinical judgments and opinions offered in court are just as flawed as any other clinical judgment.
7. To the extent that a scientist or practitioner is relying on personal experience and personal biases in drawing inferences that go beyond the data, he or she is engaging in clinical decision making, despite his or her scientific training.

The Importance of a Scientifically Informed Approach

Increasingly, mental health professionals are being asked to conform their oral testimony and their written work product to standards of *evidence-based practice* (Greeno, 2001). Whether mental health professionals are providing clinical or forensic services, there is an increasing need them to base their methods and techniques upon research that supports the efficacy of those methods and techniques (Martindale & Gould, 2006; Tippins & Wittmann, 2005).

A careful reading of our ethical responsibilities and best practices aspirations (Committee on Ethical Guidelines for Forensic Psychologists, 1991; Association of Family and Conciliation Courts, 2007; American Psychological Association, 1992, 2002; American Psychiatric Association, 1994) and of documents reflecting the current state of forensic mental health and law clearly indicates that child custody evaluators need to base their work products on scientifically informed methods and research (Amundson, Duda, & Gill, 2000; Austin, 2001; Galatzer-Levy & Krauss, 1999; Gould & Stahl, 2000; Otto et al., 2003; Roseby, 1995; Wingspread Conference Report and Action Plan, 2001).

Science and Practice

Ideally, clinical psychology should be based on scientifically and empirically validated principles, techniques, and theory. Pope (1996) wrote:

> Science works best when claims and hypotheses can be continually questioned. That which tends to disallow doubt and discredit anyone who disagrees is unlikely to foster the scientific venture or promote public policies and clinical practices based on scientific principles. Each scientific claim should prevail or fail on its research validation and logic. (p. 971)

The Forensic Model

Kuehnle (1998a) has applied the forensic model of assessment to evaluating allegations of child sexual abuse. Although she has used the term *scientist practitioner model*, we believe that her operational definitions of the role of the evaluator and of the scope and purpose of an investigation of sexual abuse allegations are analogous to our concept of the forensic model as applied to child custody evaluations.

Another term recently introduced at conferences that purports to describe a more child-sensitive model of custody evaluations is the *clinical/child-based evaluation model* (Calloway & Lee, 2002). We conducted a literature search on this term and found no citations. We also asked colleagues on several professional forensic and clinical listservs if anyone had heard of the model or could lead us to literature that described the model, but we received no information.

We were curious about both the origin and the conceptual underpinnings of this model. We noted earlier in this chapter that the first guideline of the American Psychological Association's child custody guidelines (1994) declares, "The primary purpose of the evaluation is to assess the best psychological interests of the child" (p. 678). As we presume that most, if not all, child custody evaluators respect these guidelines and endeavor to conduct evaluations accordingly, we cannot imagine a model focused on child custody assessment that would not be child-based.

We believe that people who speak about a clinical/child-based evaluation model are creating tension where none need exist. We found two articles that appeared to address this model, neither of which used the term. The first article, written by Vivienne Roseby (1995) was a building block in our field's movement toward the use of reliable methods, its support for scientifically informed opinions based upon reliable data, and its concern for offering opinions to the court that do not go beyond the appropriate interpretations of the data. Reflecting concerns about clinical hunches offered as scientifically informed opinions, Roseby writes, "Not surprisingly, mental health professionals have at times been criticized for exceeding the limitations of empirically based scientific knowledge in their efforts to be responsive" to the needs of the court (p. 97). She provides a model for child custody evaluations that is similar to the current forensic model.

Roseby identifies four assumptions that should guide child custody evaluations:

1. Minimize the parents' sense of shame and exposure and maximize their understanding of the child's needs and experiences.
2. Explicate the causes and potential avenues for diffusing the parental conflict and its effects upon the child.
3. Evaluate each parent's concern and characterological capacity to resolve the parental conflict as well as to meet the child's needs over time.
4. Identify what custody plan, support, and/or arbitration structures will be needed to support the child's development in the short and long term.

Roseby offers some interesting observations about the use of psychological test data in child custody evaluations. She warns of the dangers of interpreting test data without understanding the context of the testing. She also stresses the need to consider "all psychological test data . . . as working hypotheses which can be disconfirmed or further supported and understood in the context of information obtained by other methods" (p. 99).

Roseby argues against evaluators using psychological tests conducted and interpreted by their colleagues. She writes,

> When psychological reports are completed and returned to the evaluator, an incongruity arises. Specifically, the testing was not conducted by the same pair of

eyes, the same mind, the same sifter and sorter as the person who conducted the rest of the evaluation. As a result, the ways in which testing confirms or disconfirms other information are not fully explained and the explicit effects of test data on the final recommendations are not elucidated. When psychological test data are not braided into the logic of the overall evaluation, the data are weakened and legitimately vulnerable in court. (p. 99)

We see *no* conflict between what Roseby described in her "child focused approach" to child custody evaluations and the forensic model. In fact, we were impressed with her ability to recognize, 10 years ago, concerns that have only recently become part of usual and customary practice among child custody evaluators.

We also found an unpublished article by John M. Palen entitled "Child Custody Evaluations: Uses and Misuses" (*www.illinoisbar.org/Sections.8uses. html*), in which he describes "the components of a child-focused evaluation." After consultation and review with Palen, we summarized his article:

1. "In a child-centered assessment the focus is on identifying the needs of the child as well as the strengths and weaknesses of each parent as they affect his or her ability to parent." Palen describes this focus as "the cornerstone to a child-centered evaluation."
2. "The goal of the evaluation is to develop a parenting plan that maximizes the child's exposure to each parent's capabilities while protecting him [or her] as much as possible from their limitations."
3. "This [goal] is accomplished with a comprehensive evaluation that investigates specific concerns—identified by the court at the outset—by tapping into multiple sources of data that include: [a] extensive individual clinical interviews with parents and children that employ both open-ended and structured questions; [b] observations of each parent with each child—sometimes at each home as well as at the office; [c] review of relevant documents and records; [d] interviews with collateral sources such as teachers, physicians, and therapists; and [e] psychological testing as needed."
4. "When the same evaluator talks with all family members, attorneys, therapists, and teachers, a more comprehensive view of the family and its needs can emerge."
5. A "child-focused custody evaluation results in specific recommendations that facilitate the continued development of both children and parents."
6. When an evaluator goes on a "pathology hunt," "the task of understanding the child's needs becomes peripheral to that of exposing the parent's imperfections, mistakes, and failures—even if these limitations lie outside of the realm of parenting. . . . [A] parent's mental health *per se* is not an indicator of parenting capacity. . . . Routine psy-

chological testing within a context that is focused on uncovering parental pathology is a misuse of an important tool. . . . "

7. The "findings of the report [should be presented] to the parents together or separately in a conference with the evaluator and with their attorneys present."

8. The "ethical guidelines of the American Psychological Association require that clients who have been evaluated for any reason be given this opportunity. In addition, the Association of Family and Conciliation Courts *Model Standards of Practice for Child Custody Evaluation* require that the results of psychological testing be discussed with the adult participants in the evaluation—especially if the results indicate the need for psychological treatment or counseling."

9. "In summary, a child-focused evaluation should: [a] minimize the parents' sense of shame and exposure and maximize their understanding of their child's needs; [b] explain the causes of the parental conflict, discuss its effects on the child, and suggest ways to diffuse it; [c] evaluate each parent's current and historical capacity to resolve the conflict as well as his or her ability to meet the child's needs over time; and [d] identify what custody and time-sharing plan and supportive services will be needed to support the child's development in the short and long term."

We see *no* conflict between what Palen has described and what we refer to as the forensic model.

We acknowledge the frustration that some mental health and legal professionals have with the adversarial context within which child custody evaluations are currently presented to the court. There are legitimate differences about how mental health professionals currently interact with the legal system and how they should optimally interact with it.

In our peer-reviewed writings, our workshops and seminars, and our professional consultations, we have sought to address ways in which the methods of behavioral science may be properly applied in the search for answers to psycholegal questions. Both in our professional publications and in our court reports, we have emphasized our responsibility as forensic specialists to offer alternative plausible hypotheses. Neither in our own nor in others' writings on the forensic model do we find any statements that might encourage forensic psychologists to characterize findings or opinions in terms such as "right" or "wrong." Martindale has pointed out that an honest expert offers an "acknowledgment of the known methodological limitations inherent in evaluations of comparative custodial suitability" (Martindale, 2001a, p. 505), and we both have written about the need for transparency in all forensic activities associated with the role and activities of an evaluator (Gould, 2006; Martindale, 2004).

There is a strong emphasis on psychological fact finding in forensic work. Greenberg and Shuman (1997) refer to the need to focus attention on *historical truth*, that is, to focus attention on finding data that helps understand how people behaved in the real world. As Gould put it, the "scrutiny applied to information used in the process and the role of historical truth" in forensic evaluations is based upon the view that "litigant information [should be] supplemented with and verified by collateral sources and scrutinized by the examiner, adversaries, and the court" (Gould, 1998, p. 17). Current texts also support the need to obtain historical truth in the manner described above (see Goldstein, 2003; Heilbrun, 2001).

It is likely that all mental health professionals involved in custody-related work would agree that child custody advisory reports should be used in the most constructive manner possible, but disagreement might exist concerning how best to accomplish this goal. Custody advisory reports should not be used as weapons in custody battles to determine who won and who lost. In our view, an advisory report should focus on the specifically defined questions posed by the court or the attorneys (Amundson et al., 2000; Gould, 1999). It should be written in a manner that respects the family system and encourages a parenting plan that accentuates each parent's positive qualities (Gould & Stahl, 2000; Roseby, 1995) while realistically describing how each parent's limitations may adversely affect each child's best psychological interests. It should also be written in a way that allows the reader to understand from the child's point of view what it is like to live with each parent (Smart, 2006) and what it is like to adjust to the new living situation (Smart, 2002; Smart & Neale, 2000). We do not support an allegations-based approach (Benjamin & Gollan, 2003) or a pathology-based approach; rather, we stress the need to help the family create a functioning system that supports not only the best psychological interests of the children, but also the establishment of healthy family functioning across households.

There may be times when cross-examination will feel adversarial and when a cross-examining attorney and an expert will feel hostile toward each other. Additionally, during legal proceedings, mental health colleagues may be directed by the court to refrain from communication with one another. Such limitations on collegial contact may create tension between colleagues with opposing views. If the "collegial exchange of ideas" is prohibited by the court (or by virtue of the agreement between a retained psychologist and the retaining attorney) and if, as a result, a "hostile environment" evolves (Calloway, 2002, p. 216), it cannot logically be declared that utilization of the forensic model by one or both psychologists has created the unpleasantness. The forensic model encourages the application of reliable and relevant research to the particular family that is the focus of the evaluation. We find no support for the notion that "individual differences are overlooked" or that the forensic model "ignores the interplay between [the] idiopathic and [the] general" (Calloway, 2002, p. 217). In fact, the excellent work of Krauss and Sales (1999), Shuman and Sales (1999), Tippins and Wittmann (2005), and others has helped us integrate the complexities of legal admissibility standards into child custody assessment. A recent article in which Gould and psychologist Phil Stahl provide a set of decision rules to use in the application of current child development research to a particular family system (Gould & Stahl, 2001) serves as an example of how current authors of the forensic model stress the importance of the interplay between idiopathic and general information.

In summary, we believe that there is great value in the forensic model. We also believe that there is overwhelming support in current behavioral science literature and in presentations offered at professional conferences for the premise that the forensic model is the most parsimonious and most useful model of data gathering that has been devised to date.

The Forensic Model in Child Custody Evaluations

The scientist-practitioner model has been at the foundation of modern training in professional psychology for almost half a century. Its strength lies in resolving tensions between the use of scientific knowledge and the use of clinical judgment. One cannot exist without the other. Scientific knowledge informs clinical and forensic decision making, of which clinical judgment is a critical component. Where science provides facts, clinical judgment integrates facts into context. Where clinical judgment provides intuitive understanding, science incorporates experiences into a theoretical framework about human behavior. We refer to this integration of scientific information and clinical judgment as *scientific expertise*. We do not suggest a formula for determining what part of scientific expertise is based on research and what part is based on clinical judgment; we merely note that each is a necessary component for the development of a competently crafted and ethical forensic work product.

Psychologists are assumed to be expert in aspects of psychological science due to their training, licensure, experience, and education. Not every psychologist is expert in all areas of psychology, and even experts within a specialized field are likely not to be familiar with everything that has been published within that field, but an expert in a specific area is expected to know more than a generalist and the expert who specializes is expected to be familiar with both the historical and the current literature in his or her field.

Advantages of a Scientifically Informed Advisory Report

Science is characterized by its utilization of methods that help reduce or eliminate the inherent bias of casual, unfiltered impressions based upon personal beliefs and expectations (Martindale, 2005a). Scientific methods also help reduce bias attributable to professional beliefs and expectations (Greeno, 2001). As Greeno states:

> Most scientific techniques improve our ability to create careful documentation that enables us to perceive our world accurately. . . . Science provides us with spe-

cific techniques for decreasing bias around a number of activities. . . . the tools of social science can be regarded as having evolved in order to create a set of techniques to help us avoid a number of systematic mistakes we will make if our perceptions are unaided . . . but these techniques do not work perfectly, and there are times when scientific techniques do not make us more accurate. . . . There are constraints and limits on what we can perceive when we apply scientific techniques. (pp. 116–119)

Psychological experts differ from most other witnesses in their application of scientific methods to analyses of data. Psychological experts have no special expertise in determination of truth. What they offer the court is a method of analyzing information that is designed to identify, control, and, at times, eliminate subjectivity.

The scientific method and the model of scientifically crafting child custody evaluations discussed in this book will help protect the evaluator from the influences of mistaken impressions, unknown or unconscious biases, confirmatory bias, and other mistakes of perception and interpretation (Martindale, 2005a). The use of a scientifically informed methodology, integrated with appropriate scientific research about factors relevant to the family under scrutiny, will provide the evaluator with a firm evidentiary ground upon which to offer interpretations, opinions, and conclusions. The scientific method applied to child custody evaluations is not perfect. Science draws on special and unnatural techniques that create their own source of bias. One source of bias inherent in the scientific method is the use of techniques that impose upon our observations of human behavior an artificiality that is necessary to conduct rigorous and controlled observations of human behavior (Greeno, 2001). The rigor and control of some scientific observational techniques may affect the behaviors being observed by robbing them of the spontaneity that makes unique the quality of the human interaction. Observing interactions between parent and child is one example. Science has not developed a means by which to measure the unique aspects of the interactions observed between a loving parent and child. Despite the need to move so much of our evaluation methodology toward a scientifically informed model, there will always be room for the art of observation and clinical description (Gould & Stahl, 2000).

The Child Custody Evaluation as a Forensic Activity

A forensic evaluation is *not* the same as a clinical evaluation. The methods and procedures, the posture of the evaluator, and the intended audience for the work product are different. Greenberg and Shuman's (1997) seminal paper clearly articulated important differences between clinical and forensic roles.

For our purposes, it must be made clear that a child custody evaluation is a forensic evaluation. The form and content of the evaluation must be useful not only for the families being evaluated but also for the courts that may need the information contained in the evaluation. Courts can only utilize this important information when it is crafted in a manner consistent with rules of evidence (rules governing admissibility) and it is for this reason that a child custody evaluation must be conceptualized as a forensic activity.

It is also the general consensus, as expressed in the professional literature, that a child custody evaluation is a forensic activity. We are perplexed by those colleagues who insist that there are no professional practice guidelines indicating the need to craft a child custody evaluation as a forensic work product. Stated simply, if a psychologist knows (or should have known) at the time of accepting an assigned task that its end product will be used in an adjudicative setting, then it is by definition a forensic task. Any evaluation the findings from which are likely to be used in a legal proceeding is, by definition, a forensic evaluation (Committee on Ethical Guidelines for Forensic Psychologists, 1991).

According to the specialty guidelines for forensic psychologists (Committee on Ethical Guidelines for Forensic Psychologists, 1991), a child custody evaluation falls within the definition of forensic psychological activity. The specialty guidelines state:

> "Forensic psychology" means all forms of professional psychological conduct when acting, with definable foreknowledge, as a psychological expert on explicitly psycholegal issues, in direct assistance to courts, parties to a legal proceeding, correctional and forensic mental health facilities, and administrative, judicial, and legislative agencies acting in an adjudicative capacity. (p. 657)

The guidelines for child custody evaluations in divorce proceedings (American Psychological Association, 1994) also consider a child custody evaluation as a forensic psychological activity. The guidelines state, "Psychological data and expertise, gained through a child custody evaluation, can provide an additional source of information and an additional perspective not otherwise readily available to the court on what appears to be in the child's best interest, and thus can increase the fairness of the determination the court must make" (p. 678).

The American Academy of Child and Adolescent Psychiatry (1997b) takes a similar position and distinguishes between treating clinicians and custody evaluators. Treating clinicians are advocates or agents for children and ideally are partners with parents or guardians in the therapeutic alliance. Child custody evaluators, while guided by the best interests of the child, have no duty to the child or to the child's parents. Custody evaluators report to the court or to retaining attorneys. The aim of the custody evaluation is not to relieve suffering or to treat symptoms but to provide objective information and informed opinions to help the court render a custody decision.

The recently published Association of Family and Conciliation Courts *Model Standards of Practice for Child Custody Evaluation* (2007) provide the most comprehensive statement addressing a child custody evaluation as a forensic activity:

(a) Child custody evaluation is a process through which information and opinions bearing upon the custody of, parenting of, and access to children can be made known to the court, to the litigants, and to the litigants' attorneys in those cases in which the parents and/or other primary caregivers are unable to develop their own parenting plans. An evaluation may be requested by the parents or by their attorneys or may be ordered by the court. . . . (b) The application of the knowledge and skills of the mental health professions to the resolution of legal matters is, by definition, a forensic endeavor and these *Model Standards* have been written from that perspective. . . . Prior to commencing evaluations, evaluators shall take reasonable steps to secure court orders or consent agreements in which they are specifically named and in which their roles, the purposes of their evaluations, and the focus of their evaluations are clearly defined. . . . (p. 6, emphasis in original)

In a footnote to the *Model Standards*, the Association of Family and Conciliation Courts task force made clear the emphasis on the forensic nature of the evaluation.

In some jurisdictions, the term "forensic" is not employed in the construction of court orders and the evaluations performed for the courts may be referred to as "clinical" evaluations. Our purpose in emphasizing the forensic nature of the evaluative task is to call attention to two aspects of custody evaluations that distinguish them from other evaluations performed by mental health practitioners. First, because custody evaluations are performed in order that evaluators will be able to assist triers of fact by formulating opinions that can responsibly be expressed with a reasonable degree of professional certainty, sufficiency of information (both from a qualitative and from a quantitative perspective) is judged by a higher standard than that which might be applied to evaluations conducted within a treatment context. Second, notwithstanding the fact that reports prepared by evaluators are used for settlement purposes more often than they are used by the judges who have ordered the evaluations, evaluations must be conducted and reports must be written with the needs of the court in mind. (p. 25)

It is our position that the reports in which we outline the findings of a custody evaluation are forensic work products and should, for that reason, meet or exceed the minimal standard of evidentiary admissibility for scientific data. As soon as the evaluator knows (or should have reason to know) that his or her work product may be used in a legal arena, the quality of psychological data, as well as the methods, procedures, and reasoning used to arrive at his or her conclusions, should conform to conventional forensic psychological practice (Committee on Ethical Guidelines for Forensic Psychologists, 1991) in the area of child custody evaluation (American Psychological Association, 1994; Association of Family and Conciliation Courts, 2007). They must also meet the evidentiary standards of Federal Rules of Evidence (in particular, FRE 703) or their state equivalents governing the admissibility of scientific evidence (Goodman-Delahunty, 1997; Gould, 2006).

Because a child custody evaluation is a forensic activity, the evaluator bears a responsibility to conduct him- or herself in a manner consistent with that of a forensic specialist. In the case of psychology, the evaluator should be aware of the specialty guidelines for forensic psychologists (Committee on Ethical Guidelines for Forensic Psychologists, 1991), the guidelines for child custody evaluations in divorce proceedings (American Psychological Association, 1994), and the ethical principles of psychologists and code of conduct (American Psychological Association, 2002). In the case of psychiatry, the evaluator should be aware of the practice parameters for child custody evaluation (American Academy of Child and Adolescent Psychiatry, 1997b).

It also places a responsibility on the evaluator to employ forensic methods and procedures. There is a growing professional consensus that a five-pronged methodology drawn from conventional forensic mental health practice may be properly applied to child custody evaluations (Kirkpatrick, 2004) and that these forensic methods and procedures should be taken into account by attorneys (McCurley, Murphy, & Gould, 2006) and judges (Gould & Bell, 2000; Gould & Lehrmann, 2002) when considering what is and what is not a competent forensic work product.

What Judges and Attorneys Want

Recently, Bow and Quinnell (2004) published the data from a survey conducted among attorneys and judges. The responding judges and attorneys reported that their top reasons for child custody evaluation referrals were parental conflict, mental instability, allegations of physical or sexual abuse, and alcohol abuse. The most important components of a custody evaluation, in order, were discussions of the strengths and weaknesses of the parents, child information drawn from history and interview data, and recommendations for custody and visitation. Least important were the list of documents reviewed, family and parental histories, psychological testing of the child, and recommendations for other services such as therapy or parenting classes.

The number-one complaint in the survey about the use of child custody evaluators was the length of time taken to complete the evaluation. Other factors that concerned judges and attorneys were evaluators' lack of objectivity, lack of knowledge of legal criteria (e.g., knowing your state's best interests statute), and conclusions lacking supporting data (Bow & Quinnell, 2004).

Judges and attorneys reported that completion of a typical evaluation should take approximately 5–6 weeks and that the optimum length of a comprehensive report should be about 10 pages for judges and 12 pages for attorneys. In a previous survey of evaluators, Bow and Quinnell (2001), reported that completion of a child custody evaluation required an average of 9.27 weeks, with the most commonly reported times being 6 weeks (14%), 8 weeks (16%), and 12 weeks (11%). Evaluators gave an average report length of 21 pages, with a range from 4 to 80 pages.

In addition to reporting the concerns expressed by attorneys and judges,

Bow and Quinnell (2004) also relayed to their readers the suggestions offered by those attorneys and judges. For judges, the most common suggestion was that evaluators include all sources of information. Attorneys suggest that evaluations would be improved if evaluators avoided bias, provided data that logically supported their conclusions, and included specific, detailed recommendations.

When asked at what age a child's custodial preference should be considered, judges reported that they begin to consider a child's preference when the child is about 7 years old, while attorneys reported that they begin to consider a child's preference when the child is about 9 years old. Both attorneys and judges agree that the weight given to a child's preference should be a function of the child's maturity. In contrast, Bow and Quinnell (2001) reported that the average age of children when *evaluators* seriously consider their preferences in regard to custody decision criteria is about 12 years old.

An overwhelming number of judges (84%) and attorneys (86%) indicated that evaluators should provide recommendations about custody (Bow and Quinnell, 2004). An even higher percentage of judges (91%) and attorneys (90%) indicated that evaluators should provide recommendations for visitation. These data are consistent with Bow and Quinnell's (2001) finding that 94% of evaluators in their survey reported making explicit recommendations about custody and visitation.

Addressing who is selected as an expert witness, attorneys rated five factors as very important: objectivity, experience conducting custody evaluations, communication skills, presentation skills, and years of professional experience (Bow & Quinnell, 2004). Among the lowest rated factors were professional membership, diplomate or fellow status, and general/custody professional publications.

The value of Bow and Quinnell's work lies in providing evaluators with an understanding of what the consumers of our work product expect from us. Judges and attorneys expect briefer reports with more case-specific information that is obtained in a shorter amount of time than is reflected in current practice.

Pros and Cons of Offering Ultimate Issue Testimony

The concept of the ultimate issue refers to explicitly legal decisions that are within the domain of the court. In the field of child custody, ultimate issue testimony often involves opinions about custodial placement and of legal decision making. There is disagreement in the field about the appropriateness of offering ultimate opinion testimony in child custody work. On the one hand, Melton and Limber (1989) point out,

> Ultimate-issue opinions by mental health professionals do not assist the fact-finder, and they constitute legal opinions by definition outside the specialized

knowledge of mental health professionals. Therefore, they do not meet the standard for admissibility of expert opinions under Rule 702 (Federal Rules of Evidence). . . . As a matter of ethics, experts should not offer opinions as if they were based on specialized knowledge when they are not. (p. 83)

On the other hand, we believe that most judges want a specific recommendation as to custodial placement and would avoid using an evaluator who refuses to offer such an opinion. In many jurisdictions, the failure to offer such an opinion would throw a wrench into the traditional method of designating responsibility for experts' fees. Often responsibility for paying the expert is borne by the party who has been favored and, for that reason, the favored party wishes the report to be entered into evidence. In some jurisdictions, the opposite is true. It is presumed that a report prepared by a court-appointed evaluator will be entered into evidence and considered by the court. The party wishing to have the expert available for cross-examination (in the hopes of convincing the court that the recommendation in the report should not form the basis for the court's decision) accepts responsibility for the expert's fees. (See discussion of *State v. Kim* in Chapter 3.)

Wisely, the American Psychological Association (1994) assisted psychologists in defining the scope and limitations of expert testimony. Its use of the term *psychological* in conjunction with the concept of best interests clearly circumscribes the area of our expertise. We can provide expert testimony about the best psychological interests of the child providing that there are adequate data to form such an opinion.

Prior to assuming the role of an evaluator for the court, psychologists working with families in transition or with attorneys may wish to guide the parties to consider alternatives other than a custody evaluation. Among the options available are referrals to therapy, mediation, or a settlement-based model of custody determination. If alternatives to an evaluation are to be suggested, they must be suggested prior to the commencement of the evaluation. If recommended alternatives to a custody evaluation are communicated prior to any legal involvement by the psychologist (such as being court-appointed as the impartial evaluator), then the psychologist is operating within his or her proper role. If the psychologist recommends alternatives coincident with or subsequent to being appointed by the court or retained by the litigants' attorneys, then he or she may be operating outside appropriate ethical and professional practice parameters.

In a recent case in which one of us (Gould) was being considered by attorneys to evaluate a family involved in a relocation case, he participated in a conference call with the mother's and father's attorneys. The primary issue was the mother's challenge to a judge's temporary order. The parents had been married about 2 years prior to their separation. They had a child who was about 6 months old at the time of separation. The judge provided the mother with permission to relocate with the child to another state 500 miles from the original family residence. The judge also ordered the child to visit with the father for 2 contiguous weeks every third month. The mother complained that the child was adjusting poorly to the arrangement, while the father wanted to maintain the arrangement and refused to allow the mother to see the child during his visitation time.

During the conference call, Gould asked the attorneys if they were aware of the current literature about residential and access arrangements for infants and early-stage toddlers. Both attorneys indicated that they were. In fact, Gould had seen both attorneys attend a local presentation on this precise issue about 6 months prior. The attorneys recalled attending the workshop that addressed residential and access arrangements for infants and early-stage toddlers, but had not read the articles upon which the presentation was based. Gould asked if they would like citations for the research articles. The mother's attorney did, and the father's attorney did not. Gould forwarded the full written citations to both attorneys anyway.

During another conference call prior to the beginning of the evaluation, Gould explained his understanding of the current research and the recommendations that typically follow from the research. Both attorneys agreed that they understood the literature and wanted to proceed. Once the decision was made to appoint Gould as the court's expert, he did not raise the issue again.

Who Is the Client?

It is imperative to understand that the custody evaluator—whether appointed by a court order or consent order—is acting as the court's agent to assess the child's best psychological interests. Family law attorney Leslie Ellen Shear (personal communication, May 5, 2002) suggests that the client paradigm is inapplicable and should be avoided. Her view is that the appointed evaluator should view him- or herself as an arm of the court—almost as though he or she were a temporary employee of the court, rather than an independent practitioner assigned to perform a task for the court.

Psychologists working as custody evaluators are acting within a forensic role (Committee on Ethical Guidelines for Forensic Psychologists, 1991; Association of Family and Conciliation Courts, 2007; American Psychological Association, 1994) that demands evaluators maintain a distance between themselves and those they are evaluating. The relationship is dramatically different from that between clinicians and their clients (Greenberg & Shuman, 1997). The scope of the evaluation and the issues to be examined are determined by the court and/or by the litigants' attorneys. The report in which the findings of the evaluation are outlined is ordinarily distributed in a manner dictated by the court's appointment order. Reports are typically filed with the court and are often made available to the litigants' attorneys. (Evaluators do not ordinarily provide their reports to those who have been evaluated.)

The concepts of confidentiality and privilege are not applicable in custody evaluations. Quite simply, there is no patient and no therapist. The forensic evaluator's role is to examine the parents and children and obtain third-party information in the form of interviews with others and records review for the specific purpose of assisting the court in determining custodial placement and visitation. It is understood at the outset that, in order to assist the court, the information gathered must be communicated to others. Refer to Greenberg and Shuman (1997) for a fuller discussion of this issue.

Courts order evaluators to obtain psychological information about the children and families. It is hoped that if the information is complete, children will be spared the distress of having to offer testimony. If parents held the privilege to the information gathered by evaluators, they would be able to prevent its disclosure to the court. If parents or attorneys were gatekeepers of the information gathered by evaluators and needed by courts, much of it would be unavailable, and the need for further information would be met through testimony, including testimony by children.

Assessing the Best Psychological Interests of the Child within the Family Context

Although the American Psychological Association's (1994) custody guidelines state that "the primary consideration in a child custody evaluation is to assess the individual *and family factors* that effect the best psychological interests of the child" (p. 678, emphasis added), some authors believe that these guidelines did not sufficiently emphasize the importance of assessing and understanding the child within the context of the family (Gould & Kirkpatrick, 2001). It is critical for the evaluator to generate an understanding of the family/relational contextual variables that may have fueled the custodial dispute and may be preventing an out-of-court resolution.

American Psychological Association's Criteria

The American Psychological Association's (1994) guidelines for child custody evaluations identify the focus of a child custody evaluation as "to assess the individual and family factors that affect the best psychological interests of the child. More specific questions may be raised by the court" (p. 677). Toward this end, the American Psychological Association recommends an evaluation of parenting fitness, the psychological and developmental needs of the child, and a consideration of the resulting fit between each parent's parenting competencies and the needs of the child. To accomplish these evaluation goals, a child custody evaluation should involve (1) an assessment of each parent's capacities for parenting, (2) an assessment of the psychological functioning and developmental needs of the child and the wishes of the child where appropriate, and (3) an assessment of the functional ability of each parent to meet the needs of the child, which includes an evaluation of the interaction between each adult and the child (American Psychological Association, 1994).

Association of Family and Conciliation Courts Criteria

The Association of Family and Conciliation Courts' *Model Standards of Practice for Child Custody Evaluation* (2007) suggest that

> The child custody evaluation process involves the compilation of information and the formulation of opinions pertaining to the custody or parenting of a child and the dissemination of that information and those opinions to the court, to the litigants, and to the litigants' attorneys. Child custody evaluators shall secure from the court and/or attorneys reasonably detailed information concerning their role and the purpose and scope of the evaluation. (p. 5)

Departing from the previous *Model Standards* (Association of Family and Conciliation Courts, 1994) and from the American Psychological Association custody guidelines (American Psychological Association, 1994), in which specific criteria were identified, the 2007 Association of Family and Conciliation Courts *Model Standards* define the scope of the evaluative task as follows:

> The scope of the evaluation shall be delineated in a Court order or in a signed stipulation by the parties and their counsel. . . . (a) Evaluators shall establish the scope of the evaluation as determined by court order or by a signed stipulation by the parties and their attorneys. If issues not foreseen at the outset of an evaluation arise and if it is the evaluator's professional judgment that the scope of the evaluation must be widened, the evaluator shall seek the approval of the court or of all attorneys prior to going beyond the originally designated scope of the evaluation. Any changes in the scope of the evaluator's assigned task shall be memorialized in writing and signed by the court or by all attorneys, as applicable. . . . (b) Evaluators shall employ procedures that are most likely to yield information that will meet the needs of the court and shall conduct the data gathering phase of their evaluations in a manner consistent with state, provincial, or territorial statutes, or with judicial rules governing such evaluations. When circumstances demand that an evaluation be limited in scope, evaluators shall take steps to ensure that the boundaries to the evaluation and the evaluator's role are clearly defined for the litigants, attorneys, and the court. (pp. 13–14)

Grisso's Competency-Based Model

Grisso (1988, 2003) has argued that forensic evaluations should focus on functional abilities. A child custody evaluation should therefore be an evaluation of parenting competencies. Grisso outlines several objectives for competency evaluations that we apply to child custody evaluations. If an evaluator is practicing in a state in which the parenting abilities to be considered in custodial placement disputes have been statutorily specified or articulated in case law, the primary objective is to assess those abilities. When those abilities that, taken collectively, constitute good parenting have not been articulated either in statutes or in case law, it is the evaluator's task to identify clearly the behaviors being assessed and to offer research support for his or her contention that the identified behaviors are related to effective parenting.

A second objective is to obtain information that suggests the causes of any observable deficits in competency abilities (Grisso, 1988). The evaluator examines the parent within a specific context or role. Knowledge of the law is particularly important with regard to this component of the evaluation. In some jurisdictions, the causes of parenting deficits are not deemed pertinent, and evaluators are discouraged from offering recommendations incorporating the presumption that certain deficits can be successfully therapeutically addressed.

A third objective addresses the degree of practical significance of the parent's specific strengths and deficits in light of the specific demands of the best interests standard. Only rarely do evaluators find, either in statutes or in case law, terminology that suggests the weight to be assigned to the various factors that collectively define the best psychological interests of the child. In preparing their advisory reports, evaluators should, in our view, address the weight they assigned to the various factors considered and articulate the rationale for their decision.

Grisso (1988) takes the position that offering testimony about the ultimate issue "offers absolutely no new information to the court about the defendant's characteristics or the implications of their deficits in competency abilities" (p. 20). Grisso's argument is similar to those offered by Melton and Limber (1989) and by Myers (1991).

Otto's Competency-Based Model

Otto and Edens (2003) build on Grisso's competency-based model and include an analysis of functional components, causal components, and interactive components. Functional components are the parent's characteristics and abilities to care for children. The evaluation must examine the caretaker's child-rearing abilities. Otto and Edens (2003, p. 250) write, "Forensic assessments that describe only diagnoses, personality characteristics, or general intellectual capacities of parents and fail to assess the care taker's childrearing abilities are of little value."

The competency concept requires an examination of a parent or caretaker's knowledge, understanding, beliefs, values, attitudes, and behaviors pertaining to parenting each child. Otto and Edens (2003) make the point that to complete a competency-based evaluation adequately, the evaluator must have "a notion of functional ability concepts or behavioral dimensions constituting the relevant domain of parenting abilities" (p. 250). They also provide a list of parenting tasks for the evaluator to consider.

In previous writings, we have commented upon the enormous task of defining the domain of parenting abilities and developing investigative hypotheses that guide the evaluation process. We have suggested that evaluators operationally define specific parenting behaviors to examine for each evaluation (Gould, 1999; Martindale & Gould, 2004). The more tailored one's investigative hypotheses to the specific needs of the court, the more likely that the focus of the evaluator will be on gathering information relevant to the needs of the family under scrutiny (Amundson et al., 2000).

Otto and Edens (2003) provide a novel integration of custody and child protection literature in their discussion of parenting factors. For example, drawing on Barnum (1977), they describe "two basic responsibilities of parents: advocacy/protection and socialization" (p. 251) and drawing on Azar, Lauretti, and Loding (1998), they describe "five broad domains of parenting" (p. 251) that include an assessment of parenting skills, social-cognitive skills, self-control skills, stress management skills, and social skills. To this list, they add the need to assess parenting style.

When parenting deficiencies are identified, Otto and Edens (2003) recommend that the evaluator examine causal explanations. They suggest examination of life-situational stress, situational or examination-related stress, ambivalence, lack of information, and mental disorder or disability, each of which is defined in their chapter.

The final component of a competency-based analysis is the interactive component or what the American Psychological Association child custody guidelines refer to as the goodness-of-fit criteria. Children vary in their needs and differ in their developmental readiness. Parents also vary in their abilities to parent children adequately at different stages of the children's development. In the 1989 movie *Indiana Jones and the Last Crusade*, recall that when Indiana Jones complained to his father that he was never around during his childhood, the elder Jones responded, "You left just when you were getting interesting." Different parents may be better parents at different stages of their children's development, just as different children may need different types of care at different stages of their lives. Otto and Edens (2003) remind us that "deficiencies in certain parenting abilities may have greater or lesser significance in various cases, depending on the needs of the specific child in question" (p. 255).

Among relevant parent variables to be assessed are:

1. Parents' prior and current relationship with the child.
2. Parents' historical and current responsibility for caretaking.
3. Parents' communication with the child about
   a. The divorce.
   b. The parents' attitudes toward each other.
4. Each parent's goals for visitation and decision making should he or she be awarded custody.

5. Parent–child interactional style.
6. Parents' current and anticipated living and working arrangements.
7. Parents' emotional functioning and mental health.
8. Child's preferences.
9. Child's description of relationship with each parent.
10. Child's emotional, social, and academic functioning and mental health prior to and during the divorce process.

Gould's Scientifically Crafted Child Custody Evaluations

Gould (1998) extended the forensic assessment model used in other areas of criminal and civil forensic mental health practice and applied it to child custody work. Others had been offering continuing education training or articles that adapted conventional forensic methodology to child custody work. His initial contribution advanced the argument for a scientific crafting of child custody evaluations (Gould, 1998). He argued that the criteria included in the *Daubert* standard were important and relevant when crafting a child custody evaluation (pp. 24–48). Whether a particular state adopted a *Daubert* or a *Frye* standard for expert witness testimony, he suggested that the *Daubert* standard, stressing scientific knowledge rather than community standards, would likely result in a more reliable, relevant, and helpful work product for the court and would better reflect the usefulness of the psychological sciences as applied to child custody decision making.

Gould (1998) wrote that the available science of forensic methods and procedures should be applied to child custody evaluations. He encouraged the use of a model of custody evaluation in which the evaluator, the attorneys, and the court would work together to define the scope of the evaluation prior to its initiation, so that both parents and the evaluator would be clear about the focus and scope of the evaluation endeavor.

He also provided an evaluation protocol that encouraged evaluators first to obtain agreement either from the attorneys or the court about a list of specific psycholegal questions to be addressed in each evaluation (Gould, 1999). Once the psycholegal questions have been defined, the examiner *operationally* defines the variables to be measured. Properly articulated questions allow the evaluator to choose measurement techniques and tools that are both reliable and relevant to the questions posed.

Gould (1998, 2006) suggested the adoption of a five-pronged methodological approach to data gathering and urged evaluators to integrate current behavioral science literature into the decision-making process with regard to custody and visitation access recommendations. Support has been voiced for the use of clearly defined psycholegal questions (Amundson et al., 2000) as well as for the forensic methodology employing the five-pronged approach to data gathering (Austin, 2000c, 2000d, 2002; Kirkland, 2002).

The Art and Science of Child Custody Evaluations

Two years after the first edition of Gould's book (1998), Gould and Stahl (2000) wrote an article that began to address the conceptual differences between a scientifically informed model and a clinical model of forensic assessment. They argued that a competent evaluation is based upon the scientific process found in forensic methods and the procedures and scientific fact found in current literature. They also opined that science without context provides a meaningless report. Scientific process and scientific facts need to be integrated into an advisory report through the judicious use of clinical judgment.

Gould and Stahl (2000) wrote, "Although competent and well-intentioned practitioners may differ in how they conduct a proper child custody evaluation, it is necessary that each practitioner logically, coherently, and competently defend his or her approach to a child custody evaluation from within the framework of the behavioral science literature" (p. 398). They challenged custody evaluators to be intellectually honest both with themselves and with the courts when offering expert testimony. They wrote:

> It is one thing for unsuspecting but well-intentioned judges to allow as evidence clinical opinions that are believed by the mental health practitioner to be an admissible scientific work product but are in fact data and recommendations based on clinical rather than forensic standards [footnote not cited]. However, it is quite another to deliberately use a quasi-forensic methodology that, as an *a priori* assumption, deliberately excludes scientific methods and procedures that are precisely designed to both increase the reliability and validity of the gathered data and meet minimal standards of admissibility as scientific evidence. (p. 410)

They suggested that one way to maintain the dignity of the family during the evaluation process is

> by providing a thorough evaluation with sensible recommendations, staying focused on the children and their needs, and avoiding the temptation to join the "he said/she said" battle of the parents. . . . Without becoming advocates of settlement, without switching roles and mediating a settlement, and without advocating for either parent, evaluators can thereby indirectly assist in efforts toward the settlement and encourage parents to reduce their litigation and conflict with one another. (pp. 408–409)

They concluded that the art of conducting a child custody evaluation lies in integration of the scientific method that includes careful attention to the entirety of the evaluation data and application of current behavioral science research to those data with one's clinical judgment about family dynamics, the child's functioning and needs, and the ability of each parent to meet the needs of the child. The art of crafting recommendations in child custody evaluations is to apply current research to creative solutions for each unique family config-uration. The evaluator is never a technician applying research results without understanding the context of each family system. There are no standard proto-cols that fit all families, and, as Gould and Stahl (2001) wrote, a competent cus-tody evaluator never paints by the numbers.

The present book moves from the integration of art and science in child custody evaluation to a more sophisticated and broader discussion of how to competently conduct a scientifically informed, clinically sound forensic evalua-tion when investigating allegations of child maltreatment in the context of a child custody dispute.

CHAPTER 2

The Best Interests of the Child Standard

In this chapter, we discuss several ideas that address the best interests of the child standard (BICS). We begin with a discussion of the ambiguities contained in legal definitions of the BICS. We then discuss how the behavioral sciences approach defining the BICS, focusing on defining and measuring the best psychological interests of the child. We end the chapter by offering several ways of addressing the best psychological interests of the child.

Development of the BICS

Research estimates suggest that more than 40% of children living in the United States will have to adjust to the legal divorce of their parents (Greene, Anderson, Hetherington, Forgatch, & DeGarmo, 2003). In most of these divorces, issues related to child custody will be settled without litigation. They will be settled out of court, through the use of mediators or parent-coordinated agreements. Somewhere between 6% and 20% of all child custody cases will be decided in a courtroom (Melton, Petrila, Poythress, & Slobogin, 1997).

It has been reported that children from divorced families experience a higher frequency of adjustment problems than children from intact families (Amato, 2000; Amato & Booth, 2001), although this relative disadvantage does not necessarily suggest clinical levels of maladjustment (Bauserman, 2002; Kelly & Emery, 2003). To assist families going through divorce, the courts have constructed and adopted the BICS legally to determine the custodial placement of children in divorce proceedings (Krauss & Sales, 2000).

Legal Criticisms of the BICS

The BICS has come under attack from legal and psychological observers. Legal criticisms include that the best interests standard (1) is poorly defined, (2) is ambiguous, leading to too much judicial discretion, (3) encourages more disputes and litigation because of its vagueness and ambiguity, and (4) offers no clear guidelines that can help in judicial decision making (Krauss & Sales, 2000).

Mnookin and colleagues (Coons, Mnookin, & Sugarman, 1993; Mnookin, 1975) have argued that the broad judicial discretion provided by the BICS leads to judicial bias in custody determinations. Since there is no social or psychological consensus about normative definitions of the BICS, judges are free to impose their biases and beliefs on their judicial determinations. They also argue that judges have no expertise in making decisions about the relative importance of the various factors included in the BICS and, therefore, should not be allowed to make judicial determinations based upon such an indeterminate standard.

Recently, an entire issue of *Family Law Quarterly* was devoted to an examination of the BICS. It is interesting to note that many current concerns about its limitations are similar to those voiced more than two decades ago by Mnookin (1975).

Others have raised concerns that the ambiguity of the BICS encourages litigation because litigants are willing to take chances on how courts will decide (Krauss & Sales, 2000). Feminist theorists (Fineman, 1991; Scott, 1992) argue that the BICS is unfair. Scott (1992) suggests that a female parent's greater interest in obtaining custody places her in an unfair position when it comes to negotiating and that mothers may be willing to make greater concessions in order to prevent the possible loss of custody. Fineman (1991) argues that the solution to this inherently unfair bargaining position lies in replacing the BICS with the primary caretaker rule, which determines custodial placement based upon each parent's predivorce involvement in the lives of his or her children.

Bartlett (2002) summarized two areas of concern about the BICS. One frequent criticism is of the standards' indeterminacy. What one judge may feel is in a child's best interests may not be what another judge determines to be in the child's best interests. As a result of the variability of the BICS, many scholars have argued that parents cannot be sure of an outcome and, therefore, are more likely to litigate custody. Litigation means increased parental conflict because parents hire experts to identify deficiencies in each other's parenting (Bartlett, 2002). The other frequent criticism of the BICS is that

> it invites qualitative judgments of parents even though they are not unfit. Here, the problem is not indeterminacy but quite the opposite. This society puts great value on both parental autonomy and family diversity. The best interests standard risks these values if judges, whose variability with respect to parenting norms

tends to stay within a certain mainstream range, penalize parents who do not conform their parenting practices within this range. (Bartlett, 2002, p. 13)

Based upon her analysis of the BICS, Bartlett (2002) concluded that it "does little to constrain or steer judges; it encourages parents to contest custody; and it leaves children vulnerable to the effects of both" (p. 14).

American Society and Child Custody Standards

American society is based, in part, on the notion of *normative pluralism*. This is the idea that no shared ideal dictates or defines proper work roles, proper family structure, or proper family values (Elster, 1987; Scott, 1992). Our society is based, in part, on the premise that individuals choose how to live and what to believe in. The U.S. Constitution and many Supreme Court decisions have afforded special protection to actions taken on the basis of family and child-rearing values. Our Constitution and our social ideology guard against the state intruding into the practices of a family unless there is a compelling state interest to protect a child from danger.

The court's involvement in child custody determinations runs counter to these firmly held societal values. As Krauss and Sales (2000) state:

> The resolution of child custody disputes forces the legal system to investigate the inner workings of the family and to oversee a restructuring of the family unit, without the level of heightened interest that is usual for the court's involvement in these matters. . . . The court must engage, to some extent, in judging the parents in a way that is antithetical to many legal and societal values. (p. 845)

The challenge is to develop a legal standard that is sensitive both to the social values of American culture and to the needs of the legal system. American society and legal tradition place a high value on the concept that different individuals are to be treated similarly by the state under law. This is also a critical component in the U.S. Constitution, the Fourteenth Amendment to which addresses equal protection and due process.

A legal standard addressing the best interests of the child should "offer effective and useful guidelines, so that similar cases are decided similarly without extralegal factors significantly affecting final dispositions" (Krauss & Sales, 2000, p. 845). Consistent and useful standards, definitions, and decision-making precedents would have to be developed and then applied in a reliable manner across different cases. A legally effective child custody standard would balance the needs of the family and society, the evolving social science research and case law precedents, and the changes in each family configuration, while minimizing state intrusions into the functioning of the family (Krauss & Sales, 2000).

History of the BICS

The historical context of custody evaluations begins with Roman law and the presumption of paternal preference. Children were viewed as the property of their father. A father had absolute power over his children and was allowed to use his children as slave labor or sell them for profit. The child's mother had no legal rights.

English common law also provided for absolute paternal power and the legal doctrine of *parental famillus* guided the disposition of custody disputes. Children were viewed as the property of the father, and he had sole discretion over where they lived, both during the marriage and after divorce. Fathers had the legal responsibility to protect, support, and educate their children. Mothers had restricted access to their children after divorce.

In 1813, in deciding on the custodial placement of two children, aged 6 and 10, the supreme court of Pennsylvania articulated the *tender age doctrine*. The court declared, "it appears to us, that considering their tender age, they stand in need of that kind of assistance, which can be afforded by none so well as a mother" (*Commonwealth v. Addicks*, 1813).

At about the same time, British barrister Thomas Noon Talfourd conceived the idea that young children needed the direct care of their mother until the age of 7. From age 7 on, the custodial responsibility of the children would revert to the father. This became known as the *tender years doctrine* and was the first legal challenge to the historical paternal preference (Black & Cantor, 1989).

During the 17th and 18th centuries, U.S. law often paralleled English common law. There was a presumption of paternal preference based on the transmission of social and legal legitimacy, power, and status from the father to his children. By the 19th century, U.S. law began to apply paternal preference less consistently than did British common law. Several states developed laws that granted equal rights and responsibilities to both parents when custody of their children was in dispute.

During the mid-1800s, the Industrial Revolution began to have an effect on legal solutions to divorce. An increasing concern for the welfare of children developed, especially as fathers worked outside the home and frequently beyond the farm or village. Mothers remained at home and functioned as the primary caretakers of children. This was the first time in history that family responsibilities were clearly divided into the role of provider–wage earner for the father and child caretaker–nurturer for the mother.

Maternal Preference

Paralleling changes in familial and workplace organization were changes in the legal status of women. Gradually, the paternal preference was replaced by a maternal preference in custodial placement decisions. By the 1920s, there was a presumption favoring mothers.

The importance of the maternal preference was given a boost by the development and popularization of psychoanalysis. Sigmund Freud's theory of child development placed heavy weight upon the mother's role as primary caretaker in a child's life. Subsequent theories of attachment such as Bowlby's (1969, 1980), added much-needed scientific backing to the emphasis on infant–mother attachment, a focus that implied infant–father attachment was somehow less important to the child's development. Thus, scientific theories of psychoanalysis and attachment theory appeared to lend credibility to the legal standard of maternal preference. Current research has demonstrated that infants form meaningful attachments to both parents by the middle of their first year, but only recently has that research altered the courts' view of the tender years doctrine and maternal preference (Bray, 1991; Kelly & Lamb, 2000; Lamb, 2002).

In the 1960s, a number of factors led the courts to reexamine the maternal preference in custody determination. Increasingly, fathers enduring divorce demanded some legally acknowledged role in the postdivorce relationship with their children, legal challenges to maternal preference raised issues such as sex discrimination and constitutional protection of equal rights, and the feminist movement and the entry of large numbers of women into the workforce played roles in creating a new perspective (Kelly, 1994). Sex-based rules, such as the tender years doctrine, were held to be unconstitutional because they violated the equal protection clause of the Fourteenth Amendment to the U.S. Constitution (see *Craig v. Boren*, 1976; *Orr v. Orr*, 1979; *Reed v. Reed*, 1971; *Weinberg v. Wiesenfeld*, 1975). The reasoning was that it was discriminatory for the state to make important decisions completely on the basis of the sex of the participants (Krauss & Sales, 2000).

In 1979, Congress passed the Uniform Marriage and Divorce Act, providing for a straight best interests standard. The tide had turned from a focus on paternal or maternal preference or rights to a focus on what was best for the child. Simultaneously, the revolutionary concept of the psychological was developed (Goldstein, Freud, & Solnit, 1979).

The Psychological Parent

A *psychological parent* has been defined as one who, "on a continuing day to day basis through interplay, and mutuality, fulfills the child's psychological needs for a parent, as well as the child's physical needs" (Goldstein et al., 1979, p. 98). The idea of one psychological parent or a primary parent took hold in legal circles and was readily embraced by evaluators (Bray, 1991). The concept of a psychological parent holds great intuitive appeal and serves well as a way to understand a child's perception of the world, but it has no empirical support to date.

The concept of the psychological parent was based upon untested assumptions drawn from psychoanalytic theory and concepts drawn from attachment theory. Attachment theory suggests that determination of child custody should be based solely upon the strength of the child's psychological attachment to each parent. The parent who historically had provided for the child's environmental stability and emotional and affection needs was identified by Goldstein et al. (1979) as the psychological parent. Because of the presumed importance of maintaining a strong attachment between children and their primary caretaker, it was deemed appropriate that the psychological parent be the exclusive custodian of the children. Goldstein and colleagues (1979) further opined that contact with the noncustodial parent should be minimized and that the psychological parent should hold the power to decide when and if the noncustodial parent should visit. They wrote, "Children have difficulty relating positively to, profiting from, and maintaining contact with two psychological parents who are not in positive contact with each other. Loyalty conflicts are normal under such conditions and may have devastating consequences by destroying positive relationships with both parents" (p. 38).

The damage done by the concept of the psychological parent continues today when it is presented to the court in expert testimony *as if* there is empirical support for it, but there is no research support for the notion that children will be harmed by maintaining contact with both parents. There is, in fact, substantial literature indicating that children are positively influenced by relatively equal access to both parents (Kelly & Emery, 2003; Kelly & Lamb, 2000; Lamb, 2002; Bauserman, 2002). Despite these research findings, the concept of the psychological parent and the potentially damaging effects of frequent contact with the noncustodial parent is still a factor in some court decisions and an element of the parenting plan recommendations offered by many mental health professionals (Krauss & Sales, 2000).

The BICS Is Poorly Defined

When the BICS was introduced, there was no agreed-upon definition. As in many other areas of the law, it evolved as individual cases were adjudicated. Mental health professionals are accustomed to working with operational definitions and empirically crafted theoretical constructs, but the factors outlined in many legal definitions of the best interests of the child are drawn at least partly from experience, intuition, cultural expectations, and preconceived notions of what is good for children's healthy development.

Among the variables considered in the emerging legal definition of the BICS were concepts such as the child's need for consistency in parenting and the importance of each parent's relative contribution to a child's well-being. The notion that children are well served by safety, security, and consistency provided an impetus for the courts to endeavor to expedite custodial placement decisions.[1]

Another shift toward the BICS was the increasing consideration of a child's feelings and desires about with whom they wanted to live. Many judges developed a recognition that children's wishes might be appropriately considered if the children were deemed to be of sufficient age to formulate an opinion based upon factors that adults would deem reasonable.

As early as the mid-1970s, concerns were being expressed about the vagueness of the BICS. Mnookin (1975) wrote:

> Deciding what is best for a child poses a question no less ultimate than the purposes and values of life itself. Should the judge be primarily concerned with the child's happiness? Or with the child's spiritual and religious training? Should the judge be concerned with the economic "productivity" of the child when he grows up? Are the primary values of life in warm, interpersonal relationships, or in discipline and self-sacrifice? Is stability and security for a child more desirable than intellectual stimulation? (pp. 260–261)

Mnookin opined that when judges look to state statutes or to professional literature defining the best interests of the child, they do not find clear consensus about what defines the best child-rearing strategies or the most relevant parenting values. One result is that different judges employ different ideas about the best child-rearing strategies and/or the most relevant parenting values, yielding a court system in which each judge defines his or her own version of the BICS and in which there is no consistency or predictability in court decisions.

Emery (1999) observed that "family law has become amoral in that the law fails to offer a prescriptive code of behavior" (p. 324). He suggests that the amorality of family law mirrors the drift in law and society in general over the last several years. Our laws have become "more vague and less determinate in order to accommodate increasing pluralism in our society" (p. 324).

Joint Custody Decisions

Beginning in the 1970s, the concept of *joint custody* was forwarded by a combination of forces that included the newly developed fathers' rights movement. Fathers in this movement objected strongly to the reduction in their parental rights that often accompanied divorce. Researchers were increasingly reporting hitherto unnoticed contributions of fathers to children's welfare and development. A belief began to develop that continuity in the father–child relationship after divorce would provide for healthier postdivorce family systems. Finally, the academic world began to take notice of positive father contributions to the family and began to argue the advantages of joint custody.

Joint custody was seen as a panacea because the rights, status, and responsibilities of both parents were preserved. The field of child development began to study fathers' contributions to family welfare beyond the role of provider (Lamb & Oppenheim, 1989). Psychology began to look at attachment, child-rearing practices, communication skills, and a host of other important factors in father–child relations (Cabrera, Tamis-LeMonda, Bradley, Hofferth, & Lamb, 2000; Lamb, 1998, 2000; Marsiglio, Amato, Day, & Lamb, 2000). Studies also began to examine divorced men's sadness, alienation, depression, and loneliness resulting from reduced contact with their children (Arendell, 1995; Madden-Derdich & Leonard, 2000; Whiteside & Becker, 2000; Dudley & Stone, 2001). The proliferation of joint custody statutes in the United States has had the effect of promoting increasingly positive attitudes among parents, lawyers, mental health professionals, and judges toward greater paternal involvement after divorce (Kelly, 1994).

The State of Michigan's BICS

For more than 30 years, the Michigan Child Custody Act of 1970 has served as a model for outlining the basic tenets of the BICS. The act has served as an example of how a state legislature can enumerate and define those factors that, taken collectively, will define the "best interests of the child" in that state. Table 2.1 summarizes elements of the act.

The factors enumerated in the act reveal a concern on the part of the

TABLE 2.1. Summary of the Michigan Child Custody Act of 1970: Factors Defining the Best Interests of the Child

- The capacity and disposition of the competing parties to provide love, affection, guidance, continuation of education, and continued religious education, if the latter be deemed necessary.
- The capacity and disposition of the competing parties to provide the children with what is regarded as "remedial care"—that is, clothing and medical care (also refers to provision of other material needs).
- The length of time that a child has lived in a stable satisfactory environment and the desirability of maintaining continuity of that environment.
- The permanence of the family unit of the existing or proposed custodial home.
- The moral fitness of the competing parties. (Note: There is no mention of fitness as a parent.)
- The mental and physical health of the competing parties.
- The home, school, and community records of the child.
- The reasonable preference of the child if the court deems the child to be of sufficient age to express a preference.
- The willingness and ability of each of the parties to facilitate and encourage a close and continuing parent–child relationship between the child and the other parent or the child and the parents.
- Domestic violence, regardless of whether the violence was directed against or witnessed by the child.
- Any other issues considered by the court to be relevant to a particular child custody suit.

Michigan legislature for the emotional, physical, educational, moral, and religious growth and development provided to a child. The act also highlights a need for a stable and satisfactory living environment within which ancillary ("remedial") needs are provided. How the child feels about living with each parent is also considered. Finally, the act addresses the overall physical and psychological welfare and stability of the parents.

The Role of Values

Values, whether they are personal values or values that an individual has long ago decided form the basis for his or her professional view of the world, are inherent in custody issues and "should not be disguised by mental health professionals as settled empirical fact" (O'Donohue & Bradley, 1999, p. 315). Many evaluators' value judgments are treated both as though they were empirically determined fact and as though they were a reflection of professional consensus. Such professional arrogance (or is it naivete?) allows the often hidden values of those involved in assessing comparative custodial suitability to play a large role in the subsequent decision making and the resolution of the ultimate issue.

Emery (1999) calls on evaluators to examine critically the role played by personal and normative values in child custody determinations. Without having a clearly articulated paradigm of core values, professionals involved in custodial placement decisions—whether judges, attorneys, or mental health professionals—create an "illusion of neutrality" by relying on the vague best interests standard while "the standard (becomes) a vessel into which unarticulated normative values are poured" (Emery, 1999, p. 325).

Emery posits the need to identify a core set of values that best define what leads children to grow toward their psychological potential. This set of values would then help define the BICS and provide needed direction to judges and evaluators in identifying which parenting behaviors contribute to desired outcomes.

The trick, of course, is trying to define a set of values that accurately represents how best to guide children toward their psychological potential as functioning, productive citizens who will live, thrive, and contribute to society. Even as we write this chapter, we are aware of how value-laden its core concepts are. How can we get away from the "illusion of neutrality" as we strive to define a set of social values that we believe will guide our children toward actualizing their best interests?

This book is not about defining those values. As Emery (1999) suggests, the definition of a set of values that guides social behavior is the proper venue of law. Examination of the role played by behavioral science in researching the role of values in parenting and parental decision making may be critical in assisting the legal system to define the BICS further.

For the purposes of this book, we will not ask, "What values are best for children?" Rather, we will ask, "What values are embedded in the beliefs and attitudes each of us brings to the evaluation process?" Once we identify these values, we need to find ways to articulate them and understand how they guide a selective attention process in our data gathering. We need to explore how our personal and our professional values contribute to what we look for in the data obtained during the evaluation process and understand how those values influence our decision-making process, in both obvious and subtle ways.

The American Law Institute's "Approximation" Rule

Citing criticisms of the BICS similar to those described above, the American Law Institute (ALI) published a proposed final draft of principles of family dissolution (American Law Institute, 2002). The central principle of the ALI child custody recommendations was that custodial responsibility should be allocated in a way that roughly approximates the proportion of time each parent spent caring for a child when the family was intact. This has come to be known as the *approximation rule*.

The principle requires courts to determine how parents distributed child care responsibilities during the marriage and gives this rough allocation presumptive weight. The estimate of time devoted to caretaking responsibilities during the marriage must be used as a guide for allocating custodial responsibility in the postdivorce family. There are eight qualifications that might justify alteration of the parenting time allocation. As cited by Bartlett (2002), they are:

1. Each parent who has been minimally responsible with respect to a child in terms of child support or other manifestations of responsibility is guaranteed a minimal level of access. The jurisdiction chooses a specific period of time, which can be tailored to the age or other circumstances of the child, to constitute that minimum level of access;
2. A child's preferences may alter the allocation if those preferences are firm and reasonable and if the child has reached the age specified by a legislature or other rule-making body;
3. Adjustments are possible when necessary to keep siblings together for their own welfare;
4. To protect the child and to take account of a gross disparity in the quality of each parent's emotional attachment to the child, ability, or availability to meet the child's needs;
5. Prior agreement by a couple may be taken into account if necessary to protect reasonable expectations of the parents and the interests of the child;
6. Adjustments may be made if necessary to avoid extremely impractical arrangements;
7. The standard is not applied to the extent necessary to protect a child or parent from domestic abuse; and
8. The standard is not applied if it would require an allocation that would be manifestly harmful to the child. (Bartlett, 2002, p. 18)

The approximation rule has become a somewhat controversial concept (see Bartlett, Schepard, Warshak, & Howe, 2004; Bartlett, 2004; Schepard, 2004; Warshak, 2004). Some (e.g., Bartlett, 2002) have contended that the ambiguity of the BICS indirectly encourages litigation, that the litigation process takes its toll on children and parents, that a clearer standard might significantly reduce child custody litigation, and that the children, whose best interests we so often discuss, would be the primary beneficiaries of such a reduction in litigation.

Not surprisingly, the ALI proposal has encountered significant criticism. Schepard (2004) writes, "presumptions such as those advanced by the ALI are blunt tools to confine judicial decision making in an area as sensitive and diverse as reorganizing parent–child relationships" (p. 223). Further, "the approximation presumption predicts post-divorce child care patterns based upon past performance. The approximation presumption thus does not take into account the probability of post-divorce change in parenting roles" (p. 227). What the ALI has described as the tension between predictability and individualization was explored in depth by Garrison (1996), in an article in the *North Carolina Law Review*.

If we look closely at the BICS and the manner in which different states have endeavored to define it, it becomes clear that "best interests" encompasses some factors not within a psychologist's sphere of expertise. In a section of the ALI proposal dealing with the current legal context, the author declares that "what is best for children depends upon values and norms upon which reasonable people sometimes differ" (Bartlett, 2004, p. 206). Tippins and Wittmann (2005) assert that, in view of "the significant potential for specific custody recommendations to affect and limit personal liberties and the trajectory of a child's life, and given the paucity of relevant research available in this area and the profound evidentiary issues, . . . recommendations [such as those routinely offered] should now be viewed as ethically inappropriate."

In response to Tippins and Wittmann, we (Gould & Martindale, 2005) cite the observation by Otto and colleagues (2003) that research into the variables that are considered in formulating parenting plans "will always be constrained by the inability to use true experimental designs" (p. 203). Nevertheless, we believe that "by utilizing reliable procedures and by formulating opinions based upon the accumulated knowledge of their fields, mental health professionals can still meet the 'helpfulness standard' " (p. 254).

Over the years, the choices that custody evaluators have available to them have expanded considerably. Early custody evaluators felt limited to binary choices, such as choosing between mother and father. Now, evaluators examine a more complex array of choices. They consider all the issues that are involved in the development and implementation of a parenting plan likely to support the child in his or her relationship with both parents as well as to provide strong links for that child with others who are likely to support his or her emotional growth.

Determining the Best Psychological Interests of the Child

There is no clear consensus among attorneys, judges, and mental health professionals as to the dimensions to be examined in formulating opinions concerning the child's best psychological interests within the context of custodial suitability evaluations. There are advantages and disadvantages to employing the legal concept of best interests. As an evaluator, you need to consider the philosophical and practical aspects of the best *psychological* interests concept. You need to consider carefully what factors associated with the BICS you are choosing to evaluate and how each factor is relevant to the issues before the court in a particular family dispute.

As the specialty guidelines remind us:

> In offering expert evidence, [forensic psychologists] are aware that their own professional observations, inferences, and conclusions must be distinguished from legal facts, opinions, and conclusions. Forensic psychologists are prepared to explain the relationship between their expert testimony and the legal issues and facts of an instant case. (Committee on Ethical Guidelines for Forensic Psychologists, 1991, p. 665)

When we select the factors that we will consider in conducting a custody evaluation, we must be prepared to provide to the court an underlying logic and theory of science that ties the behaviors to be assessed to the specific issues of concern before the court. We also need to be prepared to explain how our choice of factors was related to the relevant psycholegal questions before the court. Our responsibility is to measure behavioral dimensions and interpret their meaning within the framework of a particular family. In this way, we provide the court with information useful in determining custody.

In his first book, Gould wrote:

> The determination of the best psychological interests of the child relies most extensively upon the child's developmental and psychological needs. It does not consider parental needs, legal tradition or cultural expectations. The discussion may include examination of these variables with regards to their effect on the child but they are not determinative. (1998, p. 64)

Today, we believe that the above statement excessively simplified the complexity of a child's world and the interconnecting set of variables that defines how best to serve a child's psychological interests in a binuclear family. The remainder of this chapter addresses what we believe to be the next step in conceptualizing the task of the custody evaluator in defining and framing the best psychological interests of the child within the context of a child custody evaluation.

Factors Associated with the Best Interests of the Child

The first step in identifying BICS factors is to recognize that some are beyond the realm of the behavioral sciences. Some best interests factors may be economic. Other factors may reflect community or educational concerns that are outside the scope of psychology. Still others may reflect statutory or other legal elements. Evaluators must confine their assessments to those factors that are within the scope of their expertise.

Before writing this chapter, we posted a general question to a child custody listserv. People who participate on this listserv are experienced custody evaluators, most of whom share our passion for discussion of current literature and professional practice issues. We wanted to invite our respected colleagues to share their ideas about the best psychological interests of the child and to call to our attention those components of the BICS that they felt were not well represented in the literature.

Psychologist Faulder Colby emphasized the need for interdisciplinary understanding. He suggested that, in considering how to define and measure the best psychological interests of the child, evaluators need to become well acquainted "not just with the child custody, developmental, and clinical literatures, but also the social psychological, bio-psychological, cross cultural, and sociological literatures" (personal communication, February 26, 2002).

Attorney Leslie Ellen Shear wrote:

> There will never be a purely scientific basis to the social, ethical, cultural construct we call the best interests of the child. Nor should there be a single answer or standard in a diverse and pluralistic society. We turn to science to help us explore those issues but we don't convert a question which is values-based into a scientific question nor do we aspire to do so. Science can't tell us what goals for children are preferable. These are social and cultural questions. This is a good thing, not something to be bemoaned. (personal communication, February 27, 2002)

As we have continued our work in the area of applied child custody evaluations, we have increasingly come to believe that the BICS was never intended to be concrete or invariable. The history of law suggests that the BICS represents an ill-defined but critical turning point. The BICS embodied a dramatic change from a focus on parental rights and preferences to a focus on children's needs and rights.

Arguably, the tender years doctrine was the first transition from an emphasis on parental rights to a focus on the right of children to have their well-being protected. At that time, the prevailing view within psychology was that children needed continued contact with the mother while the father worked outside the home. The social belief was that children were best nurtured by their mothers. The tender years doctrine was refined as the concept of the best psychological interests of the child evolved, but psychoanalytic and psychodynamic theory, prevalent at the time, still emphasized the need for children to be with the psychological parent. When most fathers worked outside the home, the psychological parent was likely to be the mother. Thus, even though change was occurring, the desire to preserve the mother–child relationship often resulted in a muting of other concerns.

Today, the evolution of the best psychological interests standard is intended to reflect several child-focused factors. The most important dimensions of the best psychological interests of the child are:

1. A focus on children's needs rather than parents' rights.
2. Gender-neutral standards.
3. Assessments focused on the needs of an individual child rather than on the generally agreed-upon needs of children as a group.

Some states are further refining the BICS, and the concept of best psychological interests also continues to evolve. Some judges are increasingly aware of the need to develop parenting plans that not only respond to the needs of each child, but also reasonably anticipate the ways in which each child's needs are likely to change as a function of age and foreseeable alterations in family circumstances and parental relationships.

An alternative to a focus on the best psychological interests of the child is a focus on the psychologically least detrimental alternative for the child. The original factors identified by Goldstein and colleagues (1979) in their outline of the best interests of the child were (1) preservation of environmental stability, (2) placement with the psychological parent, and (3) identification of the least detrimental alternative. Utilization of the psychologically least detrimental alternative concept avoids value judgments about what is "good" or "bad" (O'Donohue & Bradley, 1999). The emphasis is on avoidance of the worst placement rather than on prediction of what placement might produce the best results. Those who support the use of this concept assert that it is often easier to determine what will hurt a child than what environment will be best for a child.

Identification of what is psychologically least detrimental may be easier, but it is still tainted by value judgments about what is "bad." Once we move beyond factors the impact of which is generally agreed upon, such as domestic violence and maltreatment, there is precious little research that examines the effects of variables identified as potential detriments to children's adjustment. Therefore, despite the intuitive appeal of the psychologically least detrimental alternative concept, there is little current research that can help guide evaluators toward making value-neutral custody recommendations to the court.

O'Donohue and Bradley (1999) suggest that a moratorium be declared on the participation of mental health professionals in child custody evaluations because of the difficulty evaluators have in separating values from science and because so many custodial recommendations are based on the former rather than the latter. We disagree, but those of us who are engaged in child custody evaluations need to be continually aware of how our values influence our behavior, including our selection of variables to examine, our decision making, and the comparative weights we assign to different types of information. The impact of values can be diminished if evaluators gather information and discuss it within the context of current behavioral science research. An evaluator leaves the task of assigning weight to different factors up to the judge. Evaluators can also embrace the responsibility to make predictions within the proper limitations of the data while explaining both the values that influenced decision making and the relative weight assigned to different variables.

As stated earlier, custody evaluators now have a wide array of choices viewed as being available to them in offering to the court opinions for parenting plans. Some of the associations to which evaluators belong have endeavored to identify the dimensions that should be the focus of custody evaluations. Two documents that are useful in this regard are the *Model Standards of Practice for Child Custody Evaluation* developed by the Association of Family and Conciliation Courts (1994) and the American Psychological Association's (1994) guidelines for child custody evaluations in divorce proceedings.

The Association of Family and Conciliation Courts' *Model Standards of Practice for Child Custody Evaluation*

Professional organizations representing specific disciplines are torn by competing responsibilities: an obligation to the public and accountability to their members. Practitioner-members seek protection from licensing board complaints and malpractice actions, and they do not want their income-generating capacity placed in jeopardy. Barnett (2003), in outlining the objectives of the APA's Ethics Code Task Force, declared: "A main goal . . . was to create a revised Ethics Code that provides *better protection for psychologists*" (p. 9, emphasis added).

In his "Reporter's Forward" to the *Model Standards,* Martindale observes that "most professional practice standards evolve from accepted ethical principles and ethical principles are derived from and are, in essence, elucidations of the ethic of reciprocity. Evaluators should treat those with whom they interact as the evaluators would wish to be treated if the roles were reversed. It is incumbent upon evaluators to view the evaluation process from the perspective of the child, the litigants, the family members, the collateral sources, the attorneys, and the judge" (p. 61). In the words of the reporter, "The Task Force focused its attention on the needs and rights of those to whom evaluators offer their services and those who are affected by the work done by evaluators. The goal was to outline procedures that are consistent with ethical and effective practice" (p. x).

The *Model Standards* place emphasis upon the obligations of evaluators to (1) be mindful that, according to Federal Rule of Evidence 702, expert testimony must be "based upon sufficient facts or data," must be "the product of reliable principles and methods," and must be offered by a witness who has "applied the principles and methods reliably to the facts of the case"; (2) recognize that the forensic nature of the custody evaluator's task demands that the evaluator have reasonable knowledge of applicable statutes, case law, and rules of the court; (3) avoid the threats to objectivity that occur when an evaluator currently has, has had, or anticipates having a relationship with those being evaluated; (4) provide information to litigants and others in written form rather than imparting important information orally; (5) explain to judges why compliance with certain requests (such as requests for interim recommendations) is ill advised; (6) decline to speculate, even when asked to do so; (7) utter the difficult words "I don't know" when that is the truth and especially when one has taken an oath to tell the truth; (8) be informed consumers of psychological assessment instruments, avoid using them reflexively, and use them as they were intended to be used; (9) focus on obtaining data that provide information concerning enduring characteristics relating to parenting in general and, more specifically, to the parenting of the specific children who are the focus of the custody dispute; (10) affirmatively acknowledge the limitations in our techniques and in our data; (11) honor obligations not only to the courts that appoint them, to the adults whom they evaluate, and to the children whose best interests are the focus of custody/access evaluations, but also to participants in their evaluations and to affected others; (12) offer opinions that rest upon a generally accepted knowledge base or upon supportable inferences drawn from that knowledge base; and (13) refrain from offering opinions concerning the psychological characteristics of individuals whom the evaluators have not evaluated using techniques producing data sufficient to substantiate the opinions offered.

The American Psychological Association's Child Custody Guidelines in Divorce Proceedings

The American Psychological Association's child custody guidelines in divorce proceedings (1994) provide an outline of the issues that are considered the most relevant in a comprehensive evaluation. Among their most critical contributions to both the literature and professional practice was the ingenious modification of the legal concept of best interests. The child custody guidelines introduced a term (*psychological*) that permitted psychologists to provide information to the courts about child custody matters while remaining within the proper boundaries of competence of mental health professionals. Rather than addressing the ultimate issue of the best interests of the child, psychologists were advised to address only those areas that were related to the psychological aspects of the best interests of the child.

The custody guidelines state that "the primary consideration in a child custody evaluation is to assess the individual and family factors that affect the best psychological interests of the child" and that the focus of a child custody evaluation be on "parenting capacity, the psychological and developmental needs of the child, and the resulting fit" (p. 678). To accomplish this goal, a child custody evaluation should involve (1) an assessment of each parent's capacities for parenting; (2) an assessment of the psychological functioning and developmental needs of the child and the wishes of the child where appropriate; and (3) "an assessment of the functional ability of each parent to meet these needs including an evaluation of the interaction between each adult and each child" (American Psychological Association, 1994, Guideline 3).

Concerns about the Child Custody Guidelines

Krauss and Sales (2000) summarize criticisms of the custody guidelines and contribute that the presumption that mental health professionals can assess the best psychological interests of children is unsupported by any empirical evidence. Further, they believe it is unethical to offer expert testimony on matters for which there is no scientific foundation. Other writers posit that mental health professionals can provide useful information about uniquely psychological factors that can assist the court (Ackerman, 2001; Gould, 1999, 2006).

Krauss and Sales (2000) identify several more specific concerns about the principles set forth in the American Psychological Association's custody guidelines. They argue that there is no research support nor statutory authority for assessing the parenting capacity of each parent, the psychological and developmental needs of the child, or the fit between the child's needs and the abilities of the parents.

Psychologists, as a group, have not been asked to define parenting capacity. It is likely that, if asked, we would agree that it comprises numerous components, but not on the components themselves. What defines parenting skill? Which parenting attitudes are supportive of healthy development in a child? Can we agree upon what constitutes healthy development? Of what importance is congruence between community standards and each parent's approach to parenting? What weight should be given to each parent's ability and willingness to support the children's relationship with the other parent? The bottom line is that there is no empirical research that addresses the relationship between any of these variables and children's best psychological interests.

Gould and Kirkpatrick (2001) have opined that the American Psychological Association guidelines do not adequately emphasize the importance of assessing and understanding the child within the context of the family. They wrote

> We believe it is critical for the evaluator to generate an understanding of the family/relational contextual variables that may fuel the custodial dispute and its lack of

resolution. We encourage evaluators to consider the relational context. . . . Then, to systematically explore the variables identified either by the American Psychological Association (1994) or the Association of Family and Conciliation Courts. (p. 2)

Krauss and Sales (2000) posit that

perhaps one of the most useful ways that psychologists can participate in the resolution of child custody disputes is by investigating current relationships between parents, children, and significant others involved in the custody case, assessing the current psychological maladjustment of all the important parties, and exploring each party's wishes concerning an appropriate child custody arrangement. (p. 871)

In other words, it may be more productive to focus attention on the manner in which current relationships have been developed and are maintained and forego evaluative endeavors aimed at the prediction of future behavior.

The Evaluator's Focus

What does this mean for evaluators? It means that we need to consider a wide range of factors, from the intrapsychic to the extended social system. For example, we need to consider how a child's relationship with his stepmother may be affected when his biological mother relocates to another state and how such a disruption of the child–stepparent relationship may adversely affect the father's marriage to his new wife and the degree of stress that may enter into the blended family. Providing the mother with sole decision-making power may so anger the father that he believes his parental voice has been silenced and chooses to have less involvement with their son. Or the mother's remarriage and the relocation of her new husband's two teenage sons into her home may significantly affect the mother's 13-year-old daughter's comfort in the home.

Historically, we have thought about the concept of the best psychological interests of the child as a list of things to assess. The American Psychological Association suggests that we look at three specific dimensions: child, parent, and child–parent fit. The Association of Family and Conciliation Courts suggests five areas of exploration. The state of Michigan identifies 11 factors (Michigan Child Custody Act of 1970, Act 91 of 1970, Section 722.23), while the federal government points to five (Uniform Marriage and Divorce Act of 1970, Section 402). The legal terms that define the BICS have not been translated, either by our professional guidelines or by statutes, into terms and factors within the behavioral sciences that would lend themselves to empirical exploration (Jameson, Ehrenberg, & Hunter, 1997).

We have written elsewhere about the usefulness of defining questions that guide the evaluation process (Gould, Kirkpatrick, Austin, & Martindale, 2004), but we must be cognizant of how targeted questions (and their answers) fit into larger contextual dynamics that affect both the child and the families in which the child lives. Shear reminds us, "The distinction between custody and visitation is illusory. We need to focus on the parenting plan" (personal communication, March 1, 2002).

Conducting a thorough evaluation requires that evaluators be in compliance with statutes, follow the guidance offered by case law, and attend to factors specific to the family that is the focus of the evaluation. Often statutes or case law will identify certain issues *a priori*. These issues, in combination with those specifically identified by the court and those that may arise during the course of the evaluation, delineate the scope of the evaluation.

Change the Rules or Play by the Rules

O'Donohue and Bradley (1999) observed that, in child custody work, the rules by which mental health professionals are accustomed to playing may differ from those that guide the tactics of legal professionals. In their view, child custody work should be conducted in accordance with the rules of the legal profession, and mental health professionals should either play by those rules or decline to play. Emery (1999) challenges this notion: "I advocate for a different option. Change the rules. . . . I believe that psychology, the law, and divorcing families will be better served if we work to improve the system rather than refusing to participate in it" (pp. 323–327). In different jurisdictions and within different professional disciplines, there is much debate that focuses on these different perspectives concerning the occasional conflicts between "our" rules and "theirs."

Many distinguished colleagues support Emery's position that working to change the rules is appropriate (Peter Salem, personal communication, May 29, 2003). They argue that mental health professionals should not participate in the adversarial dynamics that characterize litigation and hurt families, and they posit the existence of a moral responsibility to guide families toward mediated rather than litigated solutions to their disputes.

We have no problem with advocating for mediated settlements to child custody disputes. Research into its efficacy strongly suggests that mediation encourages both parents to remain involved in their children's lives after divorce without increasing coparenting conflict (Kelly & Emery, 2003). Mediation is generally a useful and productive avenue for resolution of custodial conflict.

Where we take issue with our settlement-focused colleagues is that once families have been through mediation, settlement conferences, and other dispute-resolution procedures and have *still failed* to come to a fair resolution, *and* the court has directed that a child custody evaluation be conducted for the purpose of informing the court about the psychological aspects of family functioning, *then* the evaluator needs to follow the ethical system set forth in the child custody guidelines (American Psychological Association, 1994) and respect the important differences between clinical and forensic roles.

Let's tease this out a bit more. When parents are involved in custody disputes, several effective nonadversarial procedures are available. We believe mental health professionals and legal professionals have a moral obligation to assist families to solve their problems without intervention by the court. The more we can support parental competence in solving family disputes, the more we can empower families to do what is best for children without intrusions from outside the family system. Once the measures built into the system have failed, however, we need to acknowledge that outside assistance may be required in order to resolve the family's dispute. Once the court orders an evaluation and the evaluator has accepted the task, he or she should not also be trying to find settlement solutions.

Generally speaking, the court does not order an evaluation unless dispute resolution by other means has been deemed unworkable. The court orders the evaluation because the parents have been unable to find a compromise position to end their dispute. It is our experience that courts ask for evaluations in a very small number of the cases that come before them. When evaluations are ordered by the court, it is because the court needs additional information in order to adjudicate the matter. The evaluator's responsibility is to obtain the data requested by the court in an efficient and appropriate manner, answering the questions of concern to the court in a manner consistent with the highest standards of forensic psychological practice.

Once the evaluative process has begun, participation by the evaluator in settlement discussions would represent a departure from the assigned role and the acceptance of a competing role. The investigator's role is that of a data gatherer. When parents talk about settlement of their dispute, they are inviting intervention, not investigation. Intervention, at least in this context, is a clinical role. It may be a clinical role conducted within a forensic context (Greenberg & Gould, 2001), but it is surely not a forensic examination role.

What is wrong with switching roles if the family indicates a desire to settle? The answer is that the family has had many prior opportunities to resolve their dispute. They are in your office in order to participate in an objective, neutral evaluation. When the evaluator begins to assist the family in moving toward settlement and the settlement fails, then what does the evaluator do? Should he or she move back into an investigative role? If yes, what does the evaluator do with the information and impressions obtained while working with the parents in attempting the failed settlement? Do the information gathered and impressions formed reveal anything about their parenting? If not, then how do we ensure that such information does not affect how we think about each parent during the investigative process?

In many states, information disclosed within the context of settlement discussions cannot be revealed by a mediator to an evaluator. If an evaluator, within the context of a mediation role, hears one parent say, "I'll let you have the kids if you let me have the house," that offer says something about that parent's priorities. As the evaluator was working as a mediator at that point, can he or she use this information or must he or she pretend that the offer was never made?

If the evaluator participates in settlement discussions after the parents have begun the evaluation process, we believe that the evaluator must withdraw if efforts at settlement fail, and a new evaluator must be appointed.

Let us take another potential scenario. The evaluator has been successful in moving from the investigative role to the settlement/mediator role. The parents settle the custody dispute. Two years later, the mother wants to move, and the father petitions the court for a hearing to stop her from moving. The evaluator/mediator is subpoenaed to testify concerning the information obtained about the mother from the psychological test data administered to her before the evaluator stepped into a mediation role. How should the evaluator respond to the subpoena? *Should* the evaluator testify since he or she functioned both as an investigator and as a mediator? If the evaluator does testify, how does he or she interpret the test data, as they are supposed to be used in conjunction with other information typically obtained in the course of a full evaluation? *Should* the evaluator offer an interpretation of the test data? Can the evaluator support the decision to move from evaluator to mediator based upon currently published ethical standards and professional practice guidelines?

We encourage evaluators to take a conservative approach to custody evaluations. Making informed decisions concerning scenarios such as the ones described above requires that evaluators be familiar with the published articles in which role-boundary issues are discussed (Greenberg & Shuman, 1997; Greenberg & Gould, 2001). Understanding current thinking about forensic methods and procedures is also a critical component of competent and ethical practice in the area of child custody evaluation (Gould & Lehrmann, 2002; Martindale & Gould, 2004). Familiarity with forensic ethics and risk management issues is critical in the performance of child custody work (American Psychological Association, 1994; Bersoff, 1999; Ceci & Hembrooke, 1998; Martindale, 2001a; Weissman & DeBow, 2003).

Summary

In this chapter, we discussed legal and behavioral science concepts related to the BICS. We described limitations of current definitions and argued that evaluators should be aware of how personal and professional values may affect how they think about the best psychological interests of the child. Finally, we contended that clearly defined questions serve to focus investigative energies on relevant issues before the court.

Note

1. There are some states (e.g., New York) in which there are no defining criteria for best interests.

PART II

The Art
of Child Custody Evaluations

CHAPTER 3

Ethics and Methods

There is a strong connection between the role of ethics and the related role of appropriate methodology in child custody evaluations. Psychologists who offer to assist courts in adjudicating disputes concerning the custodial placement of children should set goals for themselves that go beyond the standard of care criterion. The authors of *Standards for Educational and Psychological Testing* (American Educational Research Association, American Psychological Association, & National Council on Measurement in Education, 1999) have observed, "The greater the potential impact on test takers, for good or ill, the greater the need to identify and satisfy the relevant standards" (p. 112). Extending that obligation further, the greater the potential impact on consumers of psychological services, for good or ill, the greater the need to adhere to established standards, to be responsive to applicable guidelines, and to endeavor to identify and subsequently utilize the best methodology possible.

Methods and procedures outlined here are those that we believe to be the most effective and for which we believe there to be the strongest rationale. Readers are reminded that the involvement of psychologists in the adjudication of custody disputes is a recent development. It will neither surprise us nor cause us dismay if better methods than those we propose here are ultimately developed. We view our education in this field as ongoing and strongly encourage readers to take the same view.

Clarity and Specificity in Ethics Codes

There is an increasing awareness that the interests of society, consumers of psychological services, well-intentioned practitioners, and the profession of psychology are best met when our ethical standards are reasonably specific and clearly written (Bala, 2005; Tippins & Wittmann, 2005). We recognize that no ethics code will ever be able to address all the thorny situations in which mental health practitioners are likely to find themselves and that all ethics codes must afford individual practitioners some leeway. For example, avoiding multiple relationships—an issue of great importance to us—is extraordinarily difficult and impossible in certain geographic areas. Ethics codes are most useful to *all* who are affected by them when a path to be chosen and a path to be avoided can be easily identified.

Practitioners who want to do the right thing but are not entirely clear concerning what practices constitute "the right thing" are offered more effective guidance when ethical standards are articulated with clarity. It's easier to do what's expected of you when what's expected of you is clearly stated. The public is also better served when standards of practice for service providers in any field are clearly articulated. The public then has a better understanding of what is to be expected and more effective recourse when providers of a service deviate from standards. The ethical standards by which we are judged are those that we have developed ourselves. Our society has become increasingly litigious, and it is not surprising that psychologists revising an ethics code might contemplate how ethical standards might be used to their disadvantage in litigation.

In a recent commentary on the new ethics code (American Psychological Association, 2002), Barnett (2003) offered several observations that we found troubling. Barnett asserted, "A main goal of the ECTF [ethics code task force] was to create a revised ethics code that provides better protection for psychologists" (p. 9) and further, "The intention is also that the ethics code not supersede each psychologist's professional judgment or create a rigid set of rules that must be followed to the letter by all for fear of adverse consequences" (p. 10). He concluded that, as the standards "were not intended by [American Psychological Association] to be applied by others when evaluating psychologists' actions, it is hoped that this statement will help reduce the chances that other individuals and bodies will misuse the ethics code against psychologists" (p. 9).

In our view, no task force at work on an ethics code for one of the helping professions should set as a "main goal" the provision of "better protection" for members of the profession. If psychologists as a group could be relied upon consistently to demonstrate good judgment, the profession could dispense with an ethics code and, in its place, periodically publish a three-word reminder to the profession: "Use good judgment." An ethics code *should* supercede each psychologist's independent judgment. What Barnett refers to as a "rigid set of rules" we would probably describe as a well-articulated, unambiguous set of standards in which professional behaviors are described as operationally as possible.

Any professional ethics code that is substantive—that is worth reading and useful as a reference on an ongoing basis—may occasionally be held aloft and pointed to by those who believe that a practitioner has failed to conform his or her professional behavior to the articulated standards. Psychologists cannot prevent our ethics code from being used as evidence of substandard practice by those who choose to ignore it.

The 2002 Psychologists' Ethics Code: New and Improved or Just New?

Whether the observations offered by Barnett (2003) are factually correct or not, the new ethics code (American Psychological Association, 2002) represents an unfortunate capitulation to psychologists who wish to blur role boundaries or not to have their work subjected to appropriate scrutiny. In its discussion of multiple relationships (Standard 3.05), a point is made of narrowing the definition. It is stated that "[a] multiple relationship occurs when a psychologist is in a professional role with a person and (1) *at the same time* is in another role with the same person" (p. 1065, emphasis added). Supporters of the new code may call attention to Standard 3.06, which more broadly covers the area of conflict of interest. Here it is stated that

> psychologists refrain from taking on a professional role when personal, scientific, professional, legal, financial, or other interests or relationships could reasonably be expected to (1) impair their objectivity, competence, or effectiveness in performing their functions as psychologists or (2) expose the person or organization with whom the professional relationship exists to harm or exploitation. (p. 1065)

We believe that the emphasis placed upon temporal correspondence by the words "at the same time" in Standard 3.05 confuses the meaning of "relationships" when that word appears in Standard 3.06. Should forensic psychologists evaluate individuals with whom they have had a treating (or other) relationship in the past but with whom they no longer interact?

With regard to the matter of receptivity to scrutiny, the 1992 American Psychological Association, ethics code (in Standard 1.23: Documentation of Professional and Scientific Work) reminded psychologists that when they "have reason to believe that records of their professional services will be used in legal proceedings . . . , they have a responsibility to create and maintain documentation in the kind of detail and quality that would be consistent with reasonable scrutiny in an adjudicative forum" (p. 1602). No similar admonition appears in the 2002 ethics code, and we believe the elimination of this standard to have been a serious error. Within the context of forensic work, due process becomes unobtainable if a forensic psychologist's records are incomplete, inaccurate, illegible, or inaccessible. With specific reference to custody litigation, those who are displeased with the findings reported or opinions offered by evaluators have an unequivocal right to scrutinize the manner in which the evaluation was conducted, to verify the accuracy of information relied upon, and to question the manner in which opinions were formulated. Without records of reasonable "detail and quality," the rights of the dissatisfied party are violated.

A Sequential Examination of Ethical Issues and Methodology

Many ethical issues arise in custody work. We endeavor, here, to examine the applicable issues in the sequence in which they are likely to emerge.

Preparation, Part 1: Knowing Enough Psychology

Prior to offering to perform evaluations of comparative custodial suitability, psychologists should attend workshops in which custody-related issues are specifically addressed. We recommend the workshops offered by the American Academy of Forensic Psychology and that psychologists interested in custody work obtain at least 21 continuing education credits (the number earned in three full-day workshops).

Psychologists in clinical practice who wish to offer their services as custody evaluators must recognize that work in this area is, by definition, forensic work. They must also recognize that many of the procedures with which they have grown comfortable will have to be modified to meet the needs of the judicial system. Forensic interviews are unlike clinical interviews. Tests that are acceptable in clinical settings may not meet the evidentiary demands associated with forensic work. Psychologists interested in custody work should be familiar with forensic interviewing of adults, forensic use of psychological tests and measures, ethics as specifically applied to forensic contexts, forensic risk management, theory and assessment of domestic violence, theory and assessment of child alienation, theory and assessment of high-conflict postdivorce families, theory and assessment of child sexual abuse, and distinctions between forensic and clinical evaluation.

We strongly recommend that *before* taking on their first case, psychologists interested in custody work read at least three major texts on custody matters and we advise newcomers to obtain individualized, paid supervision. Informal guidance offered by friends or supervision in a group context are not, in our view, good substitutes for supervision provided by experts in the field. Establishing a professional relationship with a supervisor before taking on one's first case is strongly advised. A supervisor can lead a newcomer to necessary books and articles and, perhaps most important, many potential pitfalls can be avoided by having good advice available.

Last but certainly not least, knowing enough psychology includes being intimately familiar with the ethics code, the specialty guidelines for forensic psychologists (Committee on Ethical Guidelines for Forensic Psychologists, 1991), the American Psychological Association's custody evaluation guidelines,

Standards for Educational and Psychological Testing (American Educational Research Association et al., 1999) and several texts or articles in which issues of reliability and validity are explored (e.g., Heilbrun, 1992, 1995; Otto, Edens, & Barcus, 2000).

Preparation, Part 2: Knowing Enough Law

Some psychologists feel that it is the job of attorneys and judges to know the law and the job of psychologists to know psychology. Life in the world of custody litigation is not that simple. Attorneys who know little if any psychology are ineffective when they must cross-examine psychologists. The consequences are costly. Either they struggle without assistance, often to the detriment of their client, or they retain psychologists to assist them, adding significantly to the financial burden borne by their client. Psychologists who know little if any law may make errors that will cause them to be removed from the case, may focus on issues that—by case law or by statute—are to be ignored, may neglect issues that the law requires them to address, may offer recommendations that conflict with the law, may violate the civil rights of litigants, or may inadvertently display their ignorance of the law in a way that will cause considerable embarrassment.

Psychologists preparing to offer their services as custody evaluators should be able to decipher legal citations and know how to obtain judicial decisions of interest to them. In order to appreciate the ways in which courts dissect the various elements in a custody dispute, psychologists should read several trial court and several appellate decisions in custody matters. Familiarity with the pertinent statutes and case law governing custody matters in the state in which they intend to practice is critical. The concept of the best interests of the child is one with which most psychologists have some familiarity, but an alarmingly high number of custody evaluators are unaware of the manner in which that concept is translated by the courts to which they submit their advisory reports. In some states, the criteria to be considered are clearly specified in statutes; in others, no statutorily defined criteria exist, but guidance is offered in the form of case law. In some states, the Board of Psychological Examiners has outlined standards or factors to be considered by psychologists performing custody evaluations. In others, no guidance is offered at all, and evaluators must decide for themselves how they will formulate their opinions concerning what parenting plan is most likely to serve the child's best interests.

Reference was made, above, to the offering of recommendations that conflict with law. We offer an illustrative example. A psychologist recommends that parent A be designated as the child's primary custodian but that she be required to continue raising the child in the religion of parent B. The U.S. Supreme Court has specifically ruled that parental authority in matters of religious upbringing may be encroached upon, only upon a showing of a substantial threat of harm to the physical or mental health of the child or to the public safety, peace, order, or welfare (*Wisconsin v. Yoder*, 1972, 406). A recommendation that parent A's designation as the child's custodian be made contingent upon parent A's agreement to continue raising the child in the religion of parent B is a recommendation that conflicts with established law.

Psychologists, as a group, are not reputed to have unwavering respect for the status quo, while the law changes slowly, often begrudgingly, and frequently in response to external pressure. Advocates for children might remind us that at one time children were treated as property. We call attention to this difference between the fields because the dynamics of a particular case may lead a psychologist to conclude that the arrangement most likely to be in the best psychological interests of the child is an arrangement that is inconsistent with current law. In this situation, the evaluator might consider communicating his or her awareness of the legal standard(s), acknowledging the apparent inconsistency between the recommended course of action and the legal standard(s), and cogently articulating the bases for viewing the recommended course of action as being superior to the legally preferred alternatives.

Preparation, Part 3: Knowing What You Don't Know

A recognition of one's limitations is essential, both ethically and for reasons related to risk management. Many of the issues that emerge during what initially appears to be a routine custody evaluation may require specialized knowledge and training. Few evaluators have the expertise necessary to assess allegations of sexual abuse appropriately. In many jurisdictions evaluators may be in violation of the law if they endeavor to assess such allegations and may be required as a matter of law to accept as accurate the findings of the agency charged with the responsibility of investigating such allegations. Custody disputes that involve same-sex relationships, new reproductive technologies, litigants from cultures with which the evaluator is unfamiliar, and so on may require consultation.

Preparation, Part 4: Planning to Know More

As psychologists prepare themselves to offer services as custody evaluators, they should think about the ways in which they will maintain their skills, keep themselves abreast of developments in research and in law, and establish links with other professionals involved in the same work.

The Art of Self-Promotion

Notwithstanding our emphasis on lofty matters such as ethics, we have not lost sight of the fact that the independent practice of psychology (in whatever specialty one chooses) is a business. In order for any business to be a success, there must be an appropriate means by which the availability of the product or service can be made known to potential consumers. When the service being offered is evaluations of comparative custodial suitability, the potential consumers are lawyers and judges. Though the ways in which psychologists might make their availability known to lawyers and judges are many, individuals wishing to offer forensic psychological services must not lose sight of the fact that they are obligated to take reasonable steps to ensure that their expertise is not misused.

Just Say "No"

An individual who wishes to sell a service in a geographic area in which others are already offering the same service and have established themselves faces a daunting task. It is more likely than not that newcomers will be asked to perform services that established practitioners have declined to perform. Entry-level evaluators may be asked to evaluate individuals with whom they have had prior relationships, to complete evaluations in such a brief period of time as to make the performance of adequate assessment impossible, or to perform evaluations under conditions that pose a clear threat to their objectivity and impartiality. If established practitioners have declined to perform a requested service, it is likely that the decision was well reasoned. Newcomers place their careers in jeopardy when they perform services that their more experienced colleagues have declined to perform.

Disclose Prior Contacts

Aside from the possible inconvenience, there is *no* downside to disclosing or offering to disclose every social contact, shared professional endeavor, previous case, and so on.

1. It will be felt that you are bending over backwards to avoid potential conflict and the appearance of conflict.
2. You will be viewed as ethical and forthright.
3. In almost all cases, approval will be given to your participation. When people give informed consent to your appointment at the outset of the evaluation, they are committed to the approval that they have given.
4. When there has been no disclosure, the attorney representing the nonfavored party can appear before the court and declare, "If I had known about Dr. Smith's previous contacts with my adversary, I would have asked that he be removed from the list of evaluators being considered."

Information concerning previous cases in which particular attorneys have been involved should be readily accessible. Contacts can be recorded by imaginative use of any of the various money management programs that are ordinarily included with the purchase of a computer. Where the payee would ordinarily be entered, enter the name of the person with whom time has been spent. Where a description of a purchased item or service would ordinarily be entered, enter a description of the activity (lunch, copresenter at a symposium, etc.). Where an amount would ordinarily be entered, enter the time expended. Once the data have been entered, you can, in less than a minute, find out exactly how much time has been expended with a particular attorney and in what activities.

Getting Off to a Good Start

Getting off to a good start means explaining the evaluation process to both sides in sufficient detail that they may make an informed decision about participation. The trend, at least in some jurisdictions, is toward greater evaluator disclosure regarding the scope of the evaluation and the tools used in the evaluation process.

A recent California case has been interpreted to direct evaluators to stay within the scope of the evaluation focus as defined by the court's order (In re Marriage of Seagondollar, 2006). Another recent California case decision requires evaluators to disclose the names of the tests that they intend to administer to a litigant undergoing forensic evaluation (*Carpenter v. Yamaha*, 2006).

Fairness to All

Though research suggests that many factors play a role in determining whether people will view a process as having been fair or unfair (Lind, Kanfer, & Early, 1990), it is likely that most custody litigants would not be comfortable if the competing litigant (or the attorney representing the competing litigant) were to get first crack at the evaluator. We therefore discourage evaluators from taking background information by phone either from the litigants themselves or from their attorneys.

In some jurisdictions, court orders appointing evaluators routinely contain a prohibition against *ex parte* communication between the evaluator and the attorneys representing the parties. Even where such communication is not specifically prohibited, we advise against it. We recommend making one's initial contact with the attorneys by means of identical introductory letters in which brief information is provided outlining the documents that the evaluator would like the attorneys to supply and indicating how the submission of additional documents should be handled. Evaluators should enclose with this letter a copy of the document that outlines the evaluator's policies, procedures, and fees, so that the attorneys can review the document and discuss it with their respective clients.

The initial contact with the litigants should also be by letter, and the document that outlines the evaluator's policies, procedures, and fees should also be sent to them, accompanied by the suggestion that they review it with their attorneys before signing and returning it. We believe there are significant advantages to presenting an evaluator's policies, procedures, and fees in this particular manner. A document received by mail can be reviewed in an unhurried manner. A review conducted with one's attorney affords the litigant an opportunity to obtain input from someone who is an ally, who is trained in law, and who is able to compare the outlined policies, procedures, and fees with those of other evaluators with whom the attorney has interacted. In our view, requesting that litigants sign the evaluator's policies and procedures document during the initial meeting with the evaluator and in the evaluator's presence is ill advised. It is reasonable to expect that litigants will feel rushed and pressured by the evaluator's presence, and the validity of an agreement signed under such circumstances is questionable.

Statements of Understanding

We believe it to be generally accepted that a mental health professional embarking upon child custody evaluations should provide to the litigants detailed information concerning the evaluator's policies, procedures, and fees. The American Psychological Association's ethics code refers to this obligation more than once. It is our impression that most custody evaluators present the requisite information to litigants in the form of a written document, identified in many different ways. The American Psychological Association custody evaluation guidelines confuse matters, in our view, by making reference to "informed consent" (American Psychological Association, 1994, Guideline 9). Many of the individuals being evaluated are complying with the terms of court orders to which they are strongly opposed. The concept of *consent* seems to us not applicable. For ethical reasons, it is essential that those being evaluated understand the evaluator's policies, procedures, and fees. For risk management reasons, it is essential that the evaluator be able to document (if called upon to do so) that the needed information was provided, that the litigants were encouraged to consult with their attorneys, that the litigants were given ample time in which to consider the information provided before making their decisions, and that both litigants asserted that they understood the evaluator's policies, procedures, and fees. All these requirements are best accomplished by providing to the parties and to their attorneys a descriptive document that we have elected to call a statement of understanding; by doing this prior to the commencement of the evaluation, thereby giving them ample time in which to review it; and by awaiting the return of signed copies before making arrangements to commence the evaluation. In the Appendix we outline what we believe to be the essential ingredients of this descriptive statement. We also provide examples of several other descriptive documents that may be useful to include with the statement of understanding.

Consent and Assent

If, as we have asserted, litigants are often in our presence against their will, why is it so important that we meticulously outline our policies, procedures, and fees and satisfy ourselves that they have been understood? Just as individuals convicted in criminal trials have the right to appeal, litigants in custody disputes have the right to seek modifications in orders issued by the court. A litigant who is disturbed by some aspect of an evaluator's described procedures has the right to request the appointment of a different evaluator.

Not infrequently, evaluators who take great care to provide appropriate information to the litigants become inexplicably careless in their dealings with others (such as collateral sources of information or third parties who are evaluated). Treating people fairly includes telling them what they need to know in order to make informed choices. Our obligation to take reasonable steps to avoid harming those with whom we interact professionally is not limited to those whom we see in our offices nor to those who pay our fees. (The interested reader is referred to Lind et al., 1990, for a discussion of the perceived fairness issue.)

In dealing with children, it is useful to ask what the child already knows. In explaining what they already know about the evaluation, children often unintentionally provide information suggesting that they have been coached. Also, by ascertaining what information a child already has, evaluators can correct misunderstandings and not spend time discussing matters that the child is already familiar with.

Who Is the Client?

The obligations of forensic psychologists might be better understood if we were to jettison the client model. Most evaluators are well aware that the litigants are not viewed as the clients even though it is often the litigants who are directed to pay the evaluator's fees. In the effort to force square pegs into round holes, some evaluators will assert that the court is the client; others will assert that the child is the client. Either of these misconceptions can cloud an evaluator's decision making when contemplating his or her obligations.

"My Insurance Covers Psychological Evaluations"

The primary purpose of health insurance is to provide reimbursement for expenditures related to treatment of conditions (physical or mental/emotional) that *require* treatment. A secondary purpose is to provide reimbursement for expenditures related to diagnostic evaluations, the goal of which is to assist a practitioner in evaluating a condition prior to commencing treatment, determining the correct treatment modality, and/or evaluating the progress of treatment.

The sessions that evaluators conduct with individuals whom they are evaluating (whether for a court or for an attorney) are not psychotherapy sessions, and to record them as such would be fraudulent. Custody evaluators are not providing treatment of anyone for anything. Though child custody evaluators conduct a psychological evaluation, and though many individuals who are evaluated have insurance policies that provide coverage for psychological evaluations, evaluations conducted for purposes related to treatment are significantly different from forensic psychological evaluations. Specifically, forensic psychological evaluations are conducted within the context of litigation for the purpose of providing information that will be of assistance to the court. The intended consumer of the evaluation is the court. Clinical psychological evaluations, on the other hand, are conducted within a treatment context with the purpose of providing information useful to a treating practitioner.

It should be mentioned here that standard insurance forms now contain the following statement: "Any person who knowingly and with intent to defraud any insurance company or other person files a statement of claim containing any materially false information, or *conceals for the purpose of misleading* [emphasis added] information concerning any fact material thereto, commits a fraudulent insurance act, which is a crime."

What Is Your Model?

Few evaluators have given much thought to the issue of an evaluative model. Benjamin and Gollan (2003, p. 173) describe their method as "allegation-focused" and present two checklists to litigants, one of "divorce-related allegations" (pp. 205, 206) and one of "child-focused allegations" (p. 207). Each checklist presents 19 allegations for the litigants to endorse or not endorse. In our view, such a procedure encourages each parent to focus on the negative characteristics of the other parent. If successful postdivorce adjustment demands that each parent develop an appreciation for the other parent's importance in the life of the child, a focus on deficiencies sets a destructive tone.

Strochak (2003) advocates the use of what he refers to as a conciliation/evaluation model, which "includes educational, conciliation, and counseling interventions and goals in addition to evaluation methods" (p. 1). Calloway and Lee (2002) advocate the use of what they refer to as a "clinical/child-based evaluation model."

We advocate the use of a forensic model. The concepts that we apply in this book to services performed within the legal arena have been discussed in earlier works addressing primarily clinical endeavors (Beutler, Williams, &

Entwistle, 1995; Frank, 1984; Kanfer, 1990; O'Donohue, 1989; Stricker, 1992; Stricker & Trierweiler, 1995) and by Kuehnle (1998a) in her in-depth examination of procedures to be employed in assessing allegations of child sexual abuse. As applied to child custody evaluations, the essential components of the forensic model as we conceptualize it, are:

1. The evaluator's role, the purpose of the evaluation, and the focus of the evaluation are defined by the court.
2. Where possible, the evaluator obtains (at the outset) a list of specific psycholegal issues concerning which the court seeks advisory input.
3. The evaluator conducts all professional activities in accordance with regulations and/or guidelines of state regulatory boards.
4. The procedures employed by the evaluator are informed by the psychologists' ethics code, the specialty guidelines for forensic psychologists (Committee on Ethical Guidelines for Forensic Psychologists, 1991), the American Psychological Association's custody evaluation guidelines, and similar documents developed by organizations that conceptualize the child custody evaluation as an inherently forensic psychological activity.
5. The selection of assessment instruments is guided by the 1985 and 1999 editions of *Standards for Educational and Psychological Testing* (American Educational Research Association, American Psychological Association, & National Council on Measurement in Education) and particular attention is given to the established reliability and validity of instruments under consideration (Heilbrun, 1992, 1995; Otto et al., 2000).
6. Detailed records of all aspects of the evaluation are created and preserved and are made available in a timely manner to those with the legal authority to inspect or possess them.
7. All professional activities are performed with a recognition of the investigative nature of the task, an acknowledgment of the limitations inherent in the evaluative procedures, an understanding of the distinction between psychological issues and the specific psycholegal questions before the court, and an appreciation of the need not to engage in therapeutic endeavors before, during, or after the evaluation.

Doing the Best You Can

Several years ago, Gould and Stahl (2000) wrote an article that, in part, discussed the moral foundation for expert witness testimony in which they argued that child custody evaluators have a moral responsibility to do the very best they can. Ignorance of the limitations inherent in evaluating comparative custodial suitability may contribute to sound sleep but not to better evaluations. It is essential that we recognize the many threats to objectivity and take reasonable steps to address them (Arkes, 1981; Borum, Otto, & Golding, 1993; Garb, 1994). In our view, doing the best we can (Lavin & Sales, 1998) requires that we be familiar with the concept of *mental set* (Leeper, 1935), *expectancy effects* (Rosenthal, 1966, 1967, 1968), the principles of sampling (Anastasi & Urbina, 1997), and the research on our ability (or lack thereof) to detect deception through interviews (DePaulo, Charlton, Cooper, Lindsay, & Muhlenbruck, 1997; Ekman & O'Sullivan, 1991; Feeley & Young, 1998; Frank & Feeley, 2003).

Address the Question: No More; No Less

Child custody evaluators are admonished by the American Psychological Association's child custody guidelines and by the Association of Family and Conciliation Courts *Model Standards* to conduct their evaluations within the scope of the court's order. Many custody evaluators have been intermittently reinforced for answering questions other than those that were asked and for articulately communicating opinions not supported by facts. Unfortunately, such intermittent reinforcement may continue after they begin filing reports and offering testimony in custody matters. Nevertheless, we strongly discourage providing information not pertinent to the issues before the court, offering personal opinions in the guise of professional ones, or neglecting (either by carelessness or by design) to provide information needed by the court.

In some jurisdictions, it is customary for court orders to enumerate specific issues to be addressed by an evaluator. A prudent evaluator reviews the court's order periodically during the course of the evaluation to ensure that the information needed to address the specified issues is being gathered. In other jurisdictions, no focus is provided to the evaluator by the court. When no specific issues have been identified to in the court's order, evaluators should, in the initial stages of the evaluation, determine what each party views as the main issues in the dispute. When evaluations have been completed and reports are being prepared, evaluators should take care to articulate what data were gathered, how those data bear upon the criteria that were utilized, and how each of the criteria relates to the BICS. Evaluators should resist the temptation to opine on matters concerning which they have been unable to gather sufficient information, decline to comment on matters whose pertinence to the BICS cannot be established, and exercise great care not to mingle personal opinions with professional opinions. Psychological experts draw upon published knowledge from the field of psychology in formulating their opinions. If the accumulated knowledge from the field has not been utilized in the formulation of an opinion, it is a personal opinion, irrespective of the credentials of the person expressing it. Consider the ethics code's Standard 2.04: Bases for Scientific and Professional Judgments: "Psychologists' work is based upon established scientific and professional knowledge of the discipline" (American Psychological Association, 2002, p. 1064)

What Is Basic? What Is "Extra"?

Standard 9.01 of the ethics code addresses "Bases for Assessments," and we are reminded in it that "psychologists base the opinions contained in their recommendations, reports, and diagnostic or evaluative statements, including forensic testimony, on information and techniques sufficient to substantiate their findings" (American Psychological Association, 2002, p. 1071). This strikes us as a reasonable admonition. In the opening section of the ethics code, psychologists are informed that "*reasonable* means the prevailing professional judgment of psychologists engaged in similar activities in similar circumstances, given the knowledge the psychologist had or should have had at the time" (American Psychological Association, 2002, p. 1061, emphasis added). What may have seemed clear now seems murky. Among those who devote their professional lives to custody-related work, there does not seem to be a consensus concerning either the quantitative or the qualitative features of sufficient information. For example, evaluators have been unable to reach professional consensus as to how many interviews suffice, how many collateral sources suffice, and whether the information gathered in a home visit is useful or not. Our advice, therefore, is that newcomers to the field of custody work make their decisions in consultation with experienced colleagues and have a well-thought-out rationale for those decisions.

The Virtues of Not Being Helpful, Part 1

Forensic psychology is a relatively new area of specialization, and the vast majority of the psychologists who have taken an interest in performing custody evaluations were initially trained as clinicians. Some of the most serious problems that forensic psychologists create for themselves stem from an inability or unwillingness to control the impulse to think and act like helpers when they are contractually obligated to function as examiners. One cannot, for example, evaluate someone's parenting skills while simultaneously offering advice concerning how best to improve those parenting skills. Evaluators who intervene, however obvious the need for intervention may be, indirectly become evaluators of the success or failure of their own interventions. In the course of obtaining education and training in forensic psychology, some psychologists digest a significant amount of family law and become quite confident that their knowledge of the law enables them to be helpful to litigants who may be receiving inadequate or misguided advice from their attorneys or who may have elected to represent themselves. Some psychologists have even obtained degrees in law. No matter how much law psychologists may know, offering legal advice compromises one's ability to conduct an impartial evaluation. The task that was accepted by the forensic psychologist was evaluative. Performing unassigned tasks that diminish one's effectiveness at the assigned task is imprudent and increases the risk of litigant complaints. The parent whom you have assisted is likely to view you as an ally. If you then favor the other parent in your evaluation, the parent whom you assisted may feel betrayed and angry. Anger undoubtedly fuels as many complaints as does evidence of professional error.

Interview and Observational Techniques

We noted earlier that there are aspects of custody work concerning which no consensus has been achieved. Reasonable and well-trained experts will disagree. We believe there to be agreement within the profession concerning the essential objectives of interviews with parents and with children, but there are disagreements concerning interviewing methods. In interviews with parents, questions should be posed that will enable evaluators to assess what are generally referred to as *parenting skills*. These may include the assignment of age-appropriate chores to children the use of appropriate methods for encouraging admirable behavior, and the ability to maintain effective parent–child communication in both good times and bad. Questions posed to a child should provide an opportunity to obtain the child's perspective on such issues as parental consistency, discipline, behaviors that encourage (or discourage) the child's efforts to achieve age-appropriate independence, etc.

Among skilled evaluators, there are differences of opinion concerning the degree to which interviews with parents or with children should be structured. However strongly a psychologist may feel concerning the advantages of a structured approach, it is essential, that he or she not lose sight of the skills for which he or she is being paid. Psychologists are not well-paid stenographers with doctoral degrees. It can be reasonably expected that psychologists will formulate appropriate follow-up questions (i.e., depart from the structure) when it is likely that doing so will elicit relevant information.

Few independent practitioners have either the funds or the space to construct adjoining rooms separated by one-way viewing screens, enabling them to remain unseen as they observe parent–child interactions. It is, however, the clear responsibility of evaluators to be aware of the fact that in any situation in which a human observer is in the same physical environment as the person or people being observed, the risk is always present that the observer will influence what he or she is endeavoring to observe. The evaluative task is to function as an observer of each parent's parenting behaviors, to record those behaviors, to formulate opinions concerning those behaviors, and to report both the observations and the subsequently formulated opinions to the court. During observational sessions, evaluator involvement should be minimal and, except under the most extraordinary circumstances, no comments should be made concerning the behaviors being observed.

Record Keeping and Transparency

Standard 1.23 of the 1992 American Psychological Association's ethics code addresses "Documentation of Professional and Scientific Work." Psychologists were reminded that when they "have reason to believe that records of their professional services will be used in legal proceedings . . . , they have a responsibility to create and maintain documentation in the kind of detail and quality that would be consistent with reasonable scrutiny in an adjudicative forum." Much to our dismay, as covered briefly earlier in this chapter, no similar admonition appears in the new ethics code (American Psychological Association, 2002). It remains our view that the responsibility alluded to in Standard 1.23 is a reasonable one for psychologists to accept whether or not our new ethics code obligates us to do so. The perspective provided in the specialty guidelines for forensic psychologists (Committee on Ethical Guidelines for Forensic Psychologists, 1991) is strongly worded and unambiguous. It is stated in section VI.B. that

> forensic psychologists have an obligation to document and be prepared to make available, subject to court order or the rules of evidence, all data that form the basis for their evidence or services. The standard to be applied to such documentation or recording *anticipates* that the detail and quality of such documentation will be subject to reasonable judicial scrutiny; this standard is higher than the normative standard for general clinical practice. When forensic psychologists conduct an examination or engage in the treatment of a party to a legal proceeding, with foreknowledge that their professional services will be used in an adjudicative forum, they incur a special responsibility to provide the best documentation possible under the circumstances. (p. 661, emphasis in original)

Reference in the specialty guidelines to "a special responsibility to provide the best documentation possible under the circumstances" fuels debate concerning the obligation (or lack thereof) to audio- or videotape one's sessions. Though we do not believe that tape-recording in either form is expected of psychologists, the advantages of creating and maintaining such records outweigh the disadvantages. James Wulach was the chair of the Committee on Professional Practice and Standards (COPPS) at the time that the American Psychological Association's record keeping guidelines (Committee on Professional Practice and Standards, 1993) were being developed. Wulach has expressed the view that "clearly, the videotape of a session is a vital record and, once taken, should not be destroyed. Even if agreed to by the parties, destruction of any portion of the record creates the risk of sanctions by ethics boards, regulatory agencies, or the legal system" (personal communication, February 26, 2003, quoted with permission). In our view, *any* record, in any form, must be preserved.

Martindale (2005a) writes, "child custody evaluations are often conducted in an atmosphere of distrust and animosity. In order to be effective, evaluators must utilize procedures designed to avoid fueling suspicion and contributing to the acrimony" (p. 34). During the course of an evaluation and while testifying, openness increases an evaluator's effectiveness. Disclosure of prior and current relationships before commencing an evaluation, diligence in the creation and maintenance of records during the course of an evaluation, and cooperation with those who are legally entitled to review one's files serve those who utilize an evaluator's services and enhance the evaluator's professional reputation.

Bumps in the Road

In this section, we discuss ways to address what we call "bumps in the road," areas of practice that often challenge evaluators' understanding of how best to conduct an evaluation. Sometimes we are challenged to consider whether to accept certain types of evidence. Other times we are challenged to consider whether to discuss in the body of the report information attributed to specific sources. Here, we discuss ways to think about some of these bumps in the road.

In our view, evaluators should make clear in a statement of understanding that, unless specific direction has been provided by the court, all decisions concerning who must be evaluated (and how extensively) and what information should be obtained and reviewed will be made by the evaluator. There may be instances in which evaluators will be asked to review information that they reasonably believe is likely to be more prejudicial than probative and instances in which they will be asked to contact individuals whom it would, in their judgment, be inappropriate to contact. Evaluators must be the final arbiters in such situations. When they are presented with information (diaries, documents, photographs, tapes, etc.) that they have reason to believe may have been obtained illegally, it is prudent for them to seek guidance from the attorneys or, if the attorneys are unable to agree, from the court. Evaluator requests for direction from the court inevitably entail delay and increase the cost of the evaluative process. While it is always our wish to conduct evaluations as expeditiously as possible and to avoid adding unnecessarily to the cost of evaluations, we believe that evaluators are taking a needless risk when they take it upon themselves to pass judgment on what is, in essence, a legal matter concerning which the attorneys for the parties cannot agree.

"But It's Not in the Code"

Not all professional behaviors that demonstrate negligence, incompetence, or unethical practice can be enumerated in statutes that define professional obligations, in a profession's ethics code, or in any other document. Some professional behaviors are too rarely encountered to warrant inclusion in such documents. On the other hand, in the eyes of those who develop descriptions of appropriate professional behavior, the obligation to take certain professional actions may seem so self-evident that discussion seems superfluous. Such is the case, in our view, with regard to the obligation to endeavor to resolve discrepancies in data. Not infrequently, evaluators will find that data from one source lend support to one hypothesis while data from another source lend support to an entirely different hypothesis. On occasion, obtaining the additional data that might provide clarification is not feasible. When it can be logically presumed that obtaining clarifying information will require no more than the expenditure of a reasonable amount of additional time, failure to seek the additional data is a failure to be thorough. As psychologists commence custody evaluations, it is always hoped that data from a variety of sources will be congruent, thereby offering clear support for one of the hypotheses being explored. On occasion, data generate questions the answers to which are only likely to be found if additional (and, in all likelihood, unanticipated) time is expended. We can think of no circumstances under which failure to seek the needed answers is acceptable.

Investigating Allegations

We discourage the use of an evaluative model that actively promotes the creation by each litigant of a list of allegations concerning the other parent. It is likely, however, that in most custody disputes, allegations of one type or another will spontaneously be registered. The specialty guidelines, section VI.C., remind us that "the forensic psychologist maintains professional integrity by examining the issue at hand from all reasonable perspectives, actively seeking information that will differentially test plausible rival hypotheses" (Committee on Ethical Guidelines for Forensic Psychologists, 1991, p. 661). Section VI.F. adds, "Where circumstances reasonably permit, forensic psychologists seek to obtain independent and personal verification of data relied upon" (p. 662).

Data collected in recent studies (Ackerman & Ackerman, 1997; Bow & Quinnell, 2001) suggest that approximately one-quarter of evaluative time was devoted to information verification (obtaining information from documents, from disinterested collateral sources, and from other nonparties). Newcomers to forensic work are strongly encouraged to reflect upon the two words "actively seeking." Custody evaluators cannot be passive recipients of offered information. They must know what questions to pose to parents, children, and collateral sources; must know what methods are likely to yield confirming or disconfirming data; and must maintain an investigative mind-set.

"Where'd You Get That?"

When the findings reported and recommendations offered by evaluators are challenged, all sources of data are likely to be challenged as well. Evaluators must not only be certain that information they have reviewed has been legally obtained, but they must also ensure that they do not inadvertently consider information provided by one side without the knowledge of the other side. When information obtained by an evaluator casts a parent in a negative light, that parent must be afforded the opportunity to offer a denial, an explanation, or a response. Some evaluators will not accept documents offered by litigants but only from the attorneys and insist that any documents forwarded to them be accompanied by a written assurance that the other side has been provided with a copy. Whatever method evaluators elect to employ, they should ensure that both sides know (in time to offer a response, if necessary) what information is being used in the formulation of the evaluators' opinions. When documents are received, note should be made of the date of their receipt, the manner in which they were delivered, and by whom they were delivered.

Is It Time for a Consultation?

In all probability, insecure individuals are not tempted to perform custody evaluations. It takes a certain amount of confidence to offer one's wisdom from the witness box after having been declared an expert. Confidence is an often overrated characteristic. All of us have, from time to time, been quite confident while being quite incorrect, we introduce here the concept of *constructive insecurity*. A modicum of insecurity may lead evaluators who encounter special problems to seek consultation with more experienced colleagues. Neither ethics committees nor licensing boards nor most jurors in malpractice actions expect professionals never to make errors. They merely expect professionals to take reasonable steps to prevent errors, and consultation with more experienced colleagues is one such reasonable step. When hindsight reveals a particular course of action to have been inadvisable, having enlisted appropriate assistance in deciding upon that course of action increases the likelihood that you will not be judged harshly by your peers.

Choosing Assessment Instruments

The question to ask is: "Do those instruments you have elected to utilize reliably measure *functional* abilities that bear directly upon the matter before the court?" LaFortune and Carpenter (1998, p. 222) list the seven most frequently used assessment instruments that "focus on parenting skill and the parent–child relationship" and that are "touted by their authors as helpful in clinical determinations of parental fitness." They then declare, "the validity of these measures is unestablished at best and seriously flawed at worst" (p. 222). Though the hope is expressed that improvements in these instruments may make them useful in the future, the authors conclude that their use at present "cannot be recommended" (p. 222).

Frequency of use by surveyed mental health professionals is not listed anywhere as an acceptable measure of either the reliability or the validity of an assessment instrument. It is reasonable to expect that evaluators will obtain, review, and critically examine the documentation concerning assessment instruments under consideration and that they will select only those the reliability and validity of which is acceptable when used for the purpose intended.

Consider the following, from *Standards for Educational and Psychological Testing* (American Educational Research Association et al., 1999):

1. Tests are to be accompanied by documentation that will provide test users with "the information needed to make sound judgments about the nature and quality of the test, the resulting scores, and the interpretations based on the test scores" (p. 67).
2. "Presentation and analyses of validity and reliability evidence often are not needed in a written report, but the professional strives to understand, and prepares to articulate, such evidence as the need arises" (p. 121).
3. "The greater the potential impact on test takers, for good or ill, the greater the need to identify and satisfy the relevant standards" (p. 112).

In 1971, a case came before the U.S. Supreme Court that had nothing whatsoever to do with custody work but the reverberations of which have been dramatically felt by evaluators. *Griggs v. Duke Power Company* (1971) involved procedures employed in the selection, placement, and promotion of personnel in an industrial setting. In deciding the case, the court ruled that any testing procedures must be demonstrably reasonable measures or predictors of job performance. We believe experienced evaluators agree that it is advisable to conceptualize parenting as a job and to be guided by the *Griggs* decision. In particular, evaluators must focus their attention and their assessment efforts on functional abilities that bear directly upon the attributes, behaviors, attitudes, and skills that published research suggests are reliably associated with effective parenting. Examining an attribute in the absence of evidence of its connection to parenting effectiveness leaves a psychologist open to criticism on several fronts.

The Report

In this section, we talk about ways in which to prepare a report to have maximum impact on the reader. We believe that everything and anything that has influenced the evaluator in his or her decision making is subject to disclosure and to examination by either side in the dispute. We believe that anything in the evaluator's file, anything that has affected the evaluator's thinking, and anyone with whom the evaluator has spoken may be disclosed at deposition and at trial.

In Praise of Clarity

With an awareness that some readers may view a paragraph on the merits of clarity as extraneous at best, we will continue undeterred. It is not at all uncommon to encounter reports in which assorted facts are presented unaccompanied by even a hint of their relative importance or the ways in which they shed light on one or more of the evaluative criteria. Statements appear without attribution and without needed modifiers that would identify them as allegations or as independently verified conclusions. When complex dynamics give rise to multifaceted recommendations, it must be made clear that certain components of the recommended course(s) of action are interdependent—that those contemplating them cannot pick and choose. We are not engaging in hyperbole when we express the view that whether or not a trial is necessary will in some instances hinge upon the clarity (or lack thereof) of an evaluator's report. It is hard to know whether you agree or disagree when you are not certain what has been said.

Privacy

Section 4.04 of the ethics code declares, in part, "Psychologists include in written and oral reports and consultations only information germane to the purpose for which the communication is made" (American Psychological Association, p. 1066). Even when evaluators are performing a court-ordered task and in the course of doing so are describing the behaviors or characteristics of a parent, they do not have carte blanche to include any information. The gray areas must be recognized. Does one's behavior on the job reflect upon one's parenting capacity? It depends upon what that behavior is. Questions concerning what to include in one's report become particularly thorny when the subject of discussion is a voluntary participant, such as a significant other.

"Isn't There a Name for That, Doctor?"

The American Psychological Association's custody evaluation guidelines remind evaluators (Guideline 3) that "psychopathology may be relevant to [their assessments], insofar as it has impact on the child or the ability to parent, but it is not the primary focus" (p. 668). In our view, it is advisable when describing pathology to include those attitudes, beliefs, and behaviors that are likely to interfere with effective parenting and to explain why they limit parenting capacity. Even psychologists who intentionally avoid assigning diagnostic labels should be familiar with the diagnostic criteria enumerated in the DSM-IV-TR (American Psychiatric Association, 2000). When cases are tried, attorneys wishing to accentuate a particular parent's pathology may endeavor to extract diagnostic labels from reluctant evaluators.

Nix *Ipse Dixit*[1]

There is a postscript to the *Daubert* case with which far too many psychologists are unfamiliar and that bears upon the defining characteristics of an expert opinion. The *Daubert* case was returned to the 9th Circuit Court and, again, the scientific evidence proffered by the plaintiffs was rejected. *Daubert v.*

Merrell Dow Pharmaceuticals, Inc. (on remand, 1995). Judge Alex Kozinski, writing for the court, declared that "something doesn't become 'scientific knowledge' just because it's uttered by a scientist" (at 1315–16). The court's task, Kozinski wrote, "is to analyze not what the experts say, but what basis they have for saying it" (at 1316). This was not the first time that a respected jurist had emphasized the importance of experts articulating the bases for their opinions. In 1967, David Bazelon, in his opinion in *Washington v. United States* (1967), declared that the court was "deeply troubled by the persistent use of labels and by the paucity of meaningful information" presented by experts (at 447). He added that, in the case at bar, the experts had provided "only the conclusions without any explanation of . . . what facts . . . [were] uncovered, and why these facts led to the conclusions" (at 447).

The "Ultimate-Issue" Issue

A case from Hawaii (*State v. Kim*, 1982) provides an interesting perspective. In the course of testimony, an expert expressed an opinion concerning a matter to be decided by the trier of fact. The Hawaii Supreme Court, in ruling on the admissibility of the testimony, declared that the opinion expressed "cannot be considered to be substantially more prejudicial than the testimony which led to the conclusion" (at 1335). Slobogin (1989, p. 263) has reported that "the available research strongly indicates that judges, lawyers, and juries all want ultimate issue testimony from the expert." Additionally, it is noteworthy that FRE 704 declares "testimony in the form of an opinion or inference otherwise admissible is not objectionable because it embraces an ultimate issue to be decided by the trier of fact." (There is an exception to this rule, but it applies to criminal proceedings and not to matters such as the resolution of custody disputes.) Finally, courts are generally granted wide discretionary power to decide how they will operate, particularly with regard to matters such as the assignment to litigants of financial responsibility for various fees. In many jurisdictions, by rules of the court, responsibility for payment of a testifying expert's fees is a function of the expert's opinion on the ultimate issue. In some jurisdictions, the party wishing to introduce the expert's report into evidence must pay the expert's court fees, while in others the party wishing to contest the expert's findings must pay the fees. Guideline 14 of the American Psychological Association's custody evaluation guidelines states, in part, "psychologists are obligated to be aware of the arguments on both sides of [the ultimate-issue] issue and to be able to explain the logic of their position concerning their own practice" (p. 679).

"Show Me the Money"

Koocher (1995, p. 479) declares that "it is clear that records that are needed to serve the client's imminent welfare cannot be held hostage to unpaid bills," but he points out that there is no requirement that a psychologist generate reports or summaries the production of which would demand the expenditure of additional time when agreed-upon fees have not been paid. From Koocher's perspective, "the client's imminent welfare" includes the legitimate need to expeditiously resolve an ongoing custody dispute (personal communication, March 11, 2000). Koocher's perspective on a psychologist's obligation is somewhat stricter than the perspective communicated in our ethics code's reference to records needed for purposes of "emergency treatment" (American Psychological Association, Standard 6.03, p. 1068).

Most states have tailored their laws concerning subpoenas after Rule 45 of the *Federal Rules of Civil Procedure*. It is likely that an already prepared report could be obtained by subpoena, but Shuman (1994, 6:16), in describing "the conflicting tension between the expert's proprietary interest in the knowledge that serves as the basis for that expertise and the judicial system's need for probative evidence to resolve disputes accurately," reports that most courts are reluctant to protect the asserted rights of the expert. We suggest that evaluators obtain payment in advance of the reasonably anticipated fees associated with report preparation.

Postevaluation Issues: The Virtues of Not Being Helpful, Part 2

Whatever psychologists' reasons may have been for becoming involved in custody work, we presume that a desire to be helpful to families was among them. The desire to be helpful may prompt psychologists to participate in settlement discussions. In most states, rules of admissibility bar the introduction into evidence of statements made or information produced during the course of discussions aimed at settlement. Let's assume that in the course of settlement discussions, the wife/mother offered to withdraw her petition for custody if the husband/father would relinquish any rights to the furniture contained within the marital residence. Would this offer influence an evaluator's view of the mother's custodial suitability? If settlement discussions were to prove unfruitful and the case were to proceed to trial, the evaluator would be called to testify. Would the evaluator be able to cite the mother's offer in the course of explaining the manner in which his or her opinion was formulated?

Pretrial Issues: The Virtues of Not Being Helpful, Part 3

Grisso (1990, p. 37) has observed that we "can be seduced by collaborative relationships having a subtle and almost irresistible pull toward advocacy. Often this will be at the expense of the objective attitude for which [we] must strive, as required by [our] professional ethical principles." LaFortune and Carpenter (1998, p. 213), reporting on the results of a survey of 165 licensed mental health professionals performing custody evaluations, concluded that impartiality was considered the most important of 13 "characteristics important in a child custody expert." David Shapiro (1991, p. 206) has opined that preparation *by* the expert *of* the attorney who will be directly examining him or her is appropriate.

In order to be of maximum assistance to the trier of fact, evaluators must be afforded the opportunity to relate all pertinent information and to articulate, in an organized fashion, the manner in which their opinions have been formulated. In particular, the court should be told what information was gathered, what procedures were utilized in gathering it, what criteria were employed in assessing comparative custodial fitness, and how the information gathered pertains to those criteria. The most effective way to accomplish this goal is for the expert to inform the attorney who will be conducting the direct examination of the questions that must be posed. In examining the balance of advantages and disadvantages, however, we have concluded that the risk of a perceived "collaborative relationship" and the resulting risk that the evaluator will be viewed as an advocate for one of the parties makes pre-trial preparation with an attorney inadvisable. We offer another proposal for consideration. An orderly direct examination can be ensured by providing a script to the attorney who will be conducting it as well as copies to the opposing attorney and to the attorney for the children. Providing the script instead of meeting to prepare removes the risk that the expert will be viewed as an advocate for the favored parent. Having the script may enable the opposing attorney to prepare more effectively for cross-examination, but a skilled evaluator whose assessment has been thorough should have nothing to fear.

The Virtues of Being Helpful, Part 1

Because both of us review the work of other evaluators, we acknowledge some subjectivity with regard to our views on the importance of review. The most effective manner in which to protect the rights of the nonfavored party in a custody dispute is to afford him or her and his or her counsel every reasonable opportunity to scrutinize the findings of *any* evaluation (even when the evaluator has been appointed by the court to assist the trier of fact). Evaluators should cooperate fully with those wishing to review their work. Foot dragging is self-injurious behavior. Uncooperative evaluators secure little if any protection for themselves by placing obstacles in the paths of those seeking information to which they are lawfully entitled. Such evaluators tarnish their professional reputations, inflict harm upon the image of psychology, and increase the probability that cross-examination will be vigorous and blistering.

The Big Day: The Virtues of Being Helpful, Part 2

We have urged newcomers to seek guidance from experienced colleagues. When issues of pretrial preparation and trial-related professional behavior are concerned, one is likely to encounter conflicting advice. We advise evaluators to bring the entire case file, including items they have *considered* but not *utilized* in formulating their opinions. If a litigant presents an evaluator with a document, it can reasonably be inferred that the litigant both believes the document to be pertinent and believes that the evaluator should consider its contents in formulating an opinion. If the evaluator, upon reviewing the document, decides that its contents are not pertinent, that decision—like any other decision that might affect the opinions offered by the evaluator—may be subject to examination. In our view, a cross-examining attorney is entitled to inquire about the bases for decisions not to consider certain information and is similarly entitled to inspect that information (in order to see if notations of any kind have been made on it, etc.).

The Virtues of Not Being Helpful, Part 4

If Yogi Berra were a psychologist, he might say: "Even if you're ad libbing, stick to the script." If you have done your job well, the opinions that you formulated prior to entering the courtroom were based upon sufficient information, pertinent to the BISC, and derived support from published knowledge in the field of psychology. Psychologists who have been testifying quite effectively and persuasively have been known to self-destruct when asked to provide an opinion on matters concerning which they have insufficient information, the pertinence of which is dubious, or that invite the inadvertent blending of personal opinions with professional opinions. When in doubt, decline to opine.

Return of the Big Day: It Ain't Over Even When It's Over

It is not without reason that we think the American Psychological Association erred significantly in weakening its position concerning multiple relationships. When it comes to relationships, time is of little consequence; last year's relationship affects today's decision making. Though carefully collected data are not available, relitigation is not uncommon in custodial placement matters. Just as a previous therapist should not offer to perform a custody evaluation, a custody evaluator should not offer clinical services simply because a judicial decision has been handed down. The evaluator-turned-therapist may be called upon again to offer opinions concerning issues of visitation or custodial placement.

The Shelf-Life of Your Data

Standard 9.08 (a) of the ethics code reads, "Psychologists do not base their assessment or intervention decisions or recommendations on data or test results that are outdated for the current purpose" (American Psychological Association, 2002, p. 1072). Not surprisingly, experts may hold differing views concerning the factors that render data "outdated for the current purpose." The temporal stability of the pictures that emerge from our data vary. Some intrapersonal characteristics and some interpersonal dynamics are more stable over time than others. Standard 9.06 admonishes psychologists to "indicate any significant limitations of their interpretations" (p. 1072).

It may be difficult for testifying psychologists to marshal their assertiveness skills when the individual instructing them to respond is a judge. When told that there is neither time nor funds for an update and instructed to offer an opinion based upon whatever is available, be certain to articulate with care the limitations that must be placed upon whatever opinions are offered and do not pass up any opportunity to explain the importance of the articulated limitations.

Ethical Dilemmas

Reasonable minds will disagree, so document your reasoning. Most psychologists have had enough exposure to medical settings to be aware of the adage that if it's not in the chart, it didn't happen. In the course of offering workshops to psychologists at all levels, we have become aware that many are surprised to learn that the adage applies not only to behavior (actions taken; words spoken), but also, in some contexts, to thought processes. The best evidence that a thorny issue has been thought through is a written record of one's reasoning. When a dilemma or ethical question occurs, we recommend that psychologists take the following steps:

1. Identify it in your notes.
2. Seek consultation and document having done so.
3. Seek information, if available, from applicable material appearing in the various documents that guide us in our work (the ethics code, the specialty guidelines, etc.) and record having done so.
4. Seek information, if available, from applicable material appearing in professional journals and document having done so.
5. Seek information from the materials retained by you following attendance at continuing education workshops.
6. Record the steps taken to resolve the dilemma.
7. Articulate, in your notes, the manner in which the final decision was made.

When faced with an ethical dilemma, consider using and documenting your use of a decision-making process such as this one,

1. Briefly describe the ethical dilemma and list the various issues (if there is more than one).
2. Identify all those who are likely to be affected by the decision.
3. Specify what consideration is owed to each individual affected and the basis for it.
4. List the ethical standards and/or practice guidelines that appear to be applicable.
5. For each issue, outline alternative actions, list the reasonably anticipated consequences and benefits of each action, and list any published research that sheds light on the anticipated consequences and benefits.
6. Identify the smallest change in circumstances that would cause you to choose a different action from the one tentatively chosen and identify what that different action would be.
7. Identify what action(s) must be taken in the event that there are unanticipated consequences and/or in the event that negative consequences that were considered are more serious than were anticipated.

When Law and Ethics Clash

Section IV.G. of the specialty guidelines for forensic psychologists declares, "When conflicts arise between the forensic psychologist's professional standards and the requirements of legal standards, a particular court, or a directive by an officer of the court or legal authorities, the forensic psychologist has an obligation to make those legal authorities aware of the source of the conflict and to take reasonable steps to resolve it" (Committee on Ethical Guidelines for Forensic Psychologists, 1991). Most psychologists preparing to offer forensic psychological services learn in the earliest stages of their re-education that law trumps ethics, but there are times when it can reasonably be expected that psychologists will not reflexively capitulate when directed to engage in behaviors that are disapproved of by the profession. Consider the scenario outlined below.

> Under the terms of an agreement entered into with his soon-to-be-ex-wife, Peter Parent's visitation with the couple's son, PJ, is supervised. He appears before the court seeking a modification of the agreement and, in particular, seeking unsupervised visitation. The court appoints an evaluator. The evaluation commences, but Mr. Parent is less cooperative than one might anticipate in light of his position before the court. As the Christmas holiday period approaches, Mr. Parent's attorney requests an emergency conference with the court, in the hope that it will authorize some unsupervised visitation between Mr. Parent and PJ. The court contacts the evaluator and is informed that, though a Minnesota Multiphasic Personality Inventory—2 (MMPI-2) has been administered and scored, interviews with Mr. Parent have not yet been conducted and no collateral source information has been gathered. The court directs the psychologist to fax the MMPI-2 data. The psychologist persuades

the court that it would be more appropriate if the scores were to be sent to the chief psychologist of the county's court consultation unit. The scores are sent to the chief psychologist; the court asks its on-staff psychologist to interpret the scores; and, not surprisingly, the chief psychologist endeavors to explain why this should be done. Next, the court leaves a phone message for the evaluator and asks that he or she appear in court to offer an interim recommendation and explain the test scores. The evaluator writes the letter reprinted below to the court.

[Law clerk] has left a phone message for me in which it is indicated that my presence is desired at a conference to be conducted on December 17th; that my voluntary participation is anticipated; but, that if I decline to participate voluntarily, a subpoena will be issued. I respectfully request that you consider that which follows.

I ask that the court recognize that I have not completed my assessment of Mr. Parent. *The official position of the American Psychological Association concerning statements that I can and cannot make is expressed quite unambiguously in its ethics code (American Psychological Association, 1992). Section 7.02, subsection b reads, "psychologists provide written or oral forensic reports or testimony of the psychological characteristics of an individual only after they have conducted an examination of the individual adequate to support their statements or conclusions." My brief contacts to date with Mr. Parent do not constitute "an examination of the individual adequate to support" any statements or conclusions.*

While it is always my desire to assist the court in adjudicating matters such as this, it would be inappropriate for me to offer opinions concerning the significance of any particular test scores without first having obtained pertinent background information, without having interviewed Mr. Parent, and without having obtained collateral source information.

In a text described by its authors as having been written in order "to help those who testify about the Minnesota Multiphasic Personality Inventory (MMPI) and attorneys who encounter their testimony" (p. 1), Pope, Butcher, and Seelen (1993) "emphasize . . . that the MMPI, even when scored and interpreted by a computer, produces hypotheses *[emphasis in original] that must be considered in light of other sources of information" (p. 26). In a text described as "a deskbook for judges," the authors declare that judges "must be aware of the risk of overreliance upon test scores when making assessments and judgments about people" (National Interdisciplinary Colloquium on Child Custody, 1998, p. 362).*

Even if Mr. Parent's test data were suggestive of psychopathology, the pertinence of the apparent pathology to the matter at bar would have to be investigated. The American Psychological Association's guidelines for child custody evaluations in divorce proceedings (1994, section I-3) declares, "Psychopathology may be relevant to such an assessment, insofar as it has impact on the child or the ability to parent, but it is not the primary focus." Clearly, not all pathology in parents leads them to engage in behaviors that place a child at risk for either physical or emotional harm. Where the matter before the court involves the need (or lack thereof) for supervision of visitation, a forensic psychologist is obligated to focus on the parent's actions while in the company of the child and not to be distracted by test data that may be more prejudicial than probative.

For those fearful of being found in contempt of court, there is an important difference between ignoring a subpoena and filing a motion either (1) to reargue, (2) to have the subpoena quashed, or (3) to have the subpoena modified. On occasion, psychologists are justified in not doing what a subpoena commands them to do. They must, nevertheless, respond in some appropriate manner. With the exception of rulings emanating from the Supreme Court of the United States, there are appropriate means by which directives from other courts can be appealed. If a *judicial subpoena* directs you to do something that you believe you should not do, you can inform the court of your intention to file a motion to reargue (a motion that asks the court to provide you with the opportunity to present information apparently not previously considered and reconsider its own order on the basis of the new information). To the best of our knowledge, courts always warn people before finding them in contempt. The difficult decisions must be made after the court issues such warning.

Ethics and Your Other Job

After having established themselves as evaluators, psychologists will often be asked to review work performed by other evaluators. It is not uncommon for psychologists who have been scrupulously ethical as evaluators to become inadvertently less attentive to ethical issues when they function as a consultant to an attorney. The ethical obligations of an impartial examiner are clear to almost all who function in that role. The ethical obligations of a consultant to an advocate for one side are less clear, but, though the tasks are quite different, very few of the ethical obligations are so.

The obligation to report what we believe to be unethical behavior by others "does not apply when . . . psychologists have been retained to review the work of another psychologist whose professional conduct is in question" (American Psychological Association, 2002, Standard 1.05, p. 1063). When functioning as consultants to attorneys, psychologists must respect the litigation strategies of those who have retained them. Calling attention to perceived ethical infractions may undermine attorneys' trial plans. The responsibility to those who have retained us as consultants does not, however, alter "our essential role as expert to the court" nor our obligation to "assist the trier of fact to understand the evidence" (from VII.F. of the specialty guidelines [Committee on Ethical Guidelines for Forensic Psychologists, 1991, p. 665]). In the section of the specialty guidelines that addresses public and professional communications (section VII, p. 664) one finds references to our obligation to "promote understanding and avoid deception" (subsection A) and to "correct misuse or misrepresentation of [our] products, evidence, and testimony" (A.1.); to our "special responsibility for fairness and accuracy" (subsection B); and to our responsibility not to engage in either active or passive involvement in "partisan distortion or misrepresentation" (subsection D).

Our effectiveness as experts is increased when our credibility has been established. Establishing that credibility is linked to openness, and openness suggests bringing one's entire file when making a court appearance, but there are also exceptions to these general rules. For examples, when you are functioning as a consultant to an attorney, portions of your file may be protected by attorney work product privilege and the retaining attorney may have views that differ from yours.

Summary

In this chapter, we discussed many of the bumps in the road and challenges often faced by custody evaluators throughout the evaluation process. We emphasized the need for evaluators to provide clear information about the evaluation process to parents and their attorneys prior to beginning the evaluation. Defining the scope of the evaluation and identifying specific questions to be investigated are important first steps in the process. We discussed the need to document all investigative endeavors and to be prepared to explain how data support opinions offered to the court.

Note

1. *Ipse dixit* is from the Latin meaning "he himself said it; an assertion by one whose sole authority for it is the fact that he himself said it" (Gifis, 1991, p. 252). It is used in this context to refer to the historical tendency of courts to accept an expert's pronouncement simply because the individual was qualified as an expert by a court. The *Joiner* decision made clear that an expert's opinion must be tied to the data generated by a reliable methodology.
In *General Electric Co. v Joiner* (1997), the U.S. Supreme Court bridled expert opinions by noting the following:

> But conclusions and methodology are not entirely distinct from one another. Trained experts commonly extrapolate from existing data. But nothing in either *Daubert* or the *Federal Rules*

of Evidence requires a district court to admit opinion evidence that is connected to existing data only by the ipse dixit of the expert. A court may conclude that there is simply too great an analytical gap between the data and the opinion proffered. (p. 146)

In other words, the court may not allow an expert to state something simply because of his or her *ipse dixit*; that is, credence is not lent to something based solely upon the explanation that the expert "says it's so." There must be some empirical or logical argument that ties together the data and the opinion.

CHAPTER 4

Minimizing and Correcting for Bias

One of the most serious challenges to evaluators relates not to decisions concerning methodology or to selection of assessment instruments, but to guarding against various sources of bias. Because bias in any form is internal, and because most of the biases affecting evaluators are likely to operate unconsciously, there is no way to gather meaningful data concerning the types of bias evaluators have struggled with. It seems likely to us that the most prevalent form of bias is *confirmatory bias*—the inclination to seek information that will confirm an initially generated hypothesis and the disinclination to seek information that will disconfirm that hypothesis (Martindale, 2005a).

Though it has not been studied in a custody evaluation context, research conducted in other contexts suggests that confirmatory bias is quite prevalent (see Arkes, 1981; Borum et al., 1993; Dailey, 1952; Davies, 2003; Garb, 1994; Greenwald & Pratkanis, 1988; Greenwald, Pratkanis, Leippe, & Baumgardner, 1986; Haverkamp, 1993; Hogarth, 1981; Klayman & Ha, 1987; Mahoney, 1977; Otto, 1989; Strohmer, Shivy, & Chiodo, 1990; Tversky & Kahneman, 1974).

The susceptibility of trained mental health professionals to confirmatory bias was dramatically illustrated by Rosenhan (1973) in his classic study *On Being Sane in Insane Places*. Though not described by Rosenhan as a research study of confirmatory bias, it demonstrates how a diagnosis, once made, affected the manner in which experienced mental health professionals perceived and processed additional information. Rosenhan's subjects presented themselves at 12 different hospital admissions offices in five different states. The subjects described atypical auditory hallucinations—specifically, voices that uttered the words *empty, hollow,* and *thud.* In 11 cases, a diagnosis of schizophrenia was made, and in one case a diagnosis of manic-depressive disorder was made. After having been admitted, the subjects (referred to by Rosenhan as "pseudopatients") behaved normally. An examination of their files revealed that ordinary behaviors were perceived as being related to their presumed psychiatric disorders and that unremarkable histories and family dynamics were also interpreted as being related (in some cases, causally) to the presumed disorders. Information taken and behaviors observed were construed as supporting the intake diagnosis.

Confirmatory Bias and Confirmatory Distortion

Social psychologists and policy makers believe it is important that we distinguish between prejudice (an attitude) and discrimination (a pattern of behaviors presumably motivated by prejudice). Whether conscious or unconscious, confirmatory bias, like prejudice, can be difficult to identify and, as a result, difficult to address. Martindale (2005a) has proposed that we endeavor to distinguish between the internal processes referred to as confirmatory bias and *confirmatory distortion*—a process by which an evaluator, motivated by the desire to bolster a favored hypothesis, intentionally engages in selective reporting or skewed interpretation of data, thereby producing a distorted picture of the family whose custody dispute is before the court. Some might presume that such premeditated misrepresentation of data is rare, but Golding (1995), in commenting on the involvement of mental health professionals in custodial suitability evaluations, has opined that "biased advocacy is . . . rampant" (p. 422).

Cognitive Dissonance and Bias

Uncovering information that supports one's initial impressions is inherently gratifying, while uncovering information that calls into question one's initial impressions generates discomfort. In mentioning this dynamic, we are merely reminding readers of a phenomenon originally described by Leon Festinger and his colleagues more than four decades ago (Aronson, 1968, 1992; Brehm & Cohen, 1962; Cooper & Fazio, 1984; Elliot & Devine, 1994; Festinger, 1957; Festinger & Carlsmith, 1959; Festinger, Riecken, & Schachter, 1956; Steele, Spencer, & Lynch, 1993; Wicklund & Brehm, 1976).

Strohmer and colleagues (1990) have demonstrated that mental health professionals are also susceptible to the power of suggestion. In their study, counselors were asked to consider a particular clinical hypothesis and, in doing so, to reflect upon a narrative report they had read 1 week earlier. The counselors recalled more confirmatory information than disconfirmatory information, even though the report contained more of the latter. In a second study reported in the same article, counselors were asked to consider a particular clinical hypothesis and, using a narrative report available to them as they contemplated the hypothesis, to list "confirmatory and disconfirmatory pieces of information" (p. 469). More confirmatory pieces of information than disconfirmatory pieces of information were listed even though the narrative report contained more pieces of disconfirmatory information. We should emphasize that the hypothesis suggested to the counselors was offered by those conducting the research (not a peer, supervisor, or more experienced colleague).

Positive Test Strategy and Bias

In their discussion of confirmatory bias, Klayman and Ha (1987) hypothesize the operation of what they refer to as a *positive test strategy*, a tendency to pose questions the answers to which are more likely to yield confirmatory information than nonsupportive information. For example, Parent A alleges that Parent B is an "angry person." The custody evaluator, meeting with Parent B after having heard this allegation, poses questions to Parent B concerning feelings experienced during divorce litigation; specifically, inquiries are made concerning situations in which experiencing anger would be more likely than not. The evaluator, both in posing the questions and in reporting Parent B's responses, makes no distinction between the internal emotional experience of anger and the overt expression of anger. Further, in formulating the questions, the evaluator selects situations whose connection to matters of parenting is tenuous.

Particularly when the initial evaluative session is conducted with a litigant who is perceived as both likable and credible, hypotheses formulated on the basis of information provided by this litigant may play an important role in the evaluator's conceptualization of the family, the sources of discord, and the characteristics of the not-yet-seen second litigant. For example, the evaluator sees the mother first, and during the initial session she expresses concern that her husband, with his greater financial resources, "may have been coached for this." Early in the initial session with the father, the evaluator poses several hypothetical questions to which the father provides well-reasoned responses. In the margin of the evaluator's contemporaneously taken notes appears the word "Coached!!!" For all intents and purposes, the evaluator has made his or her call. Allegations registered by the father and his denials of allegations registered by the mother will not be deemed credible, test data that cast him in a favorable light will be viewed with suspicion, and healthy interactions between him and the children will be seen as further evidence of coaching.

Anchoring

Mental health professionals should not underestimate the potentially distorting effects of *anchoring*—the perceptual and cognitive dynamic in which information that may not be pertinent and may even be false is presented in a manner that gives it salience. Information that is perceptually and cognitively prominent functions as a reference point (an anchor) and is used in the processing of other information. Operating by means of an attentional mechanism that Arkes (1991) refers to as *priming*, the anchor leads us to attend selectively. In a study conducted by Chapman and Johnson (1999), subjects considering the features of various apartments were more attentive to positive features when they had first been told that the rental fee was high and were more attentive to negative features when they had been informed that the rental fee was low. As cognitive dissonance theory suggests, we like things to make sense. It makes sense if an expensive apartment has many positive features and few negative features. It makes sense if an inexpensive apartment has many negative features and few positive features. If two pieces of a puzzle fail to fit but one of those pieces is malleable, we will endeavor to manipulate that piece. The price of each apartment is presented as a given. Perceptions of the positive and negative features of each apartment, however, can be shaped to fit that given. Through the operation of selective attention, perceptions of the apartments are constrained by the anchor (the rental fee). Northcraft and Neale (1987) conducted a similar study, including real estate appraisers among their subjects and asking that a house with a predetermined listing price (the anchor) be appraised. Even the professional appraisers were affected in their judgments by the stated listing price.

Haverkamp (1993) has found that when hypotheses are "self-generated," a significant risk is created that "information relevant to alternative hypotheses will not be elicited" (p. 313). It is noteworthy that Haverkamp reports a "lack of significant differences for experience and training levels" (p. 313).

Selective Attention and Bias

What we see depends upon the direction in which we look (Kuhn, 1962). Within the context of custody work, theory testing does not proceed as promoters of the scientific method would wish it to. Too often, the presentation of a hypothesis by a persuasive litigant can create an expectation on the part of the evaluator (Rosenthal, 1966) that can lead to selective attending as the evaluation progresses and to selective recall as the evaluator begins mentally to assemble the information that will appear in his or her report.

Overconfidence and Bias

Evaluators whose work has been contaminated by confirmatory bias may express high levels of confidence in the opinions that they express and may, as a result, be quite persuasive. Confirmatory bias contributes to overconfidence, as when new information calls a hypothesis into question, uncertainty follows. Section VI.C. of the specialty guidelines for forensic psychologists (Committee on Ethical Guidelines for Forensic Psychologists, 1991) admonishes us to examine "the issue at hand from all reasonable perspectives, actively seeking information that will differentially test rival hypotheses" (p. 661). When faced with competing hypotheses, each of which is supported to some extent by the data that have been collected, the critical thinker is unable to achieve complete certainty (Koriat, Lichtenstein, & Fischhoff, 1980). When called upon to support an opinion that has been offered, the expert who has never seriously contemplated more than one hypothesis engages in a confirmatory mental search process. Data supportive of the focal hypothesis readily come to mind; non-supportive data are not encountered.

Research suggests that, where conflicting information must be contemplated in order to formulate an opinion, information received earlier in the deliberative process has greater impact than information received later (Crano, 1977; Belsky & Gilovich, 1999). As applied to custody evaluations, the research suggests that unless something immediately arouses suspicion, there is a natural (albeit unintentional) tendency to accept the essential accuracy of the fact pattern as related by the individual from whom background information is initially obtained.

Human beings are not passive recipients of sensory input; we cannot avoid endeavoring to make sense of what we perceive. A computer can hold information in a not-yet-assigned space until further instructions are provided, but humans integrate new information with information already stored as stimuli are perceived. No human evaluator can take information from Parent A and avoid processing that information until Parent B has been heard from.

In their survey of psychologists' practices and procedures in child custody evaluations, Bow and Quinnell (2001) found that 31% of respondents conducted the initial evaluative session with both parents. There are significant methodological advantages to this choice. If an evaluator meets with one parent before the other, the risk is created that the evaluator will frame the interview questions for the second parent around the impressions and hypotheses generated from the data gathered during the initial interview with the first parent. The evaluator may use the information gathered from one parent in constructing a mental framework within which subsequently gathered information will be placed.

Under certain circumstances, conducting the initial session with both parents may not be prudent. In such cases, we suggest that the evaluator thoroughly review the pleadings and create a set of interview questions to be utilized with each parent during their individual interviews. In this way, each parent's perspectives, concerns, and allegations are processed as the evaluator formulates hypotheses and constructs the cognitive framework within which subsequently gathered information will be placed.

Even if the framework is a temporary mechanism for sorting information, it is during the initial session that an evaluator develops an understanding of the premarital relationship, the marital relationship, the sources of marital conflict, the obstacles to voluntary and cooperative dispute resolution, and the strengths and deficiencies of each party's parenting ability. Though first impressions are not cemented, the research evidence suggests that they are strong. Belsky and Gilovich (1999) found that if potential stock buyers were provided with a mix of information about a company, the decision to purchase the company's stock or not was significantly influenced by the sequence in which information was presented. When positive information preceded negative information, a "buy" decision was more likely. A decision not to buy was more likely when negative information preceded positive information.

There are no current survey data that might identify the point in the evaluative process at which evaluators formulate their initial hypotheses; however, three decades ago, Sandifer, Hordern, and Green (1970) reported that psychiatrists formulated their initial diagnostic hypotheses only minutes into their intake interviews. Our review of custody evaluators' contemporaneously taken notes suggest that evaluators occasionally record hypotheses in the early pages of their first session notes and, at times, record what can only be described as premature conclusions.

Stephen Behnke, the ethics director for the American Psychological Association, has observed that "Principle A [of the American Psychological Association ethics code] recognizes the influence that psychologists have over others and exhorts psychologists to use that influence responsibly and with care. In few places of our profession is this influence felt more than in psychological assessment" (Behnke, 2004, p. 58). The portion of an advisory report in which evaluators outline assessment data and offer interpretations of those data is fertile ground for the operation of confirmatory bias and confirmatory distortion. It is not uncommon, for example, to encounter discussions of assessment data under a heading labeled "Test Results." Readers of reports may mistakenly presume that there is no room for deliberate distortion in the reporting of test results and only minimal room for subjectivity.

Use of Psychological Tests and Bias

Referring to an instrument as a *test* creates in the minds of readers a certain aura of precision. Evaluators may describe as tests assessment devices that are far from precise. The *Standards for Educational and Psychological Testing* state, "A test is an evaluative device or procedure in which a sample of an examinee's behavior in a specified domain is obtained and subsequently evaluated and scored using a standardized process" (American Educational Research Association et al., 1999, p. 3). The importance of standardization is emphasized: "In all cases . . . tests standardize the process by which test taker responses to test materials are evaluated and scored" (p. 3). Further, those who utilize various assessment devices are reminded that "the applicability of the *Standards* to an evaluation device or method is not altered by the label applied to it" (p. 3, italics in original). Presumably, this reminder is intended to exhort mental health professionals to choose assessment instruments based upon "written documentation on the validity and reliability of [those instruments] for the specific use intended" (American Educational Research Association et al., 1985, p. 41). We are also reminded that "the greater the potential impact on test takers, for good or ill, the greater the need to identify and satisfy the relevant standards" (American Educational Research Association et al., 1999, p. 112).

Projective Techniques

Some of the instruments utilized by evaluators are not accompanied by any documentation relating to validity or reliability. In commenting on projective devices, Anastasi (1988) writes "the final interpretation of projective test responses may reveal more about the theoretical orientation, favorite hypotheses, and personality idiosyncrasies of the examiner than it does about the examinee's personality dynamics" (p. 614). Even those who feel that Anastasi has overstated the case would presumably agree that, in the interpretation of a test taker's responses, there is ample room for confirmatory bias or confirmatory distortion.

Self-Report Inventories

The use of self-report inventories (often referred to as objective tests) and computer-generated interpretive reports has been the subject of considerable discussion (Butcher, 2003; Eyde, Kowal, & Fishburne, 1991; Fowler, 1969; Moreland, 1985; Otto & Butcher, 1995; Otto & Collins, 1995; Otto et al., 2000). Millon, Davis, and Millon (1997) comment on self-report inventories,

> there are distinct boundaries to the accuracy of the self-report format; by no means is it a perfect data source. Inherent psychometric limits, the tendency of similar patients to interpret questions differently, the effect of current affective states on trait measures, and the effort of patients to affect certain false appearances and impressions all lower the upper boundaries of this method's potential accuracy. (p. 7)

Rarely do evaluators include in their advisory reports all the data that are generated when such instruments are administered to litigants. As might be expected, evaluators tend to cite those data that they deem pertinent. As evaluators decide what is pertinent, confirmatory bias can influence the decision-making process. When confirmatory distortion is involved, we find that all the pertinent data (those that appear in the report) are supportive and all the nonsupportive data (identified in a review of the file) have been excluded from the report.

Computer-Generated Interpretive Report Data

Evaluators who utilize computerized scoring services but who interpret the data independently can be selectively attentive to supportive data if they are so inclined. The problem is not resolved by the use of computer-generated interpretive reports. For many reasons, not the least of which is "the effect of current affective states on trait measures" (referred to by Millon, above), evaluators must review interpretive reports with great care. Standard 9.09(c) of the ethics code reminds psychologists that they "retain responsibility for the appropriate application, interpretation, and use of assessment instruments, whether they score and interpret such tests themselves or use automated or other services" (American Psychological Association, 2002, p. 1072). The responsibility alluded to presents an opportunity for confirmatory bias or confirmatory distortion. The evaluator can select from a lengthy narrative report those passages that are in accord with the evaluator's impressions, omit passages that would call into question those impressions, and explain both of these editorial actions by referring to the expert's ultimate responsibility for the interpretation of test data.

Note Taking and Bias

Martindale (2001b) writes, "The search for indications of bias is most efficiently begun by comparing the contents of an evaluator's contemporaneously taken notes with the evaluator's description of factors supporting the opinion(s) offered" (p. 488). We can easily see confirmatory bias or confirmatory distortion where there is a discernible pattern of discrepancies between the information that appears in the evaluator's process notes and the information that he or she includes in the advisory report. For example, if parenting strengths in the nonfavored parent are described in the contemporaneously taken notes but are nowhere to be seen in the advisory report, either bias or outright distortion is at work. Bias or distortion is also operating when parenting deficiencies in the favored parent are noted in the contemporaneously taken notes but not alluded to in the advisory report.

Transparency and Due Process

Child custody evaluations are often conducted in an atmosphere of distrust and animosity. In order to be effective, evaluators must utilize procedures designed to avoid fueling suspicion and contributing to the acrimony. The integrity of the evaluative process is dependent upon transparency and the degree to which actions by evaluators are subject to scrutiny. Unless otherwise informed by the court, evaluators should presume that everything in the file is subject to disclosure. Withholding or destroying components of the file undermines an essential element of our system of justice; courts, not psychologists, decide what is and what is not discoverable.

In order to be effective, forensic examiners must be credible, must recognize that credibility is earned and that complete openness is one means by which an expert establishes credibility, and must respect the rights of those wishing to question an expert's opinions and the manner in which they were formulated. That is the gist of the philosophy of transparency. The pattern of behavior that flows from this philosophy includes diligence in the creation and maintenance of one's records and prompt production of the complete contents of one's file (in response to lawful requests).

An evaluator should create a file at the time of initial contact with the disputing parents. Ideally, messages left by those seeking an evaluator's services should be responded to by a member of the evaluator's secretarial staff. When this is not possible, only the most basic information should be taken during an initial phone contact, but all information should be recorded with care. It is not uncommon (nor is it unreasonable) for a cross-examining attorney to inquire concerning the initial contact with an evaluator. An evaluator's records should indicate when the initial contact was made and both what information was provided and by whom. Prior to agreeing to accept an assignment, an evaluator should determine who the participants are and disclose prior involvements with any of them. Keeping track of contacts is relatively easy, making such contacts known sets the stage for an open process, and preevaluation disclosure eliminates one of the more unpleasant avenues of cross-examination. With the exceptions of dishonesty and displays of ignorance, there is no greater threat to an expert's credibility than the appearance of trying to hide how he or she conducted the evaluation.[1]

Preserve the Complete Record

The Association of Family and Conciliation Courts' *Model Standards of Practice for Child Custody Evaluation* outlines just what constituted the record of an evaluation. In Standard 3.1, the position is taken that the term *record*

> applies to all notes, documents, recordings, correspondence in any form or on any medium, tangible, electronic, hand-written, or mechanical, that are specifically related to the evaluation being conducted. The term "record," as used herein, includes, but is not limited to, all a) reports, letters, affidavits, and declarations; b) notes, recordings, and transcriptions that were created before, during, or after interactions with persons in connection with the evaluation; c) fully or partially completed assessment instruments; d) scored and un-scored raw test data, scoring reports, and interpretations; e) billing, expense, and income records pertaining to the services provided; f) mechanical, digital, physical or electronic print, film, photocopy, tape, audio, video, or photographic records; and g) all other notes, records, copies, and communications in any form that were created, received, or sent in connection with the evaluation. (p. 75)

In Standard 3.2(a), the Association of Family and Conciliation Courts admonishes evaluators to "presume that their records are created, maintained, and preserved in anticipation of their review by others who are legally entitled to possess them and/or to review them." Similarly, The American Psychological Association's guidelines for child custody evaluations in divorce proceedings (1994) remind psychologists that "all raw data and interview information are recorded with an eye towards their possible review by other psychologists or the court, where legally permitted" (Guideline 16, p. 679).

The fact that creation of an audio or video record is not required does not in any way diminish the obligation to preserve the record if it *has* been made. The American Psychological Association's record-keeping guidelines (1993, p. 984) instruct psychologists to maintain their records. The applicability of the admonition is not limited to records created in compliance with specific legal or ethical requirements. An evaluator cannot be effectively cross-examined if he or she has concealed or destroyed records that might form the basis of the cross-examination.

Judicial decisions in custody matters are more likely to serve the interests of children when court-appointed evaluators create detailed records, maintain those records, and disclose them to appropriate individuals or agencies in response to direction from the court. Psychologists are reminded in the record-keeping guidelines that "no record is free from disclosure all of the time, regardless of the wishes of the client or the psychologist" (p. 985).

Even written permission obtained from evaluees to destroy videotapes made during the course of the evaluation does not transform an unacceptable practice into an acceptable one. Those giving permission may be doing so either because they do not understand the implications or because they are reluctant to antagonize the evaluator by refusing to sign a document presented by him or her. Informed consent is predicated upon a complete knowledge of the pertinent facts, the cognitive capacity to utilize those facts in making one's decision, and the opportunity to contemplate one's decision free of coercive interference (Nolan & Nolan-Haley, 1990, pp. 305, 314, 779). Even when advised to obtain legal counsel, litigants often make decisions without having conferred with their attorneys. Litigants may fail to appreciate the importance of securing legal advice, and their desire to minimize legal expenses may tempt them to make an irrevocable decision without fully understanding its consequences. Even if parties to a custody dispute are free from coercion and have full knowledge of the consequences when they authorize the destruction of portions of the record, doing so leaves the interests of the child unrepresented and unprotected in the event of a trial.

Threats to Due Process

Without access to an evaluator's full file, a cross-examining attorney is placed at a significant disadvantage in endeavors to shed light on deficiencies in an evaluator's work. When an evaluator's alteration, concealment, or destruction of portions of the file make a thorough exploration of his or her methods and procedures impossible, the risk is increased that errors will go undetected.

When we enter the forensic arena, we implicitly accept several responsibilities. Among them is the obligation not to lose sight of both professional and personal limitations. Our documented susceptibility to bias should alert us to the importance of establishing, maintaining, and producing our records, so that bias, confirmatory distortion, methodological errors, or flawed data interpretations can be identified.

Judges are expected to render decisions only on the basis of information admitted into evidence (and, therefore, a matter of record). Forensic psychologists should formulate opinions only on the basis of information that is in their records and is available for inspection. Only in this way can psychologists be cross-examined concerning the manner in which the information was utilized in the formulation of the opinion(s) conveyed to the court. Concealment or destruction of records circumvents due process.[2]

The Honorable Stephen Hjelt, the presiding administrative law judge for the California Office of Administrative Hearings in San Diego, has observed that, more than any other, the expertise of the mental health profession "has come to be used and relied upon by the courts" (Hjelt, 2000, p. 9). He points out, however, than in the often public whining of mental health professionals concerning the problems associated with irrational litigants and zealous disciplinary boards, we have engaged in some blame avoidance (p. 12). Our efforts to secure realistic protection from frivolous complaints and suits will be fruitless unless we more effectively police ourselves. Adopting the philosophy of transparency and the pattern of professional behavior that flows from it will dispel concerns regarding our methods and increase confidence in our trustworthiness and independence. Concealment or destruction of records will generate suspicion concerning our methods, our expertise, and our integrity. If our actions produce a loss of confidence in our trustworthiness, legislators and jurists will be disinclined to insulate us from complaining litigants.

It is likely that most evaluators retain for inspection documents that they have relied upon in formulating their opinions. Some, however, feel no obligation to retain items that have been considered but *not* relied upon. In law, *considering* something involves examining it and deliberating about it (Nolan & Nolan-Haley, 1990, p. 306). Attorneys or mental health professionals reviewing an evaluator's work should have the opportunity to explore the possibility that relevant documents were ignored. On occasion, evaluators will decline to review documents that have been brought to their attention and that are reasonably viewed as pertinent. In a recently decided custody matter, the judge, in her decision, observed that the evaluator had "refused to review and consider a submission . . . [that] included an affidavit . . . containing information about [the] mental health and stability" of one of the participants in the evaluation (*Frankel v. Frankel*, unpublished decision of January 6, 2004).

Summary

In this chapter, we have noted concerns about the potentially powerful role of bias in child custody evaluation work. We discussed different types of bias and confirmatory distortion. We noted how cognitive processes such as anchoring may affect decision making during interviews, and we provided ideas for evaluators to consider that may assist in minimizing the potential effects of such bias during initial interviews. We also noted how bias may affect our use and interpretation of psychological tests and the data they generate.

We voiced concern about concealing, destroying, or altering any material reviewed during the evaluation process. Framed within the concept of transparency and due process, we talked about our legal and ethical responsibility to preserve all records obtained during the evaluation process. We noted the importance of transparency at every step in our work. We described transparency as a means of demonstrating our openness to review, as a means through which attorneys may exercise their right to review all aspects of our work, and as a means to demonstrate to the court our openness to being scrutinized so that the court can reach a more informed understanding of how the data we relied on led to the opinions we have expressed.

Notes

1. We have elected to include a fairly extensive discussion of the importance of transparency in custody-related work in order to contrast our perspective with that expressed in an American Psychological Association–published text in which the destruction of records is advocated. In this text, the authors endorse the erasure of tapes and suggest that doing so "prevents the opposing counsel from using contemporaneous material out of context during a later cross-examination at deposition or trial" (Benjamin & Gollan, 2003, p. 35).

2. All psychologists should be mindful of our history. Our ability to assist courts had to be established (*Jenkins v. U.S.*, 1962). That which we have fought hard to obtain may be lost unless we take proactive steps to preserve our integrity as a profession. To the successful evaluator, it may appear that everyone seeks our wisdom. We must not lose sight of the fact that our critics have never been far away and that respected psychologists have been among them. Melton and his colleagues (1987), commenting on our assessments of comparative custodial fitness, declared, "there is probably no forensic question on which overreaching by mental health professionals has been so common and so egregious" (p. 330). The importance of reclaiming our professional integrity and reestablishing our credibility becomes particularly apparent when our supporters become our critics.

CHAPTER 5

Increasing the Reliability and Relevance of Child Custody Evaluations

In previous chapters we suggested that the legal system's require-ments for reliable and relevant information are consistent with psy-chologists' ethical obligation to base their investigative techniques on scientific knowledge and the tools and techniques that have been developed from scientific research. The legal requirements of reliability and relevance are integrated into the methods and procedures used in scientifically informed child custody evaluations. One result is the development of methods and procedures used in child custody evaluations that are based upon a genuinely scientific foundation. A second result is that the reliability and relevance of the work product (e.g., the evaluator's report to the court) is improved.

The reliability and relevance of a scientific work product is often determined by two factors: (1) the quality of the report and the methods and procedures that lay the foundation for findings and recommendations and (2) the ability of the judge to realistically assess the quality of advisory reports prepared at his or her direction. In a recent article surveying how judges understand and use *Daubert*-type standards (Gatowski et al., 2001), judges were reported as endorsing the notion that they should function as gatekeepers. They think it is important to guard against junk science and believe that the *Daubert* criteria are useful, but some of the criteria articulated by the Supreme Court in the *Daubert* decision (*Daubert v. Merrell Dow Pharmaceuticals*, 1993) are somewhat difficult for judges to understand—in particular, the concepts of falsifiability and error rate.

In their efforts to function as responsible gatekeepers, judges are hampered by their limited understanding of science (Gatowski et al., 2001). The *Daubert* decision gave judges the discretionary authority to assess the scientific basis for proffered evidence. Unfortunately, programs designed to provide needed education in scientific methodology have been lacking. The ruling gave judges discretion, and the criteria were intended to advise them concerning the way to exercise their newfound authority most effectively. What judges need to know is how to evaluate whether expert opinions are based upon reliable methodology and are relevant in determining the facts (Gould & Lehrmann, 2002).

Over the past several years, arguably since the Supreme Court's decision in *Daubert*, one question that has drawn the attention of many in the legal and mental health professions is "What is the role of science?" There are two ways to think about science. The first way is that of the general population. In this definition, science is a collection of facts that are so well established that they are generally considered truth (Gatowski et al., 2001). The second definition of science focuses less on facts and more on process. In this definition, science comprises procedures by means of which we generate the questions that need to be posed, translate those questions (as best as we can) into observable phenomena, select methods that will facilitate the systematic study of the identified phenomena, and analyze the accumulated information in a manner most likely to produce valid answers to the questions that have been posed. Also included in this definition is the notion that scientific investigators create and maintain detailed records concerning their information gathering and make those records available for scrutiny by appropriate others.

In this chapter, we look at science as method. It is our position that, to whatever degree possible, information concerning the family drama and human experience of child custody disputes should be systematically gathered and that opinions concerning the psychological best interests of the child should be formulated on the basis of this information. If child custody evaluations are to use the methods of science in examining psycholegal questions that are of concern to the court, then we propose that the scientific reasoning expressed in *Daubert* and *Kumbo* provides a useful framework within which to structure the methods used in a child custody evaluation.

A child custody evaluation is a scientific work product and, as such, needs to be scrutinized by legal professionals under rules that guide the admissibility of scientific evidence (Gould, 1998). The evaluation should incorporate the methods and procedures of scientific inquiry that guide forensic mental health investigations (Austin, 2000d; Gould & Stahl, 2000). A satisfactory forensic work product is defined, in part, by the evaluator's use of conventional forensic methods and procedures applied to child custody examinations (Gould & Bell,

2000). Conventional forensic methods and procedures include the use of questionnaires with a semistructured format, allowing the evaluator to ask the same set of general questions to each parent while permitting deviation into areas unique to a particular parent and his or her relationship with the child. Additionally, psychological tests used within the context of custody disputes should meet the same criteria as those used in other forensic contexts (Otto et al., 2000), and established self-report measures should be employed in order to assess relevant areas of parenting. Evaluators are also urged to review pertinent records, interview others who may have relevant information, and directly observe parent–child interactions. These data collection methods provide the most robust and relevant information available about a family system.

In this chapter, we propose a more detailed structure to employ when considering the admissibility of and weight assigned to the information obtained from child custody evaluation. That is, we provide a means by which evaluators can assess the strengths and deficiencies of their evaluative procedures with the hope that such anticipatory questioning will lead to a more methodologically sound work product. We also offer a series of questions for you to consider when assessing the forensic value of your evaluation. These questions are offered as a type of inner map for you to use in the preparation of an advisory report and, subsequently, in anticipation of testimony. We conceptualize the examination as comprising five stages:

1. Preevaluation planning.
2. Evaluation.
3. Postevaluation analysis.
4. Advisory report.
5. Preparation for testimony, including having the answers to questions that might be asked in cross-examination.

Our proposed questions are presented sequentially, beginning with questions relevant to the preevaluation stage of planning and extending through the anticipation of examination and cross-examination. Although not all areas described below have questions drawn from each stage of the evaluation process, we have organized the questions presented in each section to reflect the sequence of the evaluation process.

The Standard of Relevance and the Formulation of Questions

It is generally agreed that an evaluator's first step should be the formulation of psycholegal questions that will guide the evaluation (Amundson et al., 2000; Austin, 2000d; Gould, 1999). The next step is a series of forensic interviews focused on relevant issues of concern both to the family and to the court (Ackerman, 2001; Gould, 1998; Schutz, Dixon, Lindenberger, & Ruther, 1989).

Self-report measures might be used to gather data (Otto & Edens, 2003; Schutz et al., 1989). An evaluator should select standardized psychological tests that are appropriately normed and are likely to produce data of relevance to the psycholegal questions posed (Brodzinsky, 1993; Committee on Ethical Guidelines for Forensic Psychologists, 1991). Data should be systematically gathered through direct observation of parent–child interactions (American Psychological Association, 1994; Ackerman, 2001; Committee on Ethical Guidelines for Forensic Psychologists, 1991; Schutz et al., 1989). Finally, information gathered through the aforementioned techniques should be checked against information obtained from pertinent records and in interviews with collateral sources (Ackerman, 2001; Austin, 2002; Heilbrun et al., 2003; Schutz et al., 1989).

Expert testimony must address the specific psycholegal issues before the court in order to satisfy *Daubert*'s relevancy standard. In custody litigation, the pertinent inquiry involves both the concept of best interests and the predictability of future outcome for children. The concept of best interests is poorly defined, both from a behavioral science perspective and from a legal perspective (see Chapter 2 of this volume). Obtaining relevant information about factors of concern in a specific family is best accomplished when evaluation questions are clearly defined at the beginning of the evaluation (Amundson et al., 2000). Clearly defined questions lead the evaluator to choose methods of assessment that measure behaviors directly relevant to the questions of concern to the court. Poorly defined questions lead to difficulty in choosing proper assessment tools.

If concepts alluded to in an appointment order are not reformulated into appropriate psychological variables, the evaluator is unable to choose measurement tools that will specifically measure the concepts identified as concerns of the court. When the issues of concern to the court are not converted into well-defined questions, the behaviors of relevance are difficult to identify. As a result, both reliability and relevance are seriously hampered from the outset of an evaluation. Where relevance is in doubt, helpfulness (Krauss & Sales, 1999) is also in question. In those instances in which relevance and helpfulness are diminished because of poorly defined questions and poorly chosen tools, it is virtually impossible to offer any scientific interpretation of the data. The resulting testimony should, therefore, be assigned less weight in the judge's decision making. Some attorneys have advanced the position that answers to ill-defined questions are unhelpful to the court and should be inadmissible. Others believe that in such situations, the deficiencies in the proffered testimony should influence the weight given to it but should not result in its being barred (Shear, personal communication, July 15, 2001).

Too often, experts in child custody are not asked to demonstrate the relevance of the factors they examined to the concerns of the court (Amundson et al., 2000). If the evaluator does not clearly articulate the questions that define the focus and scope of the evaluation, two problems occur. The first problem is that if the questions are poorly articulated, the hypotheses derived from them that serve to define the evaluation focus are poorly defined. As a result, the assessment tools selected by the evaluator may not yield the data needed by the court. Second, the issues alluded to in the court's order and concerning which the court seeks advisory input must be appropriate for psychological investigation. Consider an order that directs an evaluator to assess the parents' honesty and conscience and the safety of the home environment. There are times when we may need to take concerns expressed by the court and translate them into specific questions that we have the expertise to address and that have direct bearing on the parent–child relationship.

Honesty is a construct that can be defined in several ways, some of which may not be pertinent to an assessment of parenting capacity. Evaluators charged with assessing parental honesty must confine their investigations to those behaviors that bear upon the best interests of the child. Therefore, the first step is to define the concept of honesty within the context of this particular family system. The second step is to elucidate how the now-defined concept of honesty relates to aspects of parenting or aspects of the best psychological interests of the child. Without linking the concept to the psychological best interests of the child, the relevance of honesty to the matter before the court cannot be established. In requesting advisory input from an expert, it is the court's expectation that evidence proffered by the expert will be helpful in making "the existence of any fact that is of consequence to the determination of the action more probable or less probable than it would be without the evidence" (FRE 401). When the matter before the court involves the custodial placement of a child, such evidence must bear upon the BICS. Unless honesty has been defined, it cannot be established that data gathered by the evaluator will assist the court in understanding the family system and, ultimately, in making a more informed decision.

Questions that might be useful in examining the evaluator's formulation of the questions guiding the evaluation process are:

1. Did the court clearly define the questions for investigation in the body of the order?
2. If not, did the attorneys clearly define the questions for investigation in letters that are in your file?
3. If not, how did you determine the questions for investigation?
4. In the introductory section of the report, did you clearly define the main problems, questions, or issues to be addressed?
5. In the introductory section of the report, did you clearly identify the legal questions relevant to the behavioral data to be collected?
6. In the body of the report, did you translate the legal questions into psychologically useful dimensions that are able to be meaningfully assessed?
7. In the body of the report, did you identify the relevant best interests factors to be assessed?

8. In the body of the report, did you consider and discuss plausible alternative hypotheses?
9. In the body of the report, did you identify the link between the behavioral data collected and the issues of concern to the court?

The Standard of Reliability and the Use of Forensic Methods

Prior to the development of forensic psychology as a specialty, psychological testimony was typically offered by clinicians. As contrasted with clinical methodology, forensic psychological methodology provides a more reliable means of obtaining information useful in an adjudicative context. Historically, testimony offered by clinicians in child custody cases was based upon psychological tests, clinical interviews, and direct observation of the parent and child. The vast majority of those entering the offices of clinical psychologists are motivated to present themselves as they are and candidly to disclose personal deficiencies of which they are aware. Clinicians, as a rule, are ill equipped to identify deception. Additionally, the clinical method is noninvestigatory, and discrepancies between in-office behavior and at-home behavior are likely to go undetected. Over the past several years, increasing attention has been focused on the ways in which custody litigants may present themselves in a highly favorable light during evaluations. It has become apparent that opinions formulated entirely on the basis of test data, information obtained in interviews, and observation of in-office behavior are likely to be unreliable.

Forensic methods and procedures are designed to balance in-office observations with information obtained from external sources. Among the unique sources of data used in a forensic evaluation are collateral record review; interviews with professional collateral informants such as teachers, doctors, therapists, and youth counselors; and interviews with lay collateral informants such as neighbors, family members, and friends (Austin, 2002; Heilbrun et al., 2003).

The degree to which the different sources of information converge is a measure of the reliability of the data. When the views of parent and child that develop from each data source considered independently are congruent, there is a very strong probability that the opinions drawn from these data reflect an accurate picture of the family. Reliability decreases as fewer of the independent sources of information support a particular opinion.

How the evaluator integrates the information obtained from these independent methods of data gathering is critical in understanding how he or she assigns it relative weight. If the information is used to generate hypotheses, if additional data sources are subsequently examined, and if the subsequent examination enables the evaluator to confirm or disconfirm the hypotheses drawn from the assessment data, then information obtained through the use of valid self-report measures can be viewed as helpful. If the results from these self-report measures are utilized for anything other than hypothesis generation, then the court needs to consider carefully whether such information should be admissible. Viewing self-report data with skepticism is particularly important when the inventory used is unaccompanied by evidence of reliability and validity or when neither empirical nor logical relevance to the concerns of the court has been demonstrated.

Some questions it might be useful to ask are:

1. In the planning stage of the evaluation, did you choose reliable self-report measures that are related to the psycholegal questions that are the focus of the evaluation? If not, why not?
2. In the planning stage of the evaluation, did you choose self-report measures that meet the criteria by which assessment instruments used in a forensic context should be gauged? If not, why not?
3. During the evaluation, did you obtain self-report data from each parent about the specific areas of functioning that are the focus of the court's concern?
4. In the body of the report, did you clearly explain the direct or indirect relationship between choice of self-report measures and the relevant psycholegal questions?
5. In the body of the report, did you explain how the credibility of the self-report data was assessed?
6. In the body of the report, did you clearly identify the hypotheses drawn from the self-report measures?
7. In the body of the report, did you compare the information obtained from the self-report measures to information obtained from third-party collateral sources?
8. In the body of the report, did you discuss how information from self-report measures was compared to information obtained from other independent data sources?

The Use of Direct Behavioral Observations of Parent and Child

Experienced and knowledgeable evaluators differ among themselves with respect to the most effective manner in which to conduct the observational component of the evaluation. There are some procedures for systematic observation that have been developed for use in assessing parent–child interactions (e.g., Nims Observational Checklist; Nims, 2000). Also, there are some commonsense concerns that need to be explored, such as whether the evaluator became involved in the interaction being observed and, if so, to what degree. The evaluator's involvement in the observation may significantly alter how the family members relate to each other. Each report should contain an explanation of the parent–child observation and a description of the role the evaluator played in the observation.

Another important area of examination is the specific aspect of parent–child interaction assessed, the basis for the selection of that particular aspect, and the manner in which the assessment was conducted. It is often useful for the evaluator to take contemporaneous notes or make an audio recording of parent–child observations. Contemporaneously taken notes should be devoid of inferences. Notes that state, "mother and child interacted warmly" are of little use when a case comes to trial 6 months later and an evaluator is asked exactly what it was that the mother and child did. Notes should contain descriptions of observable behaviors and, to whatever extent possible, verbatim statements made by the participants to one another. Inferences can always be drawn later. An example of useful notes would be

> The parent sat next to the child, looking at the child and smiling. The child responded by smiling and reaching toward the parent for a hug. The parent responded by hugging the child. Both parent and child kissed each other on the cheek. The child let go of the parent and asked to be placed back on the floor. The parent placed the child on the floor and the child returned to the dolls.

Some questions it might be useful to ask are:

1. In planning the evaluation, did you choose a behavioral observation system that organizes observed data in a manner consistent with the psycholegal questions that address the court's concerns? If not, why not?
2. During the evaluation process, did you directly observe the behavioral interaction between parent and child?
3. During the evaluation process, did you use a similar behavioral observation rating system for each parent? If not, why not?
4. During the parent–child observations, did you interact with the parent or with the child? How you discuss how your participation in the observation may have changed the representativeness of the obtained data?
5. During the evaluation process, did people other than the parent and child participate in the observations? If yes, who and why not?
6. During the evaluation process, did you observe parent–child interaction for more than one observational period in order to assess for consistency of the nature and quality of parent–child interactions?
7. During the evaluation process, were there opportunities for observation of parent–child interaction in a natural and familiar environment? If yes, was this done?
8. In the postevaluation analysis, did you consider how your physical presence and/or participation might have affected the observed parent–child interaction?
9. In the postevaluation analysis, if other people were present during the

parent–child observation, how did you consider their influence on the observed parent–child interactions?

10. In the postevaluation analysis, what hypotheses were drawn from the observed parent–child interactions?
11. In the postevaluation analysis, was information obtained from third parties used to explore confirmation or disconfirmation of these hypotheses?
12. In the body of the report, did you describe the observed behavioral interactions between parent and child?
13. In the body of the report, did you compare your observational data about parent–child interactions to other independent sources of data in which similar parent–child interactions are described?

The Use of Collateral Record Review and Collateral Interviews

The acquisition of reliable and relevant collateral information is arguably the most important component of a child custody evaluation. Obtaining information about the real-life parenting of those involved in the evaluation is critical (Austin, 2002; Austin & Kirkpatrick, 2004; Heilbrun et al., 2003). A satisfactory forensic evaluation report should include information about how the parent and child operate in the real world, outside of the environment of the evaluator's office. Information from people who have direct observational knowledge of the parent and child in different situations may be among the most important data obtained in a child custody evaluation. Similarly, historical records may shed light on important aspects of parental cooperation and conflict; parenting challenges, difficulties, or triumphs; and other components of the parent–child relationship.

Some questions it might be useful to ask are:

1. During the planning stage of the evaluation, did you organize a set of general questions to be posed to each collateral source?
2. During the planning stage of the evaluation, did you develop a set of common questions that explored parenting skills and specific questions focused on issues of concern in this case?
3. During the evaluation process, did each parent provide a list of collateral interview sources knowledgeable about each parent's relationship with the child?
4. During the evaluation process, were the collateral sources interviewed in a consistent manner—that is, did you pose a common set of questions to allow you to compare collateral informants' responses?
5. During the evaluation process, did you pose to the interviewees general questions concerning parenting skills and specific questions focused on issues of concern to this particular evaluation? If both types

of questions were not posed, are you prepared to answer the question "Why not?"

6. During the evaluation process, did you obtain from the collateral sources the names of other people who may be useful to interview about areas relevant to the investigation? Were these people interviewed? If not, why not?

7. During the evaluation process, were the choices of collateral interview sources representative of the people involved in the child's life across a wide range of activities, or were interviews limited to family and friends?

8. In the postevaluation analysis, what hypotheses were generated as a result of the collateral information?

9. In the body of the report, did you describe similarities and differences across interviewee data in order to assess convergent validity?

10. In the body of the report, did you describe how credibility of the collateral interviewees was assessed?

11. In the body of the report, if the range of people interviewed was limited, were the resulting limitations of the obtained collateral data discussed?

Offering Conclusions and Recommendations

The final step is to organize the information gathered during the evaluation process around the questions-turned-hypotheses. For each hypothesis, the information gathered should be articulated. A discussion should follow addressing the degree to which the data confirm or disconfirm the hypothesis.

In a recent case, the evaluator was asked to address each parent's personality style and its effect on parenting. In the example below, the discussion summarizes different sources of data bearing upon relevant aspects of each parent's personality style and its effect on parenting.

> Ms. Smith's test data, parent–child observations, and in-office interviews reveal that she is someone who is somewhat rigid, methodical, and does not adapt easily to change. She displays little insight into her tendency toward rigidity and does not believe it to be a factor in her parenting. Collateral interview data are less consistent. People who have known Ms. Smith over the past 3 years noted a change in the direction of greater flexibility toward her children since her separation from her husband. People who knew Ms. Smith prior to the marital separation describe her as inflexible. There is some indication that Ms. Smith's more structured approach to parenting has led to power struggles with each minor child.
>
> Mr. Smith's test data and some collateral interview data suggest that he might have some difficulty with the appropriate expression of anger. He did not show insight into his difficulties with anger management, even when he

was presented with statements by his children suggesting that they often feel afraid of his temper and view him as unpredictable. When his oldest child, Ben, talked with him about his temper, Mr. Smith changed topics and told his son that the evaluation context was not the time to discuss "private matters."

This example shows how the evaluator integrates information from various sources to form the foundation for an opinion, in this case about each parent's personality style and its effect on parenting. By summarizing each methodological component, the evaluator is able to demonstrate the degree of convergence of different sources of data and provide a statement about the degree of psychological certainty of the offered conclusion.

Evaluators may want to describe areas for further assessment or propose means by which specific areas of concern might be more scientifically examined. Some questions it might be useful to ask are:

1. In the body of the report, did you explain how the interpretations reasonably fit the data described in the report?
2. In the body of the report, did you clearly address how the obtained information provides answers to the psycholegal questions that are relevant to the legal issues before the court?
3. In the body of the report, did you address the limitations of the data?
4. In the body of the report, did you address inconsistencies in the data?
5. In the body of the report, did you discuss the degree to which data from different methods provide a convergent (reliable) view of each parent's parenting competencies?
6. In the body of the report, did you discuss how relevant research findings are related to factors observed within this particular family?
7. In the body of the report, did you discuss how relevant research findings are used to facilitate explanations and predictions?

Finally, the evaluator should include a discussion of the limitations of the data. No report is perfect, and the known limitations of the evaluator's work product need to be described to the court in a clear and open manner.

Summary

This chapter integrated the methods and procedures of a scientifically informed child custody evaluation with criteria for legal admissibility of a scientific work product, specifically focusing on issues of reliability and relevance (Krauss & Sales, 1999). When evaluators use such an analytic paradigm to guide the construction of their evaluations, families and courts are better served. The reliability and relevance of the forensic evaluation are increased when the *Daubert* criteria are satisfied.

As a concluding comment, we recognize that the *Daubert* criteria are not truly criteria of admissibility. If they were, evidence not meeting the criteria could not be admitted, and admitting such evidence would be considered reversible error by an appellate court. The criteria are intended only to assist the judge in determining if the proffered evidence is or is not likely to be "of assistance." If a judge feels that a particular report will be of assistance, the judge can admit it into evidence even if none of the *Daubert* criteria has been met, and a report that is excluded has, by definition, probative value. Evidence has probative value if it tends to prove an issue (*United States v. Ball*, 1896). Something not admitted into evidence provides no useful information to the court.

CHAPTER 6

Interviewing Children

There are few forensic mental health areas that are as poorly understood or in which deficiencies in practitioner training are as apparent as the interviewing of young children. One reason is that the literature summaries describing the forensic interviewing of young children available in child custody and other professional practice books often provide little specific information about how children use language, how children view their worlds, or how each child describes a different world. For example, there are several books describing general principles for interviewing young children (Ackerman, 2001; Gould, 1998), but none of the current child custody books integrates these principles with linguistics aimed at helping the evaluator understand how children use specific language concepts. This chapter provides information about how to interview young children in a manner that increases the probability of obtaining reliable and relevant information. Chapter 7 focuses on children's use of language and our interpretation of their language.

Questions concerning the reliability and credibility of children's accounts often have emerged in adversarial legal proceedings and have fostered a highly contentious debate concerning the value and limitations of children's testimony (Crossman, Powell, Principe, Gabrielle, & Ceci, 2002; Lyon, 1999; Martindale, 2001b; Poole & Lamb, 1998; Underwager & Wakefield, 1998). For example, one recent child custody book included the advice "Typically, the evaluator does not interview a pre-adolescent child" (Benjamin & Gollan, 2003, p. 86). Based upon their reading of current literature that included the work of Stephen Ceci, Benjamin and Gollan concluded that *not* conducting such an interview "remains the best practice approach in light of the validity and reliability concerns adequately documented in the literature" (citations omitted, p. 86).

We disagree with Benjamin and Gollan's assertion that best practice is *not* to interview a preadolescent. Ceci (personal communication, February 23,

2002) states, "Benjamin and Gollan correctly cite our work as documenting the heightened vulnerability of very young children to suggestibility. However, these authors appear to move beyond the scientific literature by arguing that preadolescent children should not be interviewed. There is nothing in the scientific literature to justify such a blanket assertion."

We also recognize the importance of evaluators heeding Ceci and Bruck's (1995) warning that the field of forensic interviews of children is expanding so quickly that reviews of the literature published only a few years ago may now be out of date. Assertions about research results widely considered state-of-the-art 5 years ago may no longer be valid. It is incumbent upon the evaluator to maintain awareness of current literature.

Factors to Consider in Interviewing Children

We believe it is important for evaluators to obtain training, experience, and supervision in forensic interviewing and to be mindful of the research demonstrating the limited effectiveness of training programs in forensic interviewing. One line of research focused on teaching interviewers to reduce the number of leading questions and yes–no questions. Gilstrap, Nunno, Thomas, and Toglia (cited in Krackow & Lynn, 2003) and Warren and colleagues (1999) found that after a 10-day professional training seminar conducted by leading child witness researchers that about 70% of participants' interview questions were yes–no questions. In the Gilstrap and colleagues study, 34.6% of questions asked were categorized as suggestive. Lamb, Orbach, Sternberg, Hershkowitz, and Horowitz (2000) reported that forensic interviewers in child abuse cases were inaccurate 66% of the time concerning the format of the questions they asked and that interviewers tended to inflate estimates of the number of open-ended (as opposed to closed-ended) questions they asked during the interviews. Warren and Woodall (1999) found that even when interviewers had their interview notes available, they had difficulty reconstructing interview data with children. Conclusions that we have drawn from these studies are that custody evaluators need to monitor continually the format of their interview questions with children and that evaluators will be best served by audio- or videotaping interviews.

One important step in examining the trustworthiness of child interview data is to obtain information about who interviewed the child. Taking this step raises the question "What defines an interview?" Ceci and Bruck (1995) define an *interview* as any discussion with any person, whether it is a parent, a teacher, a social worker, an attorney, or a law enforcement officer, and we believe this is a useful working definition.

Current research indicates that certain interview conditions create a high risk of contaminating young children's reports. Contrary to previously held beliefs, errors made by children in reporting sexual abuse are not limited to errors of omission (i.e., failure of the child to report important events). Under certain conditions, young children can also make errors of *commission* about personally experienced events involving their own bodies, such as reporting that an event occurred that, in fact, did not (Adams, 1997). Young children, especially preschoolers, are more likely than older children to respond erroneously to suggestive questions about their experiences and to select erroneous options when responding to forced-choice questions (Crossman et al., 2002; Poole & Lamb, 1998). Young children tend to remember fewer details and make briefer accounts of their experiences than older children, but their primary information is no less accurate (Crossman et al., 2002).

Research has shown that oral testimony from children, especially young children, may be influenced by the number of interviews, the number of interviewers, the types of questions, and the types of responses to answers expressed by the interviewer (Ceci & Bruck, 1995; Poole & Lamb, 1998). When engaged in a forensic evaluation of allegations of child maltreatment, it is imperative that the evaluator determine the number of interviews in which the child has participated, the number of interviewers who have interviewed the child, and the nature and quality of interview questions posed to the child.

Examining Reliability of Interview Data

Reliability is similar to accuracy. If a child has been repeatedly interviewed using suggestive or coercive interview techniques, the child's memory of alleged events may be altered in ways that change the meaning of these events. When this happens, the child's statements are not reliable (Underwager & Wakefield, 1998).

Timeline analysis entails following the chronology of a child's statements over time. Evaluators should examine the conditions under which the interview was conducted, the number of interviews in which the child participated, and how the child's description of the alleged events evolved over time. As Underwager and Wakefield (1998) remind us,

> When the person's memory of events is changed or lost, the person may not know what is true or false. When the person then gives unreliable information, the person may not be aware of it. In such cases, the person cannot be said to be lying. A child who has been suggestively interviewed may be unable to distinguish the memory for a real event from the one that has been taught by the interviewer. Therefore, the testimony the child gives is not reliable. (p. 1)

Crossman et al. (2002) noted several factors that affect the likelihood of children giving misinformation about personal events. Among those most often cited are interviewing methods used in obtaining the testimony. Repeated questioning, delayed questioning, suggestive and misleading interviewing, the emotional tone of the interview, and the status of the person conducting the interview can all have a significant negative impact on the accuracy of the testimony obtained from the child. The preexisting belief on the part of the interviewer that sexual abuse occurred will often affect the interviewer's methods of questioning, thereby influencing the child's response (Ceci & Bruck, 1995; Poole & Lamb, 1998).

Improper Interviewing Methods and Their Negative Effect on Children's Testimony

Interviews with children suspected of maltreatment too often are conducted using improper interviewing techniques. In the following pages, we describe several factors shown not to be useful in competently conducting an interview of a young child.

Repeated Questions

Researchers have identified a continuum of questioning methods, ranging from nonleading techniques to maximally leading techniques (Crossman et al., 2002). When a child is presented with inaccurate postevent information, interpretations, or explanations, the misleading information will often modify the child's memory of the event. In general, younger children are more likely to accept someone else's interpretation of an event if it bears a resemblance to the original event (Ceci & Bruck, 1995).

Many factors appear to affect the accuracy of children's recall ability. Several studies have shown that asking a child the same question repeatedly both within an interview and across interviews often results in the child changing his or her answer (Ceci & Bruck, 1995; Poole & Lamb, 1998). Preschool-age children are particularly vulnerable to the contaminating effects of repeated questioning. Children seem to reason, "The first answer I gave must be wrong, that is why they are asking me again. Therefore, I should change my answer" (Ceci & Bruck, 1995, p. 279). Several studies (Ceci & Bruck, 1995; Ceci & Hembrooke, 1998) have shown that some interview techniques result in children quickly changing their stories to conform to the suggestions and beliefs of the interviewer. Suggestions planted in the first interview were quickly picked up, and the stories told during the second interview reflected changes that were congruent with the earlier placed suggestions.

Research suggests that when young children are provided with information during a contaminated interview, they clearly understand that the information does not come from memory. This is called *source monitoring*. Children are able successfully to identify the source of the information that formed the memory. Upon retesting, young children accurately recall the information provided during the initial contaminated interview but do not accurately recall whether it came from memory or from someone else. This is called *source misattribution* and refers to children's inability accurately to recall the original memory source (Ceci & Bruck, 1995). Young children, as contrasted with older children, are less capable of recalling the sources of their memories. Therefore, what children recall in a third interview may be intrusive memories that they now believe are their own. Once a memory has been contaminated, one cannot determine what components are accurate representations of an event and what components are contaminated representations that a child falsely believes are accurate representations of an event.

Lyon (1999) has argued that the introduction into evidence of research on the suggestibility of child witnesses is not of assistance to triers of fact and is critical of the large body of research on the subject conducted by Stephen Ceci, Maggie Bruck, and others (summarized in Ceci & Bruck, 1995; Ceci & Hembrooke, 1998; Crossman et al., 2002). Lyon's primary criticisms are:

1. That the researchers have overstated the frequency with which suggestive questioning occurs and, in their proposals for methodological changes, have failed to address the risk that abusers will be acquitted.
2. That new-wave research conditions have failed to replicate real-world phenomena closely enough, thereby making it unreasonable to presume that we have gained meaningful knowledge of real-world phenomena through the research on their artificial analogues.
3. That Bruck in particular has erred in statements made during testimony and that her decision to offer didactic as opposed to case-specific testimony is flawed.
4. That jurors are already aware that children are suggestible and that testimony concerning the new-wave research causes jurors to overestimate the probability that testimony from a particular child witness has been distorted by suggestive questioning.

Martindale (2001b) has pointed out that "some of the emotional distress experienced by children involved in sexual abuse investigations is attributable to the methods we employ in the course of our interactions with them" (p. 9). Skilled interviewers are likely to obtain more reliable information and do minimal harm. Unskilled interviewers are likely to cause significant harm and have unreliable information to show for their efforts. We are strong supporters of *didactic testimony* (also referred to as *framework testimony*), in which the testifying expert endeavors to educate the trier of fact concerning phenomena about which he or she may be insufficiently knowledgeable. Such testimony provides a context within which evidence can be evaluated. With specific regard to the need for such testimony when children have testified concerning their memories, Martindale (2001b) has observed,

> It has been well established that a proffer of evidence must be accompanied by confirmation of its authenticity. It must be shown that it is what it is presented as

being. If the prosecution wishes to introduce testimony concerning what is purported to be a memory of an actual event, the defense should be afforded the opportunity to question the authenticity of the memory. (p. 10)

Unfortunately, repeated interviewing is far more likely to be the rule than the exception in investigations of allegations of child maltreatment. The competent evaluator should aggressively explore who interviewed the child and how often and obtain and review copies of all video- or audiotapes of the interviews.

When evaluators pursue these aggressive investigation tactics in order to obtain relevant information, political issues about community relationships inevitably come into play. A court-appointed evaluator may ask for a court order directing the Department of Social Services (DSS) to cooperate in the investigation and to provide a copy of the full file to the evaluator. The order may direct the DSS investigator to be available for interviews with the evaluator. How the evaluator handles the information contained in the DSS file and works with DSS investigators may set the tone for future DSS cooperation.

Suggestive or Misleading Questioning

Several studies have shown that repeatedly giving children misleading information in a series of interviews can have serious effects on the accuracy of their later reports (Crossman et al., 2002). When misinformation becomes incorporated into children's subsequent reports, it can lead to fabrications or inaccuracies that do not even directly mirror the content of the misleading information or questions (Lamb, Sternberg, & Esplin, 2000).

Emotional Tone of the Interview

Children respond to the tone of an interviewer's questions (Ceci & Bruck, 1995), for example, providing incorrect information in response to misleading questions when the interviewer creates an emotional tone of accusation (Crossman et al., 2002). For this reason, we strongly advocate creating an audio- or videotape record of the interview to allow for a proper examination of such tonal factors.

Effects of Interviews by Adults with High Status

Young children are sensitive to the status and power of their interviewers (Crossman et al., 2002) and may be more likely to comply with the implicit and explicit agenda of high-status interviewers. It is important to consider that young children are more likely to believe adults than other children, that they are more willing to go along with the wishes of adults, and that they are more apt to incorporate adults' beliefs into their reports (Poole & Lamb, 1998). Several factors account for the susceptibility of children's testimony to contamination. There may be substantial time between the alleged events and completion of the evaluation or beginning of the trial. It is not unusual for a child to experience multiple preevaluation interviews by parents and other family members, police, counselors, teachers, DSS personnel, and pediatricians. Simultaneously with the evaluation process or in preparation for trial, the child may experience pretrial interviews by many of the same people. Research on children's responses to authority figures such as police officers, prosecutors, judges, parents, attorneys, and counselors has suggested that many children alter their testimony without being aware that they are doing so (Wakefield, 2006).

Effects of Interviewer Bias on Children's Reports

Confirmatory bias refers to the process of selective attention to information that is supportive of a preconceived idea about what has happened. Some people may approach an allegation of child maltreatment with the preconceived belief that abuse has occurred and that the purpose of the interview is to obtain from the child the information needed to support the reported allegations. Some interviewers focus the search for information in a manner that virtually assures uncovering support for their only hypothesis—that an alleged event has occurred. By failing to explore rival hypotheses that might explain the behavior of the child, such interviews may find abuse where none has occurred (Borum et al., 1993).

Though there is always some risk that inaccurate information will be obtained during interviews with children, several studies have shown that children interviewed by biased interviewers are more likely to offer inaccurate information than are children interviewed by neutral interviewers. When an interviewer's belief was contrary to what the child experienced, interviews were characterized by an abundance of misleading questions, leading children to provide highly inaccurate information (Ceci & Bruck, 1995; Poole & Lamb, 1998).

It is generally recognized that the most reliable and accurate information is obtained from children who are responding to open-ended questions designed to elicit free narrative accounts of events that they have experienced (Crossman et al., 2002; Poole & Lamb, 1998). Direct questions are best presented as nonsuggestively as possible, using developmentally and individually appropriate vocabulary and sentence construction. Repeated questions, leading questions, or suggestive questions asked in an accusatory manner are most likely to promote distortion on the part of the child. The child's responses to these types of questions may result in the introduction of details into the child's narrative that are incorporated into and contaminate subsequent accounts. Lamb and colleagues have developed a reliable structured investigative protocol that enhances young children's responses to free recall prompts in the course of forensic interviews (Orbach, Hershkowitz, Lamb, Sternberg, &

Horowitz, 2000; Orbach, Hershkowitz, Lamb, Sternberg, Esplin, & Horowitz, 2000; Orbach & Lamb, 2000). A similarly innovative approach is the Cognitive Interview modified for use with children (Saywitz, 1992). Saywitz states, "the Cognitive Interview improves the quantity of useful information gained from children 7 to 12 years of age without creating heightened inaccuracy" (p. 10). Although originally developed for use with abused children, the Cognitive Interview minimizes interview-related influence and may help children elaborate upon memories that are more difficult to recall.

Risks of Inaccuracies in Evaluators' Recording or Recollection of Child Interview Data

Concerns about the accuracy with which child statements are recorded or recalled by evaluators have prompted demands that investigative interviews be recorded electronically (Ceci & Bruck, 2000). In testifying about statements made to them by children, mental health professionals and child welfare workers often refer to contemporaneously taken notes or to notes entered after an interview with the child. Often, this practice is accepted because it is assumed that such notes are relatively accurate representations of the information exchanged during the investigative interview. Increasingly, research is demonstrating that when notes of this type are relied upon by testifying experts, the resulting testimony can be highly inaccurate (Ceci & Bruck, 2000).

In one study (Bruck, Ceci, & Francoeur, 1999), mothers were asked to recall recent conversations they had with their children. The mothers had been told in advance that they would be asked about their conversations. Foreknowledge that they would be asked questions concerning their conversations did not improve the mothers' performance. The mothers' memories for general meaning (*gist memory*) were better than their memories for the exact wording or structure of the conversation (*verbatim memory*). They had difficulty recalling how information was elicited from their children, specifically whether their children's statements were spontaneous or prompted and whether specific utterances were spoken by the mothers or by the children.

In a related study, mental health trainees who interviewed four children about experienced events had difficulty remembering which of the children made certain statements as well as which details were spontaneously produced and which were prompted using leading questions (Ceci & Bruck, 2000). In another study, experienced interviewers who participated in an analog study claimed to have asked few if any leading or even specific questions of the 5-year old children they interviewed, although a review of tape recordings of the interviews revealed that more than 80% of the questions they asked were, in fact, specific or leading. In addition, the notes the interviewers made shortly after the interview included only 20% of the questions that they actually asked (Warren & Woodall, 1999).

Another study examined verbatim contemporaneous accounts—that is, records in which the interviewer attempts to record every word—of 20 investigative interviews compared with audiotaped recordings of the same interviews (Lamb, Orbach, et al., 2000). All interviews were conducted by eight of the most senior and experienced forensic interviewers in Israel who knew that the interviews were being audiotaped, and were therefore motivated to record them as accurately as possible. Results showed that investigators' notes misrepresented both the information elicited from the young interviewees and the way the information was elicited.

> An alarming number of incident-relevant details (25% of the total) were not recorded at all in the investigators' notes, with 17.8% of the central, i.e., allegation specific details not reflected in the investigators' notes ... more than half of the substantive interviewer utterances were ignored completely and the types of prompts used to elicit information from the children were misrepresented. (Lamb, Orbach, et al., 2000, p. 704)

The researchers concluded that "such errors very likely distort judgments about the extent of interviewer contamination, the accuracy of children's testimony, the validity of children's allegations, the severity of the alleged abuse, and perhaps even children's credibility" (Lamb, Orbach, et al., 2000, p. 704).

According to McGough (1995), there are several primary dangers when hearsay is received as trial evidence: faulty memory, ambiguity, misperception, and lack of candor. McGough briefly explains the dangers:

1. *Faulty memory*: The danger that the child reporting the information to another person will forget key material.
2. *Ambiguity*: The danger that the meaning intended by the child will be misinterpreted by the witness and, hence, reported incorrectly by the witness to the fact finder.
3. *Misperception*: The danger that the child misjudged, misinterpreted, or misunderstood what he or she heard or saw.
4. *Lack of candor*: The danger that the child will consciously lie.

We believe evaluators should be concerned about faulty memory, ambiguity, and misperception. Lack of candor is less of an issue when interviewing children in these cases.

Faulty Memory

A number of researchers (Bruck & Ceci, 1995; Ceci & Bruck, 1993; Crossman et al., 2002) have provided scientific evidence that bears on the potential danger of faulty memory on the part of the child witness. There is also concern about the possibility of faulty memory on the part of the mental health professional who is reporting to the court. Bruck and Ceci (1995) point out that a child's statements and reporters' accounts of a child's statements are likely to be affected by faulty memory. According to these authors, adult interviewers are often inaccurate in recalling what was said or what took place in an interview. Inaccuracies may be found both in interviewer reports offered from memory and in notes taken contemporaneously by interviewers. In general, adult memory of interviews is inaccurate. When asked to recall conversations, most adults recall the gist of the conversation, but they often do not recall the exact words used or the sequences of interactions between speakers such as who said what to whom. Bruck and Ceci (1995) observe that written summaries of unrecorded interviews are subject to a number of distortions, and they conclude that summaries of missing interviews do not substitute for an audio or video recording.

Ambiguity

Ambiguity, the second danger affecting hearsay testimony, is also prominent in child maltreatment investigations. Children may provide responses to interview questions the meanings of which are ambiguous to the interviewer. A child may state that she was "touched on her private parts" or that a parent "rubbed her bottom." The meaning of the communication may be clear to the child but unclear to the interviewer. Unless the child is able to provide a more detailed description of the actions, the interviewer makes inferences that may or may not be accurate interpretations of the child's statements. Interviewers should ask the child developmentally appropriate follow-up questions to facilitate his or her recall of more detailed information. For example, an unreliable response is virtually assured when a mental health professional asks a 4-year-old child if he or she has been "touched" by a particular person. A 4-year-old often cannot distinguish a general, affectionate touch from a sexualized touch and may honestly reply, based on a concrete interpretation of the word *touch*, that she was "touched." The investigator may interpret this to mean that the child was touched in a sexual way, whereas the child may have been referring to a nonsexual touching. Ambiguity is also present in questions such as, "Did he or she hurt you?"; "Was it a good touch or a bad touch?"; and "Did the hug make you feel yucky?" When the results of such ambiguous questioning in an interview are presented at trial, the risks of inaccuracy are increased. Often what follows is an allegation of sexual abuse, with tremendous personal and social costs to all involved.

Ceci and Bruck (1995) provide several examples of ambiguity. Some interview summaries are written in such a way as to convince one that children made spontaneous and detailed statements about maltreatment. Often, a review of transcripts reveals that children only responded "yes" or "no" to a series of leading questions. The lesson is to review the verbatim transcript of child interviews when possible.

Misperception

The third danger to the accuracy of hearsay identified by McGough (1995) is the risk of misperception, defined as the danger that a person misjudged, misinterpreted, or misunderstood what he or she heard or saw. Recent research indicates that "if the interviewer has a bias that the child was sexually abused, this can color his interpretation of what the child said or did; and it is this interpretation that appears in the summary rather than a factual account of what transpired" (Ceci & Bruck, 1995, p. 243). Bruck and Ceci (1995) note that failure to have audio- or videotaped records of interviews with children makes it impossible to determine the accuracy of the children's subsequent statements. In reviewing the methodologies used to interview children when repeated or other improper questioning methods have been used, it is crucial to know whether and how often the interviewer asked the child leading questions. Evaluators reviewing previous interview data must know whether the interviewer "prodded the child's report" (Bruck & Ceci, 1995, p. 307).

Due Process Considerations Related to Improper Interviewing and Inaccurate Hearsay

Evaluators must be aware of and respect the rights of those being evaluated and those likely to be affected by the evaluator's findings and opinions. The issues raised in this chapter and elsewhere in this text pertaining to interviewing and child sexual abuse investigation are related to concerns about due process, fairness, and scientific reliability.

According to Riffe (1993), child abuse cases present a delicate balance of conflicting interests, including the protection of the alleged victim from further harm and the right of the accused to confront the accuser. Legislatures have attempted to provide the courts with guidance in balancing these conflicting interests by broadening allowable evidence to include more than a child's live courtroom testimony. Such legislative efforts, notes Riffe, run dangerously afoul of the accused's right under the Confrontation Clause of the United States Constitution, which requires that the accuser testify face-to-face before the accused and the trier of fact in the courtroom.

Courts have been concerned about reliability of expert testimony based upon data obtained from child interviews when there is no record of the interview to examine. The U. S. Supreme Court ruled that admissibility of a pediatrician's oral testimony describing a 3-year-old child's out-of-court interview responses resulting from a forensic interview violated the respondent's federal constitutional right to confrontation because the pediatrician's testimony was based on an interview that lacked procedural safeguards (*Idaho v. Wright*, 1990). In the Idaho case, a mother was criminally charged with two counts of lewd conduct with her 5-year-old and 3-year-old daughters. At the trial, it was agreed that the 3-year-old child was incompetent to testify. A pediatrician conducted interviews with the child and was then called to the stand to testify about the interviews.

Among other concerns, the Idaho court found the pediatrician's interview technique inadequate because "the questions and answers were not recorded on videotape for preservation and perusal by the defense at or before trial; and blatantly leading questions were used in the interrogation." The Idaho court ruled that the statements also lacked trustworthiness because "this interrogation was performed by someone with a preconceived idea of what the child should be disclosing." Noting that expert testimony and child psychology texts indicated that children are susceptible to suggestion and likely to be misled by leading questions, the court found that "the circumstances surrounding this interview demonstrate dangers of unreliability which because the interview was not [audio or video] recorded, can never be fully assessed."

The Need to Audio- or Videotape All Interviews with Children

Several authors have argued that one possible answer to the question of reliability of children's interview data is to audiotape or videotape all investigatory interviews with children, arguing that such recording of interviews allows review of questioning methods, shelters the child from subsequent stressful court proceedings, and is useful from a legal perspective (e.g., Bruck & Ceci, 1995; Ceci & Bruck, 1995, 2000; McGough, 1995). Until recently, audiotape and videotape recording of interviews did not have substantial support from a legal viewpoint. McGough (1995) notes that there is little authority from U.S. Supreme Court precedent to support an assertion that a prosecutor has a constitutional duty to mechanically record and preserve an account of a pretrial interview with a potential child witness. In fact, failure to record interviews (*Idaho v. Wright*, 1990) and discarding of investigators' notes (*Arizona v. Youngblood*, 1988) were not found by the Supreme Court to violate due process.

While there has been no U.S. Supreme Court determination requiring audiotape or videotape recording, several states have moved closer to such requirements. For example, the Supreme Court of Florida decided:

> Experts generally agree that contacts between a child and an expert evaluating the child for sexual abuse should be videotaped to ensure the trustworthiness of the communications and to ensure that the expert did not lead the child during the evaluation. . . . We can only hope that in the future greater care will be taken to properly preserve testimony in this type of case and that judges will carefully adhere to the trustworthiness and reliability requirements set forth in [our statutes]. (McGough, 1995, p. 379)

Similarly, the Idaho Supreme Court considered the failure to preserve any reviewable record of an evaluative interview with the child to be unprofessional conduct, and that failure clearly inclined it to find the hearsay report of the child's allegation to be untrustworthy and inadmissible (*Idaho v. Wright*, 1990). These decisions call into question the reliability of hearsay testimony taken from investigative interviews of children. We believe that evaluators who utilize video- or audiotaping of all interviews with children will reduce the dual risks of improper interviewing and inaccurate hearsay.

From a scientific as well as a legal standpoint, audiotaping or videotaping is advisable. Bruck and Ceci (1995) assert that "the failure to record initial interviews with child witnesses rules out the possibility of ever reaching any firm conclusion as to whether any abuse actually occurred. In other words, the primary evidence has been destroyed" (p. 272). Evaluators must also obtain verbatim transcripts of the investigative interviews. Absent an audio- or videotaped record, the fact finder cannot discern what actually happened during the investigative interviews.

Audio- or videotaping investigative interviews is also recommended for the sake of the child, as it can reduce the number of interviews in which the participates, with each interview likely to produce some stress to the child (Lamb, 1994). Therefore, it should be viewed as advisable by child advocates who are interested in protecting children from the trauma of repeated, confusing, and possibly leading or coercive questioning (Adams, 1997; McGough, 1995).

Some states, notably New Jersey, have been hesitant to enact statutes authorizing or requiring videotape recording requirements for fear that the use of a videotape as trial evidence would be found unconstitutional. The account of the interview, if related under oath, is an *ex parte*, or out-of-court, affidavit purposely created as a testimonial memorial for use at trial (McGough, 1995). The appellate courts of six states (Kansas, Louisiana, Minnesota, Missouri, Texas, and Wisconsin), however, have upheld the constitutionality of their state videotaped evidence statutes when faced with confrontation or due process questions.

Some professionals have urged that interviews not be recorded because of misgivings that a videotape could be used inappropriately to discredit a child and to exaggerate inconsistencies. McGough (1995) responds to that argument by stating that the desire to protect a child cannot justify the suppression of information simply because it might somehow detract from the child's credibility.

These arguments are not new, and the utility of videotaping pretrial interviews was assessed by the California Child Victim Witness Judicial Advisory Committee. Beginning in 1988, two pilot programs tested the effectiveness of the use of multidisciplinary teams and videotaping of interviews (Myers, 1994). The California pilot project found little to support the fear that defense attorneys received "too much ammunition" to attack the child and little support for the claim that videotaping shifts the focus away from the child's account to the interviewer's mistakes. When adequate protocols were established ensuring videotape quality, fears about the adequacy of the record disappeared (McGough, 1995; Myers, 1994).

Summary

This chapter described common pitfalls of forensic interviewing of young children. Interviewer questions may influence children's memory of events, and characteristics of the interview setting may influence children's responses. Forensic mental health professionals who have only their memory or notes of the interview may introduce hearsay; we recommend audio- or videotaping interviews.

CHAPTER 7

Children's Voices

In this chapter, we examine two critical components of a forensic evaluation of children. First, we discuss a child's perspective on life in a binuclear family. Drawing on the work of Carol Smart (2002), we describe some factors that children report affect their sense of well-being, comfort, happiness, and overall adjustment to their new family life. Then, we present information about young children's use of language. Through forensic psycholinguistics, we provide a framework for evaluators to use when listening to and interpreting children's statements.

Learning to Hear Children's Experience of Divorce

There is a growing awareness of the need to talk to children about their wishes and feelings (or, at the very least, to ascertain through other means children's wishes and feelings) about changes in their lives resulting from their parents' divorce. Talking to children in a meaningful manner and integrating their experiences in each parent's home into a description for the court pose many challenges to evaluators and to the legal system. Smart (2002) writes, "There is, for example, the fear that listening to children will become a kind of token process, a box that needs to be ticked rather than a genuine consultation. . . . there are problems of *how* to hear what is being said and then *what* to do with the diversity of accounts likely to be expressed" (p. 307, emphasis in original). Reporting results from several studies that involved speaking with children of divorce and their parents, she writes,

> One of the most significant outcomes for us was the way in which talking to children, and analyzing their stories, had the effect of jolting us into a child's

worldview. . . . We were acutely aware of how different the experiences of the "same" divorce was for parent and child. . . . Even the most caring parent could find it very difficult to see divorce from the standpoint of his or her child. (Smart, 2002, p. 308)

Smart concluded that children's voices often were not heard. Children's accounts of family life frequently were overshadowed by their parents' interpretations. Smart found that children and their parents often offered vastly different accounts of many aspects of family experiences: "It is not that children's accounts obliterate or correct the parents' accounts; nor is it the other way around. Rather, it is to acknowledge that people stand in different relationships to one another, have access to different resources, and regard different things as important" (Smart, 2002, p. 309). Smart argues that taking children's stories seriously means giving the same legitimacy to their experiences as to parents' experiences. One is not necessarily more important than the other, but each experience needs to be thoroughly understood.

When adults attempt to place themselves in the shoes of children, they often project onto the children memories of their own childhoods. They hear children's stories as reconstructions of their own childhoods, recalled through many layers of personal history. Evaluators need to be aware of the need for reflection on and sensitivity to children's stories. Smart (2002) writes, "It is not simply a matter of allowing the child to speak; it is also a matter of being attentive to what it is that we hear the child say" (p. 309).

Among the most relevant factors to examine when talking with children about their experiences in a divorced family are the following:

1. *Physical space* refers to the practical issues of getting from one place to another. Physical space includes examining concerns that the child has about organizing clothes, toys, and schoolwork. It entails letting children's friends know where they are and letting children voice their concerns about remembering where to be at certain times.

2. *Emotional space* refers to different emotional climates that exist at each parent's home. Children are moving not only from one physical home to another, but also from one emotional landscape to another. Children may react to changes in emotional climate between their mother's and their father's home. Children also may feel differently at different homes. Smart (2002) found that the geographical distance between parental homes can create an emotional distance between child and parent. Interestingly, Smart noted that even children who are equally happy to be with either parent or in either parent's home experienced transitions between homes as a journey requiring regular emotional adjustment.

3. *Psychological space* refers to differences in household structure, organization, and functions. There may be changes between homes in routines, codes of behavior, expectations, standards of living, and more. Children may

find it difficult to adjust to a home that does not fit their psychological narrative about who they are and where they are supposed to live.

4. *Equal time* refers to parents', judges', and attorneys' tendency to think about parenting time in exact amounts. Whether children spend 1 week with one parent and another week with the other parent or are on a 4 days with one parent and 3 days with the other parent schedule, the rigidity of timeshare schedules often affects children's need for flexibility between homes. For example, Smart (2002) found that if a child was scheduled to be with her father but needed to spend time with her mother on a particular day, the rigidity of the schedule became a more important decision-making element than the child's needs. If it was Tuesday, the child had to be at her father's house. Smart reported that children felt frustrated with the rigidity of their access schedules and were reluctant to talk about this frustration with their parents. Children were aware of their parents' competing needs for their time and they did not want to disappoint either parent nor did they want to cause tension because of their discontent. The result was that children did not talk about their feelings and often experienced the parenting schedule as oppressive.

5. *Time apart* refers to children's time away from one parent. Some children did not like time away from a particular parent, and other children did not like feeling that they were forced to spend time with a parent. Other children liked the time away from their residential parent because it provided them with opportunities to gain some perspective on the nonresidential parent. Smart (2002) referred to this time away from the residential parent as a *sabbatical*.

Some children worried about one parent when they were with the other parent. Children worried when their parents remained single and had no romantic partner. These children felt that time away from a single parent meant that the parent was lonely. Some children reported that time passed more slowly at one parent's home than at the other's, usually because one parent was less available, less involved, or had a home with fewer creature comforts.

6. *Time to oneself* refers to children's lack of private time. Children of divorce felt that their time was always scheduled. They felt that they had less time for themselves and less time to spend with their friends.

7. *Time and hurting* refers to an experience of a subgroup of children who had to deal with waiting for the nonresidential parent to come to visit them or wait for the nonresidential parent to take them out. These children often felt powerless and viewed time spent waiting for the parent to show up as a measure of how much that parent cared.

8. *Time and sharing* refers to those situations where both parents enjoyed plenty of time with their children and where each parent was on good terms with the other parent. Sharing parenting time became a way of continuing family life. Children felt happy with timesharing arrangements because of the quality of their relationship with each parent. Children felt that the most important issues were sustaining and managing their relationships with parents.

We believe that a unique contribution of Smart's research is its focus on aspects of *children's* experiences within the binuclear family. Smart's research may be most helpful for evaluators in reminding them that a true understanding of a child's experience of divorce comes from seeing the world through the eyes of the child. Recognizing parents' tendencies to project adult interpretations of children's experiences onto children's narratives may help evaluators focus attention on factors associated with children's experiences of divorce through children's perspectives. When it is added to the evaluator's emerging understanding of children's use of language as described in the following section of this chapter, evaluators should find themselves becoming increasingly child-centered in evaluating children's emotional, developmental, and psychological experiences of their new life.

Linguistic Principles to Guide Forensic Interviews of Children

As described in the preceding chapter, research has addressed characteristics of forensic interviewing of children (Berliner & Barber, 1984; Ceci & Bruck, 1995; Ceci & Hembrooke, 1998; Lyon, 1999; Lyon & Saywitz, 1999; Martindale, 2001b; Poole & Lamb, 1998). There is less attention in the mainstream child custody literature to how children use language. The literature examining forensic interviews of children focuses on ways in which interviewer style, questions, language, tone, and behavior and interview context may affect the reliability of the information obtained from children. This literature does not appear to address how children use language.

A competent child custody evaluator needs to understand not only how interviewer factors may affect the reliability of children's self reports, but also how young children use language to assess accurately children's meanings. Interviewing young children is a difficult task because of the linguistic complexities of questioning them (that is, how we frame the questions) and because of the nuances of understanding the language construction of young children (i.e., how children respond to our questions). Walker (1999, p. 1) reminds us, "children in our courts today are being denied a right that should belong to everyone who enters the legal system: to have an equal opportunity not only to understand the language of the proceedings, but to *be understood* [emphasis in original]."

Different Children Use Language Differently

Young children may be more likely to use language in an idiosyncratic manner, while older children may be more likely to use language in a manner consistent with social expectations. There are no rules for interviewing children that can be applied to all children. Each child has a unique growth pattern and unique family experiences, both of which shape the child's learning of language. Understanding the particular qualities of each child and his or her familial background will greatly assist evaluators in structuring interviews for that child.

Language shapes experience, and experience shapes language (Piaget, 1926; Vygotsky, 1962). Children learn how to use language in many different ways. Children learn word use through their exposure to the world (real-world context) and by observing how others use words in sentences (linguistic context). Children learn social expectations and the use of language through trial and error and adult modeling. They learn to identify what can and should be talked about and how different topics should be talked about. Different families place different emphasis and meaning on similar words and how these words should be used. For example, asking a child "Do you want to get ice cream with your friends?" is likely a request for information. Asking a child, "Do you want to be punished?" is not. In most situations, the child will provide information to the first question and clearly understand the implied admonition in the second one. Very young children, however, may provide information in response to the second question, displaying their inability to understand the metamessage contained in the communication.

Children and Adults Do Not Speak the Same Language

The meanings adults ascribe to words and phrases are often very different from the meanings children ascribe to the same words and phrases. Preschool children frequently use words that sound like the words adults use, leading to the assumption that adults and children speak the same language. This is not so. Often, children's use of adult language is tied to their idiosyncratic definition of adult language despite its proper placement in sentence structure. A word like *yesterday* means something very different to a 3-year-old than it does to an adult.

Language learning is far from complete at age 5. Important aspects of word usage are still being developed at age 10 and later. Teenagers may continue to develop an understanding of how to provide complete and coherent accounts of personal events. Some adults may never acquire the ability to detect and correct reasoning flaws in other people's statements. Use of language develops gradually and often involves children's acquisition of parts of a linguistic rule before their acquisition of the whole rule. Newly learned rules, such as the use of *yesterday, today*, and *tomorrow*, can be "fragile, operating well when they are used in familiar sentence structures to talk about familiar things, but operating uncertainly in novel or stressful circumstances" (Walker, 1999, p. 10).

It is common to find inconsistencies in children's statements. Children may use language inconsistently because they misuse a rule. Such misuse does not always indicate that there is a fundamental inconsistency in their understanding of their description of an event. It may signal only an inconsistency in their use of language to describe that particular event.

Young children are very literal in their early use of language. Children, especially young children, narrowly define words.

> Lack of experience both with language and with the world contribute to this problem, but cognitively, the ability of young children (up to about age 6 or 7) to move from the general (house) to the particular (apartment), and vice versa, is not well developed. . . . Neither is their ability—particularly for children under five—to group objects and events together according to characteristics which adults would recognize as similar. . . . Since young children interpret the world based on what they themselves have seen and heard (thus the term "concrete" thinking), they are unlikely to be able to interpret a question that asks them "What does this picture say?" since pictures can say nothing. This literal approach to language is pervasive in young and even some older children, and adults who are not aware of it can put the fact-finding process into considerable jeopardy. (Walker, 1991, pp. 11–12)

Children do not think as adults, and they often do not use language as adults. Adult-like use of language does not necessarily reflect adult-like linguistic or cognitive capabilities, as language and thinking do not develop simultaneously. Children may appear to understand adult sentences and to use words and sentences in adult ways while they are operating on a different level of understanding. Children often use words before they understand their adult meanings. This may result in adults' misunderstanding what a child is saying or thinking.

Young children in particular may have difficulty attending to more than one or two things at once. This is important to remember when interviewers present children with multipart, multi-idea questions. Forensic interviewers need to frame their questions to children in short and simple sentences. Multipart questions may confuse a child or direct a child's attention to one aspect of the question rather than to the entire question. Questions such as "Did you see your sister drop the ice cream and then see your brother cry?" may result in the child answering, "Yes." Further examination might reveal that the child attended to the first part of the question while ignoring the second part. In this real-life example, the child observed his sister drop the ice cream but did not see his brother cry. The child's response may suggest a "yes" to both questions when, in fact, the child provides information only about one aspect of the question. A good rule of thumb is that the fewer ideas there are in a question, the greater the chance that a child will recall, process, and accurately answer it.

Pausing is productive. People pause during conversation to allow the brain more time to process information. Pauses provide time for listeners to process the spoken thought. Children take more time than adults to process incoming information. Young children, ages 7 to 9, can take as much as 1.9 times as long as adults to process incoming information. Interviewers need to pause between phrases, between sentences, and after questions to allow children the processing time they need (Walker, 1999).

Children often do not indicate that they do not understand a question. Some children do not know that it is acceptable to tell others that they do not understand. Other children may believe that they understand the question when they do not. Differences between the adult's use of vocabulary and a child's understanding of the adult's words may also lead to misunderstanding.

Preparing children for interviews by letting them know what the topic will be and why we will be asking questions may help them respond more accurately to questions. Providing a framework for the interview may also be useful, but interviewers must avoid giving children suggestions about their expected answers. A good framework should introduce general topics, make bridges between different topics, and direct children's attention from one area of inquiry to another.

Children's responses to adult questions are not always answers to the questions posed for several reasons. First, children's responses may be inaccurate because they do not supply the kind and amount of information required. Second, the child and the adult may have a different understanding of the meaning of a question. Third, the child or the adult may fail to recognize that a question or an answer was ambiguous. Fourth, a child may accurately understand a question but use imprecise or idiosyncratic language in providing an answer. Of these four problems, the second and third may never be discovered if one of the parties is a child who has not yet developed the ability to detect and correct misunderstandings.

Children are often asked to recite lists as a measure of their ability to understand and properly respond to questions, but this method may not provide an accurate measure of their ability to describe an event or of their ability to recount the time, place, or frequency of an event. Reciting culturally familiar lists such as the alphabet may show acquisition of specific vocabulary, but it does not necessarily show anything about understanding of meaning. The level of accuracy displayed by a child in reciting a list does not provide a measure of the child's comprehension of the items that makeup the list.

Children are not born with the ability to give adult-like accounts of their personal experiences. It appears that children initially learn to provide autobiographical accounts by responding to questions about past events from parents and others. The questions posed tend to require "yes" or "no" answers and often follow one after the other. It is in this way that children acquire the ability to provide information in a logical sequence. As children grow older, adults often ask them questions that are more open-ended. One result of these interactions is that children learn their parents' internalized rules for narrative. The rules that children use in storytelling and how those rules are applied in storytelling may be very different from the rules that evaluators use and apply.

Children's Narratives

Walker (1999) proposes a six-stage, chronological model to explain children's development of narratives. First, children develop a *setting* that introduces both place and players. In steps two and three, children learn to describe actions within the setting, beginning with an *initiating action* followed by a *central action*. Fourth, children learn to describe the *motivations and goals* of the actors and their *internal responses*. The descriptions of internal responses may include discussion of attitudes and emotions of the actors. Finally, children learn to discuss the *consequences or conclusions*. Details provided at each stage may give additional description of sights, smells, sounds, feelings, beliefs, and reports of what each actor said. As children progress through these steps, they develop encoding structures that enhance retention of memories and facilitate recall.

At approximately age 2, children begin to develop simple narrative. Children often develop better narrative skills as they acquire other cognitive, linguistic, and conversational abilities. Refinements in their understanding of time make it possible for children to describe consistently the chronology of an event. Children also develop the ability to monitor their speech for errors, monitor the understanding of the listener, provide appropriate pronoun reference, and use language to identify old and new information. Some of these abilities are not acquired until the teenage years. Until these complex skills have been acquired, children's narratives are incomplete and may be viewed as disorganized by adult standards. Walker (1999) writes, "Incomplete narratives are harder to judge for believability, and believability is the crucial test these narratives face in the court context" (p. 19).

In some families, conversation is spontaneous, frequent, and comfortable; in other families, it is not. Children exposed to more verbally interactive parents tend to produce more complex sentence structures, and these more advanced verbal interactions facilitate the establishment of concept development (Walker, 1999). We refer to this concept as *elaborative language use* (Boland, Haden, & Ornstein, 2003; Porath, 1996; Walker, 1999).

In these elaborative language use families, thoughts tend to be articulated and parents are likely to encourage their children to articulate their thoughts and feelings and to express themselves with gradually increasing clarity. Parents who interact with their children in these ways assist their children in recalling and recounting shared past experiences by confirming correct memories and by using questions as prompts, thereby facilitating the children's ability to construct more complex and complete narratives about their experiences (Porath, 1996).

Other families provide little instruction to their children about the nature of objects and persons. Such families tend to use more pronouns, are less specific in describing objects and people, and to take more for granted about what the listener in a conversation knows (Walker, 1999). Parents who display a nonelaborative style tend not to provide reinforcement when their children recall and recount shared experiences. In these families, the parents tend not to use questions as prompts and ask the same question repeatedly in attempts to get the "right" answer. Walker posits that the overall effect of a nonelaborative style of parent–child communication delays the development of communication skills and vocabulary, discourages inquisitiveness, and leads children to exhibit passivity in learning.

Understanding a family's propensity for elaborative or nonelaborative language use may guide an evaluator in formulating questions when children are vague, reticent, or silent. As this discussion reveals, it is important for evaluators to examine ways in which children's families use language *before* interviewing children. Evaluators might consider evaluating family communication style in anticipation of structuring a developmentally appropriate child interview.

Familiarity

Familiarity matters in a wide array of situations. People are more comfortable when they are familiar with their surroundings and when they are with people whom they know. Familiarity creates expectations about events and people and is based on experience. Familiarity matters when it comes to how we use and understand language. Children are best served when they are familiar with how language is used in an interview. When children describe familiar, everyday events, they are often accurate in their use of grammar to express temporal, causal, and logical relations. They are less accurate when asked to describe events that they have not experienced.

Familiarity may affect children's responses to questions. It is likely that young children will respond to questions from an interviewer in a manner dictated more by their family's language and question use than by the interviewer's language and question use. Children are more accurate and more complete in their responses when they have become familiar with the interviewer, the setting, the language used by the interviewer, and the customs of the context in which they are going to be talking (Walker, 1999). That is, children may profit from exposure to an evaluator's office or to a courtroom environment prior to the primary information-gathering interviews (Feller, Davidson, Hardin, & Horowitz, 1992).

Culture and Language

Evaluators who interview children need to be aware of the potential effects of culture on children's use of language. Not only does one family differ from another in their use of language, but family members from different cultures may also use language differently than family members raised in American culture. Children who come from cultures with different languages may have a working knowledge of English but a reduced ability to comprehend the subtleties and nuances of our cultural use of language.

Evaluators should not interpret verbal and nonverbal expression as if all children use language and understand cultural expression the same way. Walker (1999) states:

Unless we are aware of cultural differences, it is tempting to believe that the chief function of questions for everyone is to gain information, that silence is often not golden, but bad, and that families are families everywhere. We not only tend to believe these things, we react to children as if they were true. . . . When children of all descriptions do not seem to be able to answer questions the way our *own* children do, we are not apt to think about the fact that in some cultures, questions are not to be "answered" as much as they are to be obeyed as an order or to be absorbed as models of how to see the world. (Walker, 1999, p. 23, emphasis in original)

Much research attention has been devoted to the competency of children as witnesses. It is important for custody evaluators, who rely so much on the use of language in all aspects of their work, to remember that language can also be a barrier between children and adults in forensic investigations. Evaluators need to understand how children use language and how to create interviews that will assist children in the production of accurate representations of their experiences. Walker (1999) concludes: "Until those skills have fully matured at some point in the mid-teens, the responsibility for getting at what children know rests *squarely on the adult*, and in particular, on the language of the question, and not on the language of the answer" (p. 24, emphasis in original).

Common Linguistic Problems in Interviewing Children

In this section, we discuss some of the problems that research has shown to be prevalent in children's use of language. Each of these problems has the potential to adversely to affect children's understanding of questions and/or evaluators' understanding of children's responses.

Potential Problems in Evaluators' Use of Language

Evaluators and attorneys are often guilty of using psychobabble and legalese. Children are often confused by terms of art used by attorneys or mental health professionals. What may hold rich meaning for an adult may have little, if any, meaning to a child.

Complex sentences reduce a child's ability to understand what is being asked. Walker (1999) suggests that among factors that adversely affect children's understanding of adults' questions are the following:

1. *Use of abstract and low-frequency words*—Words that express abstract concepts move beyond the grasp of children 7 and younger. It is not until about age 11 that children can begin to understand the kind of abstract reasoning often required for court testimony.

2. *Ambiguous phrases*—Young children do not have the experience with

language to know that words and sentences can be interpreted in more than one way.

3. *Embedding*—Putting potential sentences inside another sentence is called embedding. For example, the sentence "The news that he had sung a song surprised his mother" contains information about "he had sung a song" and information about his mother's reaction, "surprised his mother."

4. *Left branching*—Sentences in which something is placed in front of the subject are left branching. Most English sentences are right branching, beginning with the subject and moving right toward the verb and then the object. For example, a right-branching sentence is: "I rode a plane last night." An example of a left-branching sentence is: "Although I would have liked to have stayed in San Diego last night, the fact is that I rode a plane last night." The subject–verb–object order follows an introductory clause and is embedded in the latter part of the sentence. The meaning of such sentences is difficult for young children to follow.

5. *Negation*—Sentences that contain negatives are common to cross-examination questioning. For example, a negation is, "Did you not say that you saw your father walk the dog?" Perry and colleagues (1993) report that children, on average, gave correct answers only 50% of the time to questions that had either single ("Did you not see the car outside?") or double negatives ("Is it not true that you didn't see the car outside?").

6. *Nominalization*—Changing a verb into a noun, usually by adding a suffix. Examples of nominalization include changing *hear* to *hearing* or *appear* to *appearance*. Walker (1999) states, "The change is not just a matter of shifting from one word class to another: These single words can replace whole clauses. . . . In terms of processing time, this is one instance in which shorter is not better" (p. 43).

7. *Passive voice*—The passive voice is difficult at times for people of all ages to process, especially when it is contained in a subordinate clause—for example, "Most math problems become difficult to solve, particularly *when the problem is heard rather than read.*" Three-year-olds tend to ignore passives and focus attention on word order, 4- and 5-year-olds may better understand the adult meaning of the sentence but still make mistakes with nonaction passives, and some researchers report that children do not consistently understand the use of the passive form until they are at least 10 to 13 years old.

Walker (1999) posits that the words that most frequently create confusion for children include:

Ahead of/behind	*Know/think/guess/sure*
Always/never	*Let/make*
Any	*More/less*
Ask/tell	*Move*
Before/after	*Neither/either/another/each*
Big	*Promise*

Different/same	*Remember*
Forget	*Some/all*
First/last	*Touch*
Inside	*Yesterday/today/tomorrow*

Compound questions may be very confusing to children because they do not know what part of the question to answer. Children often do not ask for clarification when confused by a question, which may result either in responses that focus on one part of the question or in a failure to respond at all. In order for children to respond accurately to questions, they must be able to remember the questions from beginning to end and to understand what is being asked. It may be confusing for children to field questions such as "Did you tell your mother what happened when she was in the kitchen talking with your father during dinner?" or "Do you recall when your father said your mother was a lousy mother? Was it during your last visit or 2 weeks ago?" Children must recognize the multiple possibilities in the question, separate them mentally, and provide individual answers to each question. Children under the age of 12 are busy acquiring skills needed to process and understand such complex questions and almost surely will become confused.

Another area of potential difficulty is the interviewer's use of restricted-choice questions, in which two or more possibilities are linked by the word *or*. Asking a child to describe an object provides the child with numerous options. The quality of the information received is reduced when a child must respond to an interviewer who asks whether something was "little or big." Restricted-choice questions are likely to have the same effect upon children as yes/no questions. When interviewed by evaluators, young children in particular may assume that, as an adult is asking the question, there may be no options other than those presented. It is also possible that some children will feel compelled to answer any question posed by an adult. When the range of acceptable responses is perceived as having been limited, children may provide answers that they think fit an evaluator's expectation of a proper response. Thus, responses to restricted-choice questions may not meet an investigator's need for accurate information about the child's perspective. Preschool children have the most difficulty responding accurately to restricted-choice questions. When one of the two options is correct, preschool children reliably choose the correct answer; when neither choice is correct, preschool children will often confine themselves to the choices offered by the interviewer (Walker, 1999).

Often, evaluators ask about past events, beginning the questions with "Do you remember . . . ?" Walker (1999) suggests that "Do you remember?" questions are complex for children to process and may result in errors. When adults hear a "Do you remember" question, they recognize from the opening phrase that they are being asked to answer "yes" or "no." Most adults understand that they are either affirming or denying all propositions that follow the word *remember*. Adults typically follow, process, and remember all parts of the question. Children, even school-aged children, are not good at performing this comprehension task.

Evaluators may believe that children are able to follow such questions and often ask "Do you remember?" questions. This is a significant problem in interviews because while children do not process these questions the same way as adults, they often answer the question with a response that does not reveal that they have failed to comprehend the question. Another problem is the inherent ambiguity that often typifies both the question and the response. For example, a child might be asked, "Do you remember telling your mother that, during your birthday party, Uncle Lou took off Marsha's shirt and touched her private areas with his hands and his tongue?" If the child answers, "yes," which part of the question is the child affirming? There are several information choice points in the sentence yet the child responds with a single "Yes." Evaluators are more effective in their questioning when they break questions into their simplest components (Orbach & Lamb, 2000). For example:

1. "I want you to tell me all about the birthday party."
2. "What else can you tell me about the party?"
3. "Tell me a little bit more."
4. "Then what happened?"
5. "Tell me who came to your birthday party?"
6. "Tell me about Marsha."
7. "What else can you tell me about Marsha?"

Questions such as these, when asked of a young child, are more likely to elicit useful, uncontaminated information for use in an evaluation.

Another form of questioning that has the potential to influence a child's truthful response is the use of tag questions. A tag question makes a statement and then adds a short question that invites corroboration. An example of a tag question is "It's sunny, isn't it?" Tag questions are among the most powerfully suggestive forms of speech in the English language, and evaluators are encouraged to avoid use of such suggestive questioning.

Children tend to live in the here and now, and changing tense may cause them confusion. Children may provide more accurate answers when questions about present events are clustered together and questions about past events are clustered together. Minimizing the number of topic or tense changes may increase children's ability to understand what is being asked.

Another potential source of confusion is asking children about relative concepts, such as age, dimension, number, time, and kinship. Children's understanding of relative concepts matures over time. For young children, the concept of age is connected to size, particularly to height. Evaluators need to be sensitive to developmental changes both between children and within the same child over time.

Too often, evaluators ask children about the difference between a lie and the truth Investigators frequently incorporate a series of questions designed to test the ability of the child to distinguish between truth and lies. It is hard to say when children understand the difference between lies and truth because the concept of a lie is multifaceted (Poole & Lamb, 1998). Children's understanding of truth and lies improves noticeably around age 4 and continues to develop for many years afterward. Preschool children often equate a lie with a factually incorrect statement, failing to understand the role that intent plays in an adult's definition of what constitutes a lie. By the time children are about 9 years old, they often consider the speaker's intent to deceive and realize that honest mistakes are not lies (Ceci, Leichtman, & Putnick, 1992).

Researchers have identified three major limitations to incorporating truth–lie discussions into investigative interviews. The first is that children who pass such tests are not more accurate or less suggestible than same-aged peers who fail such tests. These discussions therefore do not seem helpful in predicting which children will be accurate informants. Second, there is no evidence that typical truth–lie discussions encourage children to filter out inaccurate information. Third, when young children misreport events, it is often because they misunderstand the purpose of the questions or fail to monitor the source of their knowledge rather than because of a lack of understanding of the difference between truth and lies. That is, the preschool child may be recalling the story of an event rather than the event itself (Poole & Lamb, 1998).

When children are asked to define what truth is, what a lie is, or when they are asked to explain differences between telling the truth and telling a lie, they fail "to demonstrate the real competence of young children." Asking children to identify statements as true or false through the use of hypothetical questions "If I tell you X, . . .), however, allowed almost all of the 5-year-olds to demonstrate credibly their understanding of truths and lies" (Lyon & Saywitz, 1999, cited in Walker, 1999, p. 58, emphasis in original).

Interviewers are notorious for asking children if they understand the interviewer and explain to children that if they do not understand a question, they need to ask for clarification. In practice, children often do not ask. Children may believe that they understand when they do not, or they may choose not to ask for clarification because they may believe that they should understand. Asking a child if he or she understands may not be the most useful way to explore the child's understanding. Instead, the interviewer may ask, "I want to be sure I said that question the right way. So, what do you think that I asked you?" or ask the child to use his or her words to summarize the question.

Another form of questioning to avoid with young children is asking "Why?" questions. "Why?" questions come in two forms: objective and subjective. An objective "Why?" question might be "Why is the dog barking?" A subjective why question might be "Why did you keep this secret for so long?" Both kinds of "Why?" questions may be perceived by children as accusatory and may result in them feeling that the question is critical of their action prior to producing an answer. Subjective "Why?" questions in particular inhibit accurate answers.

Answering "Why?" involves several metacognitive, cognitive, and linguistic operations, including:

a. Self-reflection
b. Reasoning from effect back to cause
c. Understanding that one has motivations
d. Figuring out what those motivations were at the time
e. Recapturing reasoning that may have taken into account possible consequences of an act and its effect on someone else
f. Putting all that awareness into language and representing fully the reasoning behind the answer. (Walker, 1999, pp. 61–62)

Children under the age of 7 are poorly equipped to meet this linguistic challenge, and even children as old as 13 may not reliably respond to questions that require inference about their internal processes.

Interviewers also need to be careful about asking "How?" questions. Some "How?" questions are easily answered by young children. Those that are troublesome usually involve complex operations not acquired until the child is older. "How old are you?" requires a memorization task. Answering "How long did it last?" requires more complex operations, such as the ability to reason from the initial effect back to the cause, and mastery of concepts such as time. Other "How?" questions require the child to internally manipulate narrative, to compare current to past experience, and to perform other complex metacognitive tasks.

When working with young children, evaluators obtain the most useful information when asking questions about concrete actions. Rather than asking a child to explain how another person touched him or her, the evaluator might say, "Show me what he did." Translating abstract questions into simple, concrete statements often allows young children to explain their experiences more accurately.

Care is also needed when asking children to provide complete answers to nonspecific questions such as "Did anything happen?" Children may need additional guidance beyond that provided in open-ended questions. Young children may need cooperative dialogue to develop a narrative of the story. After an initial disclosure of physical abuse by the mother, questions might focus on the following:

1. "Tell me in your own words what happened."
2. "Show me where your mother hit you."
3. "Show me how your mother hit you."
4. "Who did you tell about being hit?"
5. "Did anything else happen to you that you want to talk about?"

Helping children develop a narrative that is logically integrated and chronologically consistent is an important task fraught with the danger of interview contamination (Orbach & Lamb, 2000). Certain types of questions may influence children to create stories that do not accurately reflect events yet sound internally consistent (Poole & Lamb, 1998). Such questions may lead to contamination based on source misattribution (Chapter 6). A child's story may provide accurate general descriptions but include inaccurate peripheral details. This is not uncommon, and it is important for the evaluator to recognize that small inaccuracies do not mean the central events are inaccurate.

Simple as it may be for adults to provide information about who said what to whom, asking children to track the same events is often very difficult. Young children are poor reporters of who said what to whom. They often report who said what in ways that are sequentially incorrect, incorrectly report what was said, and use their own words in describing an adult conversation. Young children do not have the vocabulary, the ability to sequence a conversation from beginning to end, or the ability reliably to report the sequence of a conversation from one interview to another. Although older children are better able to perform this task, research shows that people are generally poor at remembering verbatim statements but good at recalling the gist of a conversation (Bruck et al., 1999). When asked to recall who initiated a question and who responded, performance in all age groups is poor, and confusion concerning who was the questioner and who was the responder is often noted.

Potential Problems in Children's Use of Language

Children use words that make sense to them even when the words do not make sense to others. Most young children use language in an idiosyncratic manner, assigning meanings based on factors that are important to them yet may be irrelevant to the evaluator's use of the word (Gould, 2006). Walker (1999) reminds us that in some cases of child sexual abuse, children report being stabbed despite the absence of a knife or injury. To these children, "'stab' apparently describes what the experience felt like" (p. 67) rather than actually being stabbed by a knife.

Children may overgeneralize a word, applying it to related issues that make sense to the child but are inconsistent with an adult's use of language. For example, the word *mommy* may be used to describe a teacher who is taking care of an ill first-grade child. The observing child describes the action rather than the person. Children also make up words by combining what they know. Walker (1999) describes how a child observed a small caterpillar and called it a *kittenpillar*, importing the term for a young cat and combining it with part of the word *caterpillar*.

A child's use of pronouns is often problematic. Young children become confused in accurately assigning pronouns. It is not uncommon for a young child to say "my house" when he or she intends to indicate "your house."

Children up to the age of 8 may begin a sentence with a pronoun that does not refer to the most recently mentioned noun (or person). Thus, "I saw my dad and my granddad do it. He helped me get away" could refer to a child indicating that her father assisted her in getting away, even though according to the rules of grammar, "He" points to the grandfather.

Often, children say "I don't know" when they are confused, embarrassed, or do not understand what they are expected to say. Some researchers have suggested that saying "I don't know" is related to the child's comfort in taking a risk. It is important that evaluators learn to explore critically a child's use of "I don't know" before accepting that a child, in fact, does not know the answer to a question.

Repetition by children presents another problem. A child as young as 2 years old understands that when an adult asks "What?" the child has not been understood and needs to restate her response. However, children under 9 or 10 often do not have the linguistic skills to restate the information that they are trying to impart even when they realize that they have been misunderstood.

Children often respond to the literal meaning of questions. An interviewer's poor choice of words may elicit information that is either irrelevant or incorrect. For example, asking a 5-year-old girl if she has visited the doctor may result in a "No" response because, for this child, the idea of visiting is related to playing with a friend. Asking the child if she was taken to the doctor's office might elicit a different response, as might asking the child to describe what the doctor did. Much of what we obtain from children is dependent upon the precision of our questions in relationship to their experiences and developmental level.

Children often change their answers when repeatedly questioned. They may infer that their first answer was incorrect and that that is why the evaluator is asking the question again. Some children, when presented with a question that they do not understand, will provide a different answer each time it is asked. Other children may change their answers because they focus on different parts of the sentence or understand the question differently due to their emerging yet unreliable understanding of adult words. Incomplete acquisition of a linguistic rule may cause a child to apply the rule either inconsistently or inaccurately.

Children's use of prepositions begins during the toddler years, and most children acquire most, but not all, prepositions by the time they are 5 years old (Clark & Clark, 1977). Three-year-old children tend to use *in* to mean *between* and *on* to mean *above*. Four-year-old children may become confused about the use of *above, below, at the bottom of,* and *in front of.* Preschoolers sometimes have difficulty properly using the words *before* and *after* (Walker, 1999).

Pronouns and other pointing words that have nothing close by to which to refer often present problems for children. Indexical words focus on something in the sentence. The most familiar indexical words are the pronouns "I," "him," and "that." Words like "here" and "come" also belong to this category. One problem with the use of indexicals is their inherent ambiguity because their meaning depends upon who is using them. For example, "here" can only be understood by knowing where the speaker is, and words like "it" and "that" lack clarity unless their referents have been clearly identified (Walker, 1999).

Proper use of indexicals requires that the listener understand speech roles, how people fit into these speech roles, and how to gauge what the listener knows. Children as young as preschool age understand aspects of indexical use. Mastery of the proper use of words such as *this/that* develops about age 5 while mastery of the proper use of *come/go* and *bring/take* does not develop for some children until age 7 or 8. Understanding that the pronoun and the following noun refer to the same person often does not develop until the middle school years.

Summary

In this chapter, we have discussed the importance of listening to children's stories about separation and divorce. We talked about the tendency for evaluators to understand children's experiences of separation and divorce through the stories of their parents, and we provided ideas about how to interview children to gain a better appreciation for the experience of separation and divorce through their eyes. We also described aspects of young children's use of language, with particular emphasis on the often idiosyncratic and inconsistent ways in which they understand and use language.

Evaluators need to take care systematically to explore the meaning of children's responses. It is important never to make assumptions about children's meanings without examination. Evaluators are urged to ask follow up questions that assist children in explaining what their words were intended to represent and without suggesting an answer. As discussed throughout this chapter, it is never advisable to take at face value children's responses to complex questions or to questions that involve concepts such as size, age, and time. Learning about children's emerging and dynamic understanding of the world as it is imprecisely expressed through language is among the most difficult tasks for a custody evaluator.

PART III

The Science of Child Custody Evaluations

FACTORS TO ASSESS IN CHILD CUSTODY EVALUATIONS

CHAPTER 8

Assessment of Child Developmental Factors

In this chapter, we urge evaluators to consider the purpose of parenting. Evaluators need to evaluate how, through implementation of different parenting strategies, parents guide children toward appropriate developmental goals. An important goal of parenting is to produce competent children. We define the concept of competence and a set of variables related to child competence, then discuss their relevance to the best psychological interests of the child. In Chapter 9, we examine parenting behaviors shown to facilitate a child's progress toward healthy development. In Chapter 10, we examine factors associated with risk to children's development from family system variables.

An important area of assessment should be the fit between parent and child, or what we call the relational dimension of custodial assessment. Although we acknowledge that there are times when assessment of individual factors may be critical in determining the goodness of fit between a parent and a child, we believe that more often than not the primary evaluative focus should be on the quality of the parent–child relationship and the parent's understanding and implementation of competent parenting skills. Our experience, however, has been that only in a minority of cases are recommendations for custodial placement based primarily upon specific characteristics of the child. Reflecting concerns about lack of investigative focus in child custody evaluations, a recent set of articles addresses what evaluators, judges, and attorneys need to consider when assessing special needs children in the context of custody litigation (Jennings, 2005; Kraus, 2005; Perryman, 2005; Saposnek, 2005; Saposnek, Perryman, Berkow, & Ellsworth, 2005).

We also have found that recommendations for custodial placement often do not include an analysis of the goodness of fit between the characteristics and parenting style of the parent and the developmental needs of the child. Too often, recommendations for custodial placement are based upon characteristics of the parent.

Evaluators should assess factors associated with the child, the parent, the parent–child dyad, the parent–parent dyad, and the sibling subsystem. The single-parent family system, the binuclear family system, the extended family system, and their subsets all need to be assessed. Other relational systems that may contribute to understanding the best psychological interests of a child include the school system, the peer group system, the church/youth group system, and the neighborhood in which the child lives. We strongly believe that when evaluators understand the breadth and depth of a child's life within the context of the broader relational systems in which the child exists, a fuller and more accurate understanding of the child and his or her best psychological interests will emerge.

Setting the Stage

Philosopher of science Karl Popper (1972) suggested that a theory is like a searchlight, able to focus attention on a narrow range within a larger set of possibilities. We believe that systems theory (Walsh, 2003) is useful as a searchlight in custody work because of its robustness.

Sameroff (1992) wrote that the study of *behavior in context* was the most important advance in developmental research over the last 50 years. In the past several years, there has been an increasing awareness of the importance of context in understanding the behavior of children and parents in separation and divorce. Previously, we noted Mnookin's (1975) concerns abut the lack of clear standards for judges in considering decisions that involve identifying and applying a consistent standard regarding the best interests of the child. O'Donohue and Bradley (1999) remind us that "the criteria that the courts and mental health professionals have used (in defining what should be used to assess the Best Interests of the Child) involve complex constructs . . . and that these legal and psychological constructs have *value* issues embedded in them in that they also contain evaluative judgments concerning what is desirable or undesirable" (p. 314, emphasis in original). Tippins and Wittmann (2005) point out that the "best interests standard is a legal and socio-moral construct, not a psychological construct [so] . . . there is no empirically supportable method or principle by which an evaluator can come to a conclusion with respect to best interests entirely by resort to the knowledge base of the mental health profession" (p. 215).

The Role of Values in Custodial Placement Recommendations

It is important for evaluators to be aware of how personal and professional values may affect their work (Emery, 1999; Tippins & Wittmann, 2005). For example, evaluators should be aware of how personal, professional, sociomoral, and sociocultural values may influence behaviors identified by the evaluator as desirable for child or parent. We have commented elsewhere (Gould & Martindale, 2005) about the role played by value judgments offered by evaluators under the guise of scientifically informed opinions, and Martindale (2005a) has cautioned about the need for evaluators to be aware of the potential influence of personal and professional biases in the evaluation process. We agree with Tippins and Wittmann (2005), who voice concern about the role of values in making ultimate issue recommendations, yet we take a position more closely aligned with Bala (2005), who states that "the evaluator is expected to be a *delegated fact finder and opinion former* for the court, though the factual findings and the opinions are subject to full challenge at a later hearing" (p. 556, emphasis in original). We also agree with O'Donohue and Bradley (1999), who voiced frustration over the relative lack of open interdisciplinary discussion about the role of values in custody decision making:

> We need to explicate the value issues that are embedded in custody decisions. What are detriments that ought to be avoided? At what cost? What are the magnitudes of these detriments? What are legitimate interests that ought to be maximized? What is "good" or "bad" parenting? How much attachment is "good" and how much is "bad"? What is "desirable" child development and what is "undesirable" development? Parents, children, legal personnel, and mental health practitioners may all hold differing values. Whose values should be honored? (p. 315)

Value judgments made by evaluators help define desirable and undesirable behaviors. Scholars in the field of child custody assessment have not given enough thought to nor have they engaged in enough public debate about identifying desirable and undesirable child behaviors and desirable and undesirable parenting behaviors.

In an examination of the relationship between personal values and their effect on custody decision making, we consider it useful to ask, "What outcomes do we want to see in our children's development, and what type of parenting can best facilitate movement toward that development?" We suggest throughout this section that the primary role of parenting is to help children develop into competent adults who are functional members of society.

Children's Reactions to Separation and Divorce

Most children experience the initial period of family separation as quite stressful. They have little emotional preparation for their parents' separation and may experience a variety of emotional reactions, including distress, anxiety, and anger (Kelly & Emery, 2003). Although these "crisis-engendered responses" diminish or disappear within a 12- to 24-month period (Wallerstein & Kelly, 1980), evaluators must take into account that children who are being evaluated may be emotionally adapting to their parents' separation and divorce. Evaluators must be mindful of drawing conclusions from behaviors observed during the initial separation period that may be neither representative of predivorce functioning and interactional patterns nor predictive of postresolution functioning and interactional patterns.

It is important for evaluators to examine how parents informed children about the separation and divorce and how children talked about the separation and divorce among themselves. Most children are poorly informed by their parents about the reasons for their divorce (Kelly & Emery, 2003) and are left alone to figure out its meaning and its short-term and long-term implications (Smart & Neale, 2000). A majority of parents do not talk with each other about effective custody and access arrangements (Kelly, 1993) and do not talk with their children about the immediate and far-reaching changes in family structure resulting from the divorce (Kelly & Emery, 2003).

How parents and children react to the abrupt departure of one parent, which in American culture is usually the father, should be assessed in terms of four factors:

1. How the remaining parent frames the departure of the other parent for the children.
2. What type of emotional outlet the remaining parent provides for the children.
3. How the moving parent frames his or her departure for the children.
4. How he or she provides an emotional outlet for the children.

In the beginning stages of divorce, some children may not see their nonresidential parent for weeks or months. For those children who have had strong, positive relationships with that parent, lack of contact may be very distressing and painful.

In addition, evaluators need to assess how these children adjust to new physical environments, new emotional environments, and new relationships with each parent, each sibling, each member of the extended family, and their peer and neighborhood friendship groups. We believe it is important for evaluators to examine the adjustment of children to these different changes.

Children from divorced families are at least twice as likely as children from continuously married families to have more behavioral, internalizing, social, and academic problems (Hetherington, 1999). They also are more likely to have lower academic performance and lower achievement scores. Children from divorced families have, as young adults, more difficulties in their intimate relationships. They tend to marry earlier, report less marital satisfaction, and are more likely to divorce (Amato, 2000). Relationships between adult children of divorce and their parents tend to be less affectionate and less supportive than those relationships in continuously married families (Amato & Booth, 1996). When divorced parents spoke negatively about the other parent in front of their adult children, young adults were more likely to report angry and less close relationships with the denigrating parent (Fabricius & Hall, 2000).

An important contribution is the role played by older siblings. Younger children are inoculated from some of the stress of parental divorce when they maintain strong and positive relationships with older siblings. As discussed later in this chapter, evaluators need to examine changes in the sibling subsystem resulting from parental divorce and to investigate the impact of those changes on the children's adjustment to divorce.

Children's Adjustment and the Need for Competent Parenting

There is an emerging consensus that children's risk of poor adjustment is reduced by living in the custody of a competent, adequately functioning parent. When competent custodial parents provide warmth, emotional support, adequate supervision, and monitoring; discipline authoritatively; and maintain age-appropriate expectations, children and adolescents are better adjusted compared with children whose divorced custodial parents are inattentive, less supportive, and use coercive discipline (Amato, 2000; Kelly & Emery, 2003).

Divorced children are better adjusted when they have timely and appropriate parenting from nonresidential parents. In the context of low parental conflict, frequent contact between father and children is associated with better child adjustment. Where parental conflict is high, more frequent contact is associated with poorer adjustment (Kelly & Emery, 2003). Frequent contact with nonresidential parents has a beneficial effect on children when fathers help with homework and projects, provide authoritative parenting, and hold appropriate expectations for their children. Children with involved fathers show more positive adjustment and better academic performance than children with less involved fathers. Increased paternal involvement is also associated with better grades, fewer repeated grades, and fewer suspensions (Nord, Brimhall, & West, 1997).

The psychological well-being of the primary caretaker, usually the mother, is an important factor that influences adjustment of preschool- and school-age children. Mothers whose marriages were characterized by intense conflict and/ or violence are more likely to be rejecting and cold. They tend to discipline in a harsher and more inconsistent manner than mothers who come from low-conflict marriages (Kelly & Lamb, 2003). Competent parenting by a nearby nonresidential parent does not appear to buffer against the primary caretaker's less competent parenting (Hetherington, 1999), resulting in these children being placed at a higher risk for poor adjustment (Kelly & Lamb, 2003).

A Reminder about Evaluating Children and Their Families

As we begin the process of assessing child factors, parental factors, and family factors in child custody evaluations, we need to be mindful of the extraordinary changes that have occurred in the lives of these children. We must concern ourselves with understanding how children, parents, and larger familial systems adapt to change. Through our evaluation procedures, we attempt to make sense of an evolving family system that has begun its process of change long before our examination procedures commence, and we need to remember that these changes will continue long after we have completed our assessment.

We need to remember that not all development is linear or neatly predictable. In our experience, developmental psychology texts generally emphasize regularities in child development and offer only minimal information concerning individuality, but the rhythm and pace of development are unique to each child.

Research Examining Relevant Child Development Factors

Too often, evaluators do not consider theoretical models of child development to guide their thinking in the preparation of advisory reports. We have reviewed several hundred evaluations over the years and found at least three ways in which mental health professionals have approached assessing child developmental factors in custody advisory reports. Some evaluators give no thought to operationally defining child factors to be examined. Among the most egregious examples is recent courtroom testimony from a licensed psychologist who was court appointed to conduct a custody evaluation examining a parent's request to relocate. The psychologist was asked, "Dr. Smith, for this evaluation, how did you define the best psychological interests of the child?" His response was, "I have not given that any thought. I was asked to evaluate the children." Attempting to rehabilitate the good doctor's testimony, the father's attorney asked on redirect examination, "What child-related factors did you assess that were relevant to the court's interest in the possible effects on these children of the mother's relocation to Texas?" He answered, "Factors that might affect the children if they relocate? I didn't look at that. I looked at whether they were healthy, you know, emotionally healthy and doing well in school and other aspects of life. I gave the children several tests, interviewed them individually, and my conclusions were that they were healthy kids. I found nothing abnormal in these results." The evaluator never identified a set of factors to be examined in a relocation case. Relevant factors were never identified, were never assessed, and were never used in formulating his opinions about the degree of risk to these children of the mother's move to Texas. (For a discussion of factors to consider in relocation cases, see Austin, 2000a, 2000b, 2000c; Austin & Gould, 2006; and Kelly & Lamb, 2003.)

Another limitation is evaluators' strict adherence to only assessing factors articulated in state statutes defining the best interests of the child. We believe it is important to provide information about the statutorily required factors of the best interests of the child, but these factors often do not focus on issues specific to the family under scrutiny. We encourage evaluators to provide data not only on statutorily required factors, but also on factors specifically related to questions of concern to the particular family (Amundson et al., 2000; Gould, 1999).

A third limitation is that evaluators often do not integrate findings within a comprehensive theory of development. For example, we have seen many advisory reports provide a wealth of information about how the child interacts with each parent, how each parent views the child, how the child views each parent, and how collateral informants view parent–child interactions. What is missing from these reports is a discussion of how specific parent–child factors are associated with development of healthy and positive child outcomes.

Evaluators should consider a comprehensive model of child development that has as its focus the fostering of healthy and positive functioning associated with developing competent citizens. Evaluators need to define (1) factors in a child that need to be developed and nurtured; (2) factors *in* the parent and factors *provided by* a parent to a child that need to be present and nurtured; and (3) factors in a family system that need to be present and nurtured.

In this chapter, we discuss factors associated with the development of competence in children and describe how children's successful acquisition of these competence-based behaviors, attitudes, beliefs, and values is associated with healthy, positive outcomes for children and how these healthy, positive outcomes are associated with competent functioning as adults. We do not believe this is the only model one may use to guide thinking in child custody evaluations, nor do we believe that it is the most comprehensive model. It is, we believe, a logically consistent, scientifically informed model about how children develop competence.

Developing Competence in Children

One of the most challenging aspects of child custody work is to define a set of child behaviors associated with healthy, positive outcomes for children. Stated differently, evaluators must ask, "What developmental factors do parents and/ or caregivers need to help develop and nurture best to assist children in becoming competent and productive citizens?" Once we are able to identify child factors associated with prediction of healthy, positive outcomes for children, then we may be in a better position to identify parent characteristics and parenting competencies that facilitate children's development along these dimensions of competence and productivity.

We believe that defining an empirically based set of factors associated with healthy, positive outcomes for children is consistent with the American Psychological Association's orienting guidelines for custody evaluation (1994). The orienting guidelines state, in part, that the "primary purpose of the evaluation is to assess the best psychological interests of the child" and that "the child's interests and well-being are paramount" (American Psychological Association, 1994, p. 677). The guidelines also focus attention on "an assessment of the psychological functioning and developmental needs of each child and of the wishes of each child where appropriate" (p. 678). We believe that an assessment of child factors shown to be associated with healthy, positive outcomes is consistent with the guidelines' goals of cultivating the psychological best interests of the child.

We have described parenting factors associated with the cultivation of competence in children and family factors associated with undermining the development of competence in children. We argue that the assessment of child factors, parenting factors, and family factors must be integrated into a comprehensive model of competence development in children.

The American Psychological Association's orienting guidelines include attention to "the resulting fit between parenting capacity and the psychological and developmental needs of the child" (American Psychological Association, 1994, p. 678). Our position that is this fit is organized around long-term outcomes that support and optimize a child's development into a healthy, functional citizen. Current custody literature focuses much attention on children's adjustment to postdivorce family functioning. An additional focus should be on factors associated with development of competent adult functioning. The guidelines' focus on fit between parenting capacity and psychological and developmental needs of the child should reflect a view that the parent–child fit must help children become healthy, functioning citizens.

We base this argument upon the work of Masten and Coatsworth (1998), who wrote: "It is critical to the future of a society that its children become competent adults and productive citizens. Thus, society and parents share a stake in the development of competence and in understanding the processes that facilitate and undermine it" (p. 205). Evaluation-involved families often display higher levels of conflict and higher levels of adversity than families not divorcing and families divorcing but not involved in custody litigation. Children of evaluation-involved families are likely to face a different set of challenges than children whose parents are able to settle their custodial concerns outside of court, including but not limited to individual and family obstacles to positive adjustment and consistent, high-quality parental supervision.

Divorce has the potential to become a developmental insult to a child. It may disrupt a child's world at all levels, becoming a significant obstacle in his or her life. How his or her parents and other supportive persons cultivate and nurture a child through these transitional times may be critical to his or her healthy short- and long-term adjustment. Research has not adequately addressed differences and similarities between children raised in two-parent families and children raised in divorced families, but there is a cultural bias that divorce is inherently bad for children. Research supports the view that how children adjust and grow often depends on their parents' ability to parent competently whether or not the parents are married. We suggest that much of a child's adjustment to divorce may depend upon each parent's ability to manage the adult factors associated with divorcing and to view as separate those factors associated with parenting. Children do not have to be any more adversely affected by separation and divorce than by living in a two-parent family when their parents find ways to continue to parent their children competently and create a feeling of family continuity. Children will likely be relatively unaffected in their adjustment when their parents find ways to separate and divorce minimal conflict and with minimal obstructions to their children's access to each parent (Eidman, personal communication, September 20, 2006).

There are also many normal developmental progressions that, when they happen in two-parent families, are not identified as problem behavior, yet, when observed in a divorcing family, are attributed to the result of the divorce or, in high-conflict families, the result of one parent's incompetent parenting (Eidman, personal communication, September 15, 2006).

It is particularly important to understand how competence is achieved in the context of adversity (Masten & Coatsworth, 1998). Therefore, we propose that understanding what behaviors, attitudes, beliefs, and/or values a child may need to increase the probability of his or her later success in life is critical for custody evaluators.

Definitions of Competence and Resilience

Competence is operationally defined as

> a pattern of effective adaptation in the environment, either broadly defined in terms of reasonable success with major developmental tasks expected for a person of a given age and gender in the context of his or her culture, society, and time, or more narrowly defined in terms of specific domains of achievement, such as academics, peer acceptance, or athletics. (Masten & Coatsworth, 1998, p. 205)

Competence carries the dual meaning that the individual has a track record of achievement (competent performance) and the capability to perform well in the future. Competence refers to good adaptation, not necessarily to superb achievement.

Competence develops from complex interactions between a child and her environment. Competence changes over time as a child develops or a context changes. As a child grows, her environment changes, and she learns to cope with challenges at each stage of development. Skills needed to negotiate these challenges will differ for each child and developmental level. Both a child's capabilities and the nature of the contexts in which she lives will influence the development of competence (Masten & Coatsworth, 1998).

One factor observed in healthy children is resilience. Resilience has many meanings and, in this context, reflects a manifest competence in the context of significant challenges to adaptation or development. We have all observed children undergoing divorce who appear of equal developmental readiness, yet one progresses through developmental steps effortlessly while the other needs significant support to accomplish routine tasks. What makes one child resilient and the other vulnerable to adversity?

Masten and Coatsworth (1998) suggest that to identify resilience, two judgments are required. The first judgment is whether there has been a significant threat to the child, typically indexed by high-risk status (e.g., high-conflict postseparation custodial battle) or exposure to severe adversity or trauma (e.g., family violence, loss of a relationship with a parent, relocation after divorce). The second is whether the quality of adaptation or development is good.

Developmental Tasks

Evaluations of how a child is doing in life generally reflect expectations based on pooled knowledge about child development that is both culturally transmitted from one generation to the next and responsive to changes in our understanding of what children need to succeed in the future. Important information about how each child is meeting these expectations is obtained from third-party informants such as parents, teachers, pediatricians, and others important in the child's life (Heilbrun et al., 2003). In a child custody evaluation, obtaining information from these third-party informants is critical to a complete understanding of a child, including how he or she relates to his or her world (Austin, 2002).

General concepts often are difficult to define, and competence is no exception. For our purposes, one way to define competence is the child's progression through age-appropriate developmental tasks (Havighurst, 1972). Numerous lists of developmental tasks have appeared over the years, reflecting several broad domains of competence in the environment and developmental progression.

For example, one fundamental developmental domain is conduct. It is important for children to learn how to follow rules. How well one follows the rules is an important marker of healthy development. Early in childhood, children are expected to begin controlling their behavior and complying with parental directives. Later, as they enter elementary school, they are expected to learn and to follow rules for classroom conduct and to refrain from striking out at people with whom they disagree. By adolescence, children are expected to follow rules of middle and high school, home, and society, increasingly without direct supervision.

By middle childhood, academic achievement is an important domain of success for children. It continues to be important in adolescence, with the quality of expected performance continually rising. Developing social relationships and belonging to a peer group become salient issues. Children seek peer acceptance and display age-appropriate social competence when they learn to develop and maintain friendships and romantic relationships.

How each parent supports and encourages a child's acquisition of age-appropriate developmental tasks contributes to a belief that the parent is acting in the child's best psychological interests. Evaluators often assess a child's general level of development and whether there are delays. They may examine how these delays are best ameliorated and which parent is best equipped to assist the child along his or her projected developmental path. Evaluators also may suggest parenting arrangements that best facilitate healthy child development.

Sensitivity to Different Cultures

Deciding whether a child is competent can be difficult when a child lives in a cultural or community context that differs markedly from the larger society in which the community or cultural group is embedded. Ethnographic studies have suggested that urban African American adolescents and their parents may use different criteria for successful developmental outcomes than suburban white/European Americans (Coll & Pachter, 2002; McAdoo, 2002). It is important that evaluators working with culturally diverse populations remember that families in a given community may have different values and expectations for competence.

Foundations of Competence in Early Development

Rapidly expanding knowledge about early child development indicates the importance of the early years as a foundation for later competence. The early development of motor skills, language, self-confidence, play, and problem-solving abilities, for example, is relevant to understanding competence in the school years. Underlying these capabilities is a developing brain. Recent studies of humans and other species have made it clear that the developing brain is profoundly responsive to experience (Nelson & Bloom, 1997). Both structure and function are affected by experience, a phenomenon known as *plasticity* (Cicchetti & Tucker, 1994; Nelson & Bloom, 1997). Intervention depends on plasticity because lasting changes in behavior depend on the modifiability of brain function (Masten & Coatsworth, 1998).

Motivational systems also are clearly central to human competence. Babies appear to be delighted by exercising newfound skills like blowing bubbles, making sounds, or dropping things, whereas older children find pleasure in activities like singing nonsense songs, making jokes, solving puzzles, or riding a bike. White (1959) argued that there is a mastery motivation system inherent in our species that is readily observable in the inclination of young children to engage actively with the environment and to experience pleasure (feelings of efficacy) from effective interactions. In other words, competence is motivated by pleasure in mastery. Studies have shown that babies not only exhibit the behaviors associated with mastery motivation but that their behavior begins to be affected by cognitive appraisals of likely success at an early age. Thus, a 2-year-old shows distress when an adult models a task the child realizes that he or she cannot do (Kagan, 1984). The role of perceived self-efficacy and other perceptions about one's ability and control have been the subject of considerable research among older children; it is clear that children's beliefs about their own success affect their behavior (Henderson & Dweck, 1990; Skinner, 1995).

All of the relevant systems for competence that develop in early childhood could not possibly be addressed in this chapter. We focus on two that have received considerable attention in recent years, have shown significance for competence in multiple domains, and have potential as modifiable influences on a child's competence: relationships with caring adults and self-regulation.

Attachments and Parenting

Attachment refers to an affectional tie between parent and child. It is not linked to any specific parenting behaviors, practices, or styles (Ainsworth, Blehar, Waters, & Wall, 1978). Attachment is a relational construct, the examination of which entails observation of mutual interaction of parent and child in various contexts in order to assess attachment security (Ainsworth et al., 1978). Interestingly, although attachment by definition is not a parenting style or practice, past and current research examining attachment has generally focused on parenting. Attachment, however, develops from the child's experiential history of parenting and does not affect a child's development in isolation from other influences from within the family (Cummings & Cummings, 2002).

Attachments are shaped by experience and understanding the development of attachment relationships requires observing day-to-day experiences of interactions between a parent and a child (Bowlby, 1969). "Consistent with theory, patterns of attachment are classified to distinguish parent-child relationships in terms of strategies for using the parent as a secure base and the coherency of children's attachment behavior. Of the various contexts for the child, separations are typically the most stressful, and thus, parent-child interactions on reunion are potentially the most informative with regard to the functioning of the attachment system" (Cummings & Cummings, 2002, p. 40).

The *secure base* concept is a central tenet of attachment theory. The primary dimension in attachment is the parent's relative effectiveness in providing security to his or her child, particularly during times of stress. Too often we have seen evaluators talk about attachment as if it applies to all aspects of the parent–child relationship. It is critically important that evaluators not lose sight of the core definition of attachment as the provision of emotional security. "The term secure attachment refers both to skillful secure-base use over time and contexts in naturalistic settings and to confidence in a caregiver's availability and responsiveness" (Waters & Cummings, 2000, p. 165). Ainsworth et al. (1978) posited the central importance of sensitivity, accessibility, acceptance, and cooperation as parenting behaviors that significantly contribute to a child's security of attachment to parents, with each parenting behavior viewed as a component of sensitive responsiveness of the parent to infant communications and behavioral signals. "Thus, the core prediction of attachment theory from its initial formulation was that the child's sense of emotional security would derive from the responsiveness, warmth, and emotional availability of the parent" (Cummings & Cummings, 2002, p. 43).

Four major attachment classifications have been identified (Ainsworth et al., 1978): (1) secure, (2) insecure–avoidant, (3) insecure–resistant, and (4) disorganized/disoriented. The distribution of secure, insecure–avoidant, and insecure–resistant attachments is similar for mothers and fathers (Colin, 1996). Research findings suggest that children are equally likely to form secure attachments to fathers and mothers, regardless of who works outside the home and who is a home maker (Kelly & Lamb, 2000).

A child who is *securely attached* uses his or her attachment figure (usually one or both parents) as a secure base. The child employs a coherent, organized strategy for using one or both parents as a source of security. For example, a securely attached child will, upon the return of a parent into the child's space, make an emotional connection with the parent by seeking physical contact, by seeking closer physical proximity, or through effective use of signals to the parent such as greeting the parent. The parent responds to the child's security seeking with greater responsiveness and warmth to the child's actions. Once such responsiveness, warmth, and sensitivity is obtained from the parent, the child returns to a nondistressed state.

A child who has developed an *insecure–avoidant attachment* diverts his or her attention away from anything that would activate attachment behavior. He or she learns not to rely on attachment figures during times of stress. Research evidence suggests that parents of insecure–avoidant attached children are more rejecting, tense, and irritable, and avoidant of close bodily contact toward their children in day-to-day interactions in the home (Cummings & Cummings, 2002). Other research findings suggest that mothers of avoidant infants tend to be more intrusive and overstimulating (Belsky, Rovine, & Taylor, 1984). These parent behaviors are believed to foster less confidence in the child about the parent as a reliable source of security during times of stress.

A child who displays an *insecure–resistant attachment* behavior pattern tends to display an ambivalence toward the attachment figure. Prior to separation, these infants are often observed to be clingy and uninterested in toys or play. On reunion with their parents, these children may show a combination of angry behavior and excessive contact and proximity seeking. Often, parents of insecure–resistant children are found to behave inconsistently toward their children and report problematic parent–child interactions in the home.

The child with a *disorganized/disoriented attachment* (Main & Solomon, 1990) has failed to develop a coherent strategy for coping with stress and for relying on the attachment relationship. Cummings and Cummings (2002) write: "These children may exhibit a variety of behaviors indicative of disturbance and lack of organization during reunion with the parent, including unusual sequences of behavior, both avoidant and resistant reactions in the context of the same reunion, and/or highly apprehensive or depressive behavior" (p. 41). Disorganized attachments have been found to be particularly evident among maltreated and traumatized children (Hesse & Main, 1999, 2000; Hesse, Main, Abrams, & Rifkin, 2003) and among children of parents with psychopathology (Zahn-Waxler, Duggal, & Gruber, 2002).

Attachments are believed to provide influential models for later close relationships. Past attachments remain important throughout the lifespan. It is believed that "attachment is an organizational construct that motivates and directs a relatively complex and sophisticated behavioral control system in response to the contextual demands of situations faced by the child" (Cummings & Cumming, 2002, p. 39). The attachment system is activated when an infant feels the need for safety and security. Activation of the attachment system of a securely attached infant results in the infant seeking out the parent for warmth, responsiveness, and sensitivity. Securely attached children seek the attachment figure and insecurely attached children avoid or resist seeking the attachment figure. In both secure and insecure attachments, the child's behavior reveals a coherent or organized strategy for coping with stress. No such organized or cohesive pattern of behavior is evident among children who show disorganized/disoriented attachments.

Attachment and Development of Internal Working Models

A developing knowledge base recognizes the important role of early development, including attachment, on the organization and later process and structure of the brain (Schore, 2001). A healthy and secure attachment forms as the caregiver responds sensitively and consistently to the child's needs (Bowlby, 1969). Over time, children internalize this security within the attachment relationship, forming internal working models (IWMs) of these relationships that are themselves encoded as neural pathways in the brain (Siegel, 2003). These IWMs are internalized representations of the child's perception of the relationship between the caregiver and the child. It is believed that during the first 36–48 months of life these IWMs form, providing for attachment to become stable. A child with a secure attachment develops an IWM of secure attachment and, as a result, is more competent to approach the world with a greater sense of relationship stability. A child with an insecure attachment develops an IWM of insecure attachment and, as a result, is more likely to approach the world with greater anxiety toward or avoidance of others. A child can form a secure attachment with one parent and an insecure attachment with another parent, because attachment originates from relationship-specific behaviors.

Children's Relationships with Caring Adults: The Attachment System

Under normal conditions, infants have considerable power to elicit assistance from parents in securing help for negotiating the demands of their environments, in regulating their emotions and behaviors in reaction to environmental stimulation, and in honing skills they will need for success in later developmental tasks. Infant competence is embedded in the caregiving system (Ainsworth & Bell, 1974). The caregiving or attachment system is widely believed to serve multiple functions beyond physical care, including soothing and stimulation of emotions by the caregiver, who helps to teach the infant self-regulation of emotion. The caregiving system also provides a secure base of operations for young children to explore the environment (Carlson & Sroufe, 1995).

There is evidence that the quality of these attachment relationships has predictive significance for success in later developmental tasks, such as better problem solving in *toddlers* and better peer relations in middle childhood (Carlson & Sroufe, 1995; Kelly & Lamb, 2000). Longitudinal studies of competent children and adolescents who have experienced severe adversity also strongly indicate the importance of caregiver relationships for successful adaptation (Masten, 1994).

When there is little observable evidence that a specific attachment bond has formed between an infant or toddler and the caregiver(s), as may occur in cases of autistism spectrum disorder or in situations of extreme neglect, the evaluator should become concerned. This attachment system is so basic and universal that lack of behavior associated with attachment usually occurs only when there is something fundamentally wrong with the child or the environment, leading to a high risk for adaptive failure (Kelly & Lamb, 2003). The emergence of the attachment system is clearly a critical foundation for competence in children. It is important to understand how to assess properly a strong and healthy relationship between children and their caregivers and to provide recommendations for appropriate interventions that can foster and/or remediate a dysfunctional or damaged attachment relationship.

Normative Development of Infants and Toddlers

Children confront specific developmental challenges as they grow. Depending upon the age and stage of psychological development, the emotional tasks that confront the child will vary. Disruption in the opportunity for the child to accomplish some of these tasks may result in developmental deficiencies (Whiteside, 1998).

Infants

In the first 12 months of life, infants accomplish an impressive number of developmental tasks. Their sleeping, waking, and eating cycles become regular, and they learn varied and clear ways of communicating their needs. They begin to develop a view of the world that is organized, with object permanence and concepts of causality. They learn to develop control over all parts of their bodies, learn that their actions can be goal-directed, and begin to anticipate consequences (Kelly & Lamb, 2000).

Infants need regularity and to be picked up consistently when they seek contact. They need to be comforted when distressed and require gentle and appropriately responsive caregiving (Whiteside, 1998). Most important in the infant's development is the establishment of a positive, smoothly functioning relationship based upon a secure attachment to the primary caregiver (Kelly & Lamb, 2000).

INFANCY AND THE NEED FOR SECURE ATTACHMENT

According to attachment theory (Bowlby, 1969), attachment is defined as a child's insistence on maintaining closeness to a protective caregiver. An attachment behavioral system in infants regulates infant safety and survival in the environment. Attachment systems are viewed as equally important to other primary regulatory systems such as feeding and reproduction. Infants continually monitor the availability of one or more *attachment figures* (usually parents) in an effort to seek safety and protection; when confronted with alarm, infants seek out their attachment figures (Main, 1996).

The primary developmental task of infants is to develop a trusting relationship with the world. Toddlers' primary focus is to learn to seek independence from primary attachment figures. Disruptions to safety and predictability that accompany separation and divorce may significantly affect children's ability to negotiate successfully the developmental priorities of toddlerhood. Thus, attachment theory may be important to consider when evaluating infant and early childhood adjustment to separation and divorce (Solomon & Biringen, 2001; Kelly & Lamb, 2000; Lamb & Kelly, 2001).

An infant's attachment to his or her primary caregivers is increasingly seen as the most critical factor in fostering healthy development (Main, 1996). Infant attachment behavior develops slowly during the first year of life (Biringen, 1991). Although parental attachment to the infant may develop quickly after birth, the child's attachment to the primary caregiver develops slowly, taking typically 6 months or more to establish a preferential relationship to that caregiver (Lamb, 1987; Main, 1996; Sroufe, 1983, 1991).

Healthy development results from *secure* attachment between the infant and primary caregiver. Disruptions to proper infant–caregiver attachment may result in one of several kinds of insecure attachments (Main, 1996). Separation and divorce affect children's attachment to at least one primary caregiver. Johnston and Roseby (1997) state that "parents need to understand that the security of their child's primary relationship is the essential basis for his or her sense of security in other relationships, both now and in the future. . . . The child's need for predictability is the final and essential consideration" (pp. 105–106).

Disruptions to infant–caregiver secure attachments have negative effects on several aspects of a child's development. Infants who experience disruptions in relationships with primary caregivers are at risk to develop insecure attachment behaviors (Main, 1996). Insecure attachment in infancy is related to unfavorable social development in preschool and adolescence (Belsky, 1996; Rosen & Rothbaum, 1993) and is associated with maladjustment and emotional problems throughout childhood (Davies & Cummings, 1994). Insecurely attached infants are at risk for increased aggressive behavior (Lyons-Ruth, 1996), poor peer relationships (Fagot, 1997), and other significant types of maladjustment that negatively affect the child (Main, 1996). Securely attached infants are reported to have better peer relationships (Fagot, 1997) and display higher levels of positive affect and social competence (Sroufe, 1983).

Toddlers

Toddlers, children aged 12 to 36 months, are in a period of rapid cognitive, social, and motor growth. They face the task of achieving a sense of independent mastery. They are beginning to explore their world actively, increasingly taking steps toward autonomy from their primary caregiver, yet seeking out his or her protection and comfort to ensure their safety. Securely attached toddlers are more likely to comply with parental directives and to engage in constructive problem solving (Whiteside, 1998). Securely attached toddlers tend to be enthusiastic and persistent and are less aggressive and negative than are insecurely attached children (Main, 1996). Toddlers need help in learning how to anticipate transitions. They may struggle with making sense of their experiences. When upset, young children need help from their primary caregiver in learning how to soothe and control themselves. The foundation for the child's ability to focus appropriately on how to manage his emotional arousal is associated with the degree to which he has available caregivers to whom he is securely attached. In the face of high levels of conflict in families, young children can become passively frozen or actively oppositional, as indicated by increased tantrums and bossiness. They become less able to control their actions and feelings than is typical for their age group (Johnston & Campbell, 1988). High levels of parental conflict in the toddler's world may lead to frantic, uncontrolled reactions and poor intellectual progress (Johnston & Campbell, 1988; Main, 1996).

Infants' and Toddlers' Needs for Secure Attachment

During times of family transition, infant's and toddler's needs for safety, security, predictability, and consistency are paramount (Baris & Garrity, 1988; Garrity & Baris, 1994; Johnston & Roseby, 1997; Main, 1996; Whiteside, 1998). Compared to older children, infants and toddlers are more vulnerable to changes in their environment because of the challenges and potential threats to maintaining their developing attachments (Main, 1996) and their basic trust (Baris & Garrity, 1988). Infants and toddlers build strong attachments to primary caregivers. When separated from these caregivers, they may experience a profound sense of loss, depression, and behavioral and emotional regression (Bowlby, 1969; Main, 1996).

Table 8.1 describes some developmental guidelines for the infant and toddler.

Similar to infants, toddlers may feel a strong sense of loss as a result of diminished contact with a primary caregiver. Disruption in a toddler's child's attachments may lead to depression, confusion, cognitive and linguistic disorganization, and overall maladjustment. Toddlers who are separated too long from their primary caretakers may demonstrate difficulty with attachment (reunion), separation, and with the developing need to explore the environment independently and the development of healthy relationships in later stages of development (Baris & Garrity, 1988). Kelly and Lamb (2000, 2003) make the point

TABLE 8.1. Developmental Guidelines from Infancy to 2½ Years

Primary developmental tasks
- Infants need to build trust and attachments.
- Toddlers need to balance opportunities for independence with security of caregiver presence.

Challenges to well-being
- Infants may experience a profound sense of loss, depression, and behavioral and emotional regression resulting from disruption in attachment to primary caregivers.
- Toddlers may experience similar reactions based upon loss of diminished contact with caretakers. Toddlers may also show confusion, cognitive and linguistic disorganization, and overall maladjustment. They may demonstrate difficulty in attachment (reunion).

---

that it is often difficult to rebuild a disrupted relationship to its previous level of strength, suggesting that avoiding disruption to the child's primary attachments should be a major focus of custody recommendations.

Application of Child Development Research to Custody and Access Decision Making about Young Children

Kelly and Lamb (2000, 2003; Lamb & Kelly, 2001; Lamb, 2002) have written extensively about the application of child development research to decision making about custody and access in young children. In general, the ways in which mothers and fathers establish relationships with their children and influence their children's development are quite similar. Although much has been made of research showing that mothers and fathers have distinctive styles of interaction with their young children, the differences are quite small and do not appear to be formatively significant (Kelly & Lamb, 2000). There is an emerging consensus that the benefits of maintaining contact with both parents exceed any special need for relationships with the mother or the father (Bauserman, 2002).

An alternative viewed is expressed by Solomon and her colleagues, who argue that critical attachment processes are developing at least through the first 18 months that require the child to maintain continuous contact with the primary caregiver (Solomon & Biringen, 2001). Both Solomon and Biringen (2001) and Kelly and Lamb (2000, 2003; Lamb, 2002; Lamb & Kelly, 2001) would argue that the empirical literature also shows that young children need regular interaction with both of their parents in order to foster and maintain their attachments. Where theoretical differences are most prominent is in recommendations about overnight visitation for children under 18 months old. Kelly and Lamb (2000) argue that extended separations from either parent are undesirable because they unduly stress developing attachment relationships. Solomon and colleagues argue that the primary focus should be not to unduly stress the mother–child attachment relationship during the period of time that the child is developing an internal model of his or her caregiver.

Recent research shows that young children's successful adjustment to overnight stays with noncustodial parents is associated with the quality of parent–child relationships (Pruett, Ebling, & Insabella, 2004) and that children are better adjusted when they have strong positive relationships with both parents (Kelly & Emery, 2003; Kelly & Lamb, 2003).

It is necessary for the interactions with both parents to occur in a variety of contexts (feeding, playing, diapering, soothing, putting to bed, etc.) to ensure that relationships are consolidated and strengthened. In the absence of such opportunities for regular interaction across a broad range of contexts, young child–parent relationships fail to develop and may instead weaken. It is extremely difficult to reestablish relationships between young children and their parents once they have been disrupted. Young children are best served by relationship continuity and by minimizing or avoiding relationship disruptions in the first place (Kelly & Lamb, 2000, 2003).

Maintaining Children's Attachments after Separation or Divorce

If a child's relationships with both parents were at least of adequate quality, the central challenge is to maintain these attachments after separation. In general, relationships with parents play a crucial role in shaping children's social, emotional, personal, and cognitive development, and there is a substantial literature documenting the adverse effects of disrupted parent–child relationships on children's development and adjustment. Kelly and Lamb (2003) state:

> Children who are deprived of meaningful relationships with one of their parents are at greater risk psychosocially, even when they are able to maintain relationships with their other parent. . . . there is substantial evidence that children are more likely to attain their psychological potential when they are able to develop and maintain meaningful relationships with both of their parents. (p. 196)

The most common practice in custody and access decisions has been to emphasize and preserve continuity in the relationships between young children and mothers, with children living with their mothers and having limited contact with their fathers. There is an emerging awareness of the adverse effects of severed father–child relationships as well as the positive contributions that fathers make to their children's development (Lamb, 2002; Warshak, 2000c).

Lamb (2002; Kelly & Lamb, 2000; Lamb & Kelly, 2001) argues that there is ample evidence young children become accustomed to regular separations without adverse effects on the quality of attachments to their parents. He argues that the same should be true of separations in the context of parental separation or divorce. Kelly and Lamb (2000) talk about the need for young children to have multiple contacts each week with both parents in order to minimize separation anxiety and maintain continuity in the children's attachments. They argue that the concept of residential stability (one home, one bed) has been incorrectly overemphasized for young children, without consideration for the greater significance to the child of the emotional, social, and cognitive contributions of both parent–child relationships. Living in one location (geographic or residential stability) ensures only one type of stability. Stability is also created for young children by the predictable comings and goings of both parents, by regular feeding and sleeping schedules, by consistent and appropriate care, and by affection and acceptance. Further, postseparation access or contact schedules that are predictable and can be managed without stress or distress by young children provide stability.

The Issue of Overnights with the Nonresidential Parent

Until the 1990s, conventional wisdom was that children were best served by maintaining the mother–child attachment above all else. There was less focus on the quality of father–child attachment. In their seminal article arguing that infants and young children need to maintain healthy and positive relationships with both parents, Kelly and Lamb (2000) recommended custodial arrangements include frequent visits with and overnight access for the noncustodial parent. They described both psychoanalytic theory and the tender years legal doctrine as focusing attention on preserving mother–young child attachments. The most influential psychology work addressing custodial arrangements (Goldstein et al., 1979) posited the psychological parent as the most important person in the young child's life. Until the mid-1990s, there was little focus on regular contact with the nonresidential parent and even less attention paid to the value of overnight or extended visitation with the nonresidential parent. In fact, such overnight or extended visitation for young children was often forbidden or strongly discouraged by judges, custody evaluators, therapists, mental health professionals, family law attorneys, and, not surprisingly, many mothers (e.g., Baris & Garrity, 1988; Goldstein et al., 1979; Hodges, 1991).

Such unnecessarily restrictive and prescriptive guidelines were not based on child development research and reflected an outdated view of parent–child relationships. Further, they did not take into account the quality of the father–child or mother–child relationships, the nature of both parents' involvement, or the child's need to maintain and strengthen relationships with both parents after separation. Research and experience with infant daycare, early preschool, and other stable care arrangements indicate that young children readily adapt to such transitions and also sleep well, once familiarized. Indeed, they thrive socially, emotionally, and cognitively if the care arrangements are predictable and the parents are both sensitive to the child's physical and developmental needs and emotionally available (Kelly & Lamb, 2000).

The evening and overnight periods (like extended days with naptimes) with nonresidential parents are now viewed as especially important psychologically for infants, toddlers, and young children. They provide opportunities for crucial social interactions and nurturing activities, including bathing, soothing hurts and anxieties, bedtime rituals, comforting in the middle of the night, and the reassurance and security of snuggling in the morning after awakening that 1- to 2-hour visits cannot provide. These everyday activities promote and maintain trust and confidence in the parents, while deepening and strengthening parent–child attachments (Kelly & Lamb, 2000; Lamb, 2002; Warshak, 2000a, 2000b).

Kelly and Lamb (2000) state, "There is absolutely no evidence that children's psychological adjustment or the relationships between children and their parents are harmed when children spend overnight periods with their other parents" (p. 306). There is substantial evidence regarding the benefits of these regular experiences on children's attachment to their primary caretakers. Aside from maintaining and deepening attachments, overnights provide children with a diversity of social, emotional, and cognitively stimulating experiences that promote adaptability and healthy development. In addition, meaningful father–child relationships may encourage fathers to remain involved in their children's lives by making them feel enfranchised as parents. Other advantages of overnights are the normal combination of leisure and real time that extended parenting affords, the ability to stay abreast of the constant and complex changes in the child's development, opportunities for effective discipline and teaching that are central to good parenting, and chances to reconnect with the child in a meaningful way. In contrast, brief 2-hour visits remind young children that the visiting parents exist but do not provide the broad array of parenting activities that anchor the relationships in their minds (Kelly & Lamb, 2000; Lamb, 2002; Warshak, 2000b).

Young children are able to adapt quickly to different physical characteristics of residential homes and to different physical characteristics of their bedrooms. Seeking some continuity across households in feeding and sleep routines may be more important in order to ensure stability. Thus, parents should share information about bedtimes and rituals, night awakenings, food preferences and feeding schedules, effective practices for soothing, illnesses, and changes in routine as the child matures.

In contrast to Kelly and Lamb (2000), Solomon and Biringen (2001) suggest that very young children (younger than 2 years old) do not profit from overnight parenting by the noncustodial parent. They argue that such experiences injure the primary attachment between the child and the primary caretaker. It is thought that, during their first 18 months, children develop internal models of their attachment figures. Disruption to children's developing internal models is believed to cause children undue stress and to weaken these developing models of secure attachment. *Family Court Review* has published several articles in which these two opposing theoretical models about children's overnights have been discussed. After considering the Solomon and Biringen (2001) argument, Lamb and Kelly (2001) again opined that there was substantial research support for recommending overnight contact between very young children and their noncustodial parents.

In what appears to be the first empirical examination of overnight access for young children of divorced parents, Pruett and colleagues (2004) examined how the occurrence and structure of overnight access with the nonresidential parent and parenting plans with multiple caretakers were related to psychological and behavioral problems in children 6 and younger. Data from 132 divorcing families were collected on several variables related to psychological and behavioral problems in young children who had access to both parents. Results indicated that, according to mothers and fathers, "children with overnights and those with more caretakers had fewer social problems, whereas children with inconsistent schedules had more social problems" (p. 53). When parents maintained consistent schedules, fathers reported that their children showed fewer social problems. Mothers reported that boys with inconsistent schedules showed more externalizing behaviors and that children who had overnight visits with their father had fewer attention problems. Mothers also reported that children with multiple caretakers displayed more sleep disturbances and more depression and anxiety.

Pruett and colleagues (2004) found that overnights per se were not potentially problematic for children. Children showed more difficulties with overnight visits when they had poorer parent–child relationships. Problems in parent–child relationships were the most powerful indices of child behavior problems, as reported by mothers and fathers.

Girls benefited from parenting plans with overnight access and from parenting plans with multiple caretakers, becoming less socially withdrawn (Pruett et al., 2004, p. 54). Boys did not derive the same benefit. Pruett and colleagues concluded, "Having overnights and multiple caretakers were beneficial for children preschool age and older (aged 4 to 6) when their parents first filed in the legal system. . . . It stands to reason that it is easier to be 'born' into parenting plans that require overnights and multiple caregivers than to adjust to it once the child has habituated to a different family pattern" (p. 54).

There was a lack of findings for children younger than 4 who showed neither negative nor positive effects from overnights and multiple caregivers. Pruett and colleagues hypothesize that infants and toddlers are probably too young to manifest symptoms that are more likely to emerge as children age and develop greater memory and linguistic competence. They write "the worry about implementing overnights and parenting plans with multiple caretakers for infants and toddlers is misplaced, as preschoolers may bear the brunt of such arrangements" (pp. 54–55). The conclusions drawn from this preliminary investigation suggest that young children who have strong and positive relationships with a nonresidential parent may have few, if any, negative results stemming from parenting plans with overnight contact or from parenting plans with multiple caretakers.

Developing Plans for Individual Families

Gould and Stahl (2001) suggested that the primary focus for evaluators is to understand the child development research and then apply the relevant research to each case. They proposed a multipart analysis. The first step is to examine the parenting history of the child. If the child has had a history of joint caretaking and has shown little, if any, difficulty being cared for by each parent while the family was intact, then one might predict little risk to the young child in continuing such a parenting arrangement.

The second step is to investigate the attachment history between the child and each parent. Evaluators should assess each parent's involvement in caretaking activities at each stage of attachment formation in early childhood

(Kelly & Lamb, 2000, 2003). Particular emphasis should be on exploring the skills that each parent brings to the task of parenting a young child. As summarized by Kelly and Lamb (2003), "parental sensitivity is the most reliable correlate of attachment security yet identified" (p. 194).

The third step is assessment of each parent's parenting strengths and weaknesses. Gould and Stahl (2001) write, "Examine the complementary fit that existed during the marriage in order to understand the advantages and disadvantages each parent brings to the infant or toddler when parenting the child alone" (p. 374). Additional dimensions are the temperament of the child, the communication between the parents over child-related issues, and the care being given to the child by people other than the parent when both parents are unavailable.

They concluded their article by reminding evaluators that

> research results are important in their ability to guide our thinking about how specific results might be relevant to a particular family system. However, there is never any substitute for exploring parenting history and the relevant dynamics of a particular family and then integrating that data with current research. (Gould & Stahl, 2001, pp. 374–375)

Self-Regulation

In the context of their relationships with adults, young children also begin to acquire another set of tools that enable them to control their behavior in numerous ways. They gain increasing control over their attention, emotions, and behavior through the development of a set of skills known as self-regulation (Cicchetti & Tucker, 1994; Pennington & Welsh, 1995; Rothbart & Bates, 1998).

In their first few years, children ordinarily become better at directing their attention, enabling them to shift or focus their attention more readily or to persist in attending. These are skills that will help them function in a classroom or in a play activity with peers. Later in development, good attention regulation has been linked to prosocial behavior and peer popularity, whereas difficulties in attention regulation have been linked to attention-deficit/hyperactivity disorder (ADHD), antisocial behavior, and academic problems (Eisenberg, Fabes, et al., 1997; Eisenberg, Guthrie, et al., 1997; Lynam, 1996; Rothbart & Bates, 1998; Zahn-Waxler, Cole, Welsh, & Fox, 1995). Thus, attention regulation appears to be linked with the development of competence in multiple domains from an early age.

Difficulty regulating negative emotions, such as anxiety and distress, also has been linked to problems in children. Some children are easily upset and do not calm down as readily from stressful experiences. Aggressive and disruptive behavior problems have been directly linked to negative emotional reactivity, irritability, or temperamental difficulties in infancy and childhood (Rothbart & Bates, 1998). Social competence, on the other hand, is associated with a history of lower stress reactivity and higher self-control of attention and behavior (Eisenberg, Fabes, et al., 1997) and with a tendency to express positive emotion, to be sociable, and to be agreeable (Rothbart & Bates, 1998).

Compliance and prosocial behavior are additional areas of self-regulation fundamental to successful functioning in society. Two other factors associated with development of rule-following behavior—self-control and expressed concern for others—begin to emerge in the second year of life (Eisenberg & Fabes, 1998; Sroufe, 1996; Zahn-Waxler, Radke-Yarrow, Wagner, & Chapman, 1992, as parents begin to communicate rules and expectations. The first requests often focus on safety, while later requests tend to focus more on compliance with social, family, and cultural standards (Gralinski & Kopp, 1993). Children learn early rules through the routines of daily life (Schaffer, 1996), and it is important for children of divorce to learn how to follow rules at each parent's home.

Children are expected to become reasonably compliant with parental requests and to internalize the family standards for behavior so that they comply in the absence of supervision. Self-control of this kind becomes evident during the third year of life (Schaffer, 1996). Sensitive and consistent caregiving and warm but firm parenting styles are associated with the development of self-control and compliance with social rules, whereas power-assertive methods of controlling child behavior (especially with hostile affect) generally are associated with less compliance and less internalization of standards in children (Schaffer, 1996).

Young children of divorce who are exposed to two households may need to learn two different sets of family rules. As with children's acquisition of linguistic rules, young children may have difficulty learning two sets of family rules. They may have inconsistently learned two different sets of family rules or they may inconsistently apply the rules because they are confused regarding which set of rules from which family apply in a specific instance. It is important for evaluators to investigate how family rules are developed and the consequences to young children when rules are not followed. Evaluators also need to consider who participates in developing family rules and the degree of flexibility/rigidity with which family members follow the rules. Finally, the age appropriateness of family rules and the manner in which such rules are explained and consistently encouraged are important areas of investigation.

Failure to develop compliance in the early years of life may seriously compromise later social functioning at school and with peers. Scholars have found that extreme noncompliance is related to coercive interactions between parents and children and sets the stage for aggressive, disruptive behavior in classrooms and peer interactions that can lead to peer rejection and academic problems. For some children, this may lead to associations with deviant peers who support further antisocial behavior (Patterson, 1986; Patterson, Reid, & Dishion, 1992).

Research on self-regulation suggests that these skills are extremely important for the development of competence, begin to emerge in early childhood, and are shaped by a child's experience as well as his or her disposition. A cranky baby may elicit a different care response from each parent, and different parental behaviors may increase or decrease how prone an infant is to distress (van den Boom, 1994). When parental response to infant distress is vastly different, these differences can help or hinder the development of self-regulation (Goldsmith & Harman, 1994; Jacobvitz & Sroufe, 1987; Kochanska & Aksan, 1995).

Competence in the School Years

When children enter school, they face new challenges and a new world of expectations outside the family. Some children bring a strong set of skills, motivations, and self-perceptions that will facilitate learning and relationships. Other children bring behavior or self-regulation problems and negative expectations for self or others that will hinder learning and friendships. This section highlights research on three general factors associated with success in middle childhood and adolescence: development of social competence and sibling and peer relationships, rule-governed behavior, and academic achievement. A final area of discussion is the role played by extracurricular activities in the development of social competence.

Social Competence with Siblings

How children get along with other children has been studied for many years as an indicator of current and future competence (Hartup, 1983). One of the most important relationships across a lifetime is a child's relationship with his or her siblings. Divorce may affect how siblings relate to each other and how they relate to each parent. Despite the fact that previous books on child custody evaluation have not focused attention on the sibling subsystem (e.g., Galatzer-Levy & Krauss, 1999; Gould, 1998; Stahl, 1994, 1999), we believe that a comprehensive evaluation must include an evaluator's understanding of the sibling subsystem including changes in it.

The Sibling Subsystem

Research shows that children benefit from growing up with brothers and sisters and from siblings remaining together after their parents divorce. Siblings spend more time interacting with one another than they do with their parents (Stormshak, Bellanti, & Bierman, 1996). Some researchers have found that the sibling bond may become stronger and even more important than a child's preference for a parent (Cicirelli, 1991). Siblings provide psychological, psychosocial, and emotional support to one another. Stability and continuity in sibling relationships are perhaps more important to a child's well-being than even a stable physical environment (Cicirelli, 1991; Nichols, 1986; Weithorn, 1987), and having a sibling may act as a buffer under high-stress conditions (Lockwood, Gaylord, Kitzmann, & Cohen, 2002).

The sibling relationship is important in later life. The degree of closeness between siblings is associated with the extent of contact earlier in life (Cicirelli, 1989, 1991). Thus, separating siblings may affect their long-term relationship. The earlier in the child's life that the sibling separation occurs, the more likely is severe impairment to the sibling bond. Siblings turn to each other for support when their parents divorce. Older siblings often serve as role models and/ or comforters for younger siblings, especially when the older siblings are able to assess the family situation more realistically (Nichols, 1986). There are gender differences in sibling relationships. Girls are more influenced by siblings, more nurturing with younger siblings, and more likely to view themselves as caretakers than boys. Bank and Kahn (1982) conclude that sibling bonds are influenced by the *degree of access* between siblings. This is defined by how close in age and how involved they are with one another's lives, the level of anxiety in the early mother–child attachment for each child, and the availability of auxiliary parenting resources.

Developmental Stages of Sibling Relationship Development

Sibling bonds follow a predictable developmental course that is related to stages in the family life-cycle. During the preschool years, siblings are often constant companions whose interactions shape their intellectual and personality development. At this age, siblings act as socializing agents for each other. They practice social interactions by playing different roles and, in this manner, develop a fundamental approach to learning.

Later during the school years, siblings take different roles within the family and extend familial social skills to non-family members. Adolescents often turn to their siblings for counsel, despite growing ambivalence toward the family. The sibling relationship is a primary socializing agent for moral development and the development of empathy and prosocial behavior. It provides opportunities to learn conflict resolution techniques (Perozynski & Kramer, 1999), social competence (Stormshak et al., 1996), and communication and intimacy-sharing skills.

Current Social Changes and Sibling Relationships

Several facets of contemporary family and social conditions are thought to make sibling attachments more important than ever. These include (1) the shrinking size of the extended family, (2) longer lifespans, (3) increased divorce rates, (4) expanded geographic mobility, (5) more full- and part-time working mothers, and (6) increasing numbers of parents without adequate parenting skills (Bank & Kahn, 1982; Coolahan, Fantuzzo, Mendez, & McDermott, 2000; Stormshak et al., 1996).

Social Competence and Peer Relationships

For young children, relating successfully to classmates and peers is a critical task that is considered a primary indicator of healthy development. Just as young children are more likely to reach their psychological and emotional potential when involved in healthy sibling relationships, they are likely to do so when involved in healthy peer relationships (Coolahan et al., 2000). The development of positive peer relationships during the preschool years has been associated with positive adjustment in kindergarten as well as academic success in elementary grades and high school. In contrast, poor peer relationships have been linked with detrimental consequences during later developmental periods, including emotional maladjustment, delinquent behavior, school failure, loneliness, and poor self-esteem (Ladd, 1990; Ladd, Kochenderfer, & Coleman, 1996). Children from families with higher levels of stress show higher levels of aggression, which lead to more peer rejection (Lockwood et al., 2002).

Peer relationships help children develop social competence, moral competence, and self-mastery. Peer play is the primary context in which young children acquire and express peer social competencies. The repeated interpersonal interactions that occur in peer play, especially those involving prosocial behavior or aggressive encounters, are important experiences that affect children's social development. Exposure during play to the opinions, ideas, feelings, and feedback of peers enables children to move beyond egocentric thought to consider the point of view of others. This capacity serves as a foundation for developing conflict resolution and cooperative-learning skills (Coolahan et al., 2000). This factor is particularly important in light of recent research showing that maltreated children are more likely to be isolated and less interactive in peer play than nonmaltreated children (Fantuzzo et al., 1996).

In school-aged children, peer acceptance and popularity are associated with better achievement, higher IQ, and many other positive attributes, including a history of positive parenting (Masten, 1994; Masten, Best, & Garmezy, 1990; Masten, Morison, & Pellegrini, 1985). Positive peer reputation predicts future social competence with peers, achievement, job competence, extracurricular activities, self-worth, and better mental health (Masten & Coatsworth, 1995; Parker, Rubin, Price, & DeRosier, 1995). Concomitantly, peer rejection has been associated with aggressive and disruptive behavior, externalizing disorders such as ADHD and conduct disorder, poor achievement, and a history of negative parenting (Cicchetti & Bukowski, 1995; Masten & Coatsworth, 1995). Peer difficulties also predict future maladjustment (Parker et al., 1995).

Rejected children are typically aggressive, although in some peer contexts aggressive behavior is popular (Coie & Jacobs, 1993). Rejected children appear to process social information in maladaptive ways—for example, making attributions of hostile intent that could lead to negative defensive behaviors or preemptive strikes against peers (Coie & Dodge, 1998). Recent theories about children with ADHD plus aggressive behavior suggest that problems in self-regulation of attention and emotion may contribute to the social problems of these children (Barkley, 1996).

Developmental theorists have argued that peer relations have roots in family relationships, and there is good evidence to support this view (Elicker, Englund, & Sroufe, 1992; Patterson, 1986; Patterson et al., 1992; Chapter 10, this volume). Much less attention has been given to the bidirectional influence of peers and family on the development of social competence. Parental influence on achievement and prosocial conduct, for example, may be contingent on the nature of an adolescent's crowd affiliation. Brown and Huang (1995) found that positive parenting influences were constrained by the adolescent's affiliation with deviant peers. In contrast, given a prosocial or neutral crowd, good parenting was strongly related to achievement and prosocial behavior. Their findings point to the importance of efforts by parents or intervention programs to steer children toward prosocial peers earlier in childhood.

Peer social competence also illustrates how children can influence their own development by the choices they make. Prosocial children tend to choose peers who have prosocial influences, and aggressive children tend to choose peers who exacerbate their negative behavior. Friendship can be viewed as a gateway through which the child gains passage to the rest of the world (Newcomb, Bukowski, & Bagwell, 1999), in that a child's understanding of the world and his or her connectedness to larger social networks will be influenced by friendship choices.

Recent thinking about peer relations reflects the possibility that peers may serve a protective role in development, similar to the role of siblings (Masten & Coatsworth, 1998). Having friends, for example, may help a child adjust to a new classroom or school. Studies of kindergartners (Ladd, 1990; Ladd et al., 1996) and the junior high transition (Berndt, 1989) suggest that having friends is associated with a positive attitude toward school or peers. Thus, friends may provide emotional support. They may also support academic achievement, as discussed below. Friends may also encourage deviant behavior (Lykken, 1998; Newcomb et al., 1999). Antisocial children usually develop friendships with other antisocial children that serve to escalate antisocial behavior (Coie & Dodge, 1998; Dishion, Andrews, & Crosby, 1995). Competent parents need to recognize the complexity of roles that peers may play in development. Encouraging children to become part of prosocial peer groups or to develop friendships with rule-abiding and socially competent children may be a good parenting strategy; however, parents who do not supervise who their children develop friendships with may encourage the development of relationships with deviant peer groups that may well become counterproductive.

For the evaluator, examining a child's history of peer relationship development may be important. Providing recommendations that seek to give stability to a child in the maintenance of his or her friendship and peer group affiliations may also be an area for evaluative consideration.

Rule-Governed Behavior and the Development of Socially Appropriate Conduct

One of the most important criteria by which children are evaluated by adults is their conduct with respect to rules or social norms of behavior. These include rules parents have for family behavior, expectations teachers have for conduct in the classroom and on the playground, and laws of society governing conduct. Children are described as well behaved rather than disobedient, antisocial, or delinquent according to their compliance with norms of social behavior.

Much of the research in this area has focused on negative behavior rather than rule-governed behavior. Aggressive behavior and broader antisocial behavior patterns show considerable stability over time from childhood through adolescence into the adult years (Coie & Dodge, 1998). In one of few studies examining a bipolar dimension of rule-following versus rule-breaking conduct, Masten and colleagues (1995) found rule-governed behavior to be highly stable over a 10-year interval but the nature of rule-breaking behavior changing. Moreover, antisocial behavior appeared to undermine academic and job competence. On a more positive note, if behavior improved, there was no evidence of lasting consequences of conduct problems in childhood.

There is a strong connection between academic achievement and rule-governed behavior (Masten & Coatsworth, 1995). Parenting quality, IQ, and attentional functioning all have been linked to competence and may play a role in how achievement and rule following become connected in development. For example, self-regulation problems could interfere with both learning and conduct. Academic failure could produce anger, distress, or disengagement that could lead to disruptive behavior or drifting to deviant peer groups. Alternatively, antisocial behaviors could interfere with learning or acceptance by teachers and peers or result in academic placements with fewer opportunities for learning or affiliation with competent peers. For older children and adolescents, the preponderance of data supports a conduct-to-academic direction of influence more than the reverse (Masten et al., 1995), although academic success does predict resistance to delinquency (Maguin & Loeber, 1996). For younger children, academic difficulties may play a larger role in the development of conduct problems, suggesting that early tutoring programs could produce improvements in behavior as well as in reading skills.

Both intellectual functioning and parenting behavior have been strongly implicated in the development of rule-governed conduct in children. Studies of resilience also point to the significance of good parenting quality in preventing antisocial problems among children exposed to high levels of psychosocial adversity (Masten & Coatsworth, 1998). In the United States, parents who are warm but structured with consistent rules and high expectations for behavior, often described as *authoritative* in style, have children with better conduct as well as better social competence with peers and academic achievement (Kelly & Emery, 2003). Antisocial children often have a history of harsh, punitive, rejecting, inconsistent parenting (Coie & Dodge, 1998).

Antisocial children and criminal adults have been found to have lower intellectual functioning, and children who make it out of high-risk environments often have strong intellectual skills (Masten & Coatsworth, 1998). One way higher intellectual functioning may result in better competence is through facilitating academic achievement in elementary school. Children who succeed in school may be more likely to adopt and willingly comply with social norms and to find their way into prosocial peer groups (Lykken, 1998).

Research points to the importance of three adaptive systems in the development of competence: parenting, self-regulation skills, and cognitive functioning. These resources also predict school success.

Academic Achievement

Among the most important social environments for child development is the school. Static factors such as academic achievement—indicated by grades, test scores, years in school, and whether a student has dropped out—are gauges of an individual's success in adapting to this developmental context. Typically, children with more individual resources and social support perform best in school (Masten & Coatsworth, 1998).

Individual resources associated with academic success include cognitive abilities, motivation, and beliefs, while IQ is one of the most powerful predictors of academic success. Academic competence is also influenced by beliefs and attitudes about school (Stevenson, Chen, & Lee, 1993), self-perceptions about one's academic abilities (Harter, 1982), and motivations to succeed or attributional style (Henderson & Dweck, 1990). Successful students typically attribute their successes to hard work and attribute their failings to lack of effort. Students who believe that ability and performance are fixed tend to have lower achievement (Stipek & Gralinski, 1996; Stevenson et al., 1993).

Problems in academic achievement have been associated with problems of self-regulation such as attentional problems, impulsive behavior, and antisocial behavior (Baumrind & Thompson, 2002; Maguin & Loeber, 1996; Masten & Coatsworth, 1995). Children with behavior problems tend to drop out of school more frequently than children without behavior problems, even after controlling for academic achievement (Masten & Coatsworth, 1998).

Social resources associated with academic competence include school, family, and peer systems. Schools that effectively promote academic achievement share many characteristics, including a clear mission, capable and well-qualified instructors, attention to staff development, and careful monitoring of student progress. Similarly, Kelly and Emery (2003) describe the importance of residential and nonresidential parental involvement in school supervision and school activities as promoting academic success.

Family factors associated with academic competence include parenting styles and parental involvement. Authoritative parenting has been associated with academic success from early childhood through adolescence across sex and socioeconomic status (Baumrind & Thompson, 2002; Kelly & Emery, 2003), but cultural and other contextual factors may be important. European and Hispanic American adolescents appear to benefit more from this type of parenting than African American or Asian American adolescents (Steinberg, Mounts, Lamborn, & Dornbusch, 1991). It may be that children raised in more dangerous environments may require stricter parenting styles (Baldwin, Baldwin, & Cole, 1990). Evaluators need to be mindful of conducting a comprehensive examination of parenting style with the recognition that more rigid styles of parenting may be socially appropriate responses to the child's larger family environment.

Parental involvement in education is also related to a child's academic achievement (Kelly & Emery, 2003), and short-term longitudinal evidence suggests that increasing parental involvement leads to academic improvement (Steinberg, Lamborn, Dornbusch, & Darling, 1992). Parents influence the development of academic achievement through direct involvement with schools, such as when they contact the school about their child or attend parents' functions (Steinberg, 1996). They also affect achievement through their attitudes and behavior by communicating strong educational values (Marjoribanks, 1987), conveying the value of effort (Stevenson et al., 1993), expecting and encouraging their children to succeed academically (Reynolds & Wahlberg, 1991), monitoring or helping with their child's schoolwork at home (Clark, 1993; Scott-Jones, 1995), and assisting in their school projects (Kelly & Emery, 2003). The apparent significance of parents' behavior and their belief in their children's school success has led intervention programs to target parental involvement as a key to improving academic success in children. (Also see the section entitled "Father Involvement and Children's Educational Involvement" in Chapter 9.) Evaluators may wish to list several of the school-related parenting behaviors above when developing an evaluation protocol of parental activity and school involvement.

Peers also may influence academic achievement either positively or negatively, and for some children and adolescents, their peer group may be a more powerful determinant of their school competence than their parents. High-achieving peers can influence satisfaction with school, expectations, grades, and test scores. Parents of academically competent peers also reinforce achievement, providing an ecological network of peers and adults who support educational achievement. Research suggests that parents may wish to consider selectively increasing peer involvement that promotes competence to take advantage of the influence that high-achieving peers and their parents can exert on academic competence. At the same time, it is important to be cautiously aware that there can also be negative influences when peers are not achievement-oriented (Masten & Coatsworth, 1998).

Extracurricular Activities

The significance of extracurricular activities as a competence domain also has been a neglected area of study even though a child's participation in them is often an area of examination for evaluators. Little is known about involvement in extracurricular activities and what roles it may play in development. Limited evidence indicates some benefits, such as lower rates of dropping out of school (Mahoney & Cairns, 1997) and more positive engagement in school (Braddock, Royster, Winfield, & Hawkins, 1991; Nettles, 1991). Theoretically, extracurricular involvement should have positive socializing effects on participants, and some evidence supports this contention (Mahoney & Cairns, 1997). Involvement in extracurricular activities may foster and showcase individual talents, thereby contributing to an individual's global sense of competence, efficacy, self-esteem, and well-being. Such activities may also serve to facilitate involvement in conventional social networks, promoting achievement or rule-abiding conduct (Csikszentmihalyi, Rathunde, & Whalen, 1993; McNeal, 1995). There could be risks, however, and long-term effects are still in question. The significance of extracurricular activities for competence development needs further exploration, particularly to test the popular belief that such involvement can function as a protective factor for high-risk youth by connecting them in more positive ways to school, to positive adults, to positive peer groups, or by engendering self-efficacy (Masten & Coatsworth, 1998).

Resilience in Children at Risk

Results of studies examining resilience in children have been remarkably consistent in pointing to qualities of child and environment associated with competence or with better psychosocial functioning during or following adverse experiences. The two most widely reported predictors of resilience appear to be relationships with caring prosocial adults and good intellectual functioning.

The data linking IQ or good problem-solving skills to better outcomes among children at risk appear to reflect the central importance of cognition and language as predictors of adaptability. IQ may be a broad indicator that brain development and associated cognitive development are proceeding normally despite adversity. When adversity hinders cognitive development, the consequences are likely to be more serious and long-lasting than for adversity that does not affect the major cognitive systems (Masten & Coatsworth, 1998). This finding may be particularly noteworthy when assessing maltreated or neglected children.

It appears that intellectual functioning operates as a moderator of risk for prosocial/antisocial behavior. Intellectual functioning appears to have specific protective or vulnerability roles in the processes linking adversity to social behavior. In very adverse child-rearing environments, a child's good intellectual skills appear important for development. Good intellectual functioning requires a variety of information-processing skills that may also be useful for coping with adversity. More intelligent children may solve problems or protect themselves better. They may attract the interest of teachers. They may have better self-regulation skills that help them function at school and avoid behavior problems. On the other hand, children with lower-than-average intellectual skills may find it difficult to negotiate threatening situations, disengage from school because of feelings of failure, or fail to learn as much from their experiences (Masten & Coatsworth, 1998).

When evaluating children from maltreating families, it may be important to assess a range of intellectual abilities associated with adaptive coping skills. Evaluators may need to assess three components. The first is evaluation of children's problem-solving and prosocial behavior. The second is evaluation of each parent's ability to foster in his or her children problem-solving and prosocial behavior. The third is to assess which other adults in different environments are available to foster these behaviors in children.

Children have different vulnerabilities and protective systems at different ages and at different points in their development (Lyons-Ruth, Zeanah, & Benoit, 2003). Infants, because of their total dependence on caregivers, are highly vulnerable to the consequences of lost or distressed parents or mistreatment by caregivers. At the same time, infants are protected from experiencing some of the worst atrocities of war or major disasters by their lack of understanding of what is happening. Adolescents, on the other hand, have much more advanced capabilities for adaptation in the world on their own, but they also are vulnerable to the experiences of loss or devastation concerning friends, faith, schools, and governments and what these mean for their future, which would be well beyond the understanding of young children.

Good parenting has numerous components. What good parents do depends on child and situation characteristics. The expectations and structure provided by parents may be particularly important for academic success, warmth and emotional support may be important for social competence, and a good balance of the two may be important for the development of good conduct, which in turn influences the other two (Barber, 2002). The exact nature of what parents do will change with development and will reflect the context within which the parent–child interaction occurs. Parents in a dangerous neighborhood will monitor their children more closely than the same parents in a safer area. Assessment of parenting must take such complexities into account.

Efforts to understand resilience have made it clear that children typically have multiple risk factors and multiple resources contributing to their lives (Greene et al., 2003; Lyons-Ruth et al., 2003; Masten & Coatsworth, 1998), which are often loaded with many risks and recurring stressors. Intervention models emerging from this realization describe cumulative protection efforts to address cumulative risk processes (Coie & Jacobs, 1993).

Research points to parent–child relationships as a crucial context for the development of competence, both for children with ordinary lives and for children facing extraordinary challenges (Lamb, 2002). When adversity is high and no effective adult is connected to a child, risk for maladaptation is high (Lyons-Ruth et al., 2003). The development of competence requires the involvement of caring, competent adults in a child's life (Kelly & Emery, 2003).

Self-regulation of attention, emotion, and behavior make up a third major set of adaptation skills implicated as central to the development of competence across domains and modifiable through experience, particularly in early development. Moreover, good parent–child relationships serve as scaffolds for building these skills. Intervening early to encourage self-regulation may be an important strategy to assist children in reaching their psychological potential.

Studies of competence, psychopathology, and resilience all point to the importance of establishing a good start early in development (Mash & Barkley, 2003). Children who enter school with significant problems in self-regulation, who are distrustful of adults, or who have impaired learning abilities have a substantial disadvantage for meeting the developmental tasks of middle childhood (Lyons-Ruth, Zeanah, & Benoit, 2003).

Cascading effects are also suggested by the literature highlighted here. Children who have good internal and external resources tend to get off to a good start in school, become connected to normative peers, maintain positive self-perceptions, and face the developmental tasks of adolescence with the advantages represented by success in these domains. Children who enter school with few resources, cognitive difficulties, and self-regulatory problems often have academic problems, get into trouble with teachers, are more likely to be rejected by peers, and are at risk for disengaging from normative school and peer contexts, which sets them up for considerable difficulty in the transition to adolescence (Lykken, 1998; Masten & Coatsworth, 1998).

Organizing the Advisory Report around Children's Voices

We end this chapter with a recommended set of factors to consider when evaluating children's experience of their parents. We have found in our review work that too often evaluators focus attention on the fight between the parents and pay little attention to the children's experience of living with each parent, of traveling to and from each parent's home, and of communicating with each parent.

Over the past few years, one of us (Gould) has begun to write reports that start off with the children's story told from the children's perspective. We believe it is important for the court to hear the children's description of their experiences across a wide variety of activities in a manner that is free from the frameworks placed on their experiences by their parents.

Here is an example of how to begin the discussion section of the report by focusing attention on the children's stories as told by the children:

> When divorce occurs between a couple who has children, each family member has a unique experience of the family that may or may not coincide with the perception of the mother or that of the father. Each child develops a perception of the family and a perception of the role of each member in the life of the family.
>
> This section provides a description of each child's perception of each parent. Children's accounts do not obliterate or correct the parents' accounts, nor should the reverse be true. Rather, the inclusion of these accounts serves to acknowledge that people have different relationships with each other, have access to different resources, and regard different things as important. The purpose of their inclusion is not to give primacy to children over adults but to give the same legitimacy to children's experiences that is afforded the parents'. Since the primary goal of this evaluation is to provide assistance to the court in determining the best interests of the children, I begin with the voices of each of the [fill in name of family] children.

It is important to begin a discussion of conclusions based on data obtained from children by focusing on their relationship with each parent. For example:

> The most important conclusion to be reached in this evaluation is that each of the four children have strong and loving relationships with each parent and with each stepparent. As discussed below, there are differences in how each child experiences each parent's parenting style, and parenting style differences have led each child to feel differently about each parent. Overall, however, each of these children has a strong and loving relationship with each parent that reflects age-appropriate interactions.

The remainder of the report would then provide information to the court about each child's experience of each parent's parenting style.

It may be useful to contrast each parent's perspective of the parent–child relationship with each child's perspective. For example:

> The mother and father respectively paint very different pictures of each other's parenting ability than those painted by the children. One factor apparently affecting how these parents hold so tightly to their respective beliefs in the "rightness" of their parenting style is the differing criteria used by each parent to evaluate the other's caregiving style, parenting rules, and ways of conceptualizing how children *should* develop. Another important factor contributing to perceived parenting effectiveness may be the relative lack of communication between the parents regarding (1) their parenting decisions and (2) their lack of open discussion about differences in their parenting models. A

third factor may be the weight each parent gives to information provided by the children after visiting with the other parent combined with the assumption each parent makes about the accuracy of the children's self-reports. It is my opinion that too often Mother and Father assume that the children's stories about events at the other parent's home accurately reflect not only the events themselves but also the other parent's motivation, as inferred by the children.

Children's View of Each Parent's Fairness, Caring, and Respect

In Chapter 5, we discussed aspects of Carol Smart's research about children's experiences of their parent's divorce. In the "Discussion" section of the advisory report, we recommend presenting first the children's views of their experiences with each parent and their views of the effect these experiences have had on their sense of safety, comfort, and security with their respective parents.

Recent research has examined children's view of their parents' post-divorce behavior (May & Smart, 2004; Smart, 2002, 2005, 2006; Smart, Wade, & Neale, 1999; Wade & Smart, 2002) and has focused attention on what it is like for children to be shared between their parents and to live their lives in more than one household. Three primary concepts have emerged from this research: They are children's perception of (1) fairness, (2) caring, and (3) respect.

Fairness refers to children's continual awareness of the need to be fair to both parents and their continual evaluation of the fairness of each parent's behavior toward each child and the other parent. Although many children are upset and worried for themselves when their parents' separate, the emphasis on fairness suggests that they still have a strong moral awareness of the position of both parents in relation to each other. Children want to be fair to their parents regarding the apportionment of themselves between their parents. Consider organizing the information obtained from each child around his or her perception of each parent's fairness toward the child, toward the other parent, toward the other children, and toward other issues or activities relevant to the child's experience.

It is generally assumed that parents care for their children and not vice versa. The child's perception of *caring* focuses attention on ways in which each child is cared for by each parent and on the ways in which each child in fact cares for his or her parent. Older children see their parents as separate individuals with their own needs and interests. Children of all ages expect their parents to care for them and often criticize and/or put up with a parent who does not know what they like to eat or how to talk to them. Consider organizing the information obtained from each child around his or her perception of each parent's caring of the child, each child's caring of the parent, each child's perception of the parent's caring of siblings, and each child's view of the parent's ability to place the needs of the child ahead of the parent's need.

Respect refers to children's wish for their parents to listen to them, to take their stated concerns seriously, and to include them in the information-gathering phase of decision making. Consider organizing the information around each child's experience of being listened to and being taken seriously by each parent.

Finally, organize the information obtained from the children around the eight concepts discussed in Chapter 5, including discussion of each child's experience of the following:

1. The practical issues of getting from one place to another, referred to as "physical space"
2. The different emotional climates that exist at each parent's home, referred to as "emotional space"
3. The differences in household structure, organization, and functions, referred to as "psychological space"
4. The degree to which each parent displays a rigid versus flexible attitude toward the time the child spends at the other parent's home, referred to as "equal time"
5. Spending time apart from each parent referred to as "time apart"
6. Having private time referred to as "time to oneself"
7. Having time to feel distress and discomfort, referred to as "time and hurting"
8. Having time to share, referred to as "time and sharing"

Our experience with organizing children's experiences around these variables is that it results in a clear and robust picture for the judge of how each child experiences each parent and the degree to which each child finds support from each parent.

Summary

This chapter presented a model of child development based upon competence and resilience factors. We recognize there are many other models of child development around which one might organize factors that help to define the psychological best interests of the child. We chose competence and resilience because of their contribution to predicting children's life success and productivity.

Several variables were discussed, with research results demonstrating the usefulness of these variables in predicting the psychological best interests of the child. Each of these variables has its complement in parenting behavior. That is, there is a direct relationship between the development of competence and resilience factors in children and the nature and quality of parenting that supports and nurtures such factors.

As an evaluator, you might decide to choose factors drawn from psychodynamic theory of child development or from a systems theory formulation of child factors that predict future competence and productivity. Whatever you choose, we encourage you to think through the underlying scientific beliefs of your theory and to ensure that there are some research data for the factors that you believe lay the groundwork for a child to be productive and successful in life.

CHAPTER 9

Assessment of Parent Factors

A challenging aspect of child custody evaluations is defining parenting behaviors, attitudes, beliefs, and values that make up "good-enough" parenting. Debate has raged for years about what "good-enough" parenting is, including what factors it comprises and whether psychologists, rather than social policy makers, should define the dimensions. One way to approach these challenges is first to define what children need to be healthy and successful in life. In Chapter 8, we identified the general construct of *competence* and discussed several of its dimensions. Once desired child behaviors are identified, then the dimensions of "good-enough" parenting might be conceptualized as those parenting behaviors that facilitate the development of competence. In this chapter, we examine parenting competence from several different perspectives and discuss the construct of parental emotional competence, its component parts as related to understanding parental competence, and ;parenting style variables, including those associated with authoritarian parenting.

In the majority of court decisions about custodial placement, judges continue to place children in the residential care of their mothers and provide scheduled parenting time between children and their fathers. There is an increasingly robust research literature about the importance of nonresidential parent involvement in the lives of divorced children. Therefore, we address the importance of postdivorce contact between child and nonresidential parent and variables associated with positive child adjustment. The chapter ends with a discussion of factors that we believe help define parental competence.

Defining Parenting

Lykken (1998) describes how

> good parents, who are able to maintain the affection and respect of their children and whose offspring admire them and value their good opinion, can be reasonably certain that their values and ways of socialized behaving will be adopted by the next generation. The children of less effective, less competent parents will be more likely to adopt the customs and values of the peer group; however, if the community is small, close-knit, and well socialized generally, this will achieve the same result. In urban or suburban middle-class communities, the offspring of less competent parents will be somewhat more at risk. Most of the available peer group will be well socialized because their parents are, but as the community grows in size and mutual estrangement, the likelihood increases that there will be a few neglected, undisciplined, or feral children in the peer group—faux-adult role models to whom a child not closely tied to home and parents may be drawn, and by whom that child will be influenced. (p. 131)

Lykken (1998) concludes that the relative importance of peer group influence in shaping values and behaviors of a given child is inversely proportional to the competence of that child's parents. Competent parenting not only promotes child growth along typical developmental lines, but also acts as a channel, guiding child and adolescent energies toward prosocial goals. Without appropriate parental supervision, children find this guidance from others, mostly likely from their peer group. Those less well supervised tend to find others also less well supervised. The result often is a child whose primary socialization influence is drawn from his or her peer group rather than from his or her family. Lykken (1998) makes the point that a lack of competent parental supervision leads to children who are unsocialized and more likely to become problem children and adolescents.

Identifying Good Parenting

Lykken (1998) does not define the domain of competent parenting behaviors. Turning to current behavioral science research, we find a lack of consensus about what defines competent parenting. There is little consistent information about the impact of different parenting activities on child development. For example, we do not know the short- or long-term effects on later development of exposing a child to art museums or pornography. Each of us holds beliefs about what is best for children, what provides more intellectually, morally, and culturally relevant experiences, yet there is little or no empirical research to support such beliefs.

Taken in part from Schutz and colleagues (1989), we define a group of parenting behaviors purported to facilitate the development of childhood competence. Table 9.1 lists dimensions of parenting found in the literature that appear consistent with notions of competent parenting.

Good parenting appears to include the parent's active and positive involvement in the child's life. A good parent understands and plans for the inclusion of the child in appropriate functions and encourages the sharing of mutually satisfying activities. Good parenting helps the child feel involved, a part of the family, and both special and wanted in his or her relationship with each parent (Kelly & Emery, 2003).

Direct, open, and cooperative dialogues between parent and child are also important for good parenting. Communication in good parenting is characterized by a two-way exchange of feelings of closeness, warmth, interest, and care (Fisher & Fisher, 1986). Good parenting also includes cooperative communication with the other parent. Each parent needs to understand and be aware of each child's needs, interests, and wants. Each parent needs to communicate his or her experience with the child to the other parent to provide for continuity of the child's needs across homes.

Flexibility in behavior is also characteristic of good parenting. Parents take responsibility for setting appropriate limits between themselves and their children as well as among children. This includes appropriate modulation of intimacy by avoiding the extremes of psychological closeness and distance and is characterized by the development and maintenance of interpersonal closeness that feels comfortable to both parent and child and is consistently experienced.

A competent parent sets clear boundaries between the child and the environment and, when necessary, may act as a buffer between the child and environmental challenges. Sometimes the parent may act upon such challenges in ways that may impede or enhance developmental growth. It is important for

TABLE 9.1. Good Parenting Behaviors

- Parent is actively and positively involved in child's life.
- There are direct, open, and cooperative dialogues between parent and child.
- Parent cooperatively communicates with other parent.
- Parent is flexible in behavior and limit setting.
- Parent appropriately modulates expressions of love and intimacy.
- Parent sets clear boundaries between child and environment.
- Parent identifies and understands child's needs.
- Parent accurately observes child's behavior and own behavior.
- Parent develops and nurtures independence, individuation, social responsibility, and self-confidence.
- Parent develops and nurtures child's self-esteem.
- Parent is knowledgeable about child's strengths and weaknesses.
- Parent is perceived as a positive role model.
- Parent applies appropriate discipline.
- Parent supports child's relationship with other parent.
- Parent encourages socially appropriate behaviors and respect for rules governing society.

parents to understand their personal needs and to recognize when their personal concerns may affect their judgment or behavior in guiding their child to cope with new challenges effectively.

Good parenting appears to include the ability to identify and understand the child's needs, placing them before one's own when appropriate (Ackerman & Schoendorf, 1994; Rohman, Saks, & Lou, 1987; Schutz et al., 1989), the ability accurately to observe the behaviors of the child as well as one's own, and the ability to accurately interpret the feelings of the child as well as one's own. Good parents are able to communicate these observations to their children in an empathic, sensitive, and understanding manner (Ackerman & Schoendorf, 1994; Bray, 1991; Fisher & Fisher, 1986).

Parents need to develop and nurture in their children movement toward independence, individuality, social responsibility, and self-confidence. Positive self-esteem is encouraged when parents direct their children toward alternative forms of action, and their children feel a degree of freedom when making these choices. Positive self-esteem is encouraged when parents set firm, clear, and consistent standards of behavior and when children are expected to behave in mature and respectful ways. Positive self-esteem is also bolstered when the rights of both parents and children are recognized (Ackerman, 1995; Maccoby & Martin, 1983; Maccoby & Mnookin, 1992; Schutz et al., 1989).

It is important for parents to know their children's strengths and weaknesses. Each child in a family is different from his or her siblings. A good parent knows these differences, respects them, and supports them for each child (Ackerman, 1995; Ackerman & Schoendorf, 1992; Rohman et al., 1987). Good parents help their children develop a view of them as positive role models. Good role models teach their children about limit setting, rule following, and respect of self and others (Schetky & Benedek, 1980).

Discipline is a necessary part of all development. Parental discipline takes many different forms and is often dictated by prevailing cultural expectations. A good disciplinarian sets appropriate limits, enforces transgressions, and provides guidance about the inappropriateness of the current behavior and how it may be changed (Ackerman, 1995; Bray, 1991; Derdeyn et al., 1982; Stahl, 1994; Schutz et al., 1989).

A competent parent actively encourages the needs of the child to spend time with the other parent (Schutz et al., 1989) and to participate in social groups and other extrafamilial activities that encourage social development. Finally, good parenting appears to include the teaching of socially appropriate behavior and respect for the rules that govern society. Teaching social rules and respect for social norms helps teach children about moral behavior within our society.

Identifying Deficient Parenting

Identification of deficient parenting typically is confined to behaviors our society considers dangerous, unlawful, or harmful. Anything that is judged to place a child at risk may be concerned deficient parenting. These deficiencies generally consist of abusive, addictive, or emotionally dysfunctional behaviors (see Table 9.2), but some consist of inappropriate social behaviors and attitudes (e.g., racially motivated hate speech).

Adults who fit into these groups tend to be viewed as high risk for rearing children with significant emotional, psychological, social, and educational problems. There is also an increased probability of these children having a greater than normal frequency of physical problems.

A significant body of literature examines the parameters of child maltreatment (including emotional, physical, and sexual abuse) and characterizing abusive parents. These parents show an increased likelihood of depression, low self-esteem, and dependency. They have been found to behave in less age-appropriate ways, taking fewer age-appropriate responsibilities as parents, and more likely to use anxiety- and guilt-inducing techniques as motivators with their children. Abusive parents apply discipline techniques inconsistently, make unrealistic demands of their children, and generally possess poor child management skills.

Abusive parents display a higher level of impulsive behavior. They show poor frustration tolerance, resulting in higher than normal levels of emotional distress, with which they are poorly prepared to deal. They are less emotionally and physically available to their children, tend to display immature needs for love and affection, demand their children fulfill needs normally filled by adult relationships (sometimes expecting the child to be a caretaker). Abusive parents have been found lacking awareness of their children's needs, their own needs, and how to place their children's needs ahead of their own (Gaines, Sandgrund, Green, & Power, 1978; Garbarino & Gilliam, 1980). (See Chapters 11, 12, and 13 for further discussion of variables associated with different kinds of abuse and maltreatment.)

Substance-Abusing Parents

Parental drug abuse is an important predictor of deficient parenting competencies (Jellinek et al., 1992; Schutz et al., 1989). Children prenatally exposed to il-

TABLE 9.2. Deficient Parenting Behaviors

• Substance use and abuse	• Verbal abuse
• Physical abuse	• Abuse of power and control in
• Sexual abuse	relationships
• Neglectful parenting style	• Intimate/spousal relationships
• Authoritarian parenting style	• Sibling relationships
• Alcohol use and abuse	• Parent–child relationships
• Emotional/psychological abuse	• Parent's major mental illness

legal drugs might be more difficult to parent, increasing the likelihood of abusive parental behaviors. Wasserman and Leventhal (1993) report evidence of both physical abuse and neglect in medical records of children born to cocaine-dependent mothers compared to children born to non–cocaine-dependent controls. There are also data suggesting that violent behavior (in general, not specific to child maltreatment) increases in substance-abusing individuals (Steadman et al., 1998; Mayes & Truman, 2002). (In Chapter 12, we discuss the relationship among children's exposure to spousal violence, substance and/or alcohol abuse, and increased risk for child maltreatment.)

Parental substance abuse might compromise the development and well-being of a child either by prenatal exposure to maternal drug and/or alcohol use or by impairment of parenting capabilities postnatally by either parent (Benjet, Azar, & Kuersten-Hogan, 2003). Evidence for the adverse effects of prenatal drug exposure is mixed and varies depending on the type of substance exposure. Initial reports of dramatic impairments of cocaine babies have not been confirmed by subsequent research (Carmichael-Olson & Burgess, 1997), and research findings on the effects of prenatal cocaine exposure have been inconsistent (Myers, 1992). Research on infants exposed to heroin and methadone more consistently points to early postnatal problems such as lower birth weights, higher levels of premature birth, and a greater chance for respiratory distress (Householder, Hatcher, Burns, & Chasnoff, 1982). Other studies reveal impairment in infant state regulation and responsiveness due to fetal alcohol effects and neonatal withdrawal syndrome from opiates (Mayes, 1995).

Benjet and colleagues (2003) suggest that how substance abuse might affect actual parenting behavior postnatally is more difficult to identify. Substance abuse is believed to interfere negatively with the parent–child relationship and with the quality of the environment provided by the substance-abusing parent. Kaplan-Sanoff and Fitzgerald Rice (1992) observed that addicted parents "have a primary relationship with their drug, not their child" (p. 17).

There is a social belief that parental substance abuse automatically leads to inadequate parenting. Data support the finding of increased behavioral difficulties, psychopathology, and substance abuse among offspring of such parents (Deren, 1986; West & Prinz, 1987), but research has shown that less favorable child outcomes may be the result of prenatal drug exposure rather than an impaired parenting environment. Benjet and colleagues (2003) suggest that there may be preexisting psychiatric or neuropsychological disorders or genetic vulnerabilities that predispose these parents to substance abuse and carry a genetic risk for their children.

The minimal research available on the direct effects of substance abuse on parenting behaviors or abilities has primarily involved mothers and small samples, yielding contradictory results. Some studies have found opioid-dependent mothers to be less responsive and harsher than control mothers, though there was no difference in guidance and encouragement (Hans, Bernstein, & Henson, 1999), while other studies have not found greater neglect for children of substance-abusing mothers (Harrington, Dubowitz, Black, & Binder, 1995). Heterogeneity of the substances used and the severity as well as the young age of the children limit the conclusions that can be drawn from these studies (Benjet et al., 2003). See Mayes and Truman (2002) for a summary of the effects of substance abuse on parenting.

Most studies have focused on maternal responsiveness and associated variables of restrictiveness, monitoring, or authoritarianism. Studies also have examined associated variables of warmth or involvement. Extremes of control (either being overly permissive or overly restrictive) coupled with low responsiveness have been found to undermine children's development. There are concerns about whether potential neurological impairments in memory or attention associated with long-term substance use affect parenting. There are also concerns that affect, impulse regulation, modulation of anxiety, and/or frustration tolerance may be impaired in substance-abusing parents. There is a lack of well-controlled studies examining the implications of these issues for parenting. (See Mayes, 1995, for a review of the literature on substance abuse and parenting.) In addition, there are concerns about the environments in which substance-abusing parents live that may place their children at risk (e.g., high-crime neighborhood, poverty, marital instability, neighborhood violence). Wasserman and Leventhal (1993) found that cocaine-addicted mothers and their infants had significantly more separations in the first 2 years of life than a matched control sample. Evaluators should consider the effect of frequent separations between child and mother and the development of secure attachment.

Benjet and colleagues (2003) state:

> Though parental substance abuse most probably carries risk for impaired parenting, the evidence for specific risk for any certain type of substance is quite limited, and research has yet to focus on exactly how parenting behaviors are affected and whether all parents are similarly affected. The type of substance chosen and the chronicity of usage may affect the type and level of risk. In addition, the data regarding whether parenting risk continues once substance abuse stops is very limited, but such continued risk may be of contention in court. The findings of one intervention study suggest that effects on child outcome that are not physiologically driven may be found to decrease or disappear with cessation of the substance use. . . . There is a crucial need for research that identifies exactly which parenting capacities might be compromised and whether they remain compromised if substance abuse is treated successfully or spontaneous remission occurs. (p. 242)

Parents with Major Mental Illness

Parents with major mental illness represent an area of concern for possible deficient parenting. It has long been thought that people who have been diagnosed with schizophrenia or an affective disorder are, by definition, less competent parents. Affective and cognitive disturbances seen in schizophrenic parents have been thought to influence parenting capacity by interfering with parent–child social interactions. Symptoms associated with affective disorders such as withdrawal, irritability, and anhedonia have been thought to influence parents' capacity to be warm and responsive toward their children and to control their children's behavior appropriately and consistently (Benjet et al., 2003). Evaluators need to examine whether a parent's major mental illness compromises competent parenting and be cognizant of the inconclusive research results regarding whether parents with major mental illness display incompetent parenting.

Children of parents with major affective disorders have been shown to have an increased risk of affective disorder, as well as other psychological problems, including behavior problems, attention deficits, learning disabilities, cognitive and social deficits, substance abuse, anxiety, and somatic symptoms (see, for example, Beardslee, Versage, & Gladstone, 1998; Weissman et al., 1987). Children of schizophrenic parents have an increased risk of psychiatric disorder (Watt, 1984). What remains unclear is what specifically places such children at risk.

Genetic or biological factors may play some role in placing children at risk. Children with a genetic vulnerability probably require more sensitive and more optimal parenting (Benjet et al., 2003). Children with genetic or biological risk factors may be prone to develop problems even when parenting is adequate. Benjet and colleagues (2003) report that there is some evidence that schizophrenic and depressed individuals differ in their interactions with their children compared to nondisordered parents. Summarizing research about major mental illness and parenting, they report that affectively disordered mothers tend to overreact to mild stressors they experience with their children, such as waiting in a doctor's office (Breznitz & Sherman, 1987). Other studies have found that depressed mothers tend to behave less consistently toward their children (and range from withdrawn to controlling or intrusive) with few mothers falling within the optimum range of involvement compared with nondepressed mothers (Hoffman & Drotar, 1991). Furthermore, depressed mothers have been found to use fewer questions, a less positive tone of voice, more criticism, and more coercion with their children (Cox, Puckering, Pound, & Mills, 1987). The Cox and colleagues' study suggested that the nature of the child's behavioral style or temperament should be considered. Some children have special needs, while others are more resilient when it comes to stress.

Several factors may be useful to examine in evaluating the parental competencies of individuals with major mental illness, among them (1) severity and chronicity of parental disorder, (2) child's age at time of onset, (3) child behavior, (4) parental functioning in the community, (5) social support of the parent (Oyserman, Mowbray, Meares, & Firminger, 2000), (6) degree of marital conflict, (7) degree of social isolation, and (8) economic status (poverty).

Some research has suggested that parenting differences vary across diagnosis. Goodman and Brumley (1990) reported that, compared with normal and schizophrenic mothers, parenting of depressed mothers was more variable with regard to maternal responsiveness and affective involvement. Competent children of mothers with major mental illness were more likely to have (1) an affectively disturbed parent as opposed to a schizophrenic parent, (2) a parent whose disorder was not chronic, (3) a parent whose disorder occurred later in the children's development, and (4) a mother whose lack of warmth and inactive style were compensated for by a father who was warm and active (Benjet et al., 2003).

Budd's Model of Defining Parenting Competencies

Another approach to defining parameters of competent parenting is suggested by Budd (2001). Originally developed as a guide for evaluating minimal parenting competencies in child protection cases, Budd's outline provides a useful conceptual framework. We have modified it for use in child custody evaluations.

Assessments should include a focus on a parent's capabilities and deficiencies *as a parent* and on the parent–child relationship (Budd, 2001). Adult qualities and characteristics need to be linked to specific aspects of parental fitness or unfitness, by showing how they pose a protective factor or risk to the child, respectively, or how they enable or prevent the parent from profiting from rehabilitation services. Assessments should also focus on functional capabilities of the parent and assess "what the caregiver understands, believes, knows, does, and is capable of doing related to child rearing" (Grisso, 1986, p. 201). Functional assessment embodies a constructive focus on identifying parenting strengths and areas of adequate performance rather than focusing only on parenting deficiencies. Finally, evaluators should do a comparative assessment of parenting competence, comparing parents along salient dimensions in order to determine their relative abilities among caregivers.

Minimal parenting competence is the "floor" of acceptable parenting that is sufficient to protect the safety and well-being of a child, but there are limitations to defining it. First, researchers have found pervasive differences in parenting beliefs and practices associated with socioeconomic status, race, ethnicity, and other human differences (García Coll, Meyer, & Brillon, 1995). Second, legal and child welfare criteria regarding minimal parenting competence vary from state to state and lack behavioral specificity (Melton et al., 1997). Third, consensus has not been reached on what is "good-enough" parenting (Budd & Holdsworth, 1996).

Recent work has begun to determine empirically criteria of minimal parenting competence (Budd, 2001; Budd & Holdsworth, 1996; Budd, Poindexter, Felix, & Naik-Polan, 2001; Budd, Felix, Poindexter, Naik-Polan, & Sloss, 2002; Condie, 2003). Among the relevant factors defining minimal parenting competence are: (1) Parent's intellectual functioning; (2) parent's adaptive and social functioning; (3) parent's personality and emotional functioning; (4)

parenting knowledge, attitudes, and perceptions; (5) parent–child interactions; (6) developmental needs of the child; and (7) parent's response to previous interventions and potential for change.

Budd's work may be used in several ways by custody evaluators. Information reflecting the seven criteria listed above may be used to understand a parent's minimal level of functioning. Such information may be useful in a parenting fitness evaluation where there is no comparison to another parent. Information about minimal parental functioning may be useful if there are concerns voiced by Child Protective Services or other social service agencies about a parent's risk to a child due to parenting incompetence. We also encourage evaluators to assess specific areas of concern rather than providing only global information similar to that obtained from measures of the seven criteria listed above.

Budd's work focuses attention on the identification and assessment of minimal parenting competence. We believe that it is helpful for evaluators to have considered how to define minimal parenting and what dimensions to assess to determine it. It is unlikely that many custody litigants will require an analysis of minimal parenting competence because most parents who undergo custody evaluations are minimally competent. The intellectual exercise for evaluators is to reflect upon and identify those parenting behaviors that are believed to constitute a floor of acceptable parenting competence. Then, evaluators should examine the identified minimal parenting competence for the degree to which personal or professional bias or fussy thinking about various parenting concepts may be reflected in the defined behaviors.

Emotional Competence in Adults

In this section, we posit that an important aspect of parenting is its emotional experience. Raising children involves more joy, affection, anger, and worry than do most other endeavors. Perhaps more than any other single variable, parents' emotions reflect the health of the parent–child relationship. Research supports the following conclusions about the role of emotion in parenting.

First, strong emotion is a daily component of parenting. Typical parents report feelings of anger with their children, the need to engage in techniques to control their anger, and fear that they will at some time lose control and harm their children (Dix, 1991). Strong emotion is also apparent in reports showing high rates of depression among mothers of young children (Patterson, 1982) and high rates of violence, both between parent and child and between husband and wife (Gelles & Straus, 1988). Parents' positive emotions are even more common than their negative emotions, with parents reporting two and a half times as many positive as negative interactions (Jersild, Woodyard, & Del Solar, 1949).

Second, parents' emotions often reflect the quality of the caregiving environment. Parental warmth consistently predicts favorable developmental outcomes for children. Parental conflict consistently predicts unfavorable developmental outcomes for children (Grusec & Lytton, 1988; Maccoby, 1980; Maccoby & Martin, 1983). This is true during both infancy and childhood and in both average and dysfunctional families. Even transient negative emotions between adults cause distress and aggression in infants and young children. Thus, there is considerable evidence that the caregiving environment is more favorable for children when parents express and experience more positive emotions (Dix, 1991).

Third, parents experiencing high levels of stress or low levels of social support tend to show significant parenting deficiencies, notably displaying harsher and more erratic discipline. It is assumed that these deficiencies are due, in part, to the impact that stress and support have on parents' emotions. Substantial correlations are present between stress and negative emotion as well as between support and positive emotion. Thus, there is growing evidence that parents' emotions play significantly influence parenting and children (Dix, 1991).

Fourth, chronic and intense negative emotion in parents is a sign of family dysfunction, found in families with difficult children, dysfunctional parents, or families experiencing high stress. Negative emotion is prominent in the parenting of abusive mothers, depressed mothers, mothers of aggressive boys, teenage mothers, mothers of premature infants, and mothers living in poverty (Dix, 1991).

Dix (1991) proposes that emotional processing occurs in three stages: activation, engagement, and regulation.

1. *Activation processes* precipitate emotion. Although some human emotional responses are innate or can occur with little cognitive analysis, *cognition* is an important determinant of a large percentage of human emotions. Emotions reflect how an individual chooses to appraise the benefit or harm inherent in immediate events. Parents' emotions depend on the concerns they are trying to promote, their appraisals of whether and why those concerns are promoted or are frustrated, and their appraisals of the options and resources available to ensure that their concerns are promoted.

2. *Engagement processes* help transform people's orientation to their environment. The particular form of emotional engagement depends upon which emotion is activated and on how strongly it is activated. Fear, for example, prepares people to perceive and avoid threat, while anger prepares people to perceive and remove obstructions.

3. *Regulation processes* help people understand and control emotions and their expression. Regulation processes assist people in understanding what they are feeling and why and in promoting desirable emotions, suppressing or coping with undesirable emotions, and concealing emotions, both positive and negative, that threaten to undermine their concerns.

This three-pronged emotional activation theory suggests that, during interactions with children, parents often seek to promote particular concerns or outcomes. Parents initiate plans or sequences of behavior to promote these concerns and continually appraise events to have sufficient understanding of and control to promote these concerns effectively. Finally, parents adjust their behavior based on their appraisals of whether their concerns are being met.

Behaviors and outcomes between parents and children are interdependent (Kelley & Thibaut, 1978). Whether and how parents' concerns are promoted often depend upon their children. The emotions parents experience depend upon whether their concerns and behaviors are compatible with the concerns and behaviors of their children (Maccoby & Martin, 1983). When concerns and behaviors are compatible, harmonious interaction is straightforward. When parents' and children's concerns and behaviors are incompatible, conflict and negative emotion are often experienced and expressed.

What emotions are experienced depend on the extent to which parents formulate and select concerns that children can and are willing to promote. Parents' emotions also depend on their skill at eliciting from children behaviors that allow the promotion of parental plans and concerns. Over time, parents and children develop shared representations of events, stable conceptions of each other, and interdependent behavioral dispositions that determine affective patterning characteristic of their relationship (Cummings & Cummings, 2002; Waters & Cummings, 2000). It is believed children develop dispositions to accept or resist parental influence based in large part on whether parents are sensitive and responsive to the children's needs (Maccoby & Martin, 1983).

Once aroused, the emotions parents feel when children violate or promote parental concerns influence processes basic to parental responding. Emotions influence how we think, activate monitoring and attention, orient our thinking, and help with decision making by selecting certain information to attend to and ignoring information less relevant to the issue at hand. Although emotions mobilize processes parents need to promote their concerns, they can also undermine parenting under certain circumstances. Failure to activate emotion at particular times can lead to poorly engaged, organized, or executed parenting behavior.

The impact that emotions have on parenting depends on how parents understand and control their emotions (Frijda, 1986). Emotional regulation is important to controlling what parents communicate to children and what reactions children are likely to have to those communications. It ensures that emotions occur at levels that promote organized responding and not at levels that undermine reasonable parenting. Finally, emotional regulation makes sure that parenting responses are not too positive, too negative, or badly timed. Poorly functioning regulation processes may lead parents to experience insufficient or excessive emotion or to express emotion in ways that are detrimental to children and to the coordination of parent and child behavior.

Some authors posit that parent–child conflict often occurs not because children's behavior is objectively problematic, but because parents perceive children's behavior to be inconsistent with parental goals or expectations (Maccoby & Martin, 1983). Distressed parents experience high negative affect and low positive affect because they select interactional concerns that are unrealistic and that children are unable or unwilling to promote. One source of unrealistic expectations may be parents' failure to adopt child-oriented, or empathic, concerns. Some parents have difficulty recognizing when they place their concerns and expectations ahead of those of their children. These parents often have negative emotional experiences when they expect young children to adjust to parental plans rather than the other way around. Parents' emotions depend upon their attributions about why children are promoting or violating parental concerns. Parents often become upset when they make inferences about why children are behaving in the observed manner and the degree to which parents believe the children have control over their negative behavior (Dix & Grusec, 1985).

Parents of socially competent children tend to be responsive to their children's needs. They tend to express warmth and affection, to reason and communicate openly, to make appropriate demands for mature behavior, to establish and enforce consistent rules, and to avoid arbitrary, restrictive, or punitive control (Grusec & Lytton, 1988). Such parenting increases positive emotion and reduces negative emotion because it teaches children cooperative, responsive behavior, social problem-solving skills, knowledge of social relationships, and the expectation that parents will reciprocate fairness and sensitivity.

Less competent, or distressed, parents have been found to be poorer monitors of their children's behavior. They fail to attend closely to their children's behavior and are less able to coordinate their concerns and actions with the concerns and actions of their children. They often fail to communicate clear expectations to which children can conform and are unable to formulate solutions to situations that involve incompatible parent and child behavior. These distressed parents often train their children to be noncompliant, rewarding noncompliant behavior and punishing cooperative behavior, and generally use rewards and punishments inconsistently (Dix, 1991).

Distressed parents are less likely to adopt empathic interaction strategies with their children. They are less responsive to their children's concerns and less likely to initiate actions that consider their children's concerns. Their responses are less consistent, less sensitive, and less contingent on children's prior behavior. Distressed parents are less likely to use cooperative strategies in resolving parent–child problems and less likely to engage in explaining, negotiating, and compromising with their children.

Evaluators need to understand how to assess factors associated with competent parenting and factors associated with incompetent or distressed parenting. They need to assess how parents regulate their emotional reactions toward children and whether parents place the needs of their children ahead of their own needs.

Parenting Style Variables

Parenting style variables have been analyzed along a two-factor dimension (Maccoby & Martin, 1983), a three-factor dimension (Maccoby & Mnookin, 1992), and a four-factor dimension (Baumrind, 1971, 1991; Baumrind & Thompson, 2002). Evaluators may find it useful to explore postdivorce parenting using both methods of analysis. Maccoby and Mnookin's (1992) parenting pattern styles demonstrate how parents worked with each other after divorce. In contrast, Baumrind (1971) provided a model of individual parenting style behaviors.

Maccoby and Mnookin's Three-Dimension Model

Maccoby and Mnookin (1992) estimated that 10% of families experienced "substantial" legal conflict and 15% experienced "intense" legal conflict. Thus, the majority of couples with children involved in divorce proceedings navigated the legal system without the involvement of the court or ancillary services. Those involved in high-conflict divorce, however, were found to display three types of coparenting patterns: cooperative, disengaged, and conflicted. Each coparenting pattern was assessed along dimensions of discord, frequency of communication attempts, and frequency of attempts to coordinate with the other parent. Table 9.3 shows the three parenting style factors and characteristics of each.

Cooperative coparenting was defined as parents talking frequently with each other about their children, attempting to coordinate rules in their two households, and supporting each parent's ongoing, continuous contact between the children and the other parent. Typically, cooperative parents tended to display high communication and low conflict (Maccoby & Mnookin, 1992).

Conflicted coparenting was defined as parents who often argued. Each parent tended to perceive his or her ex-spouse as attempting to upset him or her when they disagreed. Conflicted parents reported their ex-spouse to have refused or threatened to refuse to allow visitation. The other parent was viewed as undermining parenting as well as creating logistical problems in managing visits with the children (Maccoby & Mnookin, 1992).

Disengaged coparenting was defined as parents who avoided contact with each other. This resulted in parallel parenting, in which each household had its own set of rules and responsibilities. There was little, if any, coordination between parents regarding the establishment of consistent rules across households. That is, some high-conflict parents resolved their disputes by disengaging from each other and establishing separate, independent households.

Parenting Style Defined

Parenting is a complex activity that includes many specific behaviors that work individually and together to influence the ways in which children will mature

TABLE 9.3. Coparenting Patterns

Cooperative
- Frequent parental exchanges about children
- Attempts to coordinate rules in two households
- Each parent supports other parent's continuous contact with children

Conflicted
- Frequent arguments between parents
- Each parent views the other as undermining relationship between self and children

Disengaged
- Avoidance of contact between parents
- Parallel parenting, with little consistency in family rules across households

and emerge into adulthood. The construct of parenting style is used to describe normal variations in parents' attempts to control and socialize their children (Baumrind, 1991). Descriptions of parenting styles as defined by Baumrind's typology are meant to describe normal variations in parenting and should not be understood to include deviant parenting, such as might be observed in abusive or neglectful homes. Baumrind (1991; Baumrind & Thompson, 2002) assumes that normal parenting focuses upon issues of control. Although parents differ in the extent to which they exercise control upon and socialize their children. Baumrind's model assumes that the primary role of all parents is to influence, teach, and control their children.

Maccoby and Martin's Two-Dimension Model

Baumrind's research has led Maccoby and Martin (1983) to identify two parenting dimensions: parental responsiveness and parental demandingness. Parental responsiveness, characterized by parental warmth and supportiveness, refers to the degree to which parents intentionally bolster their children's individuality, self-regulation, and self-assertion by being attuned, supportive, and acquiescent to their children's unique needs and demands. Parental demandingness, characterized by degree of behavioral control exerted over children, refers to the demands parents make on children to become integrated into the entire family, by their maturity demands, supervisory actions, disciplinary efforts, and willingness to challenge the child who does not follow family rules.

Baumrind's Four-Dimension Model

Categorizing parents according to whether they are high or low on parental demandingness and responsiveness creates a typology of four parenting styles: permissive (indulgent), authoritarian, authoritative, and neglectful (uninvolved)

(Baumrind, 1971). Each of these parenting styles reflects different naturally occurring patterns of parental values, practices, and behaviors (Baumrind, 1991)
and a distinct balance of responsiveness and demandingness (Maccoby & Martin, 1983).

Permissive parents (also called "indulgent" or "nondirective") "are more
responsive than they are demanding. They are nontraditional and lenient, do
not require mature behavior, allow considerable self-regulation, and avoid confrontation" (Baumrind, 1991, p. 62). Permissive parents may be divided into
two types: democratic and nondirective. Democratic parents, though indulgent, are nevertheless more conscientious, engaged, and committed to the
child than are the more indulgent, nondirective parents. The extreme form of
permissive parenting is the neglectful parent. Neglectful or uninvolved parents
tend to be low in both responsiveness and demandingness.

Authoritarian parents tend to be restrictive, highly demanding, directive,
and not responsive to the needs or demands of children. "They are obedience-
and status-oriented, and expect their orders to be obeyed without explanation"
(Baumrind, 1991, p. 62). These parents provide well-ordered, rule-bound,
structured environments. Authoritarian parents can be divided into two types:
nonauthoritarian-directive, parents who are directive but not intrusive or autocratic in their use of power, and authoritarian-directive parents, who are highly
intrusive and autocratic in their use of power.

Authoritative parents tend to be warm, demanding, and responsive.

> They monitor and impart clear standards for their children's conduct. They are as-
> sertive, but not intrusive and restrictive. Their disciplinary methods are support-
> ive, rather than punitive. They want their children to be assertive as well as so-
> cially responsible, and self-regulated as well as cooperative. (Baumrind, 1991, p.
> 62)

The increasing professional consensus is that authoritative parenting best
serves children's growth and development (Kelly & Emery, 2003). The benefits
of authoritative parenting and the detrimental effects of uninvolved parenting
are evident as early as the preschool years and continue throughout adolescence and into early adulthood. Authoritative parents appear to be able to balance their conformity demands with their respect for their children's individuality, so children from authoritative homes appear to be able to balance the
claims of external conformity and achievement demands with their need for individuation and autonomy.

Parenting styles also differ in the extent to which they are characterized by
a third dimension: psychological control. Psychological control "refers to control attempts that intrude into the psychological and emotional development of
the child" (Barber, 1996, p. 3296) through the use of parenting practices such as
guilt induction, withdrawal of love, or shaming. One key difference between
authoritarian and authoritative parenting is in the dimension of psychological

control. Both authoritarian and authoritative parents place high demands on their children and expect their children to behave appropriately and to obey parental rules. Authoritarian parents, however, also expect their children to accept parental judgments, values, and goals unquestioningly. In contrast, authoritative parents are more open to give and take with their children and make greater use of explanations. Thus, although authoritative and authoritarian parents are equally high in behavioral control, authoritative parents tend to be low in psychological control, while authoritarian parents tend to be high (Barber, 2002).

Consequences for Children

Parenting style has been found to be predictive of child well-being. In particular, children raised by authoritative parents tend to display greater social competence, better academic performance, and fewer problem behaviors (Baumrind & Thompson, 2002). Children and adolescents whose parents are authoritative rate themselves and are rated by objective measures as more socially and instrumentally competent than those whose parents are non-authoritative (Baumrind, 1991; Weiss & Schwarz, 1996; Miller, Cowan, Cowan, & Hetherington, 1993). Children and adolescents whose parents are uninvolved perform most poorly in all domains. In general, parental responsiveness is predictive of social competence and good psychosocial functioning, while parental demandingness is associated with increased performance competence and behavioral control (i.e., academic performance and deviance) (Baumrind & Thompson, 2002). These findings indicate that children and adolescents from authoritarian families (high in demandingness, but low in responsiveness) tend to perform moderately well in school and be uninvolved in problem behavior, but to have poorer social skills, lower self-esteem, and higher levels of depression. Children and adolescents from indulgent homes (high in responsiveness, low in demandingness) are more likely to be involved in problem behavior and perform less well in school, but they have higher self-esteem, better social skills, and lower levels of depression.

Baumrind's Four-Factor Individual Parenting Style Model

Subsequent research has reported two primary styles: authoritative/democratic parenting and authoritarian/restrictive parenting. The *authoritative/democratic parenting style* is characterized by parental attempts to direct the child in a rational, issue-oriented manner by explaining the reasons for setting up the rules. It recognizes the child's individuality, encourages verbal give-and-take, and means the parent engages the child in joint decision making. There is a high degree of warmth and acceptance. The *authoritarian/restrictive parenting style* is characterized by parental attempts to exhort the child to follow rules without explanation, restrict the child's autonomy, and reserve decision making for the parent(s). Authoritarian/restrictive parents tend to be less responsive toward and accepting of the child (DeKovic & Janssen, 1992).

Authoritarian Parenting Encourages Development of Dependent Personality Styles

Authoritarian/restrictive parenting is associated with parental overprotectiveness, which is associated with increased dependency, even into adolescence and adulthood. Dependency wrought by authoritarian parenting may be characterized by increased suggestibility, conformity, compliance, interpersonal yielding, affiliative behavior, performance anxiety, and sensitivity to interpersonal cues of rejection or acceptance. Dependency predicts the onset of certain physical (e.g., ulcers, heart disease, cancer) and psychological disorders (e.g., depression, alcoholism, smoking, obesity, eating disorders). These results have been supported in cross-cultural, cross-ethnic group, and cross-methodological studies (see Bornstein, 2002, for review).

Parental authoritarianism may serve simultaneously to reinforce dependent behaviors in children and to prevent children from developing independent, autonomous behaviors they are not allowed to engage in trial-and-error learning (Baumrind & Thompson, 2002). The child of authoritarian parents may come to believe that he or she cannot function adequately without the guidance and protection of others, particularly figures of authority. These children often develop belief systems based upon the view that they need to seek out relationships in which they are nurtured and cared for by others. That is, they carry a set of beliefs that discourages independent, autonomous behavior and encourages maintaining good relationships with others by acquiescing to their requests, expectations, and demands (Baumrind, 1971; Baumrind & Thompson, 2002; Maccoby, 1980).

Dependent behaviors expressed by children may serve to encourage and reinforce overprotective, dependency-fostering behavior in parents because they evoke strong protective behaviors in mothers and fathers (Lamb, 2004). Dependent behavior in children may also contribute to an increase in parental demandingness (Maccoby, 1980).

Authoritarian Parenting Interferes with Children's Positive Placement in Social Groups

Research indicates that children's acceptance by peer groups plays an important role in their social and personality development. Peer rejection seems to be a reasonably stable phenomenon and is predictive of later social maladjustment (Parker & Asher, 1987). The role that parents play in the development and maintenance of children's fit within a social group (sociometric status) is important. Children's status in a peer group is related to socialization factors present in the parent–child relationship (DeKovic & Janssen, 1992). These factors include children's social cognition, social skills, social problem solving, and understanding of social strategies (or emotional intelligence).

Parents of children who are valued by their peer group (popular children) are more likely to adopt an authoritative/democratic parenting style when interacting with their children. Parents of children who are less well valued by their peer group (rejected children) tend to endorse an authoritarian/restrictive parenting style. Parental child-rearing style is related both to the child's status within the peer group and to the child's display of social behaviors within the peer group. That is, children from authoritative/democratic families tend more frequently to display prosocial behaviors within their peer group, high levels of social competence, and more frequently positive exchanges both with their peers and with their parents. Children from authoritarian/restrictive families tend to have more negative peer interactions and consequently do not profit from peer interaction in the way popular or average children do. The social network of these children often is characterized by disagreeable and conflicted relationships resulting in a higher level of risk for social and personal maladjustment (DeKovic & Janssen, 1992; Peterson et al., 1997).

Authoritarian/Restrictive Parents May Provide Less Developmentally Appropriate Home Environments

Authoritarian/restrictive parents are less adept at thinking about developmental issues faced by their children (Pratt, Hunsberger, Pancer, Roth, & Santolupo, 1993), and their home environments may lead children to think in simplistic, right-versus-wrong styles associated with authoritarian personality traits. It is likely that the parents passively model or actively teach approaches to problem solving based upon simplistic strategies and outcomes, modeling a rigid cognitive style that is then used by their children (Peterson et al., 1997).

Authoritarian Parents May Produce Adult Children Who Are Less Likely to Nurture the Next Generation

Children raised by authoritarian parents are more likely to develop authoritarian styles of thinking (Adorno, Frankel-Brunswik, Levinson, & Sanford, 1950) and more likely to internalize the frustration from their childhood that resulted from harsh parenting discipline, channeling it in the form of aggression toward minorities and "outsiders." In adults, authoritarianism has been linked with prejudice, rigid thinking, compliance and obedience, and threatening social conditions (Peterson et al., 1997). In contrast, those from authoritative homes are more likely to display higher levels of tolerance, cognitive flexibility, and acceptance of others. Adult children from these families are more likely to value the transmission to younger individuals of cultural ideas and ways of doing things that benefit society rather than simply passing along a rigid way of doing things. These adults, compared with authoritarian adults, carefully consider the needs of the children they mentor and guide. They equip the next generation with the tangible and ideological skills they need to negotiate the future successfully (Peterson et al., 1997).

Temperament and Parenting Style

One line of research suggests that children of different temperaments may respond differently to different styles of parenting. Kochanska (1993, 1997) examined child temperament as a moderator of the impact of parenting style on children's conscience development. He hypothesized that children's temperamental quality of fearfulness was an important factor in the development of conscience. For fearful children—those who respond with spontaneous anxious arousal to actual or potential wrongdoing—parental use of "subtle, gentle discipline deemphasizing power and instead capitalizing on that internal discomfort (of the child) should effectively foster conscience" (Kochanska, 1997, p. 228). Temperamentally fearless children appear to respond to a different style of parenting. They are hypothesized *not* to respond to transgressions with internal discomfort and may need a parenting style characterized by increased parental power to help them develop conscience. Placed into the perspective of parenting style variables, temperamentally fearful children may respond best to authoritarian parenting while temperamentally fearless children may respond best to a more authoritarian parenting style.

Parental Style of Control, Responsiveness to the Child, and Healthy Child Adjustment

Two factors associated with healthy child's adjustment are important to consider. The first is the maternal *style of control*, and the second is maternal *responsiveness to the child* (Clark, Kochanska, & Ready, 2000).

Style of control refers to a set of behaviors characterized by parental control over child behavior, limit setting, and discipline in combination with parents' expectations of how their children ought to comply with their demands. *Responsiveness to the child* refers to a set of behaviors characterized by sensitivity to the child's signals, prompt and appropriate responses to the child's needs, cooperation with and respect for the child's autonomy, emotional support, warmth and acceptance, and emotional availability to the child (DeWolf & van IJzendoorn, 1997). It is believed that children's psychological potential is best facilitated by parents who respond sensitively and promptly to their signals, provide appropriate support and comfort, follow their leads, respect their autonomy, adjust their behavior to children's current state or needs, and are skillful and affectively positive in social interactions (Clark et al., 2000).

Attachment Processes and Parenting Style Variables

Children are predisposed to form an affectionate bond with a small number of caretakers whom they are motivated to seek as a source of joy and comfort when conditions are optimal and as a haven of safety during times of stress (Ainsworth, 1979; Ainsworth & Bell, 1974; Bowlby, 1969, 1980; Condie, 2003; Kelly & Lamb, 2000; Main, 1996; Main & Solomon, 1990; Pruett et al., 2004). Research has shown that children can form either secure or insecure emotional attachments to their caretakers. Which kind of emotional attachment develops is more dependent upon the caretaker's behavior toward the child (DeWolf & van IJzendoorn, 1997) and less dependent on the child's characteristics, such as temperament (Anan & Barnett, 1999). Children with secure attachments tend to have caregivers who respond with behaviors characteristic of authoritative/democratic parenting styles that accent parental acceptance and support.

Parental Disciplinary Style

How parents discipline their children predicts critical aspects of children's positive and negative interpersonal behaviors, including the extent to which children comply with parental directives (Power & Chapieski, 1986), internalize parental values (Eisenberg & Valiente, 2002), behave altruistically (Zahn-Wexler, Radke-Yarrow, Wagner, & Chapman, 1992), and act disrespectfully or aggressively (Strassberg, Dodge, Pettit, & Bates, 1994). It is precisely because parents' behavior can have profound consequences for children's future behavior that understanding why parents choose certain disciplinary practices is an important area of examination. The following are some factors that contribute to parents' disciplinary style:

1. *The role of religion.* Many fundamentalist Christian religious belief systems support the use of corporal punishment (Ellison & Sherkat, 1993; Gershoff, 2002) as an extension of the belief in human nature as evil, human sins as requiring punishment, and the Bible as an infallible guide for parenting practices. These beliefs are codified in conservative parenting advice books that advocate the use of corporal punishment to ensure children's obedience to authority (e.g., Dobson, 1970; see review by Bartkowski & Ellison, 1995).

2. *The role of emotional reactions.* An important distinction in understanding when to apply corporal punishment lies in whether a parent selects corporal punishment because of his or her belief in its usefulness as a change agent (instrumental utility) or out of emotional arousal in response to child misbehavior (emotional utility) (Gershoff, 2002). The use of corporal punishment for emotional rather than instrumental reasons appears associated with increases in negative child behaviors (Straus & Mouradian, 1998).

3. *The role of parent–child interactions.* A third way to think about corporal punishment is the *reciprocal effects model* (Muller, 1996). It is suggested that parent and child take an active role in precipitating noncompliant behavior and that the use of physical force to resolve conflict may be a function of an aggressive microsystem in which all members are active participants.

The Intergenerational Transmission Hypothesis

The intergenerational transmission hypothesis posits that child maltreatment is transmitted across generations through a modeling process in which children learn to use physical violence as a means of resolving conflict. There is a high correspondence between being a recipient of severe corporal punishment and engaging in similar behavior with one's own children (Muller, 1996). This hypothesis explains the cycle of abuse found among maltreated children (Kempe, Silverman, Steele, Droegemueller, & Silver, 1962).

Dimensions of Effective Child Discipline

Research examining parameters of effective discipline and their effect on children has revealed that timing, intensity, length, loudness, and consistency of negative consequences can greatly influence the effectiveness of discipline. Treatment outcome studies with preschoolers show that when parents are taught to discipline with clear, firm, consistent, and appropriate consequences, their children display less noncompliant and aggressive behavior (Arnold, O'Leary, Wolff, & Acker, 1993). In the reviewed materials, the children often reported that they did not know why they were being punished.

Parenting Style and the Use of Corporal Punishment

Research has identified several areas of child functioning that often beget parental corporal punishment. It is more likely that a child will receive corporal punishment when he or she is perceived to be difficult to handle, fighting, aggressive, disobedient, or lying (Herrenkohl, Herrenkohl, & Egolf, 1983; Muller, 1996).

Drawing upon the behavioral science literature, studies indicate that more than 90% of young children receive physical discipline (Bendersky & Lewis, 1999). The definition of a spanking is a limited number of blows to the buttock as a means of discipline (Hyman, 1996). Parents punish most when children are perceived as out of control, disobedient, and disrespectful (Graziano, Hamblen & Plante, 1998). Parents have been reported to correct their young children's behavior as often as every 6–8 minutes (Minton, Kagan, & Levine, 1971). Corporal punishment is used on average less than once a month with young children (Straus, 1994) and constitutes only a small proportion of discipline parents use on a daily basis (Gershoff, Miller, & Holden, 1999).

Spanking is not recommended for children younger than 2 because of the risk of physical injury and not recommended with older children and adolescents because it has been found ineffective in managing their behavior and associated with increased risk for dysfunction and aggression. There are limited data to suggest that spanking preschool-age children with behavior problems may increase the effectiveness of less aversive disciplinary techniques (Consensus Statements, 1996) but no data to suggest that spanking older children produces positive behavior change.

In examining the potential risk to which a child may be exposed if returned to his or her parent's home, one may need to obtain information about the following variables associated with the use of corporal punishment.

FREQUENCY OF PUNISHMENT

The research examining corporal punishment in general and spanking in particular identifies the dimension of *frequency* of punishment as salient (e.g., Bugental, Lewis, Lin, Lyon, & Kopeikin, 2000). Typically, parents who spank their children tend to report a limited number of strikes per episode (Hyman, 1996).

POWER BOUTS VERSUS SINGLE ACTS OF NONCOMPLIANCE

Discipline episodes and the need for parents to undertake disciplinary action are often part of a stream of interactions that can vary along several dimensions (Ritchie, 1999). For example, discipline episodes can vary in the type of child noncompliance, the parenting goal, the length of the episode, or intensity. Some effective discipline episodes may be short, while others may involve a longer interactive process in which the parent and child become locked in a battle of wills (Ritchie, 1999). These longer interactive disciplinary episodes have been called *power relations bouts* (Holden, 1983), *conflicts* (Eisenberg, 1992), and *coercive cycles* (Patterson, 1982). In contrast, single noncompliance episodes are short and consist of only a single parenting response (Ritchie, 1999).

Power bouts appear to differ from single noncompliance episodes in several ways. First, power bouts may be common events for children, representing important developmental processes. Second, power bouts form a pattern of noncompliant behaviors and cognitions, whereas no such pattern develops in single-act transgressions (Ritchie, 1999). Third, power bouts are likely to give rise to changes in how parents think about their noncompliant child. When children engage in power bouts, it is more likely that parenting behaviors and cognitions become more negative toward the child and his or her behavior, leading to a greater likelihood of quickly interpreting behavioral missteps as noncompliance. Finally, power bouts tend to lead to more frequent, more intense, and more powerful means of parental discipline. A parent who engages in power bout struggles with his or her 4-year-old might be seen as placing the child at greater risk than if the episodes of child transgression are single episodes. As Ritchie (1999) points out, parent–child interactions and cognitions within the episode of transgression need to be carefully evaluated.

CHILD-RELATED AGGRESSIVENESS AND PARENTAL RESPONSE

An important factor in the literature is the degree to which preschool children display noncompliant behavior. Preschool children, especially boys, tend to display a higher rate of physically aggressive behaviors such as hitting, slapping, and pushing than older children. Research indicates that parents of preschoolers are more likely to respond with frustration and anger when they observe their children display noncompliant behaviors characterized by aggressive acting out.

Parents' Negative View of Their Children

There seems to be a link between parents' negative attributions of their child and risk for child abuse. Some researchers have suggested that domestic violence promotes a negative view of the child for both parents, which then increases the risk of child abuse for both parents (McGuigan, Vuchinich, & Pratt, 2000).

McGuigan and colleagues (2000) suggest that evidence for parts of this model is found in studies that demonstrate associations between certain parenting characteristics and increased risk of child maltreatment. For example, abusive mothers find infant signals and cries more disruptive than do nonabusive mothers. Abusive parents have been reported to judge their children's behavior more harshly than do nonabusive parents, and they perceive their children's behavior more negatively than do outside observers.

Parents' unrealistic expectations regarding their children's behavior increases parents' negative attributions toward their children (Azar, 1997). Parental conflict characterized by verbal arguments in the parents' relationship indirectly affects children through negative changes in the quality of the parent–child relationship (Fauber & Long, 1991). Other parenting characteristics correlated with negative outcomes for children include the perception of children as difficult or demanding (Gelles & Cornell, 1985) and diminished parental acceptance of children (Krishnakumar, Buehler, & Barber, 2003).

Research on social cognition has found that parents' attributions to their children are affected by exposure to domestic violence. Conflict between parents significantly increases their negative attributions of other family members (Fincham & Bradbury, 1990a, 1990b). Violent interactions between parents affect other family members and family relationships (Finchman, Beach, Arias, & Brody, 1998; Ehrensaft et al., 2006; Kitzmann, Gaylord, Holt, & Kenny, 2003), and parent attributions about one another are related to the attributions they make about their children (McGuigan et al., 2000).

Parents' Family of Origin

From early childhood, the child's experience of family relations, especially parenting and the relationship between parents, appears to influence his or her capacity for self-regulation of emotions and behavior and expectations about the meaning of interpersonal relationships (Gilliom, Shaw, Beck, Schonberg, & Lukon, 2002; Kopp, 1989). Children who have experienced parents who are appropriately responsive develop expectations that their needs will be met in interpersonal relationships (Bowlby, 1969) and may develop skills that allow them to cope more adaptively with negative emotions (Carlson & Sroufe, 1995). Children who have experienced parental rejection or maltreatment tend to have hostile attribution biases and social problem-solving deficiencies (Dodge, Bates, & Pettit, 1990). They appear to learn to anticipate and anxiously avoid rejection and to generalize this anticipation to interpersonal contexts beyond that with the maltreating parent (Downey & Feldman, 1996).

Early maltreatment may have the most detrimental and long-lasting effects on children's social information-processing patterns (Dodge, 1991) because these patterns are usually formed during the first 8 years of life (Dodge & Price, 1994). Maltreated children appear to be more prone to rejection by their peers because of deficiencies in interpersonal social skills. Rejection by their peers increases the likelihood that these children will gravitate to an aggressive, deviant peer group. As adolescents and emerging adults, they select their romantic partners from these groups of peers who are deficient in terms of interpersonal skills (Feiring & Furman, 2000) and experience conflicted romantic relationships (Downey & Feldman, 1996). Early child maltreatment therefore may be one pathway to involvement in abusive relationships (Wolfe, Wekerle, Reitzel-Jaffe, & Lefebvre, 1998).

Adults who experienced as children a more generally hostile, maladaptive parenting history may be at increased risk to abuse their children, and adults who experienced as children punishment that was excessively physical, power assertive, and inconsistent may be at increased risk for behavior problems, aggression, and interpersonal difficulties (Cohen & Brooks, 1995; Ehrensaft et al., 2006; Fergusson & Lynskey, 1995; Loeber & Stouthamer-Loeber, 1986). Excessively coercive punishment may serve as a model for coercive conflict resolution that is learned and generalized from the parent–child relationship to the romantic partner relationship.

Exposure to violence between parents may teach children that violence is an acceptable or effective means of resolving conflicts with partners (Jouriles, Norwood, McDonald, & Peters, 2001; Jouriles, McDonald, Norwood, & Ezell, 2001). Ehrensaft and colleagues (2006) hypothesize that the common thread linking childhood maltreatment, punitive parenting, and exposure to violent parental conflict may reside in children's significantly disrupted relationships with caregivers. They write:

> Such disruptions result in emotion regulation deficiencies, faulty social information processing, and hostile expectations about the meaning of relationships; these deficiencies may in turn increase the risk for aggressive behavior in childhood and across the lifespan [citation omitted]. Ultimately, the continuity of oppositional, ag-

gressive behavior across the lifespan may account for the relationships among child maltreatment, punishment, exposure to domestic violence, and partner abuse. (p. 742)

Patterns of emotional and behavioral self-regulation first learned and reinforced within the family are believed to be applied to early peer interactions (Gilliom et al., 2002). With repetition, these peer interaction patterns are reinforced and become reliable means for coping with emotional challenges and needs. Peer interactions in middle childhood and adolescence provide repeated opportunities to practice and shape conflict resolution skills (Hartup, 1996) that will later be applied to romantic relationships (Connolly & Goldberg, 1999). When a child's interpersonal skills are aggressive and inconsistent with those normatively displayed by his or her peers, it becomes increasingly likely that the child will be rejected by peers (Dishion, Patterson, Stoolmiller, & Skinner, 1991). Such rejection, coupled with continued parental reinforcement of coercive interpersonal skills (Cohen & Brooks, 1995; Dishion, Andrews, et al., 1995), will likely limit future opportunities for learning constructive means of relating to others (Ehrensaft et al., 2006).

Aggressive and rejected children tend to gravitate toward a deviant peer group by early adolescence (Dishion et al., 1991). The deviant peer group serves as a training ground for antisocial and violent behavior from middle to late adolescence (Dishion, Andrews, & Crosby, 1995) and increases the risk of substance abuse (Dishion, Capaldi, Spracklen, & Li, 1995), a factor that has been strongly linked to partner violence in adults (Murphy, O'Farrell, Fals-Stewart, & Feehan, 2001).

When an adolescent initiates his or her first romantic experiences, interpersonal skills and expectations about the nature of close relationships are well established within both family and peer contexts (Connolly & Goldberg, 1999). Peer groups also serve to provide feedback to adolescents about appropriate standards of behavior within romantic relationships, including partner selection, sexual behavior, and the pace of intimacy (Brown, 1999).

At least in the case of males, continued association with the deviant peer group may continue to affect relationship functioning negatively by reinforcing hostile attitudes toward women. In antisocial males, peer reinforcement of hostile talk about women has been observed and predicts aggression toward partners in young adulthood (Capaldi, Dishion, Stoolmiller, & Yoerger, 2001). Deviant peer groups bring together individuals with histories of aggressive behavior, an absence of models of interpersonal relationships as responsive and nurturing, and ineffectual conflict resolution skills.

For the evaluator, it is critically important to obtain a thorough family history of each parent, including information about early parenting history, early peer group involvement, family and peer group values, and other related factors that will help the evaluator understand the context of family and peer-relationship history that the parent brings to the current custodial context.

Postdivorce Father Involvement

While school-age and preadolescent children are beginning to develop peer and social relationships outside the home (Bray, 1991; Collins, Madsen, & Susman-Stillman, 2002), family relationships are usually the primary influence on their developing self-concepts and competence (Santrock & Yussen, 1987; Teti & Candelaria, 2002). This section describes current research findings about the importance of postdivorce contact between children and their fathers. We include a section on the importance of children maintaining postdivorce contact with their fathers because in almost 90% of divorces nationwide, mothers retain residential custody and fathers are the noncustodial parent. We also include this section because of what we believe to be misinformation contained in some recent court decisions (*Burgess v. Burgess*, 1996) and published literature (Wallerstein & Tanke, 1996) that indicated the lack of research support for the role of an active, involved father in postdivorce families.

Effects of Father Involvement in Children's Emotional Adjustment

Relationships between fathers and children following divorce often leave children feeling lonely and vulnerable (Wallerstein & Kelly, 1980). Children depend on having a continued relationship with both parents (Wallerstein & Blakeslee, 1989; Wallerstein & Kelly, 1980). Limited father contact affects various aspects of children's lives such as self-esteem, scholastic achievement, emotional stability, and psychological well-being (Bauserman, 2002; Cockett & Tripp, 1994; Wallerstein & Kelly, 1980).

Seltzer (1988) reports that research indicates most fathers and children who are separated from each other face barriers to continued interaction. In another study, Seltzer, Schaeffer, and Hong-Wen Charng (1989) report that children recover more rapidly from the emotional trauma of their parents' separation when they maintain close ties with their fathers. They also found that fathers' economic and social involvement with their children diminished some of the negative consequences of living with a single mother. Fathers who have frequent contact with their children are also more likely to discuss the children with their mother, and fathers who regularly visit their children are most likely to have a voice in major child-rearing decisions (Seltzer, 1991). When both parents share the social and economic responsibilities of child care, children appear to adapt better to their changed living arrangements than when mothers bear these responsibilities alone. The continued involvement of nonresidential fathers in families where mothers maintain physical custody is an important mediating factor in the adjustment and well-being of children of divorce (Ahrons & Miller, 1993).

Father Involvement and Prosocial Behavior

Fathers have much to offer their children in many areas, including career development, moral development, and sex role identification (Dudley, 1996). Seltzer (1991) reports a similar finding about the relationship between nonresidential fathers who spent time with their children and the development of moral judgment. Pruett (1987) reports that when both boys and girls are reared with engaged fathers, they demonstrate a greater ability to take initiative and evidence self-control, and Blankenhorn (1995) reports that children, *especially boys*, raised in a father-absent home, are more likely to behave in more aggressive ways. Fathers play the role of turning a boy's natural aggressiveness toward prosocial community and family needs. Without the influence of the father, boys' unchecked aggressiveness tends to turn toward antisocial behavior.

Father Involvement and Development of Empathy

Koestner, Franz, and Weinberger (1990) found that the single most important childhood factor in developing empathy is paternal involvement. Fathers who spent time alone with their kids performing routine child care at least twice a week raised children who were the most compassionate adults. Similar findings were reported by Bernadett-Shapiro, Ehrensaft, and Shapiro (1996), who found that fathers who participated more in child care had sons who were more empathic than sons whose fathers did not participate often in child care.

Father Involvement and Children's Educational Involvement

Children are more likely to get mostly A's and less likely to repeat a grade or be expelled if fathers are highly involved in their schools, according to a recent study by the U.S. Department of Education (1999) on fathers' involvement in their children's schools.

Summary of the U.S. Department of Education's Report

This report provided national data on the extent to which fathers and mothers are involved in their children's schools and the relationship of that involvement to five measures of how children are doing in school. Involvement in school was measured by the number of different types of activities parents had participated in since the beginning of the school year: (1) attending a general school meeting, (2) attending a regularly scheduled parent–teacher conference, (3) attending a school or class event, and (4) volunteering at the school. Parents were said to have low involvement in their children's schools if they had done none or only one of the four activities. They were categorized as having moderate involvement if they had done two of the activities. They were said to be highly involved in their children's schools if they had done three or more of the activities. In this section, we present the major conclusions that can be drawn from the report and discuss data limitations and suggestions for future research. Although some of the specifics of the analyses are lost when generalizations are made, taken together the results suggest the following broad conclusions.

1. The involvement of fathers, as well as mothers, in their children's schools is important for children's achievement and behavior. *Children do better in school when their fathers are involved in their schools, regardless of whether their fathers live with them.* The importance of parents' involvement in their children's education has been recognized for many years. Policymakers, school administrators, and families often assumed this means that *mothers'* involvement in schools is important. This assumption has some basis in truth, in the sense that mothers are more likely than fathers to be highly involved in their children's schools, and the extent of their involvement is strongly related to children's school performance and adjustment; however, fathers' involvement is also important.

In two-parent families, the involvement of fathers exerts a distinct and independent influence on whether children have ever repeated a grade, get mostly A's, enjoy school, and participate in extracurricular activities, even after controlling for mothers' involvement in school and other potentially confounding factors. In father-only families, fathers' involvement increases the likelihood that their children get mostly A's and reduces the likelihood that their children have ever been suspended or expelled. The involvement of nonresident fathers in their children's schools reduces the likelihood that their children have ever been suspended or expelled and that they have ever repeated a grade, even after controlling for the resident mothers' level of involvement and other factors.

2. *Fathers in two-parent families have relatively low levels of involvement in their children's schools.* Nearly half of fathers in two-parent families had participated in none or only one of the four school activities since the beginning of the school year. In contrast, only 21% of mothers in two-parent families, 26% of mothers in mother-only families, and 29% of fathers in father-only families had participated in none or only one of the four school activities. Structural factors, such as work commitments, do not account for fathers in two-parent families having low levels of involvement because the data reveal that single fathers with custody of their children have levels of involvement that approach those of mothers. Rather, it appears that two-parent families divide the tasks of their households so that mothers assume greater responsibility for child-related duties, including involvement in their children's schools. The low participation rates of fathers in two-parent families offer schools an opportunity to increase overall parental involvement. By targeting fathers, schools may be able to make greater gains in parental involvement than by targeting mothers or parents in general. Because mothers already exhibit relatively high levels of participation

in their children's schools, there is less room to increase their involvement. Fathers in two-parent families exhibit a tendency as their children grow older to become or remain involved in two activities: attending class or school events and volunteering at their children's schools. Schools could encourage this tendency by offering fathers more opportunities for participation in these two activities. For example, schools could offer fathers more opportunities to coach sports teams, drama clubs, or other extracurricular activities; develop special orientation events aimed at fathers; or ask fathers to talk to students about their work or about specific skills, hobbies, or interests that they have. Because many fathers do not have the flexibility of being available during school hours, opportunities for involvement in the evenings or weekends might also help increase their involvement, as well as that of working mothers.[1]

3. *Single mothers and fathers are involved in their children's schools.* Single mothers and single fathers exhibit levels of involvement in their children's schools nearly as high as mothers in two-parent families. Forty-nine percent of single mothers and 46% of single fathers are highly involved in their children's schools compared to 56% of mothers in two-parent families. Studies have repeatedly found that parental involvement is higher in two-parent than in single-parent families. While true, those findings do not acknowledge the extent to which single parents are involved in their children's schools. When the comparisons are based on parents instead of families, the extent to which single parents are involved in their schools is clear. The reason that single-parent families have lower levels of involvement than two-parent families is primarily due to the fact that there is only one parent in the household to be involved.

4. *Children benefit when their nonresident fathers participate in their schools, not when their fathers just maintain contact with them.* The active participation of nonresident fathers in their children's schools is strongly related to children's behavior as measured by whether the children had ever been suspended or expelled and whether they had ever repeated a grade. Children who see their nonresident fathers but whose fathers do not participate in any of their school activities do no better on any of the outcomes than children who have not had contact with their fathers in more than a year or who have never had contact with their fathers. The reason that existing studies are inconclusive as to the importance of nonresident fathers for their children's lives may be because days of contact are often used to measure involvement. The results from this study indicate that it is not contact per se that is important but active participation in children's school lives that matters when it comes to educational success.

5. School climate is related to parental involvement. *Mothers and fathers are more likely to be highly involved in their children's schools if the schools welcome parental involvement and make it easy for parents to be involved.* Involvement is also higher if classroom and school discipline are maintained and if teachers and students respect each other. School climate influences parental involvement even after controlling for school size and type (public or private).

6. *Limitations of the data.* There are two limitations of the data that need to be recognized. First, the Father Involvement Study is a cross-sectional survey, and, as such, it is not possible to establish definitively the direction of causation for observed associations. For example, fathers may be more likely to be highly involved because their children are doing well, *or* their children may be doing better because their fathers are highly involved. Second, the information about children's school experiences and school climate is based on parents' reports. It is possible that parents who are highly involved are more positive about how their children are doing and about the schools their children attend, which could account for some of the observed association between parental involvement and student outcomes and between parental involvement and school climate. It is unlikely that a tendency for highly involved parents to be more positive about their children's school experiences or schools is a major explanation of the findings because the association between fathers' and mothers' involvement and student outcomes is also apparent for more objective measures (e.g., grade repetition).

This study also found that children in grades 6 through 12 were more likely to enjoy school when their nonresidential father was moderately to highly involved in their school than if he had contact with them but did not participate in any of the activities (this often happens when a mother relocates). Involved nonresidential fathers tend to influence their children to enjoy school during these years. Nonresidential fathers' involvement in their children's school also tends to influence their children's involvement in extracurricular activities.

Other Findings

The results of the U.S. Department of Education study (1999) have been supported in other work. Using a sample of 4,499 children ages 7–12, Tucker, Marx, and Long (1998) report that children who were not living with both biological parents *and* who moved from one neighborhood to another tended to display lower educational performance than children living with their biological, married parents. Children living with only one parent have been reported to achieve lower grade point averages, lower college aspirations, poorer attendance records, and higher dropout rates than children living with both parents (McLanahan & Sandfur, 1994). These researchers also report that family disruption increases the risk of dropping out of high school, on average, by 150% for whites, 76% for blacks, and 100% for Hispanics. Children living in single-parent or stepfamilies report lower educational expectations on the part of their parents, less monitoring of their schoolwork by their parents, and less overall supervision of social activities (Astore & McLanahan, 1991). Biller and Kimpton (1997), in summarizing the literature on the effects on academic performance of school-age children and fathers' involvement state, "Taken together, these results suggested that involved and available fathers can have an immense impact on their children's academic performance" (p. 146).

Organizing the Advisory Report around Parenting Competencies

We end this chapter with a list of factors that we recommend evaluators consider when assessing parenting competencies. Over the years, we have categorized parenting behaviors that the previously cited research suggests facilitate effective post-divorce adjustment in children. These parenting categories can be used to organize information gathered during the evaluation process. This is not a definitive list. We urge the reader to develop a list of factors consistent with his or her understanding of the literature. The factors presented below have been useful to us in the preparation of reports and we recognize that other competent professionals may articulate a different set of criteria that may be supported by the literature.

Positive Emotional Attachment

An important dimension in developing healthy relationships with children (as well as adults) is the ability to form positive emotional attachments. Positive emotional attachments are characterized by appropriate presentation of self without distortion, behaviors of empathy, understanding, multiple perspective taking, and knowledge and use of appropriate physical and verbal behaviors demonstrated as hugging, kissing, talking softly, etc.

Bonding and Attachment

Bonding and attachment are very important for children, but they are distinct processes. Bonding refers to the parent's psychological tie to the child that usually occurs during the initial months of the child's life. Attachment is the relationship *between* parent and child. Parents must display behaviors that establish and maintain secure attachment between child and parent.

Clear Boundaries between Parent and Child

Parents take responsibility for the setting of appropriate boundaries among children and between themselves and their children. Good parenting includes appropriate modulation of intimacy and is characterized by the development and maintenance of interpersonal closeness that feels comfortable to the parents and the child and is consistently experienced. Good parenting avoids the extremes of both psychological closeness and distance. A good parent also sets clear boundaries between the child and the environment, acting as a buffer between the child and environmental challenges with which the child is unprepared to deal (Derdeyn et al., 1982; Schutz et al., 1989).

Clear Parental Priorities

Good parenting includes the ability to identify and understand the child's needs and, when appropriate, to place the needs of the child before one's own (Ackerman & Schoendorf, 1992; Rohman et al., 1987; Schutz et al., 1989).

Accurate Perceptions of Child

Parents must be able accurately to understand the educational, physical, emotional, and social needs of their children. They must be able to see beyond their beliefs about what the children need and respond to the real needs of the children.

Knowing the Child's Strengths and Weaknesses

Good parenting includes knowledge of the child's strengths and weaknesses. Each child in a family is different from his or her siblings. A good parent is aware of these differences, respects them, and supports them for each child (Ackerman, 1995; Ackerman & Schoendorf, 1992; Rohman et al., 1987).

Communication Skills

Parents need to be able to communicate with their children in an effective, clear, and honest manner. They must also provide an environment in which children learn how to communicate their thoughts and feelings in increasingly complex ways as they develop. Parents need to query their children and facilitate conversations in a manner that promotes increased cognitive sophistication.

Emotionally, children need to feel that their parents understand them and care for them. This understanding and caring needs to be communicated along several relevant dimensions, including verbal statements and acts of physical affection.

Expressive versus Restrictive Use of Language

Research shows that children who are exposed to more verbally interactive parents tend to produce more complex sentence structures and, in turn, assist in the establishment of concept development. This is sometimes referred to as *elaborative language usage* (see Chapter 7).

Elaborative or talker families (Walker, 1999) are more apt to give objects names, thereby increasing both vocabulary and the child's ability to discriminate objects in his or her environment. Elaborative families tend to articulate their thoughts and attempt to make meanings clear and encourage their children to do the same. Parents who display an elaborative style assist their children in recalling and recounting shared past experiences by confirming children's correct memories and using questions as prompts to help build a more complex and complete narrative about their life experiences.

In contrast, nonelaborative families, or pointer families (Walker, 1999), engage in less instruction with their children about the nature of objects and persons. Such families tend to use more pronouns, are less specific, and, in their conversations, take more for granted about what the listener knows. Parents who display a nonelaborative style tend not to offer support to their children in recalling and recounting shared experiences. They tend not to use questions as prompts and ask the same question repeatedly in attempts to get the "correct" response.

It is believed that, overall, a nonelaborative style of parental communication results in children developing poorer communication skills and vocabulary, less inquisitiveness about their environment, and a more passive approach to learning in general.

Nurturing Self-Esteem and Self-Efficacy

Good parenting includes the development and nurturing of independence, individuality, social responsibility, and self-confidence. Positive self-esteem is encouraged when parents direct their children's behavior toward more prosocial actions and the children feel a degree of freedom when making choices.

Good parenting inspires positive self-esteem when parents set firm, clear, and consistent standards of behavior. Children develop positive self-esteem when they are expected to behave in mature and respectful ways and when the rights of both parents and children are recognized (Ackerman, 1995; Maccoby & Martin, 1983; Maccoby & Mnookin, 1992; Schutz et al., 1989).

Moral Reasoning and Display of Moral Behavior

Good parenting includes the teaching of socially appropriate behavior and respect for the rules governing society. Teaching respect for social norms helps teach children about moral behavior within our society. Most courts are not interested in making judgments about particular moral philosophies, providing these philosophies do not place the child at risk, but they are standard bearers for social propriety and proper behavior and believe parents have a responsibility to teach their children about proper social behavior. Parents also have a responsibility to be role models for their children (Lykken, 1998).

Good Role Model

A good role model teaches the child about limit setting, rule following, and respect of self and others (Schetky & Benedek, 1980).

Parental Ability to Meet Needs of the Child

Four factors—emotional, cognitive, cultural, and physical—are of importance in determining the goodness of fit between the parenting capacities demonstrated by each parent and the psychological and developmental needs of each child. Evaluators need to examine how each parent is able to identify each child's needs and is able to appropriately provide ways to meet the child's needs. Evaluators should investigate the parent's ability to meet the needs of the child in a manner that is best for the child. Sometimes, parents correctly identify their child's needs yet provide for those needs in ways that reflect how the adult would want those needs met rather than the child. One way to assess parental ability to meet the needs of the child is to assess parenting style, as described below.

Individual Parenting Style

Parenting style is a major but often underassessed factor in post-divorce parent–child relationships development in divorced families. An authoritative parenting style is considered the most supportive of children's best psychological interests (Kelly & Emery, 2003). As discussed earlier in this chapter, an authoritative parenting style is characterized by responsiveness to children's needs, explanation and negotiation of discipline and decisions, and appropriate monitoring of children's behavior. Authoritative parenting is associated with more satisfactory post-divorce adjustment in children. (See discussion of parenting style dimensions presented earlier in the chapter.)

Parenting Knowledge

Parents need to understand basic principles of child development as those principles relate to the children's stages of development. Each parent needs to learn about their child's specific stage of child development and the parenting behaviors that are most likely to facilitate the child's growth along the relevant dimensions.

Parenting knowledge may include basic understanding of book-based child development and/or experience-based child development. Evaluators may wish to investigate how each parent has come to his or her understanding of the child's needs, with whom the parent consults when faced with questions about his or her child's behavior, and how the parent integrates such information with the information provided by the other parent.

Parenting Skills

Parents need to display at least a minimal level of parenting skill in their interactions with the child. Collateral information may be useful to evaluators as they endeavor to formulate opinions concerning how each parent displays these skills outside of the evaluation context.

Interpersonal Factors

Parents must facilitate their children's interpersonal and social development. They must help their children develop peer group membership, provide opportunities for them to participate in school and community activities, and help create positive sibling relationships within the family.

Parental Support for the Child's Relationship with the Other Parent

Most state BICS indicate that children are best served when they establish and maintain strong, secure attachments with each parent. Many state best interests statutes allude to this. Disruptions in child–parent attachments may cause the child significant short- and long-term injury to children. It is important for parents to appreciate their children's need to establish and maintain close, healthy relations with both parents. This requires that parents effectively manage whatever post-divorce anger and conflict remain.

Involvement of Extended Family

Successful post-divorce adjustment in children requires more than a healthy relationship with each parent. It also requires that children be encouraged to become involved in their extended families, sharing family experiences and building strong intra- and interfamilial relationships. Parents need to support their children in developing and maintaining relationships with both sides of the family.

Parental Conflict

Children exposed to high levels of interparental conflict have significantly more behavioral problems. Conflict interferes with the ability of parents to work together and coparent their children (Amato, 2000; Amato & Booth, 2001). The manner in which each parent handles conflict with the other parent is an important factor in considering placement recommendations.

Interparental Parenting Style

Children are best served when their parents are able to engage in direct, open, and cooperative dialogues about them. Each parent needs to understand and be aware of each child's needs, interests, and wants and to communicate his or her experience with the children to the other parent in order to provide for continuity in the way parents address various parent–child issues. Some parents' communication is characterized by conflict and others by disengagement. Evaluators need to identify the type of interparental parenting style.

Parental Supervision

Parents must supervise their children in a manner that facilitates the development of autonomy while addressing safety issues and teaching responsible social behavior. Good parenting includes the ability accurately to observe the behaviors and interpret the feelings of both child and self. Good parents are able to communicate these observations to their children in an empathic, sensitive, and understanding manner (Ackerman & Schoendorf, 1992; Bray, 1991; Fisher & Fisher, 1986).

Discipline

Good parenting includes an ability to sanction appropriately when necessary. Appropriate discipline facilitates healthy psychological development in children. Parental discipline takes many different forms and is often dictated by prevailing cultural expectations. A good disciplinarian sets appropriate limits, consistently takes appropriate action when those limits are not respected, and provides guidance about the ways in which inappropriate behaviors may be altered (Ackerman, 1995; Bray, 1991; Derdeyn et al., 1982; Stahl, 1994; Schutz et al., 1989).

Summary

In this chapter, we examined parenting competencies from several different perspectives. Information about the construct of parental emotional competence and its component parts as related to understanding parental competence in general was discussed. Parenting style variables, including behavioral correlates of authoritarian parenting, were described. The importance of noncustodial parent–child contact was discussed. The chapter concluded with a list of parenting style factors to consider when writing a child custody report.

Note

1. The reason that there were fewer differences in student outcomes from single fathers' involvement in schools compared to fathers in two-parent families may be because single fathers are not representative of all fathers.

CHAPTER 10

Assessment of Family Factors

Parents are responsible for creating a home environment that supports the best psychological interests of a child. In this chapter, we examine family factors associated with healthy family functioning. In the previous chapter, some of the individual factors that appear to affect a parent's ability to provide for the best psychological interests of a child were discussed. In this chapter, our attention is on family factors rather than individual factors. It is important to ask, "Are the family factors observed to be operating in each family under scrutiny similar to those family factors that have been associated with healthy family functioning?" One way to answer this question is to review the behavioral science literature about factors that appear to operate in families that place children at risk. We will call these *risky family factors.*

How do we define a healthy family? Repetti, Taylor, and Seeman (2002) suggest that

> good health begins early in life. In the first years of childhood, the family is charged with responsibilities for the care and development of the child. In healthy families, children learn that they can count on the environment to provide for their emotional security and their physical safety and well-being, and they acquire behaviors that will eventually allow them to maintain their own physical and emotional health independent of caregivers. From this vantage point, a healthy environment for a child is a safe environment; it provides for a sense of emotional security and social integration, and it offers certain critical social experiences that lead to the acquisition of behaviors that will eventually permit the child to engage in effective self-regulation. (p. 330)

Risky Family Factors

Repetti and colleagues (2002) argue that poor health also begins early in life. Families with certain characteristics often result in damaging outcomes for children's mental and physical health, such as overt family conflict that is displayed through recurrent episodes of anger and aggression or deficient nurturing from family relationships that are cold, unsupportive, and neglectful.

Families with these characteristics are risky because they leave their children vulnerable to a wide array of mental and physical health disorders. Risky family characteristics create a cascade of risk, beginning early in life. Families with these characteristics may create vulnerabilities or may exacerbate certain genetically based vulnerabilities that not only put children at immediate risk for adverse outcomes (as with abuse), but also lay the groundwork for long-term physical and mental health problems. Risky families create deficiencies in children's control of and expression of emotions and in their social competence. They also lead to disturbances in physiological and neuroendocrine system regulation that can have cumulative, long-term, adverse effects (Repetti et al., 2002).

Repetti and colleagues (2002) argue that

> children who grow up in risky families are also especially likely to exhibit health-threatening behaviors, including smoking, alcohol abuse, and drug abuse; the risk for promiscuous sexual activity in these children is also high. These forms of behavioral or substance abuse may represent a method of compensating for deficiencies in social and emotional development, as well as a self-medication process whereby adolescents manage the biological dysregulations produced or exacerbated by risky families. Taken together, these behavioral and biological consequences of risky family environments represent an integrated risk profile that is associated with mental health disorders across the lifespan, including depression and aggressive hostility, major chronic illnesses including hypertension and cardiovascular disease, and early death. (p. 330)

We find Repetti and colleagues' model an interesting integration of biopsychosocial factors, and we urge our colleagues to review this model and its empirical underpinnings. What drew us to their work was their identification of psychological and social factors that appear in risky families. We do not discount the potential value of a model that integrates the biological aspects of human functioning; we only note that elaboration of the biological factors is beyond the scope of this book.

Mental Health

The first factors associated with risky families we will discuss are anger and aggression. Research has demonstrated that there is a continuum of anger and aggression ranging from living with irritable and quarreling parents to being exposed to violence and abuse at home and that displays of anger and aggression show associations with mental and physical health problems in childhood with lasting effects into the adult years. The research literature overwhelmingly documents that overt conflict and aggression in the family are associated both cross-sectionally and prospectively with an increased risk for a wide variety of emotional and behavioral problems in children, including aggression, conduct disorder, delinquency and antisocial behavior, anxiety, depression, and suicide (Gelles, 1997). Empirical efforts to tie different types of maltreatment and abuse in the home to different forms of psychopathology reveal only a general association of family violence and child psychopathology (Emery & Laumann-Billings, 1998). Parenting that constrains, invalidates, and manipulates children's psychological and emotional experience and expression is also related to both internalizing and externalizing symptoms (Barber, 2002).

Families characterized by high levels of conflict, aggression, and hostility are often lacking in acceptance, warmth, and support, but there is evidence that inadequate emotional nurturance is independently associated with poor mental health outcomes. Our use of the adjectives *cold, unsupportive,* and *neglectful* covers a wide range of family characteristics and factors in the research literature, including emotional neglect of children; unresponsive or rejecting parenting; poor supervisory skills of and involvement in children's activities; poor parental availability to children's interests; lack of emotional cohesiveness, warmth, and support within the family; and experiences of alienation, detachment, or feelings of lack of acceptance by children. Research studies that assess these characteristics of family life report reliable associations between them and a broad array of mental health risks, including internalizing symptoms such as depression, suicidal behavior, and anxiety disorders (Chorpita & Barlow, 1998; Kaslow, Deering, & Racusia, 1994) and externalizing symptoms such as aggressive, hostile, oppositional, and delinquent behavior (Barber, 1996; Rothbaum & Weisz, 1994).

Whether the unit of analysis is the shared family environment or the parent–child relationship, comprehensive reviews of the research literature associate family relationships that are marked by high levels of anger and aggression or family relationships that are marked by cold, unsupportive, or neglectful parenting behaviors with mental health problems in childhood and adolescence (Repetti et al., 2002).

Physical Health

There is growing evidence that offspring of risky families have increased rates of a wide variety of physical health problems throughout life (Repetti et al., 2002). Family conflict and aggression have adverse effects on health in childhood and adulthood and on physical growth and development (Mechanic & Hansell, 1989; Montgomery, Bartley, & Wilkinson, 1997; Stein, Woolley, Cooper, & Fairburn, 1994; Walker et al., 1999; Weidner, Hutt, Connor, & Mendell, 1992).

Studies report that growing up in a cold, unsupportive, or neglectful home is also associated with poor physical health and development (Gottman, Katz, & Hooven, 1996, 1997; Wickrama, Lorenz, & Conger, 1997), including obesity in early adulthood (Lissau & Sorensen, 1994) and more serious medical conditions in midlife (Russek & Schwartz, 1997; Shaffer, Duszynski, & Thomas, 1982). Some studies find a link between cold, unsupportive, or neglectful family environments and poorer growth during infancy (M. Valenzuela, 1997), poorer general health (Gottman & Katz, 1989), and, among children with a diagnosed medical problem, less control over or more severe symptoms of the disease (Gil et al., 1987; Martin, Miller-Johnson, Kitzmann, & Emery, 1998).

In summary, research results appear consistently to support the adverse role played by two factors that exist in risky families: (1) conflict and aggression, and (2) a cold, unsupportive, or neglectful home environment.

Emotion Processing

Risky family environments also are associated with the way that children process emotions, another factor that may be implicated in the development of mental and physical health disorders. *Emotion processing* is defined as the experience, control, and expression of emotion, particularly in emotionally arousing situations. Three factors of emotion processing seem to be related to variables associated with risky family environments: emotional reactivity in emotionally arousing situations, emotion-focused coping, and emotion understanding.

Risky Family Characteristics and Emotion Processing

There appears to be an empirical link between risky family environments and the three aspects of emotion processing mentioned above. The first group of studies we discuss below are short-term reaction studies, characterized by observations of a child's immediate emotional reaction in an emotion-arousing situation.

Conflict and Aggression

Many short-term reaction studies have focused on children as they listen to or observe angry and conflictual interactions, either staged in laboratory settings or naturalistic interactions in the home. The emotional and behavioral responses of children whose home lives are characterized by conflict and aggression are then compared with the responses of children from homes with less aggression and happier marriages. The findings indicate that high levels of conflict at home sensitize children to anger. These children are reported to react with greater distress, anger, anxiety, and fear (Ballard, Cummings, & Larkin, 1993; Cummings, Zahn-Waxler, & Radke-Yarrow, 1981; Davies & Cummings, 1998; O'Brien, Margolin, John, & Krueger, 1991). Increased reactivity may result from chronic stress levels in conflictual and violent homes. Chronic or repeated stressors in the environment, such as high levels of violence and family conflict, may not allow for sufficient recovery from heightened emotional arousal. Sustained states of emotional arousal may, over time, increase reactivity. This is consistent with a model proposed by Perry and Pollard (1998) that suggests chronic stress affects neurobiological development and creates a sensitized stress-responsive system that influences arousal, emotion regulation, behavioral reactivity, and cardiovascular regulation. Thompson and Calkins (1996) suggest that hypervigilance in children from aggressive and violent homes may also contribute to increased reactivity (Repetti et al., 2002).

Emotion processing is also assessed by tasks that measure children's understanding of emotions and by self-reports of methods used to cope with stressful experiences in the past. Emotion understanding includes the ability to recognize emotional states both in self and others, the skills to express emotions in a culturally acceptable manner, and the knowledge of causal antecedents of different emotions, all factors that are integral to the processing of emotions in stressful or arousing situations. In two investigations, young children who were maltreated or whose homes were marked by high levels of anger and distress had less accurate understanding of emotions compared with their peers (Camras et al., 1988; Dunn & Brown, 1994). This may be because families with high levels of negative affect are less likely to engage in conversations about feelings (Dunn & Brown, 1994), and families with better emotion understanding in children are more likely to do so (Dunn, Brown, Slomkowski, Tesla, & Youngblade, 1991).

Although there are few studies of emotional reactivity and emotion understanding in adolescents, there is research literature on coping in adolescence. The strategies favored by teens from risky families emphasized a desire to reduce tension and escape the situation (Johnson & Pandina, 1991; Valentiner, Holahan, & Moos, 1994). Teens from high-conflict homes tried to distract their own and others' attention from interpersonal conflict (O'Brien et al., 1991). Short-term studies of younger children have found those from high-conflict homes sometimes engaged in solicitous or placating behavior (Camras & Rappaport, 1993; Cummings et al., 1981; Cummings, Pellegrini, Notarius, & Cummings, 1989). It is possible that, after repeatedly failing to change stressful events in the family through behaviors such as appeasement and placation, children growing up in angry and aggressive homes gradually abandon efforts to control difficult situations. Older children may focus, instead, on trying to escape and recover from heightened emotional arousal. In short, the legacy of growing up with high levels of overt anger and aggression at home may be not only a stronger emotional reaction in situations that involve conflict, but also a particular set of behaviors for responding in those situations (Repetti et al., 2002).

Cold, Unsupportive, and Neglectful Homes

Several studies have found that, even in very early development, deficient nurturing may be associated with dysfunctional emotion processing. Babies begin to regulate their emotional responses soon after birth, engaging in behaviors such as sucking to soothe themselves (Campos, 1998). Parental nurturing appears to facilitate the development of these primitive coping behaviors. Insecure parent–child attachment or little family cohesion or support are associated with less adaptive coping across a wide age range (Hardy, Power, & Jaedicke, 1993) and with deficiencies in emotion understanding among preschoolers (Laible & Thompson, 1998). See Chapter 8 for a more in-depth discussion of attachment processes.

Summary

Growing up in a risky family environment interferes with the development of means for processing emotions. Distress found in risky families may result in children developing high emotional reactivity, deficiencies in emotion understanding, and a reliance on unsophisticated coping responses to stressful situations. Across studies using different methodologies and age groups, findings indicate that children living in risky family environments are more likely than their peers to focus on tension reduction, distraction, and escape in stressful situations (Repetti et al., 2002).

Emotion Processing and Mental and Physical Health Outcomes

Emotion processing is also a link between risky family characteristics and adverse mental and physical health outcomes. Repetti and colleagues (2002) argue that poor regulation of emotions is implicated in more than half of the Axis I and in almost all of the Axis II psychiatric disorders in the DSM-IV (American Psychiatric Association, 1994). A small but growing research literature has tied indicators of emotion regulation both to internalizing and to externalizing symptoms in children and adolescents (Eisenberg, Fabes, & Murphy, 1996; Southam-Gerow & Kendall, 2002; Zahn-Waxler, Iannotti, Cummings, & Denham, 1990). In addition to acting as a mediator of the link between negative family environments and mental health (Valentiner et al., 1994), effective emotion processing may moderate a child's vulnerability to risky family characteristics (Katz & Gottman, 1995).

Emotion processing is also implicated in physical health, as emotional and physiological responses to stress are interrelated. For example, children who are emotionally reactive in certain situations (such as angry social interactions) are also more likely to be physiologically reactive (El-Sheikh, Cummings, & Goetsch, 1989).

Different Types of Emotional Reactivity and Health

Anger in particular appears to play a significant role in the development of coronary artery disease and hypertension, at least in some individuals (e.g., Dembroski, MacDougall, Williams, Haney, & Blumenthal, 1985; Jorgensen, Johnson, Kolodziej, & Schreer, 1996; Julkunen, Salonen, Kaplan, Chesney, & Salonen, 1994; Smith, 1992). Emotion processing may also be indirectly implicated in the onset and course of certain diseases through its link with psychopathology, particularly with respect to mental health problems that involve chronic or recurrent negative emotional states. Depression and anxiety appear to play a significant role in numerous health risks, including all-cause mortality (Martin et al., 1995). Epidemiological, psychological, and experimental evidence point to a clear dose–response relation between anxiety and coronary heart disease (Kubzansky, Kawachi, Weiss, & Sparrow, 1998). Major depression, depressive symptoms, history of depression, and anxiety have all been identified as predictors of cardiac events (Frasure-Smith, Lesperance, & Talajic, 1995), and depression is a risk factor for mortality following a myocardial infarction, independent of cardiac disease severity (Frasure-Smith et al., 1995). State depression and clinical depression also relate to sustained suppressed immunity (Herbert & Cohen, 1993).

Social Competence

Emotion processing ultimately blends into social competence. It directly affects how skilled children are at managing the often frustrating and challenging experiences they have with family and peers (Repetti et al., 2002). For example, in order to negotiate difficult social interactions, such as peer conflicts, children must learn how to respond in a socially appropriate manner while feeling frustrated and angry. The importance of emotion regulation for children's social functioning has been extensively studied, and research consistently shows that emotionally intense children who are poor regulators of their emotions are liked less by their classmates and viewed as less socially competent by observers (e.g., Cassidy, Parke, Butkovsky, & Braungard, 1992; Eisenberg et al., 1993; Gottman et al., 1996; Krevans & Gibbs, 1996). Popular and socially competent children are better able to control their angry and excited emotions in arousing situations and tend to display less overt negative emotion than other children (Hubbard & Cole, 1994). The quality of social behavior and relationships outside of the home is another factor related to risky family characteristics and social competence (Repetti et al., 2002).

Conflict and Aggression

Children living in homes with high levels of conflict and aggression have been found to have difficulty with emotion regulation. In studies, children living with hostile and aggressive parents had fewer of the positive skills that facilitate successful interactions with peers (Crockenberg & Lourie, 1996; Pettit, Dodge, & Brown, 1988) or were more likely to behave in an aggressive or antisocial manner (Hart, Nelson, Robinson, Olsen, & McNeilly-Choque, 1998; Schwartz, Dodge, Pettit, & Bates, 1997). Other studies found that sons from aggressive families were more likely to be rejected and victimized by peers (Dishion, 1990; Schwartz et al., 1997), and women who had grown up in troubled and conflicted homes had more avoidant attitudes and feelings about closeness and intimacy (Klohnen & Bera, 1998).

Cold, Unsupportive, and Neglectful Homes

Lack of warmth and nurturance is another set of factors that can have adverse effects on children's ability to form and maintain social relationships. Most studies of these factors have examined links between quality of the mother–child bond (focusing in particular on attachment security) and children's relationships with peers. The results indicate that children whose parents are less responsive, warm, and sensitive are less likely to initiate social interactions and more aggressive and critical (Brody & Flor, 1998; Hart et al., 1998; Kerns, Klepac, & Cole, 1996; Landry, Smith, Miller-Loncar, & Swank, 1998). When parents were cold, unsupportive, or neglectful, children's social relationships throughout life were more problematic and less supportive (Booth, Rose-Krasnor, McKinnon, & Rubin, 1994; Bost, Vaughn, Washington, Cielinski, & Bradbard, 1998; Kerns et al., 1996; Larose & Boivin, 1998; MacKinnon-Lewis, Starnes, Volling, & Johnson, 1997). In conclusion, the development of social competence and supportive relationships outside the family are compromised by growing up in a risky family environment.

Social Skills

There are several ways that risky families can hinder the early acquisition of social skills for initiating and maintaining friendships and for managing difficult interpersonal situations, such as those involving conflict and anger. First, young children model the social behavior that they observe in the family. Empirical evidence points to a close correspondence between social skills observed in the family and a child's behavior when interacting with peers. Children growing up in families in which complex social skills (e.g., sensitivity to the child's feelings or needs) are rarely demonstrated show fewer conflict management skills and are less sensitive and responsive with peers (Herrera & Dunn, 1997; Lindsey, Mize, & Pettit, 1997; Putallaz, 1987). Similarly, children who are the recipients of anger, aggression, and hostility from siblings and parents are described by their teachers as less socially competent and more aggressive (Carson & Parke, 1996; Stormshak et al., 1996). In addition to acting as role models, parents should engage in active efforts to shape their children's relationships and social skills through discussions of social problems and advice giving (Laird, Pettit, Mize, Brown, & Lindsey, 1994). Mothers who suggest fewer constructive techniques to solve social problems have children who have fewer social skills, engage in more aggressive and less prosocial behavior, and are less likely to generate prosocial solutions to problems (Eisenberg, Fabes, & Murphy, 1996; Mize & Pettit, 1997; Pettit et al., 1988).

Social Cognition

Social relationships in adolescence and adulthood are also shaped by aspects of social cognition first developed in childhood. On the basis of the same risky family experiences that shape social skills, children may develop and store in memory social algorithms, relationship schemas, or working models of self and others in close relationships that are activated and applied in new situations throughout life (Andersen & Berk, 1998; Bugental, 2000). For example, evidence suggests that growing up in a violent household shapes the development of the basic cognitive structures that guide social behavior and relationships in childhood and adulthood. In a study of college students, the negative effect of childhood exposure to physical aggression at home on current relationships was mediated by heightened rejection sensitivity (e.g., worries about social acceptance; Feldman & Downey, 1994). During childhood, the link between physical abuse at home and aggressive behavior with peers is partially mediated by patterns of social information processing, such as tendencies to attribute hostile motives to others, to pay less attention to relevant social cues, and to think of fewer effective behavioral responses to problematic social situations (Dodge et al., 1990).

Hostility

Hostility is an oppositional orientation toward people stemming from feelings of insecurity about oneself and negative feelings toward others (Houston & Vavak, 1991). Early family environments characterized as unsupportive, unaccepting, and conflictual contribute to the development of hostility (Houston & Vavak, 1991; Smith, Pope, Sanders, Allred, & O'Keefe, 1988; Woodall & Matthews, 1989), a link that has been documented in longitudinal studies (Matthews, Woodall, Kenon, & Jacob, 1996; Woodall & Matthews, 1993). In addition to its origins in the family environment, hostility may also have biological origins, specifically representing a psychological response to high levels of physiological reactivity (Fukudo et al., 1992; Krantz & Manuck, 1984). To the extent that hostility has a genetic basis in physiological reactivity, parents and children who share genes that predispose them to this reactivity may create and respond to the family environment in ways that foster, rather than counteract, the development of hostility.

Summary

Parents and siblings in risky families are poor models of prosocial behavior, and they do not provide other kinds of active socialization that would facilitate the early development of complex social skills. Social experiences in risky families may also contribute to social information-processing rules and biases and to mental representations of self and others that interfere with positive social interaction and the maintenance of healthy relationships. Moreover, the early and continuing impact of warped emotion processing, such as increased reactivity to anger and conflict, places added demands on the social skills of children from risky families and further impedes the development of social competence.

Social Competence and Mental and Physical Health Outcomes

Social competence is an integral component of mental health at all ages. Longitudinal studies show that school-age children who are rejected or neglected by their peers are at an increased risk for behavioral and emotional problems a few years later (Hymel, Rubin, Rowden, & Le Mare, 1990; Kupersmidt & Patterson, 1991). A lack of social integration in adults, particularly with respect to primary ties with supportive significant others, such as a spouse or children, is associated with an increased risk of depression (George, 1989). There is also a long-term association between childhood social competence and adult mental health. For example, rejected children are at an increased risk for adult psychopathology (Bagwell, Newcomb, & Bukowski, 1998; Parker & Asher, 1987).

In terms of physical health risks, social competence most clearly translates into the ability to attract and sustain social support. In more than 100 investigations, social support has been documented to reduce health risks of all kinds, affecting the likelihood of illness, the course of recovery among people who are already ill, and mortality risk more generally (House, Umberson, & Landis, 1988; Uchino, Uno, & Holt-Lunstad, 1999). Some of the social behaviors associated with risky family environments, such as a hostile interpersonal style, can also generate stress. Research suggests that conflictual social interactions may contribute as much to illness and poor health as supportive social contacts contribute to good health (e.g., Rook, 1984; Taylor, 1999). For example, hostility has been tied to high levels of low-density lipoprotein cholesterol, high levels of triglycerides, and a higher ratio of total cholesterol to high-density lipoprotein cholesterol in women (Suarez, Bates, & Harralson, 1998) as well as to the likelihood of developing coronary heart disease in adulthood (Dembroski et al., 1985). The association between hostility and cardiovascular health may be multidetermined, partly mediated by the elevated physiological reactivity that appears to be a component of hostility and partly mediated through the added stress of interpersonal conflict.

Through their impact on social competence, and the skills and cognitions it entails, childhood family environments influence the kind of interpersonal relationships that offspring have throughout life. It is through this channel, particularly because relationships can act as sources of social support and social stress, that the development of social competence in the family has a lasting impact on mental and physical health. Ewart (1991) reviewed evidence that hostile parenting produces deficiencies in social competence that foster vulnerability to emotionally charged negative interpersonal events, which, in turn, is associated with heightened cardiovascular reactivity and disease risk. With respect to mental health outcomes, evidence indicates that chronic interpersonal stress in adulthood is one of the conditions that connects exposure to family violence during childhood to recurrence of depression in adulthood (Kessler & Magee, 1994).

Substance Abuse and Risky Sexual Behavior

Adolescence brings increasing autonomy to make decisions about how and with whom to spend time. The cascade of influences impinging upon the behavior of the adolescent offspring of risky families include all of the earlier disruptions in biological regulation, emotion processing, and social competence. In this section, we discuss how a risky family environment may increase the likelihood that an adolescent will engage in behaviors that threaten his or her health. We focus on two classes of behavior—substance use (including alcohol, cigarettes, and illicit drugs) and risky sexual behavior (such as early, promiscuous, and unprotected sexual intercourse)—because of the short- and long-term risks they pose for mortality, severe illness, or serious life disruption.

The substance abuse treatment literature indicates that repair of the family social environment reduces adolescent drug use. For example, family therapy is more effective than individual or peer group counseling (Stanton & Shadish, 1997), and improvements in parenting practices over the course of family therapy are associated with reductions in drug use (S. E. Schmidt, Liddle, & Dakof, 1996). These findings highlight the important part played by the family in changing patterns of drug use, although they do not rule out the possibility that the same characteristics of a child may both undermine the development of supportive family relationships and increase his or her propensity to abuse substances (Wills, DuHamel, & Vaccaro, 1995).

Relationship to Risky Family Factors

The specific characteristics of risky families have been tied to increased rates of smoking, alcohol abuse, drug use, and risky sexual behavior in adolescence and adulthood. Some research suggests that the experience of abuse in childhood is a risk factor for these behaviors (Malinosky-Rummell & Hansen, 1993; Small & Luster, 1994). The evidence for this association is based primarily on cross-sectional analyses of data provided by a single respondent, often a retrospective description of abuse in childhood (Anda et al., 1999; Cunningham, Stiffman, Doré, & Earls, 1994; Dietz et al., 1999; Felitti et al., 1998; Harrison, Hoffmann, & Edwall, 1989). Studies with stronger research designs have found increased rates of alcohol abuse among adult women who grew up in conflictual or abusive homes (Widom & White, 1997).

Why are children who grow up in risky families more likely to abuse substances and engage in risky sexual behaviors? First, research indicates that some of the most potent ingredients in a neglectful home are inadequate parental knowledge about and inadequate parental supervision of adolescents' activities. In homes with less parental monitoring and more permissiveness, adolescents engage in more frequent sexual activity and more risky sexual behavior (Jemmott & Jemmott, 1992; Metzler, Noell, Biglan, Ary, & Smolkowski, 1994; Miller, Forehand, & Kotchick, 1999; Romer et al., 1994; Small & Luster, 1994) and smoke more (Biglan, Duncan, Ary, & Smolkowski, 1995). In a 6-year longitudinal study, the association between a lack of support and nurturance at home and adolescents' increased use of alcohol was mediated by the extent to which teens told their parents about their whereabouts and activities (Barnes, Reifman, Farrell, & Dintcheff, 2000). This finding is consistent with the suggestion that most measures of parental monitoring assess open channels of communication between parent and child that reflect child disclosure at least as much as parental efforts to control and manage children (Stattin & Kerr, 2000).

The direct impact of neglectful parents on opportunities for alcohol and drug use may be compounded through a concomitant increase in the influence exerted by peers. For example, longitudinal data suggest that the effect of peer drug use is much weaker when parenting is authoritative (i.e., when parents are involved, make demands, and supervise while demonstrating acceptance and warmth; Mounts & Steinberg, 1995) and that the impact of inadequate parental monitoring on problem behaviors, such as substance abuse and risky sexual behavior, is partially mediated by increased association with peers who engage in antisocial and deviant behavior (Ary, Duncan, Biglan, et al., 1999).

Perhaps most important, risky sexual behavior and substance abuse may compensate for deficiencies in the biological, social, and emotional functioning of adolescents from risky families. Adolescents who engage in risky sexual behavior are more likely to smoke cigarettes and abuse substances, and there is an association between drinking, smoking, and other drug use (Biglan et al., 1990; Capaldi, Crosby, & Stoolmiller, 1996; Donovan & Jessor, 1985; Kandel &

Yamaguchi, 1993; Millstein & Moscicki, 1995; Shiffman et al., 1994; Tubman, Windle, & Windle, 1996). These offspring may have more social problems than their peers, may be more reactive to stress (particularly interpersonal stress), and may have fewer coping strategies and sources of social support on which to draw. Early and promiscuous sexual behavior and substance use may help adolescents manage negative emotions and gain social acceptance in the absence of adequate emotion coping strategies or social skills (e.g., Aloise-Young, Hennigan, & Graham, 1996; Mayne & Buck, 1997; see Taylor, 1999, for a review).

Summary

By adolescence, the offspring of risky families must adapt to the cumulative consequences of years spent in a damaging home environment. Substance abuse and risky sexual behavior may help these adolescents compensate for their biological, emotional, and social deficiencies. These processes may be compounded by parents' inadequate knowledge about and supervision of teens' activities and by adolescents' weak internal barriers to certain risky behaviors and their greater susceptibility to peer influence. Patterns of substance abuse and problems in behavioral self-regulation during adolescence as a result of growing up in a risky family are also no doubt influenced by the dramatic hormonal changes that occur during puberty.

Socioeconomic Status, Family Characteristics, and Mental and Physical Health Risks

Low socioeconomic status (SES), an important dimension of a family's social ecology, has also been tied to all of the risky family characteristics described here (e.g., Dodge, Pettit, & Bates, 1994), and loss of SES has been associated with an increase in these family characteristics. Poor children are at heightened risk for physical mistreatment or abuse (McLoyd, 1998; Reid, Macchetto, & Foster, 1999) and exposure to family violence (Emery & Laumann-Billings, 1998; Garbarino & Sherman, 1980; U.S. Department of Justice, 1994) and are also more likely to be in family relationships lacking in warmth and support (Bradley, Corwyn, McAdoo, & Coll, 2001; McLeod & Shanahan, 1996). Both sustained poverty and descent into poverty appear to move parenting in more harsh, punitive, irritable, inconsistent, and coercive directions (Wahler, 1990). McLoyd (1998) reviewed evidence that descent into poverty precipitates marital and parent–child conflict that, in turn, alters parental behavior in a hostile and coercive direction, leading to the development of internalizing and externalizing symptoms in young children (e.g., Conger, Ge, Elder, Lorenz, & Simons, 1994; Duncan, Brooks-Gunn, & Klebanov, 1994). These parenting characteristics may evolve, in part, as a result of deficient coping strategies for managing the stressors associated with low SES. Poor families living in high-crime neighborhoods must accommodate to persistent, multiple, uncontrollable demands that require constant effort to meet immediate physical and psychological needs. Such heavy chronic burdens favor reactive coping skills and can exacerbate the negative effects of other vulnerabilities in the family (Aspinwall & Taylor, 1997; Repetti & Wood, 1997a, 1997b).

Low SES may be not only a contextual factor for understanding the development of risky families, but also an outcome of growing up in a risky family environment. Research literatures in developmental psychology, sociology, and public health relate the characteristics of risky families to a wide range of adverse adult outcomes that cluster with low SES, including low school achievement, low educational attainment (in years), low adult income, high likelihood of divorce in adulthood, low occupational status, and poor status on other indicators of life success (Power & Hertzman, 1997).

Low SES is not inevitably associated with risky family environments. Effective parenting may buffer children from the adverse effects of low SES. Cowen, Wyman, Work, and Parker (1990) found that so-called *stress-resilient* children, who had successfully weathered a variety of chronic problems (including poverty, family turmoil, illness, and violence) were characterized by nonseparation from the primary caregiver during infancy, positive parent–child relations during preschool and elementary years, a strong sense of parenting efficacy by the parents, and parental use of reasoned, age-appropriate, consistent disciplinary practices (see also Masten, Morison, Pellegrini, & Tellegen, 1990; Rutter, 1990; Werner & Smith, 1982).

Physical Health and Safety Factors

Recently, Hynan (2002) described several physical health and safety factors to be assessed in child custody evaluations. He rightly criticizes previous custody texts (e.g., Ackerman, 1995; Bricklin, 1995; Gould, 1998; Schutz et al., 1989; Stahl, 1994, 1999) for not including "substantive guidance about evaluating physical health considerations, except child abuse" (p. 74).

Physical Health Factors

Hynan (2002) identifies two main categories of risk to children from exposure to tobacco smoke. Secondhand smoke, or what he called environmental tobacco smoke (ETS), "places children at significantly higher risk for developing a variety of illness" (p. 75), and children who are exposed to parents who model smoking tobacco are at an increased likelihood to smoke when they are older.

Hynan (2002) cites research indicating that exposure to ETS significantly raises the risk to children of a number of common and serious childhood illnesses. These include, but are not limited to, asthma, cough, middle-ear disease, and lower respiratory infection such as bronchitis and pneumonia. Children exposed to ETS are also more likely to receive medical interventions to treat the physical symptoms of exposure. He writes:

> The risk for asthma is 40 to 50 percent higher, and surgical removal of tonsils or adenoids is 60 to 100 percent higher for children exposed to ETS. The incidence of lower respiratory tract infection and of hospitalization for respiratory problems is 50 to 150 percent higher for ETS exposed children. . . . an examination of the numbers of children actually affected medically by ETS [is reflected by the number of office visits]. For example, between 1.3 and 2 million physician visits per year for coughs are attributable to ETS. Estimates of middle ear illnesses per year due to ETS range from 200,000 to 350,000. Asthma cases caused by ETS are estimated to range from 307,000 to 522,000 [per year]. (Hynan, 2002, p. 75)

Children who begin smoking at an early age are statistically more likely to engage in drug misuse and related behavioral problems. Hynan (2002) argues that "parental smoking may increase the risk of children and adolescents experiencing a broad range of difficulties" (p. 76).

Child Safety Factors

Unintentional injury is the single most frequent cause of death among children. It also results in a large number of hospital admissions and emergency room visits (Hynan, 2002). Parental supervision has a considerable influence on the likelihood that a child may suffer an injury. Hynan (2002) argues that separated and divorced parents may be at increased risk to have an unintentional injury happen to their child because there is often less parental supervision due to only one parent being present in the home.

The highest rates of injury death for infants are by suffocation. A common cause of injury death for children 2 to 4 years old is drowning. Motor vehicle accidents are the most common cause of injury death for older children (Hynan, 2002).

Citing research about the amount of supervision needed as a function of a child's age, Hynan (2002) writes:

> Preschool children . . . require constant supervision, and early elementary school children . . . require nearly constant to very close supervision. More risky physical domains, such as being near a street, necessitated closer supervision than safer ones, such as being inside the home. . . . children appear unable to make adequate judgments about traffic until about age 7 or 8, [which] suggests that they need close supervision around motor vehicles until that age. (p. 77)

Recent advances in the empirical investigation of factors associated with home safety have culminated in the development of the Home Inventory of Dangers and Safety Precautions—2 (HIDSP-2; Tymchuk, Lang, Dolyniuk,

Berney-Ficklin, & Spitz, 1999). The HIDSP-2 has been found to be a useful inventory to assess home safety during a custody evaluation.

Assessment of Risky Family Factors

It is important to select psychological tests and measures that are reliable and that measure, either directly or indirectly, aspects of behaviors that are relevant to the issues before the court (Flens & Drozd, 2005). As Weiner (2003) notes, "The tests selected for inclusion in an assessment battery should provide information relevant to answering the questions that have been raised about the person being examined. . . . The administration of minimally useful tests that have little relevance to the referral question is a wasteful procedure that can result in warranted criticism" (p. 5).

We offer below several suggestions about psychological tests and measures that may be useful to consider in assessing several of the dimensions discussed in this chapter. There is no one assessment protocol that we recommend. In our respective forensic practices, we find that we often add and subtract tests based on currently available reviews, relevance to the issues of the particular case, and characteristics of the test taker. We have found useful the online service of test reviews offered by the Buros Institute of Mental Measurements, Test Reviews Online (*www.unl.edu/buros*). We also believe that there is no substitute for following journals and attending conferences where useful information about these tests and measures is often presented.

Our review of the literature on risky family factors identified several areas for evaluators to consider assessing in a child custody evaluation. The evaluation of anger and aggression might be accomplished through the use of self-report measures of anger control and anger expression such as the Aggression Questionnaire (AQ; Buss & Warren, 2000) distributed by Western Psychological Services (WPS, 800-648-8857) and the State-Trait Anger Expression Inventory–2 (STAXI-2; Speilberger, 1999) distributed by Psychological Assessment Resources (PAR, 800-331-8378). See reviews of the AQ by Brown (2003) and Kelley (2003) and of the STAXI-2 by Freeman (2002) and Klecker (2002).

Conflict and hostility between intimate partners may be measured through the Revised Conflict Tactics Scales (Straus, Hamby, & Warren, 2003), distributed by WPS. Conflict and hostility between parent and child may be measured through the Conflict Tactics Scale: Parent–Child Version (Straus et al., 2003), also distributed by WPS. Assessment of parental risk for physical child abuse may be measured using the Child Abuse Potential Inventory (CAPI) distributed by PAR. See review of the CAPI by Otto and Edens (2003).

We also find that assessment of interparental alliance and cooperation is useful. We use the Parental Alliance Measure (PAM; Abidin & Konold, 1999) distributed by PAR and the Parenting Satisfaction Scale (PSS; Guidubaldi & Cleminshaw, 1994) distributed by Psychological Corporation (PC, 800-872-

1726). See reviews of the PAM by Carlson (2003) and Clare (2003) and reviews of the PSS by Katz (2001) and Smith (2001).

Risky family factors such as parental acceptance, parental support, and parental warmth may be assessed by measures such as the Parent Child Relationship Inventory (PCRI; Gerard, 1994) distributed by WPS, the Parenting Stress Inventory (PSI; Abidin, 1995) and Stress Index for Parents of Adolescents (SIPA; Sheras, Abidin, & Konold, 1998) distributed by PAR. An assessment tool that we recently have begun to examine for use in child custody evaluations is the Parental Acceptance-Rejection Questionnaire (PARQ; Rohner, 1960). See reviews of the PCRI by Marchant and Paulson (1998), and Boothroyd (1998), and Otto and Edens (2003); reviews of the PSI by Ackerman and Kane (1998), Allison (1998), Barnes & Oehler-Stinnett (1998), and Otto and Edens (2003); and reviews of the SIPA by Jones (2001) and Swearer (2001).

We also recommend for those parents who have remarried that a measure of marital satisfaction or marital stability be administered to assess for risky family factors in the second marriage. We would suggest that you consider the Marital Satisfaction Inventory distributed by PAR and WPS and the NEO Couples' Compatibility Report distributed by PAR.

Adult and adolescent alcohol and substance abuse may be assessed using scales from the MMPI-2, MMPI-A and Millon inventories. These tests are distributed by NCS Pearson (800-627-7271) and may be supplemented by the adult and adolescent version of the Substance Abuse Subtle Screening Inventory (SASSI-3; Miller, 1997) distributed by PAR or the Michigan Alcohol Screening Test (MAST; Selzer, 1996) published by Melvin L. Selzer. See reviews of the SASSI-3 by Ken and Vace (2003) and Pittenger (2003) and reviews of the MAST by Conoley and Reese (2001) and Murdoch (2001).

When need occurs for diagnosis of substance abuse disorders and comorbid psychopathology, consider the Structured Clinical Interview for DSM-IV Axis I Disorders (First, Spitzer, Gibbon, & Williams, 1998) and for Axis II disorders (First, Spitzer, Gibbon, Williams, & Benjamin, 1998). For reviews of the Structured Clinical Interview for DSM-IV Axis I Disorders, see Werner (2001) and Widiger (2001). For reviews of the Axis II interview protocol, see Arbisi (2001) and Martin (2001). The webpages of the National Institute on Alcohol Abuse and Alcoholism (*www.niaaa.nih.gov*) and the National Institute on Drug Abuse (*www.nida.nih.gov*) provide additional current information on many widely used tests and measures for assessing substance use and abuse.

Young children who appear to display a higher than average number of sexual behaviors may be assessed using the Child Sexual Behavior Inventory (CSBI; Friedrich, 1997) published by PAR. See reviews of the CSBI by Berndt (2001) and McKnight (2001).

Measurement of a child's overall functioning in different environments might be a accomplished using the Conners' Rating Scale (CRS; Conners, 1997) distributed by PAR, the Behavior Assessment System for Children—Revised (BASC-R; Reynolds & Kamphaus, 1998) distributed by the American

Guidance Service (800-328-2560), or the Achenbach Child Behavior Checklist (CBCL; Achenbach, 2001) published by Riverside Publishing (800-323-9540). See reviews of the CRS by Hess (2001) and Knoff (2001); reviews of the BASC-R by DiPerna (2001) and Spies and Jones (2001); and reviews of the CBCL by Doll (1998) and Furlong and Wood (1998).

Measurement of a child's personality functioning might be accomplished through the use of a direct measure of children's personality such as the Children's Personality Questionnaire (CPQ; Porter & Cattell, 1975) published by the Institute for Personality and Ability Testing (800-225-4728) or through the use of parental measures of children's personality such as the Personality Inventory for Children–2nd Edition (PIQ; Lachar & Gruber, 2001) published by WPS. For reviews of the CPQ, see Hagin (1998) and Stinnett (1998). For reviews of the PIC see Krishnamurthy (2001) and Urbina (2001).

Summary

In this chapter, we discussed research describing "risky families." Risky families are characterized by conflict, anger, and aggression; by relationships that lack warmth and support; and by neglect of the needs of offspring. These families are risky in multiple ways. First, several of these characteristics, most notably physical abuse and neglect, represent immediate threats to the lives and safety of children. Second, the fact that children's developing physiological and neuroendocrine systems must repeatedly adapt to the threatening and stressful circumstances created by these family environments increases the likelihood of biological dysregulations that may contribute to a buildup of *allostatic load*, that is, the premature physiological aging of the organism that enhances vulnerability to chronic disease and to early mortality in adulthood (McEwen & Stellar, 1993; Seeman, Singer, Horwitz, & McEwen, 1997). Third, risky families fail to provide children with important self-regulatory skills, leaving the children unable effectively to create and enlist social support or to deal with emotion-engaging interpersonal situations (as well as a wide array of other stressful events that may require coping skills). Finally, risky families increase children's vulnerability to behavior problems and substance abuse, including smoking, alcohol, drugs, and promiscuous sexual activity. These risks are multiple and pervasive, and they are related to each other through common biological and psychosocial pathways. Separately and in concert, they place a child not only at immediate risk, but also at long-term and life-long risk for adverse mental and physical health outcomes. The chapter concluded with a discussion of various assessment tools to consider when evaluating factors associated with risky families.

The Art and Science of Child Custody Evaluations

ASSESSING ALLEGATIONS OF MALTREATMENT

CHAPTER 11

Assessing Allegations of Child Sexual Abuse

In the next three chapters, we address the complexities that arise when allegations of maltreatment are raised within the context of child custody evaluations. All child custody evaluations are complex, but when combined with other intricate forensic issues such as allegations of child sexual abuse or domestic violence, unique evaluative skills are needed. Social and political issues immensely complicate the evaluative task.

Hunt (1999) observes that, over the past 15 years, there has been a dramatic increase in efforts to impose limits on the freedom of social scientists to conduct research in socially sensitive areas, particularly when the research may generate data likely to call into question current social values or cultural beliefs. We have noted a similar trend in child custody work, especially when issues of child maltreatment or family violence are raised. There is often tension between data-derived information and politically correct positions, causing some to minimize the importance of systematically collected data. On the other hand, we must oppose the efforts of litigants to inflate the value of research data and obscure their limitations because the data are supportive of personal or ideological agendas. An evaluator's task is to focus on psycholegal issues before the court and to be appropriately guided by research data.

Current behavioral science research suggests that, in the absence of medical evidence and/or a child's spontaneously offered and clearly articulated report, there are few indicators that can lead an evaluator responsibly to formulate an opinion that a child has been maltreated. We emphasize the word *responsibly* to remind you that only opinions expressed with a reasonable degree of professional certainty are of use in forensic settings. Many behaviors often associated with maltreatment are also observed in children whom we are reasonably certain have not been maltreated, suggesting that such behaviors may be a function of nothing more than the normal variability of children's behavior, increased stress in a child's family system, and/or the emotional impact of being the prize over which one's parents are competing. Situational stress may lead to higher incidents of unusual or problem behavior, including the display of sexual behavior (Friedrich, 2002).

One challenge to custody evaluators is to inform the court and the public what we as a profession know about maltreatment. Mental health professionals need to play an active role in educating judges, parents, and other consumers of psychological information about the many ways in which psychological research data can be misinterpreted. We agree with Tippins and Wittmann (2005) and Bala (2005), who recommend better education for judges and attorneys about social science research and its limitations, better training and clearer qualification standards for those who perform court-ordered evaluations, and clearer standards of professional practice developed by professional organizations whose members perform evaluations.

There are many myths about child maltreatment, and some people who hold strongly to those myths do so because they are congruent with other beliefs in which those people are emotionally invested. Lilienfeld (2002) reminds us that psychology as a profession cannot ignore the all-too-frequent tendency of the media, politicians, and others to distort and oversimplify the findings of social science research and, perhaps just as disturbingly, to make fundamental errors in logic when attempting either to support or to discredit these findings (p. 176).

Just as the media and politicians can distort research findings, either deliberately or inadvertently, so can parents, attorneys, and judges involved in custody decisions. When framing an opinion about possible child maltreatment, the evaluator needs to provide a context—a description of how the particular family functions—and explain how the research utilized in formulating the opinion fits within the context. Without understanding the context of a family system, offering workable recommendations for intervention and treatment is difficult.

Maltreatment

As evaluators, we often encounter maltreatment both in the form of harmful acts and in the form of acts that are deemed improper. There are many adult acts that we consider egregious because there is a consensus that they injure children. An examination of empirical studies (see Friedrich, 2002, for review) in medicine and in the behavioral sciences, however, reveals a paucity of data linking specific acts of sexual maltreatment with either long- or short-term adverse effects on the victim. Some victims of abuse suffer for years while other victims show few signs if trauma (Archer, 2000a).

Emery (1999) has called on evaluators to examine the role played by personal and normative values in child custody determinations. He opines that the best interests standard often becomes "a vessel into which unarticulated normative values are poured" (p. 325). Tippins and Wittmann (2005) voice concern about the degree to which

> the court may be basing its decision on personal value judgments of witnesses who happen to have professional credentials. However, those credentials do not entitle the witness's personal, as opposed to professional or scientific, judgments to be admitted, let alone carry weight. When an expert witness "does not testify on the basis of the collective view of his scientific disciple" and where "no understandable scientific basis is stated," "personal opinion, not science, is testifying." (p. 207, citations omitted)

Their concern is that the evaluator's personal values and experiences as a parent become the standard against which each mother and father is judged. "Clinicians often present their logic and personal values under the guise of behavioral-scientific truth without disclosing that we have no reliable clinical method to do this weighing. Simple logic and subjective values do not represent specialized knowledge" (Tippins & Wittmann, 2005, p. 2002).

It is contrary to the concept of parental rights found in the Supreme Court's interpretation of the U.S. Constitution for a custody evaluator to present recommendations about a family's parenting values and parenting behavior that are based on the evaluator's personal values and beliefs but presented *as if* they were based on scientifically informed judgment. Evaluators need to be careful not to make this mistake (Gould, 2006).

Our constitution guarantees the right to raise our children as we see fit. "Government must be sharply restricted in its capacity to oversee the circumstances under which children are being raised. Precisely because childrearing means family values, interests, ideas, and religious beliefs of the next generation, we should expect American law to insist, as the Supreme Court has, that the state cannot enter the domain of family life" (Guggenheim, 2005, p. 25). "The state can neither supply nor hinder" (*Prince v. Massachusetts*, 1944, p. 166) the parent's right to teach their children values or inculcate them into religious training. "The fundamental theory of liberty upon which all governments in this Union repose excludes any general power of the State to standardize its children" (*Pierce v. Society of Sisters*, 1925, p. 535). "The home derives its preeminence as the seat of family life . . . The entire fabric of the Constitution and the purposes that clearly underlie its specific guarantees demonstrate that the rights to marital privacy and to marry and raise a family are of similar order and magnitude as the fundamental rights" (*Griswold v. Connecticut*, 1965, p. 495, quoting *Poe v. Ullman,* 1961). And, finally, the Troxil court stated that "the interests of parents in the care, custody, and control of their children is perhaps the oldest of the fundamental liberty interests recognized by the Court . . . it cannot now be doubted that the Due Process Clause of the Fourteenth Amendment protects the fundamental rights of parents to make decisions concerning the care, custody and control of their children" (*Troxil v. Granville,* 2000, p. 57).

The challenge for evaluators is to identify when parents engage in behavior that is harmful to their children rather than to identify behavior that is unusual, odd, or different from that considered normal within community standards. As a result of the constitutional protections provided parents, the state assumes a modest role in monitoring behaviors within the family. The state sets boundaries at the outer limits of what is acceptable parenting.

> Thus, laws protecting children from neglect and abuse, even at the hands of their parents, have come to be regarded as the proper exercise of the state's police power (regulating the conduct of citizens that has the potential to harm others). This means only that parents are obligated to exercise a "minimum degree of care" when raising their children. Unless parents fall below this (low) standard and are found to be "unfit" in court proceedings charging them with abuse or neglect, parental childrearing decisions are virtually immune from state oversight. (Guggenheim, 2005, p. 36)

Despite its limitations, mental health research and theory can inform public debate about what is harmful and what is improper. Books such as Barber's *Intrusive Parenting* (2002), Bancroft and Silverman's *The Batterer as Parent* (2002a), and Condie's *Parenting Evaluations for the Courts* (2003) may help define and narrow areas of concern regarding maltreatment of children within families.

Defining the Context within Which Maltreatment Occurs

When an allegation of maltreatment is registered, evaluators need to understand the interconnectedness of psychological and physical maltreatment in this specific situation. We need to assess for victims of family violence, witnesses to family violence, substance abuse, emotional abuse, physical abuse, sexual abuse, and other related areas of abuse of power and control. Each needs to be investigated separately; then, the information gathered during each inquiry needs to be integrated with other information concerning the family in order to understand its functioning and how each child fares within the family system.

Research shows a strong and consistent relationship between domestic violence and child abuse (Maiuro, 2001). Estimates are that between about 30% and 70% of families in which there is domestic violence also show child abuse

(Pulido & Gupta, 2002). The relationship between the incidence of violent acts toward a spouse and abusive acts toward a child is stronger if the perpetrator is the father (National Center for Injury Prevention and Control, 1985). Children observing parental domestic violence are more likely than children from nonviolent homes to manifest a variety of significant mental health problems (Knapp, 1998; McKay, 1994). Abused women are more likely then nonabused women to abuse their children (Pulido & Gupta, 2002), meaning children are at risk from both the perpetrator and the victim. When conducting an evaluation with allegations of maltreatment it is important for the evaluator to consider factors associated with maltreatment such as those listed above.

Other relationships to consider include those (1) between allegations of child alienation and allegations of domestic violence (Walker & Shapiro, 2003b); (2) between allegations of child alienation and allegations of parental conflict (Warshak, 2001a, 2002, 2003); (3) between child exposure to parental conflict and poorer child adjustment (Jaffe, Lemon, & Poisson, 2003; Kitzmann et al., 2003; Rossman, 1998; Rossman & Rosenberg, 1992); (4) between parental conflict, particularly around the time of marital separation, and domestic violence (Garrity & Baris, 1994; Johnston & Campbell, 1993); and (5) between the amount of time a parent victim is physically abused and sexual abuse of the parent-victim by the partner (Pulido & Gupta, 2002).

Involvement of Multiple Systems in Investigations of Allegations of Child Maltreatment

In describing difficulties inherent in an empirical definition of maltreatment, Emery and Laumann-Billings (1998) write that "the underlying problem is that our conceptualizations of violence or abuse are inherently driven by social judgment and not by immutable social standards or by empirical science" (p. 121). When, in the course of a custody evaluation, evidence surfaces of possible maltreatment, the evaluator may need to gather information from people who are familiar with the investigation.[1] These collateral sources of information may include pediatricians, therapists and counselors, ministers and youth ministers, social service agencies, police, the prosecutor's office, school personnel, after-school personnel, day care providers, and counselors.

Child sexual abuse allegations that arise in the context of a custody dispute may involve the interface of five very different systems. The judicial system is involved because of the custody matter and overall responsibility for family matters; the criminal justice system may become involved if the law has been violated (in which case information and/or opinions offered in an evaluator's report may be used in the adjudication of the criminal matter); the social services system is involved because its statutory responsibilities are to protect children's health and welfare; the private sector mental health profession may be involved if the child has been to therapy; and the medical profession may be involved if there has been a physical examination investigating medical evidence. Conflicts may arise among the various systems because of perspectives concerning investigative methodologies and goals. Added to these potential conflicts are tensions within each system about how to investigate, prosecute, and treat the victim, the victim family, and the perpetrator.

Political Advocacy Agendas and Ethical Forensic Investigations

Ambiguity about the meaning several key terms often leads to uncertainty about what should be or needs to be investigated. There is a lack of consensus within the mental health community about how to conceptualize, evaluate, and treat child maltreatment, and lawyers often advocate for their clients' positions with little understanding of the science underlying current maltreatment research. Advocates increasingly participate in the legal system as expert witnesses and bring to their testimony a passionate plea for child protection. It has been our experience, however, that often these advocate expert witnesses substitute advocacy for science and present outdated or incorrect information to the court (e.g., Goldstein, 1998), but their testimony sounds compelling because their focus is on protection of the child, independent of whether the current empirical science supports their advocacy positions.

Substituting advocacy and passion for accurate information based on empirical findings is not appropriate in forensic psychological investigations. As indicated in the specialty guidelines for forensic psychologists (Committee on Ethical Guidelines for Forensic Psychologists, 1991), there are no ethical prohibitions against strongly advocating for a position once a proper evaluation has been completed and the opinions are based upon objective interpretations of the data. Advocacy based upon the data differs dramatically from advocacy that is fueled by preexisting values and beliefs. Ethical evaluators do not, however, advocate for opinions based on values and beliefs, only for opinions based on data gathered during a comprehensive and properly conducted evaluation.

A Unified Model of Assessment of Allegations of Maltreatment and Family Violence

Current research and theory suggests that many of the variables to be examined in exploring allegations of psychological abuse are the same as those in investigations of alleged sexual abuse.

There are differences between a forensic model and models often used to evaluate allegations of maltreatment. This chapter compares and contrasts these types of models and calls for researchers and practitioners to discuss the differences with an eye toward building a more unified evaluation model that incorporates ideas from both types.

Defining Child Sexual Abuse

In the remainder of this chapter, we describe a protocol for use in the investigation of allegations of child sexual abuse. The protocol integrates two evaluation models: the forensic model and the trauma-based model. Although the evaluation protocol was developed with child sexual abuse allegations in mind, we believe it to be useful in investigating allegations of any form of maltreatment. We offer ideas about how to assess satisfactorily relevant factors associated with each area of maltreatment while recognizing that no evaluation protocol can incorporate all variables involved in all cases.

The American Psychological Association's Definition of Child Sexual Abuse

The American Psychological Association's Presidential Task Force on Violence and the Family (1996) defines child sexual abuse as

> the deliberate engagement of a child, by a parent, family member, other caretaker, or person in a position of authority and trust, in sexual activities for which the child is developmentally unprepared and cannot give informed consent. . . . *Incest* is sexual contact or sexualized behavior by relatives or quasi-relatives, such as parents, step-parents, foster parents, or siblings, when the abuser is older or holds a position of power over the victim. . . . Incest and child sexual abuse include a continuum of behaviors ranging from noncontact activities such as exhibitionism, voyeurism, sexual photography, verbal sexual propositions, and harassment, to activities involving physical contact. Contact abuse includes both penetration and other types of sexualized touching; penetration need not occur for incest or child abuse to be traumatic. (p. 49)

Ambiguity of Definitions

Haugaard (2000) believes there is no consensus regarding what acts constitute child sexual abuse. He points out that assessment of intent is critical in some allegations of child sexual abuse and that intent can be difficult to judge. The definition of a child is based upon statutory language that distinguishes between a minor child and a person who has reached the age of majority. With regard to the definition of abuse, some researchers have argued that the term *abuse* refers to the presence of harm (Rind, Tromovitch, & Bauserman, 1998) and that *child sexual abuse* may not be an appropriate term to describe adult–child sexual encounters from which no resultant harm can be readily observed (Haugaard, 2000). Most authoritative books on child custody evaluation either do not discuss the definition ambiguities involved in identifying and assessing allegations of child sexual abuse (e.g., Galatzer-Levy & Krauss, 1999; Gould, 1998; Stahl, 1994, 1999) or provide only a respectfully brief nod to concerns about definition ambiguity, then move on to other topics (e.g., Ackerman, 1995, 2001; Ackerman & Kane, 1998).

We begin by focusing on definition ambiguity because this focus is consistent with a critical theme of this book and, in our view, with the theme of forensic assessment in general. Evaluators need to define what it is they are evaluating and then formulate specific assessment questions that serve to guide the evaluation. When specific questions are identified before the evaluation task has begun, the focus of the evaluation is clearer and it is more likely to produce data directly relevant to the concerns of the court and family.

Therefore, a first step in thinking about allegations of child sexual abuse is to define, from the perspective of the referring source, the meaning of the terms to be evaluated. The term *child sexual abuse* is used in many contexts and by professionals from various disciplines who may have different mandates and goals when working with a child who is alleged to have been sexually abused. Clinicians may focus on treatment issues for the child or family and, as a result, may prefer a more inclusive, inexact definition that allows them to work with a wide range of children and families. Prosecutors and judges may see their primary role as prosecuting and incarcerating perpetrators of child sexual abuse while protecting the rights of those who were violated. They may prefer a definition that clearly identifies permitted and prohibited behaviors (Haugaard, 2000). Child welfare workers and child advocates may see their role as protecting victim-children and may prefer a more inclusive, inexact definition. Forensic evaluators may prefer a stricter definition that allows them to draw upon specific, related research.

The second step in the process of reducing definition ambiguity is to describe operationally the specific behaviors that are alleged to have occurred. Too often, when allegations of sexual abuse are registered, those taking the report do not seek unambiguous descriptions of the behaviors that are the focus of the report. Further complicating our definitional task is that fact that behavior occurs within a context. In some situations, intelligently formulating an opinion concerning whether certain described acts do or do not constitute abuse requires that we be provided with detailed information concerning the context within which the acts occurred.

Definition Ambiguity Hinders Research into Prevalence Rates

Definition ambiguity limits the usefulness of research data on the prevalence of sexual abuse. Researchers utilizing a broad definition of sexual abuse will report data that is not congruent with data reported by researchers utilizing a narrow definition. Similarly, modifiers such as *severe* have been used in different ways by different writers (Haugaard, 2000). The term has been used to describe such diverse characteristics as frequency, duration, presence of physical pain, emotional discomfort, use of physical force by the alleged sexual perpetrator, or type of sexual activity.

Careful Use of Terminology

In discussing matters not yet adjudicated, we have been careful to use the term *alleged perpetrator*. The term *sex offender* is legally defined and refers to someone who has either acknowledged guilt or has been found guilty of a sexual offense (as defined by the jurisdiction in which the act was committed). In our view, evaluators should avoid the use of legally defined terms, as the information we use in formulating our opinions is more limited than that considered by the court.

A *paraphilia* is a mental disorder involving certain non-normative sexual arousal patterns that cause the person who experiences them distress or have led to overt behavior such as pedophilia (American Psychiatric Association, 1994). *Deviant sexual interest* is a nontechnical term that has many different definitions. Sometimes it serves to define non-normative interest or non-normative behavior (Lanyon, 2001). When using a legally defined term such as *sexual offender* to describe behaviors that are outside personal or community values or practice, evaluators must take care to clearly communicate that the use of a term reflects a value judgment and not a legal conclusion.

Evaluating Allegations of Sexual Abuse

When sexual abuse allegations arise in the context of divorce custody disputes, families are particularly vulnerable to heightened emotions, increased polarization, and threats to the integrity of parent–child relationships. The evaluator must conduct the evaluation in a manner that ensures systematic and contextual elements are assessed and taken into consideration (Kuehnle, 1996, 2003). Berliner and Conte (1993) remind us that professional opinions must be formulated on the basis of reliable data and not upon personally held or collectively shared assumptions, biases, or cultural myths.

Recent estimates are that false allegations of sexual abuse arise in 23–33% of cases (Gordon, 1996; Kuehnle, 2003). As evaluators, we are confronted with three problems. First, the mental health community's ability to discriminate true from false allegations is still in its infancy. To date, researchers have been unable to identify a single behavior on the basis of which we might reliably distinguish abused from nonabused children (William Friedrich, personal communication, 2004). Second, we are unable to ascertain reliably the validity of allegations of abuse based upon analyses of components of children's reports. Third, we are unable to identify sex abuse perpetrators on the basis either of patterns of data from objective psychological tests or patterns of observable behavior (Quincey & Lalumiere, 2001). Weissman (1991) reminds us that there is

> no reliable constellation of historical, demographic, personality, or other factors . . . that accurately characterizes either the child victim or the child offender. Neither

is there any reliable psychological or physiological test or method for determining whether a child has been sexually abused or whether someone has committed an act of sexual abuse. (p. 52)

Responsibly addressing the problem of allegations of sexual abuse that arise within the context of custody cases is complicated by the fact that many clinicians lack specific training in this area. As a result, the legal profession is often confronted with an array of self-identified experts who have emerged to fill the void. Untrained evaluators often draw conclusions on the basis of inadequate or insufficient information, resulting in harm to children and irreparable damage to parent–child relationships. When children have been assessed in inappropriate ways, the resulting contamination may make it impossible for even the most skilled examiner to distinguish fact from fiction.

Texts that address the evaluation of allegations of child sexual abuse include those by Hewitt (1999) and Kuehnle (1996, 2003). There are texts that address the forensic evaluation process in a more general manner (e.g., Heilbrun, 2001; Melton et al., 1997), texts that cover the application of forensic evaluation methods and procedures to child custody evaluations and examination of allegations of child sexual abuse within visitation and custody disputes (e.g., Gould, 1998, 2006), and articles in the professional literature that suggest evaluation protocols for use in investigating allegations of child sexual abuse (Kuehnle, 1998a, 1998b; Kuehnle, Coulter, & Firestone, 2000; Weissman, 1991).

How Do Evaluators Assess Allegations of Child Sexual Abuse in Child Custody Disputes?

Bow, Quinnell, Zaroff, and Assemany (2002) write that an evaluator assessing allegations of child sexual abuse that have arisen within the context of a custody dispute must have knowledge of three forensic areas: (1) practices and procedures in the child custody area, (2)sexual abuse evaluation techniques, and (3) assessment of alleged sexual offenders.

In surveying the procedures employed by forensic psychologists as they investigated child sexual abuse allegations in the context of custody disputes, Bow and colleagues found that one-quarter of the respondents reported interviewing the alleged perpetrator and alleged victim together. Sixty-six percent of respondents indicated that they had tested the alleged victim. Bow and colleagues comment on the frequent use of projective instruments, despite their lack of support in the peer-reviewed literature (Lilienfield, Wood, & Garb, 2000) and lack of usefulness as diagnostic tools (Kuehnle, 1998a). Only 36% of respondents reported using a sexual abuse protocol, model, or professional practice guideline in conducting their evaluations of allegedly abused children. Interviewers used aids (listed in order of their frequency of use in the evaluations) such as projective drawings, play therapy, anatomical drawings, doll-house play, puppet play, and anatomically detailed (AD) dolls.

With specific reference to AD dolls, Conte, Collins, Mary, and Fogarty (1991) report that a survey of professionals performing child abuse evaluations revealed that 92% of those surveyed used them. This frequency-of-use datum is of particular significance in light of the fact that Skinner and Berry (1993), Bruck and Ceci (1995), and Koocher and colleagues (1995) have reviewed the AD doll literature and concluded that there is no empirical evidence to support the notion that one can distinguish abused children from nonabused children based upon an analysis of their play with AD dolls. Fisher and Whiting (1998, p. 174) declare that "psychologists using these dolls as a diagnostic instrument risk operating in an ethically indefensible manner." Mason (1998, p. 220), in an analysis of 122 cases involving investigations of alleged sexual abuse heard in appellate courts between 1980 and 1990 and reported in WESTLAW and LEXIS, reports that most appellate courts reject testimony in which it is asserted that certain forms of play with AD dolls constitute evidence of sexual abuse.

In general, Bow and colleagues (2002) survey data suggest that many evaluators are not guided by published research as they make decisions concerning their techniques and instruments. Research suggests that there is a relationship between sexual abuse and physical abuse, yet only 4% of the responding evaluators administered the Child Abuse Potential Inventory (CAPI) or other measures of physical abuse potential. Bow and colleagues suggest that a comprehensive model for the forensic assessment of allegations of child sexual abuse within the context of a child custody dispute should include five components. They are:

1. The forensic evaluator should have no prior involvement with the case and should be appointed by the court. The evaluator should explore rival, plausible hypotheses. Consideration may be given to a sole evaluator versus team approach.
2. The evaluator should review all relevant records.
3. The evaluator should assess the nature, sequence, and circumstances of the allegation(s).
4. The evaluator should use multiple data sources consistent with current writings about forensic methods and procedures. Several variables were recommended for assessment:
   a. The evaluator should interview the alleged victim using forensic interview protocols. The evaluator should be cautious about use of projective tools and AD dolls. The evaluator should include in his or her report the criteria used for evaluating child interview data.
   b. The evaluator should use relevant psychological testing, including MMPI-2, Millon Clinical MultiAxial Inventory, 3rd Edition

(MCMI III), and the Substance Abuse Subtle Screening Inventory—3rd Edition (SASSI-III) to screen for substance abuse. The evaluator should also use appropriate and relevant assessment tools when evaluating children.

c. The evaluator should assess the alleged perpetrator's sexual history and should assess his or her using specialized instruments.

d. The evaluator should obtain information from direct parent–child observations when such observational interviews do not place the child at risk. Bow and colleagues (2002) wisely recommend that if a parent–child observation is to be conducted, the evaluator needs to supervise the entire observation. They recommend that the observation occur at the end of the evaluation process, after determination that the procedure is unlikely to retraumatize the child. Observation of the child with the alleged perpetrator should occur after baseline information is gathered about the child's behavior with the protective parent.

e. The evaluator should interview collateral informants and review collateral records.

5. The evaluator should formulate the findings into a comprehensive report that focuses on answering the referral questions.

We would add to this model the suggestion that, at the beginning of the evaluation process, the evaluator obtain a list of referral questions from the court to guide the investigation process. We further recommend, as discussed later in this chapter, that each referral question be examined against each of the nine hypotheses suggested by Kuehnle (1996). Evaluators should always be mindful of the fact that referrals for investigation of allegations of sexual abuse require that two issues be considered: first, whether the child was sexually abused? second, if so, then by whom? In order to perform their tasks responsibly, evaluators should be familiar with the literature on normative sexual behavior in children (Friedrich, 2002) and the recent research on sexual problem behaviors in children (Silovsky & Niec, 2002).

Potential Evaluator Bias

When there are no medical findings, evaluators investigating allegations of child sexual abuse must be mindful of the many factors that are likely to influence their decisions concerning methodology and opinion formation. Such factors include the following: when the allegations surface (before, during, or following a custody dispute); by whom they are initially reported; whether previous allegations have been registered; if there have been previous allegations, whether they have been viewed as credible by those who investigated them; the child's age, gender, social and cognitive development, emotional maturity, linguistic competence, memory development, and sexual knowledge;

and the intellectual functioning, job status, access to the child, and current adult relationships of the accused and the parent who has registered the allegation.

Some of these factors (such as the linguistic competence of the child) should be taken into consideration; others may predispose an evaluator either to believe or not to believe an allegation, based on perceived correlations. Further complicating the process of separating the pertinent from the distracting are the passage of time, the number of interviews during which the child repeats his or her story, and the changing developmental competencies of the child. Berliner and Conte (1993) remind us that "assumptions about the nature of abuse reports . . . may limit accuracy of professional judgments" (p. 112). They also remind us of the complexity of the evaluative task, stating, "the empirical literature of effects of abuse in general does not support the idea that there are consistent psychological responses to sexual abuse" (p. 116).

Conceptual Models for the Assessment of Child Sexual Abuse within a Child Custody Evaluation

Though no consensus exists concerning how to conduct an evaluation of alleged child sexual abuse within the context of a custody dispute, we urge evaluators to employ methods and procedures drawn from current literature addressing forensic methodology (Ackerman & Kane, 1998; Gould, 1998, 2006; Heilbrun, 2001; Kuehnle, 1998a, 2003) and forensic interviewing methods (Crossman et al., 2002; Poole & Lamb, 1998; Walker, 1999).

Ideas drawn from professional practice guidelines may be helpful in developing an evaluation protocol when conducting a forensic evaluation of allegations of child sexual abuse in the context of a custody dispute. Such guidelines include the guidelines for psychosocial evaluation of suspected sexual abuse in young children (American Professional Society on the Abuse of Children, 1990), the guidelines for the clinical evaluation of child and adolescent sexual abuse (American Academy of Child and Adolescent Psychiatry, 1997a), and the guidelines for psychological evaluations in child protection matters (American Psychological Association, 1999).

Know the Literature

Competent evaluators should be familiar with the research on normative sexual behaviors in children (Friedrich, 2002; Friedrich, et al., 1998), variability of children's sexual development and display of sexual behaviors (Friedrich, 2002; Friedrich, Fidher, Broughton, Houston, & Shafon, 1998), display of sexual problem behaviors (Silovsky & Niec, 2002), and parent–child attachment issues (Kelly & Lamb, 2000; Lamb & Kelly, 2001) and their relationship to sexual behavior (Friedrich, 2002) and other forms of abuse and maltreatment (Drozd & Olesen, 2004). Evaluators should also be familiar with research on bathing rituals (Rosenfeld, Siegel, & Bailey, 1987) and sleep rituals (Morelli, Rogoff, Oppenheim, & Goldsmith, 1992; Rosenfeld, O'Reilly-Wenegrat, Haavik, Wenegrat, & Smith, 1982) in families, normative physical-sexual development (Kuehnle, 1996; Johnson, 1999), and normative psychosexual development (Friedrich, 2002; Johnson, 1999; Johnson & Kendrick, 1984; Okami, Olmstead, & Abramson, 1997; Sivan & Schor, 1987) in children, including children's use of sex games (Best, 1983; Lamb & Coakley, 1993), masturbatory behavior (Langfeldt, 1981; Leung & Robson, 1993), and general interest in sexual exploration (Haugaard & Tilly, 1988; Rosenfeld, Bailey, Seigel, & Bailey, 1986). They should be familiar with literature on how children at different developmental stages label different parts of the body (Johnson & Kenrick, 1984), specifically sexually related body parts (Sivan & Schor, 1987). Evaluators should be aware of literature on children's sexual play (Heiman, Leiblum, Esquilin, & Pallitto, 1998; Lamb & Coakley, 1993) and how parental values about sexual liberalness affect child behavior (Okami et al., 1997).

Additionally, there is an extensive literature shedding light on children's memory and children's testimony (Akehurst, Milne, & Koehnken, 2003; Aldridge & Cameron, 1999; Bowen & Howie, 2002; Brady, Poole, Warren, & Jones, 1999; Brainerd & Reyna, 2002; Bruck & Ceci, 1997; Bruck et al., 1999; Bruck, Ceci, & Hembrooke, 2002; Cassidy & DeLoache, 1995; Ceci & Bruck, 1998; Crossman et al., 2002; Dorado & Saywitz, 2001; Geiselman, 1999; Gilstrap, Frasier-Thill, & Ceci, 2001-2002; Goodman, Batterman-Faunce, Schaaf, & Kenney, 2002; Hershkowitz, Orbach, Lamb, Sternberg, & Horowitz, 2002; Huffman, Warren, & Larson, 1999; Lamb & Fauchier, 2001; Lamb, Sternberg, Orbach, Esplin, & Mitchell, 2002; London & Nunez, 2002; Lyon, 1999, 2001; Martindale, 2001a; Marxsen, Yuille, & Nisbet, 1995; Milne & Bill, 1996; Orbach & Lamb, 2000, 2001; Peters & Nunez, 1999; Peterson & Grant, 2001; Peterson, Moores, & White, 2001; Powell & Thomson, 1997; Reyna, Holliday, & Marche, 2002; Roberts, 2002; Roberts & Lamb, 1999; Roberts & Powell, 2001; Saywitz & Camparo, 1998; Saywitz, Snyder, & Nathanson, 1999; Waterman, Blades, & Spencer, 2001) and how adults understand children's use of language (Sutherland, Gross, & Hayne, 1996; Walker, 1999).

Much has been written regarding techniques of sexual abuse assessment (Aldridge, 1998; American Professional Society on the Abuse of Children, 1995; Boat & Everson, 1996; Bruck, Ceci, Francoeur, & Resnick, 1995; Katz, Schonfeld, Carter, Leventhal, & Cicchetti, 1995; Koocher et al., 1995), and there are important writings about investigator confirmatory bias within the evaluation procedures (Vogeltanz & Drabman, 1995).

Evaluators are urged to take note of books like *Jeopardy in the Courtroom* (Ceci & Bruck, 1995), *Expert Witnesses in Child Abuse Cases* (Ceci & Hembrooke, 1998), *Investigative Interviews of Children* (Poole & Lamb, 1998), *Assessing Allegations of Child Sexual Abuse* (Kuehnle, 1996), *Assessing Allegations of Sexual Abuse in Preschool Children* (Hewitt, 1999), and *Psychological Assessment of Sexually Abused Children and Their Families* (Friedrich, 2002).

Evaluators should familiarize themselves with the arguments on all sides of an issue, such as the susceptibility of young children to interviewer influence (e.g., Ceci & Bruck, 1995; Lyon, 1999, 2001; Martindale, 2001a).

The competent evaluator should also be familiar with the literature on forensic assessment of sexual offenders. Among recent works useful to the evaluator are *Violent Offenders: Appraising and Managing Risk* (Quincey, Harris, Rice, & Cormier, 1998), the entire issue of *Psychology, Public Policy and Law* (Winick & LaFond, 1998), and *Assessment of Sexual Offenders against Children* (Quincey & Lalumiere, 2001).

Evaluators should also be knowledgeable about current literature on family violence including *Report of the APA Presidential Task Force on Violence and the Family* (American Psychological Association, 1996), *The Impact of Family Violence on Children and Adolescents* (Kashani & Allan, 1998), *Intimate Violence in Families*, third edition (Gelles, 1997), *The Batterer as Parent: The Impact of Domestic Violence on Family Dynamics* (Bancroft & Silverman, 2002a), *Psychological Abuse in Violent Domestic Relations* (O'Leary & Maiuro, 2001), *Children Exposed to Domestic Violence: Current Issues in Research, Intervention, Prevention, and Policy Development* (Geffner, Jaffe, & Suderman, 2000), and *The Conflict Tactics Scales Handbook* (Straus, Hamby, & Warren, 2003) that provides an excellent summary of intimate partner violence research.

The Evaluation Process

We suggest that evaluators review as much background and collateral information as possible before conducting face-to-face interviews. The initial interview will be more productive if a list of hypotheses has been generated prior. The evaluator should not be limited only to questions that flow from the hypotheses, but the hypotheses should provide an initial direction to the interview. A thorough review of information from all sources prior to a child interview should help reduce the chances that evaluators will neglect to inquire about critical areas or will require multiple interviews with a child due to lack of preparedness.

Once the evaluator has gathered and reviewed information from different sources, it is time to interview the child. The child should be evaluated alone. Some evaluators believe that with children younger than 5, one can include a parent in the initial minutes of the interview to help the child become comfortable with the interviewer and the environment. If you choose to allow a parent to join the initial minutes of a child interview, you need to consider what effect a parent's presence may have on the child, both during the initial stages of the interview and during the rest. Be mindful of the fact that, in making decisions concerning how to interview the child, you should also contemplate how the child may be influenced, by whom the child may be influenced, and in what direction the child may be influenced.

When parents of young children remain in the waiting room, some children may feel that they must provide information consistent with what they believe to be the information already provided by the parent. It may be helpful to ask parents to leave the office and return after a phone call from the evaluator. The child's knowledge that the parent has left the office may make the child more comfortable and more apt to be candid. It can also be useful to have each parent bring the child in for an interview, so that consistencies and inconsistencies can be noted.

Interviewers must inform children that they are not expected to remember everything, that they may be confused about certain things (and that this is OK), that they can change something they said earlier, and that they can describe events that they have not described before to anyone else.

We suggest examination of the following variables during a structured interview:

1. Child's susceptibility to influence by others and how and/or the degree to which the child has been so influenced or coached.
2. Child's developmental understanding of counting and temporal concepts.
3. Child's developmental understanding of location of body parts, their relationship to each other on the body, and use of language to describe body parts.
4. Child's developmental understanding of colors, shapes, and textures (especially if there were allegations of ejaculation).
5. Consistency of child's self-report, including consistency over time and internal consistency.
6. Child's view of each parent's support for the child and for the child's account of the event.
7. Child's description of games and play with other children and adults that might be interpreted as sexual games or play.
8. Child's view of each parent's use of discipline to manage the child's behavior.
9. Child's view of each parent's parenting style.
10. Child's view of each parent's discipline style.
11. Child's view of parental cooperation.
12. Child's view of parental conflict.
13. Child's view of other care takers.
14. Child's view of home environment regarding sexuality.
15. Child's view of sleeping patterns and rituals at each parent's home.
16. Child's view of bathing patterns and rituals at each parent's home.
17. Child's view of daily routine at each parent's home.
18. Child's view of each parent's use of drugs or alcohol.
19. Child's view of each parent's treatment of child in relationship to siblings.
20. Child's friendship group and opportunities to play with friends.

The focus of an unstructured interview with a child is to observe the child's spontaneous play. The evaluator should note developmental milestones, characteristics of the child's independent play, and characteristics of the child's behavior when engaged in interactive play. Among areas of assessment to be investigated during an unstructured interview are:

1. Child's manner of play with toys.
2. Child's manner of play with agemates and/or siblings.
3. Child's manner of play with adults.
4. Child's choice of toys and games.
5. Child's manner of play with each toy or game.
6. Child's spontaneous drawings.
7. Child's verbal description of drawings.
8. Child's decision making ability.
9. Child's ability to follow directions.
10. Child's ability to respect limits and boundaries.

Child interviews require patience. In order to create a safe and comfortable environment for the child, evaluators must follow the child's rhythm and pace. It is likely that several interviews may be needed to establish rapport and trust and possible that most, if not all, interviews with the child may need to be conducted at the child's home in order to facilitate his or her sense of safety and comfort. All interviews with the child should be audiotaped or, if possible, videotaped (Ceci & Bruck, 2000).

There are a number of *don'ts* in interviewing of children when concerns of sexual abuse arise:

1. Don't schedule the child's interview after a physical examination or after another interview. You want to talk with the child in a way that facilitates an independent representation of his or her thoughts, emotions, and behaviors. Don't present yourself as someone to whom children talk about bad things. The child should understand that you are someone who talks to many different people about many different things and feel it is acceptable to talk about any topic that may be of importance *to the child*.

2. Be aware that empathic responses may contaminate the interview process by revealing the evaluator's beliefs, concerns, and feelings, subtly encouraging the child to make statements that are supportive of the evaluator's hypotheses rather than reflective of the child's true feelings.

3. Children should not be reminded of previous interviews or of things the evaluator is aware the child has said in previous interviews or in conversations with others.

4. Children should not be told that statements made will be kept secret. The child needs to know that your job is to report your findings to the judge. Explain at a level commensurate with the child's developmental level why the

judge needs to know all the important information the child tells you and make note of the child's permission to repeat what he or she says.

Understanding How Children Think

The process that a child must go through either to repel an abusive approach or to report an occurrence of abuse is very complex. Children must first be informed about what sexual abuse is in order to identify it properly, but, as discussed throughout this chapter, there is no clear professional agreement about what constitutes an abusive act (Haugaard, 2000; Reppucci & Haugaard, 1989). When children are taught broad definitions of sexual abuse, many nonabusive incidents may be reported. On the other hand, if a more restrictive definition is taught to a child, then acts that are abusive but do not fit the definition exactly may go unreported. The competent evaluator must explore how the child understands the behavior that is considered abusive, within what the context the behavior occurred, and how the abusive behavior was brought to the attention of the reporter.

Assessing Allegations of Maltreatment within the Context of a Child Custody Dispute

Though we are proponents of the forensic model, we encourage evaluators to read the research and incorporate some of the tools that are drawn from the *trauma-based model.*

Many writers who support the *trauma-based* model utilize descriptors such as *nonoffending parent*, victim parent, or *protective parent* in describing the parent in whose care they believe the child should be placed (e.g., Walker & Shapiro, 2003b). They often describe the other parent as the *offending parent*, the *perpetrator parent*, the *sex offender parent*, or the *accused abuser.* The use of such terms prior to the completion of a thorough evaluation suggests that the evaluator has formulated opinions prior to obtaining and dispassionately examining all pertinent information.

There may be times when the data supporting the allegation is so compelling that a child needs to be placed in a protective environment before completion of the evaluation. In most cases, however, it is only after a thorough evaluation has been conducted that we are able to ascertain from whom the child requires protection and by whom the needed protection will be provided. Reflexively curtailing a child's contact with one parent in response to an allegation against that parent can cause irreparable damage—damage that might be prevented if we humbly acknowledged that we are not always able to distinguish the good guys from the bad guys and that decisions concerning how best to protect children must be made based upon a complete set of reliable data, not upon biases and initial impressions. Forensic evaluation of allegations of child maltreatment or family violence ought to include the use of semistructured interview methods, psychological tests and measures, collateral record review and interviews, and direct parent–child observations.

The Evaluator's Cognitive Set and Attitude

Traditional methods of training for forensic evaluators include admonishments to maintain an objective, neutral, and detached cognitive set and attitude toward those being evaluated (Greenberg & Shuman, 1997). As Gould (1998) stated in his custody book:

> The forensic evaluator approaches the litigant with an attitude of objectivity, detachment, and impartiality. The forensic examiner is neutral in feeling and attitude toward the litigant. His job is not to help change the litigant's current situation, but to make a dispassionate, objective assessment of the issue at hand and to communicate those facts and opinions to the court.
>
> This is not to say that we treat litigants poorly. We treat them with respect and understand the exceptional emotional challenges they may face in enduring a custody challenge. However, no matter how strongly we may feel on a personal level about the issues at hand, no matter how much we may like the litigants on one side and dislike the litigants on the other side, it is imperative that our professional attitude and beliefs focus us on a neutral, impartial, objective, fair, and dispassionate evaluation. (p. 18)

Proponents of the trauma-based model encourage evaluators to take a more empathic approach to the alleged victims and their protectors. It is argued that, without a more empathic emotional connection between the alleged victim and evaluator, the victim will tend to disclose less relevant information during the interview (Lenore Walker, personal communication, September 17, 2003). It is presumed that an evaluator can maintain an objective and neutral cognitive set while conveying an attitude of warmth, support, understanding, and empathy. In our view, the evaluator should be able to create an alliance with the child that allows the child to feel safe, protected, and comfortable in exploring the alleged event(s) while not creating an interview environment with opportunities to distort information. The challenge, as we see it, is for evaluators to understand clearly how to interview a child forensically using the techniques and procedures known to influence child disclosures minimally (see Ceci & Bruck, 1995; Crossman et al., 2002; Poole & Lamb, 1998) while entering into an alliance with the child that involves the type of trust and comfort the child needs to talk about his or her physical and emotional experiences.

The Interview

Geffner, Goldstein, Fox, and Ducote (2002) comment on the lack of evaluator training in the forensic assessment of allegations of child maltreatment and family violence in child custody disputes. Drozd (personal communication,

June 26, 2004) suggests that evaluators are often unfamiliar with *how* to interview child and adult victims about maltreatment and family violence. In the initial stages of data gathering, it is important to obtain information about the developmental history and current developmental functioning of each child in the family.

A trauma-based approach begins the interview process with a face-to-face interview of the reporting parent. The child is not present. Walker and Shapiro (2003b) describe the importance of assessing positive parenting behaviors such as empathy and awareness of the child, predictability, nonintrusiveness, emotional availability, ability to trust and be intimate, and ability to adapt to new situations and multiple demands. They also describe the importance of assessing negative parenting behaviors such as self-centeredness and self-focus (above and beyond those that are self-protective), depression, antisocial behavior and attitudes, inconsistency with behavior toward siblings or new stepchildren, domestic violence and child abuse, and mental illness.

The next step in the trauma-based model is to interview the alleged child victim using structured and unstructured interview formats (Drozd & Olesen, 2004). The structured interview should gather information about the child's developmental performance based on age expectations, including, but not limited to, the child's knowledge and use of vocabulary and an assessment of his or her linguistic competencies. We recommend that readers refer to Drozd and Olesen (2004) for helpful ideas to be used in structuring a child interview and observing children in independent and interactive play.

Child interviews require patience. In order to create a safe and comfortable environment for the child, evaluators must follow the child's rhythm and pace. It is likely that several interviews may be needed to establish rapport and trust. Most, if not all, interviews with the child may need to be conducted at the child's home in order to facilitate the child's sense of safety and comfort. We recommend that all interviews with the child be audio- or, if possible, videotaped (Ceci & Bruck, 2000).

The third step in the trauma-based model is to interview the parent alleged to have been abusive. The first interview and possibly all others are conducted without the child present. Deciding whether to bring the child and the allegedly abusive parent together requires an assessment of the risk presented to the child by reexposure to the allegedly abusive parent.

Proponents of the forensic model encourage the interview of each parent prior to interviewing the child, while, in the trauma-based model, the examiner gathers interview data from only one parent prior to interviewing the child. Interviewing a child after gathering data from only one parent may increase the likelihood that the evaluator's questions during the child interview reflect a strong bias toward gathering information about hypotheses drawn only from the interviewed parent. Without having interviewed the allegedly abusive parent before interviewing the child, the evaluator is unable to pose questions that reflect the allegedly abusive parent's recollection of pertinent events, perspective on possibly ambiguous situations, and concerns.

Martindale (2001b) has pointed out:

> It is both arrogant and foolhardy for psychologists to presume that because we are knowledgeable concerning the principles of perception that these principles do not apply to us. . . . Unless something in a litigant's initial presentation immediately arouses suspicion, there is a strong (albeit unintentional) tendency to accept the essential accuracy of the fact pattern as it is related to us by those from whom we initially obtain background information. (p. 44)

Parent–Child Observations

Proponents of both the forensic model and the trauma-based model believe that observations of parent–child interactions enable the evaluator to gather information about the nature and quality of the parent–child relationship.

Proponents of the trauma-based model have expressed concern that children exposed to a traumatic experience such as sexual, emotional, or physical abuse perpetrated by a parent may need to begin treatment prior to or commensurate with the beginning of a forensic evaluation. They believe reexposure prior to the child being psychologically prepared to deal with an abusive parent may often lead to irreparable harm (Geffner et al., 2000; Kerig, Fedorowicz, Brown, & Warren, 2000). The primary goal of treatment with traumatized children is to facilitate the child's ability to gain mastery of the traumatic experience (Kerig et al., 2000). Traumatic experiences evoke strong and dysregulating emotions, which then come to be triggered not only by the perpetrator of the trauma, but also by places or other people associated with it (Geffner et al., 2000).

We urge forensic mental health practitioners to participate in scholarly discussion of this and related issues. We cannot ignore the possibility that attempts to use a play therapy modality to assist a child therapeutically to work through a bonafide trauma may inadvertently lead to the creation in the child's mind of a false belief about a nonexistent trauma. Readers are encouraged to familiarize themselves with research on children's suggestibility. In an issue of Court Review, Martindale (2002b) has outlined the risks; Lyon (2001), in the same issue, articulates his view that the risks have been exaggerated. Readers are also encouraged to read some articles in which research on source misattribution is outlined (e.g., Ceci & Bruck, 1995). Some writers (e.g., Campbell, 1992a, 1992b) have declared that research support for the effectiveness of play therapy is lacking. Play therapy is particularly problematic when practitioners formulate opinions concerning the child's family dynamics on the basis of the child's in-office play. Adult interpretations of children's play often tell us more about the adult than about the reality of the child's life.

What to Do in the Interim

Kleinman (2004) argues that a child's access to an allegedly abusive parent should be suspended during the course of an evaluation because reexposure to the alleged perpetrator will retraumatize the child. In our view, other factors must be considered when making decisions regarding access. The age of the child must be considered. Suspending contact between a 6-month-old child and her allegedly abusive parent and suspending contact between a 7-year-old and that parent will likely have different effects on the child's developing attachment. We have yet to see a discussion in the literature that weighs the need to protect the child from exposure to the allegedly abusive parent against the developmental needs of the child and the child's emerging attachment to that parent. We must also consider the possibility that the other parent may adversely influence the child against the alleged perpetrator parent during the time of suspended contact. Some who advocate the trauma-based model often reject outright the notion that the parent who is protecting his or her child from the alleged perpetrator parent may also be engaged in a systematic attempt to influence the child negatively against that parent (Drozd & Olesen, 2004).

As a final note to this section, we repeat our earlier agreement with Bow and colleagues (2002) that, in cases of alleged child abuse or maltreatment, parent–child observations are recommended only when comparable available data are unavailable from other reliable sources and the observation does not present an undue risk to the child. Parent–child observations that reveal cooperative parenting and good relationship interaction may not provide much information about the child's true feelings or the allegation of abuse. On the other hand, an observation demonstrating strained, angry, or negative interactions between child and parent may be useful. Bow and colleagues wisely recommend that, if a parent–child observation is to be conducted, the evaluator should supervise the entire observation. They recommend that the observation occur at the end of the evaluation process, after determination that the procedure is unlikely to retraumatize the child and only after baseline information is gathered about the child's behavior with the nonabusive parent.

The Use of Psychological Tests and Measures

Both the trauma-based model and the forensic model stress the need for reliable data, and the use of psychological tests and measures is one potential source of it. There is, however, no consensus in the field of child custody nor is there one in the subspecialty of the forensic investigation of allegations of child maltreatment and family violence about a test or group of tests that provides an optimally reliable set of data about allegations of child maltreatment.

The trauma-based model encourages use of a set of tests and measures that explore a group of constructs uniquely related to concerns about maltreatment and violence. For example, the Conflict Tactics Scale (CTS; Straus, 1979) was designed to evaluate different tactics that might be used by intimate partners in resolving a conflict. The CTS measures aspects of physical violence and psychological aggression. Straus (1979; Straus & Smith, 1990) has reported that the more psychologically aggressive partners are to each other, the more likely they are to be physically aggressive.

The Revised Conflict Tactics Scales (CTS2; Straus, Hamby, & Warren, 2003) ask respondents to describe how they settle their differences. The CTS2 has 39 questions, but the CTS actually have 78 items. For each question, respondents are asked to describe their own behavior and then to describe their partner's behavior. The dual-questioning format reflects an assumption that abuse is a form of conflict resolution and that the behavior of both people involved in a conflict is important. A strength of the CTS2 is its focus on specific behavior, but its critics argue that focusing on specific behavior ignores subtle patterns of coercion and domination that characterize abusive relationships (Schafer, 1996).

Other assessment instruments include the following:

1. The *Danger Assessment Scale* (DAS; Campbell, 1995) was developed to help women evaluate the degree of danger they face and consider how to decrease their risk for danger (Campbell, Sharps, & Glass, 2000). Refer to Jory (2004) for a critique and to Campbell and colleagues (2004) for a discussion of the predictive validity of the DAS.
2. The *Index of Spousal Abuse* (Hudson & McIntosh, 1981) was developed to measure both the physical and psychological abuse of women. A severity of physical abuse index and a severity of psychological abuse index are obtained from the scale.
3. The *Psychological Maltreatment of Women Inventory* (Tolman, 1989, 1999, 2001) was developed to assess the manner in which a male partner controls a female partner. The 58-item PMWI contains items that reflect highly controlling behaviors.
4. The *Index of Psychological Abuse* (Sullivan, Parisian, & Davidson, 1991) is a 33-item measure of the amount of ridicule, harassment, isolation, and control a woman has experienced. Factor analysis has revealed six subscales: (a) criticism and ridicule, (b) social isolation and control, (c) threats and violence, (d) emotional withdrawal, (e) manipulation, and (f) emotional callousness.
5. The *Dominance Scale* (Hamby, 1996) was developed to measure three types of dominance: authority, restrictiveness, and disparagement. Hamby viewed these forms of dominance as causes of violence rather than as examples of violence itself.

Assessment of Trauma

Trauma should be assessed in all cases of suspected maltreatment or violence. There are several tests available through psychological test publishers that purport to measure the impact of trauma on a child or an adult. These measures of trauma are built upon the belief that victims of trauma experience distress, most commonly characterized by symptoms of posttraumatic stress disorder (PTSD).

Trauma measurement instruments include the Trauma Symptom Inventory (TSI; Briere, 1995) for adults and the Trauma Symptom Checklist for Children (TSCC; Briere, 1996). The TSCC has two versions, one to be administered when sexual abuse is suspected and the other when it is not. The latter version deletes many of the questions about sexuality that would be inappropriate for young children without sexual knowledge. Because trauma research identifies dissociation as one potential outcome of maltreatment or violence, if dissociation is suspected, evaluators may wish to consider utilizing the Dissociative Experiences Scale (Carlson & Putnam, 1993). If there are concerns about lethality, use of the Suicide Probability Scales (Cull & Gill, 1990) should be considered. There are also measures of suicidal ideation on the MMPI-2 and the TSI. The Marital Satisfaction Inventory—Revised might also be useful (Snyder, 1997). Further description of these tests can be found in Geffner and colleagues (2002).

Tests and Measures Administered to the Child

When evaluators identify a data collection method as a psychological test, the test must display some or all of the characteristics described by Heilbrun (1995) and by Otto and colleagues (2000) for the use of psychological tests in a forensic context. When using a *psychological method*—as opposed to a psychological test—the data obtained from the child's responses to the stimuli should be treated only as information from which to generate hypotheses. The evaluator should be aware of the lack of reliability and validity of these methods.

Children who experience trauma may display a higher frequency of disruptive, dysfunctional, or sexual problem behaviors. Objective measures administered to the child that may assess areas of concern include the AQ, Child Anxiety Scale, Children's Depression Inventory, Children's Inventory of Anger, Piers-Harris Children's Self-Concept Scale, and Revised Children's Manifest Anxiety Scale.

Limitations of Projective Tools

Regardless of your views of the value of projective instruments, it is important to recognize that, in material prepared for the legal profession, they are described in less than glowing terms. In a text described as "A Deskbook for

Judges," projective techniques are described as "generally exhibit[ing] low reliability and poor validity" (National Interdisciplinary Colloquium on Child Custody, 1998, p. 369). The authors conclude that such instruments "are of little forensic value and are useful only for clinical speculation and hypothesis generation. . . . Some of these tests . . . [are susceptible to] egregious misuse [and are] of no more probative value than tea-leaf patterns in the bottom of a cup" (p. 369). Supporters of the Rorschach will be dismayed to learn that the authors of this deskbook describe it as "an unreliable psychological test—one of the 'rubber rulers' of psychological testing" (p. 362). They then remind the reader that "No test can be an accurate measure of an attribute if [it] is not first a reliable measurement device. Reliability sets an upper limit upon the claimed usefulness of any psychological test" (p. 362).

In a clinical setting, a psychodiagnostic assessment marks the beginning of an ongoing relationship, in the course of which there will be opportunities for subsequent reassessment. As new information disconfirms old hypotheses, appropriate adjustments can be made. In a forensic setting, the report in which one's assessment is described marks the end of the relationship. No opportunities to reassess are provided.

The vast majority of psychologists conducting evaluations of comparative custodial fitness are clinicians who have entered the forensic arena for a variety of reasons. Some have brought to their forensic work psychodiagnostic assessment instruments that they found useful in their clinical work, but some of these are ill-suited to the demands of forensic work (Garb, Wood, & Nezworski, 2000; Garb, Wood, Lilienthal, & Nezworski, 2002; Lally, 2001; Lilienfeld et al., 2000; Weiner & Kuehnle, 1998).

Choosing assessment tools with demonstrated psychometric properties increases the likelihood of gathering useful data from reliable measurement procedures. Formulating an opinion in a custody dispute requires that the examiner be attentive to both the quantitative and qualitative aspects of data gathering. The view expressed in the custody guidelines (American Psychological Association, 1994) is that "The psychologist strives to use the most appropriate methods available . . . and generally uses multiple methods of data gathering" (Guideline III-11). In order for the foundation upon which a recommendation rests to be secure, much information must be gathered, and the caliber of the information must be such that it will withstand the scrutiny of a vigorous cross-examination.

Imwinkelried (1992, p. 116) cites case law that supports a cross-examining attorney's right to "demand an affirmative showing [by the expert] of [an] instrument's accuracy." Interjudge reliability coefficients for projective tests have not been impressive. In Anastasi's (1988) view, "the final interpretation of projective test responses may reveal more about the theoretical orientation, favorite hypotheses, and personality idiosyncrasies of the examiner than it does about the examinee's personality dynamics" (p. 614).

In a clinical setting, projective tests can be of inestimable value in facilitating the formulation of hypotheses that, as treatment progresses, the clinician can further investigate. In a forensic setting, in which one is expected to formulate opinions that can be expressed with a reasonable degree of professional certainty, self-report inventories offer clear advantages. The data obtained by means of such assessment devices are insulated from possible examiner bias and, therefore, superior in forensic settings to assessment instruments constructed in such a manner as to permit examiner subjectivity to affect the data collection process or scoring.

Psychologists often speak of the Rorschach in a manner suggesting that there is only one. While the 10 projective stimuli are always the same, there are as many Rorschachs as there are systems for interpreting Rorschach protocols. Exner (1980, p. 564) has called attention to "the truly vast differences" among the various Rorschach systems and "the impact of those differences on . . . interpretation."

It is generally agreed that the superiority of the Exner system for interpreting the Rorschach has been demonstrated. It might, therefore, be considered inappropriate to utilize another system simply because you are more familiar with it. If one is using the Exner system, it should be in accordance with his instructions. It has been common knowledge for approximately four decades (Rosenthal, 1966) that what an examiner *expects* to find (based upon information provided to the examiner prior to the examination) can dramatically affect what he or she find. Exner has stated, "Sometimes even . . . simple demographic information, such as socioeconomic status, . . . [can create] premature sets" (Exner, 1993, p. 329). Elsewhere (Exner, 1986, p. 306), he states that the effect of premature sets on "the interpretation of any [Rorschach] data converts the process from science to an art form." Though Exner has confined his observations to the Rorschach, it is clear that the same pitfalls are present in interpreting other projective test data. In most forensic contexts, significant information is available to the evaluator prior to the administration of assessment instruments, and the evaluator's knowledge may affect interpretation of projective test results.

We also have concerns about the manner in which the Thematic Apperception Test (TAT) is often used in custody evaluations. When reviewing the work of others, we have often found that their use of the TAT is inconsistent with its standards of administration (Murray, 1943). According to the manual, there are 11 universal cards (1, 2, 4, 5, 10, 11, 14, 15, 16, 19, 20). There is one card to be given to adult males (12M) and one card to be given to adult females (12F). There is one card to be given to male children (13B) and one to be given to female children (13G). Card 12MF is to be given to adults regardless of their sex, and 12BG is to be given to children regardless of their sex. Seven cards are to be given to males regardless of age (3BM, 6BM, 7BM, 8BM, 9BM, 17BM, 18BM), and seven are to be given to females regardless of age (3GF, 6GF, 7GF, 8GF, 9GF, 17GF, 18GF). The total number of cards shown is 20, 11 of which are the universal cards; 9 are selected based upon the age and sex of the person taking the TAT (Murray, 1943).

As Ackerman and Kane (1998) point out, examiners seldom follow the recommended format of administering two series of 10 cards each, at least 1 day apart, with the cards chosen on the basis of the individual's sex and age. They write, "clinicians commonly use fewer than 20 cards and administer the test in a single 1 hour session. The examiner selects those cards most likely to provide information germane to the purpose of the examination" (p. 511). Because there are no generally accepted systems of TAT scoring and interpretation, it should come as no surprise that the reliability and validity of the TAT are questionable. Similar concerns are cited by Ackerman and Kane (1998) about the use of the Children's Apperception Test (CAT; Bellak & Bellak, 1949).

The Children's Apperceptive Story-Telling Test (CAST; Schneider, 1989) is an alternative to the CAT and is reported to be "the most serious and psychometrically sound effort thus far to develop an apperceptive story-telling technique for use with children" (Aronow, 1995, p. 181) ages 6 through 13. Currently, no normative data have been reported describing how children undergoing custodial evaluation perform on the CAST or comparing children from intact families with children from divorcing families.

The Roberts Apperception Test for Children (RATC; Roberts, 1982) is the first apperceptive storytelling test to provide an objective scoring system. Children between the ages of 6 and 15 are administered 16 cards. There are 11 cards for boys and 11 cards for girls and five cards for both boys and girls. As with the CAST, no normative data have been reported describing how children undergoing custodial evaluation perform on the RATC or comparing children from intact families with children from divorcing families.

Kuehnle (1996; Weiner & Kuehnle, 1998) provides a useful discussion of how to use projective tools with children when the assessment is conducted within a forensic context. Evaluators also need to be aware of arguments for and against the use of projective tools, especially human figure drawings. Those interested in obtaining authoritative information concerning the use of drawing tasks are referred to Garb et al. (2002); Hammer (1997); Hiler and Nesvig (1965); Lally (2001); Lilienfeld et al. (2000); Naglieri, McNeish, and Bardos (1991); Smith and Dumont (1995); Wakefield and Underwager (1992); and Wenck (1977). Those contemplating the use of drawings should be aware that even the strongest proponents of drawing tasks have pointed out that drawings tend to reflect "state as opposed to trait characteristics" (Knoff & Prout, 1985, p. 55).

Parent Assessment of the Child

There are several measures of a parent's perception of a child's behavior that may be useful to administer. When there are concerns about sexual abuse, the Child Sexual Behavior Inventory (Friedrich, 1997) may provide useful information about the frequency of observed sexual behavior. The CSBI was developed to assess sexual behavior better in children. An assumption of the test theory was that sexually abused children more frequently displayed sexualized behavior than nonabused children. Originally, the questionnaire was designed to be used by female caretakers of children between the ages of 2 and 12. Friedrich (1997) recommended that female caretakers who were not the accusing parent should complete the inventory. In his later writings, Friedrich (2002) recommended having male caregivers complete the inventory too: "This enables you to examine any discrepancies between caregivers" (p. 179).

Male caregivers typically report fewer observed sexual behaviors on the inventory compared with female caregivers, although this is not always the case. When there is a discrepancy between the male and female caregivers' reports, the evaluator should interview both caregivers about what each observed and what led each caregiver to categorize the observed behavior as sexual behavior.

Friedrich also stressed the importance of the evaluator asking about the context in which the alleged abusive behavior was to have occurred as well as the parent's typical response to these behaviors.

Friedrich (2002) recommended asking four additional questions that more precisely assess sexually aggressive behavior. The areas for questioning are:

1. "Touches other children's private parts after being told not to."
2. "Plans how to sexually touch other children."
3. "Forces other children to do sexual acts."
4. "Puts finger or object in other child's vagina or rectum." (p. 179)

The CSBI generates *T* scores on three different scales: Total Sexual Behavior, Developmentally Related Sexual Behavior, and Sexual-Abuse-Specific Sexual Behavior. *T* scores of 65 or higher are considered clinically elevated. A *T* score of 65 places the child at the 93rd percentile; such a high score is considered clinically significant requiring further investigation. Friedrich (2002) warned against using the CSBI as a screening tool for child sexual abuse: "Using the CSBI in this manner is inappropriate. It can never indicate absolutely whether a child has or has not been sexually abused; too many false positives result" (p. 181).

Observation of sexual behaviors in children causes concern for several reasons. Friedrich (2002) identifies seven of them:

1. Observation of a discrete behavior that may directly reflect a child's being abused causes grave concern.
2. Observation is a misinterpretation of behavior by a caregiver who decides that the child's expression of the behavior is (a) sexual in nature, (b) similar to adult behavior, and, therefore, (c) a sign of sexual abuse.
3. Observation is a misinterpretation of a behavior observed by a caregiver as bad and then negatively reinforced; often found in families where parents engage in coercive parenting and children's behaviors are misinterpreted in an overly critical and punitive manner.

4. Observation reflects exposure to erotic sexual behavior associated with abuse that introduces the child to an overly stimulating repertoire of behaviors. The child persists in these behaviors because some aspects of the abuse were pleasurable.
5. Observation reflects traumatizing sexual abuse. The child's increased sexual behavior reflects his or her confusion and anger over the abuse, and the observed sexual behavior reflects his or her mixing aggression with sexuality.
6. Observation of sexual behavior reflects the child's exposure to his or her parent's overly (or inappropriately) stimulating parenting practices, including the child witnessing sexual or aggressive acts between adults and/or teenage siblings.
7. Observation of sexual behavior reflects an already oppositional child who now incorporates sexually provocative behavior into her preexisting lying, stealing, truancy, and physical aggressiveness (Friedrich, 2002).

It is important to note that increased frequency of sexual behaviors (Friedrich, 2002) or sexual problem behaviors (Silovsky & Niec, 2002) is not found in children who have been sexually abused. Elliott and colleagues report that the highest levels of observed sexual behavior in children in their sample were from children exposed to pornography. Silovsky and Niec report that children who displayed a high frequency of sexual problem behaviors were more likely not to have a history of substantiated sexual abuse. They conclude, "If these results are supported in replications of the study, it appears that other factors are needed to explain the etiology of sexualized behavior in many young children" (p. 195). Research appears to support the view that increased sexual behavior in children is related to a variety of individual, interpersonal, and family variables and does not mean that a child has been sexually abused. Among relevant family factors that may be associated with increased frequency of sexual behavior are modeling of aggression in the home, parental rejection of the child, inconsistent parenting, and poor or inconsistent parental supervision of the child (Friedrich, 2002).

When there are concerns about a parent's possible maltreatment of a child, administration of a measure that screens for neglect and maltreatment is important. One such measure is the Parenting Stress Inventory (Abidin, 1995), which has been favorably reviewed as a useful tool in child custody evaluations (Otto & Edens, 2003). The PSI is intended to identify stressful areas in parent–child interactions. Another useful instrument is the Child Abuse Potential Inventory (Milner, 1986), a 160-item self-report measure developed to assess parental risk for child physical abuse. It was designed as a screening tool used by child protective service workers when investigating suspected cases of child abuse. Otto and Edens (2003) reviewed its use in child custody evaluations. The CAPI, they write, "was not developed as an index of dimensions of parenting attitudes or abilities generally, but specifically to identify parents who are at high risk for abuse" (p. 284). They conclude, "Thus it is not meaningful to consider how parenting dimensions on the measure might be used to compare a parent's abilities to the parallel needs of a specific child" (p. 290).

When there are concerns about the parent's perception of the nature and quality of his or her relationship with a child, administration of the Parent Child Relationship Inventory (Gerard, 1994) may be appropriate. Otto and Edens (2003) provided a favorable review of the use of the PCRI in custody evaluations. A mistake we have observed among evaluators who use the PCRI is the administration of one test to describe more than one child. We recommend administration of one PCRI per child so that the evaluator may obtain data about each parent's relationship with each child.

It may be useful to assess children's, adults', and parents' perception of parental acceptance and rejection. The Parental Acceptance-Rejection Questionnaire (Rohner, 2000; Rohner, Saavedra, & Granum, 1978), a 60-item self-report questionnaire, may be useful in doing so. Reliability and validity of the PARQ has been satisfactory and meta-analyses of the PARQ across 51 studies found that it was a reliable measure for clinical and applied purposes (Khaleque & Rohner, 2002a, 2002b; Rohner & Britner, 2002; Rohner & Khaleque, 2003).

Forensic Evaluation of an Alleged Perpetrator of Child Maltreatment

In this section, we address forensic evaluation of an alleged perpetrator of child maltreatment. Current texts addressing how to investigate allegations of child sexual abuse do not offer extensive information about how to evaluate the alleged perpetrator. Hewitt's (1999) text on assessing allegations of sexual abuse in preschool children provides no information about how to examine an alleged perpetrator. Even Kuehnle's (1996) superb work on assessing allegations of child sexual abuse does not include much information about how to assess an alleged perpetrator. Friedrich (2002) addresses the psychological assessment of sexually abused children and their families likewise does not include much information about how to assess an alleged perpetrator.

Limitations of Research

It is important that evaluators and courts understand the limited behavioral science literature directly addressing sexual offenders who molest stepchildren. Most studies describe research examining sexual offenders who have been incarcerated or hospitalized because of illegal sexual behavior involving bodily contact with a victim. Most of these people have been men who have committed rape or sexual molestation (Quincey et al., 1998). The court is advised to consider the limited nature of these studies when endeavoring to apply their findings.

There is a substantial literature supporting the finding that the frequency of offending and the likelihood of recidivism are strongly related to the type of victim and the relationship between offender and victim (Fitch, 1962; Frisbie, 1969; Frisbie & Dondis, 1965; Mohr, Turner, & Jerry, 1964). Among child molesters, heterosexual father–daughter incest offenders (who have no other victims) exhibit the lowest recidivism rate, heterosexual extrafamilial child molesters display an intermediate recidivism rate, and homosexual child molesters show the highest recidivism rates (Quincey et al., 1998). The nature of past sex offenses is related to future sex offenses in that there is a tendency for offenders to recommit the same type of offenses rather than switching among them (Hanson & Thornton, 1999). Child molesters who reoffend are more likely to be convicted of another molestation crime than of some other violent offense, whereas other types of sexual offenders tend to be about as likely to be convicted of a nonsexual violent offense as a sexual one (Quincey et al., 1998).

Sexual aggressors have been reported to endorse rape myths, traditional as opposed to egalitarian sex roles, interpersonal violence, hostility to women, adversarial sexual beliefs, sensation seeking, and generally right-wing political views (Quincey et al., 1998). The literature that specifically examines predictors of recidivism among child molesters suggests that recidivism is related to number of previous offenses, selection of male victims, and selection of unrelated victims. Recidivists are younger and are more frequently diagnosed as sociopaths (Quincey & Lalumiere, 2001). Among the best predictors are previous convictions for violent offenses and previous sexual offenses (Rice & Harris, 1995, 1997).

Factors Associated with Sexual Abuse Potential

Appraising risk for sexual maltreatment of a minor is a complex task. The science underlying its methods, procedures, tools, and predictive value are still developing. Two recently described models are those of Quincey and Lalumiere (2001) and Lanyon (2001).

The Quincey and LaLumiere model is briefly described below.

1. Data from follow-up studies of similar offenders are examined.
2. An examinee's characteristics are compared with those of individuals who have committed sex offenses against children. Among the salient factors are social competence, empathy, loneliness, social skills, attitudes toward sex and sexual behavior, and sexual preferences.
3. Situational factors are considered. Situational factors that have been found to be related to probability of reoffense include criminal companions, lack of employment, not seeing one's children, alcohol/drug use, frequent drinking, instability in living arrangements, and lack of responsiveness to supervision.

4. Consideration is given to dynamic factors such as lack of remorse, lack of empathy, procriminal sentiments, desire for and selection of physically immature children as sexual objects, unorthodox ethical values, and grave difficulties in establishing meaningful and healthy relationships with adults.

5. Specific forms of psychopathology are considered. For example, Simon (2000) reports that child molesters tend to be differentiated from other sexual offenders on measures of antisocial personality characteristics and substance abuse.

Lanyon (2001), in discussing his model, writes, "the task of conducting assessments related to sex offending would be facilitated and made more meaningful by the availability of an agreed-upon conceptual framework or model within which to understand this area" (p. 253). In Lanyon's view, we must understand the examinee's psychological characteristics, obtain knowledge of his or her deviant sexual interests, assess the risk of reoffense, assess amenability to treatment, endeavor to assess self-serving misrepresentation by the examinee, and formulate an opinion concerning whether the examinee fits specific formal criteria (either legally defined or defined by the DSM). It is important, however, to remember the limitations of using a model such as Lanyon's, which was developed for use with convicted sexual offenders, when it is applied within the context of a child custody dispute to individuals alleged to have sexually abused a child.

Lanyon (2001, p. 253) posits six questions that need be answered in a sex offender assessment:

1. What kind of person is this? What are the person's general psychological characteristics?

2. What kind of an offender is this? What are the person's deviant sexual interests?

3. What is the risk of reoffense? How dangerous is the person?

4. What is the person's amenability to treatment?

5. To what extent is the person engaging in self-serving misrepresentation during the evaluation?

6. In regard to forensic contexts, how well does the person fir specific formal criteria, either legal or other, such as "sexually violent person" or "pedophile"?

Lanyon (2001) also provides a more detailed discussion of relevant assessment dimensions for each area of examination. He includes a list of recommended tests and measures to be used in a comprehensive evaluation. The reader is encouraged to review this well-crafted article while keeping in mind its limitations.

Faller's Model of Assessment of Intrafamilial Sexual Offenders

Faller (1990) has written about prerequisite factors for and contributing factors to child sexual maltreatment and abuse. Factors that may predispose an individual to act on his or her arousal include pervasive superego deficits, specific deficits in an otherwise satisfactorily functioning superego, cognitive deficits that make the acceptance of absurd rationalizations easier, impaired impulse control, diminished capacity (caused by psychosis, the consumption of intoxicants, or limited intellectual ability. Those factors identified by Faller as contributing to the sexual abuse of children are the offender's childhood experiences, cultural norms, ambiguous role relationships (such as those that may occur in blended families), behaviors of the nonoffending parent, environmental factors, factors that jeopardize customary boundaries, life events that threaten the self-esteem of the offender, and characteristics of the child that may increase his or her vulnerability to victimization.

Kirkpatrick's Model of Evaluation of Allegations of Child Sexual Abuse within the Context of Child Custody Disputes

Another model of the forensic evaluation of allegations of child sexual abuse when custody is in dispute was developed by Kirkpatrick (1999). Kirkpatrick's ideas are organized around Kuehnle's (1996) multiple-hypotheses model, and his model integrates current research about forensic interviewing, forensic testing, use of collateral sources, and direct behavioral observations. An outline of his investigative protocol is presented below.

The evaluator obtains case background information and clearly defines the reason for the referral. Methods and procedures used in the evaluation include (1) testing and interviews of the parties, (2) interviews and observations of the child, (3) interviews and observations of the child and parties, (4) collateral interviews, and (5) home visits.

A thorough review of records is critical. Among the records to be obtained and reviewed are (1) court records, including complaints, motions, and orders; (2) criminal records check; (3) police records and complaints; (4) DSS records; (5) pediatric records; and (6) school records.

Armed with information about case history, legal history, and family and personal history, when the sexual abuse of a young child is alleged, the evaluator must consider the following possibilities (from Kuehnle, 1996).

1. The child is a victim of sexual abuse, and the allegation is credible and accurate.
2. The child is a victim of sexual abuse but, due to age or cognitive deficits, does not have the verbal skills to provide a credible description of his or her abuse.

3. The child is a victim of sexual abuse but, due to fear, will not disclose his or her abuse.
4. The child is a victim of sexual abuse but, due to misguided loyalty, will not disclose his or her abuse.
5. The child is not a victim of sexual abuse and is credible but has misperceived an innocent interaction. (A variation of this hypothesis might be that the child is truthful but has misperceived an ambiguous or innocent situation or has misidentified an alleged suspect.)
6. The child is not a victim of sexual abuse but has been unintentionally contaminated by a concerned or hypervigilant caretaker or authority figure.
7. The child is not a victim of sexual abuse but has been intentionally manipulated by a caretaker or authority figure into believing that he or she has been abused.
8. The child is not a victim of sexual abuse but knowingly falsely accuses someone of sexual abuse because of pressure by caretakers or authority figures who believe the child has been abused.
9. The child is not a victim of sexual abuse but knowingly falsely accuses someone of sexual abuse for reasons of personal aggrandizement or revenge.[2]

Describing an approximate, detailed chronology is important. The first step is to identify when the child's first spontaneous disclosure occurred and the conditions under which it occurred. The evaluation should obtain information about the initial report. In examining the usefulness of the child's initial report, the evaluator should investigate several factors that may have influenced the report (many of these have been discussed in Chapter 6), among the most important of which are:

1. Interviewer or confirmatory bias.
2. High status or perceived authority.
3. Stereotype induction.
4. Characteristics of the initial interviews to consider.
5. Use of AD dolls.
6. Memory factors.
7. Suggestive interviewing.
   a. Use of open-ended questions
   b. Use of leading or misleading questions
   c. Use of repeated questioning (within and across interviews)
   d. Emotional tone of interview (selective reinforcement, bribes, threats, rewards)
   e. Peer pressure
   f. Aggrandizement of adult status
   g. Visualization procedures

The evaluator should obtain a detailed and specific report of the alleged sexual behavior. What is the sexual behavior being described? Is it normative or atypical? The sexual problem behavior should be defined along several dimensions, including frequency of observed behavior, intent of observed behavior, effect of observed behavior (on child and on others), and compulsiveness of observed behavior.

It is important to investigate whether the initial report was spontaneous or prompted. It is best to have a video- or audiotape of the child's initial disclosure. If the initial disclosure occurred during an interview, then the evaluator should ask:

1. What did the interviewer say just prior to the disclosure?
2. What were the child's verbatim statements?
3. What did the child do/say immediately after the disclosure?
4. What did the interviewer do/say immediately after the disclosure?

The evaluator must investigate the extent to which parents or caretakers have interviewed the child and the extent to which nonfamily caretakers have interviewed the child.

Assessment of the child's behavior should include examination of symptoms of distress or sexualized behavior. This may be accomplished through interviewing, testing, collateral data, direct observations, and parent reports. Obtaining medical records and examining whether the child denied the alleged abuse are relevant areas of inquiry. Assessing the child's level of distress and reaction to trauma are also important.

There are several child-related areas to assess. Among the characteristics of the child to be considered are developmental level, language development, cognitive development, and social development. Attachment to each parent should be assessed from both a current and a historical perspective. The evaluator needs to assess relevant characteristics of the alleged perpetrator parent, characteristics of the protective parent, and characteristics of the immediate and extended families. Other factors that should be examined are the presence of alienation dynamics, preseparation maltreatment allegations, and intimate partner maltreatment.

Kirkpatrick (2001) recommends that evaluators organize the discussion section of the report around the following topic areas:

1. Maltreatment and its effect on the child.
2. Maltreatment and its effect on the family.
3. Maltreatment and its effect on the protective parent.
4. Maltreatment and the rehabilitation possibilities for the perpetrator.
5. The marriage and family context.
6. The child's best psychological interests.
7. Analysis of parenting capacities.

8. The resulting fit.
9. Recommendations.

We believe that Kirkpatrick's evaluation protocol is among the most thorough and comprehensive available to guide evaluators in gathering a robust set of data and in organizing these data around salient factors relevant to a forensic evaluation of allegations of child sexual abuse within the context of a custody dispute.

Summary

This chapter described the forensic assessment of allegations of child sexual abuse within the context of a child custody evaluation. Two specific models were discussed, the forensic model and the trauma-based model. We argued that the forensic evaluation of allegations of child sexual abuse within the context of a custody dispute must include an evaluation of the alleged victim, the alleged perpetrator parent, and the other parent. It might also include an assessment of extended family system factors that may contribute to dysfunction in the binuclear family. The chapter concluded with a description of several evaluation protocols for use in investigation of allegations of child sexual abuse in the context of custody disputes.

Notes

1. The evaluator will likely have a statutory responsibility to report suspicion of child maltreatment to the Department of Social Services.
2. Although preadolescent and adolescent children may be capable of knowingly falsely accusing someone of sexual abuse for secondary gains (e.g., escape from the family, revenge, removal of an adult from the family, etc.), preschool and young school-age children are probably not cognitively sophisticated enough to initiate a false sexual abuse allegation.

This list is reprinted by permission from Kuehnle (1996). Copyright 1996 by Professional Resources Exchange, Inc.

CHAPTER 12

Assessing Allegations of Domestic Violence

The forensic assessment of allegations of domestic violence in child custody evaluations remains among the hottest topics for research and practice in forensic psychology (Jaffe, Lemon, & Poisson, 2003; Horvath, Logan, & Walker, 2002; Logan, Walker, Jordan, & Horvath, 2002; Meier, 2003) and is of great interest to family court judges (Jaffe, Crooks, & Poisson, 2003; National Council of Juvenile and Family Court Judges, 1999). Forensic assessment of allegations of domestic violence when custody is in dispute presents a unique challenge to forensic evaluators not only because of the complexity of the psychological variables involved in a comprehensive assessment, but also because of the political and social dimensions involved in judicial decisions about it (e.g., Cuthbert et al., 2002).

In 1987, in the first edition of their much-cited work *Psychological Evaluations for the Courts*, Melton and colleagues, commenting on our assessments of comparative custodial fitness, declared, "there is probably no forensic question on which overreaching by mental health professionals has been so common and so egregious" (Melton et al., 1987, p. 330). A decade later, they reiterated their assertion in the book's second edition (Melton et al., 1997, p. 463). This observation has been applied by Austin (2000d) to the investigation of allegations of domestic violence that are made within the context of custodial placement disputes. Evaluators *have* overreached by offering to the court opinions based upon inadequate or incomplete data, outdated research, or personal beliefs and personal biases and presenting these opinions as expert (e.g., *Severson v. Hansen*, 1995).

Jaffe, Crooks, and Poisson (2003) identify several myths of domestic violence and child custody:

1. *Domestic violence is rarely a problem for divorcing couples involved in child custody disputes.* The reality is that the majority of parents in high-conflict divorces involving child custody report a history of domestic violence.
2. *Domestic violence ends with separation for abused women.* The reality is that abused women often face continuing risks from their partner after separation.
3. *As long as children are not abused directly, they are not harmed by exposure to domestic violence.* The reality is that children exposed to domestic violence may suffer from significant emotional and behavioral problems related to this traumatic experience.
4. *As domestic violence is behavior between adults, it is not relevant for the determination of child custody.* The reality is that domestic violence is highly relevant to the determination of child custody by courts and court-related services.
5. *Family courts, lawyers, and court-related services such as mediation and custody evaluation can assess the needs of abused women and their children as well as the impact of the batterer.* The reality is that the significance of domestic violence is overlooked by family courts, lawyers, and court-related services.

We begin this chapter by focusing on tensions between science and politics because we believe that evaluators need to be aware of the larger social policy and community standards factors that may influence how custody opinions and recommendations are accepted. We also believe that one can hold strong political views about issues such as the meaning of domestic violence within our society and still bring to the evaluation endeavor a clarity of method, a respect for ethics, and a commitment to fairness and due process.

Abuse Is a Violation of a Fundamental Human Right

Throughout the world, intimate partner abuse and child abuse have been recognized as violations of fundamental human rights, particularly the right to freedom from violence (Universal Declaration of Human Rights, 1948; Declaration on the Elimination of Violence Against Women, 1993). In the United States, some researchers have estimated that one-quarter of the women in this country are reported to be abused by their husbands or by men with whom they have an intimate relationship (Jaffe, Lemon, & Poisson, 2003; Tjaden & Thoennes, 2000a, 2000b). In 1998, women accounted for about 75% of U.S. victims of intimate murder and about 85% of U.S. victims of nonlethal violence (Henneburg, 2000).

About 43% of female victims of intimate partner violence live in households with children younger than 12 (Rennison & Welchans, 2000). As discussed further below, children of women who are abused by a male partner are at higher risk for being abused themselves by these same men. Some studies indicate that domestic violence and child abuse co-occur, with some researchers reporting that 40–70% of the children of battered mothers have been found to be directly abused by their mother's batterer (Ross, 1996). Researchers are identifying important links among intimate partner abuse, child abuse, and custody disputes. Child custody and visitation arrangements often provide a context for abusive men to continue their attempts to control and victimize their former intimate partners and their children (Bancroft & Silverman, 2002a, 2002b; Jaffe, Lemon, & Poisson, 2003).

In response to emerging concerns about the relationship among intimate partner abuse, child abuse, and child custody disputes, victim advocacy and child advocacy groups have begun to bring to the attention of family courts a message that a strong and dangerous bias exists in the courts (Cuthbert et al., 2002; Schafran, 2003) and that this bias is reflected in six specific categories of human rights violations:

1. Failure to protect battered women and children from abuse.
2. Discrimination and bias against battered women.
3. Degrading treatment of battered women.
4. Denial of due process to battered women.
5. Allowing the batterer to continue abuse through the family court process.
6. Failure to respect the economic rights of battered women and their children (Cuthbert et al., 2002).

Although it is unclear whether these types of alleged human rights violations occur with regularity or whether they occur across the United States, we raise these concerns to bring to your attention that many in the domestic violence arena believe that family courts do not fairly adjudicate custody disputes when issues of domestic violence are alleged.

The Importance of Research about Men and Research about Women

Previous studies suggest that women are more accurate reporters of the entire context of family violence than are men. Men are more likely to report only violent acts that they commit when they have an intent to harm (Margolin, John, & Gleberman, 1988). Walker (1995) and Straus (1999) have called attention to the need to examine the reasons women use violence against men. Though it has been acknowledged that most battered women use violence in reaction to the abuse they experience, there are some data to suggest that a small group of women initiate violence or are equal contributors to the physical violence in the family (Bow & Boxer, 2003; Hines & Malley-Morrison, 2001; Johnston & Campbell, 1993).

Forensic evaluators should maintain an awareness of current trends, methodological changes, and developments in the field of domestic violence. We wish to emphasize our strongly held belief that domestic violence is an important risk factor in many child custody cases (Jaffe, Lemon, & Poisson, 2003) and that, at the very least, evaluators should conduct initial screening for domestic violence in all custody cases, *whether or not allegations of domestic violence have been registered in previous court pleadings.*

From a scientific perspective, emphasizing research on both male and female victims *and* male and female perpetrators is important. From an empirical and practical point of view, we note that women are far more often the victims of violent actions that injure (Margolin et al., 1988; O'Leary & Maiuro, 2001; Zorza, 2002, 2006). Battered women seek medical attention for injuries sustained as a consequence of domestic violence significantly more often than men, and they sustain injuries as a consequence of domestic violence more often after separation than during cohabitation (Cuthbert et al., 2002). As many as 75% of visits to the emergency room by battered women occur after separation (Cuthbert et al., 2002). The risk for continued intimate partner violence and for children exposed to it increases during the separation period (Logan et al., 2002; Cuthbert et al., 2002).

Competing Needs of Science and Politics

Archer (2000b) acknowledged the potentially competitive needs of science and politics when he researched a socially sensitive issue exploring physical aggression in representative samples (that is, people who were not involved in mental health treatment for intimate partner violence) of heterosexual partners, generally young couples. He attempted to place his work within the context of scientific research, arguing that an evidence-based analysis would be a useful scientific contribution. Archer (2000a) also conducted meta-analyses of sex differences in physical aggression to heterosexual partners in representative samples. He found that women were slightly more likely than men to use one or more acts of physical aggression and to use such acts more frequently but that men were more likely to inflict injury and that 62% of those injured by a partner were women.

These results did not strike us particularly unusual or polarizing. For at least 20 years, researchers have reported somewhat similar results. Gelles and Straus (1988) have reported similar results since the mid-1970s about the relatively similar frequencies of physically aggressive actions in husband to wife and wife to husband intimate partner violence. They also reported that men were more likely to inflict injury on women. In their 1975 survey of American families, Straus and Gelles (1986) found that, among wives reporting violence by their husbands in the previous year, 12.1% reported that they had been the victim of some kind of violence and 3.8% reported that they had been the victim of severe violence. This rate of severe violence toward married women is equivalent to 2.1 million wives nationwide. Although Straus and Gelles's survey data revealed a 27% decrease from previous studies in reported incidents of wife beating, this number still represented 1.6 million married females experiencing severe assault by their intimate partner during marriage. As surprising as this number is, it is important for evaluators to remember that the risk for violence *increases* when couples separate and divorce.

In commenting upon Archer's (2002) reported results, O'Leary (2000) makes the point that conclusions about physically aggressive behavior in intimate relationships cannot be generalized to samples of physically abusive men and women (p. 688). He believes the frequency of physical aggression in young couples requires immediate action to prevent and deescalate physical aggression by men and women in its early stages. He concludes by saying, "The need to address physical aggression in intimate relations by both men and women is now inescapable" (p. 688).

The political context of *how* research results describing socially sensitive issues may be used by society is discussed by White, Smith, Koss, and Figueredo (2000). White and colleagues raised awareness about the social policy implications of a scientific finding that may undermine social policy initiatives to protect victims of domestic violence. They write:

> It is a serious public policy concern for psychologists to endorse a position that men and women are equally violent in relationships. Such a message is harmful in its potential to undermine empathy and public support for the plight of female survivors of male violence and to deflate the momentum of efforts to change the structural conditions that support violence against women . . . social scientists have a special obligation to consider the policy implications of their work and to exert their best efforts to present findings in a form that maximizes the potential that they will be correctly understood and applied. (p. 695)

A similar point is made by Jaffe, Lemon, and Poisson (2003) who remind us that "although the prevalence of domestic violence will be debated for another generation, it is clear that the impact of divorce cannot be meaningfully researched without considering violence and abuse" (p. 6).

Custody evaluators should be aware of the social and political context within which a custody trial occurs. Expert testimony about socially and politically charged issues such as domestic violence must be presented honestly while at the same time framed within the context of normative social, community, and cultural values. We do not suggest that an evaluator alter a conclusion or misrepresent or exclude research that is politically incorrect. The point is that evaluators need to be sensitive to how their reports may be viewed outside of the limited context of a specific custody case and how a court's decision on one case may have wide-ranging public policy implications across a state.

Models, Assumptions within Models, and Potential Bias

Traditional models of domestic violence are based on the assumption that males are most likely perpetrators and females victims (Dutton, 2005a, 2005b). Two assumptions are that patriarchy and male privilege drive domestic violence. Assessment strategies that follow from a gender-based model of domestic violence place greater emphasis on characteristics of the abuser such as personality factors including, but not limited to, impulsiveness, low frustration tolerance, narcissism, lack of empathy, and values and beliefs about the relationship between men and women based upon social and gender inequality. Research paradigms and clinical treatment models examining batterer characteristics (e.g., Bancroft & Silverman, 2002a) focus greater attention on individual factors than on family and/or relationship factors, but in the family system under scrutiny, the more useful level of analysis for the cause(s) of domestic violence may lie in relationship factors or family factors more representative of the gender-inclusive model (Dutton, 2005a; Johnson, 2005). The evaluator needs to be open to investigating all relevant factors, whether or not the examination of such factors is viewed as politically correct (Gould, Martindale, & Eidman, 2007).

Dutton (2005) posits that there is little empirical support for the notion that intimate partner violence should be framed as a gender-based issue in which men are overwhelmingly more likely to be perpetrators of domestic violence and women to be its victims. The assumptions in a gender-inclusive model are that men and women are perpetrators and victims of domestic violence and that abusive behavior in intimate relationships reflects diverse causes that may frequently interact. In this model, factors that need to be examined include relationships between and among family members, type of abuse, and the effect of familial violence on each member and his or her respective role in maintaining the dysfunction. It is possible, however, that in the family system under scrutiny, the more useful level of analysis for the causes of domestic violence may lie in specific personality factors more representative of the gender-specific model. Again, we stress that the evaluator needs to be open to investigating all relevant factors, independent of model.

We believe that an examiner engaged in the forensic evaluation of allegations of domestic violence within the context of child custody litigation ought to be familiar with as many different models of domestic violence as possible in order to anticipate which factors are the most relevant to assess in a particular family. We believe that evaluators need to be neutral with regard to the gender politics of domestic violence.

We have written elsewhere about the parameters of the forensic model (Martindale & Gould, 2004) and its application to child custody assessments (Gould, 2006). The forensic model is based upon an evaluator's neutrality and independence from bias, including bias that might occur from alignment with a particular scholarly argument. The data gathered in a forensic evaluation either do or do not support a specific hypothesis. It is not the role of the evaluator to offer to the court judgments of truthfulness or credibility. That is the unique province of the judge. Evaluators' opinions and conclusions should be based solely upon the weight of psychological information obtained during the evaluation.

There is, we believe, a motivation for many evaluators to try to be helpful to the court by offering opinions, and when the data are insufficiently reliable, these "helpful" evaluators offer opinions based upon clinical judgment rather than upon the psychological facts found in the evaluation data. These clinical judgments, intended to help, are based upon assumptions for which there is little, if any, empirical support, and they exemplify the egregious overreaching to which Melton and colleagues (1997) and Austin (2000d) have referred. No matter what model one believes in, one should investigate domestic violence allegations with a neutral, independent perspective.

For those evaluators who believe in a specific model, it is important to consider how that belief leads to inclusion or exclusion of certain variables for investigative consideration. Such inclusion and exclusion guided by the evaluator's belief in a specific domestic violence model may lead the evaluator to ignore forensically relevant variables useful to the court in determining the veracity of the allegations. We stress again that embracing a specific model may result in a bias leading to consideration of one set of variables and exclusion of another set of variables.

Evaluators Are Better Educated Than We Thought

Recent research suggests that, despite a widely held belief to the contrary (Schrafran, 2003), evaluators are involved in continuing education courses focused on domestic violence education. Bow and Boxer (2003) surveyed child custody evaluators for their education in and exposure to domestic violence assessment and found that 68.2% of their sample had no graduate courses addressing domestic violence; however, custody evaluators had taken continuing education courses on domestic violence. The average number of seminars on domestic violence was 7.4 (median = 4), and the median number of domestic violence books or articles read by evaluators was 18. Only 4.5% of the sample had attended no seminars, and 2.7% had read fewer than three books or articles.

Bow and Boxer (2003) found that 37% of custody evaluations involved allegations of domestic violence. Of these allegations, 46% surfaced around the time of separation, 29% were characterized as episodic violence, and 24% were characterized as chronic violence. Fifty-one percent of the violence was male-initiated, 11% was female-initiated, and 14% was bidirectional. The most frequently reported types of domestic violence were, in order of frequency, verbal or emotional abuse, physical aggression, coercion and threats, controlling finances, destruction of property, isolation, stalking, forced sex, and kidnapping children.

Despite the apparent increase in awareness of allegations of domestic violence on the part of custody evaluators and the relatively high frequency of occurrence of allegations of domestic violence in court-ordered custody disputes, evaluators are not using abuse-specific measures in their assessment protocols. Bow and Boxer (2003) reported that when specialized questionnaires were utilized, they were used when assessing adults. Twenty-nine percent of evaluators developed their own questionnaire, 20% used the Spousal Assault Risk Assessment Guide (SARA), 15% used the Psychopathy Checklist—Revised (PCL-R), 11% used the Historical, Clinical, and Risk Items (HCR-20), and 9% used the CTS. Abuse-specific measures such as the TSI (Briere, 1995), the TSCC (Briere, 1996), and the Detailed Assessment of Posttraumatic Stress (DAPS; Briere, 2001) that might assist the evaluator in gauging the degree of experienced trauma of the alleged child victim were not reported to have been used by evaluators.

Bow and Boxer did not provide information about the type of questionnaires used by evaluators in assessing allegations of domestic violence. It would be useful to know *how* evaluators gather information about allegations of domestic violence. There are several useful semistructured interview formats for use with alleged victims and alleged perpetrators, such as that developed by Drozd (2007). There are also useful investigative protocols that assist the evaluator in understanding the larger family context within which the alleged violence occurred (e.g., Bancroft & Silverman, 2002a).

Logan and colleagues (2002) conducted a content analysis of 82 child custody evaluations and found that evaluators do not appear to investigate the nature or extent of domestic violence, and, "more specifically, [evaluators] do not explore domestic violence as a way of attending to the child's safety interests" (p. 735). Evaluators interviewed parents together even when court documents indicated concern about allegations of domestic violence toward the mother. Logan and colleagues write: "This practice could contribute not only to distorted information from victims, but could also contribute to further harm through retribution for disclosures of violent acts or child endangerment" (p. 735). This concern is consistent with research results showing that abused women are more likely than nonabused women to report that the abuser may affect their ability to be open during court proceedings because of their fear of possible future harm (Newmark, Harrell, & Salem, 1995).

Not surprisingly, there is another perspective to be considered. If an evaluator customarily begins the evaluative process by conducting a session attended by both parents, it might be argued that a departure from the customary procedure suggests that, before having met either party, the evaluator had already taken a position (albeit tentative) on the validity of the allegations. Positions taken or hypotheses generated prior to the commencement of an evaluation can become fertile ground for the operation of confirmatory bias (Martindale, 2005a).

A related, and hotly debated, issue is whether evaluators ought to be sensitive to people's expressed fears and discomforts if being responsive entails departing from the evaluators' customary procedures. In particular, what should an evaluator do when one parent expresses a reluctance to attend a joint session and explains that the other parent is intimidating? In the Bow and Boxer (2003) survey, 25% of those responding reported that they conduct joint interviews, likely because they believe that useful (if not vital) observational data are obtained that way. Those who feel strongly about the usefulness of joint sessions might argue (1) that it is in the children's best interests that the advisory report to be utilized by the court be the product of an evaluative process that has been as free as possible from methodological flaws; (2) that any source of useful information should be tapped, unless doing so is in conflict with the law (as would be the case if an evaluator were to listen to illegally obtained tape recordings); (3) that there will be times when a procedure makes one or both parents more comfortable but deprives the evaluator of information he or she deems useful; and (4) that when the evaluator's customary procedure causes some emotional discomfort for one or both parents but preserves the integrity of the evaluative process, the parents should be expected to subordinate their needs to those of their children.

In contrast to Bow and Boxer, Logan and colleagues (2002) found that "multiple methods were not used to examine the 'best interests of the child' " (p. 735). Just over half of the evaluations reviewed provided information that collateral interviews were conducted. Only about 38% of cases included home visits, and even fewer reviewed school records, criminal histories, medical records, counseling records, or court records.

In work product review consultations, continuing education workshops, and professional seminars that we have conducted, we have found that many forensic evaluators are poorly informed about the *psychological* dynamics of domestic violence, the effects of domestic violence on children, and the potential harm to children resulting from exposure to domestic violence. Our experience is that too many forensic evaluators continue to think about domestic violence as characterized only by acts of physical aggression. We are concerned that maintaining a focus only on acts of physical aggression will lead to continued underestimates of true cases of domestic violence and, as a result, place more families at risk for maltreatment and abuse.

Foundational Concepts in Understanding Domestic Violence

In this section, we discuss historically important core concepts about domestic violence. As the reader will see in our discussion of an evaluation paradigm for familial violence, the concepts of the cycle of violence, the power and control wheel, and other historically relevant factors are incorporated.

The Cycle of Violence

In the beginning, there was the cycle of violence. Walker's (1979) work transformed understanding of how to think about the dynamics of domestic violence in order to follow a pattern of abuse. She wrote that battered women are not constantly physically assaulted nor does such violence occur at random times. Although subsequent research and clinical experience have added substantially to Walker's initial ideas, it is equally important to understand that not all domestic violence is characterized by the cycle of violence pattern. It is naive for evaluators to believe that if the cycle of violence is not readily apparent, then no domestic violence has occurred. Other models explaining domestic violence provide alternative factors to examine.

The cycle of violence represents a pattern of behavior that characterizes the abusive dance between perpetrator and victim. It comprises three phases: tension building, battering, and honeymoon.

Phase 1: Tension Building

There is an increase in tension between batterer and victim in phase 1. The batterer engages in behaviors of verbal dominance and control as well as some minor physical aggression. The verbal dominance and control may take the form of name calling, continuous criticism, verbal harassment, psychological and emotional humiliation, and psychological and emotional threat.

During this phase, the victim is aware of a change in the batterer's behavior and attitude. He becomes increasingly agitated, impatient, and angry. In response to the change in the emotional climate of the family, the victim begins to exercise caution when interacting with the batterer. Minor battering may occur, and the victim often rationalizes these events, attributing the behavior to external stressors or blaming herself and the family.

As the victim withdraws from contact with the batterer and begins slowly to protect herself, the batterer recognizes that his increased aggressiveness and dominance is wrong. He fears that the victim will leave him, triggering fears of abandonment and threats to his control over her. She reinforces his fear by further withdrawing into a protective mode, hoping that she will not be the trigger to his more explosive and dangerous battering behaviors. The tension between them builds as the batterer becomes more agitated and controlling in response to the victim's increased withdrawal.

In healthy relationships, couples may disagree or argue, but both have equal power in the relationship. In battering relationships, the abuser's need for power and control underlies anger and blaming. The tension continues to escalate. Victims of such abuse often describe feeling like they are "walking on eggshells" during this time.

The tension between victim and batterer leads to increased hostility and dissatisfaction. Phase 2 begins.

Phase 2: Battering

Phase 2 is characterized by a major destructive act of physical violence by the abuser against the victim. There is an increase in the use of severe verbal abuse, psychological control, and psychological intimidation. During this phase, the threat of physical harm to the spouse (and possibly the children) is greatest, and the most serious physical injuries occur at this time.

The perpetrator does not understand his anger and may believe that the victim deserved the abuse. It is not usual for the abused to believe that she is responsible for the abuser's actions. She may also deny the seriousness of her injuries to calm the batterer and reassure him that she will never leave.

Often, the batterer is unable to recall the abuse in any detail, while the victim has a clear memory of the details. Sometimes, she fights back, which may lead to increased serious physical injury.

Some battering incidents occur because the abuser is so angry or so drunk that he loses control of himself. Clinical observation of batterers reveals that they often make statements such as, "if she hadn't kept nagging me, I wouldn't have lost my temper," or "I was so angry, I didn't know what I was doing." The attribution by the batterer is either that the victim caused him to abuse her or that his abuse was the result of being out of control.

The cycle of violence model posits that, in fact, batterers *take* control when they batter. They take control of the immediate situation, their partner, their physical space, and usually the outcome of the situation. Domestic violence is an abuse of power and control, not a passionate response gone out of control.

Phase 3: The Honeymoon

In the honeymoon phase, the batterer is apologetic and loving toward his spouse. He may shower her with gifts and promises never to hurt her again. The purpose of his loving behavior is to ensure that she does not leave him. Such a departure might trigger his deep-seated fear of abandonment and cause him to become more of a threat to her safety. The loving behavior often entices the victim into staying in the relationship. In part, she believes she is responsible, so staying provides her an opportunity to rectify her mistake. Her staying also reflects her fear that movement away from the perpetrator may trigger another physical assault on her. Whether the movement is psychological or physical, the victim is compelled to deny her fears (or at least hide them) and move closer to the batterer.

The psychological and physical closeness that may result from the victim attempting to respond positively to the batterer's overtures begins the cycle over again, with Phase 1. The closer the parents become to each other, the more difficult it is to maintain the closeness. As the abused moves away from the abuser, seeking a more comfortable and safe distance, the abuser responds to her movement with irritation and anger. He feels threatened by her movement away, and she senses his increased irritation and takes steps to protect herself. The cycle begins anew.

The batterer is likely to have experienced a physiological release of tension. He is frequently sorry, feels guilty, and is willing to try anything to make up with his partner. He may give her flowers or gifts. The couple may even make love in an attempt to reestablish intimacy and security after the explosion. The batterer also places responsibility for his actions on his victim, blaming her for "having to hit her" or "making me do what I did because she was asking for it." He will minimize his role in the violence. Often, the victim will be in shock, emotionally distraught, and physically injured. She will feel confused and guilty that somehow she caused him to lose control and engage in violence. She will want to believe his promises that he will never become abusive again. Both partners deny how bad the abuse was and that it could happen again. In this stage, the increased intimacy and promises to get help or never do it again give the victim hope that things will change.

There are two predictable outcomes from the cycle of violence. The first is that, without intervention, the cycle does not change. The second is that, over time, the severity of the violence becomes worse and both its frequency and the magnitude of the injuries increase.

The Power and Control Wheel

We include a discussion of the power and control wheel because of the frequency with which people talk about power and control factors in relationships and because of the critical place the power and control concept has in current views of domestic violence. We believe it is important that any discussion of power and control factors recognize the important contribution made by the Duluth model.

The Duluth Model

The power and control wheel was initially developed by the Duluth Abuse Intervention Project from the experiences of more than 200 battered women and has subsequently been reaffirmed in several other studies. The wheel illustrates that violence is part of a pattern of behaviors rather than isolated incidents of abuse or cyclical explosions of pent-up anger, frustration, or painful feelings (Crichton-Hill, 2001). A batterer's use of physical assaults or sexual abuse may be infrequent but reinforces the power of the other tactics on the wheel that eventually undermine his partner's ability to act autonomously (Dutton & Starzomski, 1997).

The wheel consists of eight sections: using intimidation; emotional abuse; isolation; minimizing, denying, and blaming; using children; male privilege; economic abuse; and using coercion and threats. A second circle surrounds the first and includes physical and sexual violence. These are viewed as extreme tactics to generate power and control (Dutton & Starzomski, 1997).

The central premise on which the power and control wheel is based is that "battering is caused by a culturally supported belief that people have the right to control their partners" (Crichton-Hill, 2001, p. 204). The power and control wheel is built upon a feminist analysis of family violence that suggests that

> violence against women is a behavior approved of and sanctioned in many part of the culture. Abusive men and, often, women victims have been immersed in a culture that supports relationships of dominance, rooted in the assumption that based on differences, some people have the legitimate right to master others. (Crichton-Hill, 2001, p. 205)

Assessment of Cultural Assumptions

Four cultural assumptions have been identified supporting the belief that people have the right to control their partners: natural order, objectification of women, forced submission, and overt coercion and physical force. A comprehensive forensic evaluation of domestic violence should assess both the underlying cultural conditions as well as the areas of concern identified on the power and control wheel.

NATURAL ORDER

Natural order is a belief system that places the abuser in a position of power over the victim and makes the abuser feel that he is legitimately entitled to obedience. To determine whether the concept of natural order contributes to the current concerns about the role of power in social and intimate relationships, our attention needs to be upon the various cultures from which the person being evaluated comes. These include family of origin, workplace culture, friendship and community groups, and other relevant subcultures in which the person being evaluated participates.

OBJECTIFICATION OF WOMEN

Objectification provides continual reinforcement for abusers to see women as objects rather than as humans of equal status. The pornography and advertising industries promote objectification of women. Areas of examination for an evaluator may include cultural traditions and beliefs relating to traditional male and female roles and relationships, including leisure and entertainment activities, status and social position variables. Historical information from female associates, including former romantic and business partners, may help determine whether the person being evaluated has tended toward objectifying women.

FORCED SUBMISSION

Forced submission of victims to abusers takes place through the use of conditioned power within a culturally reinforced environment. Forced submission occurs because abusers expect to dominate. A culturally reinforced environment promotes the domination of men and persuades women to accept this domination. Examination of this variable includes the alleged victim as well as the alleged perpetrator.

For the alleged perpetrator, factors that need to be assessed include the belief that he can force another into a position of submission, the belief that he is entitled to do so and to stop the other person from attempting to escape from the dominance, and the belief that he can control access to outside resources.

Factors that need to be assessed in the alleged victim include the belief that she is being forced into a position of accepting dominance (Crichton-Hill, 2001), the belief that her efforts to escape harm would make a difference (Cribb, 1997), the knowledge of available resources (Cribb, 1997), the degree of both real and perceived isolation from others (Crichton-Hill, 2001), and the belief that the surrounding culture is understanding of domestic violence.

OVERT COERCION AND PHYSICAL FORCE

Overt coercion and physical force allows the abuser to use physical violence without significant punishment. Examination of the alleged perpetrator's use of physical violence is both historical and current and includes data from children and adults. Each of these areas may be important to assess in a comprehensive evaluation of domestic violence allegations.

Dutton's Criticism: Patriarchy Does Not Cause Family Violence

Dutton (1998, 1999, 2000; Dutton & Kropp, 2000; Dutton & Starzomski, 1997) suggests that domestic violence or, more specifically, intimate partner violence is a complex phenomenon that can occur for numerous reasons, only one of which might be belief in patriarchy or male privilege. Dutton argues that research has called into question older models of domestic violence.

As summarized in Table 12.1, Stets and Straus (1990) examined the 1975 U.S. national survey data on domestic violence and investigated violence levels

TABLE 12.1. National Survey Results for Violence by Gender

	Males	Females
Dating	12.5%	0.1%
Cohabiting	13.4%	7.3%
Married	5.7%	9.6%

Note. N = 5,242 couples. Data from Stets and Straus (1990).

in married couples compared with violence levels in couples who were cohabiting or dating obtained from other surveys. They found that 9–13% of females used severe violence when their male partner was nonviolent. They also found that married females were more likely than married males to use unilateral violence, that is, violence that is not reciprocated.

Magdol et al. (1997) conducted a longitudinal study of 1,037 people born in 1972 and 1973 in New Zealand. His sample was demographically representative of the geographic area being studied. When the subjects turned 21, Magdol et al. conducted interviews with those who had been involved in an intimate relationship within the past year. Of the original 1,037 subjects, 425 females and 436 males participated in these interviews.

The results revealed that women engaged in more abusive behavior than men. The rates of intimate partner violence were similar to U.S. rates. Perpetrators and victims presented the same demographic profiles. They were unemployed, had less schooling, were more alcohol-dependent, and had higher scores on all mental health and criminality measures, indicating greater concern for their overall mental health.

Archer's (2000a) meta-analytic study of intimate partner behaviors examined three variables associated with aggressive behavior between couples: mutual aggressiveness and male perpetrator, female victim violence. As summarized in Table 12.2, data revealed roughly equivalent frequency of aggression for males and females. The numbers in the "men" and "women" columns show the actual number of men and women reporting violence, injury, and medical

TABLE 12.2. Frequency of Aggressive Behaviors between Men and Women in Nonrepresentative Samples

	Men	Women	Effect size
Violence	30,343	34,053	–0.05[a]
Injury	7,011	7,531	0.15
Medical treatment	4,936	6,323	0.08

Note. Data from Archer (2000a).
[a]Women slightly more likely to be violent.

treatment. The effect size is significant only for male versus female violence at the .05 level, with the number of women who engaged in violence against men slightly higher than the number of men who engaged in violence against women.

Based in part on the consistency of empirical results of these studies, Dutton (1998) argues that domestic violence does not appear to be caused by patriarchy, as research demonstrates that women assault men at about the same rates as men assault women. He argues that no single-factor explanation for domestic violence sufficiently explains the available data and proposes a nested ecological theory examining interactive effects of the broader culture, the subculture, the family, and individual characteristics.

Dutton (1998) believes a complete theory of domestic violence must be able to discriminate assaultive from non-assaultive males. He suggests that in order properly to answer the question "Why do men beat their wives?" one has to examine why some men but not all beat their wives. He also contends that research needs to identify factors that distinguish why some men repeatedly and severely assault their wives while others do so sporadically and in less serious ways and others still remain nonviolent throughout their marriages (Dutton, 1998).

Dutton (1998) writes that both feminist and sociobiological models lead to predictions of violence rates that are much higher than those actually obtained. He suggests that newer models provide the empirical foundation to rethink both the focus and treatment implications lacking in the older models.

Feminist theories have made significant contributions to analyses of the social and family context within which domestic violence occurs. Dutton (2004, 2007) argues that analysis should be integrated into explorations of individual differences associated with personality factors. He suggests that the data support the conclusion that an abusive personality exists. This personality type seems to have an attachment disorder as part of its development. Neurobiological deficits that may be a result of inadequate attachment are thought to create a perpetrator who has impulsive aggression caused in part by faulty development of the brain and abnormal levels of neurotransmitters. The implications of the new model suggest a combination of drug treatment, cognitive-behavioral treatment for anger/assault, and dialectical behavior therapy for self-disturbance/borderline personality.

Dutton (2005a) argues that recent publications linking domestic violence and custody assessment (Bancroft & Silverman, 2002b; Jaffe, Lemon, & Poisson, 2003) provide a "one-sided analyses of domestic violence based on self-selected and non-representative samples" (p. 24). What is problematic, he writes, is that "while their description of the actions and consequences of abuse on the child are accurate, there is a priming of assessors to look only at the male as the abuse perpetrator, and once having done so to suspect his denial of abuse" (p. 25).

Dutton (2005a) warns evaluators of bias that is embedded in the books that teach them how to conduct assessments of allegations of domestic violence in the context of child custody disputes. He argues that Jaffe, Lemon, and Poisson (2003) and Bancroft and Silverman (2002a) present a picture to the reader that males are perpetrators, perpetrators lie, and that alleged perpetrators who deny such abuse must, therefore, be lying because highly abusive men deny their responsibility in perpetrating abusive behaviors. The evaluator is taught to be skeptical about male accounts with little, if any, warning about being skeptical of female accounts. Once the bias is laid out that males lie and deny, the evaluator is advised to use clinical judgment based, in part, on the presumption that males are perpetrators and females are victims (Dutton, 2005a).

Dutton (2005a) and Johnson (2005) point out that much of the domestic violence and custody assessment literature is based upon samples drawn from battered women's shelters or from treatment groups for men who batter and that these research results are then inappropriately generalized to the general population. Appel and Holden (1998) reported in their review of 31 studies that wife assault and physical abuse of children occurred from 20 to 100% when the sample was from battered women or abused children; when samples representative of the community were examined, the overlap between spousal abuse and child abuse was only 6%. Dutton (2005a) asserts that the assumptions drawn from a shelter sample or a male perpetrator sample do not apply to community samples. These data create a false impression that spousal assault is mainly husband to wife and that such assault has a high likelihood of being accompanied by physical child abuse. Such impressions are contrary to more accurate data (Dutton, 2005a; Johnson, 2005). Margolin and Gordis (2003) reported that cumulative stress was more likely to affect women in doing the same.

Some authors have argued that female fear of being killed by an intimate male partner creates an unsafe environment for women in custody disputes (Jaffe, Lemon, & Poisson, 2003). This level of fear is often based upon belief about the probability of harm that are inconsistent with the data. Wilson and Daly (1993) reported that abandonment homicide occurs in about 3 of 100,000 marriages. Any form of male-perpetrated partner homicide occurs at less than 0.6 per 100,000 women older than 15, while female-perpetrated partner homicide occurs at a rate of about 0.5 per 100,000 men (Browne, Dutton, & Williams, 1998). Dutton (2005a) reminds us that "spousal homicide is extremely rare regardless of the gender of the victim" (p. 32).

Dutton (2005a) cautions evaluators to be aware of how cultural bias toward the belief that males are perpetrators and females are victims may affect investigative efforts. In a recent custody case in which Gould was involved as a consultant, the court-appointed evaluator interviewed the mother and three domestic violence advocates with whom the mother had consulted once the custody evaluation began. None of the advocates conducted an independent investigation of the mother's allegations. They listened to the mother tell her story and, based only upon that story, concluded that the father presented a significant risk to both child and mother. The evaluator concluded that the mother's story was supported because three professionals with whom she consulted provided the evaluator with the same story the mother told the evaluator. When the flawed nature of the evaluator's data collection methodology was pointed out, the evaluator was unable to see how each of the collateral sources was reciting information provided only by the mother. The parent's story being told by a third party with credentials still is only the parent's story.

Among the concerns raised by the above example is the idea that often women's strongest determinants of perceived safety lie in their perception of the likelihood of assault or reassault. Evaluators may obtain information about the consistency of a parent's perceived fear, but that perception may not necessarily correlate with the likelihood of an assault. Dutton (2005a) argues that evaluators need to be aware of how the "paradigm of domestic violence literature has literally made female subjective consciousness into reality. Clearly, there will be some relationships where fear of an aggressor is justified, but to generalize this on the basis of gender alone is not warranted by the data" (p. 33). His solution is for evaluators to guard against subjective judgments drawn from gender-based assumptions and to include objective assessment checklists including questions about parental abuse that are administered equally to mothers and to fathers.

Walker's Evolving View of Domestic Violence

Walker (1995) reminds us that "it is often difficult for advocates in the battered woman's movement to shift from previously held positions, even when they are presented with new data that contradicts those positions" (p. 265). She calls on researchers, evaluators, and advocates to reflect on the emerging literature and make the shift from a unidimensional view of batterers (Pence & Paymar, 1993) to an understanding that batterers and battering relationships are multidimensional.

Walker (1995) recognizes that previous models of evaluation of batterers and victims were based on a unidimensional and somewhat simplistic idea about domestic violence. Today, we recognize that batterers, like battered women, come from all demographic groups. In fact, the label *batterer* and its subsequent description of the behavioral acts of violence has sufficed as a descriptor until now. Many recent studies challenge the one-size-fits-all descriptive definitions of domestic violence (Johnston & Campbell, 1993; Dutton & Starzomski, 1997). Studies have demonstrated that few battered women actually fit the stereotyped model of a passive and helpless woman who never fights back to protect herself or her children (Hansen & Harway, 1993; Walker, 1984). At the same time, researchers are finding that there are similarities in how people respond to trauma whether it is the result of physical violence, psychological abuse, or sexual abuse.

Models of Domestic Violence

There are several different ways to think about domestic violence. In this section, we describe some current models that may help guide thinking about the forensic assessment of allegations of domestic violence.

Holtzworth-Munroe and Stuart's Tripartite Typology of Male Batterers

One line of research examining the causes of domestic violence asks the question "What characteristics lead men to violence?" In their attempts to understand the characteristics of male batterers, several authors developed typologies of them. Holtzworth-Munroe and Stuart (1994) summarized several of these typologies and proposed a model based on their convergence. Their integration of these different models resulted in a metatypology of male batterers divided into three types on the basis of (1) severity and frequency of their violence within the relationship, (2) generality of violence (i.e., only within the relationship or also outside the relationship), and (3) psychopathology/personality disorder characteristics. Holtzworth-Munroe and Stuart argued that three types of batterers labeled generally violent/antisocial, dysphoric/borderline, and family-only can be identified from previous research and that these three types of men are influenced by different etiological factors that affect the development of violent behavior.

According to this model, *family-only* batterers engage in the least severe and frequent violence and the least amount of emotional and sexual abuse of partners and typically are not violent outside the family. They show little psychopathology; if pathology is present, it is most likely to be a passive dependent personality pattern.

The *dysphoric/borderline* type of batterer engages in moderate to severe abuse of females, including psychological and sexual abuse. They may manifest some extrafamilial violence and criminal behavior. These men are the most depressed, psychologically distressed, and emotionally volatile and show borderline and schizotypal personality patterns. They are likely to have alcohol and drug abuse issues.

The third type of male batterer is the generally *violent/antisocial* type, who engages in moderate to severe marital violence, including psychological and sexual abuse. These men engage in the most extrafamilial violence and criminal activity. They are likely to have alcohol and drug problems and antisocial and narcissistic personality patterns.

Holtzworth-Munroe and Stuart (1994) proposed a set of *distal* and *proximal* factors that might differentially identify each batterer type. They proposed that certain genetic/prenatal factors, early childhood family experiences (e.g., exposure to violence in the home), and deviant peer experiences in childhood and adolescence increase the likelihood of becoming violent and influence the type of batterer a violent man becomes. Some of these factors affect behavior in adult partner relationships by their connection to attachment problems in adulthood, impulsivity, poor social skills, and violence-supportive attitudes and beliefs.

According to the model, the greater the presence of distal risk factors such as difficult temperament, violence/abuse in family of origin, and deviant peer group, the more likely a man is to be the violent/antisocial type. Presence of these factors also indicated a greater likelihood that the man would be more frequently and severely violent, both within and outside the relationship. In terms of proximal risk factors, generally violent men were predicted to display high levels of impulsivity, attachment difficulties (avoidant/dismissing attachment style), social skills deficits, and violence-supportive attitudes.

Dysphoric/borderline batterers were predicted to display social skills deficits and moderate levels of impulsivity. They were proposed to be more likely to be preoccupied or ambivalent rather than dismissing in their attachment style and somewhat less likely to have violence-supportive beliefs.

The third type, the family-only batterers, were predicted to show moderate levels of impulsivity, secure or possibly preoccupied attachment, and some social skills deficits with their partners but generally not violence-supportive beliefs and attitudes.

Holtzworth-Munroe and Stuart's model suggests that the largest group of batterers, family-only batterers, are less likely than the other two types to seek mental health services to address violence issues. This may mean that they are underrepresented in clinical samples, particularly those including large numbers of adjudicated men.

Hamberger, Lohr, Bonge, and Tolin (1996) examined the predictive usefulness of this typology on a sample of court-referred batterers. They used cluster analysis of the Millon Clinical Multiaxial Inventory (MCMI-I) and found that approximately 85% of their sample fit into clusters defined by psychopathology in a manner generally consistent with the model. Their analysis revealed a slightly different variation of the proposed dysphoric/borderline type, the passive aggressive/dependent type, which unexpectedly had the highest frequency of spousal violence.

Tweed and Dutton (1998) also examined the predictive usefulness of the typology, seeking validation for the generally violent/antisocial type (labeled *instrumental*) and the dysphoric/borderline type (labeled *impulsive*) in a largely adjudicated sample of batterers. They found general support for this distinction using cluster analysis of the MCMI-II. The instrumental group showed an Antisocial–Narcissistic–Aggressive profile on the MCMI-II and reported more severe physical violence. The impulsive group showed a mixed profile on the MCMI-II with Passive-Aggressive, Borderline, and Avoidant elevations, high scores on a self-report of borderline personality organization, higher chronic anger, and fearful attachment.

Waltz, Babcock, Jacobson, and Gottman (2000) also explored validation of the Holtsworth-Monroe and Stuart (1994) typology. They examine three variables that might distinguish among the batterer types: severity of violence, extent of violence, and personality disorder characteristics. Results generally supported the predicted typology. Violent/antisocial batterers were significantly more violent within and outside the relationship. The dysphoric/borderline group was moderately violent both within and outside the family and endorsed many psychological symptoms. The family-only batterers endorsed the fewest symptoms and were the least violent of the three battering types. There were also differences in violence in family of origin, attachment differences, and communication skills among the three groups and a nonviolence comparison.

Gottman's Examination of Physiological Responses of Male Batterers

Acknowledging the potential usefulness of typological classifications of male batterers, Gottman and his colleagues have suggested that there may be alternative ways of conceptualizing the behavior of batterers that would prove useful for further characterizing variability among batterers. Gottman and colleagues (1995) write that one such approach involves research examining psychophysiological correlates (e.g., heart rate) of spousal abuse. Although the relationship between psychophysiological variables and general aggression and antisocial behavior is far from clear, there is evidence in research on delinquency and criminality suggesting such a link (see Scarpa and Raine, 1997, for a review). Although early work in this area found little relationship between resting heart rate and psychopathy, researchers have demonstrated an association more recently between low resting heart rate and violence perpetration.

There is a comparative paucity of evidence linking psychophysiological measures with marital violence. One exception to this is the batterer typology proposed by Gottman and colleagues (Babcock, Jacobson, Gottman, & Yerington, 2000; Berns, Jacobson, & Gottman, 1999; Gottman et al., 1995; Jacobson & Gottman, 1998; Waltz et al., 2000). Rather than using resting heart rate, Gottman et al. (1995) used husbands' heart rate reactivity to a marital conflict discussion to classify batterers. They defined reactivity as the difference in heart rate between a baseline condition and average heart rate over the first 5 minutes of a 15-minute marital conflict discussion. Men whose heart rates decreased from baseline were called Type 1 batterers, or cobras, and men whose heart rates increased from baseline were labeled Type 2 batterers or pit bulls (Gottman et al., 1995 ; Jacobson & Gottman, 1998).

The differences between Type 1 and Type 2 men found by Gottman and colleagues revealed that Type 1 men scored higher on MCMI-II scales measuring antisocial and aggressive sadistic personality characteristics and were more likely to score at clinically significant levels on the Drug Dependence scale. They were more likely to have witnessed interparental violence as children and more likely to report being violent to individuals outside of their intimate relationships. Type 1 men also engaged in higher levels of emotional aggression in marital interaction. Results revealed that, although the two types of men did not differ in frequency of violence, a larger proportion of Type 1 men had perpetrated severe violence (i.e., significant group differences were found in the proportions of men who had "threatened with a knife or gun" and "used a knife or gun"; group differences approached statistical significance for "kicked, bit, or hit" and "slapped"). In contrast, Type 2 men scored higher on the Dependent Personality scale of the MCMI-II and were more likely to be separated or divorced from their partner 2 years after the initial assessment (Gottman et al., 1995).

Jacobson and Gottman (1998) further elaborated on what they believed to be the differences between these two types. Type 1 men were described as antisocial and aggressive, probably psychopathic, cold, calculating, and manipulative. Their callousness and hostility were viewed as particularly frightening given their lack of relationship dissolution, suggesting that they may prevent their spouses from leaving, perhaps through intimidation. Type 2 men, on the other hand, were characterized as dependent, needy, and emotionally volatile.

Appel and Holden's Taxonomy of Adults' Use of Physical Aggression

Appel and Holden (1998) have described a fourfold taxonomy to explain adults' use of physical aggression toward partners and children. In *single perpetrator families*, only one parent directs aggression toward both the partner and the children. In *sequential perpetrator families*, one parent engages in physical aggression toward the partner while the victim/partner directs physical aggression toward the children. *Dual perpetrator families* are characterized by one parent engaging in acts of physical aggression toward the other parent while both parents direct physical aggression toward the children. The final category is *marital violence families* in which both parents engage in acts of physical aggression toward each other, and one or both parents may also display acts of physical aggression toward the children.

Appel and Holden (1998) also suggest two distinct pathways that explain the co-occurrence of marital and parent–child physical aggression. The first pathway is referred to as the *parent aggressor hypothesis* and entails that an adult indiscriminately directing aggression toward a parent is also more likely to hit a child. Research with families from domestic violence shelters shows that the parent aggressor pathway operates for men. Fathers' use of physical aggression toward female partners has been related to greater use of physical aggression with their children. In the two studies that have looked at the parent aggressor pathway in women, neither found support for links between women's reports of their aggression toward male batterers and aggression toward their children.

The second pathway is referred to as the *parent-victim hypothesis* and posits that adults who are targets of marital physical aggression are more likely to hit their children. Research has shown that father's use of physical aggression against mothers has been linked to greater risk and/or severity of mothers' physical aggression toward their children in families referred to domestic violence shelters.

In a recent study (Mahoney, Donnelly, Boxer, & Lewis, 2003) using parents and adolescents who were clinic-referred rather than from domestic violence shelters, the parent-victim hypothesis found support. Both mothers and fathers who were targets of physical aggression by their partners were more likely to direct severe physical aggression toward their adolescent children. The parent aggressor hypothesis found support only among fathers. Fathers were more likely to use physical aggression toward their adolescent children after perpetrating acts of physical aggression toward their partner, while mothers were not (Mahoney et al., 2003).

Johnston and Campbell's Typology of Domestic Violence

In an attempt to categorize types of domestic violence within the dynamic context of family systems, Johnston and Campbell (1993) offered an empirically derived category system identifying five types of domestic violence. They defined domestic violence as the use of physical restriction, force, coercion, or intimidation of force by one parent to force another parent to do something against his or her will. Among the violent behaviors are hitting, slapping, biting, choking, threat with a weapon, unlawful entry, destruction of property, physical injury, suicide, and murder. Violence also includes psychological intimidation such as threats, control, and inappropriate use of power tactics. These may include harassment, stalking, threats against children, and violence against pets or property. Johnston and Campbell do not include a definition of emotional abuse but note that emotional abuse often precedes, accompanies, or follows physically violent behavior.

The five basic types of domestic violence identified by Johnston and Campbell (1993) are ongoing or episodic male battering, female-initiated violence, male-controlling interactive violence, separation-engendered violence or postdivorce trauma, and psychotic and paranoid reactions. Each of these domestic violence categories will be discussed below, along with information about how children are affected by each style.

Ongoing or Episodic Male Battering

The classic battering male/battered wife syndrome is found among those categorized as ongoing and episodic batterers. It appears that the propensity for physical abuse and violence lies with the men in these relationships. Typically, these males demonstrate low frustration tolerance, poor impulse control, and a high need to dominate and control their female partners. They also show signs of significant jealousy and possessiveness. These males displayed traditional chauvinistic attitudes and an exaggerated view of their masculinity. About half of them were also found to engage in the use of drugs or alcohol as a precipitant or contributor to violence.

Johnston and Campbell (1993) described these men as displaying little restraint as they acted out their internal rage and frustration. They appeared to want to hurt their partners as much as to control them. They also tended to deny or minimize their abuse or place the blame for their violence on their wives.

When the woman separated from the relationship, the episodic male batterer tended to become extremely dangerous. They would stalk their partners, terrorizing them with threats of or attempts at murder or suicide. Accompanying these violent actions were pleas for reconciliation and forgiveness characterized by promises to change. Johnston and Campbell (1993) reported that the possibility for violence often remained very high, lasting years after the separation.

The women in these relationships reacted with one of two styles. Some women became fearful, depressed, and showed signs of helplessness. They developed (or had coming into the marriage) low self-esteem and an inadequate ability to protect themselves or their children.

The other style was one of assertiveness. These women took a stand against their husbands' physical abuse early in the marriage. Johnston and Campbell (1993) indicate that neither style of victim appeared intentionally to provoke or escalate the physical abuse they received, but some became caught up in the violence and defended themselves or their children.

PARENT–CHILD RELATIONSHIPS IN EPISODICALLY VIOLENT
DIVORCING FAMILIES

Female children younger than 8 were typically very passive and constricted. They revealed a high degree of underlying fearfulness and insecurity in relation to both parents. These young girls felt unprotected by their mothers. They showed some difficulty in knowing how to separate from their mothers, reacting whiny, regressive behaviors. They often had repressed or intrusive memories of violent experiences, which served as the foundation for realistic fears and avoidance of their fathers.

Interestingly, these young girls showed a princess-like relationship with their fathers. The fathers would intermittently lavish attention on their daughters while being focused on their own needs. These girls were confused about the nature of their relationship with their fathers, viewing them as both loving suitor and dangerous man. There were poor boundaries between these men and their daughters. The father–daughter relationship was characterized by mutual seductiveness and provocation of the father's aggressiveness. Johnston and Campbell (1993) report that these men needed validation of their attractiveness and maleness, finding ways to garner it from their young daughters, "who became watchful and oriented to managing their fathers's narcissistic equilibrium and anger" (p. 287).

Older girls (8 to 14 years old) displayed more anger, rejection, and avoidance of their fathers or aligned with their mothers as a way of taking a stand against their fathers' violence and protecting their mothers. These older girls often felt responsible for protecting their mothers and angry at their mothers for tolerating their fathers' abuse. The mothers tended to be too oppressed and depressed to be emotionally available to any of their children.

Boys younger than 8 were found to be oppositional, difficult, and aggressive. They displayed manipulative and controlling behaviors, especially toward their mothers. Similar to younger girls, these boys were often confused, anxious, and worried about their mothers' safety and experienced intermittent memories of their fathers' violence.

Boys 8 to 14 years old showed signs of modeling their behavior on their fathers'. They displayed explosive, rageful attacks upon their mothers, who typically responded in passive, ineffective, and submissive manner. Johnston and Campbell (1993) speculate that these boys wanted a closer relationship with their mothers but feared that it would result in their becoming passive, weak, and victimized like their mother.

Younger and older boys both tended to show fear and obedience in the presence of their fathers. The violent fathers were preoccupied with their own needs and inconsistently available to their sons. These boys longed for their fathers' approval, were fearful of being shamed by them, and held significant feels of anger and rage toward them. Fathers often provided mixed messages about aggressiveness. When boys displayed aggressiveness, fathers would punish it in an abusive manner.

Boys and girls who had little or no contact with their violent fathers tended to repress their memories of violence within the home. They tended to idealize their fathers, longed for contact with them, and blamed themselves or their mothers for the fathers' absence. In those instances in which the violent fathers had significant child care responsibilities, their low frustration tolerance, need to assert power and control events, and hypersensitivity to minor transgressions often resulted in episodic explosions. This display of violence toward the children resulted in a deterioration of the father–child relationship and increased the possibility of child abuse (Johnston & Campbell, 1993).

Female-Initiated Violence

There are some domestic violence situations in which the female initiates the aggression. Johnston and Campbell (1993) suggest that the violence of these women lies "primarily within their own intolerable internal states of tension" (p. 290). They are often characterized as histrionic, emotionally labile, dependent, and self-focused. They tended to display explosive temper outbursts when they believed their expectations or needs were not being properly met by their husbands. Alcohol also played a role in some of these households.

Unlike the episodic male batterer, these women often were able to admit their violent behavior. These women were reported to throw objects, destroy possessions, attack their partner, hit, bite, kick, and commit other physical assaults. These attacks might include threats to use weapons, especially when the security of the relationship was being threatened, as during marital separation.

The husbands of these women often tried to prevent or contain the violence by passively fending off the attacks. They may also attempt to restrain their wives from hurting family members. When the marriages ended, these men often ended their attempts to contain or placate their wives' aggressive reactions. These men were characterized as passive, depressed, obsessive, and intellectualizing. They felt intimidated by their wives' aggressiveness and embarrassed when they were pulled into the fight. Johnston and Campbell (1993) describe the husband's style as passive–aggressive (p. 291). Compared with the episodic male batterer, female-initiated violence tended to result in less severe damage and injury. They speculate that the lower level of destruction results from the husband being able to maintain his emotional control and "disarm his wife" (p. 291).

PARENT–CHILD RELATIONSHIPS IN DIVORCING FAMILIES WITH FEMALE-INITIATED VIOLENCE

Children in these families had erratic and unpredictable relationships with their mothers, who were described as intermittently loving and nurturing and unpredictably explosive, angry, and rejecting. Boys often took the brunt of their mothers' attacks.

Young girls were reported to be intimidated and fearful, recoiling from contact with their mothers to avoid their wrath. Some girls assumed the role of caretaker to their mothers during emotional outbursts. These girls also were found to play the role of parent and manager of household tasks and were more protected from their mothers' rage than boys.

Girls tended to be supported by emotionally closer and more protective relationships with their fathers and often were viewed by their fathers as the "good girls" in contrast to the "bad mothers." As these girls developed, however they tended to become more demanding, display temper outbursts, and enter into power struggles with both parents, suggesting identification with the aggressive female role model (Johnston & Campbell, 1993).

Boys in these female-initiated violence families displayed behaviors more similar to their fathers. They were characterized as passive–aggressive, demonstrating sadness, behavioral inhibition, and depression. Boys were found to be overtly angry with their mothers, frequently entering into power struggles.

Younger boys appeared to have more ambivalent and confused relationships with their mothers. They showed more difficulty in emotionally separating from their mothers, which interfered with their normal developmental progression toward autonomy. These boys needed their mothers' nurturing but found that their mothers' intermittent, conditional acceptance and punitiveness interfered with the boys' ability to develop secure attachments with them. Further, if their fathers were passive and intimidated by the mothers, boys were unable to be protected or rescued from their mothers' rage. This resulted in boys feeling very angry at their mothers for their aggressiveness and rejection and angry at their fathers for their inept ability to protect their children.

Male-Controlling Interactive Violence

Violence in this category appeared to arise out of increasing disagreements between spouses. There appeared to be a trend of escalating aggression from verbal insults to verbal abuse to physical violence. Johnston and Campbell (1993) reported that the most prominent aspect of this category of violence was the male's overwhelming need to assert control over his wife. Men were observed to use physical force in their attempts to dominate and overpower their wives. This aggressive behavior did not, however, involve sadistic acts or brutal beatings.

These men showed varying amounts of control over their behaviors related to the amount of resistance to their efforts to control put forth by their spouses. Psychological characteristics of the male included traditional beliefs in authoritarian and dictatorial behavior as an appropriate role within the family. Physically violent behavior within the family was an accepted way of resolving intrafamilial conflict. Such men often would become physically violent with their children, their siblings, and their parents and tended to display physically aggressive behaviors as a way of resolving interpersonal conflict outside the family.

Parents within this category of violent behavior tended to blame each other for the frequency and intensity of aggressiveness. As more stress was placed on the divorcing couple, there was a greater chance of violence. Once the spouses separated and were no longer able to provoke each other, Johnston and Campbell (1993) reported that the violence between them often ended.

PARENT–CHILD RELATIONSHIPS IN DIVORCING FAMILIES
WITH MALE-CONTROLLING INTERACTIVE VIOLENCE

Somewhat unique to this category of violence is the co-occurrence of male-dominated violence with female violence. Both parents are poor role models for nonviolent conflict resolution, ego control, and anger management. Thus, children within these family systems observed each spouse becoming violent with the other. Children of these families often displayed aggressiveness or passive aggressiveness. Families were characterized by inconsistent family rules, contradictory messages, unreliable discipline, and high levels of tension. Children's alliances were found to change frequently within the family, aligning with one parent and then the other. Physical punishment as a primary discipline style was common as well as physical fights between siblings.

Some girls living in male-controlled interactive violent families were observed to be assertive, strong willed, and demanding. They appeared ready and prepared to fill the void of parental control abdicated by their warring parents. Other girls were reported to react with passive–aggressive behaviors, varying between passiveness and subtle defiance. Their behavior often revealed a cycle of passive to overtly aggressive responding.

Younger boys showed discipline and behavior control problems. They revealed a somewhat less well-developed ability to channel their excitement appropriately when faced with minor difficulties—that is, they overreacted. Older boys tended to be defiant of authority, belligerent, and outwardly disobedient to each parent. This was particularly true between older boys and their mothers.

Fathers appeared to have peer-like relationships with their sons, creating almost a "boys club" type of atmosphere through which the boys developed a sense of identity and esteem. These boys also appeared more likely to use aggressive acting out and coercion in their attempts to get what they wanted, especially from their mothers and sisters. Fathers were reported to reward their sons' toughness and acting out, and some mothers also rewarded their sons' aggressiveness. Fathers were observed to be more controlling and punitive with their daughters compared with their sons, while mothers were reported to have difficulty managing both boys and girls.

Separation-Engendered Violence or Postdivorce Trauma

Males and females identified as belonging to this category displayed acts of violence that were uncharacteristic of their everyday lives. Increased aggressiveness was associated with increased tension around the separation and divorce. Physical violence was absent during their marriage, but either party was observed to lash out in anger during times of acute stress or symbolic importance, such as an anniversary. Violence was unpredictable and infrequent. When it occurred, it tended to cast a dark shadow of mistrust on the offending spouse precisely because it was unexpected. Johnston and Campbell (1993) reported that both men and women were able to acknowledge their aggression and expressed genuine shame over their loss of control. In general, the risk for further violence was small once the emotional and legal issues involved in the divorce were resolved.

PARENT–CHILD RELATIONSHIPS IN SEPARATION-ENGENDERED VIOLENT DIVORCING FAMILIES

Children from these families were observed to show behavioral signs similar to PTSD. They displayed anxiety, fear, difficulty concentrating, and withdrawal of verbal exchange within the family. They also showed signs of behavioral inhibition and emotional constriction. Younger children tended to report intrusive memories, nightmares, headaches, and stomachaches. Several showed a temporary fear of the parent perceived to be violent.

Mothers were observed to be more emotionally supportive of their daughters and fathers of their sons in these cases of unpredictable, infrequent violence. Although the children were frightened by witnessing parental violence, the parents generally demonstrated good judgment, good ego control, and good anger management. The damage to the parent–child relationship appeared short-lived, with rehabilitation to the relationship resolved through therapeutic treatment strategies.

Psychotic and Paranoid Reactions

A small number of divorcing parents engaging in violent family behavior were found to be experiencing significant psychopathology. The psychotic and paranoid reactions often were exacerbated by the stressors associated with the marital breakup. According to Johnston and Campbell (1993), "the marital separation often triggered an acute phase of danger wherein a disturbed spouse pieced together the rubble of their marriage and mentally rewrote history, perceiving their partner as having intentionally plotted to exploit them and cast them off" (p. 294). The disturbed spouse was likely to respond with some type of aggressiveness to his or her perceived feelings of betrayal. The violent behavior sometimes come in the form of a preemptive strike against the other spouse. Sometimes there was a series of aggressively provocative attacks resulting from no clear trigger. These attacks often were perpetrated with a sense of righteous indignation and a belief by the perpetrator that he or she was protecting either him- or herself or the children from the malicious intentions of his or her spouse.

The abnormal behavior ranged from fleeting, incoherent ideas coupled with unpredictable outbursts of verbal and physical aggression to full-blown paranoid delusions. These delusional systems often were logically coherent, linking the perceived betrayal of the spouse to a conspiracy with others. In such situations, not only was the spouse found to be at risk but also those who were perceived to be part of the conspiracy. The victim spouses appeared to react in one of two ways. Either they understood the threat and were frightened by it, seeking to avoid or calm the aggressor, or they appeared oblivious to the significant danger in which they found themselves.

PARENT–CHILD RELATIONSHIPS IN DIVORCING FAMILIES WITH PSYCHOTIC OR PARANOID REACTIONS

Johnston and Campbell (1993) reported that there were not enough children in their sample to make generalizations. Children in these family systems were either a part of the aggressive–psychotic parent's delusional system or emotionally separated from the disturbed parent. When observed to be part of the delusional system, the child was found to display psychotic-like behavior with "massive identification with the disturbed parent's affective state and reality distortion" (p. 295). When the child was able to maintain emotional distance from the disturbed parent, symptoms similar to acute or chronic trauma were observed. Johnston and Campbell (1993) reported that the trauma appeared similar to that observed in children in the separation-engendered violence or ongoing or episodic male battering categories.

Summary of the Johnston and Campbell Model

Johnston and Campbell (1993) reported that boys' adjustment tended to be most significantly affected in the ongoing or episodic male battering category. They were likely to be less disturbed in the male-controlling interactive and female-initiated violence categories and least disturbed in separation engendered violent and nonviolent divorcing families.

Girls were found to be equally disturbed in male-battering and male-controlling interactive violent families. They were less disturbed in female-initiated and separation-engendered violent families. They were least disturbed in nonviolent divorcing families.

Johnston and Campbell (1993) conclude, "it is important to differentiate among the various profiles of domestic violence when helping parents make postdivorce plans for custody of their children. . . . Parent-child relationships are likely to vary with the different patterns of violence, and children of different ages and gender are affected differently" (p. 296). Consideration of sole or joint custody is inappropriate with a father who has engaged in ongoing or episodic battering. Similarly, any parent who is psychotic or has paranoid delusions should not be awarded sole or joint custody. In fact, when the threat of violence is real, visitation may need to be supervised or suspended until the children's safety is assured. Johnston and Campbell also warn that spouses who left battering or psychotic relationships may have diminished capacity to parent children effectively as a function of their victimization. They may need assistance in rehabilitating their parenting competence to a level of satisfaction. A careful examination of the parenting capacity of a mother who is a female initiator of violence is needed before considering placing children under her care. It may be that the father is the more appropriate residential parent, but he may be too passive and unavailable to this children as a result of his victimization. When considering a male-controlling aggressor, fathers may be found to need parenting skills to manage their children assertively. Similarly, mothers from these relationships may also need such skills. Very clear, structured transition routines are needed to ensure the safety of the children as well as effectively manage the potential for conflict between the parents.

Bancroft and Silverman's Critique of Johnston and Campbell's Model

Bancroft and Silverman (2002a) have offered a critique of Johnston and Campbell's work, suggesting that Johnston and Campbell discredit the concerns raised by mothers and children regarding access to an abusive father. Bancroft and Silverman point out that missing from the various explanations offered for children's reluctance to visit with their father in postseparation, high-conflict families are concerns about the father's abusiveness during the marriage directed toward either the mother or the children. They state that Johnston and Campbell "describe such factors as the child's loyalty or protectiveness toward one parent and the child's desire to relieve ambivalent feelings by casting one parent as all good and the other as all bad. The authors make no reference to other possible causes of reluctance to visit, such as appropriate self-protectiveness" (p. 134).

Conflict-Initiated and Control-Initiated Violence

Dalton, Carbon, and Olesen (2003) describe two distinct kinds of violence that they label conflict-initiated and control-initiated violence. *Control-initiated violence* is specific to abusive relationships. The focus is on one person's domination over another. Dalton and colleagues write, "Often, abusive relationships are characterized by rules, and abuse is justified as punishment for infractions of the rules. Within this context, conflict or dispute is 'manufactured' as a way of asserting control" (p. 15).

Conflict-initiated violence focuses on the mutuality of conflict, not on use and abuse of power and control. Dalton and colleagues (2003) state:

> When both parents are immersed in ongoing conflict, the participation of each in the conflict does not provide a basis, in and of itself, for choosing one over the other as the primary physical or sole legal custodian; other factors will be determinative in that decision. When one parent has abused the other, there are strong arguments . . . for giving sole legal and physical custody to the non-abusive parent. (p. 12)

We believe that the distinction between control-initiated and conflict-initiated violence is relevant for evaluators to consider. Examination of the underlying reason for intimate partner conflict may help categorize some of the dynamics of conflict associated with marital dissolution.

Models of Psychological Assessment in the Forensic Evaluation of Allegations of Domestic Violence within a Custody Dispute

There are several important reasons a systematic exploration of allegations of domestic violence is critical in child custody evaluations. The first involves concerns about placing a child in a family context in which parental violence occurs. Research indicates that children living in homes in which parental violence occurs are more likely to be targets of violence themselves. The second is that children living in a family context in which domestic violence occurs are psychologically affected by their exposure to it. A third concern is that parents involved in domestic violence tend to be poorer parents in areas of child supervision. Typically, the victim of the violence tends to be more depressed, and depressed parents tend to be poorer supervisors of their children's activities. Another concern is that children raised in homes in which domestic violence occurs often identify with the aggressor, attributing less parenting legitimacy to the victimized parent.

The Spousal Assault Risk Assessment Guide

Several researchers have explored the empirical factors that might predict future intimate partner violence. One such tool is the Spousal Assault Risk Assessment Guide (SARA; Kropp & Hart, 1997, 2000; Whittemore & Kropp, 2002).

The SARA is a checklist of risk factors for spousal assault comprising 20 items identified by an extensive review of empirical literature and of articles written by clinicians with extensive experience in evaluating men who abuse their partners. The SARA contains four general categories, each with specific areas of inquiry:

Criminal history

1. Past assault of family members.
2. Past assault of strangers or acquaintances.
3. Past violation of conditional release or community supervision.

Psychosocial adjustment

4. Recent relationship problems.
5. Recent employment problems.
6. Victim of and/or witness to family violence as a child or adolescent.
7. Recent substance abuse or dependence.
8. Recent suicidal or homicidal ideation.
9. Recent psychotic and/or manic symptoms.
10. Personality disorder with anger, impulsivity, or behavioral instability.

Spousal assault history

11. Past physical assault.
12. Past sexual assault/sexual jealousy.
13. Past use of weapons and/or credible threats of death.
14. Recent escalation in frequency or severity of assault.

15. Past violation of no-contact order.
16. Extreme minimization or denial of spousal assault history.
17. Attitudes that support or condone spousal assault.

Alleged current offense

18. Severe and/or sexual assault.
19. Use of weapons and/or credible threats of death.
20. Violation of no-contact order.

Other considerations are also relevant to the prediction of spousal abuse. Variables include understanding the current emotional crisis; history of torturing or disfiguring intimate partners; being a victim or witness of political persecution, torture, or violence; sexual sadism; having easy access to firearms; stalking; or a recent loss of social support system.

In light of Dutton's criticism of feminist theory's overfocus on patriarchy, the SARA contains an item examining male privilege or patriarchy. Item 17 queries "Attitudes that support or condone spousal assault." It is possible that, in a particular case, this risk factor alone would support an opinion of high risk if the individual's beliefs in male privilege were of sufficient strength. It would also be likely that item 10, "Personality disorder with anger, impulsivity, or behavioral instability," would also be found to be present.

Austin's Model of Assessing Allegations of Domestic Violence

Austin (2000d) suggests that there may be a strategic advantage in child custody disputes for one party to be viewed as the victim of marital violence and the other party to be falsely accused of being a perpetrator. A high percentage of men and women in contested custody cases report being abused in their marriage (Newmark, Harrell, & Salem, 1995) and Bow and Boxer's (2003) work indicates that more than one-third of custody referrals contain allegations of domestic violence. Bow and Boxer report that among the evaluators who responded to their questionnaire, 57% of the cases in which there were allegations of domestic violence were supported. That is, more than half of the referred allegations were found to be substantiated incidents of familial violence.

Bow and Boxer (2003) also reveal that evaluators involved in assessing allegations of domestic violence utilize the forensic model described in this book. They rely on interview data, test data, observational data, and collateral record review and interviews. Austin's model helps to refine further the specific steps needed to be taken by an evaluator in a thorough evaluation of allegations of domestic violence.

Austin (2000d) suggests a six-factor test of credibility to evaluate systematically allegations of domestic violence within the context of custody disputes. He proposes:

1. Obtaining information from extensive third-party record review.
2. Examining alleged and confirmed patterns of abuse complaints prior to the start of the custody dispute.
3. Obtaining information from credible others such as former romantic partners.
4. Seeking out disconfirming verbal reports by credible third parties.
5. Examining psychological variables of and past history of abusive behavior by the alleged perpetrator of marital violence.
6. Examining psychological status of the allegedly victimized spouse.

These steps are the minimal number needed to conduct a satisfactory evaluation.

Goodmark (personal communication, April 14, 2003) indicated concern about an evaluator seeking a pattern of legal complaints prior to the custody dispute because so many victims of domestic violence do not seek assistance at all. Often these women have been so isolated from their families and friends that they believe help is not available from anyone. They do not seek assistance from outside sources because they fear that any movement toward assistance from an outside source will result in further punishment by the batterer. Goodmark also voiced concern about seeking corroboration from former romantic partners. A search for past complaints would likely result in no information about past abuse and might lead the naive evaluator to conclude that, as there is no third-party account of any past abuse, it must mean that there has been no abuse.

Goodmark also voiced concern about the investigative strategy of seeking corroboration from former romantic partners. She identified the potential danger to a former romantic partner by the batterer once it becomes known that the former partner has provided details about their past relationship. We recognize the potential safety concerns in this investigative strategy and encourage evaluators to decide who to contact on a case-by-case basis. We believe that Goodmark's important concern is best addressed by the evaluator taking time to explain painstakingly to the former romantic partner how the information gathered during the interview may be used in court and how all information obtained from the interview may be subject to full disclosure to the court and to the parties involved in the litigation.

Drozd and Olesen's Model for Assessing Allegations of Domestic Violence

Drozd and Olesen (2003) suggest that an examination of allegations of domestic violence within the context of a custody and visitation dispute needs to recognize the larger family system context with particular attention to the developmental needs of the child. The forensic assessment of allegations of domestic violence within the context of custody and divorce disputes ought to examine the allegations of violence as well as the motivation of the alleging party and the contribution of the alleged victim.

Drozd, Kleiman, and Olesen (2000) recommend that evaluators gather information from the following independent sources of information:

1. Obtaining civil and criminal complaints and judgments from police, courts, and other relevant venues.
2. Obtaining work records.
3. Assessing for weapons access.
4. Examination of substance and alcohol use.
5. Formal risk assessment.
6. Collateral contacts, including former romantic partners.
7. Examination of power and control variables in relationship.
8. Examination of how parents argued (type of interaction).
9. Examination of how parents resolved arguments (methods of resolution).
10. Examination of trigger for fights.
11. Parents' understanding of fight triggers and how to avoid them.
12. Psychological variables that may contribute to propensity toward violence, for example, impulsiveness, low frustration tolerance, rigid versus flexible thinking, authoritarian worldview, sex role perspective.
13. Parental insight into their anger and its management.
14. Parental insight into the cycle of violence within their relationship—that is, how does it start and what attributions does each parent make about the other parent's motivation?
15. Examination of psychological/emotional abuse variables.
16. Examination of financial/economic abuse variables.
17. Examination of sexual abuse variables.
18. Exposure of child to forms of violence and conflict.
19. Examination of child disciplinary techniques (what is used).
20. Examination of deployment of child disciplinary techniques (when is it used).
21. Awareness of multiple disciplinary strategies sans corporal punishment.

Drozd, Kleinman, and Olesen (2000) provide a more complex and comprehensive list of factors to consider than Austin (2000d). Both models provide a comprehensive set of data from which to address allegations of familial violence. We encourage evaluators to adopt either model to guide their information gathering and investigative procedures. We believe they offer the most comprehensive set of variables to examine for forensic evaluation. The Drozd, Kleinman, and Olesen model provides the most detailed set of factors and includes the factors articulated in Austin while Austin's model points the evaluator toward data-gathering sources necessary to acquire a satisfactory evaluation.

Bancroft and Silverman's Model of Assessment of Familial Maltreatment

Forensic evaluation of the alleged perpetrator of familial violence ought to reflect research and clinical experience with batterers and those who commit acts of maltreatment. Included in this literature base is research and clinical experience on parenting characteristics of abusive parents and characteristic behaviors and attitudes that abusive parents display toward their former intimate partners (Bancroft & Silverman, 2002b). We include a discussion of Bancroft and Silverman's work because we have found it to be a useful framework within which to organize information about the alleged abuser, his or her behaviors toward others, and his or her parenting style. We also have found their discussion about how children may be affected by exposure to domestic violence in the home and the potential risks of allowing an abusive parent unsupervised access to his or her children useful in assisting us to piece together the complexities involved in understanding how domestic violence affects children of divorce.

We also suggest caution when using Bancroft and Silverman's (2002) model, which is developed, in large part, from research drawn from women in battered women's shelters. It is unclear how this population of women and their intimate partners differ from the population of people undergoing child custody evaluations. Some, perhaps many, of the descriptions of an abusive intimate partner and his behavior within a family system may be shown to be similar to behaviors displayed by abusive parents whose partners have not sought safety in a battered women's shelter. Similarly, some of the descriptors of an abusive parent's parenting behaviors and how such attitudes and beliefs may affect children need further empirical study.

We include a discussion of their model because one of us (Gould) has found its heuristic valuable in organizing the data gathered in an evaluation of allegations of domestic violence within a custody dispute. We emphasize that further empirical work needs to be done to support the usefulness of this model.

Historical and Current Factors of the Allegedly Abusive Parent

The evaluator should examine historical and current factors of the alleged abusive parent that may pose a risk to children. Among historical factors to assess are:

1. History of physical abuse toward the children.
2. History of neglectful or underinvolved parenting.

3. History of sexual abuse or boundary violations with the children.
4. History of using the children as weapons and of undermining the mother–child relationship.
5. History of mental health.
6. History of substance/alcohol abuse.

Among current factors to assess are:

1. Level of physical danger to the current partner or former partner.
2. Level of psychological cruelty toward partner, former partner, and children.
3. Level of willingness to risk physically or emotionally hurting the children incidental to abuse of their mother.
4. Level of coercion or manipulative control exercised over the partner during the relationship.
5. Level of entitlement, self-centeredness, and selfishness.
6. Level of risk to abduct the children.
7. Level of refusal to accept responsibility for past violence or abusive actions.
8. Refusal to accept the end of the relationship.
9. Refusal to accept a former partner's decision to begin a new relationship.

Factors Associated with Allegedly Abusive Parent's Behavior toward Other Family Members

Bancroft and Silverman (2002) describe factors they believe to be characteristic of an abusive parent's behavior toward others in a family system, such as imposition of a pattern of control over an intimate partner, including undue criticism, verbal abuse, economic control, isolation, cruelty, and an array of other tactics. Evaluators should examine patterns of control over the course of the marriage as abuse of control tends to emerge gradually and to intensify during the early years of the marriage. Evaluators should explore changes in imposition of power associated with marriage, pregnancy, birth of a child, and other life transitions and assess arguments and decision making, household responsibilities, emotional caretaking and attention, sexual relations, finances, child rearing, and outside social contacts.

Evaluators should examine how the family was organized, with particular attention to whether the family was organized around meeting the needs of the allegedly abusive parent to the point of treating others like servants. Did the allegedly abusive parent hold high and unreasonable expectations, including forceful and urgent demands for catering to every wish? Alleged abusers are often preoccupied with their own needs and, as a result, are either less available or unavailable to their children's needs. Their self-centeredness often interferes with their children's ability to move toward age-appropriate autonomy and independence. Investigate how responsive the allegedly abusive parent is to the needs of the children. Examine his or her ability to place the needs of the children ahead of parental needs. Assess children's developmental movement toward age-appropriate autonomy and independence.

The quality of communication between husband and wife may reflect the husband's attitude that the wife is a willful and ignorant child whom he needs to educate and improve. He may show an attitude of contempt toward his partner, referring to her not by name but by terms such as "my girl" or "the wife," suggesting a degree of emotional distance indicative of not knowing her as a person. He may treat his loved ones as objects of possession, leading to stalking behavior and limited social contact with and access of the intimate partner to others.

Evaluators need to assess whether the allegedly abusive parent confuses strong feelings of love for his or her partner as a justification to abuse. Violence may be viewed as an expression of the depth of love. In normative populations, there is a relationship between intensity of love and intensity of anger toward an intimate partner. An abusive spouse often confuses the experience of anger with the expression of violence. It is not the experience of anger but the expression of anger through violent action that is abusive.

Evaluators should be aware that abusive parents use a wide range of manipulative tactics to coerce their children or their former partner to conform their behaviors to serve their needs. As described in the section on the cycle of violence, the abusive parent may be kind, loving, and inviting and then become violent, rageful, and dangerous. It is important to remember that the vast majority of domestic violence offenders project a public image that is in sharp contrast to the private reality of their behavior and attitudes. They tend to externalize responsibility for their actions and are successful at manipulating other family members to take responsibility for the abuse. Denial, minimization, and victim blaming are also characteristics of abusive behavior.

Factors Associated with an Abuser's Parenting Style

There are several factors that characterize a batterer's style of parenting. Abusive parents tend to use an authoritarian parenting style. They are often underinvolved or neglectful in the lives of their children. They tend to place responsibility for parenting on the other parent. Abusive parents tend to show less physical affection and consider caring for their children to be the domain of the woman. They often show a lack of knowledge about their children's lives, including their education, medical care, social involvements, and other relevant areas of child development. They are largely unaware of the effects of their violent and controlling behavior on their children's development.

Abusive parents tend to consider themselves superior in all aspects of their family life and place little positive value on the parenting of the mother, resulting in a consistent undermining of the mother's parental authority in front of the children. They also undermine the mother's parenting competence by continuous criticism.

Abusive parenting is often characterized by a lack of responsiveness to the needs of the children and an insensitivity to children's feelings and experiences resulting from the abusive parent's rigid adherence to his own ways. Children are often forced to behave in a manner that reflects well on the abusive parent, as if they were an extension of the parent. Abusive parents are often unable to view their children as separate from themselves. Children are viewed as objects, not as people with separate internal states and emotional needs. These parents often are poor supervisors of their children's activities yet are able to hold up a good public image with their children, making data obtained from parent–child observations during the evaluation process useful only when compared to information obtained from third-party informants.

Raising children in a home characterized by familial violence perpetrated by one parent toward the other may foster beliefs and attitudes that ill serve children's best psychological interests. Among them are that children may:

1. Develop the view that their mother causes the violence. That is, they develop a belief that victims of violence are to blame for it.
2. Learn that use of physical aggression or psychological control is an acceptable means to gain control over others.
3. Develop rigid ideas about gender roles. Boys, in particular, are vulnerable to developing a belief that boys and men should be in control and girls and women should submit.
4. Develop the belief that abusers do not experience consequences for their abusive actions.
5. Develop the belief that women are weak, incompetent, stupid, or violent.
6. Develop the belief and behaviors that reflect the idea that anger causes violence.
7. Develop the belief that it is safer to align with the batterer and behave like him rather than risk behaving in a manner contrary to his expectations. This increases the likelihood that the children will, themselves, become batterers in their relationships.

Criticism of the Bancroft and Silverman Model

Our criticism of the Bancroft and Silverman model focuses on its representativeness and its empirical support. Their model is based on information obtained from work with women who sought safety in battered women's shelters. This is not a representative sample of women alleging domestic violence in child custody evaluations. We acknowledge the clinical usefulness of their model when applied to family systems in which women sought shelter in battered women's shelters, but we are concerned that many of the clinical ideas and the investigative protocol that flow from those ideas have neither their foundation in empirical work on those involved in child custody disputes nor have been subject to empirical scrutiny.

We believe that further clinical and empirical work needs to be done on their model. At the same time, we believe that many of the ideas guiding it are useful to consider when investigating the potentially harmful effects of domestic violence on the family.

The American Bar Association Commission on Domestic Violence (1994) has proposed that where family violence has occurred, there be a rebuttable presumption that the perpetrator not be awarded custodial rights and responsibilities.

Evaluators need to understand the power and control dynamic of maltreatment and intimate partner violence when considering custodial arrangements. When there are genuine (as opposed to intentionally fabricated) allegations of child maltreatment or if a parent perceives a child to be at high risk for any abuse by the other parent, it will be extremely unlikely that the custodial parent will be able to maintain friendly relations with the other parent.

Summary

This chapter has reviewed the forensic evaluation of allegations of domestic violence within child custody disputes. We have discussed the social and political context within which such evaluations occur and described both historical and current conceptualizations of and research about domestic violence. We ended the chapter by discussing a variety of factors evaluators may consider using when developing an evaluation protocol to assess allegations of domestic violence within the context of child custody disputes.

CHAPTER 13

Assessing Allegations of Child Alienation

Evaluators and clinicians alike have worked with divorcing families in which one parent systematically undermines a child's relationship with the other parent. We will call this *child alienation*. Over the past 25 years, considerable understanding has evolved about the dynamics and the processes of child alienation. The professional literature contains references to several different models of alienating behavior. In this chapter, we describe many of these models and their advantages and limitations. The final portion of this chapter describes an emerging model that provides decision rules to discriminate among abuse, estrangement, and alienation.

In 1949, Reich described alienating behavior when he wrote about parents who seek "revenge on the partner through robbing him or her of the pleasure in the child" (p. 265). Thirty years later, Wallerstein and Kelly (1980) identified child alienation within a population of divorced families, describing a child's irrational rejection of a parent and resistance or refusal to visit him or her. The initial alienation formulation was a pathological alignment between an angry parent and an older child or adolescent that resulted from the dynamics of the marital separation. Child alienation was considered one of many possible reactions a child had to his or her parents' divorce (Wallerstein & Kelly, 1980).

In this chapter, we discuss the history of the concept of alienation and its more recent formulations. We include arguments for and against the concept of alienation, including some of the controversial issues generated by the concept of parental alienation syndrome. We believe that some parents in conflicted divorce situations engage in a process in which they intentionally and negatively influence their children's perception of the other parent, which results in thwarting children's relationships with target parents. Such intentional and negative distraction of parent–child relationships is, by definition, not in the best psychological interests of the child. We use the term *alienating parent* to refer to the parent who engages in attempts to negatively influence a child against the other partner. We use the term *target parent* to refer to the parent toward whom the alienation is being focused (Garrity & Baris, 1994).

Before we present a historical description of the evolution of and challenges to the concept of alienation, we must state our position about alienation dynamics. We agree with Baker (2005), who recently opined that parents who engage in alienating behaviors have the potential adversely to affect children's best psychological interests. Alienating strategies may be conceptualized as effective tools for interfering with the developing or existing attachment relationship between the child and the target parent. Current attachment theory and research suggests that infants develop strong emotional ties with each parent, the purpose of which is to ensure the infants' safety by inducing them to seek closeness to a caretaking adult when there is perceived or real danger. Certain biologically determined experiences activate the attachment system, resulting in the infant seeking comfort and closeness to the attachment relationship that historically has provided safety and comfort when needed. For infants and young children, these experiences may include illness, darkness, being alone, being in an unfamiliar environment, and having strangers present. When these signals of potential danger are activated, the attachment system is activated and the infant seeks proximity to and comfort from the attachment figure. If the attachment figure is appropriately responsive to the infant's comfort-seeking behavior, the infant learns to trust that adult and will continue to seek comfort from him or her in the future. When the attachment figure is not emotionally or physically available, the infant either becomes preoccupied with gaining comfort from that parent (if the parent is unpredictably available) or accepts that the parent is not available and ceases seeking to gain comfort from that parent (if the parent is predictably unavailable). In order for infants to desire comfort from and closeness to the caretaking adult, they have to develop a sense over time that the adult is emotionally and physically available. As children develop and mature, the types of situations that activate the need for comfort from and proximity to an attachment figure change, but the underlying function of the attachment relationship remains the same.

Parents engaged in alienating behaviors appear to understand intuitively that the way to alienate effectively a child from the other parent is to encourage the child to believe that the target parent is not emotionally or physically available so that the child will cease seeking comfort from and contact with that parent. To do this, the alienating parent tries to instill the belief in the child that the target parent is not predictable, safe, available, or comforting. In fact, alienating parents often give a more frightening message, namely that the target parent is untrustworthy, unsafe, and unavailable. In addition to the messages of emotional unavailability, the alienating parent also limits contact between the child and target parent, which limits the target parent's function as an attachment figure. The target parent has fewer opportunities to provide comfort to the child, to take care of the child when he or she is ill, to soothe the child when he or she is afraid, and to be with the child as a primary caretaking parent. Alienating parents also tend to behave in ways that suggest to their children that the alienating parent would be less emotionally and physically available if the children did develop a positive relationship with the target parent. This creates a sense of insecurity in the child about his or her relationship with both the target parent and the alienating parent. Insecurity in the alienating parent–child relationship is reduced when the child pleases the alienating parent by turning against the target parent, thereby removing the threat of the alienating parent becoming emotionally or physically unavailable. Thus, children receive double messages from the alienating parent: (1) the target parent is not safe and is unavailable for the child to have a relationship with; and (2) pursuing a relationship with the target parent would entail loss of the relationship with the alienating parent for the child. The conclusion is that alienating behavior interferes with the attachment process and, therefore, is a primary risk to children's best psychological interests.

Gardner's Parental Alienation Syndrome

In the mid-1980s, Richard Gardner began to formulate a more elaborate and detailed description of alienation by suggesting a series of criteria for assessing what he believed to be the alienation process in its most disturbing form. He also provided a label for the phenomenon, calling it parental alienation syndrome (PAS). PAS was first defined as a conscious or unconscious attempt by one parent to behave in such a way as to alienate the child or children from the other parent (Gardner, 1985). In his early writings, Gardner identified the mother as the parent who engaged most often in systematic attempts to alienate a child from the other parent (Gardner, 1992). More recently, Gardner (2002) has indicated that fathers are becoming as likely as mothers to engage in the process of alienation.

According to Gardner, the purpose of PAS is to align the child with one parent by forcing the other parent out of the child's life. PAS does not simply refer to brainwashing or programming of a child by a parent but includes a child's own contributions to the campaign of denigration. It is the *combination* of the two that warrants the term PAS.

Gardner (1992) theorized that PAS includes, but is not limited to, conscious programming techniques such as brainwashing. Time is the alienating parent's most powerful ally. The longer the alienating parent has direct control over the child, the greater the alienating influence will be. As the alienating parent is able to dominate the child's time, the target parent is unable to spend time with the child. The result is a widening of the gap between the child's strengthening alliance with the alienating parent and the child's weakening alliance with the target parent. Eventually, the child adopts the malicious, intolerant, rejecting attitude of the alienating parent toward the target parent, which results in a belief system in which the child views the target parent with hatred and fear.

PAS is an *inappropriate* label to use when abuse is real and Gardner (1999) has provided guidelines for distinguishing between abuse and alienation. Parents engaging in PAS claim that the children's alienation is not programmed by them but is the inevitable result of the target parent's bona fide abuse of them. Similarly, abusive parents claim that the children's denigration is programmed by the other parent. Prior to his death, Gardner was working to differentiate between these two types of accusations (Gardner, 1999).

Once an abuse allegation is brought against a parent, appropriate investigations are conducted by child protective services and, sometimes, by local police. The court may suspend the alleged abuser's access to the child until completion of investigations and subsequent hearings to protect the child from further risk. When there are no concerns about a parent alienating a child from the other parent, these protective actions of the court support the best interests of the child.

When there are intentionally false allegations from a parent working toward eliminating the target parent from the life of the child, the same protective steps taken by the court often result in the child being shielded from the alleged perpetrator and exposed both to the alienator and to the alienation process. The conundrum is that, as the court's investigation proceeds, the alienating parent has more time to influence the child into believing that the target parent is a fearful, bad, abusive, and dangerous person.

Eight Characteristics of PAS

Gardner (1992) has identified eight characteristics of PAS. The first is a campaign of denigration, in which the child incessantly affirms hatred and fear of the target parent. Behaviorally, the child increasingly withdraws from contact with the target parent, refusing to visit the target parent, speak to the target parent on the phone, or have any other type of contact with the target parent. When the child spends time with the target parent, the child may speak indirectly to that parent. The child may speak in the third person—for example, "You tell Daddy that I don't want to go to Disneyland because he will force me to have fun when all I want is to be home with my mother."

The child may reject presents and toys from the target parent. Gardner (1992) suggests two reasons for the rejection of gifts. One is that the child has been taught to reject everything the target parent provides because it is evil, harmful, or dangerous. In this way, the child avoids anything that may be "contaminated" by the target parent. Another reason is that the act of accepting gifts may place the child in a loyalty bind. Accepting the gifts may please the target parent and, in fact, feel pleasurable to the child, but it may anger the alienating parent, who then would threaten to unleash his or her anger upon the child as well as upon the other parent. Thus, rejection of presents and toys from the target parent is an affirmation to the alienating parent that the child has chosen sides and will continue to work toward gaining his or her favors.

A second characteristic of PAS is the display of inconsistent, illogical, weak, or absurd rationalizations by the child for devaluing the target parent.

Another component of the development of PAS is the child's use of phrases, terms, and scenarios that do not reflect the child's experience or developmental level. These phrases, terms, or scenarios may reflect more advanced development than the child has achieved or they may reflect a level of development that is inconsistent with the child's experiences. The alienated child tends to be exposed to and to accept as true the alienating parent's stories and beliefs about the target parent.

A fourth characteristic of PAS is the child's lack of ambivalence toward either parent. The child often feels that the target parent is all bad and the alienating parent is all good. Although younger children tend to think dualistically, the child experiencing parental alienation tends to maintain a dualistic belief system about each parent even when such an either–or framework represents a type of developmental immaturity.

Another aspect of PAS is an allegation on the part of the alienating parent that the decision to reject the target parent is the child's decision. An alienated child may often invoke phrases and concepts about the target parent that are duplicate the alienating parent's statements, revealing both the degree of parental influence and the child's lack of awareness of that influence. Factors associated with children's suggestibility and children's memory functioning may be important areas for an evaluator to examine in assessing PAS (Gould, 1998; Warshak, 2002, 2003).

The sixth and seventh components of the syndrome appear to be directly related to children's psychological splitting of parents into good parent and bad parent. PAS children provide unconditional and unquestioned support to the alienating parent. The alienating parent may become idealized as one who can do no wrong or as the weaker of the two parents, who needs the children's protection from the bad target parent.

There is also a lack of guilt or a lack of feelings of loss about the target parent, pointing to another area for assessment regarding the possible impact of alienation on children's cognitive development. Children's empathic responding is an important step in normal child development. PAS children often demonstrate a lack of empathy toward the target parent. Evaluators should examine the degree to which lack of empathic response toward the target parent contributes either to a delay in or a tendency to interfere in the healthy development of a child's empathy and/or social perspective taking.

Finally, the feelings and beliefs about the danger inherent in a relationship with the target parent are generalized to include extended family members and, sometimes, friends and neighbors associated with the target parent.

Virtual Allegations

Another concern is what Cartwright (1993) has termed *virtual allegations*, characterized by a parent's hints of safety concerns communicated subtly to a child about the target parent. The purpose of virtual allegations is to cast aspersions on the character of the target parent by giving the child hints that the target parent is a risk. Examples of virtual allegations are: "You'll be safe with your father. If you're not, call me at any time" or "You will only have to visit with you mother for 2 days and then you will be back at home with me, safe and secure." Virtual allegations leave lingering doubts in the minds of children that subtly shade decision making about the target parent without the target parent being aware of their influence, a concern similar to issues surrounding confirmatory bias factors discussed in Chapter 4.

Systems Theory and PAS

In their early writings, Ward and Harvey (1993) viewed the alienation process as a form of family system disturbance. They viewed alienation as a means of maintaining the alienating parent's dependence on the child, as a means of assisting in managing the anger and desire for revenge felt by the child or the alienating parent, as a means of protecting the alienating parent's self-esteem, or as a means of avenging the target parent's abandonment of the family.

In their later writings, Ward and Harvey (1997) suggested that investigation of allegations of PAS needed to include examination of the full family system, assessing not just the alienating parent and his or her effect on the child, but also how the target parent may contribute to the dysfunctional family system. Other factors ripe for evaluation included contributions made to the alienating system by extended family members, treating therapists, and attorneys engaged in supporting the polarized view of the family, as well as other extrafamilial influences (Greenberg & Gould, 2001).

It is critical that evaluators investigate factors that operate in the full family system, with particular emphasis on how the experience of alienation affects the child's world. The evaluator needs to understand how the child's world has been affected by the polarization in the family. The child's pain, loneliness, lack of connection to the target parent, and unbalanced view of reality are critical components to assess in an investigation of child alienation.

When there are many children in a family, an important area for investigation is how siblings influence one another. Assessment may focus on how a particular child is supported in her alienation of the target parent by her siblings or how a child may be rejected by her siblings because of her alienation of one parent. Siblings who have already bought into the alienation alignment may encourage other siblings to join against the target parent and his extended family. Often older children attempt to influence their younger siblings to accept the belief system about the target parent.

Children who resist the alienation alignment often are treated with great hostility within the family system, especially by the children who have already aligned with the alienating parent. If the nonaligned child continues to resist the alienating influence, there is some chance he or she may align with the target parent. These children often feel rejected by their siblings and by the alienating parent, increasing the chances that the nonaligned child will develop emotional difficulties related to rejection, depression, and anxiety.

Self-Concept and PAS

Arendell's (1995) research into fathers' reactions to divorce shows that the relative importance of different self-concepts is related to amount of activity connected to each concept. Arendell suggests that a man often will view himself as a worker and therefore place the concept of "worker" high in his self-concept hierarchy, in part because it is an activity in which he engages every day. A man may also place the concept of "fatherhood" high within his self-concept hierarchy when he frequently engages in positive, rewarding fatherhood activities. The less often an activity occurs, the less likely it is to be placed high within a man's self-concept hierarchy. Concepts that placed lower in the self-concept hierarchy tend to have a lower frequency of occurrence, and it becomes less likely for the man to engage or want to engage in those less frequently occurring activities.

Divorced fathers' beliefs about the importance of fatherhood and the resulting time they devote to their fathering activities are related directly to the frequency of contact with their child. Divorced men appear to want to be involved with their children and rate higher their association with the concept of fatherhood when they are in continuous contact with their child. PAS interrupts this needed continuous contact and may contribute to the reevaluation of the concept of fatherhood within the target parent's self-concept hierarchy. The result may be a lessening of the importance of the role of father and a reduction in the number of attempts to contact the child.

A reduction in father-initiated attempts to contact the child serves two purposes for the alienating parent. The first is that fewer attempts to reach out to the child help fortify the alienating parent's argument that the target parent is uncaring, selfish, and uninterested. The second is that less contact between father and child results in less knowledge about the child. When a target parent and child spend time together after a long separation, the father is less familiar with the child. The child may have been influenced by the alienating parent to interpret the father's unfamiliarity as further indication of his lack of caring, selfishness, or disinterest. As the child becomes older, the alienating parent's influence in successfully thwarting the father–child relationship appears more and more to others as though it is the child's independent, reasoned decision to have little if any contact rather than a result of the original alienation influence.

This shift in appearances is particularly important in cases in which the alienation continues for years and the father continues his battle to maintain a relationship with his child. A judge may be less influenced by the testimony of a 7- or 9-year-old child. That same child brought before the same judge at age 13 or 15 may be perceived as providing a clearer, wiser, more fully integrated preference about what is in his or her best psychological interest. What is overlooked is how the powerful alienating influence that began when the child was 6 now has become a fully integrated personal belief for the teenager. In an unfortunate irony, the process designed to protect the child—the deliberate, slow nature of the court system—may significantly harm the child by contributing to the sturdiness of the child's belief about the target parent (Gould, 1998).

Support for PAS

Several authors have supported the concept of PAS, most notably Dunne and Hedrick (1994); Kopetski (1998); Kopetski, Rand, and Rand (2006); Rand (1997a, 1997b); and Warshak (2001b, 2003). Dunne and Hedrick reported that cases of PAS appeared to result from the pathology of the alienating parent and from the alienating parent's relationship with the children.

We believe that the best current arguments in favor of PAS are offered by Warshak (2000b, 2001a, 2001b, 2002, 2003), who discusses three essential elements in the identification of PAS. The first element is rejection or denigration of a parent that reaches the level of a campaign. The second element is that the rejection is unjustified; that is, it has no basis in past behavior of the parent toward the child. The third element is that the alienation process is a partial result of the alienating parent's influence. If any of these three elements is absent, the term PAS is not applicable.

An interesting observation offered by Warshak reminds us of the importance of context. What we know about a context and how we understand it often affects how we express our ideas. He points out that there are many scholars who write about alienation have much in common. Writers' formulation of varying alienation models may create an appearance of differences in how these authors conceptualize PAS when, in fact, there are few differences among the models in their explanation of the process of alienation. Warshak reminds us that Gardner is trained as a physician and formulates within a medical model. Kelly is a psychologist and Johnston is a sociologist, and together they formulate alienation dynamics from a family systems approach with more detail given to a wider range of factors that affect the family and each member.

Warshak recognizes the legal issues involved in the use of the term *syndrome* in Gardner's model of alienation. He believes that PAS properly refers to a cluster of observed symptoms rather than to a set of ideas about etiology, incidence, prognosis, and treatment. He describes a concern that the designation *syndrome* conveys to the court an established stature and legitimacy that may be more appropriate following the publication of rigorous empirical research. In court, the term may strengthen confidence in the scientific basis of the witness's testimony and, by implication, in the value and reliability of that testimony.

Warshak voices concern that, from the standpoint of trial strategy, in some cases it may be preferable for experts to avoid using the term PAS when testifying. He suggests that experts rely on descriptions of the behavior and statements of the child and the behavior and statements of each parent. By describing behavior and statements, the expert is able to educate the court about how children are susceptible to manipulation by adults to develop negative attitudes and false memories about other adults. This information may be used to illustrate for the court the significance of specific facts in the case at hand. Warshak (2001a) writes:

> Dropping the term "syndrome" when referring to irrationally alienated children, and limiting oneself to behavioral descriptions, does avoid legal issues surrounding the admissibility of expert testimony on PAS. But it is not clear how changing the term from PAS to "alienated child" would lead to fewer misidentifications of children who are unreasonably alienated from a parent. As with PAS, the term "alienated child" can be misapplied to children who are not alienated, or whose alienation is warranted. (p. 35)

We believe that Warshak's focus on proper identification is the most important issue to consider when investigating allegations of child alienation in the context of a child custody evaluation. How the alienation dynamic is labeled is less important than developing a reliable method of identification and a reliable method of assessment.

Warshak acknowledges that a major limitation of Gardner's model is the lack of empirical support for the interrater reliability of the diagnosis. PAS is a clinical model, and there is little empirical research examining the reliability of the eight diagnostic criteria offered by Gardner. Warshak (2001a) writes:

> The description of PAS symptoms [citation omitted], and the description of the behaviors seen in the alienated child, appear on the surface to be clear cut and intelligible. We await empirical research, however, that tests the ability of clinicians to apply these symptoms to case material and agree on whether or not a particular symptom is present in a particular child. (p. 38)

Gould (1998) provided a similar suggestion to child custody evaluators:

> Use of the concept of PAS within a clinical setting presents few problems for practitioners. Whether the clinician can definitively establish a "syndrome" or not is less important than the task of helping divorced families heal or establishing a fact pattern of systematic negative influence by one parent upon a child that significantly interferes with that child's ability to form a healthy bond with the other parent.
>
> When the concept of PAS is presented in a court of law, one must ask, "Upon

what empirical foundation does the syndrome exist?" The answer to date is that there is little, if any, research establishing the empirical foundation for the existence of Parental Alienation Syndrome. Thus, use of the PAS concept may not be admissible scientific testimony because there is no underlying theory of science, its psychometric characteristics have yet to be demonstrated, there are no established protocols to follow when attempting to measure it and it has yet to be shown to be falsifiable.

I am not suggesting that the concept of parental alienation does not show itself frequently in the context of custody determination. I believe it does. However, since the premise of this book is that the competent evaluator is able to present to the court a clear underlying theory of science, statistical properties of the tools being used and evidence that its primary assumptions are testable (falsifiable), using the term "Parental Alienation Syndrome" should be carefully applied. Until PAS has developed an established research base, it is wiser to describe the behaviors and their effect on a child rather than present the same data as indicative of a scientifically accepted, empirically established syndrome. (p. 173)

Warshak (2001a) argues that PAS may be admissible both under *Frye* and under *Daubert*. Addressing admissibility under *Frye*, PAS may be framed within the context of clinical rather than scientific testimony. Warshak argues that "when clinically based testimony is proffered, courts 'are limited to judging qualifications of the experts and the acceptability of that testimony to other similar practitioners . . . [citation omitted]" (p. 43). He argues that PAS would pass the general acceptance test.

He also argues that PAS would pass a *Daubert* challenge based upon "growing professional literature on PAS in peer-review journals" (Warshak, 2001a, pp. 43–44). Warshak reported that at least 94 publications on PAS not authored by Gardner have appeared in the literature and passed the peer review process.

We believe that Warshak's writing should be read by those involved in child custody evaluations. We neither endorse nor challenge his position on PAS. We wish for evaluators to reach their own opinions about the usefulness of PAS and other formulations of alienation dynamics. We find his attempts further to define genuine alienation from other forms of family alignment (Warshak, 2002, 2003) to be very useful in informing evaluators how to think about polarized family systems.

Challenges to PAS

Few concepts in the psychological literature generate as much passionate debate as PAS. We offer a criticism of the PAS debate that mirrors our criticism of the debate over child-based models of child custody evaluation (discussed in Part I of this volume). Too often, the debate over PAS has placed advocacy over science and personal attack over professional debate and dialogue. We find this both a distraction from debate about the significant issues that need scrutiny and a disservice to our profession and the different professional communities we serve. Focusing attention on personal attacks rather than professional differences makes it more difficult for non-mental health professionals to identify areas of genuine professional disagreement.

We agree with Warshak that "debate about the existence, conceptualization, and treatment of pathological alienation has suffered from the tactics and tone of gender politics and polemics. Such an atmosphere obscures rather than clarifies and impedes the examination for and against the various positions" (personal communication, December 28, 2003). In this section, we discuss some of the professional debate about PAS.

The American Psychological Association Presidential Task Force on Violence and the Family

Criticisms of PAS began with the *Report of the American Psychological Association Presidential Task Force on Violence and the Family* (1996), when a learned group of colleagues looked at the role of violence in custody and access decisions. Research results began to reveal that many mothers lost custody in cases in which there were concerns about domestic violence. Drawing on Liss and Stahley's (cited in American Psychological Association, 1996) research showing that fathers were awarded custody in most contested domestic violence custody cases led, in part, to the task force's conclusions that the concept of PAS was being used by abusive fathers to obtain custody of their children. They reported that a parent's concern about custody and visitation may keep that parent in an abusive relationship. They found that battered mothers who protected their children from exposure to abusive fathers were cast as alienating these children from their fathers. Courts unfamiliar with abuse dynamics were awarding custody of these children to the abusing fathers who made claims of PAS.

The task force report found that fathers who battered mothers were twice as likely to seek sole custody of their children than were nonviolent fathers. These abusive fathers were also more likely to dispute custody if there were sons involved.

The task force observed that many children from these high-conflict homes maintained loyalties to only one parent, choosing either to identify with the aggressor or with the victim. Children's rejection of their abusive father or their alignment with their victimized mother often resulted in the father and his supporters blaming the mother for alienating the children. Only with more recent scholarship has a more accurate understanding of protective parenting behaviors been widely disseminated (e.g., Drozd & Olesen, 2004).

The task force also opined that there was no empirical support for the concept of PAS. They wrote, "Although there are no data to support the phenomenon called *parental alienation syndrome*, in which mothers are blamed for interfering with their children's attachment to their fathers, the term is still used by some evaluators and courts to discount children's fears in hostile and psychologically abusive settings" (p. 40, emphasis in original).

The task force drew attention to the ways in which batterers were successfully posing allegations of PAS in court to obtain custody from mothers who were not alienating their children, but protecting them from exposure to a battering parent. The courts heard evidence of the mother's unwillingness to provide access to a battering parent as support for her attempts to thwart a father's right to see his children. One finding that caused members of the task force concern was their discovery that court decisions awarding an allegedly abusive father custody of his children increasingly appeared to be relying on inaccurate and unsupported theories such as PAS offered by mental health experts.

At the same time, several of Gardner's works on PAS are cited in the references of the child custody guidelines (American Psychological Association, 1994) suggesting that, at the time of its publication, the authors believed that PAS was an important concept with which evaluators ought to be familiar.

Myers's Critique of Syndrome Evidence Applied to PAS

Myers (1993) wrote one of the seminal articles in the field of psychology and law about syndrome evidence. He writes that the word *syndrome* is a literal translation into Greek of the word *concurrence*. The concept of *syndrome* is defined variously, each definition suggesting "a set of symptoms which occur together." He says:

> "Syndrome" is defined somewhat loosely in medicine and psychology.... The concepts of disease and syndrome overlap, but are not synonymous. With diseases, the cause of the malady is usually, although not always, known.... With syndromes, by contrast, the cause of the patient's symptoms is often unknown or poorly understood. (pp. 1451–1452)

Myers concludes his discussion of diseases and syndromes by pointing out that the former tend to carry more diagnostic certainty than the latter. The relationship between symptoms and etiology is clear with many diseases but varies much more with syndromes. Syndromes are on a continuum of certainty, with some having greater certainty as to their causes than others.

Myers's argument focuses on the probative value of syndrome evidence. If a syndrome has low diagnostic value—that is, if there is a relatively low certainty of relationship between symptoms and etiology—then the probative value of the syndrome is low. If there is a high certainty of relationship between symptoms and etiology, then the probative value is high.

Testimony about syndromes may confuse the court because judges often do not know that "there is a continuum of certainty along which syndromes are arrayed" (p. 1455). Syndrome evidence may also confuse judges because psychological syndromes arise from application of the word "syndrome" to situations that differ markedly from the meaning of syndromes in medicine and psychology. . . . Some so-called syndromes depart from this accepted meaning in that they do *not* point with *any* degree of certainty to a particular cause. (p. 1455, emphasis in original)

Myers uses the term *nondiagnostic syndrome* to refer to a syndrome that does not fall within the traditional meaning of the word and that does not have a particular etiology.

Applying his argument to PAS, we believe Myers would argue that PAS is an example of a nondiagnostic syndrome. The eight criteria identified by Gardner have not been subjected to empirical analysis to determine their usefulness in predicting alienating behavior. Because there are no empirical studies of the diagnostic criteria of PAS as predictors of child alienation, courts cannot determine the reliability of the diagnostic criteria as predictors of the syndrome. If a nondiagnostic syndrome such as PAS is presented to the court unchallenged, the court may infer that it is sufficiently reliable to warrant consideration at trial. Myers and others (e.g., Bruch, 2001) argue that there are no empirical studies demonstrating the psychometric integrity of the diagnostic criteria.

Gardner (1998) and Warshak (2001a) argue that the concept of a syndrome is appropriately applied to PAS because, like other psychiatric syndromes, the diagnostic criteria of PAS result from an interplay of psychological, social, and biological factors. PAS, like other psychiatric syndromes, may be defined as multifactored. On the other hand, Warshak acknowledges concern about the potential prejudicial effect of a syndrome that conveys "an established stature and legitimacy that may be more appropriate following more rigorous empirical research. In court, the term 'syndrome' may strengthen confidence in the scientific basis of the witness' testimony and, by implication, in the value and reliability of that testimony" (p. 42).

In an argument surprisingly similar to that forwarded by Myers (1993) about child sexual abuse accommodation syndrome (see pp. 1456–1458), Warshak argues that, although PAS may not be used

> as a test of whether the aligned parent promulgated the child's alienation, it can provide the court with an alternative explanation of a child's negative or fearful conduct and attitudes. Also, PAS testimony can assist the court in evaluating a child's ability to perceive, recollect, or communicate. When PAS has been misdiagnosed . . . expert testimony on PAS may be proffered in rebuttal. (p. 42)

We believe that Myers (1993) and Warshak (2001a, 2003) agree on the use of testimony about alienation dynamics. Testimony about alienation dynamics may be useful to the court as an alternative explanation of a child's behavior, but it should not be offered as a diagnostic syndrome or based only upon observation of a child's behavior without third-party verification. We agree with Warshak's (2001a) view that

> Testimony by an expert knowledgeable about the strategies that parents use to promulgate and support alienation, the extent to which children can be manipulated to reject and denigrate a parent, the extent to which children are suggestible, the mechanics of stereotype induction, and the psychological damage associated with involving children in parental hostilities, may assist the court in determining the proper amount of weight to give a child's explicitly stated preferences and statements regarding each parent. (p. 42)

Walker and Drozd's Critiques of PAS

Walker and Shapiro (2003b) summarized concerns about PAS by suggesting that Gardner's argument is a circular one: if a parent acts a certain way, he or she is alienating and the child is an alienated child, and if a child is alienated, the alienating parent should be punished by limiting or eliminating that parent's contact with the child. They believe that Gardner's work is too simplistic. Drozd and Walker (2001) argue that children's behaviors vary over time. Therefore, it is important for evaluators to be able to address behavior variability and reliably differentiate behaviors by one parent or the other and directly tie them to the child's reactions without calling it a syndrome.

Drozd and Olesen (2004) have reconceptualized alienation by looking at children's behaviors and attachments and then assessing whether their parents' behaviors may be alienating in nature. They have offered a series of questions to ask children, and they recommend a number of areas to explore in determining whether abuse and/or alienation are present in a custody case.

According to Drozd and Olesen (2004), the first thing to assess is the child's behavior:

1. Is there a problem with the child's attachments?
2. Is there a problem with his or her behavior?
3. If yes, is there a reality-based reason for the child's troubled behavior?
4. Are there reasons to believe that the child has been exposed to some form of abuse? (Observation of abuse to another person.)
5. Are there reasons to believe that the child has been the victim of some form of abuse? (Child has been a victim of abuse.)
6. Are there reasons to believe that the child has interpreted events as abusive? (Child interprets an event or family environment as abusive.)
7. If the child has been exposed to or a victim of abuse, is the abuse *pure abuse* or is it combined with alienation dynamics?

Without a proper evaluation of family history, the evaluator may conclude that the present behaviors reveal alienation. Some alienating parents may appear as if they are alienating their children from a caring, nonabusive parent when they are, in fact, protecting their children from exposure to an abusive parent or an abusive environment, or from reexposure to people or environmental cues that cause a child to reexperience a traumatic event.

Some protective mothers may be unaware they are protecting their children. They may thwart access to the father out of their own fear of contact with the abuser or out of their fear for their children. They may thwart children's contact with their abusive father out of anger. Protective parents who inadvertently demonstrate some alienating behaviors can be easily educated to stop the alienating behaviors and to find other ways to protect their children (Drozd & Olesen, 2004).

Walker (personal communication, September 18, 2003) argues that

> more times than not the batterer or abusive parent is the one who alienates the children from the other nonviolent parent. After all, by definition, the abusive parent has the power, and the children frequently will follow what he says to do, including disliking, disrespecting, and/or being abusive with their other parent. If there's no abuse and yet if there are still problems with the child's behavior and/or attachments, it is possible that the child is simply aligned with one parent more than the other, or that one child has more of an affinity towards one parent as opposed to the other. These may be normal developmental variations that will in time be ameliorated without intervention. It is also possible for some children to be subject to pure alienation—in which the alienating parent demonstrates alienating behaviors toward the target parent.

Her concern is that judges and advocates who observe behaviors used by one parent against the other (almost always the woman against the man, which should arouse suspicion) that could be interpreted as attempts to keep the father away from the child or cause the child to dislike the father are almost always classified as PAS without tying the behavior of that parent to the child's reactions. Drozd and Walker (2001) have suggested that, quite often, protective behavior is mislabeled as alienating.

Bruch's Critique of PAS

Law Professor Carol Bruch (2001) criticized Gardner's work on PAS, citing several areas of concern: "Gardner confounds a child's developmentally related reaction to divorce and high parental conflict (including violence) with psychosis. In doing so, he fails to recognize parents' and children's angry, often inappropriate, and totally unpredictable behavior following separation" (p. 530). She criticizes Gardner for positing that PAS occurs primarily in young children, suggesting that the current literature does not support the notion that young children are most vulnerable to alienation pressures.

She also challenges Gardner on the base rate of false allegations of abuse in custody cases. There is no professional consensus on base rates of false allegations of abuse in child custody disputes. Current estimates range from the single digits to approximately one-third of cases.

Bruch's third criticism of Gardner's PAS model focuses attention on the custodial parent. Her argument is similar to Walker's cited above, suggesting that there are many times when a custodial parent is protecting self or child from an abusive parent yet such behaviors are viewed by the court only as alienating the child from the father.

A fourth criticism focuses on Gardner's view that the relationship between a child and an alienated parent will be irreparably harmed if drastic action is not taken. Bruch believes that Gardner's oft-cited remedies to alter fundamentally the relationships between the child and each parent, including changing custody, can endanger the child.

It is interesting to note that Kelly and Johnston's (2001) reconceptualization of the alienation concept is applauded by Bruch. Bruch's main criticism focuses attention on recommendations leading to judicial interventions. She writes, "these mental health professionals, like Gardner before them, go far beyond their data as they craft recommendations for extended, coercive, highly intrusive judicial interventions" (p. 543). Some states have mental health or legal professionals who work with postdivorce parents to implement the court order regarding custody and parenting time or to assist the parents in communicating about the needs of their children. Some states refer to this role as a "special master" and other states refer to this role as a "parent coordinator." There are differences in the responsibilities of each role and your specific state may have published rules for such a role. In general, a special master or parent coordinator is a professional who is appointed by the court to act in a quasi-judicial manner and make day-to-day decisions for divorced families in conflict. They typically are mental health professionals with significant experience working with families in litigation about custody matters. A primary task of the special master is to assist parents in decision making about their children and a secondary task is to assist parents to stay out of court. Bruch's concerns focus on the use of a Special Master, the quasijudicial powers embodied in that role, and the limited understanding of the law by the mental health professional appointed to that role.

Gardner (2002) responds to Bruch's critique by arguing that Bruch's PAS critique was one-sided: "Bruch makes consistent choices by quoting professionals and articles with only one point of view, and does not vary from this" (p. 1). He writes that Bruch did not capture his true statements, using language that tended subtly to misrepresent his position on important issues such as the inappropriateness of PAS applied to cases of actual abuse.

We believe that such point–counterpoint dialogue is useful to the mental health field in general, as it forces opposing sides to articulate their positions clearly and make literature-based arguments.

Criticism of Gardner's View on Pedophilia

Some authors have criticized Gardner for his writings about the historical and current prevalence of child–adult sexual activity. Part of this criticism appears to result from Gardner's description of historical child–adult sexual contact without providing an accompanying condemnation of such behavior, which appears to his critics as consent or support for child–adult sexual contact. Similarly, his writings about the current acceptance of pedophilia in certain cultures appear to some critics to be descriptive but not condemnatory. For example, Dallam (1999) offers examples of Gardner's writings that she believes suggest that he supports sexual activity between children and adults. Dallam writes

> Gardner [citation omitted] considers sexual activities between adults and children to be part of the natural repertoire of human sexual activity and suggests that pedophilia may enhance the survival of the human species by serving "procreative purposes." According to Gardner [citation omitted], "pedophilia has been considered the norm by the vast majority of individuals in the history of the world" and "it is widespread and accepted practice among literally billions of people." (p. 3)

Similar views of Gardner is found on several websites critical of PAS. One such site offers a critical review of some of Gardner's concepts. Included among them are quotes about pedophilia from some of his books. (See *cincinnatipas.com/richardgardner-pas.html*.)

Gardner has argued, however, that pedophilia is an abominable exploitation of children:

> I believe that pedophilia is a bad thing for society. I do believe, however, that pedophilia, like all other forms of atypical sexuality, is part of the human repertoire and that all humans are born with the potential to develop any of the forms of atypical sexuality (which are referred to as paraphilias by DSM-IV). My acknowledgment that a form of behavior is part of the human potential is not an endorsement of that behavior. Rape, murder, sexual sadism, and sexual harassment are all part of the human potential. This does not mean I sanction these abominations. (*www.rgardner.com/refs/misperceptions_versus_facts.html*)

He vehemently maintains that there has been a gross misunderstanding of his position. He writes:

> I consider pedophilia to be a psychiatric disorder, an abominable exploitation of children. I have never supported a pedophile in his (or her) quest for primary child custody . . . , there are some who claim that I am reflexively protective of pedophiles and sympathetic to what they do. There is absolutely nothing in anything I have ever said or written to support this absurd allegation. When I conclude in a custody dispute that an accused father has pedophilic tendencies, I will advise the court to provide protection for the children. I never have recommended

primary custody for such a parent, nor can I imagine myself ever doing so. (*www.rgardner.com/refs/misperceptions_versus_facts.html*)

PAS Is Biased

Another criticism of PAS is that it is biased against women and against a neutral, objective means of assessment. Myers (1997) writes that gender bias infects the syndrome, making it a powerful tool to undermine the credibility of women who allege child sexual abuse. Faller (1998) makes a similar point, writing that "research findings from large samples with defined methodology do not support Gardner's assertion that large numbers of mothers (or others) involved in divorce make false allegations either by design or because they are mentally ill" (p. 108).

Amaya-Jackson and Everson (1996) raise concerns about apparent bias in the assessment procedures used to determine PAS. They argue that the assessment procedures Gardner advances are slanted to arrive at conclusions that the mother is alienating and the father is the victim of false allegations. Recently, Gardner (2002) has written that he believes the incidence of PAS perpetrated by mothers is about the same as the incidence of PAS perpetrated by fathers. Berns's (2001) study found about equal numbers of mothers and fathers as alienators, while Kopetski and Rand (cited in Warshak, 2003) report about one-third of alienators are fathers.

Criticism of the Sex Abuse Legitimacy Scale

Many researchers have criticized Gardner's Sex Abuse Legitimacy Scale (SALS) for its lack of reliability and validity. Berliner and Conte (1993) and Myers (1993) have been highly critical of it. Conte wrote that the SALS is "probably the most unscientific piece of garbage I've seen in the field in all my time. To base social policy on something as flimsy as this is exceedingly dangerous" (cited in Moss, 1988, p. 26).

We agree with Conte's professional criticism of the scale. Gould (1998) has previously criticized the SALS for its lack of research, specifically for its lack of psychometric characteristics. We also agree that data obtained from use of the scale should be viewed with great caution, as there is no consensus about the meaning of that information. We point to Conte's harsh criticism of the SALS as an example of the manner in which unprofessional attacks are often intertwined with useful professional critique.

Criticism of the Polemics of the Alienation Debate

We believe that the use of inflammatory language does not help create dialogue. We also believe that the use of respectful and professional dialogue tends to encourage those engaged in both the political and scientific sides of this debate to consider more constructive language intended to invite professional debate rather than personal attack. We object to personal attacks offered under the guise of scientific debate, and we wish to make clear our concern that, on occasion, people on both sides of these issues have allowed their passion and advocacy to speak louder than their scholarship. We believe that scholarship and critical thinking ought to lead the way for advocacy and that when advocacy leads the way for scholarship—when a particular position speaks louder than the science upon which it is based—many in the mainstream stop listening. The result is that important points and counterpoints that evaluators need to understand and integrate into their thinking fall on deaf ears.

We applaud Warshak (2000b, 2001a, 2001b, 2002, 2003), Myers (1993), Lyon (1999), and Drozd and Olesen (2004) for their scholarship and Bruch (2001) for stimulating debate on the proper role of the courts in dealing with alienated children. What we found missing from Bruch's argument was a more balanced review of cogent arguments put forth by those such as Warshak (2000b, 2001a, 2001b, 2002, 2003), Rand (1997a, 1997b), and Baker (2005) about aspects of alienation dynamics that may be useful for evaluators to consider.

We find the family systems/developmental model of Kelly and Johnston (2001) most useful in assessing child alienation. When evaluators use it in combination with Drozd and Olesen's (2004) decision-making model that guides discrimination among abuse, estrangement, and alienation, they are likely to develop a comprehensive model for investigating these challenging issues.

Kelly and Johnston's Child Alienation Model

Kelly and Johnston (2001) propose the concept of the *alienated child* as a more useful conceptualization of alienation dynamics at work in high-conflict families. They define an alienated child as "one who expresses, freely and persistently, unreasonable negative feelings and beliefs (such as anger, hatred, rejection and/or fear) toward a parent that are significantly disproportionate to the child's actual experience with that parent" (p. 251). Their model refocuses alienation assessment dynamics to examine the child, his or her observable behaviors, and parent–child relationships. They argue that the emphasis on an alienating parent wrongly focuses our attention on adult behavior when our concerns should be how the child is influenced and how the child's relationships with each parent are affected. They write, "This objective and neutral focus enables the professionals involved in the custody dispute to consider whether the child fits the definition of an alienated child, and if so, to utilize a more inclusive framework for assessing *why* the child is now rejecting a parent and refusing contact" (p. 251, emphasis added).

Distinguishing Alienated Children from Other Children Who Resist Visitation

An important task for evaluators is distinguishing the alienated child (who persistently refuses and rejects visitation because of unreasonable negative views and feelings) from children who resist contact with a parent after separation for a variety of normal, realistic, and/or developmentally predictable reasons. Echoing Warshak's (2002, 2003) caution, Kelly and Johnston (2001) note their concern about the frequency with which children are inappropriately labeled alienated and how a parent who questions the wisdom of visitation often is labeled an alienating parent. They cite several reasons children may resist visitation and state, "only in very specific circumstances does this behavior qualify as alienation" (p. 251). Among the reasons children may resist visits are:

1. Concerns rooted in normal developmental processes (e.g., normal separation anxieties in the very young child).
2. Concerns rooted primarily in the high-conflict marriage and divorce (e.g., fear or inability to cope with the high-conflict transition).
3. Concerns rooted in a child's response to a parent's parenting style (e.g., rigidity, anger, or insensitivity to the child).
4. Concerns rooted in the child's worries about an emotionally fragile custodial parent (e.g., fear of leaving this parent alone).
5. Concerns rooted in the remarriage of a parent (e.g., behaviors of the parent or stepparent that alter willingness to visit).

A Continuum of Child–Parent Relationships after Separation and Divorce

Kelly and Johnston (2001) propose a continuum of child–parent relationships after separation and divorce. The five-point continuum ranges from positive to negative, with the most negative being alienation. We provide a brief discussion of each below.

Positive Relationships to Both Parents

At the healthiest end of the continuum are the majority of separated children, who have positive relationships with both parents. They value both parents and wish to spend significant (often equal) amounts of time with each of them.

Affinity with One Parent

The next step along the continuum are children who have an affinity for one parent while also desiring continuity and contact with both parents. Affinity for one parent is characterized by children feeling closer to one parent than the other. It may result from temperament, gender, age, shared interests, sibling preferences of parents, and parenting practices. Such affinities may shift over time with changing developmental needs and situations. Kelly and Johnston write, "Although these children may occasionally express an overt preference for a parent, they still want substantial contact with and love from both parents" (p. 252).

Allied Children

The third step along the continuum are children who have developed an alliance with one parent. During the marriage or separation, these children demonstrate or express a consistent preference for one parent over the other. They often want limited contact with the nonpreferred parent after separation. Allied children generally do not fully reject the other parent nor do they seek to terminate all contact. They tend to express some ambivalence toward this parent, including anger, sadness, and love, as well as resistance to contact.

Kelly and Johnston (2001) note that such alliances may have their roots in the family dysfunction that preceded the divorce. Children may have been encouraged to take sides or to carry hostile messages between parents. Alliances appear to occur more often in older children in response to the dynamics of the marital breakup. Older children tend to make moral assessments and judgments about which parent caused the breakup, who is most hurt, who is most vulnerable, and who needs and/or deserves the child's help and support. These strong alliances and children's accompanying expressions of moral outrage and contempt are usually short-lived if the child has an opportunity to process the separation with a therapist or trusted adult or fade when the conflict subsides. Some of these children may also develop more hardened alignments or even alienation in the context of a bitter divorce with protracted litigation, which may result in strong resistance to visiting the parent they are not allied with.

Evaluators need to distinguish allied children from alienated children. Most allied children acknowledge (sometimes begrudgingly) that they love the other parent, yet focus attention on not enjoying time with that parent. They do not engage in the fierce, brittle remonstrations and cruel behaviors toward the rejected parent commonly observed in the alienated child, but they often protect the preferred parent, whom they perceive as wounded and needing their full attention (Kelly & Johnston, 2001).

Estranged Children

A fourth step along the continuum finds children who are realistically estranged from one of their parents as a consequence of that parent's history of family violence, abuse, or neglect. These children need to be clearly distinguished from alienated children. They have taken sides in the family because of a fact-based history of observing repeated violence or explosive outbursts of a parent during the marriage or after separation. Sometimes these children have been victims of violence and abusive behavior from an abusive parent. The only time they feel safe enough to reject the violent or abusive parent is after the separation, when protected by their custodial parent.

These children do not have to witness violence directly. They may witness the aftermath of intimate partner violence or be traumatized by an act of violence that from an adult's perspective may not have been very serious or injurious. Kelly and Johnston (2001) write, "The mix of intense anger towards the abusive parent, and phobic reactions to that parent caused by subconscious fear of retaliation looks like alienation. But unlike alienated children, the estranged children do not harbor *unreasonable* anger and/or fear" (p. 253, emphasis in original).

Children who have suffered exposure to or been victims of abuse generally suffer from some type of traumatic stress reaction. Evaluators need to assess for trauma reactions. If no trauma reaction is identified, then one might wish to consider alienation, among other alternative hypotheses.

Among the reasons children become estranged from a parent are:

1. Severe parental deficiencies, including persistent immature and self-centered behaviors.
2. Chronic emotional abuse of the child or preferred parent.
3. Physical abuse that goes undetected.
4. Characterologically angry, rigid, and restrictive parenting styles.
5. Psychiatric disturbance or substance abuse that grossly interferes with parenting capacities and family functioning.

The responses of these realistically estranged children following separation are commonly and incorrectly interpreted and played out in custody disputes as alienation. The deficient, abusive, or violent parent frequently accuses the protective parent of alienating the child against him or her, but does not acknowledge how marital violence or severe parenting deficiencies negatively affected his or her parent–child relationship.

The Alienated Child

At the extreme end of the continuum are children who are alienated from a parent after separation and divorce. They tend to express their rejection of that parent (1) stridently, and (2) without apparent guilt or ambivalence, and (3) strongly resist or completely refuse any contact with that parent.

Often, a target parent has been less involved in his or her children's lives compared with the other parent or displays less robust parenting competencies. The child's complaints and allegations about the rejected parent may reflect some true incident that has been grossly distorted and exaggerated, resulting in the child holding highly negative views and feelings. It is the gross distortion and exaggeration that makes this a *pathological* response. Child alienation is a severe distortion on the child's part of the previous parent–child relationship. These children display an intensity, breadth, and ferocity of behavior toward the target parent they are rejecting that go far beyond alliance or estrangement. They are responding to complex and frightening dynamics within the divorce process itself that include an array of parental behaviors combined with their own vulnerabilities that make them susceptible to becoming alienated. Child alienation most often occurs in high-conflict custody disputes and is an infrequent occurrence among the larger population of divorcing children.

Systemic Processes That Potentiate Child Alienation

Kelly and Johnston (2001) recommend an evaluation model based upon systems theory and suggest two broad factors to consider. *Background factors* are viewed as directly or indirectly affecting the child. These may include, but are not limited to,

1. A history of intense marital conflict.
2. A humiliating separation.
3. Subsequent divorce conflict and litigation that can be fueled by professionals and extended family.
4. Personality dispositions of each parent.
5. Child-related factors such as age, cognitive capacity, and temperament.

The second broad factor is *intervening variables*, which moderate or intensify the child's response to critical background factors. Intervening variables may include:

1. Parenting beliefs and behaviors.
2. Sibling relationships.
3. The child's own vulnerabilities within the family dynamics.

Kelly and Johnston (2001) believe that children may be groomed to be alienated. Children may be exposed to several of these factors, resulting in an increased risk for alienation in the future. Evaluators need to assess fully the influence of these alienating processes in order for preventive action to be taken, especially when children are younger. The presence of alienating processes and the display of typical alienating behaviors of parents do not reliably predict that a child will become alienated. It is hypothesized that alienation results from the intensity and longevity of children's exposure to these alienating processes in combination with other important parent and child variables.

Kelly and Johnston (2001) suggest a set of "risk factors that may potentiate alienation" (p. 255). Among these risk factors are:

1. Triangulation of the child in intense marital conflict.
2. The child's experience of separation as deeply humiliating.
3. The parents' involvement in highly conflicted divorce and litigation.
4. Tribal warfare or the contributions of new partners, extended kin, and professionals.

Common Behaviors and Organizing Beliefs of the Aligned Parent

Continuous and negative representation of one parent undermines the child's relationship with, confidence in, and love for that parent. One result is intolerable confusion for the child, most easily resolved by the child choosing to take sides with one parent rather than the other. The influence of these alienating behaviors on a child constitutes a form of emotional abuse (Kelly & Johnston, 2001).

There are several organizing beliefs held by the aligned parent that help alienate the child from the other parent. These organizing beliefs are born out of the aligned parent's deep psychological issues and reflect his or her deep distrust and fear of the ex-spouse. Often, the aligned parent is "absolutely convinced that [the ex-spouse] is at best irrelevant and at worst a pernicious influence on the child" (Kelly & Johnston, 2001, p. 257). The three major organizing beliefs are:

1. Children do not need the other parent in their lives.
2. The rejected parent is dangerous to the child in some way(s), either violent, physically or sexually abusive, or neglectful.
3. The rejected parent does not and has never loved or cared about the child.

Aligned parents often create alliances with professionals who mobilize and enable these parents to present themselves in a coherent, organized manner. In addition, the nature of the adversarial process tends to polarize positions and parties, leading to increased hostility and dualistic thinking with little challenge. There is often significant pathology and anger in the aligned parent, and he or she often has problems with boundaries and differentiation from the child, severe separation anxieties, impaired reality testing, and projective identifications with the child (Dunne & Hedrick, 1994; Johnston & Roseby, 1997; Lampel, 1996; Lund, 1995; Wallerstein & Kelly, 1980).

Normal parenting does not include encouraging complete rejection of the other parent. Even when there is a history of child abuse, a history of parental mental illness, or when the child's safety is endangered, the average parent will seek different avenues and more rational means of protecting the child. Most parents recognize that their child loves the other parent despite that parent's destructive behavior.

Behaviors of the Rejected Parent That Contribute to Child Alienation

Although it was lightly touched upon in previous formulations of alienation, Kelly and Johnston (2001) focus attention on the contribution of the rejected parent to the alienation process. They contend that the rejected parent's behaviors do not by themselves warrant the disproportionately angry response of the child nor the refusal to have contact. The rejected parent's involvement and parenting capacities are generally within a normative range, though possibly compromised by marital conflicts, divorce disputes, and the child's problematic response.

Characteristics of rejected parents that may contribute to the alienation process are:

1. A tendency to become passive and withdraw in the face of conflict.
2. A tendency to react to the child's harsh and unjustified treatment by becoming highly affronted and offended by the lack of respect and ingratitude afforded them.
3. Display of a parenting style characterized by a harshness, lack of empathy, and rigidity that does not, however, rise to the level of emotional or physical abuse.
4. A tendency to display a self-centered, immature personality.
5. A history of having displayed critical and demanding behaviors in parent–child interactions during the marriage, leading to the aligned parent counterreacting to the perceived harshness and overcompensating by becoming even more lenient or overprotective with the child.
6. A tendency to have difficulty differentiating the needs and behaviors of the alienated child from the motivations and behaviors of the aligned parent.

Kelly and Johnston (2001) provide a more thorough explanation of each of these tendencies and how both the alienated child and the aligned parent may react to the rejected parent's behaviors. It is the richness of the family systems interpretation of each family member's interaction that provides a significantly more complex and subtle understanding of alienation dynamics.

Developmental Stage and Vulnerability of the Child to the Alienation Process

Not all children are subject to alienation. There are certain individual differences that may make some children more vulnerable, including differences in children's psychological, cognitive, and developmental strengths and vulnerabilities and external arrangements involving the rejected parent. Among the most critical are:

1. The child's age and cognitive capacity.
2. The child's feeling of abandonment by the rejected parent.
3. The child's temperament and personality style.
4. Other parent–child relationship factors that may include the dependency of the child on the aligned parent, threats of abandonment by the aligned parent, the child's belief that he or she needs to protect and take care of the aligned parent, and an enmeshed parent–child relationship.
5. Lack of external support for the child, including the child not being allowed to spend time with the rejected parent or that parent's extended family.

Consistent with descriptions offered by Clawar and Rivlin (1991), Gardner (1992, 1998), Wallerstein and Kelly (1980), and Warshak (2001a, 2002, 2003), Kelly and Johnston (2001) offer a typical presentation of an alienated child:

> The core feature of alienated children is the extreme disproportion between the child's perception and beliefs about the rejected parent and the actual history of the rejected parents' behaviors and the parent–child relationship. Unlike most aligned or estranged youngsters, alienated children freely express hatred or intense dislike toward the rejected parent. They demonize and vilify that parent, often present trivial reasons to justify their hatred, and are usually not reticent about broadcasting the perceived shortcomings of the parent to others. (p. 262)

Kelly and Johnston also describe how the target parent may respond to a child's rejection. They write:

> This is particularly baffling to the rejected parent, extended family, and other adults knowledgeable about the prior parent–child relationship. Most often, as stated above, rejected parents have had at least an adequate relationship with these children, and the angry rejection is not merited, even when contributions of the rejected parent are taken into account. (p 263)

There are several common behaviors among alienated children, including:

1. The child strongly expresses resistance to visiting the rejected parent and, in more extreme cases, absolutely refuses to see the parent in any setting, including a therapeutic one, and desires unilaterally to terminate the parent–child relationship.
2. The child may wish only to talk to lawyers who represent his or her viewpoint, and to custody evaluators and judges whom they believe will fully support his or her efforts to terminate the parent–child relationship.
3. The child's manner of telling his or her story reveals replicas or slight variants of the aligned parents' allegations and stories about the rejected parent yet has little if any underlying substance, texture, or detail to support the allegations.

4. The child may act in a hostile and disrespectful manner toward the rejecting parent, grandparents, and other relatives.
5. The child often idealizes or speaks glowingly of the aligned parent and refuses to consider any information that might undermine this viewpoint of his or her perfect companion and parent. The child vigorously rejects any suggestion that his or her obsessive hatred of the rejected parent has any relationship to the views or behaviors of the aligned parent.
6. The child's social relationships are often impaired due to a polarized thinking style. He or she is likely to hold simplistic, black-and-white views of the world and may express harshly strident views and feelings toward others that are reflected in his or her dealings with peers and those in authority.
7. The child's behavior in the rejected parent's home is severely problematic and disturbed.

We believe that Kelly and Johnston's (2001) reformulation of alienation dynamics is an important contribution to the literature. Earlier, we cited Bancroft and Silverman's (2002) criticisms of this model, and we believe that evaluators may find it useful to incorporate relevant criticisms of the model, but we find the combination of a family systems perspective that includes individual factors, dyadic factors, group factors, and extrafamilial factors to provide a more robust approach to the evaluation of alienation dynamics.

We also point to the need for empirical research on Kelly and Johnston's model. Similar to PAS, the child alienation model has developed from clinical observations rather than systematic empirical support. We strongly urge a comprehensive research program aimed at developing an empirical foundation that supports what we believe to be a uniquely important set of clinical observations.

Drozd and Olesen's model of assessment of child alienation takes into account many of robust features of Kelly and Johnston's model while also addressing concerns voiced by Bancroft and Silverman.

Drozd and Olesen's Model for Discriminating Alienation from Domestic Violence

Few investigation questions are as difficult to examine as distinguishing among allegations of child abuse, domestic violence, and a child's unnecessary alienation from an otherwise good parent. On the one hand, placing a child with a violent, intimidating, or abusive parent while severing ties with the more nurturing and more protective parent may result in harsh consequences for the child and is counter to the child's best interests. At the same time, limiting or eliminating a child's contact with a good-enough parent based on the other parent's allegations that that parent is dangerous or evil results in similarly harsh consequences for the child and also is considered counter to the child's best interests. In the latter case, the child's experience of reality becomes distorted. His or her ability to judge the quality of relationships with others and experiences of being with other people become impaired (Stoltz & Ney, 2002; Lampel, 2003).

Drozd and Olesen (2004) recommend an evaluation strategy for distinguishing among allegations of child abuse, domestic violence, and a child's unnecessary alienation from an otherwise good parent. The first step is to assess the nature of the child's attachment to and relationship with each parent. The evaluator should take an extensive history from each parent and from the child, then gather information on past and current observed child problem behaviors. The evaluator should directly observe the child across several settings to determine whether the alleged distressing behavior shows rejection of a parent or whether it represents some other form of disruption in the parent–child relationship (that is, in the child's attachment to either parent). For example, in a recent case, historical information revealed that a toddler experienced several residential moves, changes in babysitters, and significant disruptions to her daily routine. Several hypotheses were generated to explore the toddler's display of distress, among them her developmental age; her reaction to externally imposed stressors that resulted in her significantly reduced sense of safety, security, and predictability; and her temperament, a factor that may be independent of the contextual changes she has endured.

It is important for evaluators to determine whether a child's behavior problems are artifacts of the current situation, such as a child's reaction to her parent's separation. The evaluator should examine factors that operate across other levels of system functioning, such as individual, relationship, family, and extended family factors. Evaluators may also ask questions that probe deeper into each of these areas. That is, the evaluator may need to probe both across a broader set of factors and deeper within each factor.

If there are problems with a child's relationship with either parent and/or if a child is displaying behavior problems, the evaluator must investigate whether there is a realistic basis for the child's behaviors. There are many types of family situations and many types of parenting behaviors other than alienating parenting behavior that may lead a child to refuse contact with or express anger and rejection toward a parent. There are situations in well-functioning families that could result in a child's behavior change. There may have been a preseparation family dynamic characterized by one parent's physical or emotional absence from the family that resulted in the child developing an insecure attachment to that parent.

Evaluators need to examine how infants and toddlers developed attachments to each parent. They may need to assess individual factors such as a child's temperament or a child's affinity for one parent over the other parent that contribute to the child's feeling significantly closer to one parent. Sometimes, a parent may feel particularly possessive of a very young child because of the child's preexisting illness, disability, or vulnerability but not actively attempt to interfere with the child's relationship with the other parent.

In addition to nonpathological causes of a child's refusal to visit or have contact with one parent, there are cases in which the child's avoidance of a parent is a reasonable, healthy, and rational response to violence in the family and its resulting trauma. Abusive relationships within these families are difficult to observe, leaving only the child's strong desire to avoid contact with the dangerous parent as an indicator that something within the family is unhealthy. It is difficult to determine what is unhealthy. For example, when a parent has been violent toward the other parent or abusive to the child, the child may wish to avoid contact, especially being alone with the feared parent, and may try to avoid weekend visits or travel away from home with the feared parent. The challenge is to be sensitive to child protection while also conducting a thorough evaluation of all reasonable hypotheses explaining the child's behavior.

Questions about the Child's Behaviors and Relationships

Evaluators need to examine allegations of domestic violence and other forms of abuse from the perspective of the child. Some questions we believe are critical to ask in a competently conducted evaluation are:

- Are there any problems with the child's behaviors?
- What type of problems?
- Under what conditions or context are the behaviors observed?
- During what time are the behaviors observed?
- Who has observed the behaviors?
- How often have the behaviors been observed?
- How consistently over time and place have the behaviors been observed?
- Where and when do these behaviors occur?
- Under what circumstances are the behaviors *not* observed?
- Who observes and reports them?
- Are there any problems with the child's relationship with either parent?
- If yes, what type of problems?
- When did the problem behaviors start?

Questions about Whether or Not There Has Been Abuse

Once the evaluator has gathered information that leads to a preliminary hypothesis that a child displays problem behaviors or that there is a problem in the parent–child relationship, the next area of investigation is whether there is a factual or reality-based reason for the problem. Among the questions to ask are:

- Has the child been exposed to any kind of abuse—as the direct victim or as a secondary victim?
- Has there been child abuse?
- Has there been alcohol or drug abuse?
- Has there been family violence?
- Has there been emotional or psychological abuse?
- Has there been physical abuse?
- Has there been sexual abuse?
- Has the child interpreted an event as abusive?
- If there is abuse, who is the alleged aggressor?
- Who is the alleged victim?

When there are allegations of abuse, a thorough assessment of all elements of the alleged abuse is critical. It is important to examine the particular dynamics and behaviors of alleged abuse. Among the factors to be investigated are abuse severity, chronicity, and context.

Children exposed to abuse are affected differently based upon their age and their stage of development, the support that they have from others, and their general level of resilience. Evaluators should assess the ways in which the child is safeguarded by the protective parent and the risk posed to the child by the alleged abusive parent.

Drzod and Olesen (2004) recommend that, after careful evaluation of the basis for a child's rejection of a parent, evaluators need to look more broadly at both parents and their parenting of the child in question. Such behavior should be investigated using careful interviews with the parties, collateral witnesses, and written records of letters, faxes, voicemail messages, and emails. Any investigation of alleged alienating behavior by one parent toward the other parent should be separate from an investigation of the behavior of the alleged abusive parent. The evaluator should explore questions about how the child may have been influenced. Among the questions to ask are the following:

- Has the child been exposed to a campaign of excessive denigration of the other parent?
- Has one parent engaged in any behaviors associated with alienation of the child from the other parent, such as rejecting the child when the child expresses love for the other parent?
- Does the parent believe the things he or she says about the other parent?
- Is he or she genuinely frightened and protective, even if mistakenly so?
- Is there a financial or other kind of gain that would help explain the reason for the behavior if genuine fear does not seem to be present?
- Is there a personal or family history of rejection being repeated in the current family system?

- Is the parent displaying polarized thinking for reasons not related to a past or present history of abuse?
- Does the parent see most things and/or most situations as win–lose or all-or-nothing?
- Is there documented psychopathology that would explain any of the parent's existing problems with flexible and clear thinking?
- Is the parent prone to form enmeshed relationships?
- Does the parent tend to view the child as an extension of him- or herself?

If there is no campaign of alienation, the evaluator should consider examining questions such as:

- Is the observed child problem behavior or the observed parent–child problem behavior associated with situation-specific factors around separation?
- Is there a greater affinity for one parent because of gender, shared interests, or temperament?

Relationship Typology

Drozd and Olesen (2004) propose a classification system for pathological and nonpathological parent–child relationships. They point out that both abuse and alienation may lead to parent–child relationship problems. Kelly and Johnston (2001) add that medical problems, developmental difficulties, psychological issues, school or learning problems, and family problems may cause or contribute to relationship problems.

Drozd and Olesen (2004) propose four nonpathological and six pathological parent–child relationships. The nonpathological parent–child relationships include equal relationships, affinity in nonabusive families, alignment in nonabusive families, and protective parenting found in abusive families. The pathological parent–child relationships include identification with the aggressor, estrangement as a result of abandonment or poor parenting, estrangement as a result of abuse in the family, alienation in nonabusive families (by the mother or by the father), alienation by the abuser in families where there is abuse, and alienation by the victim mother in families where there is abuse.

Nonpathological Relationships

Equal Relationships

Many, if not most, children in nonabusive families have equal relationships with their parents—relationships that are not identical but relatively equal.

Affinity in Nonabusive Families

Affinity consists of a child being emotionally closer to one parent than to the other, perhaps because the parent to whom the child feels closer has interests that are more in tune with the child's interests. Affinity relationships may also develop because a child's personality is more similar to the parent with whom he or she has an affinity or because the child has spent significantly more time with that parent. When a child has an affinity toward one parent, it is likely that the child also has a strong and positive affectional bond with the other parent.

Alignment in Nonabusive Families

In families where there is no abuse, the child may have an exaggerated connection with one parent at the expense of the other parent. The affectional bond with one parent is strong, and the affectional bond with the other parent is weaker or nonexistent. It is possible that the parent with whom the child is aligned has neither directly nor indirectly promoted or manipulated the child into the alignment, and, if this is the case, most likely the alignment is nonpathological. A pathological alignment not caused by direct parental abuse or alienation occurs when the child is unable to tolerate tension surrounding his or her parents' high-conflict divorce. The child may opt out of the unbearable conflict by choosing sides, thereby reducing his or her sense of conflict.

Protective Parenting in Abusive Families

Some parents' concerns and fears about the safety of their children are reality-based. These parents have a fact-based reason to protect their children from the other parent. Research shows that when there is one kind of abuse in a family, there is an increased risk there will be other kinds of abuse. Evaluators need to be aware of a strong relationship between the existence of domestic violence in a family and increased risk for child abuse. Husbands who abuse their wives are more likely to abuse their children. (See Chapter 12 for a more in-depth discussion of these relationships and of potential risk to children.) Therefore, a victim parent may engage in healthy protective parenting to keep a child out of harm's way. The evaluator should assess the parent's ability to protect the child in healthy ways. When protective parenting inhibits a child's normal development, it is important that evaluators provide recommendations about how a parent can learn healthy protective parenting behaviors.

Pathological Relationships

Identification with the Aggressor

Identification with the aggressor refers to a type of alignment that occurs in abusive families. It begins with a child being fearful of the aggressor parent, either consciously or unconsciously. The child then has a counterphobic reaction to the fear and aligns with the aggressor. The child thinks, "If I stay close to him, stay on his good side, I will be safe, and I will not be hurt like he has hurt my mother and my sisters." Often, the abuser promotes this kind of alignment. Sometimes the abuser actively capitalizes on the child victim's identification by encouraging the child to view his or her mother as weak and disempowered and to dislike her.

Estrangement as a Result of Abandonment or Poor Parenting

There are situations in nonviolent families where a child may develop an estranged relationship with a parent. For example, estrangement may occur when a child has not seen her father for 2 years because he was stationed overseas during wartime. From the child's perspective, the parent has abandoned her. Another form of estrangement may result when a parent abuses drugs and becomes emotionally unavailable to the child. From the child's perspective, the parent has abandoned him or her.

Estrangement as a Result of Abuse in the Family

Some children may not develop emotional attachments with one parent for good reasons. A parent may have abused them or their other parent. These children may be traumatized from what they have been exposed to, experienced, or witnessed. They may be afraid of the abusive parent and have few or no positive emotions toward that parent, usually while maintaining a relationship with the other parent. The estrangement is caused by something the estranged parent has done or failed to do and is the child's reaction to the parent's actions. The child's reasons are reality-based. According to Drozd and Olesen (2004), cases of estrangement with domestic violence are most at risk of being mislabeled as cases of alienation. The abusive parent claims that the victim parent has made the children not want to be around him by making allegations of abuse. He does this to take the focus off of him and to put the blame for the child's rejection of him on the victim parent.

Alienation in Nonabusive Families

With alienation, the child develops strong and unambivalent feelings toward the target or rejected parent. Although the rejected parent has not been abusive, the child refuses contact with that parent for irrational reasons. There is no reality-based reason for the child's rejection of the parent. Genuine cases of alienation are rare (Johnston, 2003).

Alienation by the Abuser in Families Where There Is Abuse

Another type of alienation in families with domestic violence or abuse occurs when the abusive parent alienates the child against the victim parent. The abuser is in a better position to promote a division that might be developing between the victim parent and the child because the abusive parent holds the power in the family system. To the evaluator, the abusive parent appears calm, rational, and a good parent, while the victim parent appears emotionally distraught and inadequate in her parenting. The evaluator must examine underlying reasons for the observed behaviors in both parents and children.

Alienation by Victim Mothers in Families Where There Is Abuse

Drozd and Olesen (2004) observe that some mothers may be more pathological, and more entrenched in their hatred of the abusive father. In these cases, the victim mother engages in protective parenting and alienating behaviors.

Summary

In this chapter, we reviewed many current conceptual models of alienation dynamics, from the initial work of Richard Gardner through the recent work of Leslie Drozd and Nancy Olesen. Criticisms of alienation concepts were presented, including challenges to the concept of parental alienation syndrome. Reformulation of alienation was described, and an evaluation model that helps distinguish allegations of abuse from allegations of child alienation was presented.

CHAPTER 14

Another Call for Humility

W e use this concluding chapter to step up on our soapbox and voice our concerns, described in several of our previously published articles, about the need for humility in the administration of our evaluation services and in the oral and written testimony that we offer (Gould, 2006; Gould & Martindale, 2005; Martindale, 2005b; Martindale & Gould, 2004). We begin with the premise that mental health professionals who are engaged in offering forensic services are guests of the legal system. We have been invited into the legal arena because the courts believe that we can offer information and/or analysis that is beyond the scope of the judge, the lay witnesses, and the attorneys.

Stay within the Lines

We have been invited into the legal field, and we believe it is important to respect and to play by its rules. This means forensic experts need to learn about rules of evidence and to keep up with changes in case law relevant to their areas of practice. There are times, however, when judges and attorneys invite mental health professionals to opine on matters that are beyond the scope of our expertise. In these circumstances, it is incumbent upon us to refuse politely.

Example 1

In a custody case, the judge asked the evaluator to assess a family and to offer an opinion about the most developmentally appropriate parenting plan for a 3-year-old and a 5-year-old. Between completing the evaluation and testifying at trial, the mother sought to relocate to another state. A relocation analysis was never part of the evaluator's initially assigned task. At trial, the judge asked the evaluator to comment on the possible effects of the mother's intended move on the children's attachment with each parent. The evaluator complied. An opinion about relocation and its risk to children's attachment ought to be offered to the court only after an appropriate evaluation has been conducted.

Example 2

An evaluator has been asked to assess the potential risk of physical harm to a child by a father who has a history of alcohol abuse. At trial, the judge asks the evaluator to consider the potential risk to the child of the mother's upcoming marriage and the child's subsequent living arrangements with stepsiblings. Without having considered what data must be included in such an evaluation in order to render a reliable opinion, it is inappropriate for the testifying expert to provide an opinion.

Know State Statutes and Case Law

It is important for evaluators to know the standards for admissibility of evidence in the jurisdictions in which they practice and to appreciate the importance of using reliable and valid techniques in their forensic assessments. We urge evaluators to read case law about the admissibility of scientific evidence. Obtain the case that set the precedent in the jurisdiction in which you practice and follow any clarifications or modifications that may have appeared in subsequent decisions. Develop your methodology to be consistent with your state's legal definitions of reliability and relevance.

Do Not Offer Ultimate-Opinion Testimony Concerning the Credibility of the Litigants

Each state has case law that helps define the limits of expert testimony. An issue before the court that experts are expected not to testify about is the credibility of litigants, yet they often do so.

Recently, we were involved as consultants on a case in which an expert analyzed the credibility of the litigants and based her recommendations on that analysis. Neither the psychological needs of the children nor the ability of each parent to meet those needs was discussed. The specialty guidelines for forensic psychologists (Committee on Ethical Guidelines for Forensic Psychologists, 1991) urge psychologists actively to seek "information that will differentially test plausible rival hypotheses" and, where circumstances reasonably permit, . . . [to] seek to obtain independent and personal verification of data relied upon" (p. 661). The American Psychological Association custody guidelines (1994) declare, "Important facts and opinions are documented from at least two sources whenever their reliability is questionable" (p. 679). In seeking the information alluded to, evaluators will often find that one litigant's version of certain events is accurate and that the other litigant's version of those same events is inaccurate. Though the temptation may be strong to offer opinions concerning the comparative credibility of the two litigants, evaluators must recognize that such judgments are the province of the court.

Follow Peer-Reviewed Methods and Procedures

The criteria often used in establishing a community standard among practitioners from a specific profession are found in the writings that appear in peer-reviewed books and journals and in professional practice guidelines. We believe that there is little, if any, disagreement among scholars and teachers of forensic psychology about the use of forensic methodology, exemplified by the use of interviews, psychological tests, direct behavioral observations, third-party record review, and collateral interviews. We can only hypothesize concerning the reasons some evaluators fail to utilize accepted procedures. Some may believe that their individual knowledge exceeds the collective knowledge of the profession in which they have trained. Some may be unfamiliar with generally accepted procedures. (Their lack of familiarity may be related to a failure to read the professional literature, which, in turn, may stem from a mistaken belief that they already know whatever they need to know.) Finally, some evaluators may feel that their clinical skills are sufficient and that they need not use the methods employed by others.

In another evaluation, the evaluator conducted a home study of each parent's house and observed the children. The information provided in the report described the father's interactions with the children in glowing terms and the mother's interactions with the children in more neutral terms. The opinions expressed in the report created the impression that the father's interactions with the children were extraordinary. When the evaluator's notes were reviewed, there were no descriptions of the child's behavior, of the parents' behavior, or of the parent–child interactions. The notes contained written statements such as "good interaction" or "enthusiastic play." There was no information that might have provided a reviewer with the descriptive information that would have made it possible to understand the underlying basis for the praise that was expressed in the report. Evaluators should not lose sight of the fact that "[a]ll raw data and interview information are [to be] recorded with an eye towards their possible review by other psychologists or the court" (American Psychological Association, 1994, p. 679).

Do Not Make Complex That Which Is Simple

We have also been impressed by the tendency of some of our colleagues to make the simple complex. The following is from an advisory report filed by an evaluator: "The interparental dyad is replete with distrust, negative emotionality, suboptimal conflict containment skills, distance, some degree of mutual dislike, as well as at times with fault-finding and dismissiveness, interlaced with bidirectional underinforming about particulars pertinent to the child's activities." A more user-friendly statement would be: "The parents are poorly skilled at resolving conflict over their child and do not provide each other with information about their child."

Here is another example of overly complex phrasing: "The following recommendations resting on the foundation of amassed information from a variety of child and adult-derived sources have been explicitly conceptualized to operate as pragmatic, problem-targeted, and responsive solutions directly linked to identified needs that pertain to but also go above and beyond the child custody and parenting access issues." In a report we reviewed, a father who tended to lose his temper was described as follows: "His capacity to modulate his emotional experience appears tenuous such that he may not utilize cognitive strategies to adequately inhibit intense emotions from being enacted behaviorally at times." Finally, the following is the opening paragraph of the "Conclusions and Recommendations" section of a report prepared by a psychologist who identifies herself as a child-centered evaluator:

> This evaluation has been conducted employing a child-centered approach, which necessitates expert professional thinking that takes into account the psychological, legal, and emotional aspects, utilizing the best resources of the attorneys, the evaluator, family therapists, and the teachers involved with the family, in order to formulate a multipronged plan from the consortium of professional input. In this report I have put the differential developmental needs of the children into the forefront of my professional recommendations. The child-centered evaluator must protect children from the extended polarizing fray and cannot allow the evaluation process to turn the evaluator into yet another denigrating, opinionated adult who chooses to side with one of the parents and prolong the conflict. The recommendations offered will promote emotional symmetry and help the family with the postdivorce adjustments and transitions that often cause children to display disturbed behavior and incomplete adjustment.

Know Current Literature

It is not uncommon to encounter reports or testimony in which evaluators explain their procedures or opinions by referring to writings that are decades old, the deficiencies of which have been identified in more recent writings. We have a far better understanding of the dynamics of domestic violence today than we had two decades ago, yet we continue to encounter discussions in which evaluators explain violence by one partner on the basis of the alleged precipitating behaviors of the other partner.

Appreciate the Distinction between Clinical Assessment and Forensic Assessment

Martindale (2001a) writes,

> In a clinical setting, a psychodiagnostic assessment marks the beginning of an on-going relationship in the course of which there will be opportunities for subsequent reassessment. As new information disconfirms old hypotheses, appropriate adjustments can be made. In a forensic setting, the report in which one's assessment is described marks the end of a relationship. No opportunities to reassess are provided. Because of this critical difference between clinical assessment and forensic assessment, it cannot be presumed that instruments popular among clinicians are suitable in forensic work. (p. 498)

Recognize That Conducting Custody Evaluations Is an Inherently Forensic Endeavor

When we are acting with definable foreknowledge as mental health experts on issues being adjudicated by the court, we are rendering a forensic mental health service. The primary goal is to assist the court.

Recognize That the Court Shall Be Conceptualized as the Primary Recipient of the Report That the Evaluator Prepares

Notwithstanding the irrefutable reality that, more often than not, our reports are used by the litigants and their attorneys in pretrial settlement negotiations and the related reality that such settlements cause most of our reports never to be seen by the judges for whom they were prepared, it is incumbent upon us to prepare reports with the needs of the court in mind. In particular, this means that we cannot omit from our reports important information about parenting deficiencies that we may have identified in order to protect the deficient parent from the hurt that will be experienced when he or she reads the report. It is unrealistic to believe we can facilitate a family's postdispute adjustment by preparing reports in which we address parental strengths but omit parental shortcomings.

Create and Preserve Detailed Records

Evaluators must recognize that, with rare exceptions, their records are created with the needs of the legal system in mind. This means that records should be created in anticipation of their review by others and in reasonable detail, should be carefully maintained, and should be made available to others who are legally entitled to examine them.

Attend Continuing Education Seminars

The field of child custody evaluation is rapidly changing, and it is important for evaluators to participate in continuing education endeavors that will expose them to new empirical findings and facilitate the exchange of ideas with colleagues. We have found that continuing education programs in which several different workshops are presented over several days provide opportunities for meeting and establishing collegial relationships that may serve you well over the years. Discussions after workshops, over dinner, or while having drinks in the lounge afford opportunities to hash out ideas, inquire about new trends, share war stories, and learn from colleagues.

Another useful experience is membership in a local professional group focused on child custody matters. Several communities have such groups. Becoming a member of the child custody listserv is another way to keep current. If you are interested in signing up for it, contact Vicky Campaigna, PhD, at drvicky@rcn.com or Jonathan Gould at jwgould@aol.com.

Summary

In this chapter, we provided an evolving list of dos and don'ts for custody evaluators. Our primary concern is to focus attention on the obligation of mental health professionals engaged in child custody evaluations to present themselves and their work product in as transparent a manner as possible. Included in this transparency are acknowledgment of the strengths and limitations of one's opinions and conclusions, availability of one's full file for review by attorneys and the court, and knowing and abiding by rules of court, rules of evidence, and rules of professional conduct.

We also stressed the need to remain current regarding literature that addresses empirical research, conceptual models, evaluation methods and procedures, ethical developments, case law decisions, and statutory amendments. Attending continuing education programs, participating in peer review and peer supervision groups, and belonging and actively contributing to a child custody listserv are important elements in the evaluator's ongoing development.

A Final Word

Over the past few years, a number of psychologists have written and spoken a good deal about scientifically informed child custody evaluations (e.g., Ackerman & Kane, 2003; Emery, Otto, & O'Donohue, 2005), and about the application of the forensic model to child custody evaluations (Gould, 2006; Martindale & Gould, 2004), including the two of us (e.g., Gould, 1998, 1999, 2004; Gould & Bell, 2000; Gould & Stahl, 2000; Gould & Lehrmann, 2002; Gould, Kirkpatrick, Austin, & Martindale, 2004; Galatzer-Levy, Baerger, Gould, & Nye, 2002; Baerger, Galatzer-Levy, Gould, & Nye, 2002; Martindale, 2001a, 2005b; Martindale & Gould, 2004, 2005).

From our perspective, the forensic model is evolving. Contrary to what we would like to believe about our colleagues, survey data have shown that few practitioners undertake research or even read about it. Nathan (2000) writes that our collective professional behavior reflects little involvement in research and little involvement in reading to keep current with research and that these behaviors continue "to be a disappointment and an embarrassment to the discipline" (p. 250).

We urge forensic psychologists to maintain an active interest in current, relevant literature. More than 25 years ago, Barlow (1981) opined, with dismay, that it did not appear that clinical practice was being influenced by clinical research. Our concern is similar. It seems that far too many forensic mental health practitioners are unfamiliar with the research findings that should be guiding them.

The jump from a clinical model to a forensic model need not trigger another debate about the relative contribution of actuarial or scientifically informed methods versus clinical judgment. Yet, there are forensic practitioners who continue to argue that, despite empirical studies showing a lack of reliability and validity of specific assessment tools, in the right hands such tools provide information that may be presented in court (Trubitt, 2004).

Martindale (2006) has recently addressed this issue in his review of Trubitt's (2004) book, in which she suggests including play therapy modalities in comprehensive child custody evaluations. Despite research evidence to the contrary, Trubitt contends that children's play in an office setting is a reliable indicator of their psychological life or, as Martindale puts it in his article, that "office play does not lie" (p. 77).

This state of affairs should be particularly distressing to a discipline (psychology) and a specialty area (forensic psychology) whose goals over the last several decades have been to produce professionals who integrate the methods of science into forensic practice, to produce new knowledge, to respect the needs of the court and the rules of admissibility for scientific evidence, and to use already existing knowledge in a manner that scientifically informs assessment methods and psychological opinions presented to the court.

We believe that the greatest threat to the practice of child custody evaluation and to testimony on the subject is sweeping conclusions based only on years of experience and clinical judgment, intuition, or hunches. We need to move away from conclusions reflected by impressionistic testimony captured by phrases like "I know good parenting when I see it" or "My years of experience have taught me what good parenting is." Although clinical judgment is an important component of child custody assessment, it is reliable methods and relevant research that inform our conclusions and our opinions.

We do a disservice to families in conflict, to the court system, and to the professional image of child custody evaluators when we confuse perceived helpfulness with actual helpfulness (Martindale, 2006). In *Daubert*, the Supreme Court described Federal Rule of Evidence 702 as setting forth a helpfulness standard (at 2796). FRE 702, as amended April 17, 2000, declares that expert testimony must be "based upon sufficient facts or data," must be "the product of reliable principles and methods," and must be offered by a witness who has "applied the principles and methods reliably to the facts of the case." Experts who rely on clinical hunches (Calloway, 2002) or intuition (Trubitt, 2004) have formulated opinions that are not "the product of reliable principles and methods" and have the potential to mislead the court. Such insensitivity to the rules of evidence and wanton misdirection of the court serves no one well.

As is true elsewhere in our society, the services offered by child custody evaluators and the methods employed in providing those services are, to a large extent, consumer-driven. Tippins and Wittmann (2005, p. 193) have called for "clinical humility and judicial vigilance." At the risk of appearing immature by stating you go first, it seems to us that when judges and attorneys become more vigilant, clinical humility from child custody evaluators will quickly follow. If judges and attorneys (as the consumers of forensic mental health services) encourage evaluators to ignore the limits of an empirically established specialized knowledge base, only the atypically conscientious will resist the economic incentive to provide that which has been sought (Gould & Martindale, 2005).

We have previously written that there are three possible positions that evaluators, as a group, can take.

1. We can conclude that in order for evaluators to be of meaningful assistance to the court, *all* evidence we offer must be scientifically derived; that evaluators who offer evidence relating to custody matters are, therefore, doing a disservice to the judicial system, to parents and children, and to the mental health profession; and that we should stop offering this service.

2. We can encourage those who engage our services in custody-related matters to play "don't ask; don't tell"; that is, cross-examining attorneys will not inquire about the empirical bases for our opinions and we will not volunteer information concerning the known deficiencies in our current procedures. This tactic is in violation of our obligation to inform others of the known limitations of our procedures and undermines the legal process by keeping information from the court that, if it had been known at the time of the court's ruling, might have been useful in the court's decision making.

3. We can be diligent in acknowledging the known limitations of our procedures and dedicate ourselves to improving them (Gould & Martindale, 2005). Knowledge is derived through inquiry, and professional activity stimu-

lates inquiry. If mental health professionals stop performing custody evaluations, the interactions that catalyze empirical research will not occur and no progress will be seen. If we are to provide the assistance that the legal system seeks, we must persevere, but we must be mindful of our limitations and respond to the call for clinical humility by articulating those limitations and working diligently both in developing more scientifically informed methods and procedures to be used in child custody evaluations and in crafting our advisory reports to reflect more accurately the experiences and needs of children.

APPENDIX

Sample Statements of Understanding and Letters

Note. These documents are also available at the authors' website: *www.child-custody-consultants.com.*

Statement of Understanding to Be Signed by the Litigants Prior to the Commencement of the Evaluation

It is generally agreed that, even when evaluations have been court-ordered, litigants should be provided with information concerning the evaluator's policies, procedures, and fees prior to the commencement of the evaluation. We favor the descriptive term *Statement of Understanding*, as does the New York Matrimonial Commission.

The following is a tweaked version of the statement of understanding that we have used in custody evaluations. Be mindful of the fact that some of the references may not be applicable to the jurisdiction in which you practice. Statements we make concerning compelled expert testimony are an example.

Statement of Understanding of [Date]

General Information

I have been appointed by the court to conduct an impartial evaluation of comparative custodial fitness. My purpose in conducting this evaluation is to gather information that will enable me to formulate an opinion concerning what custody/visitation arrangement is most likely to be in the best interests of your child(ren). Though the manner in which my fees will be paid has been determined either by the court or through negotiations among the parties and their attorneys, and though my fees are not paid by the court, the work that I will be doing will be done for the court. Regardless of the source from whom an impartial evaluator receives remuneration, an impartial evaluator is expected to operate as though s/he were employed by the court. It is particularly important that this position be understood when fees are being paid only by one of the two parties. The fee-paying party cannot simply call a halt to the evaluation. The authority to instruct an evaluator to perform no further services rests with the court, not with the party who bears the financial responsibility for payment of the evaluator's fees (nor with that party's attorney).

I do not presume that those whom I am evaluating are lying; however, neither do I presume that they are being truthful. Forensic psychologists are expected to secure verification of assertions made by those whom they are evaluating. Your cooperation will be expected as verification of assertions made by you is sought.

Ordinarily, unless otherwise directed by the court, at the conclusion of the evaluation I will meet with both litigants and review a draft of my advisory report. You will be asked to make notations on your copy, initial each page, and return the draft after having reviewed it. Shortly after this meeting, the final report (incorporating your notations) will be prepared and sent to the court. Unless otherwise instructed by the court, copies will be

(cont.)

sent to the attorneys for both litigants and to the attorney representing the child(ren). If an individual is representing him/herself, I will follow direction from the court concerning whether or not to provide that individual with a copy of the report. Your signature on the last page of this document will authorize me to release information to the attorneys and to the court at any point in the evaluative process, to release to them my final advisory report, and to release my file to anyone who is authorized by law to review it. With the exception of information presented to you in order to afford you an opportunity to respond, information gathered by me is ordinarily not disclosed prior to the completion of the evaluation. Under certain circumstances, however, disclosure of information may be deemed advisable by me or may be requested by the attorneys or by the court. If disclosure is deemed appropriate, only *information* will be shared. Interim recommendations will *not* be offered.

Authority to release to others (such as treating practitioners) my advisory report and/ or any of the information utilized by me in preparing the report rests with the court. If a review of the report in my office is deemed inadvisable by me, I will notify the court that copies will be delivered to the court with a recommendation that they be distributed to the litigants and to their attorneys at a meeting to be held with the presiding judge.

Privilege, Confidentiality, and Privacy

Principles of confidentiality and privilege do not apply within the context of an assessment such as the one being conducted. Information provided by you, regardless of the form in which it has been provided (your statements, tape recordings, diaries, correspondence, photographs, etc.) may be shared with others involved in the evaluation (including, where necessary and appropriate, children and collateral sources). By presenting information to others, verification of information provided can be sought, and the other party can be afforded the opportunity to respond to allegations that may have been made. Statements made by children may have to be cited in an advisory report, and it is therefore important that you not mislead your child(ren). Do not tell a child that what is said is confidential. It is not. Information concerning your payments (amounts, source of payments, form of payments) is also not confidential.

Office staff must check my telephone messages, read my mail, and type my correspondence and reports. Those who work for me receive instruction in matters relating to confidentiality.

The need may arise for me to discuss the evaluation with other professionals and/ or provide a copy of the final advisory report and pertinent supporting documents to colleagues for their review and comments. In either case, all names and identifying information will be changed. In discussions with my partner, names are not changed.

Fees

Fees are as shown on the cost sheet that has been attached. Note that I reserve the right to increase fees (with appropriate notice to you). Also note that fees for an assessment of this type are not reimbursable by health insurance.

It must be emphasized that the $_____ figure shown on our cost sheet does *not* represent the total cost of the evaluation. It represents only those fees that it is possible to specify in advance. A comprehensive evaluation inevitably entails additional services, fees for which cannot be specified in advance. If you wish to examine an account statement on which typical fees are itemized, one will be furnished upon request.

My services as an evaluator commence with my acceptance of the assignment to conduct an evaluation. Though I do not actively seek information prior to our first evaluative session, information may come to me in the form of statements made in telephone interactions, etc. Even information not actively sought by me will be considered by me in the formulation of my opinions (in my view, ignoring unsought information is not a viable option). Additionally, in most cases, some time will have been expended by me prior to your receipt of this document (for example, phone time with the court and correspondence time). For these reasons, fees are charged retroactively; that is, from the time of my notification by the court of my appointment to conduct this evaluation.

If, in my judgment, it is advisable that I consult with other mental health professionals, attorneys, or other professionals, time expended by me in such consultations will be billed for. Any fees charged to me by those with whom I consult will *not* be passed along to the person(s) financially responsible for the cost of the evaluation.

The record-keeping requirements of forensic work make it necessary to log each telephone message and make a record of even the briefest telephone call. For this reason, there will be a minimum fee of $____ (5 minutes @ $____/hour) charged for any phone contact.

Once an evaluation has been concluded, fees paid may be reapportioned through negotiations among the parties and their attorneys or by court order; however, while the evaluation is in progress, fees cannot be apportioned based upon what was done for whom. All work relating to the assessment (obtaining and reviewing documents, contacting others for information, etc.) is done in order to obtain as much relevant information as possible and cannot be viewed as work done for one party or the other. Similarly, fees cannot be apportioned in a manner that involves assigning financial responsibility for fees associated with certain services to one party and responsibility for fees associated with other services to the other party.

There may be times when an individual being evaluated will be required to pay fees for time expended by me in obtaining and reviewing information that the individual would have preferred that I not obtain or review. Similarly, there may be times when the financially responsible party (parties) will be required to pay fees in connection with the evaluation of a third party whom the financially responsible party (parties) would have preferred that I not evaluate.

If it should become necessary for me to report allegations of abuse/neglect to Child Protective Services (CPS), the financially responsible party (parties) will be billed for any time expended in filing the report, being interviewed by CPS, etc. This may mean that a financially responsible party will have to pay for time expended in reporting him/her to CPS.

There may be times when the actions of one party will make it necessary for me to make phone calls and/or write letters. In calculating fees for my services, no distinction is made between time expended in administrative matters and time expended in providing psychological services. Fees for time expended in administrative matters are apportioned as are all other fees. In summary, fees are charged for time expended in any/all professional activities associated with the evaluative process or arising from the evaluative process. This includes time expended in addressing fee-related matters.

It is to your advantage to organize any material that you submit for my consideration. You are paying for my time and more time, is required to review material if it has been poorly organized. Any items submitted to me should be clearly identified with your name. This is particularly important in the case of photographs, audiotapes (including microcassettes), diary pages, and notes.

The performance of evaluation-related services by me does not cease with the issuance of my report. Fees for all postevaluation services (correspondence, phone time, attendance at conferences, etc.) are the responsibility of the party requesting the services, unless other arrangements have been made in advance or the court has ordered that responsibility for these fees be apportioned in some other manner.

If there is a trial or if an evaluator is called to be deposed, an expert cannot be compelled to offer opinions without remuneration. [*Note*: Though this is true in New York, it may not be applicable elsewhere.] If one wishes an expert to make a court appearance or appear at a deposition, one must pay the expert's fees for time expended, including reasonable fees for time expended in preparation. Though the judicial system [in New York] protects experts from being compelled to appear without remuneration when their opinions are being sought, the law does not protect experts from being subpoenaed as fact witnesses (for example, to describe, as an eye-witness to an accident might, events that transpired in their presence). I must, therefore, require that you agree that if my presence is requested for *any* reason, the fees specified on our cost sheet will be paid by the party requesting my presence, unless other arrangements have been made in advance or the court has ordered that responsibility for these fees be apportioned in some other manner. Additionally, the scheduling of my testimony will be done in consultation with me and with an appropriate recognition of possible conflicting personal or professional commitments. In the unlikely event that an appearance by me is requested by the court or by the law guardian, my fees will be paid by the party (parties) responsible for the other costs associated with my evaluation and in the same proportions.

Some courts have begun ordering that the evaluator's fees for trial-related expenses be paid by the nonfavored party. If that should occur, the nonfavored party will be required to pay the *same* fees that would otherwise have been paid by the favored party, including fees for time expended in preparation for trial. If this portion of the statement of understanding raises any questions concerning your possible financial obligations, please bring your questions to my attention and to the attention of your attorney.

Return of Fees

Though fees paid for services rendered are not returned even when an evaluation has not been completed, you are not expected to pay for services that have never been performed. Since fees for certain services (such as the report outlining the findings of the evaluation) are paid in advance, certain circumstances (such as a settlement) may make it unnecessary to perform services for which fees have already been paid. Under such circumstances, fees paid in advance will be refunded. It must be understood, however, that no refunds will be made until I have been formally notified, either by the court or by the attorneys for both parties, that it is the position of all involved that my task has been completed, that no further services will be requested, and that I am discharged. Upon receipt of such formal notice, a final account statement will be prepared and any funds owed by me to the financially responsible party (parties) will accompany the final account statement.

Limitations, Risks, and Services *Not* Provided

The profession of psychology has not developed specific methods and procedures for use in assessing comparative custodial fitness, and neither the profession of psychology nor the state of New York has established specific criteria. The criteria that I employ and the methods and procedures that I utilize have been chosen by me. The evaluative procedure is outlined briefly on our cost sheet. Any questions that you may have will be responded to during our initial evaluative session.

Unless instructed otherwise by the court, I will, as the evaluation progresses, share information (including preliminary impressions) with a law guardian if one has been appointed. Subsequent to the completion of my evaluation and prior to the preparation of my advisory report, I am willing to confer with the attorneys if such a conference is desired by all involved and not objected to by the court. Detailed information concerning my findings, however, will be communicated in writing only. Be aware that the dispute is not resolved with the issuance of my report. Though the information provided and opinions expressed are intended to assist the court, the court may reject all or portions of the information provided and/or may reject the opinions offered. Also recognize that, though it has not yet occurred, the possibility exists that, even after having completed a thorough examination of the issues, I may not be able to offer an opinion with a reasonable degree of professional certainty. Neither under this circumstance nor under circumstances in which completion of the evaluation becomes either impossible or unnecessary are fees for services already rendered refunded. (If an evaluation has not begun, fees for time expended in attempts to commence the evaluation, document review, etc., will be subtracted from any retainer fee paid and the balance will be refunded.)

It is not possible to guarantee that an evaluation will be concluded by a specific date. Ordinarily, judges who have requested that forensic evaluations be performed wish to have advisory reports prepared prior to the commencement of a trial. Though quite unlikely, it is possible that a judge will begin trial prior to receiving an advisory report.

Reasonable steps are taken to minimize the distress associated with the evaluation process. Nevertheless, although approximately 97% of the cases in which I have been involved have been resolved without judicial intervention, I must presume that there will be a trial and must conduct myself accordingly. This means that information that you provide will be questioned and, at times, you may feel as though you are being interrogated rather than interviewed. In order to perform my court-ordered function, I must be an examiner, not a therapist.

It must be understood that I cannot provide psychological advice to individuals whom I am evaluating. If counseling or psychotherapy services are desired, I will be pleased to provide the names of appropriate professionals. My pager is for use only in emergencies and only by my patients. Since I cannot provide emergency assistance to someone whom I am evaluating, my pager is *not* to be used either by those whom I am evaluating or by their attorneys. If an emergency situation arises, assistance should be sought through the police, the nearest hospital, or your attorney (depending, of course, on the nature of the emergency).

Unless I have been directed otherwise by the court, I will presume that all items in the case file are discoverable (that is, subject to examination) by both parties, their attorneys, the attorney for the child(ren), and any expert(s) who may have been retained by counsel for either party. In the event of a trial, unless I have been directed otherwise by the court, all items in the case file will be brought with me to court any day that I am scheduled to offer testimony.

If there is a trial and if you should request that I testify, it is important that you understand my obligations as an evaluator and as a testifying expert. I am obligated to maintain my impartiality and openness to new information throughout the course of the evaluation and during the trial. It is *not* my obligation to defend the precision of facts reported, the accuracy of data interpretations made, or the validity of opinions offered in the face of newly introduced information that might reasonably call them into question. Though it is more likely than not that testimony offered by me will explain and be supportive of the contents of my report, no assurances can be offered that this will be the case. A cross-examining attorney may bring to my attention information of which I was unaware (either because it was not brought to my attention during the course of my evaluation or because it pertains to events occurring subsequent to the issuance of my report). The attorney may ask how the new information might affect my professional opinion of you and/or your spouse. I will, of course, respond honestly. You must recognize that I am not an advocate for the person who seeks my testimony and that I am obligated to offer any/all pertinent information that might be of assistance to the trier of fact. I must, for example, provide information concerning your parenting deficiencies and your spouse's parenting strengths. Put most simply, fees paid to me represent compensation for time expended. The person paying my fees cannot be assured that my testimony will be helpful to his/her case.

Opinions expressed by me in my advisory report will be formulated on the basis of information provided to me between the day on which I was initially contacted and the day on which the report is prepared.

If any questions arise concerning legal matters, you must consult with your attorney. It is inappropriate for someone not trained in the law to attempt to respond to questions concerning legal matters.

Psychological Testing

It is expected that when individuals being evaluated come to our office for the purpose of taking psychological tests, they will arrive unaccompanied. Spouses, children, companions, and friends can serve as sources of distraction. If someone must transport the test taker, that person will be asked to leave and not return until the test taker has finished.

Submission and Retention of Documents

Ordinarily, in consultation with your attorney, it will be possible for you to anticipate what documents I am likely to require. Obtaining pertinent documents prior to the commencement of the evaluation will expedite the evaluative process. Documents that you wish me to consider must be delivered in a manner that ensures their safe transfer into my custody and I must receive written assurance that documents submitted for my review have been provided to the other party. Under no circumstances are litigants or others to make unannounced visits to our office in order to deliver documents. Because I may be called upon to produce all items (documents, tapes, photographs, etc.) that I have considered in formulating my professional opinion, it is my policy to retain any items that are presented to me for my consideration. You are therefore strongly encouraged to make copies of any materials that you intend to turn over to me. If you neglect to make copies and if you later require copies, you will be charged for time expended in preparing copies. Documents and other items will be returned only after I have been informed either by the court or by attorneys for both parties that it is no longer necessary for me to retain them. If, prior to trial, a lawful request is made that I copy and release items in my file for examination by an attorney or by an appropriate reviewing mental health professional, all involved will be notified. Unless an objection to the release of the requested items is brought before the court and honored by the court, the requested items will be released. (You are reminded that your signature on this document will constitute an authorization to release requested items to those lawfully entitled to receive them. Under most circumstances, those lawfully entitled to receive them include the court, the attorneys for both parties, and any consultants retained by the attorneys.) The attorney requesting copies will pay the costs associated with producing the copies. (Currently, the standard fee for photocopying is ____¢/page. I reserve the right to charge a higher fee for pages both sides of which must be copied and/or for items on non-standard-size pages, that is, other than 8.5" x 11".)

Out-of-Session Contact

Out-of-session contact (casual waiting-room conversation, telephone calls, etc.) should be avoided. It is to your disadvantage to communicate information to an evaluator in an informal manner. Phone contact should be limited to scheduling appointments and addressing other procedural matters. Information concerning matters pertinent to the evaluation itself should not be communicated by phone. Our phone is answered by machine at *all* times. If you must contact me by phone, leave a message clearly stating the reason for your call, provide a telephone number at which you can be reached, and specify the times at which you can be reached.

Obtaining Additional Information

Individuals being evaluated must agree to authorize me to obtain any documents that I may wish to examine and to authorize communication between me and any individuals who, in my judgment, may have information bearing upon the subject of the assessment. In most cases, information needed from professionals (teachers, other mental health practitioners, etc.) will be obtained by telephone. Individuals who are likely to be advocates for one party or the other will be expected to provide information in writing (though I reserve the right to contact such individuals by phone if clarification and/or additional information is required).

Where specific instructions concerning those to be evaluated (and how extensively they are to be evaluated), information to be obtained, etc. has not been included in the order appointing me, the decisions concerning these matters will be made by me. There may be instances in which I will be asked to review information that I reasonably believe is likely to be more prejudicial than probative and instances in which I will be asked to contact individuals whom it would, in my judgment, be inappropriate to contact. I must be the final arbiter in such situations.

I reserve the right to consider any information regardless of the manner in which it has been obtained (unless it has been obtained illegally). If I am asked to consider information that may have been illegally obtained, I will follow instructions from the attorneys if they are in agreement. If they cannot agree, I will request direction from the court.

If you wish to have individuals write to me on your behalf, you will be provided with stick-on labels that read: "I understand that the information I have provided is *not* confidential." The statement must be signed, the label must be affixed to the flap of the envelope, and the letter must be mailed directly to me. (Letters are not to be forwarded to me by you or by your attorney.) Letters received by me will be reproduced by me and furnished to the attorneys for the parties and the attorney for the child(ren). It is your responsibility to explain to anyone from whom you solicit a letter that the information contained in the letter may be revealed to *any* of the individuals involved in the evaluation (including children, if necessary and appropriate) and may be quoted in the advisory report. Unless advance approval is obtained, any information transmitted via fax by anyone other than the attorneys or the court will be discarded unread.

Contact with Attorneys

Once I have received word that I will be conducting an impartial evaluation of comparative custodial fitness, I endeavor to avoid *ex parte* communication with the attorneys representing the litigants. If a law guardian has been appointed, I will speak periodically to him/her and will exchange information with him/her (unless instructed not to do so by the court). In my judgment, our roles are similar and it is, therefore, appropriate that we share information. During the evaluation, oral communication with attorneys for the parties will occur only if it is not in contravention of a court directive, only if it can be done by means of a conference or conference call, and only if unusual circumstances make such communication necessary. If correspondence becomes necessary, it must be on a copies-to-all basis. Once the evaluation has been completed and my report has been released, I *will* engage in oral discussions with the attorneys if I deem it advisable to do so, if no objections to such discussions are raised, and if such discussions are not in contravention of the court's order or subsequent directives.

Allegations of Abuse/Neglect

It must be understood that *I am required by law to report allegations of abuse or neglect* (even if they have been previously reported). The penalties imposed on mandated reporters who fail to report such allegations are severe. If allegations are made, they will be reported, and my action in reporting them must not be interpreted as a display of support for the individual who has made the allegations or as an indication that I disapprove of the alleged actions of the person who has been accused. Most important, it must not be inferred that my reporting of such allegations suggests that I find them credible.

Postevaluation Developments

Following the meeting at which a draft of my report is reviewed, I will take reasonable steps to avoid contact with the litigants and with counsel. No substantive response will be provided to letters, faxes, e-mails, or phone messages. If a trial has been scheduled and either party feels that new information should be considered by me, this will be done only if a formal request is made by both attorneys or ordered by the court and only if each party is afforded an opportunity to present his/her perspective on the additional information. Ordinarily, if the need for an updated evaluation is agreed upon or ordered by the court, psychological tests will not be readministered. The time-related limitations to the applicability of the test data will be addressed in my testimony.

I do not participate in postevaluation settlement discussions unless (1) the law permits litigants to waive privilege; (2) both litigants, with written approval by counsel, have done so; and (3) this postevaluation role has been agreed to, in writing, at the outset of the evaluation.

A litigant who believes an evaluator's findings and/or recommendations to be flawed is entitled to request that the evaluator's work be reviewed by another mental health professional. Though the favored party may not wish the evaluator's work to be critically examined, such scrutiny is entirely appropriate, and the evaluator's entire file should be made available to the consultants retained by the attorneys for the purpose of conducting such a review. It is my policy to cooperate with those seeking to review my work. An exception: Mental health professionals who are related to or involved in social or professional relationships with litigants should not offer their services either as evaluators or as reviewers. Efforts by such individuals to obtain my file will be resisted, and the file will be released only in response to a court order.

I ask that you thoroughly review this document with your attorney. The evaluation will not proceed until both of the parties have expressed their understanding of and willingness to abide by the policies and procedures set forth in this document. Please initial pages __, __, __, __, and __ and sign this page in the space provided below. [As sent to the parties, this is a seven-page document.]

Your signature below indicates (1) that you have received, read, and understood my policies and procedures; (2) that you recognize that neither the principle of confidentiality nor the principle of privilege applies to any information in my file concerning this matter; and, (3) that you are authorizing the release by me, either orally or in written form, of any/all information in my file, including my advisory report, to the court, the law guardian, the attorneys for both parties, and qualified mental health professionals retained to review my work.

With specific regard to information that might ordinarily be protected from disclosure by HIPAA provisions, in signing this document, you acknowledge that pursuant to HIPAA Section 164.512(e)(1)(i) of the Code of Federal Regulations, disclosures of otherwise protected health information may be provided in the course of judicial or administrative proceedings. Your authorization for the release of my file is not qualified; it includes an authorization to release information provided to me by health service providers who may have been collateral sources of information. You also acknowledge that once records have been released by me to the court, to the attorneys, or to consultants retained by the attorneys, I no longer exercise control over who may access the information contained in those records.

It is not to be inferred that you agree with these policies and procedures. Further, by signing this document, you are not waiving any rights you may have to raise objections to any policies or procedures. Though this copy must be signed and returned, you are urged to make a photocopy and retain it for your reference during the course of the evaluation. [Fee information appears on page __.]

Signature

Revisions in the Statement of Understanding
[Inserted When the Court's Order Alters My Methodology]

The following information appears in our statement of understanding: "Ordinarily, unless otherwise directed by the court, at the conclusion of the evaluation I will meet with both parents and review a draft of my advisory report. You will be asked to make notations on your copy and return it. Shortly after this meeting, the final report (incorporating your notations) will be prepared and copies will be sent to the court, attorneys for both parents, and the law guardian (if one has been appointed)."

The court has directed that I *not* review my report with you and, additionally, has directed that copies not be provided to the attorneys. Your signatures below will document your acknowledgment of this procedural change.

DO NOT SIGN THIS DOCUMENT UNLESS YOU HAVE READ IT AND UNDERSTAND IT.

_____

Signature

Statement of Understanding to Be Signed by Non-Party Participants Prior to Their Participation in the Evaluation

Many evaluators overlook their ethical obligation to inform non-party participants in evaluations that principles of confidentiality and privilege do not apply and of the foreseeable uses of the information gathered by the evaluator. We believe that a document similar to that presented to the litigants should be presented to non-party participants.

Statement of Understanding for Non-Party Participant in a Custodial Suitability Evaluation

It is my customary policy to review with those whom I have evaluated all test data (and the meaning that I have attached to those data), all impressions formed by me on the basis of my own observations, all information gathered by me from collateral sources, and all opinions formulated by me on the basis of these sources of information.

The circumstances of your involvement in this matter are unusual. You are not one of the litigants, yet you have been asked to participate in this evaluation because of your relationship with one of the litigants. It is important that you understand that neither statements made by you nor the results of the tests you will be taking will be kept confidential. Your statements, your test data, my observations concerning you, and any professional opinions I may formulate concerning you will be included in my advisory report. Under ordinary circumstances, that report will be viewed by both litigants, their attorneys, the law guardian (if one has been appointed), and the court. It will not, however, be made available to you, even though you may be discussed in a portion of it. You should also be aware that, if this matter proceeds to trial, my testimony may include information and opinions concerning you. Though I will ordinarily meet with the litigants at the conclusion of the evaluation and will discuss *their* test data with *them*, I will not be meeting with you. If you wish to have the test data explained to you by a qualified mental health professional, I will, with your signed authorization, forward the test data to a mental health professional who is qualified to interpret the data for you, explain their implications, and answer any questions you might have.

You are encouraged to consult with an attorney if you have any questions or concerns with regard to this document. If you wish to consult with an attorney but fees are of concern, please inform me. Arrangements will be made for a free consultation with an attorney familiar with these matters. Your signature below signifies your understanding of the conditions described above and your acceptance of these conditions.

_____

Signature

_____

(*cont.*)

[Commentary: Section 4.04 (a) of the 2002 ethics code declares, "Psychologists include in written and oral reports and consultations, only information germane to the purpose for which the communication is made." Even when an evaluator is describing the behaviors or characteristics of a parent, the evaluator does not have carte blanche to include any information. The gray areas must be recognized. Does one's behavior on the job reflect upon one's parenting capacity? Answer: It depends upon what the behavior is. Questions concerning what to include in one's report become particularly thorny when the subject of discussion is a significant other. Great care must be exercised because there is always the risk that the individual who is romantically involved with the competing mother or father may assert that information provided by you created embarrassment (i.e., emotional distress) and that it was not germane (i.e., not needed by the trier of fact).]

Statement of Understanding
to Be Signed by a Parent Not Attending the Review Session

If evaluators review their data and reports with litigants prior to releasing their reports, there will be times when one of the litigants will decline to attend the review session. In such situations, we believe it to be advisable to obtain the litigant's signature on a statement expressing recognition of the rights being waived by nonattendance.

Statement of Understanding for Parent Refusing to Attend Final Session

I do not wish to attend a meeting with Dr. _____ and [the other parent] at which a draft of Dr. _____'s advisory report in the matter of [Parent v. Parent] will be reviewed.

    I recognize that by not attending I am forfeiting the following rights: (1) My right to offer comments and/or register objections prior to the release of the report; (2) my right to have Dr. _____ explain to me the results of psychological tests taken by me and to explain any interpretations made by him on the basis of those results; (3) my right to have Dr. _____ explain to me the bases for conclusions drawn and recommendations offered in his advisory report to the court; and (4) my right to obtain the information contained in Dr. _____'s report at the same time that it is obtained by [the other parent].

    Dr. _____ has urged me to consult with my attorney concerning my decision and has clearly stated his belief that it is his ethical obligation to guarantee the above-mentioned rights. I, nevertheless, relieve him of this obligation.

_____

Signature

[Commentary: If this form is not signed and returned, consider alternative means by which it can be documented that the information was provided. Such alternatives include (but are not limited to) resending the form using a service that obtains the signature of the recipient, using the services of a process server, or faxing the information to the litigant's attorney using a fax machine that provides a report verifying receipt of the fax.]

Statement of Understanding to Be Signed by Litigants Reviewing the Report

Before litigants are presented with a report for their review, we believe it to be advisable to have each litigant sign a document in which the purpose of the review session is described and in which the litigants agree not to discuss the contents of the report with their children.

Statement of Understanding Concerning Reviewing Draft of Advisory Report

I understand that the document I am about to receive is a draft of Dr. _____'s advisory report and that his purpose in providing me with this draft is to afford me the opportunity to correct any factual errors, offer comments, register objections, and ask questions concerning any portions of the report that I do not understand.

I understand that the draft is not mine to take with me when I leave. The report contains information the disclosure of which should occur only in an appropriate forum. The report, therefore, is not to be removed from Dr. _____'s office. I agree to return my copy (with whatever notations I may have made) to Dr. _____ when asked to do so.

I recognize that discussing the contents of this report with our children would be to their emotional detriment, and I therefore agree not to do so. Additionally, I agree not to question our children concerning any statements they may have made to Dr. _____ that may be alluded to in the advisory report.

Directions: Please initial each page as you review the report. Brief comments and/or corrections can be made directly on the report. Longer comments and/or corrections can be made on a comment/correction form such as the one attached. You will be provided with as many of these forms as you need.

_____
Signature

Statement of Understanding and Fee Agreement to Be Signed by the Litigant Requesting Testimony

When a litigant bears responsibility for payment of fees for testimonial services, we believe it to be advisable to ensure that the litigant understands the manner in which fees will be calculated and understands that payment for testimonial services does not ensure that testimony will be helpful to that litigant's position before the court.

Statement of Understanding and Fee Agreement to Be Signed by Parent Requesting the Expert's Testimony

Dr. _____, the court-appointed evaluator in this matter, has filed an advisory report with the court. My attorney and I believe that the information provided and opinions expressed in that report are likely to advance my position in the matter(s) being adjudicated. For that reason, I have asked Dr. _____ to offer testimony.

I understand that Dr. _____ is obligated to maintain his impartiality and openness to new information throughout the course of his testimony. It is *not* his obligation to defend the precision of facts reported, the accuracy of data interpretations made, or the validity of opinions offered in the face of newly introduced information that might reasonably call them into question. Though it is more likely than not that testimony offered by him will explain and be supportive of the contents of his report, no assurances can be offered that this will be the case.

A cross-examining attorney may bring to Dr. _____'s attention information of which he was unaware (either because it was not brought to his attention during the course of the evaluation or because it pertains to events occurring subsequent to the issuance of his report). The attorney may ask how the new information might affect his professional opinion of me and/or my spouse. I understand Dr. _____'s obligation to respond honestly and recognize that he is not an advocate for me and must offer any/all pertinent information that might be of assistance to the trier of fact. In particular, I understand that Dr. _____ must, for example, provide information concerning my parenting deficiencies and my spouse's parenting strengths. Fees paid to Dr. _____ represent compensation for time expended. No assurance is offered that Dr. _____'s testimony will be helpful to my case.

From the time Dr. _____ is initially contacted and told to anticipate that testimony will be requested, time expended in corresponding with attorneys and/or the court, consulting with attorneys, preparing for trial, traveling to and from meetings with

(cont.)

attorneys and/or to and from court, and waiting are all billed at the rate of \$_____/hour. (It is likely, therefore, that time will have already been expended prior to my receipt of this document. I agree to be charged retroactively for time already expended.)

It is understood that Dr. _____ offers no assurances concerning his availability to testify on specific dates unless his availability on those dates has been ascertained in advance and an agreed-upon retainer has been paid.

If testimony from Dr. _____ has been anticipated and if time has been expended in preparation for trial, all such time will be charged for, whether or not testimony is given. (If, for example, an agreement is reached prior to Dr. _____'s scheduled testimony, obviating the need for his testimony, time expended will still be charged for.) Though testimony time is billed at the rate of \$_____/hour, if Dr. _____ comes to court (whether or not testimony is offered) a minimum fee of \$_____ will be charged.

I understand that if Dr. _____ has reserved time in which to testify, and is notified less than 48 hours in advance that he will not be called to testify, I will still be charged a fee for the time reserved. The fee for time reserved will be one-half of the fees that would have been generated if office hours had not been canceled.

I find these fees to be reasonable, payment in the amount of \$_____ accompanies this document, and I agree to pay any additional fees in payments not lower than \$____ per month until any balance has been paid in full. I also agree that a service/interest charge shall accrue on any unpaid balance at the rate of 1.2% per month. If payment is not made in the manner specified, Dr. _____ is authorized to utilize the services of a collection agency or an attorney and all reasonable costs associated with their collection efforts shall be added to my bill. Within 1 week of the conclusion of the trial my account will be calculated by Dr. _____ and sent to me. If money is owed to me, Dr. _____'s check will accompany the account statement.

_____
Signature

Introductory Letter to the Attorneys

In this introductory letter, the evaluator briefly outlines policies and procedures and the ways in which each attorney can assist in furnishing the evaluator with needed information.

Introductory Letter to Attorneys (Sent after Having Received Court Order)

I have, today, learned of my appointment by the Honorable [Name of Judge] to conduct an impartial evaluation of comparative custodial fitness in connection with the above-referenced matter. Though it is my wish to commence the evaluation without delay, it is important that the parties be familiar with our procedures before we begin.

Enclosed herewith is a copy of our statement of understanding—a document that those whom we evaluate must review and sign. Please review the statement with your client. We ask that your client sign the statement after having reviewed it with you and that you countersign, indicating that you have no objections to the policies, procedures, and fees outlined. Once a signed copy of the statement of understanding has been returned by each party and the required retainer has been advanced, the initial evaluative session (attended by both parties) will be scheduled.

If there is anything in the statement about which you wish clarification, please call our office. Your call will be returned by Dr. _____, and she will provide whatever information you desire. (Your call will not be returned by me as it is my desire—and the court's—that there be no *ex parte* communication with attorneys representing individuals whom I have been assigned to evaluate.) A copy of our cost sheet constitutes page 7 of our statement of understanding.

Though I wish to avoid speaking with the attorneys representing the parents, it is my policy to exchange information with the law guardian unless I have been directed by the court not to do so. I have found sharing information with law guardians to be quite helpful.

It is my wish to be thorough, and I have found that the pleadings frequently provide information pertinent to the issues about which the court is seeking my advisory input. In order that the burden of reproducing the documents be shared in some reasonably equitable manner, I suggest that each of you reproduce and forward to me those documents filed by you on behalf of your client. If, in addition to the pleadings, you have any documents containing material information that you feel I ought to consider, you are herewith invited to provide copies of such documents. Please be certain that copies of materials submitted for my consideration are forwarded to your adversary and to the attorney for the child(ren). If, as the evaluation progresses, new information

(cont.)

comes to your attention that you wish to share with me, please forward any new information to me in writing and confirm that copies have also been sent both to your adversary and to the attorney representing the child(ren). Prior to concluding the evaluation, I will notify all three attorneys of my intention to begin preparation of my report.

Collateral source information is of particular importance in an evaluation such as this. For that reason, each party will be asked to provide a list of individuals from whom useful information might be obtained. You are encouraged to assist your clients in the preparation of this document. (Generally, professionals—other mental health professionals, for example—will be contacted by telephone, whereas neighbors, family members, colleagues, and others who are likely to be allied with one party or the other will be asked to provide their information in written form and must clearly state that they understand that the information being provided is not confidential.)

Introductory Letter to the Litigants

In this introductory letter to the litigants, brief procedural information is provided and the litigants are encouraged to review the enclosed statement of understanding with their respective attorneys.

Introductory Letter to Parents (Sent after Having Received Court Order)

I have been informed of my appointment by the Honorable [Name of Judge] to conduct an impartial evaluation of comparative custodial fitness, and it is my wish that you be familiar with our procedures before we begin.

A copy of our statement of understanding—a document that those whom we evaluate must review, sign, and return—has been sent to your attorney. Please arrange to meet with him/her so that you can review the document together. As soon as you and [the other parent] have returned the signed statement and the required retainer has been paid, I will contact you to schedule the initial evaluative session, which will be attended by both of you. (Your children will not attend the initial session.) In order to facilitate the scheduling of the initial session, I have also enclosed a meeting time preference sheet for you to complete.

In order to move things along more quickly, I have also enclosed two questionnaires and a short information sheet to be completed. It is *not* necessary for you to complete these at this time; however, they should be completed prior to our initial meeting and should be brought with you to that meeting.

Letter Sent to Attorneys When Allegations of Abuse Have Been Registered

Evaluators who commence the evaluative process with a joint session are faced with a dilemma when one party expresses an unwillingness to attend a joint session, citing alleged abuse by the other party as the basis for this position. This letter outlines the evaluator's reluctance to alter his/her procedures based upon unsubstantiated allegations, thereby indirectly suggesting that those allegations are viewed as credible.

Letter to Attorney Representing Parent Alleging Abuse by Other Parent (Re: Handling of Initial Conjoint Session)

Mrs. Smith has contacted our office and has expressed to [my partner] her reluctance to attend a joint session with Mr. Smith. She asserts that she has been the victim of abuse by Mr. Smith and, for this reason, feels that she should not be compelled to be in his company. She has acknowledged that there has been no judicial finding with regard to her allegations.

You are, I believe, familiar with the manner in which I conduct an impartial evaluation of comparative custodial fitness and, specifically, with the fact that the process is begun by conducting a session attended by both parents. I believe that the integrity of the evaluative process is compromised when it is begun in any other manner. I request that you discuss this with your client and determine the extent of her discomfort with a joint session. Certainly, arrangements can be made for her and Mr. Smith to arrive and depart at different times and she can, if she wishes, have someone accompany her.

It is in the children's best interests that the advisory report to be utilized by the court be the product of an evaluative process that has been as free as possible from methodological flaws. When one procedure makes the parents more comfortable but is methodologically unsound and a different procedure causes some emotional discomfort for the parents but preserves the integrity of the evaluative process, it has always been my policy to urge parents to subordinate their needs to those of their children.

If Mrs. Smith feels strongly about the matter, I will ask that you, your adversary, and [the guardian *ad litem*] resolve the issue of which parent is to be interviewed first and I will ask, further, that I be provided with a directive from the court.

Where there has been a *finding of fact* that one parent has been the victim of abuse by the other, I am (albeit, with some reluctance) receptive to modifying my procedure. Where I have been presented with allegations (not yet substantiated), it is appropriate that I seek direction from the court. I cannot commence an impartial evaluation of comparative custodial fitness accepting as established fact that Mr. Smith has been abusive to Mrs. Smith (and that her abuse by him forms the basis for her reluctance to attend a joint session with him). *If* I were to do so and *if* I were subsequently to prepare an advisory report in which I favored your client, [Mr. Smith's attorney] could cogently argue that I commenced the evaluation having prejudged his client.

Letter Sent to Attorneys When One of the Litigants Is Inarticulate

When more time must be spent with one litigant than with the other, it is advisable to explain the reasons for this imbalance and to do so in advance.

Letter to Attorneys When Dealing with One Articulate and One Inarticulate Litigant

All three of you are, I believe, aware that Mrs. Smith has earned a master's degree in English and that Mr. Smith did not complete high school. Additionally, while Mr. Smith was attending high school, it was concluded (on the basis of an evaluation performed by school personnel) that his academic efforts were being hampered by an expressive language disorder. Mrs. Smith has presented her position and has responded to my questions in a clear, concise manner. Mr. Smith has displayed a tendency to be discursive.

Suggestions: (1) More sessions for Mr. Smith; (2) The attorneys be permitted to submit position statements for their clients.

Letter Sent to Collateral Sources

In this letter sent to collateral sources prior to contacting them, potential sources are informed of the evaluator's role, purpose, and procedure and are informed that information obtained from collateral sources must be disclosed.

Letter to Collateral Source (Sent Prior to Requesting Information)

I have been court-appointed to perform an impartial evaluation of comparative custodial fitness in connection with the above-referenced matter. My task is to evaluate Mr. and Mrs. Doe and prepare an advisory report for the court. I have reason to believe that you may have information that would be useful to me.

Enclosed are a release-of-information authorization form and a photocopy of the court order appointing me to conduct an evaluation. You will note that both Mr. and Mrs. Doe have authorized us to communicate with one another either orally or in writing.

Though some time may pass before you are contacted by me (because I prefer to gather information from other sources only after I have formed my own preliminary impressions), I want you to be aware that if you agree to speak with me, I will record our conversation and it is likely that information provided by you will appear in my report (which both Mr. and Mrs. Doe will read). You must also be aware that if information provided by you is utilized, you will be identified as the source of that information. [Refer to specialty guidelines for forensic psychologists (Committee on Ethical Guidelines for Forensic Psychologists, 1991), Section VII-E.]

Advising the court in situations such as this is an extremely difficult task, and I am to some degree dependent upon the willingness of people such as you to share information with me. I recognize that sharing information, knowing that it cannot be kept confidential, is difficult. I ask, nevertheless, that you recognize that the best interests of the Doe children are served by a thorough evaluation.

You are encouraged to consult with an attorney if you have any questions or concerns with regard to the information provided in this letter. If you wish to consult with an attorney but fees are of concern, please inform me. Arrangements will be made for a free consultation with an attorney familiar with these matters.

Pretrial Letter to the Attorney for the Nonfavored Party

In this letter sent to the attorney representing a litigant wishing to challenge an evaluator's report, the evaluator assures the attorney of the evaluator's intention to cooperate in the attorney's endeavors to obtain copies of the evaluator's file items.

Pretrial Letter to Attorney for the Nonfavored Party

I have been contacted by [attorney for favored party] and have been asked to anticipate that I will be providing expert testimony in the above-referenced matter, scheduled for trial before the Honorable [judge's name] on [trial date]. In order to obviate the need for your serving me with a *Subpoena Duces Tecum*, I offer the assurance that follows.

I recognize the right of opposing counsel to conduct a thorough cross-examination concerning the bases for opinions expressed by me and recognize the concomitant right of access to all relevant materials, Section VII-E of the specialty guidelines for forensic psychologists states: "Forensic psychologists . . . actively disclose which information from which source was used in formulating a particular written product or oral testimony" (Committee on Ethical Guidelines for Forensic Psychologists, 1991), More importantly, New York's *Civil Practice Law and Rules* require that I "specify the data and other criteria supporting [my] opinion" (CPLR # 4515, p. 71). In my view, when I offer an opinion concerning comparative custodial suitability, I am obligated to articulate what data were utilized, how those data bear upon the criteria that I have employed, and how the criteria bear upon the established best interests standard. For these reasons, it is my practice to bring with me the entire contents of my file.

If, in order to facilitate your preparation for trial, you wish to be provided with a copy of the contents of my file, this can be accomplished in one of two ways. (1) I will copy the file and forward it to you accompanied by an affidavit attesting to its completeness and accuracy. The cost of copying will be established in advance; an itemized bill will be sent; and, upon receipt of payment, the file will be promptly copied and delivered to you by Airborne Express. (2) You or your representative can copy the file at my office under my supervision. If this option is chosen, you will be charged 10 cents per page for the use of my equipment and paper and will be charged _____ per hour for the time expended by me in supervising the process. Original documents will remain in my custody and will be brought with me to court on the day(s) of trial.

You are assured that, in keeping with my role as an impartial examiner, I will endeavor to be cooperative with counsel for *both* parties.

References

Abidin, R. R. (1995). *Parenting Stress Inventory* (3rd ed.). Odessa, FL: Psychological Assessment Resources.

Abidin, R. R., & Konold, T. R. (1999). *Parenting alliance measure*. Odessa, FL: Psychological Assessment Resources.

Achenbach, T. M. (2001). *Child Behavior Checklist*. Burlington, VT: University of Vermont.

Ackerman, M. J. (1995). *Clinician's guide to child custody evaluations*. New York: Wiley.

Ackerman, M. J. (2001). *Clinician's guide to child custody evaluations* (2nd ed.). New York: Wiley.

Ackerman, M. J., & Ackerman, M. (1997). Custody evaluation practices: A survey of experienced professionals (revisited). *Professional Psychology: Research and Practice, 28*, 137–145.

Ackerman, M. J., & Kane, A. W. (1998). *Psychological experts in divorce actions* (3rd ed.). New York: Aspen Law & Business.

Ackerman, M. J., & Kane, A. W. (2004). *Psychological experts in divorce actions* (3rd Ed.): *2003 cumulative supplement*. New York: Aspen Law & Business.

Ackerman, M. J., & Schoendorf, K. (1992). *The Ackerman–Schoendorf Parent Evaluation of Custody Test (ASPECT)*. Los Angeles, CA: Western Psychological Services.

Adams, J. K. (1997). Interviewing methods and hearsay testimony in suspected child sexual abuse cases: Questions of accuracy. Retrieved from *www.ipt-forensics.com/journal/volume9/j9_1_4.htm*.

Adorno, T. W., Frenkel-Brunswik, E., Levinson, E., & Sanford, R. N. (1950). *The authoritarian personality*. New York: Harper.

Ahrons, C. R., & Wallisch, L. (1987). The relationship between former spouses. In D. Perlman & S. Duck (Eds.), *Intimate relationships: Development, dynamics, and deterioration* (pp. 269–296). Newbury Park, CA: Sage.

Ahrons, C. R., & Miller, R. B. (1993). The effect of post divorce relationship on paternal involvement: A longitudinal analysis. *American Journal of Orthopsychiatry, 63*(4), 498–512.

Ainsworth, M. D. S. (1979). Infant–mother attachment. *American Psychologist, 34*, 932–937.

Ainsworth, M. D. S., & Bell, S. M. (1974). Mother–infant interaction and the development of competence. In K. Connolly & J. Bruner (Eds.), *The growth of competence* (pp. 97–118). New York: Academic Press.

Ainsworth, M. D. S., Blehar, M. C., Waters, E., & Wall, S. (Eds.). (1978). *Patterns of attachment: A psychological study of the Strange Situation*. Hillsdale, NJ: Erlbaum.

Akehurst, L., Milne, R., & Koehnken, G. (2003). The effects of children's age and delay on recall in a cognitive or structured interview. *Psychology, Crime and Law, 9*, 97–107.

Aldridge, J., & Cameron, S. (1999). Interviewing child witnesses: Questioning techniques and the role of training. *Applied Developmental Science 3*, 136–147.

Aldridge, N. C. (1998). Strengths and limitations of forensic child sexual abuse interviews with anatomical dolls: An empirical review. *Journal of Psychopathology and Behavioral Assessment, 20*, 1–41.

Allison, J. A. (1998). Review of the Parenting Stress Index. In J. C. Impara & B. S. Plake (Eds.). *The thirteenth mental measurements yearbook*. Lincoln, NE: Buros Institute of Mental Measurements.

Aloise-Young, P. A., Hennigan, K. M., & Graham, J. W. (1996). Role of the self-image and smoker stereotype in smoking onset during early adolescence: A longitudinal study. *Health Psychology, 15*, 494–497.

Amato, P. R. (2000). The consequences of divorce for adults and children. *Journal of Marriage and the Family, 62*, 1269–1287.

Amato, P. R., & Booth, A. (1996). A prospective study of divorce and parent-child relationships. *Journal of Marriage and the Family, 58*, 356–365.

Amato, P. R., & Booth, A. (2001). The legacy of parents' marital discord: Consequences for children's marital quality. *Journal of Personality and Social Psychology, 81*(4), 627–638.

Amaya-Jackson, L., & Everson, M. D. (1996). Book reviews: Protocols for the sex-abuse evaluation. *Journal of the American Academy of Child and Adolescent Psychiatry, 35*(7), 966–967.

American Academy of Child and Adolescent Psychiatry. (1997a). Practice parameters for the forensic evaluation of children and adolescents who may have been physically or sexually abused. *Journal of the American Academy of Child & Adolescent Psychiatry, 36*, 423–442.

American Academy of Child and Adolescent Psychiatry. (1997b). Practice parameters for child custody evaluation. *Journal of the American Academy of Child and Adolescent Psychiatry, 36*(10, Suppl.), 57S–68S.

American Bar Association Commission on Domestic Violence. (1994). *Model code on domestic and family violence*. Washington, DC: Author.

American Educational Research Association, American Psychological Association, & National Council on Measurement in Education. (1985). *Standards for educational and psychological testing*. Washington, DC: American Psychological Association.

American Educational Research Association, American Psychological Association, & National Council on Measurement in Education. (1999). *Standards for educational and psychological testing*. Washington, DC: American Psychological Association.

American Law Institute. (2002). *Principles of the law of family dissolution: Analysis and recommendations*. Washington, DC: Author.

American Professional Society on the Abuse of Children. (1990). *Guidelines for psychosocial evaluation of suspected sexual abuse in young children*. Chicago: Author.

American Professional Society on the Abuse of Children. (1995). *Practice guidelines: Use of anatomical dolls in child sexual abuse assessments*. Chicago: Author.

American Psychiatric Association. (1994). *Diagnostic and statistical manual of mental disorders* (4th ed.). Washington, DC: Author.

American Psychiatric Association. (2000). *Diagnostic and statistical manual of mental disorders* (4th ed., text rev.). Washington, DC: Author.

American Psychological Association. (1992). Ethical principles of psychologists and code of conduct. *American Psychologist, 47*, 1597–1611.

American Psychological Association. (1993). *Record keeping guidelines.* Washington, DC: Author

American Psychological Association. (1994). Guidelines for child custody evaluations in divorce proceedings. *American Psychologist, 49*, 677–680.

American Psychological Association. (1996). *Report of the APA Presidential Task Force on Violence and the Family*. Washington, DC: Author.

American Psychological Association. (1999). Guidelines for psychological evaluations in child protection matters. *American Psychologist, 54*, 586–593.

American Psychological Association. (2002). Ethical principles of psychologists and code of conduct. *American Psychologist, 57*, 1060–1073.

Amundson, J. K., Duda, R., & Gill, E. (2000). A minimalist approach to child custody evaluations. *American Journal of Forensic Psychology, 18*(3), 63–87.

Anan, R. M., & Barnett, D. (1999). Perceived social support mediates between prior attachment and subsequent adjustment: A study of urban African American children. *Developmental Psychology, 35*(5), 1210–1222.

Anastasi, A. (1988). *Psychological testing* (6th ed.). New York: Macmillan.

Anastasi, A., & Urbina, S. (1997). *Psychological testing* (7th ed.). Upper Saddle River, NJ: Prentice-Hall.

Anda, R. F., Croft, J. B., Felitti, V. J., Nordenberg, D., Giles, W. H., Williamsion, D. F., et al. (1999). Adverse childhood experiences and smoking during adolescence and adulthood. *Journal of the American Medical Association, 282*, 1652–1658.

Andersen, S. M., & Berk, M. S. (1998). The social–cognitive model of transference: Experiencing past relationships in the present. *Current Directions in Psychological Science, 7*, 109–115.

Appel, A. E., & Holden, G. W. (1998). The co-occurrence of spouse and physical child abuse: A review and appraisal. *Journal of Family Psychology, 12*, 578–599.

Arbisi, P. A. (2001). The structured clinical interview for DSM-IV Axis II personality disorders. In B. S. Plake & J. C. Impara (Eds.), *The fourteenth mental measurements yearbook*. Lincoln, NE: Buros Institute of Mental Measurements.

Archer, J. (2000a). Sex differences in physically aggressive acts between heterosexual partners: A meta-analytic review. *Psychological Bulletin, 126*, 651–680.

Archer, J. (2000b). Sex differences in physical aggression to partners: A reply to Frieze (2000), O'Leary (2000), and White, Smith, Koss, and Figueredo (2000). *Psychological Bulletin, 126*, 697–702.

Arendell, T. (1995). *Fathers and divorce*. Thousand Oaks, CA: Sage.

Arizona v. Youngblood, 488 U.S. 51 (1988).

Arkes, H. R. (1981). Impediments to accurate clinical judgment and possible ways to minimize their impact. *Journal of Consulting and Clinical Psychology, 49*, 323–330.

Arkes, H. R. (1991). Costs and benefits of judgment errors: Implications for debiasing. *Psychological Bulletin, 110*, 486–498.

Arnold, D. S., O'Leary, S. G., Wolff, L. S., & Acker, M. M. (1993). The parenting scale: A measure of dysfunctional parenting in discipline situations. *Psychological Assessment, 5*(2), 137–144.

Aronow, E. (1995). Review of the Children's Apperceptive Story Telling Test. In J. C. Conley (Ed.), *The twelfth mental measurements yearbook* (pp. 180–181). Lincoln: University of Nebraska Press.

Aronson, E. (1968). Dissonance theory: Progress and problems. In R. P. Abelson, E. Aronson, W. J. McGuire, T. M. Newcomb, M. J. Rosenberg, & P. H. Tannenbaum (Eds.), *Theories of cognitive consistency: A sourcebook* (pp. 5–27). Chicago: Rand McNally.

Aronson, E. (1992). The return of the repressed: Dissonance theory makes a comeback. *Psychological Inquiry, 3*, 303–311.

Ary, D., Duncan, T. E., Biglan, A., Metzler, C., Noell, J. W., & Smolkowski, K. (1999). A developmental model of adolescent problem behavior. *Journal of Abnormal Child Psychology, 27*(2), 141–150.

Aspinwall, L. G., & Taylor, S. E. (1997). A stitch in time: Self-regulation and proactive coping. *Psychological Bulletin, 121*, 417–436.

Association of Family and Conciliation Courts. (1994). Model standards of practice for child custody evaluation. *Family and Conciliation Courts Review, 32*, 504–513.

Association of Family and Conciliation Courts. (2007). Model standards of practice for child custody evaluation. *Family Court Review, 45*(1), 70–91.

Astore, N. M., & McLanahan, S. S. (1991). Family structure, parental practices, and high school completion. *American Sociological Review, 56*(3), 309–320.

Austin, W. G. (2000a). Relocation law and the threshold of harm: Integrating legal and behavioral perspectives. *Family Law Quarterly, 34*(1), 63–82.

Austin, W. G. (2000b). Risk reduction interventions in the child custody relocation case. *Journal of Divorce and Remarriage, 33*(1–2), 65–73.

Austin, W. G. (2000c). A forensic psychology model of risk assessment for child custody relocation law. *Family and Conciliation Courts Review, 38*(2), 192–207.

Austin, W. G. (2000d). Assessing credibility in allegations of marital violence in the high-conflict child custody case. *Family and Conciliation Courts Review, 38*(4), 462–477.

Austin, W. G. (2001). Partner violence and risk assessment in child custody evaluation. *Family Court Review, 39*(4), 483–496.

Austin, W. G. (2002). Guidelines for utilizing collateral sources of information in child custody evaluations. *Family Court Review, 40*(2), 177–184.

Austin, W. G., & Gould, J. W. (2006). Exploring three functions in child custody evaluation for the relocation case: Prediction, investigation, and making recommendations for a long-distance parenting plan. *Journal of Child Custody, 3/4*, 63–108.

Austin, W. G., & Kirkpatrick, H. D. (2004). the investigation component in forensic mental health evaluations: Considerations in the case of parenting time evaluations. *Journal of Child Custody, 1*, 23–43.

Azar, B. (1997). Poor recall mars research and treatment. *The APA Monitor, 28*(1), 1, 29.

Azar, S. T., Lauretti, A. F., & Loding, B. V. (1998). The evaluation of parental fitness in termination of parental rights cases: A functional–contextual perspective. *Clinical Child and Family Psychology Review, 1*, 77–100.

Babcock, J. C., Jacobson, N. S., Gottman, J. M., & Yerington, T. P. (2000). Attachment, emotional regulation, and the function of marital violence: Differences between secure, preoccupied, and dismissing violent and nonviolent husbands. *Journal of Family Violence, 15*, 391–409.

Baerger, D. R., Galatzer-Levy, R., Gould, J. W., & Nye, S. (2002). A methodology for reviewing the reliability and relevance of child custody evaluations. *Journal of the American Academy of Matrimonial Lawyers, 18*(1), 35–73.

Bagwell, C. L., Newcomb, A. F., & Bukowski, W. M. (1998). Preadolescent friendship and peer rejection as predictors of adult adjustment. *Child Development, 69,* 140–153.

Baker, A. J. L. (2005). The long-term effects of parental alienation on adult children: A qualitative research study. *American Journal of Family Therapy, 33*(4), 289–302.

Bala, N. (2005). Tippins and Wittmann asked the wrong question: Evaluators may not be "experts," but they can express best interests opinions. *Family Court Review, 43*(4), 554–562.

Baldwin, A. L., Baldwin, C., & Cole, R. E. (1990). Stress-resistant families and stress-resistant children. In J. Rolf, A. S. Masten, D. Cicchetti, K. H. Nuechterlein, & S. Weintraub (Eds.), *Risk and protective factors in the development of psychopathology* (pp. 257–280). New York: Cambridge University Press.

Ballard, M., Cummings, E. M., & Larkin, K. (1993). Emotional and cardiovascular responses to adults' angry behavior and to challenging tasks in children of hypertensive and normotensive parents. *Child Development, 64,* 500–515.

Bancroft, L., & Silverman, J. G. (2002). *The batterer as parent: The impact of domestic violence on family dynamics.* Thousand Oaks, CA: Sage.

Bank, S., & Kahn, M. (1982). *The sibling bond.* New York: Basic Books.

Barber, B. K. (1996). Parental psychological control: Revisiting a neglected construct. *Child Development, 67*(6), 3296–3319.

Barber, B. K. (2002). *Intrusive parenting: How psychological control affects children and adolescents.* Washington, DC: American Psychological Association.

Baris, M. A., & Garrity, C. N. (1988). *Children of divorce: Guidelines for residence and visitation.* DeKalb, IL: Psytec.

Barkley, R. A. (1996). Behavioral inhibition, sustained attention, and executive functions: Constructing a unifying theory of ADHD. *Psychological Bulletin, 121,* 65–94.

Barkley, R. A. (2003). Attention-deficit/hyperactivity disorder. In E. J. Mash & R. A. Barkley, *Child psychopathology* (2nd ed., pp. 75–143). New York: Guilford Press.

Barlow, D. H. (1981). On the relation of clinical research to clinical practice: Current issues, new directions. *Journal of Consulting and Clinical Psychology, 49,* 147–155.

Barnes, G. M., Reifman, A. S., Farrell, M. P., & Dintcheff, B. A. (2000). The effects of parenting on the development of adolescent alcohol misuse: A six-wave latent growth model. *Journal of Marriage and the Family, 62,* 175–186.

Barnes, L. L. B., & Oehler-Stinnett, J. J. (1998). Review of the Parenting Stress Index. In J. C. Impara & B. S. Plake (Eds.), *The thirteenth mental measurements yearbook.* Lincoln, NE: Buros Institute of Mental Measurements.

Barnett, J. E. (2003, Spring). APA's revised ethics code: Implications for professional practice. *The Register Report, 29,* 9–11.

Barnum, R. (1997). A suggested framework for forensic consultation in cases of child abuse and neglect. *Journal of the American Academy of Psychiatry and Law, 25,* 581–593.

Barsky, A. E., & Gould, J. W. (2002). *Clinicians in court: A guide to subpoenas, depositions, testifying and everything else you need to know.* New York: Guilford Press.

Bartkowski, J. P., & Ellison, C. G. (1995). Divergent models of childrearing in popular manuals: Conservative Protestants v. the mainstream experts. *Sociology of Religion, 56*(1), 21–34.

Bartlett, K. T. (2002). Preference, presumption, predisposition, and common sense: From traditional custody doctrines to the American Law Institute's Family Dissolution Project. *Family Law Quarterly, 36*(1), 11–25.

Bartlett, K. T., Schepard, A., Warshak, R. A., & Howe, W. (2004, May 14). *The Approximation Rule: Are predictability, presumptions, and best interests compatible?* Presentation at the 41st annual conference of the Association of Family and Conciliation Courts, San Antonio, TX.

Baumrind, D. (1971). Current patterns of parental authority. *Developmental Psychology Monograph,* (P. 2,4) (1), 1–103.

Baumrind, D. (1991). The influence of parenting style on adolescent competence and substance use. *Journal of Early Adolescence, 11*(1), 56–95.

Baumrind, D., & Thompson, R. A. (2002). The ethics of parenting. In M. Bornstein (Ed.), *Handbook of parenting: Vol. 5. Practical issues in parenting* (2nd ed., pp. 3–34). Mahwah, NJ: Erlbaum.

Bauserman, R. (2002). Child adjustment in joint-custody versus sole arrangements: A meta-analytic review. *Journal of Family Psychology, 16*(1), 91–102.

Beardslee, W. R., Versage, E. M., & Gladstone, T. R. G. (1998). Children of affectively ill parents: A review of the past 10 years. *Journal of the American Academy of Child and Adolescent Psychiatry, 37,* 1134–1141.

Behnke, S. (2004). Ethics rounds: Test scoring and interpretation services. *Monitor on Psychology, 35,* 58–59.

Bellak, L., & Bellak, S. (1949). *Children's Apperception Test.* Berkeley, CA: Consulting Psychologists Press.

Belsky, G., & Gilovich, T. (1999). *Why smart people make big money mistakes and how to correct them.* New York: Simon & Schuster.

Belsky, J. (1996). Parent, infant, and social-contextual antecedents of father–son attachment security. *Developmental Psychology, 32*(5), 905–913.

Belsky, J., Rovine, M., & Taylor, D. G. (1984). The Pennsylvania Infant and Family Development Project, 3: The origins of individual differences in infant–mother attachment—Maternal and infant contribution. *Child Development, 55,* 718–728.

Bendersky, M., & Lewis, M. (1999). Prenatal exposure and neonatal condition. *Infant Behavior Development, 22*(3), 353–366.

Benjamin, A., Gould, J. W., & Rotman, A. (2005, May 19). *Ethical infractions and malpractice in child custody evaluations.* Conference presentation at the 42nd annual Conference of the Association of Family and Conciliation Courts, Seattle, WA.

Benjamin, G. A. H., & Gollan, J. K. (2003). *Family evaluation in custody litigation: Reducing risks of ethical infractions and malpractice.* Washington, DC: American Psychological Association.

Benjet, C., Azar, S. T., & Kuersten-Hogan, R. (2003). Evaluating the parental fitness of psychiatrically diagnosed individuals: Advocating a functional–contextual analysis of parenting. *Journal of Family Psychology, 17*(2), 238–251.

Berliner, L., & Barber, M. K. (1984). The testimony of the child victim of sexual assault. *Journal of Social Issues, 40*(2), 125–137.

Berliner, L., & Conte, J. R. (1993). Sexual abuse evaluations: Conceptual and empirical obstacles. *Child Abuse and Neglect, 17,* 111–125.

Bernadett-Shapiro, S., Ehrensaft, D., & Shapiro, S. (1996). Father participation in childcare and the development of empathy in sons: An empirical study. *Family Therapy, 23,* 77–93.

Berndt, T. J. (1989). Obtaining support from friends during childhood and adolescence. In D. Belle (Ed.), *Children's social networks and social supports* (pp. 308–331). New York: Wiley.

Bernet, F. M. (2001). Review of the Child Sexual Behavior Inventory. In B. S. Plake & J. C. Impara (Eds.), *The fourteenth mental measurements yearbook*. Lincoln, NE: Buros Institute of Mental Measurements.

Berns, S. (2001). Parents behaving badly: Parental alienation syndrome in the family court—Magic bullet or poisoned chalice? *Australian Journal of Family Law, 15*(3), 191–214

Berns, S. B., Jacobson, N. S., & Gottman, J. M. (1999). Demand–withdraw interaction in couples with a violent husband. *Journal of Consulting and Clinical Psychology, 67*, 666–674.

Bersoff, D. N. (1999). *Ethical conflicts in psychology* (2nd ed.). Washington, DC: American Psychological Association.

Best, R. (1983). *We've all got scars: What boys and girls learn in elementary school.* Bloomington: Indiana University Press.

Beutler, L. E., Williams, R. E., & Entwistle, S. R. (1995). Bridging scientist and practitioner perspectives in clinical psychology. *American Psychologist, 50*(12), 984–994.

Biglan, A., Duncan, T. E., Ary, D., & Smolkowski, K. (1995). Peer and parental influences on adolescent tobacco use. *Journal of Behavioral Medicine, 18*, 315–330.

Biglan, A., Metzler, C. W., Wirt, R., Ary, D., Noell, J., & Ochs, L. (1990). Social and behavioral factors associated with high-risk sexual behavior among adolescents. *Journal of Behavioral Medicine, 13*, 245–261.

Biller, H. B., & Kimpton, J. L. (1997). The father and the school-age child. In M. E. Lamb, *Role of the father in child development* (pp. 143–161). New York: Wiley.

Biringen, Z. (1991). Attachment theory and research: Application to clinical practice. *American Journal of Orthopsychiatry, 64*(3), 404–420.

Black, J. C., & Cantor, D. J. (1989). *Child custody.* New York: Columbia University Press.

Blankenhorn, D. (1995). *Fatherless America: Confronting our most urgent social problem.* New York: Basic Books.

Boat, B. W., & Everson, M. D. (1996). Concerning practices of interviewers when using anatomical dolls in child protective services investigations. *Child Maltreatment, 1*, 96–104.

Boland, A. M., Haden, C. A., & Ornstein, P. A. (2003). Boosting children's memory by training mothers in the use of an elaborative conversational style as an event unfolds. *Journal of Cognition and Development, 4*, 39–65.

Booth, C. L., Rose-Krasnor, L., McKinnon, J.-A., & Rubin, K. H. (1994). Predicting social adjustment in middle childhood: The role of preschool attachment security and maternal style. *Social Development, 3*, 189–204.

Boothroyd, R. A. (1998). Review of the Parent–Child Relationship Inventory. In J. C. Impara & B. S. Plake (Eds.), *The thirteenth mental measurements yearbook*. Lincoln, NE: Buros Institute of Mental Measurements.

Bornstein, M. H. (Ed.). (2002). *The handbook of parenting: Vol. 4. Social Conditions and Applied Parenting.* Mahwah, NJ: Erlbaum.

Borum, R., Otto, R. K., & Golding, S. (1993, Spring). Improving clinical judgment and decision making in forensic evaluation. *Journal of Psychiatry and Law*, 35–76.

Bost, K. K., Vaughn, B. E., Washington, W. N., Cielinski, K. L., & Bradbard, M. R.

(1998). Social competence, social support, and attachment: Demarcation of construct domains, measurement, and paths of influence for preschool children attending Head Start. *Child Development, 69,* 192–218.

Bow, J. N., & Boxer, P. (2003). Assessing allegations of domestic violence in child custody evaluations. *Journal of Interpersonal Violence, 18,* 1394–1410.

Bow, J. N., & Quinnell, F. A. (2001). Psychologists' current practices and procedures in child custody evaluations: Five years after American Psychological Association guidelines. *Professional Psychology: Research and Practice, 32*(3), 261–268.

Bow, J. N., & Quinnell, F. A. (2002). A critical review of child custody evaluation reports. *Family Court Review, 40*(2), 164–176.

Bow, J. N., & Quinnell, F. A. (2004). Critique of child custody evaluations by the legal profession. *Family Court Review, 42*(1), 115–127.

Bow, J. N., Quinnell, F. A., Zaroff, M., & Assemany, A. (2002). Assessment of sexual abuse allegations in child custody cases. *Professional Psychology: Research and Practice, 33*(6) 566–575.

Bowen, C. J., & Howie, P. M. (2002). Context and cue cards in young children's testimony: A comparison of brief narrative elaboration and context reinstatement. *Journal of Applied Psychology, 87,* 1077–1085.

Bowlby, J. (1969). *Attachment and loss: Vol. 1. Attachment.* London: Hogarth.

Bowlby, J. (1980). *Attachment and loss: Vol. 2. Loss.* New York: Basic Books.

Braddock, J. H., Royster, D. A., Winfield, L. F., & Hawkins, R. (1991). Bouncing back: Sports and academic resilience among African-American males. *Education and Urban Society, 24,* 113–131.

Bradley, R. H., Corwyn, R. F., McAdoo, H. P., & Coll, C. G. (2001). The home environments of children in the United States: I. Variations by age, ethnicity, and poverty status. *Child Development, 72,* 1844–1867.

Brady, M. S., Poole, D. A., Warren, A. R., & Jones, H. R. (1999). Young children's responses to yes–no questions: Patterns and problems. *Applied Developmental Science, 3,* 47–57.

Brainerd, C. J., & Reyna, V. F. (2002). Recollection rejection: How children edit their false memories. *Developmental Psychology, 38,* 156–172.

Bray, J. H. (1991). Psychosocial factors affecting custodial and visitation arrangements. *Behavioral Sciences and the Law, 9,* 419–437.

Brehm, J. W., & Cohen, A. R. (1962). *Explorations in cognitive dissonance.* New York: Wiley.

Breznitz, Z., & Sherman, T. (1987). Speech patterns of natural discourse of well and depressed mothers and their young children. *Child Development, 58,* 395–400.

Bricklin, B. (1995). *The custody evaluation handbook: Research-based solutions and applications.* New York: Brunner/Mazel.

Briere, J. (1995). *Trauma Symptom Inventory (TSI).* Odessa, FL: Psychological Assessment Resources.

Briere, J. (1996). *Trauma Symptom Checklist for Children (TSCC).* Odessa, FL: Psychological Assessment Resources.

Briere, J. (2001). *Detailed Assessment of Posttraumatic Stress (DAPS).* Odessa, FL: Psychological Assessment Resources.

Brody, G. H., & Flor, D. L. (1998). Maternal resources, parenting practices, and child competence in rural, single-parent African-American families. *Child Development, 69,* 803–816.

Ceci, S. J., & Bruck, M. (1993). The suggestibility of the child witness: A historical review and synthesis. *Psychological Bulletin, 113*, 403–439.

Ceci, S. J., & Bruck, M. (1995). *Jeopardy in the courtroom*. Washington, DC: American Psychological Association.

Ceci, S. J., & Bruck, M. (1998). The ontogeny and durability of true and false memories: A fuzzy trace account. *Journal of Experimental Child Psychology, 71*, 165–169.

Ceci, S. J., & Bruck, M. (2000). Why judges must insist on electronically preserved recordings of child interviews. *Court Review, 37*, 8–10.

Ceci, S. J., & Hembrooke, H. (Eds.). (1998). *Expert witnesses in child abuse cases: What can and should be said in court*. Washington, DC: American Psychological Association.

Ceci, S. J., & Leichtman, M. D. (1992). "I-know-you-know-I know": Recursive awareness in 3-year-olds. In S. J. Ceci, M. Leichtman, & M. Putnick (Eds.), *Cognitive and social factors in early deception* (pp. 16–25). Hillsdale, NJ: Erlbaum.

Ceci, S. J., Leichtman, M., & Putnick, M. (Eds.). (1992). *Cognitive and social factors in early deception*. Hillsdale, NJ: Erlbaum.

Chapman, G. B., & Johnson, E. J. (1999). Incorporating the irrelevant: Anchors in judgments of belief and value. In T. Gilovich, D. Griffin, & D. Kahneman (Eds.), *Heuristics and biases: The psychology of intuitive judgment* (pp. 120–138). Cambridge, U.K.: Cambridge University Press.

Child Pornography Prevention Act of 1996, Public Law 104–208, 110 Stat. 3009–3026.

Chorpita, B. F., & Barlow, D. H. (1998). The development of anxiety: The role of control in the early environment. *Psychological Bulletin, 124*, 3–21.

Cicchetti, D., & Bukowski, W. (Eds.). (1995). Developmental processes in peer relations and psychopathology [Special issue]. *Development and Psychopathology, 7*(4), 587–774.

Cicchetti, D., & Tucker, D. (Eds.). (1994). Neural plasticity, sensitive periods, and psychopathology [Special issue]. *Development and Psychopathology, 6*(4).

Cicirelli, V. G. (1989). Feelings of attachment to siblings and well-being later in life. *Psychology and Aging, 4*, 211–216.

Cicirelli, V. G. (1991). Sibling relationships in adulthood. *Marriage and Family Review, 16*, 291–310.

Clare, M. (2003). Review of the Parenting Alliance Measure. In B. S. Plake, J. C. Impara, & R. A. Spies (Eds.), *The fifteenth mental measurements yearbook*. Lincoln, NE: Buros Institute of Mental Measurements.

Clark, H., & Clark, E. (1977). *Psychology and language*. New York: Harcourt.

Clark, L. A., Kochanska, G., & Ready, R. (2000). Mother's personality and its interaction with child temperament as predictors of parenting behavior. *Journal of Personality and Social Psychology, 79*, 274–285.

Clark, R. M. (1993). Homework-focused parenting practices that positively affect student achievement. In N. F. Chavkin (Ed.), *Families and schools in a pluralistic society*. Albany: State University of New York Press.

Clawar, S., & Rivlin, B. (1991). *Children held hostage*. Chicago: American Bar Association.

Cockett, M., & Tripp, J. (1994). *The Exeter Family Study: Family breakdown and its impact on children*. Exeter, UK: University of Exeter Press.

Cohen, P., & Brook, J. S. (1995). The reciprocal influence of punishment and child behavior disorder. In J. McCord (Ed.), *Coercion and punishment in long-term perspectives* (pp. 154–164). Cambridge, UK: Cambridge University Press.

Coie, J. D., & Dodge, K. A. (1998). Aggression and antisocial behavior. In N. Eisenberg (Ed.), *Handbook of child psychology: Vol. 3. Social, emotional, and personality development* (5th ed., pp. 779–862). New York: Wiley.

Coie, J. D., & Jacobs, M. R. (1993). The role of social context in the prevention of conduct disorder. *Development and Psychopathology, 5*, 263–275.

Colin, L. V. (1996). *Human attachment.* New York: McGraw-Hill.

Coll, G., & Pachter, L. M. (2002). Ethnic and minority parenting. In M. H. Bornstein (Ed.), *Handbook of parenting* (Vol. 4, pp. 1–20). Hillside, NJ: Erlbaum.

Collins, W. A., Madsen, S. D., & Susman-Stillman, A. (2002). Parenting during middle childhood. In M. H. Bornstein (Ed.), *The handbook of parenting* (2nd ed.). *Vol. 1: Children and parenting* (pp. 73–102). Mahwah, NJ: Erlbaum.

Committee on Ethical Guidelines for Forensic Psychologists. (1991). Specialty guidelines for forensic psychologists. *Law and Human Behavior, 15*(6), 655–665.

Committee on Professional Practice and Standards, American Psychological Association. (1993). *Record keeping guidelines.* Washington, DC: Author.

Committee on Training in Clinical Psychology. (1950). Standards for practicum training in clinical psychology: Tentative recommendations. *American Psychologist, 5*, 594–609.

Commonwealth v. Addicks, 5 Binney 520 (Pa. 1813).

Condie, L. O. (2003). *Parenting evaluations for the courts: Care and protection matters.* New York: Plenum Press.

Conger, R. D., Ge, X., Elder, G. H., Jr., Lorenz, F. O., & Simons, R. L. (1994). Economic stress, coercive family process, and developmental problems of adolescents. *Child Development, 65*, 541–561.

Conners, K. C. (1997). *Conners' Rating Scales–Revised.* New York: Multi-Health Systems.

Connolly, J. A., & Goldberg, A. (1999). Romantic relationships in adolescence: The role of friends and peers in their emergence and development. In W. Furman, B. B. Brown, & C. Feiring (Eds.), *The development of romantic relationships in adolescence* (pp. 266–290). New York: Cambridge University Press.

Conoley, J. C., & Reese, J. (2001). Review of the Michigan Alcohol Screening Test. In B. S. Plake & J. C. Impara (Eds.), *The fourteenth mental measurements yearbook.* Lincoln, NE: Buros Institute of Mental Measurements.

Consensus Statement. (1996). The short- and long-term consequences of corporal punishment. *Pediatrics, 98*(Suppl.), 853.

Conte, J. R., Collins, M., & Fogarty, L. (1991). National survey of professional practice in child sexual abuse. *Journal of Family Violence, 6*(2), 149–166.

Coolahan, K., Fantuzzo, J., Mendez, J., & McDermott, P. (2000). Preschool peer interactions and readiness to learn: Relationships between classroom peer play and learning behaviors and conduct. *Journal of Educational Psychology, 92*(3), 458–465.

Coons, J. E., Mnookin, R. H., & Sugarman, S. D. (1993). Deciding what's best for children. *Notre Dame Journal of Law, Ethics and Public Policy, 7*, 465–474.

Cooper, J., & Fazio, R. H. (1984). A new look at dissonance theory. In L. Berkowitz (Ed.), *Advances in experimental social psychology* (Vol. 17, pp. 229–264). Orlando, FL: Academic Press.

Cowen, E. L., Wyman, P. A., Work, W. C., & Parker, G. R. (1990). The Rochester Child Resilience Project: Overview and summary of first-year findings. *Development and Psychopathology, 2*, 193–212.

Cox, A. D., Puckering, C., Pound, A., & Mills, M. (1987). The impact of maternal depression on young children. *Journal of Child Psychology and Psychiatry, 28*, 917–928.

Craig v. Boren, 429 U.S. 190 (1976).

Crano, W. D. (1977). Primacy vs. recency in retention of information and opinion change. *Journal of Social Psychology, 101,* 87–96.

Cribb, J. (1997). "Being bashed is something I have to accept": Western Samoan women's attitudes towards domestic violence in Christchurch. *Social Policy Journal of New Zealand, 9,* 164–170.

Crichton-Hill, Y. (2001). Challenging ethnocentric explanations of domestic violence: Let us decide, then value our decisions—A Samoan response. *Trauma, Violence, and Abuse: A Review Journal, 2*(3), 203–214.

Crockenberg, S., & Lourie, A. (1996). Parents' conflict strategies with children and children's conflict strategies with peers. *Merrill–Palmer Quarterly, 42,* 495–518.

Crossman, A. M., Powell, M. B., Principe, G. F., Gabrielle, F., & Ceci, S. J. (2002). Child testimony in custody cases: A review. *Journal of Forensic Psychology Practice, 2*(1), 1–32.

Csikszentmihalyi, M., Rathunde, K., & Whalen, S. (1993). *Talented teenagers: The roots of success and failure.* New York: Cambridge University Press.

Cull, J. G., & Gill, W. S. (1990). *The Suicide Probability Scales.* Beverly Hills: Western Psychological Services.

Cummings, E. M., & Cummings, J. S. (2002). Parenting and attachment. In M. H. Bornstein (Ed.), *Handbook of parenting: Vol. 5. Practical issues in parenting* (2nd ed., pp. 35–58). Mahwah, NJ: Erlbaum.

Cummings, E. M., Zahn-Waxler, C., & Radke-Yarrow, M. (1981). Young children's responses to expressions of anger and affection by others in the family. *Child Development, 52,* 1274–1282.

Cummings, J. S., Pellegrini, D. S., Notarius, C. I., & Cummings, E. M. (1989). Children's responses to angry adult behavior as a function of marital distress and history of interparental hostility. *Child Development, 60,* 1035–1043.

Cunningham, R. M., Stiffman, A. R., Doré, P., & Earls, F. (1994). The association of physical and sexual abuse with HIV risk behaviors in adolescence and young adulthood: Implications for public health. *Child Abuse and Neglect, 18,* 233–245.

Cuthbert, C., Slote, K., Driggers, M. G., Mesh, C. J., Bancroft, L., & Silverman, J. (2002). *Battered mothers speak out: A human rights report on domestic violence and child custody in the Massachusetts family courts.* Wellesley, MA: Wellesley Centers for Women.

Dailey, C. A. (1952). The effects of premature conclusions upon the acquisition of understanding of a person. *Journal of Psychology, 33,* 133–152.

Dallam, S. J. (1999). Parental alienation syndrome: Is it scientific? In E. St. Charles & L. Crook (Eds.), *Expose: The failure of family courts to protect children from abuse in custody disputes.* Los Gatos. CA: Our Children Charitable Foundation.

Dalton, C., Carbon, S., & Olesen, N. (2003). High-conflict divorce, violence, and abuse: Implications for custody and visitation decisions. *Juvenile and Family Court Journal, 54*(4), 11–34.

Daubert v. Merrell Dow Pharmaceuticals, 113 S. Ct. 2786 (1993).

Daubert v. Merrell Dow Pharmaceuticals, Inc. 43 F. 3d. (9th Cir. 1311, 1995).

Davies, M. F. (2003). Confirmatory bias in the evaluation of personality descriptions: Positive test strategies and output interference. *Journal of Personality and Social Psychology, 85*(4), 746–744.

Davies, P. T., & Cummings, E. M. (1994). Marital conflict and child adjustment: An emotional security hypothesis. *Psychological Bulletin, 116*(3), 387–411.

Davies, P. T., & Cummings, E. M. (1998). Exploring children's emotional security as a mediator of the link between marital relations and child adjustment. *Child Development, 69*, 124–139.

Declaration on the Elimination of Violence Against Women (DEVAW), G. A. Res. 48/104, A/48/49, 1993.

DeKovic, M., & Janssen, J. M. A. M. (1992). Parents' child-rearing style and child's sociometric status. *Developmental Psychology, 28*, 925–932.

Dembroski, T. M., MacDougall, J. M., Williams, R. B., Haney, T. L., & Blumenthal, J. A. (1985). Components of Type A, hostility, and anger-in: Relationship to angiographic findings. *Psychosomatic Medicine, 47*, 219–233.

DePaulo, B. M., Charlton, K., Cooper, H., Lindsay, J. J., & Muhlenbruck, L. (1997). The accuracy–confidence correlation in the detection of deception. *Personality and Social Psychology Review, 1*, 346–357.

Derdeyn, A. P., Levy, A. M., Looney, J. G., Westman, J. C., Scott, E., & Spurlock, J. (1988). *Child custody consultation: Report of the Task Force on Clinical Assessment in Child Custody.* Washington, DC: American Psychiatric Association.

Deren, S. (1986). Children of substance abusers: A review of the literature. *Journal of Substance Abuse Treatment, 3*, 77–94.

DeWolf, M. S., & van IJzendoorn, M. H. (1997). Sensitivity and attachment: A metaanalysis on parental antecedents of infant attachment. *Child Development, 68*(4), 571–591.

Dietz, P. M., Spitz, A. M., Anda, R. F., Williamson, D. F., McMahon, P. M., & Santelli, J. S. (1999). Unintended pregnancy among adult women exposed to abuse or household dysfunction during their childhood. *Journal of the American Medical Association, 282*, 1359–1364.

DiPerna, J. C. (2001). Review of the Behavior Assessment System for Children–Revised. In B. S. Plake & J. C. Impara (Eds.), *The fourteenth mental measurements yearbook.* Lincoln, NE: Buros Institute of Mental Measurements.

Dishion, T. J. (1990). The family ecology of boys' peer relations in middle childhood. *Child Development, 61*, 874–891.

Dishion, T. J., Andrews, D. W., & Crosby, L. (1995). Antisocial boys and their friends in early adolescence: Relationship characteristics, quality, and interactional process. *Child Development, 66*, 139–151.

Dishion, T. J., Capaldi, D., Spracklen, K., & Li, F. (1995). Peer ecology of male adolescent drug use. *Development and Psychopathology, 7*, 803–824.

Dishion, T. J., Patterson, G. R., Stoolmiller, M., & Skinner, M. L. (1991). Family, school, and behavioral antecedents to early adolescent involvement with antisocial peers. *Developmental Psychology, 27*, 172–180.

Dix, T. (1991). The affective organization of parenting: Adaptive and maladaptive processes. *Psychological Bulletin, 110*, 3–25.

Dix, T., & Grusec, J. E. (1985). Parent attribution processes in the socialization process of children. In J. Sigel (Ed.), *Parental belief systems* (pp. 201–234). Hillsdale, NJ: Erlbaum.

Dobson, J. (1970). *Dare to discipline.* Wheaton, IL: Tyndale House.

Dodge, K. A. (1991). Emotion and social information processing. In J. Garber & K. A. Dodge (Eds.), *The development of emotion regulation and dysregulation* (pp. 159–181). Cambridge, UK: Cambridge University Press.

Dodge, K. A., Bates, J. E., & Pettit, G. S. (1990). Mechanisms in the cycle of violence. *Science, 250*(4988), 1678–1683.

Dodge, K. A., Pettit, G. S., & Bates, J. E. (1994). Socialization mediators of the relation between socioeconomic status and child conduct problems. *Child Development, 65*, 649–665.

Doll, B. (1998). Review of the Child Behavior Checklist. In J. C. Impara & B. S. Plake (Eds.), *The thirteenth mental measurements yearbook*. Lincoln, NE: Buros Institute of Mental Measurements.

Donovan, J. E., & Jessor, R. (1985). Structure of problem behavior in adolescence and young adulthood. *Journal of Consulting and Clinical Psychology, 53*, 890–904.

Dorado, J. S., & Saywitz, K. J. (2001). Interviewing preschoolers from low- and middle-SES communities: A test of the Narrative Elaboration Recall Improvement technique. *Journal of Clinical Child Psychology, 30*, 568–580.

Downey, G., & Feldman, S. I. (1996). Implications of rejection sensitivity for intimate relationships. *Journal of Personality and Social Psychology, 70*(6), 1327–1343.

Drozd, L. (2007). *Domestic violence in child custody (DVCC)*. Newport Beach, CA: Author.

Drozd, L., Kleinman, T., & Olesen, N. (2000). Alienation or abuse? *Proceedings of the Fourth International Symposium on Child Custody Evaluations* (pp. 169–181). Madison, WI: Association of Family and Conciliation Courts.

Drozd, L., & Olesen, N. (2003, May 31). *Attachment in divorcing families: Problems and solutions*. Workshop presented at the 40th anniversary Conference of the Association of Family and Conciliation Courts, Ottawa, Ontario, Canada.

Drozd, L. M., & Olesen, N. W. (2004). Is it abuse, alienation, and/or estrangement? A decision tree. *Journal of Child Custody, 1*(3), 65–105.

Drozd, L., & Walker, L. (2001, September). *Protective mothers*. Paper presented at the International Conference on Family Violence. Family Violence and Sexual Assault Institute, San Diego, CA.

Dudley, J. R. (1996). Noncustodial fathers speak about their parental role. *Family and Conciliation Court Review, 34*(3), 410–426.

Dudley, J. R., & Stone, G. (2001). *Fathering at risk: Helping nonresidential fathers*. New York: Springer.

Duncan, G. J., Brooks-Gunn, J., & Klebanov, P. K. (1994). Economic deprivation and early childhood development. *Child Development, 65*, 296–318.

Dunn, J., & Brown, J. (1994). Affect expression in the family, children's understanding of emotions, and their interactions with others. *Merrill–Palmer Quarterly, 40*, 120–137.

Dunn, J., Brown, J., Slomkowski, C., Tesla, C., & Youngblade, L. (1991). Young children's understanding of other people's feelings and beliefs: Individual differences and their antecedents. *Child Development, 62*, 1352–1366.

Dunne, J., & Hedrick, M. (1994). The parental alienation syndrome: An analysis of sixteen selected cases. *Journal of Divorce and Remarriage, 21*, 21–37.

Dutton, D. G. (1998). *The domestic assault of women: Psychological and criminal justice perspectives*. Vancouver: University of British Columbia Press.

Dutton, D. G. (1999). Traumatic origins of intimate rage. *Aggression and Violent Behavior, 4*, 431–447.

Dutton, D. G. (2000). Witnessing parental violence as a traumatic experience shaping the abusive personality. *Journal of Aggression, Maltreatment and Trauma, 3*, 59–67.

Dutton, D. G. (2004, January 23–24). Domestic violence: New perspectives on assessment and treatment. Workshop material presented by Donald Dutton, San Diego, CA.

Dutton, D. G. (2005a). Domestic abuse assessment in child custody disputes: Beware the domestic violence research paradigm. *Journal of Child Custody, 2*(4), 23–42.

Dutton, D. G. (2005b). On comparing apples with apples deemed nonexistent: A reply to Johnson. *Journal of Child Custody, 2*(4), 53–64.

Dutton, D. G., & Kropp, P. R. (2000). A review of domestic violence risk instruments. *Trauma Violence and Abuse, 1*, 171–181.

Dutton, D. G., & Starzomski, A. J. (1997). Personality predictors of the Minnesota Power and Control Wheel. *Journal of Interpersonal Violence, 12*, 70–82.

Ehrensaft, M. K., Cohen, P., Brown, J., Smailes, E., Chen, H., & Johnson, J. G. (2003). Intergenerational transmission of partner violence: A 20-year prospective study. *Journal of Clinical and Consulting Psychology, 71*(4), 741–753.

Eisenberg, N. (1992). *The caring child.* Cambridge, MA: Harvard University Press.

Eisenberg, N., & Fabes, R. A. (1998). Prosocial development. In N. Eisenberg & W. Damon (Eds.), *Handbook of child psychology* (5th ed., Vol. 3, pp. 701–778). New York: Wiley.

Eisenberg, N., Fabes, R. A., Bernszweig, J., Karbon, M., Poulin, R., & Hanish, L. (1993). The relations of emotionality and regulation to preschoolers' social skills and sociometric status. *Child Development, 64*, 1418–1438.

Eisenberg, N., Fabes, R. A., & Murphy, B. C. (1996). Parents' reactions to children's negative emotions: Relations to children's social competence and comforting behavior. *Child Development, 67*, 2227–2247.

Eisenberg, N., Fabes, R. A., Shepard, S. A., Murphy, B. C., Guthrie, I. K., Jones, S., et al. (1997). Contemporaneous and longitudinal prediction of children's social functioning from regulation and emotionality. *Child Development, 68*, 642–664.

Eisenberg, N., Guthrie, I. K., Fabes, R. A., Reiser, M., Murphy, B. C., Homgren, R., et al. (1997). The relations of regulation and emotionality to resiliency and competent social functioning in elementary school children. *Child Development, 68*, 295–311.

Eisenberg, N., & Valiente, C. (2002). Parenting and children's prosocial and moral development. In M. H. Bornstein (Ed.), *Handbook of parenting: Vol. 5. Practical issues in parenting* (pp. 111–142). Mahwah, NJ: Erlbaum.

Ekman, P., & O'Sullivan, M. (1991). Who can catch a liar? *American Psychologist, 46*, 913–920.

Elicker, J., Englund, M., & Sroufe, L. A. (1992). Predicting peer competence and peer relationships in childhood from early parent–child relationships. In R. D. Parke & G. W. Ladd (Eds.), *Family-peer relationships: Modes of linkage* (pp. 77–106). Hillsdale, NJ: Erlbaum.

Elliot, A. J., & Devine, P. G. (1994). On the motivational nature of cognitive dissonance: Dissonance as psychological discomfort. *Journal of Personality and Social Psychology, 67*, 382–394.

Ellison, C. G., & Sherkat, D. E. (1993). Obedience and autonomy: Religion and child-rearing orientations reconsidered. *Journal for the Scientific Study of Religion, 32*, 13–29.

El-Sheikh, M., Cummings, E. M., & Goetsch, V. L. (1989). Coping with adults' angry behavior: Behavioral, physiological, and verbal responses in preschoolers. *Developmental Psychology, 25*, 490–489.

Elster, J. (1987). Solomonic judgments: Against the best interest of the child. *University of Chicago Law Review, 54*, 1–40.

Emery, R. E. (1999). *Marriage, divorce, and children's adjustment* (2nd ed). Thousand Oaks, CA: Sage.

Emery, R. E., & Laumann-Billings, L. (1998). An overview of the nature, causes, and consequences of abusive family relationships: Toward differentiating maltreatment from violence. *American Psychologist, 53*(2), 121–135.

Emery, R. E., Otto, R. K., & O'Donohue, W. T. (2005). A critical assessment of child custody evaluations: Limited science and a flawed system. *Psychological Science in the Public Interest, 6*, 1–29.

Ewart, C. K. (1991). Familial transmission of essential hypertension, genes, environments, and chronic anger. *Annals of Behavioral Medicine, 13*, 40–47.

Exner, J. E., Jr. (1980). But it's only an inkblot. *Journal of Personality Assessment, 44*, 563–577.

Exner, J. E., Jr. (1986). *The Rorschach: A comprehensive system: Vol. 1. Basic foundations* (2nd ed.). New York: Wiley.

Exner, J. E., Jr. (1993). *The Rorschach: A comprehensive system: Vol. 1. Basic foundations* (3rd ed.). New York: Wiley.

Eyde, L., Kowal, D. M., & Fishburne, F. J. (1991). The validity of computer-based test interpretations of the MMPI. In T. B. Gutkin & S. L. Wise (Eds.), *The computer and the decision-making process* (pp. 75–123). Hillsdale, NJ: Erlbaum.

Fabricius, W. V., & Hall, J. (2000). Young adults' perspectives on divorce: Living arrangements. *Family and Conciliation Courts Review, 38*, 446–461.

Fagerstrom, D. (1997). *Divorce: A problem to be solved not a battle to be fought*. Orinda, CA: Brockwood.

Fagot, B. I. (1997). Attachment, parenting, and peer interactions of toddler children. *Developmental Psychology, 33*(3), 489–499.

Faller, K. C. (1990). *Understanding child sexual maltreatment*. Thousand Oaks, CA: Sage.

Faller, K. C. (1998). The parental alienation syndrome: What is it and what data support it? *Child Maltreatment, 3*(2), 100–115.

Fantuzzo, J., Sutton-Smith, B., Atkins, M., Meyers, R., Stevenson, H., Coolahan, K., et al. (1996). Community-based resilient peer treatment of withdrawn maltreated preschool children. *Journal of Consulting and Clinical Psychology, 64*, 1377–1386.

Fauber, R. L., & Long, N. (1991). Children in context: The role of the family in child psychotherapy. *Journal of Consulting and Clinical Psychology, 59*, 813–820.

Federal Rules of Civil Procedure. United States Code.

Federal Rules of Evidence. United States Code. Title 28.

Feeley, T. H., & Young, M. J. (1998). Humans as lie detectors: Some more second thoughts. *Communication Quarterly, 46*(2), 109–126.

Feiring. C., & Furman, W. C. (2000). When love is just a four-letter word: Victimization and romantic relationships in adolescence. *Child Maltreatment, 5*(4), 293–298.

Feldman, S., & Downey, G. (1994). Rejection sensitivity as a mediator of the impact of childhood exposure to family violence on adult attachment behavior. *Development and Psychopathology, 6*, 231–247.

Felitti, V. J., Anda, R. F., Nordenberg, D., Williamson, D. F., Apitz, A. M., & Edwards. (1998). Relationship of childhood abuse and household dysfunction to many of the leading causes of death in adults. *American Journal of Preventive Medicine, 14*, 245–258.

Feller, J. N., Davidson, H. A., Hardin, M., & Horowitz, M. (1992). *Working with the courts in child protection.* Washington, DC: Department of Health and Human Services.

Fergusson, D. M., & Lynskey, M. Y. (1995). Childhood conduct problems, attention-deficit behaviors and adolescent alcohol, tobacco and illicit drug use. *Journal of Abnormal Psychology, 23*(3), 379–396.

Festinger, L. (1957). *A theory of cognitive dissonance.* Stanford, CA: Stanford University Press.

Festinger, L., & Carlsmith, J. M. (1959). Cognitive consequences of forced compliance. *Journal of Abnormal and Social Psychology, 58,* 203–210.

Festinger, L., Riecken, H. W., & Schachter, S. (1956). *When prophecy fails.* Minneapolis: University of Minnesota Press.

Fincham, F. D., & Bradbury, T. N. (1990a). Preventing marital dysfunction: Review and analysis. In F. D. Fincham & T. N. Bradbury (Eds.), *The psychology of marriage: Basic issues and applications* (pp. 375–401). New York: Guilford Press.

Fincham, F. D., & Bradbury, T. N. (Eds.). (1990b). *The psychology of marriage: Basic issues and applications.* New York: Guilford Press.

Finchman, F. D., Beach, S. R., Arias, I., & Brody, G. H. (1998). Children's attributions in the family. The children's relationship attribution measure. *Journal of Family Psychology, 12*(4), 481–493.

Fineman, M. (1991). *The illusion of equality: Rhetoric and reality of divorce reform.* Chicago: University of Chicago Press.

First, M. B., Spitzer, R. L., Gibbon, M., & Williams, J. B. W. (1998). *The structured clinical interview for DSM-IV Axis I disorders: Clinical version.* Washington, DC: American Psychiatric Press.

First, M. B., Spitzer, R. L., Gibbon, M., Williams, J. B. W., & Benjamin, L. S. (1998). *The structured clinical interview for DSM-IV Axis II personality disorders.* Washington, DC: American Psychiatric Press.

Fisher, C. B., & Whiting, K. A. (1998). How valid are child sexual abuse validations? In S. J. Ceci & H. Hembrooke (Eds.), *Expert witnesses in child abuse cases: What can and should be said in court* (pp. 159–184). Washington, DC: American Psychological Association.

Fisher, S., & Fisher, R. L. (1986). *What we really know about parenting.* Northvale, NJ: Jason Aronson.

Fitch, J. H. (1962). Men convicted of sexual offenses against children: A descriptive followup study. *British Journal of Criminology, 3,* 18–37.

Flens, J. R., & Drozd, L. (Eds.). (2005). *Psychological testing in child custody evaluations.* New York: Haworth Press.

Fowler, R. D. (1969). Automated interpretation of personality test data. In J. N. Butcher (Ed.), *MMPI: Research developments and clinical applications.* New York: McGraw-Hill.

Frank, G. (1984). The Boulder model: History, rationale, and critique. *Professional Psychology—Research and Practice, 15*(3), 417–435.

Frank, M. G., & Feeley, T. H. (2003). To catch a liar: Challenges for research in lie detection training. *Journal of Applied Communication Research, 21*(3), 58–75.

Frankel v. Frankel, Index No. 350741/01 N.Y. (2004).

Frasure-Smith, N., Lesperance, F., & Talajic, M. (1995). The impact of negative emotions on prognosis following myocardial infarction: Is it more than depression? *Health Psychology, 14,* 388–398.

Freeman, S. J. (2002). Review of the State–Trait Anger Expression Inventory—2. In B. S. Plake, J. C. Impara, & R. A. Spies (Eds.), *The fifteenth mental measurements yearbook*. Lincoln, NE: Buros Institute of Mental Measurements.

Friedrich, W. (1997). *Child Sexual Behavior Inventory*. Odessa, FL: Psychological Assessment Resources.

Friedrich, W. N. (2002). *Psychological assessment of sexually abused children and their families*. Thousand Oaks, CA: Sage.

Friedrich, W. N., Fisher, J., Broughton, D., Houston, M., & Shafran, C. R. (1998). Normative sexual behavior in children: A contemporary sample. *Pediatrics, 101*, 1–9.

Frijda, N. H. (1986). *The emotions*. Cambridge, UK: Cambridge University Press.

Frisbie, L. V. (1969). Another look at sex offenders in California. *California Mental Health Research Monograph, 12*. Sacramento, CA: Department of Mental Hygiene.

Frisbie, L. V., & Dondis, E. H. (1965). Recidivism among treated sex offenders. *California Mental Health Research Monograph, 5*. Sacramento, CA: State of California Department of Mental Hygiene.

Frye v. United States, 293 F. 1013 (D. C. Cir. 1923).

Fukudo, S., Lane, J. D., Anderson, N. B., Kuhn, C. M., Schanberg, S. M., & McCown, N. (1992). Accentuated vagal antagonism of beta-adrenergic effects on ventricular repolarization: Evidence of weaker antagonism in hostile Type A men. *Circulation, 85*, 2045–2053.

Furlong, M. J., & Wood, M. (1998). Review of the Child Behavior Checklist. In J. C. Impara & B. S. Plake (Eds.), *The thirteenth mental measurements yearbook*. Lincoln, NE: Buros Institute of Mental Measurements.

Gaines, R., Sandgrund, A., Green, A. H., & Power. E. (1978). Etiological factors in child maltreatment: A multi-variate study of abusing, neglecting, and normal mothers. *Journal of Abnormal Psychology, 87*, 531–540.

Galatzer-Levy, R. M., & Krauss, L. (1999). *The scientific basis of child custody decisions*. New York: Wiley.

Galatzer-Levy, R., Baerger, D. R., Gould, J. W., & Nye. S. (2002). Evaluating the evaluation: How to understand and critique custody evaluations. In R. Brown & L. Morgan (Eds.), *2003 Family Law Update*, (pp. 139–211). Baltimore: Aspen.

Garb, H. N. (1994). Cognitive heuristics and biases in personality assessment. In L. Heath, R. S. Tindale, J. Edwards, E. Posavac, F. Bryant, E. Henderson, et al. (Eds.), *Applications of heuristics and biases to social issues* (pp. 73–90). New York: Plenum Press.

Garb, H. N., Wood, J. M., Lilienfeld, S. O., & Nezworski, M. T. (2002). Effective use of projective techniques in clinical practice: Let the data help with selection and interpretation. *Professional Psychology: Research and Practice, 33*, 454–463.

Garb, H. N., Wood, J. M., & Nezworski, M. T. (2000). Projective techniques and the detection of child sexual abuse. *Child Maltreatment: Journal of the American Professional Society on the Abuse of Children, 5*(2), 161–168.

Garbarino, J., & Gilliam, G. (1980). *Understanding abusive families*. Lexington, MA: Lexington Books.

Garbarino, J., & Sherman, D. (1980). High-risk neighborhoods and high-risk families: The human ecology of child maltreatment. *Child Development, 51*, 188–198.

García Coll, C. T., Meyer, E. C., & Brillon, L. (1995). Ethnic and minority parents. In M. H. Bornstein (Ed.), *Handbook of parenting* (Vol. 2, pp. 189–209). Mahwah, NJ: Erlbaum.

Gardner, R. A. (1985). Recent trends in divorce and custody litigation. *Academy Forum (A Publication of the American Academy of Psychoanalysis), 29*(2), 3–7.

Gardner, R. A. (1992). *The parental alienation syndrome*. Creskill, NJ: Creative Therapeutics.

Gardner, R. A. (1998). *The parental alienation syndrome and the evaluation of child abuse accusations*. Creskill, NJ: Creative Therapeutics.

Gardner, R. A. (1999). Guidelines for assessing parental preference in child custody disputes. *Journal of Divorce and Remarriage, 30*, 1–9.

Gardner, R. A. (2002). Denial of the parental alienation syndrome also harms women. *American Journal of Family Therapy, 30*(3), 191–202.

Gardner, R. A., Sauber, R., & Lorandos, D. (Eds.). (2006). *The international handbook of parental alienation syndrome: Conceptual, clinical, and legal considerations*. Springfield, IL: Charles C Thomas.

Garrison, M. (1996). How do judges decide divorce cases? An empirical analysis of discretionary decision making. *North Carolina Law Review, 74*, 401–435.

Garrity, C., & Baris, M. (1994). *Caught in the middle: Protecting the children of high-conflict divorce*. New York: Lexington Books.

Gatowski, S. I., Dobbin, S. A., Richardson, J. T., Ginsburg, G. P., Merlino, M. L., & Dahir, V. (2001). Asking the gatekeepers: A national survey of judges on judging expert evidence in a post-*Daubert* world. *Law and Human Behavior, 25*(5), 433–458.

Geffner, R. A., Goldstein, S., Fox, N., & Ducote, R. (2002, July). *Conducting custody evaluations in the best interests of the child: Techniques, new legal and ethical requirements, and child sexual abuse issues*. Three-day workshop presented by the Family Violence and Sexual Assault Institute at the California School of Professional Psychology, San Diego, CA.

Geffner, R. A., Jaffe, P. G., & Suderman, M. (Eds.). (2000). *Children exposed to domestic violence: Current issues in research, intervention, prevention, and policy development*. New York: Haworth.

Geiselman, R. E. (1999). Commentary on recent research with the cognitive interview. *Psychology, Crime and Law, 5*, 197–202.

Gelles, R. J. (1997). *Intimate violence in families* (3rd ed.). Thousand Oaks, CA: Sage, Inc.

Gelles, R. J., & Cornell, C. P. (1985). *Intimate violence in families*. Beverly Hills: Sage.

Gelles, R. J., & Straus, M. A. (1988). *Intimate violence*. New York: Simon & Schuster.

George, L. K. (1989). Stress, social support, and depression over the life-course. In K. Markides & C. Cooper (Eds.), *Aging, stress, social support, and health* (pp. 241–267). London: Wiley.

General Electric Co. v. Joiner, 522 U.S. 136 (1997).

Gerard, A. B. (1994). *Parent–Child Relationship Inventory*. Los Angeles, CA: Western Psychological Services.

Gershoff, E. (2002). Corporal punishment by parents and associated child behaviors and experiences: A meta-analytic and theoretical review. *Psychological Bulletin, 128*(4), 539–579.

Gershoff, E., Miller, P. C., & Holden, G. W. (1999). Parenting influences from the pulpit: Religious affiliation as a determinant of parental corporal punishment. *Journal of Family Psychology, 13*(3), 307–320.

Gil, K. M., Keefe, F. J., Sampson, H. A., McCaskill, C. C., Rodin, J., & Crisson, J. E. (1987). The relation of stress and family environment to atopic dermatitis symptoms in children. *Journal of Psychosomatic Research, 31*, 673–684.

Gilliom, M., Shaw, D. S., Beck, J. E., Schonberg, M. A., & Lukon, J. L. (2002). Anger regulation in disadvantaged preschool boys: Strategies, antecedents, and the development of self-control. *Developmental Psychology, 38,* 222–235.

Gilstrap, L. L., Fraser-Thill, R. L., & Ceci, S. J. (2001–2002). Children's source monitoring. *Imagination, Cognition and Personality, 21,* 176–180.

Golding, S. L. (1995). Mental health professionals and the courts. In D. N. Bersoff (Ed.), *Ethical conflicts in psychology* (pp. 421–422). Washington, DC: American Psychological Association.

Goldsmith, H. H., & Harman, C. (1994). Temperament and attachment: Individuals and relationships. *Current Directions in Psychological Science, 3,* 53–57.

Goldstein, A. M. (Ed.). (2003). *Handbook of psychology: Vol. 11. Forensic psychology.* New York: Wiley.

Goldstein, J., Freud, A., & Solnit, A. (1979). *Beyond the best interests of the child.* New York: Free Press.

Goldstein, S. L. (1998). *The sexual exploitation of children: A practical guide to assessment, investigation, and intervention* (2nd ed.). New York: CRC Press.

Goodman, G. S., Batterman-Faunce, J. M., Schaaf, J. M., & Kenney, R. (2002). Nearly 4 years after an event: Children's eyewitness memory and adults' perceptions of children's accuracy. *Child Abuse and Neglect, 26,* 849–884.

Goodman, S. H., & Brumley, H. E. (1990). Schizophrenic and depressed mothers: Relational deficits in parenting. *Developmental Psychology, 26,* 31–39.

Goodman-Delahunty, J. (1997). Forensic psychological expertise in the wake of *Daubert. Law and Human Behavior, 21*(2), 121–140.

Gordon, B. N. (1996, November 26). A framework for assessing children's allegations of sexual abuse in juvenile, criminal and custody cases. Workshop presented at the Charlotte Area Health Education Center Continuing Professional Education Program, Charlotte, NC.

Gottman, J. M., Jacobson, N. S., Rushe, R. H., Shortt, J. W., Babcock, J., La Taillade, J. J., et al. (1995). The relationship between heart rate reactivity, emotionally aggressive behavior, and general violence in batterers. *Journal of Family Psychology, 9,* 227–324.

Gottman, J. M., & Katz, L. F. (1989). Effects of marital discord on young children's peer interaction and health. *Developmental Psychology, 25,* 373–381.

Gottman, J. M., Katz, L. F., & Hooven, C. (1996). Parental meta-emotion philosophy and the emotional life of families. Theoretical models and preliminary data. *Journal of Family Psychology, 10,* 243–268.

Gottman, J. M., Katz, L. F., & Hooven, C. (1997). *Meta-emotion: How families communicate emotionally.* Hillsdale, NJ: Erlbaum.

Gould, J. W. (1998). *Conducting scientifically crafted child custody evaluations.* Thousand Oaks, CA: Sage.

Gould, J. W. (1999). Professional interdisciplinary collaboration and the development of psycholegal questions guiding court-ordered child custody evaluations. *Juvenile and Family Court Journal, 50*(1), 43–52.

Gould, J. W. (2004). Evaluating the probative value of child custody evaluations: A guide for forensic mental health professionals. *Journal of Child Custody, 1*(1), 77–96.

Gould, J. W. (2006). *Conducting scientifically crafted child custody evaluations* (2nd ed.). Sarasota, FL: Professional Resource Press.

Gould, J. W., & Bell, L. C. (2000). Forensic methods and procedures applied to child custody evaluations: What judges need to know in determining a competent forensic work product. *Juvenile and Family Court Journal, 38*(2), 21–27.

Gould, J. W., & Greenberg, L. R. (2000). Merging paradigms: The marriage of clinical treatment with forensic thinking. *Newsletter of the Academy of Family Psychology, 3*(2), 3–7.

Gould, J. W., & Kirkpatrick, H. D. (2001, August). *Conducting scientifically crafted child custody evaluations.* Continuing education workshop presented at the annual convention of the American Psychological Association, San Francisco.

Gould, J. W., Kirkpatrick, H. D., Austin, W., & Martindale, D. A. (2004). A protocol for offering a critique of a colleague's forensic work product. *Journal of Child Custody, 1*(3), 37–64.

Gould, J. W., & Lehrmann, D. (2002). Evaluating the probative value of child custody evaluations. *Juvenile and Family Court Journal, 53*(2), 17–30.

Gould, J. W., & Martindale, D. A. (2005). A second call for clinical humility and judicial vigilance: Comments on Tippins and Wittmann (2005). *Family Court Review, 43*(2), 253–259.

Gould, J. W., Martindale, D. A., & Eidman, M. H. (2007). Domestic violence and child custody assessment. *Journal of Child Custody.* Manuscript submitted for publication.

Gould, J. W., & Stahl. P. M. (2000). The art and science of child custody evaluations: Integrating clinical and mental health models. *Family and Conciliation Courts Review, 38*(3), 392–414.

Gould, J. W., & Stahl, P. M. (2001). Never paint by the numbers: A response to Kelly & Lamb (2000), Solomon (2001), and Lamb & Kelly (2001). *Family Court Review, 39*(4), 372–376.

Gralinski, J. H., & Kopp, C. B. (1993). Everyday rules for behavior: Mothers' requests to young children. *Developmental Psychology, 29*, 573–584.

Graziano, A. M., Hamblen, J. L., & Plante, W. A. (1998). Subabusive violence in child rearing in middle-class American families. *Pediatrics, 98*(4), 845–888.

Greenberg, L. R., & Gould, J. W. (2001). Merging paradigms: Clinical treatment in a forensic context. *Professional Psychology: Research and Practice, 32*(5), 469–478.

Greenberg, L. R., Gould, J. W., Gould-Saltman, D. J., & Stahl, P. M. (2001, Winter). Is the child's therapist part of the problem?: What attorneys, judges, and mental health professionals need to know about court-related treatment for children. *Association of Family and Conciliation Courts-California Newsletter*, pp. 6–7, 24–29.

Greenberg, L. R., Gould, J. W., Gould-Saltman, D. J., & Stahl, P. M. (2004). Is the child's therapist part of the problem? Retrieved from *www.abanet.org/genpractice/magazine/Sept2004/domestic.html*.

Greenberg, L. R., Martindale, D. A., Gould, J. W., & Gould-Saltman, D. J. (2004). Ethical issues in child custody and dependency cases: Enduring principles and emerging challenges. *Journal of Child Custody, 1*(1), 9–32.

Greenberg, S. A., & Shuman, D. W. (1997). Irreconcilable conflict between therapeutic and forensic roles. *Professional Psychology: Research and Practice, 28*, 50–57.

Greenberg, S. A., & Shuman, D. W. (2007). When worlds collide: Therapeutic and forensic roles. *Professional Psychology: Research and Practice, 38*(2), 129–133.

Greene, S. M., Anderson, E., Hetherington, E. M., Forgatch, M. S., & DeGarmo, D. S. (2003). Risk and resilience after divorce. In F. Walsh (Ed.), *Normal family processes: Growing diversity and complexity* (3rd ed., pp. 96–120). New York: Guilford Press.

Greeno, C. G. (2001). Introduction to the technical series: What is science, and how does it help us? *Family Process, 40*(1), 115–120.

Greenwald, A. G., & Pratkanis, A. R. (1988). On the use of "theory" and the usefulness of theory. *Psychological Review, 95*(4), 575–579.

Greenwald, A. G., Pratkanis, A. R., Leippe, M. R., & Baumgardner, M. H. (1986). Under what circumstances does theory obstruct research progress? *Psychological Review, 93*, 216–229.

Griggs et al. v. Duke Power Company, 401 U.S. 424 (1971)

Grisso, T. (1986). *Evaluating competencies: Forensic assessment and instruments*. New York: Plenum Press.

Grisso, T. (1988). *Competency to stand trial evaluations: A manual for practice*. Sarasota, FL: Professional Resource Exchange.

Grisso, T. (1990). Evolving guidelines for divorce/custody evaluations. *Family and Conciliation Courts Review, 28*(1), 35–41.

Grisso, T. (2003). *Evaluating competencies: Forensic assessments and instruments* (2nd ed.). New York: Plenum Press.

Griswold v. Connecticut, 381 U.S. 479, 495 (1965).

Grusec, J. E., & Lytton, H. (1988). *Social development: History, theory, and research*. New York: Springer-Verlag.

Guggenheim, M. (2005). *What's wrong with children's rights*. Cambridge, MA: Harvard University Press.

Guidubaldi, J., & Cleminshaw, H. K. (1994). *Parenting Satisfaction Scale*. Odessa, FL: Psychological Assessment Resource.

Hagin, R. A. (1998). Review of the Children's Personality Questionnaire. In J. C. Impara & B. S. Plake (Eds.), *The thirteenth mental measurements yearbook*. Lincoln, NE: Buros Institute of Mental Measurements.

Hamberger, L. K., Lohr, J. M., Bonge, D., & Tolin, D. F. (1996). A large-sample empirical typology of male spouse abusers and its relationship to dimensions of abuse. *Violence and Victims, 11*, 277–292.

Hamby, S. L. (1996). The Dominance Scale: Preliminary psychometric properties. *Violence and Victims, 11*, 199–212.

Hammer, E. F. (1997). Editor's comment. In E. F. Hammer (Ed.), *Advances in projective drawing interpretation* (p. 377). Springfield, IL: Charles C Thomas.

Hans, S. L., Bernstein, J., & Henson, L. G. (1999). The role of psychopathology in the parenting of drug-dependent women. *Development and Psychopathology, 11*, 957–977.

Hansen, M., & Harway, M. (1993). *Battering and family therapy*. Thousand Oaks, CA: Sage.

Hanson, R. K., & Thornton, D. (1999). *Static 99: Improving actuarial risk assessments for sex offenders*. Ottawa, Ontario: Public Works and Government Services Canada.

Hardy, D. F., Power, T. G., & Jaedicke, S. (1993). Examining the relation of parenting to children's coping with everyday stress. *Child Development, 64*, 1829–1841.

Harrington, D., Dubowitz, H., Black, M., & Binder, A. (1995). Maternal substance use and neglectful parenting: Relations with children's development. *Journal of Clinical Psychology, 24*(3), 258–263.

Harrison, P. A., Hoffman, N. G., & Edwall, G. E. (1989). Sexual abuse correlates: Similarities between male and female adolescents in chemical dependency treatment. *Journal of Adolescent Research, 4*, 385–399.

Hart, C. H., Nelson, D. A., Robinson, C. C., Olsen, S. F., & McNeilly-Choque, M. K. (1998). Overt and relational aggression in Russian nursery-school-age children: Parenting style and marital linkages. *Developmental Psychology, 34,* 687–697.

Harter, S. (1982). The perceived competence scale for children. *Child Development, 53,* 87–97.

Hartup, W. W. (1996). The company they keep: Friendships and their developmental significance. *Child Development, 67,* 1–13.

Haugaard, J. J. (2000). The challenge of defining child sexual abuse. *American Psychologist, 55*(9), 1036–1039.

Haugaard, J. J., & Tilly, C. (1988). Characteristics predicting children's responses to sexual encounters with other children. *Child Abuse and Neglect, 12,* 209–218.

Haverkamp, B. E. (1993). Confirmatory bias in hypothesis testing for client-identified and counselor self-generated hypotheses. *Journal of Counseling Psychology, 40*(3), 303–315.

Havighurst, R. J. (1972). *Developmental tasks and education* (3rd ed.). New York: Longman.

Heilbrun, K. (1992). The role of psychological testing in forensic assessment. *Law and Human Behavior. 16*(3), 257.

Heilbrun, K. (1995). Child custody evaluations: Critically assessing mental health experts and psychological tests. *Family Law Quarterly, 29*(1), 63–78.

Heilbrun, K. (2001). *Principles of forensic mental health assessment* (Perspectives in Law and Psychology, Vol. 12). New York: Kluwer/Plenum.

Heilbrun, K., Warren, J., & Picarello, K. (2003). Third-party information in forensic assessment. In A. M. Goldstein (Ed.), *Handbook of psychology: Vol. 11. Forensic psychology* (pp. 69–86). New York: Wiley.

Heiman, M. L., Leiblum, S., Esquilin, S. C., & Pallitto, L. M. (1998). A comparative survey of beliefs about "normal" childhood sexual behavior. *Child Abuse and Neglect, 22*(4), 289–299.

Heltzel, T. (2007). Compatibility of therapeutic and forensic roles. *Professional Psychology: Research and Practice, 38*(2), 122–128.

Henderson, V. L., & Dweck, C. S. (1990). Motivation and achievement. In S. S. Feldman & G. R. Elliott (Eds.), *At the threshold: The developing adolescent* (pp. 308–329). Cambridge, MA: Harvard University Press.

Henneberg, M. (2000, August). *Bureau of Justice statistics, 2000: At a glance* (Pub. #NCJ183014). Washington, DC: Department of Justice.

Herbert, T. B., & Cohen, S. (1993). Stress and immunity in humans: A meta-analytic review. *Psychosomatic Medicine, 55,* 364–379.

Herrenkohl, R. C., Herrenkohl, E. C., & Egolf, B. P. (1983). Circumstances surrounding the occurrence of child maltreatment. *Journal of Clinical and Consulting Psychology, 51*(3), 424–431.

Herrera, C., & Dunn, J. (1997). Early experiences with family conflict: Implications for arguments with a close friend. *Developmental Psychology, 33,* 869–881.

Hershkowitz, I., Orbach, Y., Lamb, M. E., Sternberg, K. J., & Horowitz, D. (2002). A comparison of mental and physical context reinstatement in forensic interviews with alleged vicitms of sexual abuse. *Applied Cognitive Psychology, 16*(4), 429–441.

Hess, A. K. (2001. Review of the Conners' Rating Scales–Revised. In B. S. Plake & J. C. Impara (Eds.), *The fourteenth mental measurements yearbook*. Lincoln, NE: Buros Institute of Mental Measurements.

Hesse, E., & Main, M. (1999). Second-generation effects of unresolved trauma in nonmaltreating parents: Dissociated, frightened, and threatening parental behavior. *Psychoanalytic Inquiry, 19*(4), 481–540.

Hesse, E., & Main, M. (2000). Disorganized infant, child, and adult attachment: Collapse in behavioral and attentional strategies. *Journal of the American Psychoanalytic Association, 48*(4), 1097–1127.

Hesse, E., Main, M., Abrams, K., & Rifkin, A. (2003). Unresolved states regarding loss or abuse can have "second generation" effects: Disorganization, role inversion, and frightening ideation in the offspring of traumatized, non-maltreating parents. In M. F. Solomon & D. Siegel (Eds.), *Healing trauma: Attachment, mind, body, and brain* (pp. 57–106). New York: Norton.

Hetherington. E. M. (1999). Should we stay together for the sake of the children? In E. M. Hetherington (Ed.), *Coping with divorce, single parenting, and remarriage* (pp. 93–116). Mahwah, NJ: Erlbaum.

Hewitt, S. K. (1999). *Assessing allegations of sexual abuse in preschool children: Understanding small voices*. Thousand Oaks, CA: Sage.

Hiler, E., & Nesvig, D. (1965). An evaluation of criteria used by clinicians to infer pathology from figure drawings. *Journal of Consulting Psychology, 29*, 520–529.

Hines, D. A., & Malley-Morrison, K. (2001). Psychological effects of partner abuse against men: A neglected research area. *Psychology of Men and Masculinity, 2*, 75–85.

Hjelt, S. (2000). Professional psychology: A view from the bench. *Register Report, 26*(1), 8–13.

Hodges, W. (1991). *Interventions for children of divorce: Custody, access, and psychotherapy* (2nd ed.). New York: Wiley

Hoffman, Y., & Drotar, D. (1991). The impact of postpartum depressed mood on mother–infant interaction: Like mother like baby? *Infant Mental Health Journal, 12*, 65–80.

Hogarth, R. M. (1981). Beyond discrete biases: Functional and dysfunctional aspects of judgmental heuristics. *Psychological Bulletin, 90*, 197–217.

Holden, G. W. (1983). Avoiding conflict: Mothers as tacticians in the supermarket. *Child Development, 54*, 233–240.

Holtzworth-Munroe, A., & Stuart, G. L. (1994). Typology of male batterers: Three subtypes and the differences among them. *Psychological Bulletin, 116*(3), 476–497.

Horvath, L. S., Logan, T. K., & Walker, R. (2002). Child custody cases: A content analysis of evaluations in practice. *Professional Psychology: Research and Practice, 33*(6), 557–565.

House, J. S., Umberson, D., & Landis, K. R. (1988). Structures and processes of social support. *American Review of Sociology, 14*, 293–318.

Householder, J., Hatcher, R., Burns, W., & Chasnoff, I. (1982). Infants born to narcotic addicted mothers. *Psychological Bulletin, 92*, 453–468.

Houston, B. K., & Vavak, C. R. (1991). Cynical hostility: Developmental factors, psychological correlates, and health behaviors. *Health Psychology, 10*, 9–17.

Hubbard, J. A., & Cole, J. D. (1994). Emotional correlates of social competence in children's peer relationships. *Merrill–Palmer Quarterly, 40*, 1–20.

Hudson, W. W., & McIntosh, S. (1981). The index of spouse abuse. *Journal of Marriage and the Family, 43*, 873–888.

Huffman, M. L., Warren, A. R., & Larson, S. M. (1999). Discussing truth and lies in interviews with children: Whether, why, and how? *Applied Developmental Science, 3*, 6–15.

Hunt, M. (1999). *The new know-nothings: The political foes of the scientific study of human nature*. New Brunswick, NJ: Transaction.

Hyman, I. A. (1996). Using research to change public policy: Reflections on 20 years of effort to eliminate corporal punishment in schools. *Pediatrics, 98*(4), 818–821.

Hymel, S., Rubin, K. H., Rowden, L., & Le Mare, L. (1990). Children's peer relationships: Longitudinal prediction of internalizing and externalizing problems from middle to late childhood. *Child Development, 61*, 2004–2021.

Hynan, D. J. (2002). Child health and safety factors in custody evaluations. *Journal of Forensic Psychology Practice, 2*, 73–80.

Idaho v. Wright, 497 U.S. 805 (1990).

Imwinkelried, E. W. (1992). *The methods of attacking scientific evidence* (2nd ed.). Charlottesville, VA: Michie.

In re Marriage of Seagondollar, 2006 Cal. App. LEXIS 779 (May 25, 2006).

Jacobson, N. S., & Gottman, J. (1998). *When men batter women: New insights into ending abusive relationships*. New York: Simon & Schuster.

Jacobvitz, D., & Sroufe, L. A. (1987). The early caregiver–child relationship and attention-deficit disorder with hyperactivity in kindergarten: A prospective study. *Child Development, 58*, 1488–1495.

Jaffe, P. G., Crooks, C. V., & Poisson, S. E. (2003). Common misconceptions in addressing domestic violence in child custody disputes. *Juvenile and Family Court Journal, 54*(4), 57–68.

Jaffe, P. G., Lemon, N. K. D., & Poisson, S. E. (2003). *Child custody and domestic violence: A call for safety and accountability*. Thousand Oaks, CA: Sage.

Jameson, B., Ehrenberg, M. F., & Hunter, M. A. (1997). Psychologists' understanding of the Best Interests of the Child Criterion in custody and access disputes. *Professional Psychology: Research and Practice, 28*(3), 253–262.

Jellinek, M. S., Murphy, J. M., Poitrast, F., Quinn, D., Bishop, S. J., & Goshko, M. (1992). Serious child mistreatment in Massachusetts: The course of 206 children through the courts. *Child Abuse and Neglect, 16*, 179–185.

Jemmott, L. S., & Jemmott III, J. B. (1992). Family structure, parental strictness, and sexual behavior among inner-city black male adolescents. *Journal of Adolescent Research, 7*, 192–207.

Jennings, S. (2005). Autism in children and parents: Unique considerations for family court professionals. *Family Court Review, 43*(4), 582–595.

Jenkins v. U.S., 307 F.2d. 637 (1962).

Jersild, A. T., Woodyard, E. S., & Del Solar, F. C. (1949). *Toys and problems of child rearing*. New York: Bureau of Publication, Teacher College, Columbia University.

Johnson, C. N., & Kenrick, K. (1984). Body partomony: How children partition the human body. *Developmental Psychology, 20*(5), 967–974.

Johnson, M. P. (2005). Apples and oranges in child custody disputes: Intimate terrorism vs. situational couple violence. *Journal of Child Custody, 2*(4), 43–52.

Johnson, T. C. (1999). *Understanding your child's sexual behavior: What's natural and healthy*. Oakland, CA: New Harbinger Publications.

Johnson, V., & Pandina, R. J. (1991). Effects of family environment on adolescent substance use, delinquency, and coping styles. *American Journal of Drug and Alcohol Abuse, 17*, 71–88.

Johnston, J. R. (2003). Parental alignments and rejection: An empirical study of alienation in children of divorce. *Journal of the American Academy of Psychiatry and the Law, 31*(2), 158–170.

Johnston, J. R., & Campbell, L. E. G. (1988). *Impasses of divorce: The dynamics and resolution of family conflict*. New York: Free Press.

Johnston, J. R., & Campbell, L. E. G. (1993). A clinical typology of interparental violence in disputed custody divorces. *American Journal of Orthopsychiatry, 63*(2), 190–199.

Johnston, J. R., & Roseby, V. (1997). *In the name of the child: A developmental approach to understanding and helping children of conflicted and violent divorce*. New York: Free Press.

Jones, E. L. (2001). Review of the Stress Index for Parents of Adolsecents. In B. S. Plake & J. C. Impara (Eds.), *The fourteenth mental measurements yearbook*. Lincoln, NE: Buros Institute of Mental Measurements.

Jorgensen, R. S., Johnson, B. T., Kolodziej, M. E., & Schreer, G. E. (1996). Elevated blood pressure and personality: A meta-analytic review. *Psychological Bulletin, 120*, 293–320.

Jory, B. (2004). The Intimate Justice Scale: An instrument to screen for psychological abuse and physical violence in clinical practice. *Journal of Marital and Family Therapy, 30*(1), 29–44.

Jouriles, E. N., McDonald, R., Norwood, W. D., & Ezell, E. (2001). Issues and controversies in documenting the prevalence of children's exposure to domestic violence. In S. A. Graham-Bermann & J. L. Edleson (Eds.), *Domestic violence in the lives of children: The future of research, intervention, and social policy* (pp. 12–34). Washington, DC: American Psychological Association.

Jouriles, E. N., Norwood, W. D., McDonald, R., & Peters, B. (2001). Domestic violence and child adjustment. In J. Grych & F. Fincham (Eds.), *Interparental conflict and child development: Theory, research, and applications* (pp. 315–336). Cambridge, UK: Cambridge University Press.

Julkunen, J., Salonen, R., Kaplan, G. A., Chesney, M. A., & Salonen, J. T. (1994). Hostility and the progression of carotid artherosclerosis. *Psychosomatic Medicine, 56*, 519–525.

Kagan, J. (1984). *The nature of the child*. New York: Basic Books.

Kandel, D., & Yamaguchi, K. (1993). From beer to crack: Developmental patterns of drug involvement. *American Journal of Public Health, 83*, 851–855.

Kanfer, F. H. (1990). The scientist-practitioner connection: A bridge in need of constant attention. *Professional Psychology—Research and Practice, 21*(4) 264–270.

Kaplan-Sanoff, M., & Fitzgerald Rice, K. (1992). Working with addicted women in recovery and their children: Lessons learned in Boston City Hospital's Women and Infants Clinic. *Zero to Three, 13*, 17–22.

Kashani, J. H., & Allan, W. D. (1998). *The impact of family violence on children and adolescents*. Thousand Oaks, CA: Sage.

Kaslow, M. H., Deering, C. G., & Racusia, G. R. (1994). Depressed children and their families. *Clinical Psychological Review, 14*, 39–59.

Katz, I. S. (2001). Review of the Parenting Satisfaction Scale. In B. S. Plake & J. C. Impara (Eds.), *The fourteenth mental measurements yearbook*. Lincoln, NE: Buros Institute of Mental Measurements.

Katz, L. F., & Gottman, J. M. (1995). Vagal tone protects children from marital conflict. *Development and Psychopathology, 7*, 83–92.

Katz, S. M., Schonfeld, D. J., Carter, A. S., Leventhal, J. M., & Cicchetti, D. V. (1995). The accuracy of children's reports with anatomically correct dolls. *Journal of Developmental and Behavioral Pediatrics, 16,* 71–76.

Keith-Spiegel, P., & Koocher, G. P. (1985). *Ethics in psychology: Professional standards and cases.* Hillsdale, NJ: Erlbaum.

Kelley, H. H., & Thibaut, J. (1978). *Interpersonal relations: A theory of interdependence.* New York: Wiley.

Kelley, M. L. (2003). Review of the Aggression Questionnaire. In B. S. Plake, J. C. Impara, & R. A. Spies (Eds.), *The fifteenth mental measurements yearbook.* Lincoln, NE: Buros Institute of Mental Measurements.

Kelly, J. B. (1993). Current research on children's postdivorce adjustment: No simple answers. *Family and Conciliation Court Reviews, 31*(1), 29–49.

Kelly, J. B. (1994). The determination of child custody. *Children and Divorce, 4*(1), 121–142.

Kelly, J. B., & Emery, R. E. (2003). Children's adjustment following divorce: Risk and resilience perspectives. *Family Relations, 52,* 352–362.

Kelly, J. B., & Johnston, J. R. (2001). The alienated child: A reformulation of parental alienation syndrome. *Family Court Review, 39*(3), 249–266.

Kelly, J. B., & Lamb, M. E. (2000). Using child development research to make appropriate custody and access decisions for young children. *Family and Conciliation Courts Review, 38*(3), 297–311.

Kelly, J. B., & Lamb, M. E. (2003). Developmental issues in relocation cases involving young children: When, whether, and how? *Journal of Family Psychology, 17,* 193–205.

Kempe, C. H., Silverman, F., Steele, B., Droegemueller, W., & Silver, H. (1962). The battered child syndrome. *Journal of the American Medical Association, 181,* 17–24.

Ken, B., & Vacc, N. A. (2003). Review of the Substance Abuse Subtle Screening Inventory–3rd edition. In B. S. Plake, J. C. Impara, & R. A. Spies (Eds.), *The fifteenth mental measurements yearbook.* Lincoln, NE: Buros Institute of Mental Measurements.

Kerig, P. K., Fedorowicz, A. E., Brown, C. A., & Warren, M. (2000). Assessment and intervention for PTSD in children exposed to violence. *Journal of Aggression, Maltreatment and Trauma, 3,* 161–184.

Kerns, K. A., Klepac, L., & Cole, A. K. (1996). Peer relationships and preadolescents' perceptions of security in the child–mother relationship. *Developmental Psychology, 32,* 457–466.

Kessler, R. C., & Magee, W. J. (1994). Childhood family violence and adult recurrent depression. *Journal of Health and Social Behavior, 35,* 13–27.

Khaleque, A., & Rohner, R. P. (2002a). Reliability of measures assessing the pancultural association between perceived parental acceptance–rejection and psychological adjustment: A meta-analysis of cross-cultural and intracultural studies. *Journal of Cross-Cultural Psychology, 33,* 87–99.

Khaleque, A., & Rohner, R. P. (2002b). Perceived parental acceptance–rejection and psychological adjustment: A meta-analysis of cross-cultural and intracultural studies. *Journal of Marriage and Family, 64,* 54–64.

Kirkland, K. (2002). The epistemology of child custody evaluations. *Family Court Review, 40*(2), 185–189.

Kirkland, K., & Kirkland, K. L. (2001). Frequency of child custody evaluation complaints and related disciplinary action: A survey of the Association of State and Provincial Psychology Boards. *Professional Psychology: Research and Practice*, 32(2), 171–174.

Kirkpatrick, H. D. (1999). *Forensic assessment of child sex abuse allegations*. Workshops presented for the American Academy of Forensic Psychology, Toronto and Chicago.

Kirkpatrick, H. D. (2004). A floor, not a ceiling: Beyond guidelines—An argument for minimum standards of practice in conducting child custody and visitation evaluations. *Journal of Child Custody*, 1(1), 61–77.

Kitzman, K., Gaylord, N., Holt, A. R., & Kenny, E. D. (2003). Child witness to domestic violence: A meta-analytic review. *Journal of Consulting and Clinical Psychology*, 71(2). 339–352.

Klayman, J., & Ha, Y-W. (1987). Confirmation, disconfirmation, and information in hypothesis testing. *Psychological Review, 94*, 211–228.

Klecker, B. M. (2002). Review of the State–Trait Anger Expression Inventory—2. In B. S. Plake, J. C. Impara, & R. A. Spies (Eds.), *The fifteenth mental measurements yearbook*. Lincoln, NE: Buros Institute of Mental Measurements.

Kleinman, T. (2004). Child protection and child custody: Domestic violence, abuse, and other issues in child protection. *Journal of Child Custody*, 1(1), 115–126.

Klohnen, E. C., & Bera, S. (1998). Behavioral and experiential patterns of avoidantly and securely attached women across adulthood: A 31-year longitudinal perspective. *Journal of Personality and Social Psychology, 74*, 211–223.

Knapp, J. F. (1998). The impact of children witnessing violence. *Pediatric Clinics of North America, 45*, 355–364.

Knoff, H. M. (2001). Review of the Conners' Rating Scales–Revised. In B. S. Plake & J. C. Impara (Eds.). *The fourteenth mental measurements yearbook*. Lincoln, NE: Buros Institute of Mental Measurements.

Knoff, H. M., & Prout, H. T. (1985). The Kinetic Drawing System: A review and integration of the Kinetic Family and Kinetic School Drawing Techniques. *Psychology in the Schools, 22*, 50–59.

Kochanska, G. (1993). Toward a synthesis of parental socialization and child temperament in early development of conscience. *Child Development, 64*, 325–347.

Kochanska, G. (1997). Multiple pathways to conscience for children with different temperaments from toddlerhood to age 5. *Development Psychology, 33*, 228–240.

Kochanska, G., & Aksan, N. (1995). Mother–child mutually positive affect, the quality of child compliance to requests and prohibitions, and maternal control as correlates of early internalization. *Child Development, 66*, 236–254.

Koestner, R., Franz, C., & Weinberger, J. (1990). The family origins of empathic concern: A 26-year longitudinal study. *Journal of Personality and Social Psychology, 58*, 709–717.

Koocher, G. P. (1995). The commerce of professional psychology and the new ethics code. In D. N. Bersoff (Ed.), *Ethical conflicts in psychology* (2nd ed., pp. 479–481). Washington, DC: American Psychological Association.

Koocher, G. P., Goodman, G. S., White, C. S., Friedrich, W. N., Sivan, A. B., & Reynolds, C. R. (1995). Psychological science and the use of anatomically detailed dolls in child sexual-abuse assessments. *Psychological Bulletin, 118*, 199–222.

Kopetski, L. M. (1998). Identifying cases of parental alienation syndrome, part II. *The Colorado Lawyer*. Retrieved from *www.fact.on.ca/Info/pas/kopet98b.htm*.

Kopetski, L. M., Rand, D. R., & Rand, R. (2006). Incidence, gender, and false allegations of child abuse: Data on 84 parental alienation syndrome cases. In R. A. Gardner, R. Sauber, & D. Lorandos (Eds.), *The international handbook of parental alienation syndrome: Conceptual, clinical and legal considerations*. Springfield, IL: Charles C Thomas.

Kopp, C. B. (1989). Regulation of distress and negative emotions: A developmental view. *Developmental Psychology, 25*, 343–354.

Koriat, A., Lichtenstein, S., & Fischhoff, B. (1980). Reasons for confidence. *Journal of Experimental Psychology: Human Learning and Memory, 6*, 107–118.

Krackow, E., & Lynn, S. J. (2003). Is there touch in the game of Twister? The effects of innocuous touch and suggestive questions on children's eyewitness memory. *Law and Human Behavior, 27*(6), 589–604.

Krantz, D. S., & Manuck, S. B. (1984). Acute psychophysiologic reactivity and risk of cardiovascular disease: A review and methodologic critique. *Psychological Bulletin, 96*, 435–464.

Kraus, M. B. (2005). Planning is important even when life doesn't go the way we plan. *Family Court Review, 43*(4), 607–611.

Krauss, D. A., & Sales, B. D. (1999). The problem of helpfulness in applying *Daubert* to expert testimony: Child custody determination in family law as an exemplar. *Psychology, Public Policy, and Law, 5*(1), 78–99.

Krauss, D. A., & Sales, B. D. (2000). Legal standards, expertise, and experts in the resolution of contested child custody cases. *Psychology, Public Policy, and Law, 6*(4), 843–879.

Krevans, J., & Gibbs, J. C. (1996). Parents' use of inductive discipline: Relations to children's empathy and prosocial behavior. *Child Development, 67*, 3263–3277.

Krishnakumar, A., Buehler, C., & Barber, B. K. (2003). Youth perceptions of interparental conflict, ineffective parenting, and youth problem behaviors in European American and African American families. *Journal of Social and Personal Relationships, 20*, 239–260.

Krishnamurthy, R. (2001). Review of the Personality Inventory for Children–2nd Edition. In B. S. Plake & J. C. Impara (Eds.), *The fourteenth mental measurements yearbook*. Lincoln, NE: Buros Institute of Mental Measurements.

Kropp, P. R., & Hart, S. D. (1997). Assessing risk of violence in wife assaulters: The Spousal Assault Risk Assessment Guide. In C. D. Webster & M. A. Jackson (Eds.), *Impulsivity: Theory, assessment, and treatment* (pp. 302–325). New York: Guilford Press.

Kropp, P. R., & Hart, S. D. (2000). The Spousal Assault Risk Assessment (SARA) Guide: Reliability and validity in adult male offenders. *Law and Human Behavior, 24*, 101–118.

Kubzansky, L. D., Kawachi, I., Weiss, S. T., & Sparrow, D. (1998). Anxiety and coronary heart disease: A synthesis of epidemiological, psychological, and experimental evidence. *Annals of Behavioral Medicine, 20*, 47–58.

Kuehnle, K. (1996). *Assessing allegations of child sexual abuse*. Sarasota, FL: Professional Resource Press.

Kuehnle, K. (1998a). Child sexual abuse evaluations: The scientist–practitioner model. *Behavioral Sciences and the Law, 16*(1), 5–20.

Kuehnle, K. (1998b). Ethics and the forensic expert: A case study of child custody involving allegations of child sexual abuse *Ethics and Behavior, 8*(1), 1–18.

Kuehnle, K. (2003). Child sexual abuse evaluations. In A. M. Goldstein (Ed.), *Forensic psychology* (pp. 437–460). New York: Wiley.

Kuehnle, K., Coulter, M., & Firestone, G. (2000). Child protection evaluations: The forensic stepchild. *Family and Conciliation Courts Review, 38*(3), 368–391.

Kuhn, T. S. (1962). *The structure of scientific revolutions*. Chicago: University of Chicago Press.

Kumho Tire Company Ltd. et al. v. Carmichael et al., 256 U.S. 137 (1999).

Kupersmidt, J. B., & Patterson, C. J. (1991). Childhood peer rejection, aggression, withdrawal, and perceived competence as predictors of self-reported behavior problems in preadolescence. *Journal of Abnormal Child Psychology, 19,* 427–503.

Lachar, D., & Gruber, C. P. (2001). *Personality Inventory for Children–2nd Edition.* Los Angeles: Western Psychological Services.

Ladd, G. W. (1990). Having friends, keeping friends, making friends, and being liked by peers in the classroom: Predictors of children's early school adjustment? *Child Development, 61,* 1081–1100.

Ladd, G. W., Kochenderfer, B. J., & Coleman, C. C. (1996). Friendship quality as a predictor of young children's early school adjustment. *Child Development, 67,* 1103–1118.

LaFortune, K. A., & Carpenter, B. N. (1998). Custody evaluations: A survey of mental health professionals. *Behavioral Sciences and the Law, 16,* 207–224.

Laible, D. J., & Thompson, R. A. (1998). Attachment and emotional understanding in preschool children. *Developmental Psychology, 34,* 1038–1045.

Laird, R. D., Pettit, G. S., Mize, J., Brown, E. G., & Lindsey, E. (1994). Mother–child conversations about peers contributions to competence. *Family Relations, 43,* 425–432.

Lally, S. J. (2001). Should human figure drawings be admitted into court? *Journal of Personality Assessment, 76*(1), 135–149.

Lamb, M. E. (1987). Predictive implications of individual differences in attachment. *Journal of Consulting and Clinical Psychology, 55,* 817–824.

Lamb, M. E. (1994). The investigation of child sexual abuse: An interdisciplinary consensus statement. *Journal of Child Sexual Abuse, 3,* 93–106.

Lamb, M. E. (1998). Fatherhood then and now. In A. Booth & A. C. Crouter (Eds.), *Men in families: When do they get involved? What difference does it make?* (pp. 47–52). Mahwah, NJ: Erlbaum.

Lamb, M. E. (2000). The history of research on father involvement: An overview. *Marriage and Family Review, 29*(2–3), 23–42.

Lamb, M. E. (2002). Placing children's interests first: Developmentally appropriate parenting plans. *Virginia Journal of Social Policy and the Law, 10*(1), 98–119.

Lamb, M. (Ed.). (2004). *The role of the father in child development* (4th ed.). New York: Wiley.

Lamb, M. E., & Fauchier, A. (2001). The effects of question type on self-contradictions by children in the course of forensic interviews. *Applied Cognitive Psychology, 15*(5), 483–491.

Lamb, M. E., & Kelly, J. B. (2001). Using empirical literature to guide the development of parenting plans for young children: A rejoinder to Solomon and Biringen. *Family Court Review, 39,* 365–371.

Lamb, M. E., & Oppenheim, D. (1989). Fatherhood and father–child relationships: Five years of research. In S. H. Cath & A. Gurwitt (Eds.), *Fathers and their families* (pp. 11–26). Hillsdale, NJ: Analytic Press.

Lamb, M. E., Orbach, Y., Sternberg, K. J., Hershkowitz, I., & Horowitz, D. (2000). Accuracy of investigators' verbatim notes of their forensic interviews with alleged child abuse victims. *Law and Human Behavior, 24*(6), 699–708.

Lamb, M. E., Sternberg, K. J., & Esplin, P. W. (2000). Effects of age and delay on the amount of information provided by alleged sex abuse victims in investigative interviews. *Child Development, 71*(6), 1586–1596.

Lamb, M. E., Sternberg, K. J., Orbach, Y., Esplin, P. W., & Mitchell, S. (2002). Is ongoing feedback necessary to maintain the quality of investigative interviews with allegedly abused children? *Applied Developmental Science, 6,* 35–41.

Lamb, S., & Coakley, M. (1993). "Normal" childhood sexual play and games: Differentiating play from abuse. *Child Abuse and Neglect, 17,* 515–526.

Lampel, A. K. (1996). Children's alignment with parents in highly conflicted custody cases. *Family and Conciliation Courts Review, 34*(2), 229–239.

Lampel, A. K. (2003). Assessing for alienation and access in child custody cases: A response to Lee and Olesen. *Family Court Review, 40*(2), 282–298.

Landry, S. H., Smith, K. E., Miller-Loncar, C. L., & Swank, P. R. (1998). The relation of change in maternal interactive styles to the developing social competence of full-term and preterm children. *Child Development, 69,* 105–123.

Langfeldt, T. (1981). Childhood masturbation: Individual and social organization. In L. L. Constantine & F. M. Martinson (Eds.), *Children and sex: New findings, new perspectives* (pp. 63–72). Boston: Little, Brown.

Lanyon, R. I. (2001). Psychological assessment procedures in sex offending. *Professional Psychology: Research and Practice, 32,* 253–260.

Larose, S., & Boivin, M. (1998). Attachment to parents, social support expectations, and socioemotional adjustment during the high school–college transition. *Journal of Research on Adolescence, 8,* 1–27.

Lavin, M., & Sales, B. D. (1998). Moral justifications for limits on expert testimony. In S. J. Ceci & H. Hembrooke (Eds.), *Expert witnesses in child abuse case: What can and should be said in court* (pp. 59–81). Washington, DC: American Psychological Association.

Leeper, R. W. (1935). A study of a neglected portion of the field of learning: The development of sensory organization. *Journal of Genetic Psychology, 46,* 41–75.

Leung, A. K. C., & Robson, W. L. M. (1993, April). Childhood masturbation. *Clinical Pediatrics, 32*(4), 238–241.

Lilienfeld, S. O. (2002). When worlds collide: Social science, politics, and the Rind et al. (1998) child sexual abuse meta-analysis. *American Psychologist, 57,* 176–188.

Lilienfeld, S. O., Wood, J. M., & Garb, H. N. (2000). The scientific status of projective techniques. *Psychological Science in the Public Interest, 1,* 27–66.

Lind, E. A., Kanfer, R., & Early, P. C. (1990). Voice, control, and procedural justice: Instrumental and noninstrumental concerns in fairness judgments. *Journal of Personality and Social Psychology, 59,* 952–959 .

Lindsey, E. W., Mize, J., & Pettit, G. S. (1997). Mutuality in parent–child play: Consequences for children's peer competence. *Journal of Social and Personal Relationships, 14,* 523–538.

Lissau, I., & Sorensen, T. I. A. (1994). Parental neglect during childhood and increased risk of obesity in young adulthood. *Lancet, 343,* 324–327.

Lockwood, R. L., Gaylord, N. K., Kitzmann, K. M., & Cohen, R. (2002). Family stress and children's rejection by peers: Do siblings provide a buffer? *Journal of Child and Family Studies, 11*(3), 331–345.

Loeber, R., & Stouthamer-Loeber, M. (1986). Family factors as correlates and predictors of juvenile conduct problems and delinquency. *Crime and Justice, 7,* 29–149.

Logan, T. K., Walker, R., Jordan, C. E., & Horvath, L. S. (2002). Child custody evaluations and domestic violence: Case comparisons. *Violence and Victims, 17*(6), 719–742.

London, K., & Nunez, N. (2002). Examining the efficacy of truth/lie discussions in predicting and increasing the veracity of children's reports. *Journal of Experimental Child Psychology, 83,* 131–147.

Lund, M. (1995). A therapist's view of parental alienation syndrome. *Family and Conciliation Courts Review, 33*(3), 308–316.

Lykken, D. T. (1998). The case for parental licensure. In T. Millon, E. Simonsen, M. Birket-Smith, & R. D. Davis (Eds.), *Psychopathy: Antisocial, criminal, and violent behavior* (pp. 122–143). New York: Guilford Press.

Lynam, D. R. (1996). Early identification of chronic offenders: Who is the fledgling psychopath? *Psychological Bulletin, 120,* 209–234.

Lyon, T. D. (1999). The new wave in children's suggestibility research: A critique. *Cornell Law Review, 84,* 1004–1105.

Lyon, T. D. (2001). Let's not exaggerate the suggestibility of children. *Court Review, 28*(3), 12–14.

Lyon, T. D. (2002). Scientific support for expert testimony on child sexual abuse accommodation. In J. R. Conte (Ed.), *Critical issues in child sexual abuse* (pp. 107–138). Newbury Park, CA: Sage.

Lyon, T. D., & Saywitz, K. J. (1999). Young maltreated children's competence to take the oath. *Applied Developmental Science, 3,* 16–27.

Lyons-Ruth, K. (1996). Attachment relationships among children with aggressive behavior problems: The role of disorganized early attachment patterns. *Journal of Consulting and Clinical Psychology, 64*(1), 64–74.

Lyons-Ruth, K., Zeanah, C. H., & Benoit, D. (2003). Disorder and risk for disorder during infancy and toddlerhood. In E. J. Mash & R. A. Barkley (Eds.), *Child psychopathology* (2nd ed., pp. 589–631). New York: Guilford Press.

Maccoby, E. (1980). *Social development: Psychological growth and the parent–child relationship.* New York: Harcourt.

Maccoby, E. E., & Martin, J. A. (1983). Socialization in the context of the family: Parent–child interaction. In P. H. Mussen & E. M. Hetherington (Eds.), *Handbook of child psychology: Vol. 4, Socialization, personality, and social development* (4th ed., pp. 1–101). New York: Wiley.

Maccoby, E. E., & Mnookin, R. H. (1992). *Dividing the child: Social and legal dilemmas of custody.* Cambridge, MA: Harvard University Press.

MacKinnon-Lewis, C., Starnes, R., Volling, B., & Johnson, S. (1997). Perceptions of parenting as predictors of boys' sibling and peer relations. *Developmental Psychology, 33,* 1024–1031.

Madden-Derdich, D. A., & Leonard, S. A. (2000). Parental role identity and fathers' involvement in coparental interaction after divorce: Fathers' perspectives. *Family Relations: Interdisciplinary Journal of Applied Family Studies, 49*(3), 311–318.

Mahoney, J. L., & Cairns, R. B. (1997). Do extracurricular activities protect against early school dropout? *Developmental Psychology, 33,* 241–253.

Mahoney, A., Donnelly, W. O., Boxer, P., & Lewis, T. (2003). Marital and severe parent-to-adolescent physical aggression in clinic-referred families: Mother and adolescent reports on co-occurrence and links to child behavior problems. *Journal of Family Psychology, 17,* 3–19.

Magdol, L., Moffitt, T. E., Caspi, A., Newman, D. L., Fagan, J., & Silva, P. A. (1997). Gender differences in partner violence in a birth cohort of 21-year-olds: Bridging the gap between clinical and epidemiological approaches. *Journal of Consulting and Clinical Psychology, 65*, 68–78.

Maguin, E., & Loeber, R. (1996). Academic performance and delinquency. In M. Tonry (Ed.), *Crime and justice: A review of research* (Vol. 20, pp. 145–264). Chicago: University of Chicago Press.

Mahoney, M. J. (1977). Publication prejudices: An experimental study of confirmatory bias in the peer review system. *Cognitive Therapy and Research, 1*, 161–175.

Main, M. (1996). Introduction to the special section on attachment and psychopathology: 2. Overview of the field of attachment. *Journal of Consulting and Clinical Psychology, 64*(2), 237–243.

Main, M., & Solomon, J. (1990). Procedures for identifying infants as disorganized/disoriented during the Ainsworth Strange Situation. In M. T. Greenberg, D. Cicchetti, & E. M. Cummings (Eds.), *Attachment in the preschool years* (pp. 121–160). Chicago: University of Chicago Press.

Maiuro, R. D. (2001). Sticks and stones may break my bones, but names will also hurt me: Psychological abuse in domestically violent relationships. In K. D. O'Leary & R. D. Maiuro (Eds.), *Psychological abuse in violent domestic relations* (pp. ix–xx). New York: Springer.

Malinosky-Rummell, R., & Hansen, D. J. (1993). Long-term consequences of childhood physical abuse. *Psychological Bulletin, 114*, 68–79.

Marchant, G. J., & Paulson, S. E. (1998). Review of the Parent–Child Relationship Inventory. In J. C. Impara & B. S. Plake (Eds.), *The thirteenth mental measurements yearbook*. Lincoln, NE: Buros Institute of Mental Measurements.

Margolin, G., & Gordis, E. B. (2003). Co-occurrence between marital aggression and parents' child abuse potential: The impact of cumulative stress. *Violence and Victims, 18*(3), 243–258.

Margolin, G., John, R. S., & Gleberman, L. (1988). Affective responses to conflictual discussions in violent and nonviolent couples. *Journal of Consulting and Clinical Psychology, 56*, 24–33.

Marjoribanks, K. (1987). Ability and attitude correlates of academic achievement: Family group differences. *Journal of Educational Psychology, 79*, 171–178.

Marsiglio, W., Amato, P., Day, R. D., & Lamb, M. E. (2000). Scholarship on fatherhood in the 1990s and beyond. *Journal of Marriage and the Family, 62*(4), 1173–1191.

Martin, L. R., Friedman, H. S., Tucker, J. S., Schwartz, J. E., Criqui, M. H., Wingard, D. L., et al. (1995). An archival prospective study of mental health and longevity. *Health Psychology, 14*, 381–387.

Martin, M. T., Miller-Johnson, S., Kitzmann, K. M., & Emery, R. E. (1998). Parent–child relationships and insulin-dependent diabetes mellitus: Observational ratings of clinically relevant dimensions. *Journal of Family Psychology, 12*, 102–111.

Martin, S. G. (2001). The structured clinical interview for DSM-IV Axis II personality disorders. In B. S. Plake & J. C. Impara (Eds.), *The fourteenth mental measurements yearbook*. Lincoln, NE: Buros Institute of Mental Measurements.

Martindale, D. A. (2001a). Cross-examining mental health experts in child custody litigation. *Journal of Psychiatry and Law, 29*(4), 483–511.

Martindale, D. A. (2001b). On the importance of suggestibility research in assessing the credibility of children's testimony. *Court Review, 38*(3), 8–10.

Martindale, D. A. (2004). Integrity and transparency: A commentary on record keeping in child custody evaluations. *Journal of Child Custody, 1*(1), 33–42.

Martindale, D. A. (2005a). Confirmatory bias and confirmatory distortion. *Journal of Child Custody, 2*(1/2), 31–48.

Martindale, D. A. (2005b). Psychological assessment: Evaluating the evaluations. *The Matrimonial Strategist, 22*(12), 3–5.

Martindale, D. A. (2006). Play therapy doesn't play in court. *Journal of Child Custody, 3*(1), 77–86.

Martindale, D. A. (2007). Reporter's forward to the Association of Family and Conciliation Court's *Model Standards of Practice for Child Custody Evaluation. Family Court Review, 45*(1), 61–69.

Martindale, D. A., & Gould, J. W. (2004). The forensic model: Ethics and scientific methodology applied to child custody evaluations. *Journal of Child Custody 1*(2), 1–22.

Martindale, D. A., & Gould, J. W. (2005). A second call for clinical humility and judicial vigilance: Comments on Tippins and Wittman (2005). *Family Court Review, 43*(2), 253–259.

Martindale, D. A., & Gould, J. W. (2006). Evaluating the evaluators in custodial placement disputes. In H. Hall (Ed.), *Forensic psychology and neuropsychology for criminal and civil cases.* Boca Raton, FL: CRC Press.

Marxsen, D., Yuille, J. C., & Nisbet, M. (1995). The complexities of eliciting and assessing children's statements. *Psychology, Public Policy, and Law, 1*, 450–460.

Mash, E. J., & Barkley, R. A. (Eds.). (2003). *Child psychopathology* (2nd ed.). New York: Guilford Press.

Mason, M. A. (1998). Expert testimony regarding the characteristics of sexually abused children: A controversy on both sides of the bench. In S. J. Ceci & H. Hembrooke (Eds.), *Expert witnesses in child abuse case: What can and should be said in court* (pp. 217–234). Washington, DC: American Psychological Association.

Masten, A. S. (1994). Resilience in individual development: Successful adaptation despite risk and adversity. In M. Wang & E. Gordon (Eds.), *Risk and resilience in inner city America: Challenges and prospects* (pp. 3–25). Hillsdale, NJ: Erlbaum.

Masten, A. S., Best, K. M., & Garmezy, N. (1990). Resilience and development: Contributions from the study of children who overcome adversity. *Development and Psychopathology, 2*, 425–444.

Masten, A. S., & Coatsworth, J. D. (1995). Competence, resilience, and psychopathology. In D. Cicchetti & D. Cohen (Eds.), *Developmental psychopathology: Vol. 2. Risk, disorder, and adaptation* (pp. 715–752). New York: Wiley.

Masten, A. S., & Coatsworth, J. D. (1998). The development of competence in favorable and unfavorable environments: Lessons from research on successful children. *American Psychologist, 53*(2), 205–220.

Masten, A. S., Coatsworth, J. D., Neemann, J., Gest, S. D., Tellegen, A., & Garmezy, N. (1995). The structure and coherence of competence from childhood through adolescence. *Child Development, 66*, 1635–1659.

Masten, A. S., Morison, P., & Pellegrini, D. S. (1985). A revised class play method of peer assessment. *Developmental Psychology, 21*, 523–533.

Masten, A. S., Morison, P., Pellegrini, D., & Tellegen, A. (1990). Competence under stress: Risk and protective factors. In J. Rolf, A. S. Masten, D. Cicchetti, K. Neuchterlein, & S. Weintraub (Eds.), *Risk and protective factors in the develop-*

ment of psychopathology (pp. 236–256). Cambridge, UK: Cambridge University Press.

Matthews, K. A., Woodall, K. L., Kenon, K., & Jacob, T. (1996). Negative family environment as a predictor of boys' future status on measures of hostile attitudes, interview behavior, and anger expression. *Health Psychology, 15,* 30–37.

May, V., & Smart, C. (2004). Silence in court?—Hearing children in residence and contact disputes. *Child and Family Law Quarterly, 16*(3), 305–316.

Mayes, L. (1995). Substance abuse and parenting. In M. H. Bornstein (Ed.), *The handbook of parenting* (Vol. 4, pp. 101–125). Hillsdale, NJ: Erlbaum.

Mayes, L., & Truman, S. D. (2002). Substance abuse and parenting. In M. H. Bornstein (Ed.), *The handbook of parenting* (2nd ed.): *Vol. 4. Social conditions and applied parenting* (pp. 329–360). Mahwah, NJ: Erlbaum.

Mayne, T. J., & Buck, R. W. (1997). Sex, emotion, and the triune brain. *The Health Psychologist, 19,* 8–23.

McAdoo, H. (2002). African American parenting. In M. H. Bornstein (Ed.), *Handbook of parenting* (2nd ed.): *Vol. 4. Social conditions and applied parenting* (pp. 47–58). Mahwah, NJ: Erlbaum.

McCurley, M. J., Murphy, K. J., & Gould, J. W. (2006). Protecting children from incompetent forensic evaluations and expert testimony. *Journal of the American Academy of Matrimonial Lawyers, 19*(2), 277–320.

McEwen, B. S. (1998). Protective and damaging effects of stress mediators. *New England Journal of Medicine, 338,* 171–179.

McEwen, B. S., & Stellar, E. (1993). Stress and the individual: Mechanisms leading to disease. *Archives of Internal Medicine, 153,* 2093–2101.

McGough, L. S. (1995). For the record: Videotaping investigative interviews. *Psychology, Public Policy, and Law, 1*(2), 370–386.

McGuigan, W. M., Vuchinich, S., & Pratt, C. (2000). Domestic violence, parents' view of their newborn, and child abuse risk. *Journal of Family Psychology, 14*(4), 613–624.

McKay, M. M. (1994). The link between domestic violence and child abuse: Assessment and treatment considerations. *Child Welfare League of America, 73,* 29–39.

McKnight, T. (2001). Review of the Child Sexual Behavior Inventory. In B. S. Plake & J. C. Impara (Eds.), *The fourteenth mental measurements yearbook.* Lincoln, NE: Buros Institute of Mental Measurements.

McLanahan, S., & Sandfur, G. (1994). *Growing up with a single parent: What hurts, what helps?* Cambridge, MA: Harvard University Press.

McLeod, J. D., & Shanahan, M. J. (1996). Trajectories of poverty and children's mental health. *Journal of Health and Social Behavior, 37,* 207–220.

McLoyd, V. C. (1998). Socioeconomic disadvantage and child development. *American Psychologist, 53,* 185–204.

McNeal, R. B. (1995). Extracurricular activities and high school dropouts. *Sociology of Education, 68,* 62–81.

Mechanic, D., & Hansell, S. (1989). Divorce, family conflict, and adolescents' well-being. *Journal of Health and Social Behavior, 30,* 105–116.

Meier, J. (2003). Domestic violence, child custody, and child protection: Understanding judicial resistance and imagining the solutions. *American University's Journal of Gender, Social Policy, and the Law, 11,* 657–731.

Melton, G. B., & Limber, S. (1989). Psychologists' involvement in cases of child maltreatment: Limits of role and expertise. *American Psychologist, 44,* 1225–1233.

Melton, G. B., Petrila, J., Poythress, M. G., & Slobogin, C. (1987). *Psychological evaluations for the courts: A handbook for mental health professionals and lawyers*. New York: Guilford Press.

Melton, G. B., Petrila, J., Poythress, M. G., & Slobogin, C. (1997). *Psychological evaluations for the courts: A handbook for mental health professionals and lawyers* (2nd ed.). New York: Guilford Press.

Metzler, C. W., Noell, J., Biglan, A., Ary, D., & Smolkowski, K. (1994). The social context for risky sexual behavior among adolescents. *Journal of Behavioral Medicine, 17,* 419–438.

Michigan Child Custody Act, Act 91 of 1970.

Miller v. California, 413 U.S. 15 (1973).

Miller, G. A. (1997). *Substance Abuse Subtle Screening Inventory–3rd Edition (SASSI-3)*. New York: SASSI Institute.

Miller, K. S., Forehand, R., & Kotchick, B. A. (1999). Adolescent sexual behavior in two ethnic minority samples: The role of family variables. *Journal of Marriage and the Family, 61,* 85–98.

Miller, N. B., Cowan, P. A., Cowan, C. P., & Hetherington, E. M. (1993). Externalizing in preschoolers and early adolescents: A cross-study replication of a family model. *Developmental Psychology, 29*(1), 3–18.

Millon, T., Davis, R. D., & Millon, C. (1997). *MCMI-III manual* (2nd ed.). Minneapolis: NCS Pearson.

Millstein, S. G., & Moscicki, A.-B. (1995). Sexually transmitted disease in female adolescents: Effects of psychosocial factors and high risk behaviors. *Journal of Adolescent Health, 17,* 83–90.

Milne, R., & Bull, R. (1996). Interviewing children with mild learning disability with the cognitive interview. *Issues in Criminological and Legal Psychology, 26,* 44–51.

Milner, J. S. (1986). *The Child Abuse Potential Inventory manual* (2nd ed.). Webster, NC: Psytec Corporation.

Minton, C., Kagan, J., & Levine, J. A. (1971). Maternal control and obedience in the two-year-old. *Child Development, 42,* 1873–1894.

Mize, J., & Pettit, G. S. (1997). Mothers' social coaching, mother–child relationship style, and children's peer competence: Is the medium the message? *Child Development, 68,* 312–332.

Mnookin, R. (1975). Child custody adjudication and judicial function in the face of indeterminacy. *Law and Contemporary Problems, 39,* 226–293.

Mohr, J. W., Turner, R. E., & Jerry, M. B. (1964). *Pedophilia and aggression*. Toronto: University of Toronto Press.

Montgomery, S. M., Bartley, M. J., & Wilkinson, R. G. (1997). Family conflict and slow growth. *Archives of Disease in Childhood, 77,* 326–330.

Moreland, K. L. (1985). Validation of computer-based interpretations: Problems and prospects. *Journal of Consulting and Clinical Psychology, 53,* 816–825.

Morelli, G. A., Rogoff, B., Oppenheim, D., & Goldsmith, D. (1992). Cultural variation in infants' sleeping arrangements: Questions of independence. *Developmental Psychology, 28,* 604–613.

Moss, D. C. (1988). Abuse scale: Point system for abuse claims. *Journal of the American Bar Association, 74,* 26.

Mounts, N. S., & Steinberg, L. (1995). An ecological analysis of peer influence on adolescent grade point average and drug use. *Developmental Psychology, 31,* 915–922.

Muller, R. T. (1996). Family aggressiveness factors in the prediction of corporal punishment: Reciprocal effects and the impact of observer perspective. *Journal of Family Psychology, 10,* 474–489.

Murdoch, J. W. (2001). Review of the Michigan Alcohol Screening Test. In B. S. Plake & J. C. Impara (Eds.), *The fourteenth mental measurements yearbook.* Lincoln, NE.: Buros Institute of Mental Measurements.

Murphy, C. M., O'Farrell, T. J., Fals-Stewart, W., & Feehan, M. (2001). Correlates of intimate partner violence among male alcoholic patients. *Journal of Consulting and Clinical Psychology, 69*(3), 528–540.

Murray, H. A. (1943). *Thematic Apperception Test manual.* Odessa, FL: Psychological Assessment Resources.

Myers, B. (1992) Cocaine-exposed infants: Myths and misunderstandings. *Zero to Three, 13,* 1–5.

Myers, J. E. B. (1991). *Evidence in child abuse and neglect cases* (3rd ed.). New York: Aspen.

Myers, J. E. B. (1993). Expert testimony describing psychological syndromes. *Pacific Law Journal, 24,* 1449–1464.

Myers, J. E. B. (1994, July). *Child victim witness investigative pilot projects: Research and evaluation final report.* Sacramento, CA: California Department of Justice.

Myers, J. E. B. (1997). *A mother's nightmare—Incest: A practical legal guide for parents and professionals.* Thousand Oaks, CA: Sage.

Naglieri, J. A., McNeish, T. J., & Bardos, A. A. (1991). Performance of disruptive behavior disordered and normal samples on the Draw a Person Screening Procedure for Emotional Disturbance. *Psychological Assessment, 4,* 156–159.

Nathan, P. E. (2000). The Boulder model: A dream deferred—or lost? *American Psychologist, 55,* 250–251.

National Center for Injury Prevention and Control. (1985). *The co-occurrence of intimate partner violence against mothers and abuse of children.* Retrieved from *www.cdc.gov/ncipc/factsheets/dvcan.htm.*

National Council of Juvenile and Family Court Judges. (1999). *Effective intervention in domestic violence and child maltreatment cases: Guidelines for policy and practice.* Reno, NV: Author.

National Interdisciplinary Colloquium on Child Custody. (1998). *Legal and mental health perspectives on child custody law: A deskbook for judges.* Danvers, MA: Westgroup.

Nelson, C. A., & Bloom, F. E. (1997). Child development and neuroscience. *Child Development, 68,* 970–987.

Nettles, S. M. (1991). Community involvement and disadvantaged students: A review. *Review of Educational Research, 61*(3) 379–406.

Newcomb, A. F., Bukowski, W. M., & Bagwell, C. L. (1999). Knowing the sounds: Friendship as a developmental context. In W. A. Collins & B. Laursen (Eds.), *Relationships as developmental contexts: The Minnesota Symposia on Child Psychology* (Vol. 30, pp. 63–84). Mahwah, NJ: Erlbaum.

Newmark, L., Harrell, A., & Salem, P. (1995). Domestic violence and empowerment in custody and visitation cases. *Family and Conciliation Courts Review, 33*(1), 30–62.

Nichols, W. C. (1986). Sibling subsystem therapy in family system reorganization. *Journal of Divorce, 9*(3), 13–31.

Nims, J. (2000). *Nims Observation Checklist.* Los Angeles: Western Psychological Services.

Nolan, J. R., & Nolan-Haley, J. M. (1990). *Black's law dictionary* (6th ed.). St. Paul, MN: West.

Nord, C. W., Brimhall, D., & West, J. (1997). *Fathers' involvement in their children's schools.* Washington, DC: National Center for Education Statistics.

Northcraft, G. B., & Neale, M. A. (1987). Experts, amateurs, and real estate: An anchoring-and-adjustment perspective on property pricing decisions. *Organizational Behavior and Human Decision Processes, 39,* 84–97.

O'Brien, M., Margolin, G., John, R. S., & Krueger, L. (1991). Mothers' and sons' cognitive and emotional reactions to simulated marital and family conflict. *Journal of Consulting and Clinical Psychology, 59,* 692–703.

O'Donohue, W. (1989). The (even) bolder model: The clinical psychologist as metaphysician–scientist–practitioner. *American Psychologist, 44*(12), 1460–1468.

O'Donohue, W., & Bradley, A. R. (1999). Conceptual and empirical issues in child custody evaluations. *Clinical Psychology: Science and Practice, 6*(3), 310–322.

Okami, P., Olmstead, R., & Abramson, P. R. (1997). Sexual experiences in early childhood: 18-year longitudinal data from the UCLA family lifestyles project. *The Journal of Sex Research, 34*(4), 339–347.

O'Leary, K. D. (2000). Are women really more aggressive than men in intimate relationships? Comment on Archer (2000). *Psychological Bulletin, 126,* 685–689.

O'Leary, K. D., & Maiuro, R. D. (Eds.). (2001). *Psychological abuse in violent domestic relations.* New York: Springer.

Orbach, Y., Hershkowitz, I., Lamb, M. E., Sternberg, K. J., Esplin, P. W., & Horowitz, D. (2000). Assessing the value of structured protocols for forensic interviews of alleged child abuse victims. *Child Abuse and Neglect, 24*(6), 733–752.

Orbach, Y., Hershkowitz, I., Lamb, M. E., Sternberg, K. J., & Horowitz, D. (2000). Interviewing at the scene of the crime: Effects on children's recall of alleged abuse. *Legal and Criminological Psychology, 5*(Pt. 1), 135–147.

Orbach, Y., & Lamb, M. E. (2000). Enhancing children's narratives in investigative interviews. *Child Abuse and Neglect, 24*(12), 1631–1648.

Orbach, Y., & Lamb, M. E. (2001). The relationship between within-interview contradictions and eliciting interviewer utterances. *Child Abuse and Neglect, 25*(3), 323–333.

Orr v. Orr (No. 77–1119) 351 So.2d 904 (1979).

Otto, R. K. (1989). Bias and expert testimony of mental health professionals in adversarial proceedings: A preliminary investigation. *Behavioral Sciences and the Law, 7*(2), 267–274.

Otto, R. K., Buffington-Vollum, J. K., & Edens, J. F. (2003). Child custody evaluations. In A. M. Goldstein (Ed.), *Handbook of psychology,* Vol. 11. *Forensic psychology* (pp. 179–208). New York: Wiley.

Otto, R. K., & Butcher, J. N. (1995). Computer-assisted psychological assessment in child custody evaluations. *Family Law Quarterly, 29*(1), 79–96.

Otto, R. K., & Collins, R. P. (1995). Use of the MMPI-2/MMPI-A in child custody evaluations. In Y. S. Ben-Porath, J. R. Graham, G. C. N. Hall, R. D. Hirschman, & M. S. Zaragoza (Eds.), *Forensic applications of the MMPI-2.* New York: Sage.

Otto, R. K., & Edens. J. F. (2003). Parenting capacity. In T. Grisso (Ed.), *Evaluating competencies: Forensic assessments and instruments* (2nd ed., pp. 229–307). New York: Plenum Press.

Otto, R. K., Edens, J. F., & Barcus, E. H. (2000). The use of psychological testing in child custody evaluations. *Family and Conciliation Courts Review, 38*(3), 312–340.

Oyserman, D., Mowbray, C. T., Meares, P. A., & Firminger, K. B. (2000). Parenting among mothers with a serious mental illness. *American Journal of Orthopsychiatry, 70,* 296–315.

Palen, J. M. *Child custody evaluations: Uses and misuses.* Retrieved on September 25, 2002, from *www.illinoisbar.org/Sections.8uses.html.*

Parker, J. G., & Asher, S. R. (1987). Peer relations and later personal adjustment: Are low-accepted children at risk? *Psychological Bulletin, 102*(3), 357–389.

Parker, J. G., Rubin, K. H., Price, J. M., & DeRosier, M. E. (1995). Peer relationships, child development, and adjustment: A developmental psychopathology perspective. In D. Cicchetti & D. J. Cohen (Eds.), *Developmental psychopathology: Vol. 2. Risk, disorder, and adaptation* (pp. 96–161). New York: Wiley.

Patterson, G. R. (1982). *Coercive family process.* Eugene, OR: Castalia.

Patterson, G. R. (1986). Performance models for antisocial boys. *American Psychologist, 44,* 432–444.

Patterson, G. R., Reid, J. B., & Dishion, T. J. (1992). *A social learning approach: Vol. 4. Antisocial boys.* Eugene, OR: Castalia.

Pence, E., & Paymar, M. (1993). *Education groups for men who batter: The Duluth model.* New York: Springer.

Pennington, B. F., & Welsh, M. (1995). Neuropsychology and developmental psychopathology. In D. Cicchetti & D. J. Cohen (Eds.), *Developmental psychopathology: Vol. 2. Risk, disorder, and adaptation* (pp. 254–290). New York: Wiley.

Perozynski, L., & Kramer, L. (1999). Parental beliefs about managing siblings conflict. *Developmental Psychology, 35,* 489–499.

Perry, B. D., & Pollard, R. (1998). Homeostasis, stress, trauma, and adaptation. *Stress in Children, 7,* 33–51.

Perry, N. W., Claycomb, L., Tam, P. McAuliff, B., Dostal, C., & Flanagan, C. (1993). When lawyers question children: Is justice served? *Law and Human Behavior, 19,* 606–629.

Perryman, H. P. (2005). Parental reaction to the disabled child: Implications for family courts. *Family Court Review, 43*(4), 596–606.

Peters, W. W., & Nunez, N. (1999). Complex language and comprehension monitoring: Teaching child witnesses to recognize linguistic confusion. *Journal of Applied Psychology, 84,* 661–669.

Peterson, B. E., Smirles, K A., & Wentworth, P.A. (1997). Generativity and authoritarianism: Implications for personality, political involvement, and parenting. *Journal of Personality and Social Psychology, 72,* 1202–1212.

Peterson, C., & Grant, M. (2001). Forced-choice: Are forensic interviewers asking the right questions? *Canadian Journal of Behavioural Science, 33,* 118–127.

Peterson, C., Moores, L., & White, G. (2001). Recounting the same events again and again: Children's consistency across multiple interviews. *Applied Cognitive Psychology, 15,* 353–371.

Pettit, G. S., Dodge, K. A., & Brown, M. M. (1988). Early family experience, social problem-solving patterns, and children's social competence. *Child Development, 59,* 107–120.

Piaget, J. (1926). *The language and thought of the child.* New York: Harcourt.

Pierce v. Society of Sisters, 268 U.S. 510, 535 (1925).

Pittenger, D. J. (2003). Review of the Substance Abuse Subtle Screening Inventory–3rd Edition. In B. S. Plake, J. C. Impara, & R. A. Spies (Eds.), *The fifteenth mental measurements yearbook.* Lincoln, NE: Buros Institute of Mental Measurements.

Poe v. Ullman, 367 U.S. 497, 551–551 (1961) (Harlan, J. dissenting).

Poole, D. A., & Lamb, M. E. (1998). *Investigative interviews of children: A guide for helping professionals*. Washington, DC: American Psychological Association.

Poole, D. A., & Lindsay, D. S. (2002). Reducing child witnesses' false reports of misinformation from parents. *Journal of Experimental Child Psychology, 81*, 117–140.

Pope, K. S. (1996). Memory, abuse, and science: Questioning claims about the false memory syndrome epidemic. *American Psychologist, 51*(9), 957–974.

Pope, K. S., Butcher, J. N., & Seelen, J. (1993). *MMPI, MMPI-2 and MMPI-A in court: A practical guide for expert witnesses and attorneys*. Washington, DC: American Psychological Association.

Popper, K. (1972). *Objective knowledge*. New York: Oxford University Press.

Porath, M. (1996). Narrative performance in verbally gifted children. *Journal for the Education of the Gifted, 19*, 276–292.

Porter, R. B., & Cattell, R. B. (1975). *Children's Personality Questionnaire*. Champaign, IL: Institute for Personality and Ability Testing.

Powell, M. B., & Thomson, D. M. (1997). The effect of an intervening interview on children's ability to remember one occurrence of a repeated event. *Legal and Criminological Psychology, 2*, 247–262.

Power, T. J., & Chapieski, M. L. (1986). Childrearing and impulse control in toddlers: A naturalistic investigation. *Developmental Psychology, 22*, 271–275.

Power, C., & Hertzman, C. (1997). Social and biological pathways linking early life and adult disease. *British Medical Bulletin, 53*, 210–221.

Pratt, M. W., Hunsberger, B., Pancer, S. M., Roth, D., & Santolupo, S. (1993). Thinking about parenting: Stage and complexity of reasoning about developmental issues across the lifespan. *Developmental Psychology, 29*, 585–595.

Prince v. Massachusetts, 321 U.S. 158 (1944).

Pruett, K. D. (1987). *The nurturing father*. New York: Warner Books.

Pruett, M. K., Ebling, R., & Insabella, G. (2004). Critical aspects of parenting plans for young children: Interjecting data into the debate about overnights. *Family Court Review, 42*(1), 39–59.

Pulido, M. L., & Gupta, D. (2002). Protecting the child and the family: Integrating domestic violence screening into a child advocacy center. *Violence Against Women, 8*, 917–933.

Putallaz, M. (1987). Maternal behavior and children's sociometric status. *Child Development, 58*, 324–340.

Quincey, V. L., Harris, G. T., Rice, M. E., & Cormier, C. A. (1998). *Violent offenders: Appraising and managing risk*. Washington, DC: American Psychological Association.

Quincey, V. L., & Lalumiere, M. (2001). *Assessment of sexual offenders against children* (2nd ed.). Thousand Oaks, CA: Sage.

Rand, D. C. (1997a). The spectrum of parental alienation syndrome (Part I). *American Journal of Forensic Psychology, 15*(3), 23–52.

Rand, D. C. (1997b). The spectrum of parental alienation syndrome (Part II). *American Journal of Forensic Psychology, 15*(4), 39–92.

Reed v. Reed, 404 U.S. 71 (1971).

Reich, W. (1949). *Character Analysis* (3rd ed., trans. by Theodore P. Wolfe). New York: Orgone Institute Press.

Reid, J., Macchetto, P., & Foster, S. (1999). *No safe haven: Children of substance-abusing parents*. New York: Center on Addiction and Substance Abuse.

Rennison, C., & Welchans, S. (2000). *U. S. Department of Justice, Bureau of Justice Statistics, Intimate Partner Violence: A special report to the Office of Justice Programs*. Washington, DC: Department of Justice.

Repetti, R. L., Taylor, S. E., & Seeman, T. E. (2002). Risky families: Family social environments and the mental and physical health of offspring. *Psychological Bulletin, 128*(2), 330–366.

Repetti, R. L., & Wood, J. (1997a). Effects of daily stress at work on mothers' interactions with preschoolers. *Journal of Family Psychology, 11*(1), 90–108.

Repetti, R. L., & Wood, J. (1997b). Families accommodating to chronic stress: Unintended and unnoticed processes. In B. H. Gottlieb (Ed.), *Coping with chronic stress* (pp. 191–220). New York: Plenum Press.

Reppucci, N. D., & Haugaard, J. J. (1989). Prevention of child sexual abuse: Myth or reality. *American Psychologist, 44*, 1266–1275.

Reyna, V. F., Holliday, R., & Marche, T. (2002). Explaining the development of false memories. *Developmental Review, 22*, 436–489.

Reynolds, C. R., & Kamphaus, R. W. (1998). *Behavior Assessment System for Children– Revised*. Circle Pines, MN: American Guidance Services.

Reynolds, A. J., & Wahlberg, H. J. (1991). A structural model of science achievement. *Journal of Educational Psychology, 83*, 97–107.

Rice, M. E., & Harris, G. T. (1995). Violent recidivism: Assessing predictive validity. *Journal of Consulting and Clinical Psychology, 63*, 737–748.

Rice, M. E., & Harris, G. T. (1997). Cross-validation and extension of the Violence Risk Appraisal Guide for child molesters and rapists. *Law and Human Behavior, 21*, 231–241.

Riffe, G. H. (1993). Children's testimony in criminal physical and sexual abuse cases. *The Oklahoma Bar Journal, 64*(35), 2749–2760.

Rind, B., Tromovitch, P., & Bauserman, R. (1998). A meta-analytic examination of assumed properties of child sexual abuse using college samples. *Psychological Bulletin, 124*, 22–53.

Ritchie, K. L. (1999). Maternal behaviors and cognitions during discipline episodes: A comparison of power bouts and single acts of noncompliance. *Developmental Psychology, 35*, 580–589.

Roberts, G. E. (1982). *Roberts Apperception Test for Children*. Beverly Hills: Western Psychological Services.

Roberts, K. P. (2002). Children's ability to distinguish between memories from multiple sources: Implications for the quality and accuracy of eyewitness statements. *Developmental Review, 22*, 403–435.

Roberts, K. P., & Lamb, M. E. (1999). Children's responses when interviewers distort details during investigative interviews. *Legal and Criminological Psychology, 4*, 23–31.

Roberts, K. P., & Powell, M. B. (2001). Describing individual incidents of sexual abuse: A review of research on the effects of multiple sources of information on children's reports. *Child Abuse and Neglect, 25*, 1643–1659.

Rohman, L. W., Sales, B. D., & Lou, M. (1987). The best interests of the child in custody disputes. In L. A. Weithorn (Ed.), *Psychology and child custody determinations: Knowledge, roles, and expertise*. Lincoln: University of Nebraska Press.

Rohner, R. P. (1960). *Child acceptance-rejection and modal personality in three Pacific societies*. Unpublished master's thesis, Stanford University.

Rohner, R. P. (2000). *The warmth dimension: Foundations of parental acceptance-rejection theory*. Storrs, CT: Author.

Rohner, R. P., & Britner, P. A. (2002). Worldwide mental health correlates of parental acceptance-rejection: Review of cross-cultural and intracultural evidence. *Cross-Cultural Research: The Journal of Comparative Social Science, 36*, 15–47.

Rohner, R. P., & Khaleque, A. (2003). Reliability and validity of the parental control scale: A meta-analysis of cross-cultural and intracultural studies. *Journal of Cross-Cultural Psychology, 34*, 643–649.

Rohner, R. P., Saavedra, J. M., & Granum, E. O. (1978). Development and validation of the Parental Acceptance-Rejection Questionnaire. *Catalog of Selected Documents in Psychology, 8*, 7–8.

Romer, D., Black, M., Ricardo, I., Feigelman, S., Kaljee, L., & Galbraith, J. (1994). Social influences on the sexual behavior of youth at risk for HIV exposure. *American Journal of Public Health, 84*, 977–985.

Rook, K. S. (1984). The negative side of social interaction: Impact of psychological well-being. *Journal of Personality and Social Psychology, 46*, 1097–1108.

Rosenhan, D. L. (1973). On being sane in insane places. *Science, 179*, 250–258.

Rothbaum, F., & Weisz, J. R. (1994). Parental caregiving and child externalizing behavior in nonclinical samples: A meta-analysis. *Psychological Bulletin, 116*, 55–74.

Rothbart, M. K., & Bates, J. E. (1998). Temperament. In N. Eisenberg (Ed.), *Handbook of child psychology: Vol. 3. Social, emotional, and personality development* (5th ed., pp. 105–176). New York: Wiley.

Roseby, V. (1995). Uses of psychological testing in a child-focused approach to child custody evaluations. *Family Law Quarterly, 29*(1), 97–110.

Rosen, K. S., & Rothbaum, F. (1993). Quality of parental care giving and security of attachment. *Developmental Psychology, 29*(2), 358–367.

Rosenfeld, A., Bailey, R., Seigel, B., & Bailey, G. (1986). Determining incestuous contact between parent and child: Frequency of children touching parents' genitals in a nonclinical population. *Journal of the American Academy of Child Psychiatry, 25*(4), 481–484.

Rosenfeld, A., Siegel, B., & Bailey, R. (1987). Familial bathing patterns: Implications for cases of alleged molestation and or pediatric practice. *Pediatrics, 79*, 224–229.

Rosenfeld, A., O'Reilly-Wenegrat, A. O., Haavik, D. K., Wenegrat, B. G., & Smith, C. R. (1982). Sleeping patterns in upper-middle-class families when the child awakens ill or frightened. *Archives of General Psychiatry, 39*(8), 943–947.

Rosenthal, R. (1966). *Experimenter effects on behavioral research*. New York: Appleton-Century-Crofts.

Rosenthal, R. (1967). Covert communications in the psychological experiment. *Psychological Bulletin, 67*, 356–367.

Rosenthal, R. (1968). Self-fulfilling prophecy. *Psychology Today, 2*, 44–57.

Ross, S. M. (1996). Risk of physical abuse to children of spouse abusing parents. *Child Abuse and Neglect, 20*(7), 589–598.

Rossman, B. B. R. (1998). Descartes' error and posttraumatic stress disorder: Cognition and emotion in children who are exposed to parental violence. In G. W. Holden, R. Geffner, & E. N. Jouriles (Eds.), *Children exposed to marital violence: Theory, research, and applied issues* (pp. 223–256). Washington, DC: American Psychological Association.

Rossman, B. B. R., & Rosenberg, M. S. (1992). Family stress and functioning in children:

The moderating effects of children's beliefs about their control over parental conflict. *Journal of Child Psychology and Psychiatry, 33,* 699–715.

Russek, L. G., & Schwartz, G. E. (1997). Feelings of parental caring can predict health status in mid-life: A 35-year follow-up of the Harvard Mastery of Stress study. *Journal of Behavioral Medicine, 20,* 1–13.

Rutter, M. (1990). Psychosocial resilience and protective mechanisms. In J. Rolf, A. S. Masten, D. Cicchetti, K. H. Nuechterlein, & S. Weintraub (Eds.), *Risk and protective factors in the development of psychopathology* (pp. 181–214). New York: Cambridge University Press.

Sameroff, A. (1992). Systems, development, and early intervention: A commentary. In J. Sameroff, P. Hauser-Cram, M. W. Kraus, & C. C. Upshur (Eds.), *Development of infants with disabilities and their families. Monographs of the Society for Research in Child Development, 57*(6, Serial No. 230), 154–163.

Sandifer, M., Hordern, A., & Green, L. (1970). The psychiatric interview: The impact of the first three minutes. *American Journal of Psychiatry, 126,* 968–973.

Santrock, J. W., & Yussen, S. R. (1987). *Child development.* Dubuque, IA: William C. Brown.

Saposnek, D. T. (2005). Preface to the special issue: Special needs children in the family court. *Family Court Review, 43*(4), 563–565.

Saposnek, D. T., Perryman, H. P., Berkow, J., & Ellsworth, S. (2005). Special needs children in family court cases. *Family Court Review, 43*(4), 566–581.

Saywitz, K. J. (1992, Summer). Enhancing children's memory with the Cognitive Interview. *The APSAC Advisor,* 9–10.

Saywitz, K., & Camparo, L. (1998). Interviewing child witnesses: A developmental perspective. *Child Abuse and Neglect, 22,* 825–843.

Saywitz, K. J., Snyder, L., & Nathanson, R. (1999). Facilitating the communicative competence of the child witness. *Applied Developmental Science, 3,* 58–68.

Scarpa, A., & Raine, A. (1997). Psychophysiology of anger and violent behavior. *Psychiatric Clinics of North America, 20,* 375–394.

Schafer, J. (1996). Measuring spousal violence with the Conflict Tactics Scale: Notes on reliability and validity issues. *Journal of Interpersonal Violence, 11,* 572–585 .

Schaffer, H. R. (1996). *Social development.* Oxford, UK: Blackwell.

Schafran, L. H. (2003). *Understanding sexual violence.* Los Angeles: California Center for Judicial Education and Research.

Schepard, A. (2004). The Approximation Rule: Are predictability, presumptions, and best interests compatible? *Proceedings of the 41st annual Conference of the Association of Family and Conciliation Courts* (pp. 220–235). Madison, WI: Association of Family and Conciliation Courts.

Schetky, D. H., and Benedek, E. P. (Eds.). (1980). *Child psychiatry and the law.* New York: Brunner/Mazel.

Schmidt, S. E., Liddle, H. A., & Dakof, G. A. (1996). Changes in parenting practices and adolescent drug abuse during multidimensional family therapy. *Journal of Family Psychology, 10,* 12–27.

Schneider, M. F. (1989). *Children's Apperceptive Story Telling Test.* Austin, TX: Pro Ed.

Schore, A. N. (2001). Minds in the making: Attachment, the self-organizing brain, and developmentally oriented psychoanalytic psychotherapy. *British Journal of Psychotherapy, 17*(3), 299–328.

Schutz, B. M., Dixon, E. B., Lindenberger, J. C., & Ruther, N. J. (1989). *Solomon's sword: A practical guide to conducting child custody evaluations*. San Francisco: Jossey-Bass.

Schwartz, D., Dodge, K. A., Pettit, G. S., & Bates, J. E. (1997). The early socialization of aggressive victims of bullying. *Child Development, 68*, 665–675.

Scott, E. (1992). Pluralism, parental preference, and child custody. *California Law Review, 80*, 615–672.

Scott-Jones, D. (1995). Parent–child interactions and school achievement. In B. A. Ryan, G. R. Adams, T. P. Gullotta, R. P. Weissberg, & R. L. Hampton (Eds.), *The family–school connection: Theory, research and practice* (Vol. 2, pp. 75–107). Thousand Oaks, CA: Sage.

Seeman, T. E., Singer, B., Horwitz, R., & McEwen, B. S. (1997). The price of adaptation—Allostatic load and its health consequences: MacArthur studies of successful aging. *Archives of Internal Medicine, 157*, 2259–2268.

Seltzer, J. A. (1991). Relationships between fathers and children who live apart: The father's role after separation. *Journal of Marriage and the Family, 53*(1), 79–101.

Seltzer, J. A. (1998). Father by law: Effects of joint legal custody on nonresident fathers' involvement with children. *Demography, 35*(2), 135–146.

Seltzer, J. A., Schaeffer, N. C., & Hong-Wen Charng, H. W. (1989). Family ties after divorce: The relationship between visiting and paying child support. *Journal of Marriage and the Family, 51*(4), 1013–1031.

Selzer, M. L. (1996). *The Michigan Alcohol Screening Test*. LaJolla, CA: Author.

Severson v. Hansen, 529 N.W.2d 167 (N.D. 1995).

Shaffer, J. W., Duszynski, K. R., & Thomas, C. B. (1982). Family attitudes in youth as a possible precursor of cancer among physicians: A search for explanatory mechanisms. *Journal of Behavioral Medicine, 5*, 143–163.

Shapiro, D. L. (1991). *Forensic psychological assessment: An integrative approach*. Boston: Allyn & Bacon.

Sheras, P. L., Abidin, R. R., & Konold, T. R. (1998). *Stress Index for Parents of Adolsecents*. Odessa, FL: Psychological Assessment Resources.

Shiffman, S., Fischer, L. A., Paty, J. A., Gnys, M., Hickcox, M., & Kassel, J. D. (1994). Drinking and smoking: A field study of their association. *Annals of Behavioral Medicine, 16*, 203–209.

Shuman, D. W. (1994). *Psychiatric and psychological evidence* (2nd ed.). New York: McGraw-Hill.

Shuman, D. W., Greenberg, S., Heilbrun, K., & Foote, W. E. (1998). An immodest proposal: Should treating mental health professionals be barred from testifying about their patients? *Behavioral Sciences and the Law, 16*(4), 509–523.

Shuman, D. W., & Sales, B. D. (1998). The admissibility of expert testimony based upon clinical judgment and scientific research. *Psychology, Public Policy and Law, 4*(4), 1226–1252.

Shuman, D. W., & Sales, B. D. (1999). The impact of *Daubert* and its progeny on the admissibility of behavioral and social science evidence. *Psychology, Public Policy, and Law, 5*(1), 3–15.

Siegel, D. (2003). An interpersonal neurobiology of psychotherapy: The developing mind and the resolution of trauma. In M. F. Solomon & D. Siegel (Eds.), *Healing trauma: Attachment, mind, body, and brain* (pp. 1–56). New York: Norton.

Silovsky, J. F., & Niec, L. (2002). Characteristics of young children with sexual behavior problems: A pilot study. *Child Maltreatment, 7*(3), 187–197.

Simon, L. M. (2000). An examination of the assumptions of specialization, mental disorder, and dangerousness in sex offenders. *Behavioral Sciences and the Law*, *18*, 275–308.

Sivan, A. B., & Schor, D. P. (1987, August). *Children's labels for sexually related body parts*. Poster session presented at the annual meeting of the American Psychological Association, New York.

Skinner, E. A. (1995). *Perceived control, motivation, and coping*. Thousand Oaks, CA: Sage.

Skinner, L. J., & Berry, K. K. (1993). Anatomically detailed dolls and the evaluation of child sexual abuse allegations: Psychometric considerations. *Law and Human Behavior*, *17*, 399–421.

Slobogin, C. (1989). The ultimate-issue issue. *Behavioral Sciences and the Law*, *7*(2), 259–266.

Small, S. A., & Luster, T. (1994). Adolescent sexual activity: An ecological, risk-factor approach. *Journal of Marriage and the Family*, *56*, 181–192.

Smart, C. (2002). From children's shoes to children's voices. *Family Court Review*, *40*, 307–319.

Smart, C. (2005). Textures of family life: Further thoughts on change and commitment. *International Journal of Social Policy*, *34*(4), 541–556.

Smart, C. (2006). Children's narratives of post-divorce family life: From individual experience to ethical disposition. *Sociological Review*, pp. 155–170.

Smart, C., & Neale, B. (2000). "It's my life, too"—Children's perspectives on post-divorce parenting. *Family Law*, *30*, 163–169.

Smart, C., Wade, A., & Neale, B. (1999). Objects of concern?—Children and divorce. *Child and Family Law Quarterly*, *11*(4), 365–376.

Smith, D., & Dumont, F. (1995). A cautionary study: Unwarranted interpretations of the Draw-A-Person test. *Professional Psychology: Research and Practice*, *23*, 298–303.

Smith, J. V. (2001). Review of the Parenting Satisfaction Scale. In B. S. Plake & J. C. Impara (Eds.), *The fourteenth mental measurements yearbook*. Lincoln, NE: Buros Institute of Mental Measurements.

Smith, T. W. (1992). Hostility and health: Current status of a psychosomatic hypothesis. *Journal of Personality and Social Psychology*, *48*, 813–838.

Smith, T. W., Pope, M. K., Sanders, J. D., Allred, K. D., & O'Keefe, J. L. (1988). Cynical hostility at home and work: Psychosocial vulnerability across domains. *Journal of Research in Personality*, *22*, 525–548.

Snyder, D. K. (1997). *Manual for the Marital Satisfaction Inventory—Revised*. Sarasota, FL: Professional Resource Press.

Solomon, J., & Biringen, Z. (2001). Another look at the developmental research: Commentary on Kelly & Lamb's "Using child development research to make appropriate custody and access decisions." *Family Court Review*, *39*(4), 355–364.

Southam-Gerow, M. A., & Kendall, P. C. (2002). Emotion regulation and understanding: Implications for child psychopathology and therapy. *Clinical Psychology Review*, *22*, 189–222.

Speilberger, C. D. (1999). *State–Trait Anger Expression Inventory—2 (STAXI-2) professional manual*. Tampa, FL: Psychological Assessment.

Spies, R., & Jones, C. F. (2001). Review of the Behavior Assessment System for Children–Revised. In B. S. Plake & J. C. Impara (Eds.), *The fourteenth mental measurements yearbook*. Lincoln, NE: Buros Institute of Mental Measurements.

Sroufe, L. A. (1983). Infant–caregiver attachment and patterns of adaptation in preschool: The roots of maladaptation and competence. In M. Perlmutter (Ed.), *Minnesota symposium in child psychology* (Vol. 16, pp. 129–135). Hillsdale, NJ: Erlbaum.

Sroufe, L. A. (1991, Winter). Sorting it out: Attachment and bonding. *Early Report of the Center for Early Education and Development, 18*(2), 3–4.

Sroufe, L. A. (1996). *Emotional development: The organization of emotional life in the early years.* New York: Cambridge University Press.

Stahl, P. M. (1994). *Conducting child custody evaluations: A comprehensive guide.* Thousand Oaks, CA: Sage.

Stahl, P. (1997). *Evaluation issues re: parental alienation syndrome.* Paper presented at the Third International Symposium on Child Custody Evaluations. Breckenridge, CO.

Stahl, P. M. (1999). *Complex issues in custody evaluations.* Thousand Oaks, CA: Sage.

Stanton, M. D., & Shadish, W. R. (1997). Outcome, attrition, and family–couples treatment for drug abuse: A meta-analysis and review of the controlled, comparative studies. *Psychological Bulletin, 122,* 170–191.

State v. Kim, 64 Haw. 645 P.2d 1330 (1982).

Stattin, H., & Kerr, M. (2000). Parental monitoring: A reinterpretation. *Child Development, 71,* 1072–1085.

Steadman, H., Mulvey, E., Monahan, J., Robbins, P., Appelbaum, P., Grisso, T., et al. (1998). Violence by people discharged from acute psychiatric inpatient facilities and by others in the same neighborhoods. *Archives of General Psychiatry, 55,* 393–401.

Steele, C. M., Spencer, S. J., & Lynch, M. (1993). Self-image resilience and dissonance: The role of affirmational resources. *Journal of Personality and Social Psychology, 64,* 885–896.

Stein, A., Woolley, H., Cooper, S. D., & Fairburn, C. G. (1994). An observational study of mothers with eating disorders and their infants. *Journal of Child Psychology and Psychiatry, 35,* 733–748.

Steinberg, L. (1996). *Beyond the classroom: Why school reform has failed and what parents need to do.* New York: Simon & Schuster.

Steinberg, L., Lamborn, S. D., Dornbusch, S. M., & Darling, N. (1992). Impact of parenting practices on adolescent achievement: Authoritative parenting, school involvement, and encouragement to succeed. *Child Development, 63,* 1266–1281.

Steinberg, L., Mounts, N. S., Lamborn, S. D., & Dornbusch, S. M. (1991). Authoritative parenting and adolescent adjustment across varied ecological niches. *Journal of Research on Adolescence, 1,* 19–36.

Stern, M., & Zevon, M. A. (1990). Stress, coping, and family environment: The adolescent's response to naturally occurring stressors. *Journal of Adolescent Research, 5,* 290–305.

Sternberg, K. J., Lamb, M. E., Hershkowitz, I., Esplin, P. W., Redlich, A., & Sunshine, N. (1996). The relation between investigative utterance types and the informativeness of child witnesses. *Journal of Applied Developmental Psychology, 17,* 439–451.

Stets, J. E., & Straus, M. A. (1990). Gender differences in reporting of marital violence and its medical and psychological consequences. In M. A. Straus & R. J. Gelles (Eds.), *Physical violence in American families: Risk factors and adaptations to violence in 8,145 families* (pp. 151–165). New Brunswick, NJ: Transaction.

Stevenson, H. W., Chen, C., & Lee, S. Y. (1993). Mathematics achievement of Chinese, Japanese, and American children: Ten years later. *Science, 259*, 53–58.

Stinnett, T. A. (1998). Review of the Children's Personality Questionnaire. In J. C. Impara & B. S. Plake (Eds.), *The thirteenth mental measurements yearbook*. Lincoln, NE: Buros Institute of Mental Measurements.

Stipek, D., & Gralinski, J. H. (1996). Children's beliefs about intelligence and school performance. *Journal of Educational Psychology, 88*, 397–407.

Stoltz, J. M., & Ney, T. (2002). Resistance to visitation: Rethinking parental and child alienation. *Family Court Review, 40*(2), 220–231.

Stone, G. (2001). Father postdivorce well-being: An exploratory model. *Journal of Genetic Psychology, 162*(4), 460–477.

Stone, G. (2002). Nonresidential father postdivorce well-being: The role of social supports. *Journal of Divorce and Remarriage, 36*(3–4), 139–150.

Stormshak, E. A., Bellanti, C. J., & Bierman, K. L. (1996). The quality of sibling relationships and the development of social competence and behavior control in aggressive children. *Developmental Psychology, 32*(1), 79–89.

Strassberg, Z., Dodge, F. A., Pettit, G. S., & Bates, J. E. (1994). Spanking in the home and children's subsequent aggression toward kindergarten peers. *Development and Psychopathology, 6*, 445–462.

Straus, M. A. (1979). Measuring intrafamily conflict and violence. The conflict tactics (CT) scales. *Journal of Marriage and the Family, 41*, 75–78.

Straus, M. A. (1994). *Beating the devil out of them: Corporal punishment in American families*. San Francisco: New Lexington Press.

Straus, M. A. (1999). The controversy over domestic violence by women: A methodological, theoretical, and sociology of science analysis. In X. B. Arriaga & S. Oskamp (Eds.), *Violence in intimate relationships* (pp. 17–44). Thousand Oaks, CA: Sage.

Straus, M. A., & Gelles, R. J. (1986). Societal change and change in family violence from 1975 to 1985 as revealed by two national surveys. *Journal of Marriage and the Family, 48*, 465–479.

Straus, M. A., Hamby, S. L., & Warren, W. L. (2003). *The Conflict Tactics Scales handbook: Revised Conflict Tactics Scales (CTS2) and CTS—Parent–Child Version (CTSPC)*. Los Angeles: Western Psychological Services.

Straus, M. A., & Mouradian, V. E. (1998). Impulsive corporal punishment by mothers and antisocial behavior and impulsiveness of children. *Behavioral Sciences and the Law, 16*, 353–374.

Straus, M. A., & Smith, C. (1990). Violence in Hispanic families in the United States: Incidence rates and structural interpretations. In M. A. Straus & R. J. Gelles (Eds.), *Physical violence in American families: Risk factors and adaptations in violence in 8,145 families* (pp. 341–363). New Brunswick, NJ: Transaction.

Stricker, G. (1992). The relationship of research to clinical practice. *American Psychologist, 47*(4) 543–549.

Stricker, G., & Trierweiler, S. J. (1995). The local clinical scientist: A bridge between science and practice. *American Psychologist, 50*(12), 995–1002.

Strohmer, D. C., Shivy, V. A., & Chiodo, A. L. (1990). Information processing strategies in counselor hypothesis testing: The role of selective memory and expectancy. *Journal of Counseling Psychology, 37*, 465–472.

Suarez, E. C., Bates, M. P., & Harralson, T. L. (1998). The relation of hostility to lipids and lipoproteins in women: Evidence for the role of antagonistic hostility. *Annals of Behavioral Medicine, 20*, 59–63.

Sullivan, C. M., Parisan, J. A., & Davidson, W. S. (1991, August). *Index of psychological abuse: Development of a measure*. Poster presentation at the annual conference of the American Psychological Association, San Francisco.

Sutherland, R., Gross, J., & Hayne, H. (1996). Adults' understanding of young children's testimony. *Journal of Applied Psychology, 81,* 777–785.

Swearer, S. M. (2001). Review of the Stress Index for Parents of Adolsecents. In B. S. Plake & J. C. Impara (Eds.), *The fourteenth mental measurements yearbook*. Lincoln, NE: Buros Institute of Mental Measurements.

Taylor, S. E. (1999). *Health psychology* (4th ed.). New York: McGraw-Hill.

Taylor, S. E., Repetti, R. L., & Seeman, T. E. (1997). Health psychology: What is an unhealthy environment and how does it get under the skin? *Annual Review of Psychology, 48,* 411–447.

Tesler, P., & Thompson, P. (2006). *Collaborative divorce: The revolutionary new way to restructure your family, resolve legal issues, and move on with your life*. HarperCollins.

Teti, D. M., & Candelaria, M. A. (2002). Parenting competence. In M. H. Bornstein (Ed.), *The handbook of parenting* (2nd ed.): *Vol. 4. Social conditions and applied parenting* (pp. 149–180). Mahwah, NJ: Erlbaum

Thompson, R. A., & Calkins, S. D. (1996). The double-edged sword: Emotional regulation for children at risk. *Development and Psychopathology, 8,* 163–182.

Tippins, T. M., & Wittmann, J. P. (2005). Empirical and ethical problems with custody recommendations: A call for clinical humility and judicial vigilance. *Family Court Review, 43*(2), 193–222.

Tjaden, P., & Thoennes, N. (2000a). *Full report of the prevalence, incidence, and consequences of intimate partner violence against women: Findings from the National Violence Against Women Survey*. Washington, DC: National Institute of Justice.

Tjaden, P., & Thoennes, N. (2000b). *Extent, nature, and consequences of intimate partner violence: Findings from the National Violence Against Women Survey*. Washington, DC: National Institute of Justice.

Tolman, R. M. (1989). The development of a measure of psychological maltreatment of women by their male partners. *Violence and Victims, 4,* 159–178.

Tolman, R. M. (1999). The validation of the psychological maltreatment of women inventory. *Violence and Victims, 14,* 25–37.

Tolman, R. M. (2001). The validation of the Psychological Maltreatment of Women Inventory. In K. D. O'Leary & R. D. Maiuro (Eds.), *Psychological abuse in violent domestic relations* (pp. 47–60). New York: Springer.

Troxil v. Granville, 530 U.S. 57 (2000).

Trubitt, A. (2004). *Play therapy goes to court: Implications and applications in contested child custody* (2nd ed.). Kailua, HI: Author.

Tubman, J. G., Windle, M., & Windle, R. C. (1996). The onset and cross-temporal patterning of sexual intercourse in middle adolescence: Prospective relations with behavioral and emotional problems. *Child Development, 67,* 327–343.

Tucker, C. J., Marx, J., & Long, L. (1998). Moving on: Residential mobility and children's school lives. *Sociology of Education, 71*(2), 111–129.

Tversky, A., & Kahneman, D. (1974). Judgment under uncertainty: Heuristics and biases. *Science, 185,* 1124–1131.

Tweed, R., & Dutton, D. G. (1998). A comparison of instrumental and impulsive subgroups of batterers. *Violence and Victims, 13*(3), 217–230.

Tymchuk, A. J., Lang, C. M., Dolyniuk, C. A., Berney-Ficklin, K., & Spitz, R. (1999). The

Home Inventory of Dangers and Safety Precautions—2: Addressing critical needs for prescriptive assessment devices in child maltreatment and in healthcare. *Child Abuse and Neglect, 23,* 1–14.

Uchino, B. N., Uno, D., & Holt-Lunstad, J. (1999). Social support, physiological processes and health. *Current Directions in Psychological Science, 8,* 145–148.

Underwager, R., & Wakefield, H. (1998). The Taint Hearing. Retreived from *www.ipt-forensics.com/journal10/j10_7.htm.*

Uniform Marriage and Divorce Act (UMDA) § 308, 9A ULA 160 (1970).

U.S. Department of Education. (1999). *Fathers' involvement in their children's education.* Washington, DC: U.S. Government Printing Office.

U.S. Department of Health and Human Services, Administration on Children Youth, and Families. (2001). *Child maltreatment 1999.* Washington, DC: U.S. Government Printing Office.

U.S. Department of Health and Human Services, Administration on Children Youth, and Families. (2002). *Child maltreatment 2000.* Washington, DC: U.S. Government Printing Office.

U.S. Department of Justice. (1994). *Violence against women: A national crime victimization survey report* (Bureau of Justice Statistics Selected Findings, NCJ-145325). Washington, DC: U. S. Government Printing Office.

United States v. Ball, 163 U.S. 662 (1896).

Universal Declaration of Human Rights (UDHR), G. A. Res. 217A (III), A/810 at 71, 1948.

Urbina, S. (2001). Review of the Personality Inventory for Children–2nd Edition. In B. S. Plake & J. C. Impara (Eds.), *The fourteenth mental measurements yearbook.* Lincoln, NE: Buros Institute of Mental Measurements.

Valentiner, D. P., Holahan, C. J., & Moos, R. H. (1994). Social support, appraisals of event controllability, and coping: An integrative model. *Journal of Personality and Social Psychology, 66,* 1094–1102.

Valenzuela, M. (1997). Maternal sensitivity in a developing society: The context of urban poverty and infant chronic undernutrition. *Developmental Psychology, 33,* 845–855.

van den Boom, D. C. (1994). The influence of temperament and mothering on attachment and exploration: An experimental manipulation of sensitive responsiveness among lower-class mothers with irritable infants. *Child Development, 65,* 1457–1477.

Vogeltanz, N. D., & Drabman, R. S. (1995). A procedure for evaluating young children suspected of being sexually abused. *Behavior Therapy, 26,* 579–597.

Vygotsky, L. S. (1962). *Thought and language* (trans. and ed. E. Hanfmann & G. Vakan). Cambridge, MA: M.I.T. Press.

Wade, A., & Smart, C. (2002). As fair as it can be? Childhood after divorce. In A. Jensen & L. McKee (Eds.), *Children and the changing family.* London: Falmer Routledge.

Wahler, R. G. (1990). Some perceptual functions of social networks in coercive mother–child interactions. *Journal of Social and Clinical Psychology, 9,* 43–53.

Wakefield, H. (2006). Guidelines on investigatory interviewing of children: What is the consensus in the scientific community? *Journal of Forensic Psychology, 24*(3), 57–74.

Wakefield, H., & Underwager, R. (1992). Uncovering memories of alleged sexual abuse: The therapists who do it. *Issues in Child Abuse Accusations, 4*(4), 197–213.

Walker, A. G. (1999). *Handbook on questioning children: A linguistic perspective*. Washington, DC: American Bar Association Center on Children and the Law.

Walker, E. A., Gelfand, A., Katon, W. J., Koss, M. P., Von Korff, M., Bernstein, D., et al. (1999). Adult health status of women with histories of childhood abuse and neglect. *The American Journal of Medicine, 107*, 332–339.

Walker, L. A. (1979). *The battered woman*. New York: Harper & Row.

Walker, L. A. (1984). Battered women, psychology, and public policy. *American Psychologist, 39*, 1178–1182.

Walker, L. E. (1995). Current perspectives on men who batter women—Implications for intervention and treatment to stop violence against women: Comment on Gottman et al. (1995). *Journal of Family Psychology, 9*, 264–271.

Walker, L. E., & Shapiro, D. L. (2003a) *Introduction to forensic psychology: Clinical and social psychological perspectives*. New York: Klewer.

Walker, L. E., & Shapiro, D. L. (2003b). Access to, and protection of, children. In L. E. Walker & D. L. Shapiro, *Introduction to forensic psychology: Clinical and social psychological perspectives* (pp. 219–242). New York: Klewer.

Wallerstein, J., & Blakeslee, S. (1989). *Second chances: Men, women and children, a decade after divorce*. New York: Houghton Mifflin.

Wallerstein, J. S., & Kelly, J. B. (1980). *Surviving the breakup: How children and parents cope with divorce*. New York: Basic Books.

Wallerstein, J. S., & Tanke, T. J. (1996). To move or not to move: Psychological and legal considerations in the relocation of children following divorce. *Family Law Quarterly, 30*(2), 305–332.

Walsh, F. (Ed.). (2003). *Normal family processes: Growing diversity and complexity* (3rd ed.). New York: Guilford Press.

Waltz, J., Babcock, J. C., Jacobson, N. S., & Gottman, J. M. (2000). Testing a typology of batterers. *Journal of Consulting and Clinical Psychology, 68*, 658–669.

Ward, P., & Harvey, J. C. (1993). Family wars: The alienation of children. *New Hampshire Bar Journal, 34*(1), 30–40.

Ward, P., & Harvey, J. C. (1997). *Family wars: The alienation of children*. Paper presented by the Third International Symposium on Child Custody Evaluations. Breckenridge, CO.

Warren, A. R., & Woodall, C. E. (1999). The reliability of hearsay testimony: How well do interviewers recall their interviews with children? *Psychology, Public Policy, and Law, 5*, 1–17.

Warren, A. R., Woodall, C. E., Thomas, M., Nunno, M., Keeney, J. M., Larson, S. M., et al. (1999). Assessing the effectiveness of a training program for interviewing child witnesses. *Journal of Applied Developmental Psychology, 3*, 128–135.

Warshak, R. A. (2000a). Remarriage as a trigger of parental alienation syndrome. *American Journal of Family Theragpy, 28*(3), 229–241.

Warshak, R. A. (2000b). Blanket restricitons: Overnight contact between parents and young children. *Family and Conciliation Courts Review, 38*(4), 422–445.

Warshak, R. A. (2001a). Current controversies regarding parental alienation syndrome. *American Journal of Forensic Psychology, 19*(3), 29–59.

Warshak, R. A. (2001b). *Divorce poison*. New York: HarperCollins.

Warshak, R. A. (2002). Misdiagnosis of parental alienation syndrome. *American Journal of Forensic Psychology, 19*(3), 29–59.

Warshak, R. A. (2003). Bringing sense to parental alienation: A look at the disputes and the evidence. *Family Law Quarterly, 37*(2), 273–301.

Warshak, R. A. (2004). *The Approximation Rule: Are predictability, presumptions, and best interests compatible?* Proceedings of the 41st annual Conference of the Association of Family and Conciliation Courts (p. 236). Madison, WI: Association of Family and Conciliation Courts.

Washington v. United States, 390 F.2d 444 (1967).

Wasserman, D. R., & Leventhal, J. M. (1993). Maltreatment of children born to cocaine-dependent women. *American Journal of Diseases of Children, 147,* 1324–1328.

Waterman, A. H., Blades, M., & Spencer, C. (2001). Interviewing children and adults: The effect of question format on the tendency to speculate. *Applied Cognitive Psychology, 15,* 521–531.

Waters, E., & Cummings, E. M. (2000). A secure base from which to explore close relationships. *Child Development, 71,* 164–172.

Watt, N. F. (1984). In a nutshell: The first two decades of high-risk research in schizophrenia. In D. Ricks, A. Thomas, & J. E. Roff (Eds.), *Children at risk for schizophrenia: A longitudinal perspective.* New York: Cambridge University Press.

Weidner, G., Hutt, J., Connor, S. L., & Mendell, N. R. (1992). Family stress and coronary risk in children. *Psychosomatic Medicine, 54,* 471–479.

Weinberg v. Wiesenfeld, 420 U.S. 636, 645 (1975).

Weiner, I. (2003). The assessment process. In J. R. Graham & J. A. Naglieri (Eds.), *Handbook of psychology: Vol. 10. Assessment psychology* (pp. 3–25). New York: Wiley.

Weiner, I., & Kuehnle, K. (1998). Projective assessment of children and adolescents. In C. R. Reynolds (Ed.), *Comprehensive clinical psychology: Vol 4. Assessment* (pp. 431–458). Oxford: Elsevier Science.

Weiss, L. H., & Schwarz, J. C. (1996). The relationship between parenting types and older adolescents' personality, academic achievement, adjustment, and substance use. *Child Development, 67*(5), 2101–2114.

Weissman, H. N. (1991). Forensic psychological examination of the child witness in cases of alleged sexual abuse. *American Journal of Orthopsychiatry, 61*(1), 48–58.

Weissman, H. N., & DeBow, D. M. (2003). Ethical principles and professional competencies. In A. M. Goldstein (Ed.), *Handbook of psychology: Vol. 11. Forensic psychology* (pp. 33–54). New York: Wiley.

Weissman, M. M., Gammon, G. D., John, K., Merikangas, K. R., Warner, V., Prusoff, B. A., et al. (1987). Children of depressed parents. *Archives of General Psychology, 44,* 847–853.

Weithorn, L. A. (Ed.). (1987). *Psychology and child custody determinations: Knowledge, roles, and expertise.* Lincoln: University of Nebraska Press.

Wenck, S. L. (1977). *House-tree-person drawings: An illustrated diagnostic handbook.* Los Angeles: Western Psychological Services.

Werner, E. E., & Smith, R. S. (1982). *Vulnerable but invincible: A study of resilient children.* New York: McGraw-Hill.

Werner, P. D. (2001). Review of the the structured clinical interview for DSM-IV Axis I disorders. clinical version. In B. S. Plake & J. C. Impara (Eds.), *The fourteenth mental measurements yearbook.* Lincoln, NE: Buros Institute of Mental Measurements.

West, M. O., & Prinz, R. J. (1987). Parental alcoholism and childhood psychopathology. *Psychological Bulletin, 102,* 204–218.

White, J. W., Smith, P. H., Koss, M. P., & Figueredo, A. J. (2000). Intimate partner aggression—What have we learned? Comment on Archer (2000). *Psychological Bulletin, 126*, 690–696.

White, R. W. (1959). Motivation reconsidered: The concept of competence. *Psychological Review, 66*, 297–333.

Whiteside, M. F. (1998). Custody for children age 5 and younger. *Family and Conciliation Courts Review, 36*(4), 479–502.

Whiteside, M. F., & Becker, B. J. (2000). Parental factors and the young child's postdivorce adjustment: A meta-analysis with implications for parenting arrangements. *Journal of Family Psychology, 14*(1), 5–26.

Whittemore, K. E., & Kropp, P. R. (2002). Spousal assault risk assessment: A guide for clinicians. *Journal of Forensic Psychology Practice, 2*, 53–64.

Wicklund, R. A., & Brehm, J. W. (1976). *Perspectives on cognitive dissonance*. Hillsdale, NJ: Erlbaum.

Wickrama, K. A. S., Lorenz, F. O., & Conger, R. D. (1997). Parental support and adolescent physical health status: A latent growth-curve analysis. *Journal of Health and Social Behavior, 38*, 149–163.

Widiger, T. A. (2001). The structured clinical interview for DSM-IV Axis I Disorders: Clinical Version. In B. S. Plake & J. C. Impara (Eds.), *The fourteenth mental measurements yearbook*. Lincoln, NE: Buros Institute of Mental Measurements.

Widom, C. S., & White, H. R. (1997). Problem behaviours in abused and neglected children grown up: Prevalence and co-occurrence of substance abuse, crime, and violence. *Criminal Behaviour and Mental Health, 7*, 287–310.

Wills, T. A., DuHamel, K., & Vaccaro, D. (1995). Activity and mood temperament as predictors of adolescent substance use: Test of a self-regulation mediational model. *Journal of Personality and Social Psychology, 62*, 901–916.

Wilson, M. I., & Daly, M. (1993). An evolutionary psychological perspective on male sexual proprietariness and violence against wives. *Violence and Victims, 8*, 271–294.

Wingspread Conference Report and Action Plan. (2001). High-conflict custody cases: Reforming the system for children. *Family Court Review, 39*(2), 146–157.

Winick, B. J., & LaFond, J. O. (Eds.). (1998). Sex offenders: Scientific, legal, and public policy perspectives. *Psychology, Public Policy and Law, 4*, 1–570.

Wisconsin v. Yoder, 406 U.S. 205 (1972).

Wolfe, D. A., Wekerle, C., Reitzel-Jaffe, D., & Lefebvre, L. (1998). Factors associated with abusive relationships among maltreated and nonmaltreated youth. *Development and Psychopathology, 10*(1), 61–85.

Woodall, K. L., & Matthews, K. A. (1989). Familial environment associated with Type A behaviors and psychophysiological responses to stress in children. *Health Psychology, 8*, 403–426.

Woodall, K. L., & Matthews, K. A. (1993). Changes in and stability of hostile characteristics: Results from a 4-year longitudinal study of children. *Journal of Personality and Social Psychology, 64*, 491–499.

Zahn-Waxler, C., Cole, P. M., Welsh, J. D., & Fox, N. A. (1995). Psychophysiological correlates of empathy and prosocial behaviors in preschool children with behavior problems. *Development and Psychopathology, 7*, 27–48.

Zahn-Waxler, C., Duggal, C., & Gruber, R. (2002). Parental psychopathology. In M. H. Bornstein (Ed.), *The handbook of parenting: Vol. 4. Social conditions and applied parenting* (pp. 295–328). Mahwah, NJ: Erlbaum.

Zahn-Waxler, C., Iannotti, F. J., Cummings, E. M., & Denham, S. (1990). Antecedents of problem behaviors in children of depressed mothers. *Development and Psychopathology, 2,* 271–291.

Zahn-Waxler, C., Radke-Yarrow, M., Wagner, E., & Chapman, M. (1992). Development of concern for others. *Developmental Psychology, 28,* 126–136.

Zorza, J. (Ed.). (2002). *Violence against women.* Kingston, NJ: Civics Research Institute.

Zorza, J. (Ed.). (2006). *Violence against women* (2nd ed.). Kingston, NJ: Civics Research Institute.

Index